The Computational Beauty of Nature

Gary William Flake

The Computational Beauty of Nature

Computer Explorations of Fractals, Chaos, Complex Systems, and Adaptation

A Bradford Book
The MIT Press
Cambridge, Massachusetts
London, England

First MIT Press paperback edition, 2000

Library of Congress Cataloging-in-Publishing Data
Flake, Gary William.
The computational beauty of nature: computer explorations of fractals, chaos, complex systems, and adaptation / Gary William Flake.
p. cm.
"A Bradford Book."
Includes bibliographical references and index.
ISBN-13 978-0-262-06200-8 (hardcover: alk. paper)
ISBN-13 978-0-262-56127-3 (paperback: alk. paper)
1. Electronic digital computers—Programming. 2. System analysis. I. Title.
QA76.6.F557 1998
003′.3—dc21 97-52394
CIP

For my parents

Contents

Preface

The scientist does not study nature because it is useful; he studies it because he delights in it, and he delights in it because it is beautiful. If nature were not beautiful, it would not be worth knowing, and if nature were not worth knowing, life would not be worth living. Of course I do not here speak of that beauty that strikes the senses, the beauty of qualities and appearances; not that I undervalue such beauty, far from it, but it has nothing to do with science; I mean that profounder beauty which comes from the harmonious order of the parts, and which a pure intelligence can grasp.

— Henri Poincaré

A VARIATION ON an old joke goes as follows:

> Engineers study interesting real-world problems but fudge their results. Mathematicians get exact results but study only toy problems. But computer scientists, being neither engineers nor mathematicians, study toy problems and fudge their results.

Now, since I am a computer scientist, I have taken the liberty of altering the joke to make myself and my colleagues the butt of it. This joke examines a real problem found in all scientific disciplines. By substituting experimentalist, theorist, and simulationist for engineer, mathematician, and computer scientist, respectively, the joke becomes generalized for almost all of the sciences and gets to the heart of a very real division.

A theorist will often make many simplifying assumptions in order to get to the essence of some physical process. Particles do not necessarily look like billiard balls, but it often helps to think in this way if you are trying to understand how classical mechanics says things should behave. Likewise, experimentalists often have to deal with messy processes that are prone to measurement error. So if a physicist finds that the surface temperature of an object is between 100,000 and 200,000 degrees, it doesn't matter if the units are Celsius degrees or Kelvin degrees, because the margin of error is orders of magnitude larger than the difference in the two measuring units.

A simulationist is a relatively new breed of scientist who attempts to understand how the world works by studying computer simulations of phenomena found in nature. A simulationist will always have to make some assumptions when building a computer model but will also find that the simulated results are not always a perfect match for what exists in the real world. Hence, the simulationist, having to incorporate principles from theory and experimental methodologies, straddles the fence and must deal with limiting factors found in both extreme approaches. But this is not always a bad thing.

Consider an economist who builds a simplified model of the world economy, runs the model on a computer, and reaches the conclusion that interest rates, unemployment, inflation, and growth will all reach a constant level at the end of the year and stay that way forever. For this one case, the simplified model tells us very little about how the real world works because the simplified model has failed to capture an important aspect of the real world. On the other hand, suppose that a simplified model is such that it never reaches equilibrium, turns out to be extremely sensitive to the starting conditions, and displays surprisingly complex behavior. Even if this model fails to make actual predictions about the real economy, it still has some predictive power since it may reveal a deeper truth about the inherent difficulty of predicting the economy or similar systems. In other words, the model is predictable in its unpredictability. Hence, if a simplified model can behave in a sophisticated manner, then it is not too great a leap to conclude that the real-world economy can display an even greater form of sophistication.

For the first case, if after simplifying a natural process we find behavior that is profoundly simpler than the original phenomenon, then it is likely that the model failed to capture some essential piece of the real-world counterpart. On the other hand, if an analogous form of complexity is still found even in a simplified model, then it is highly possible that a key feature of the natural system has been isolated. This illustrates that simulations—especially if they are simplifications—can yield insight into how things work in the real world.

All of this boils down to a simple but deep idea: simple recurrent rules can produce extremely rich and complicated behaviors. Pure theory often fails to make accurate predictions of complicated natural processes because the world does not always obey equations with analytical solutions. Similarly, experiments with complicated observations are often useless because they fail to bridge things from a reverse direction and correlate complex effects from simple causes. It is only through the marriage of theory and experimentation that many claims of the complexity of nature can withstand reasonable tests. Simulation, then, becomes a form of experimentation in a universe of theories. The primary purpose of this book is to celebrate this fact.

How to Read This Book

While writing this book I had three different goals in mind. Thus, I think that there are three different ways that one can read this book.

On one level, most of the chapters stand on their own and can be appreciated in isolation from the others. I've spent the better part of ten years collecting interesting examples of computer simulations. If you are the sort of person who always wanted a crisp and simple description of how to make a fractal, chaotic system, cellular automaton, or neural network, then you may wish to skip around, dive right into the example programs, and play with the simulations that look appealing.

The second way that you can read this book relates to how I learned about all of the different topics covered in the chapters. While I am trained as a computer scientist, I spent several years working among physicists and other scientists. Thus, for better or worse, I've seen many of the covered topics approached in different manners. In this context, I believe that there is a captivating and interdisciplinary connection between computation, fractals, chaos, complex systems, and adaptation. I've tried to explain each in terms of the others, so if you are interested in how one part of the book relates to the others, then a more sequential reading of the book may pay off for you.

For the third way, I believe that there is an overall pattern that ties all of the part topics together into one coherent theme. This preface, the introduction, the five postscript chapters, and the epilogue are my attempt to thread everything in the book into one overall message.

If this book is a forest, then the first way of reading it is akin to poking at individual trees. The second way is analogous to observing how nearby trees relate to each other. The third way would equate to standing back and taking in the whole forest at once. It doesn't really matter which path you take in exploring these ideas, as I expect that most readers will stick to one path in preference to the others. But if you happen to try all three paths, you may be rewarded with a special type of understanding that not only relates each topic to the others but also each topic as it is viewed from different perspectives.

Dealing with Difficult Subjects

The topics covered in this book demand varying amounts of sophistication from you. Some of the ideas are so simple that they have formed the basis of lessons for a third grade class. Other chapters should give graduate students a headache. *This is intentional.* If you are confused by a sentence, section, or chapter, first see if the glossary at the end of the book helps; if it doesn't, then by all means move on.

Regarding mathematical equations, there are many ways of looking at them. If a picture is worth a thousand words (as well as a million pixels), then—as is shown later—an equation can be worth a billion pictures. An equation can often describe something so completely and compactly that any other type of description becomes cumbersome by comparison. Nevertheless, I have done my best to make every equation somewhat secondary to the supporting text.

If a particular equation confuses you, the first thing you should do is see if the surrounding text gives you a little more insight into what the symbols mean. If that doesn't work, then look to see if there is a picture that corresponds to the equation. Finally, if all else fails, you should do what I do when I don't understand an equation: mentally substitute the sounds "blah blah blah" for the equation and keep going. You would be surprised how often this works.

Don't be discouraged if you don't understand something. And please don't write off a topic as being beyond your capabilities. If you are genuinely not interested in a difficult section, so it goes. But if you are interested, it may happen that you will retroactively understand something, given enough time and effort.

Personal Motivation

At the risk of being self-indulgent, I must admit that writing this book has been a selfish labor of love. Every writer is told at one time or another to pick a target reader and write for that one person. I wrote this book for the person I was around ten or fifteen years ago.

I always wished for a book that combined all of these topics within one cover, gave sufficient information to enable one to duplicate all of the programs, and at the same time gave enough motivation to appreciate the more fundamental themes. I also wanted this hypothetical book to have parts that could be understood on a first reading, but additionally have sections that would be beyond my capabilities for years to come. This book could be sporadically opened at a random page or read sequentially. It would serve as a cookbook of computer recipes, be mostly self-contained, be a basic primer on some common mathematics, and also serve as a pointer to more fundamental texts.

Whether or not the book you are holding lives up to the idealized version that I've had in my head is mostly a personal matter. My second most important goal for the book was for it to be a spark for those, like myself, who hack simply for the joy of hacking. Thus, while my idealized version of the book has been my "bullseye," I'll be happy just to hit the target on most counts since, in the end, the programs are the heart of the book.

Acknowledgments

Over the years many friends and colleagues have either directly or indirectly influenced the outcome of this book. The only way who I can even come close to acknowledging all that deserve it is to start from the beginning of my academic career and work up to the present.

When I was an undergrad at Clemson University, Ed Page and Gene Tagliarini brought me into their research group, gave me a slice of the funding pie, and introduced me to neural networks. During these years, Roy Pargas, Hal Grossman, Steve Stevenson, Steven Hedetneimi, and Eleanor Hare all had a hand in nudging me in the direction of graduate school and research. It's a rare department that encourages undergrads to pursue research to the point of publication, and without this early exposure I am fairly certain that things would have turned out very different for me.

During the late 1980s, the Center for Nonlinear Studies at Los Alamos National Laboratory was a hotbed of research activity that attracted some of the most original thinkers in the world. Chris Barnes and Roger Jones not only acted as mentors but also managed to slip me through the back door at CNLS, which allowed me to work with a truly amazing group of people. I would also like to single out Peter Ford for inspiring me as a hacker. During this period Chris and Roger introduced me to Y.-C. Lee, then the Senior Scientist of CNLS, whom I would later follow to Maryland for graduate school.

At the University of Maryland I was a graduate student in the Computer Science Department, a research assistant at the Institute for Advanced Computer Studies, and indirectly funded, along with Y.-C. Lee and his group, in the Laboratory for Plasma Research. I greatly benefited from working with H.-H. Chen, G.-Z. Sun, and the rest of the LPR group, which had a lot to do with honing my mathematical skills. Y.-C. served as a coadviser on my thesis along with Jim Reggia. The other members of my thesis committee, Bill Gasarch, Dianne O'Leary, and Laveen Kanal, all had a significant impact on my graduate studies.

While at Siemens Corporate Research I have had the good fortune to work on exciting applications that directly relate to some of the topics in this book. I would like to thank Thomas Grandke, our CEO, and Wolf-Ekkehard Blanz, the former head of the Adaptive Information and Signal Processing Department, for creating a laboratory environment that maintains the delicate balance between research and development, and for allowing me to pursue external academic activities such as this book. SCR's librarian extraordinare, Ruth Weitzenfeld, kindly helped me track down many of the references mentioned in this book, for which I am most grateful. I would also like to acknowledge my colleagues at SCR who have helped me to refine my thoughts on learning theory. I offer a tip of the hat to Frans Coetzee, Chris Darken, Russell Greiner, Stephen Judd, Gary Kuhn, Mike Miller, Tom Petsche, Bharat Rao, Scott Rickard, Justinian Rosca, Iwan Santoso, Geoff Towell, and Ray Watrous.

I am extremely grateful to the friends, family, and colleagues who either have read preliminary portions of this book or have indirectly contributed to it through thoughtful discussions. While it is not possible to mention all of the people who have influenced this book, I would specifically like to thank Lynn, Marilyn and Stanford Apseloff, David Bader, Bill Flake, Lee Giles, Sara Gottlieb, Stephen Hanson, Bill Horne, Barry Johnson, Gary Kuhn, Barak Pearlmutter, Bill Regli, Scott Rickard, Mark Rosenblum, Pat Vroom, Ray Watrous, and Tony Zador. Lee Giles initially tried to talk me out of writing this book, but his other good qualities more than make up for this. Special thanks go to Barak Pearlmutter, who went well beyond the call of duty by giving very detailed critiques of multiple drafts of this book. I am also grateful for all of the comments provided by the anonymous reviewers. It goes without saying that any remaining errors are all mine.

Since this book forms a core for the type of course that I have always wanted to teach, I am grateful that several educators have given me a chance to try out some of the topics in this book on their students. In particular, Yannis Kevrekidis graciously allowed me to lecture to his students at Princeton University on discrete dynamical systems, and Laura Slattery and I built a set of lessons for her third grade class that demonstrated some of the principles of self-organization.

Very special thanks go to Scott Rickard, who has easily been my most eager reader. He has read more versions of this book than anyone other than myself. I am deeply grateful for his comments—which often provided a much-needed sanity check on my writing—and for his encouragement.

Harry Stanton of the MIT Press was a very early supporter of this book. His enthusiasm was so genuine and contagious that after talking with him, I couldn't imagine going with any other publisher. Unfortunately, Harry did not live to see this book into print, but his influence on the final product is still substantial. Bob Prior and Deborah Cantor-Adams provided much critical assistance during the editorial and production stages. Beth Wilson carefully copyedited the manuscript. And the excellent production staff of the MIT Press made the project as painless as possible by doing their jobs with the highest level of skill and professionalism. To all of them, I give my thanks.

I have only the deepest thanks for my family. My parents, to whom this book is dedicated, and my brother and sister, Greg Flake and Vicki Merchel, have a long history of encouraging me to do crazy things, which has had a lot to do with giving me the endurance to work through this project to the end.

The Computational Beauty of Nature

1 Introduction

The point of philosophy is to start with something so simple as not to seem worth stating, and to end with something so paradoxical that no one will believe it.
— Bertrand Russell

Things should be as simple as possible, but not simpler.
— Albert Einstein

Reductionism is the idea that a system can be understood by examining its individual parts. Implicit in this idea is that one may have to examine something at multiple levels, looking at the parts, then the parts of the parts, and so on. This is a natural way of attempting to understand the universe. Indeed, the hierarchy of science is recognizably organized in this manner. For example, take the so-called hard sciences. Biologists study living things at various levels ranging from the whole body, to organ systems, down to cellular structure. Beyond the cellular level lie chemical interactions and agents such as enzymes, which are organic chemical catalysts, and amino acids, which are building blocks for proteins. This is the domain of the chemist. To reduce things further, one would have to start looking into how atoms and molecules interact through chemical bonds that are dependent upon the number of electrons in the outermost electron shell of an atom. But what, exactly, are atoms? The physicist probes further into the nature of things by shattering atoms into their constituent parts, which brings us to protons, neutrons, and finally quarks. Ironically, at this level of understanding, scientists are dependent on mathematical techniques that often bear little resemblance to the reality that we are familiar with.

To be sure, there is some overlap among scientific and mathematical fields that is exemplified by disciplines that use tools common to other areas (e.g., organic chemistry, biophysics, and quantum mathematics), but even these hybrid disciplines have well-defined niches. Reductionism is a powerful way of looking at the universe. But this begs a somewhat silly question: Since everything ultimately breaks down to the quantum level, why aren't all scientists mathematicians at the core? In such a world physicians would make diagnoses based on the patient's bodily quarks, which makes about as much sense as building a house particle by particle. Nevertheless, every scientist must possess some knowledge of the level one step more fundamental than his or her specialty, but at some point reductionism must stop for science to be effective.

Now, suppose that we wished to describe how the universe works. We could take a reductionist's approach and catalog all of the different types of objects that exist—perhaps starting with galaxy clusters, hitting terrestrial life forms about midway through, and then ending with subatomic particles—but would this approach really succeed in describing the universe? In making a large list of "things" it is easy to forget that the manner in which "things" work more often than not depends on the environment in which they exist. For example, we could describe the form of a duck in excruciating detail, but this gives us only half of the story. To really appreciate what a duck is, we should look at ducks in the air, in water, in the context of what they eat or what eats them, how they court, mate, and reproduce, the social structures they form, how they flock, and their need to migrate.

Looking back at the organization of the sciences, we find that at each level of understanding, traditional scientists study two types of phenomena: agents (molecules, cells, ducks, and species) and interactions of agents (chemical reactions, immune system responses, duck mating, and evolution). Studying agents in isolation is a fruitful way of discovering insights into the form and function of an agent, but doing so has some known limitations. Specifically, reductionism fails when we try to use it in a reverse direction. As we shall see throughout this book, having a complete and perfect understanding of how an agent behaves in no way guarantees that you will be able to predict how this single agent will behave for all time or in the context of other agents.

We have, then, three different ways of looking at how things work. We can take a purely reductionist approach and attempt to understand things through dissection. We also can take a wider view and attempt to understand whole collections at once by observing how many agents, say the neurons in a brain, form a global pattern, such as human intelligence. Or we can take an intermediate view and focus attention on the interactions of agents. Through this middle path, the interactions of agents can be seen to form the glue that binds one level of understanding to the next level.

1.1 Simplicity and Complexity

Let's take this idea further by examining a single ant. By itself, an ant's behavior is not very mysterious. There is a very small number of tasks that any ant has to do in the course of its lifetime. Depending on its caste, an ant may forage for food, care for the queen's brood, tend to the upkeep of the nest, defend against enemies of the nest, or, in the special case of the queen, lay eggs. Yet when we consider the ant colony as a whole, the behavior becomes much more complex. Army ant colonies often consist of millions of workers that can sweep whole regions clean of animal life. The fungus-growing ants collect vegetable matter as food for symbiotic fungi and then harvest a portion of the fungi as food for the colony. The physical structures that ants build often contain thousands of passageways and appear mazelike to human eyes but are easily navigated by the inhabitants. The important thing to realize is that an ant colony is more than just a bunch of ants. Knowing how each caste in an ant species behaves, while interesting, would not enable a scientist to magically infer that ant colonies would possess so many sophisticated patterns of behavior.

Instead of examining ants, we could have highlighted a number of interesting examples: economic markets that defy prediction, the pattern recognition capabilities of any of the vertebrates, the human immune system's response to viral and bacterial attack, or the evolution of life on our planet. All of these examples are *emergent* in that they contain simple units that, when combined, form a more complex whole. This is a case of the whole of the system being greater than the sum of the parts, which is a fair definition of holism—the very opposite of reductionism.

We also know that agents that exist on one level of understanding are very different from agents on another level: cells are not organs, organs are not animals, and animals are not species. Yet surprisingly the interactions on one level of understanding are often very similar to the interactions on other levels. How so? Consider the following:

- Why do we find self-similar structure in biology, such as trees, ferns, leaves, and twigs? How does this relate to the self-similarity found in inanimate objects such as snowflakes, mountains, and clouds? Is there some way of generalizing the notion of self-similarity to account for both types of phenomena?

- Is there a common reason why it's hard to predict the stock market and also hard to predict weather? Is unpredictability due to limited knowledge or is it somehow inherent in these systems?

- How do collectives such as ant colonies, human brains, and economic markets self-organize to create enormously complex behavior that is much richer than the behavior of the individual component units?

- What is the relationship between evolution, learning, and the adaptation found in social systems? Is adaptation unique to biological systems? What is the relationship between an adaptive system and its environment?

The answers to all of these questions are apparently related to one simple fact: Nature is frugal. Of all the possible rules that could be used to govern the interactions among agents, scientists are finding that nature often uses the simplest. More than that, the same rules are repeatedly used in very different places. To see why, consider the three attributes below that can be used to describe the interactions of agents.

Collections, Multiplicity, and Parallelism Complex systems with emergent properties are often highly parallel collections of similar units. Ant colonies owe much of their sophistication to the fact that they consist of many ants. This is obvious, but consider the implications. A parallel system is inherently more efficient than a sequential system, since tasks can be performed simultaneously and more readily via specialization. Parallel systems that are redundant have fault tolerance. If some ants die, a task still has a good chance of being finished since similar ants can substitute for the missing ones. As an added bonus, subtle variation among the units of a parallel system allows for multiple problem solutions to be attempted simultaneously. For example, gazelles as a species actively seek a solution to the problem of avoiding lions. Some gazelles may be fast, others may be more wary and timid, while others may be more aggressive and protective of their young. A single gazelle cannot exploit all of the posed solutions to the problem of avoiding lions simultaneously, but the species as a whole can. The gazelle with the better solution stands a better chance of living to reproduce. In such a case, the species as a whole can be thought of as having found a better solution through natural selection.

Iteration, Recursion, and Feedback For living things, iteration corresponds to reproduction. We can also expand our scope to include participants of an economic system, antibodies in an immune system, or reinforcement of synapses in the human brain. While parallelism involves multiplicity in a space, iteration involves a form of persistence in time. Similarly, recursion is responsible for the various types of self-similarity seen in nature. Almost all biological systems contain self-similar structures that are made through recurrent processes, while many physical systems contain a form of functional self-similarity that owes its richness to recursion. We will also see that systems are often recurrently coupled to their environment through feedback mechanisms. While animals must react according to their surroundings, they can also change this environment, which means that future actions by an animal will have to take these environmental changes into account.

Adaptation, Learning, and Evolution Interesting systems can change and adapt. Adaptation can be viewed as a consequence of parallelism and iteration in a competitive environment with finite resources. In this case the combination of multiplicity and iteration acts as a sort of filter. We see this when life reproduces because it is fit, companies survive and spawn imitations because they make money, antibodies are copied because they fight infections, and synapses are reinforced because of their usefulness to the organism. With feedback mechanisms in place between an agent and an environment, adaptation can be seen as forming a loop in the cause and effect of changes in both agents and environments.

There are certainly many more ways to describe the interactions of agents; however, multiplicity, iteration, and adaptation by themselves go a long way in describing what it is about interactions between agents that makes them so interesting. Moreover, multiplicity, iteration, and adaptation are universal concepts in that they are apparently important attributes for agents at all levels—from chemical reactants to biological ecosystems.

Looking back at our original goal of attempting to describe the universe, we find that there are a few generalizations that can be made regarding agents and interactions. Describing agents can be tedious, but for the most part it is a simple thing to do with the right tools. Describing interactions is usually far more difficult and nebulous because we have to consider the entire environment in which the agents exist. The simplest type of question that we can ask about an interaction is what will X do next, in the presence of Y? Notice that this question has a functional, algorithmic, or even *computational* feel to it, in that we are concerned not with "What is X?" but with "What will X do?" In this respect, describing an interaction is very similar to discovering nature's "program" for something's behavior. The goal of this book is to highlight the computational beauty found in nature's programs.

1.2 The Convergence of the Sciences

In a way, this book is also a story about scientific progress in the last part of the twentieth century. In the past, and even today, there is a worrisome fragmentation of the sciences. Specifically, scientists' areas of expertise have become so specialized that communication among scientists who are allegedly in the same field has become difficult, if not impossible. For example, the computer sciences can be subdivided into a short list of subdisciplines: programming languages, operating systems, software engineering, database design, numerical analysis, hardware architectures, theory of computation, and artificial intelligence. Most computer scientists can comfortably straddle two or three of the subdisciplines. However, each subdiscipline can be further divided into even more specialized groups, and it is fair to say that a recursion theorist (a subset of theory of computation) will usually have little to talk about with a connectionist (a subset of artificial intelligence). To make things worse, computer science is a new science; that is, the situation is much worse in the older sciences, such as physics and biology.

Traditionally, there has also been a subdivision in most scientific disciplines between theorists and experimentalists. Again, some notable scientists (such as Henri Poincaré, quoted in the preface) have dabbled in both areas, but as a general rule most scientists could be safely classified in one of the two classes.

It is no coincidence that the recent renaissance in the sciences also marks the introduction and proliferation of computers. For the first time, computers have blurred the line between experimentation and theory. One of the first uses of computers was to simulate the evolution of complicated equations. Someone who creates and uses a simulation is simultaneously engaging in theory and experimentation. As computers became more affordable and easy to use, they became a general-purpose tool for all of the sciences. Thus, the line between experimentation and theory has been blurred for all of the disciplines wherever computer simulations provide some benefit.

And just what sort of computer simulations have been built? Meteorologists build weather simulations. Physicists study the flow of plasma and the annealing of metals. Economists have modeled various types of economies. Psychologists have examined cognitive models of the brain. In all cases, scientists have found beauty and elegance in modeling systems that consist of simple, parallel, iterative, and/or adaptive elements. More important, scientists have been making discoveries that have been relevant to multiple fields. Thus, in many ways, the computer has reversed the trend toward fragmentation and has helped the sciences converge to a common point.

1.3 The Silicon Laboratory

Where do we begin? This book is in five parts, with the first part acting as a general introduction to the theory of computation. The remaining four parts highlight what I believe are the four most interesting computational topics today: fractals, chaos, complex systems, and adaptation. Each topic has had popular and technical books devoted to it alone. Some few books deal with two or three of the topics. I hope to convince you that the combination of the five parts is far more interesting taken together than alone. Figure 1.1 illustrates this point further by showing an association map of the book parts. The line segment between any two parts is labeled by a topic that straddles both of the joined parts. Many of the labels in the figure may be unfamiliar to you at this point, but we will eventually see how these topics not only are casually related because of the computational aspect of each but also intricately bounded together into a powerful metaphor for understanding nature's more beautiful phenomena.

An overview of the book's contents follows. Each part is relatively self-contained and can be appreciated on its own. However, this book is also designed so that each part acts as a rough introduction to the next part.

Computation What are the limits of computers and what does it mean to compute? We will examine this question with a bottom-up approach, starting with the properties of different types of numbers and sets. The key point of the first part of this book is that the theory of computation yields a surprisingly simple definition of what it means to compute. We will punctuate this fact by showing how one can construct higher mathematical functions with only a very small set of primitive computational functions as a starting place.

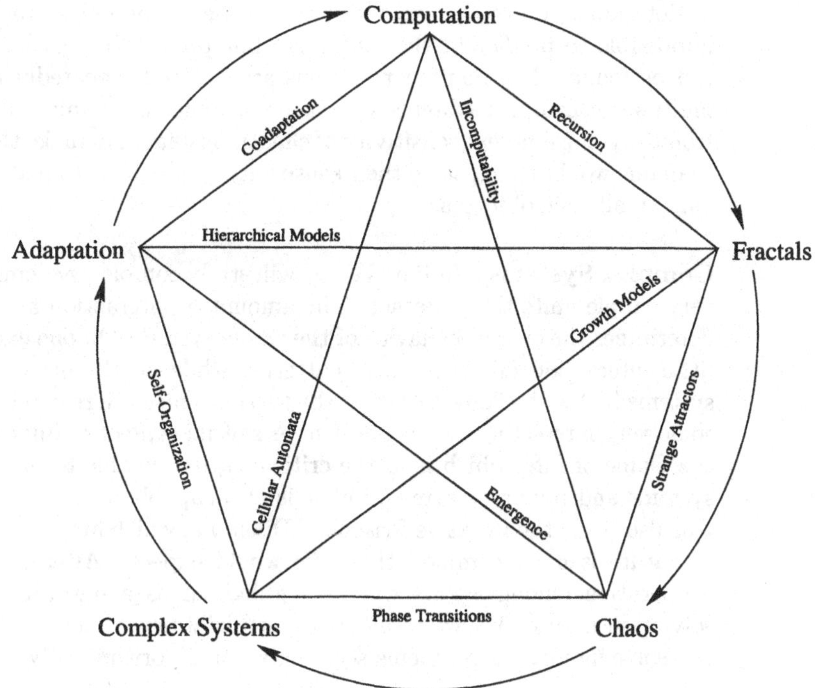

Figure 1.1 An association map of the contents of this book

However, even though the notion of computability is easy to define, it turns out that the process of computation can be extremely rich, complex, and full of pitfalls. We will examine what it means for a function to be incomputable and also see that there are more incomputable functions than computable functions.

Fractals In Part II, we will study various types of *fractals*, which are beautiful images that can be efficiently produced by iterating equations. Since fractals can be computationally described, it is interesting to see that they are often found in natural systems, such as in the way trees and ferns grow or in the branching of bronchial tubes in human lungs. Curiously, the last type of fractal that we will examine in Part II has the same sort of pathological quality that the incomputable programs in Part I have.

Chaos In Part III, we will examine a special type of fractal, known as a *strange attractor*, that is often associated with chaos. Chaos makes the future behavior of deterministic systems such as the weather, economies, and biological systems impossible to predict in the long term but predictable in the short term. Chaos can be found when nonlinear systems are iterated repeatedly but is also found in multi-agent complex systems such as ecosystems, economies, and social structures. Ironically, the inherent sensitivity of chaotic systems can make them easier to control than one would think, since their sensitivity can be used to make large changes with only small control forces.

Complex Systems In Part IV, we will study complex systems consisting of many very simple units that interact. The amount of interaction among agents partially determines the overall behavior of the whole system. On one extreme, systems with little interaction fall into static patterns, while on the other extreme, overactive systems boil with chaos. Between the two extremes is a region of criticality in which some very interesting things happen. A special type of cellular automata known as the Game of Life, which is in the critical region, is able to produce self-replicating systems and roving creatures, but it is also capable of universal computation. We will also study the Iterative Prisoners' Dilemma, which may explain why cooperation in nature is more common than one would expect. Afterward, competition and cooperation among agents will be highlighted as a natural method of problem-solving in nature. We will see how an artificial neural network with fixed synapses can solve interesting problems seemingly non-algorithmically.

Adaptation Finally, in Part V, we will allow our complex systems to change, adapt, learn, and evolve. The focus of these chapters will include evolutionary systems, classifier systems, and artificial neural networks. Genetic algorithms will be used to evolve solutions to a wide variety of problems. We will also see how a simple form of feedback coupled with evolutionary mechanisms can be used to mimic a form of intelligence in classifier systems. We will then examine how artificial neural networks can be trained by example to solve pattern classification and function approximation problems. At the end of this part, we will see how in many ways one can view learning, evolution, and cultural adaptation as one process occurring on varying time scales.

Throughout this book we will talk about physics, biology, economics, evolution, and a host of other topics, but the prevailing theme will be to use the computer as a laboratory and a metaphor for understanding the universe.

I Computation

Any discrete piece of information can be represented by a set of numbers. Systems that compute can represent powerful mappings from one set of numbers to another. Moreover, any program on any computer is equivalent to a number mapping. These mappings can be thought of as statements about the properties of numbers; hence, there is a close connection between computer programs and mathematical proofs. But there are more possible mappings than possible programs; thus, there are some things that simply cannot be computed. The actual process of computing can be defined in terms of a very small number of primitive operations, with *recursion* and/or *iteration* comprising the most fundamental pieces of a computing device. Computing devices can also make statements about other computing devices. This leads to a fundamental paradox that ultimately exposes the limitations not just of of machine logic, but all of nature as well.

Chapter 2 introduces some important properties of different types of numbers, sets, and infinities. Chapter 3 expands on this by introducing the concepts behind computation and shows how computation can be seen to operate over sets of integers. Chapter 4 ties together some of the paradoxes seen in the earlier chapters to show how they are applicable to all of mathematics.

2 Number Systems and Infinity

It is strange that we know so little about the properties of numbers. They are our handiwork, yet they baffle us; we can fathom only a few of their intricacies. Having defined their attributes and prescribed their behavior, we are hard pressed to perceive the implications of our formulas.
— James R. Newman

Our minds are finite, and yet even in these circumstances of finitude we are surrounded by possibilities that are infinite, and the purpose of human life is to grasp as much as we can out of the infinitude.
— Alfred North Whitehead

THERE ARE TWO complementary images that we should consider before starting this chapter. The first is how a painter or sculptor modifies a medium to create original structure from what was without form. The second is how sound waves propagate through a medium to travel from one point to another. Both images serve as metaphors for the motivation behind this and the next chapter. As for the first image, just as a painter adds pigment to canvas and a sculptor bends and molds clay, so a programmer twiddles bits within silicon. The second image relates to the way information within a computer is subject to the constraints of the environment in which it exists, namely, the computer itself.

The key word in both metaphors is "medium," yet there is a subtle difference in each use of the word. When a human programs a computer, quite often the underlying design of the program represents a mathematical process that is often creative and beautiful in its own right. The fact that good programs are logical by necessity does not diminish the beauty at all. In fact, the acts of blending colors, composing a fugue, and chiseling stone are all subject to their own logical rules, but since the result of these actions seems far removed from logic, it is easy to forget that the rules are really in place. Nevertheless, I would like you to consider the computer as a medium of expression just as you would canvas or clay.

As for the second metaphor, everything that is dynamic exists and changes in accordance with the environment in which it exists. The interactions among objects and environments are also governed by a well-defined set of rules. Similarly, programs executing inside of a computer are by definition following a logical path; thus one could think of a computer as a medium in which programs flow just as sound travels through matter.

There is also a sort of yin-yang duality in this idea that I find pleasing. One of the first items covered in an introductory physics course is the difference between potential and kinetic energy. You can think of potential energy as the energy stored in, say, a battery or a rock placed on top of a hill. Kinetic energy is energy that is in the process of being converted, as when the stored electricity in a battery drives a motor and when a rock rolls down a hill. Similarly, when a human designs a program, there exists a potential computation that is unleashed when the program executes within a computer. Thus, one can think of the computation as being kinetic and in motion. Moreover, just as a child with a firecracker can be surprised by the difference between potential and kinetic energy, so computer programmers are often surprised (even pleasantly) by the difference between potential and kinetic computation.

Now that we've agreed to look at the computer as a medium, and since this book is really about looking at the universe in terms of processes familiar to computer scientists, the next two chapters are devoted exclusively to the properties of numbers and computers.

2.1 Introduction to Number Properties

Sometime around the fifth century B.C., the Greek philosopher Zeno posed a paradox that now bears his name. Suppose that Achilles and a tortoise are to run a footrace. Let's assume that Achilles is exactly twice as fast as the tortoise. (Our tortoise is obviously a veritable Hercules among his kind.) To make things fair, the tortoise will get a head start of 1000 meters. After the start of the race, by the time Achilles runs 1000 meters, the tortoise is still ahead by 500 meters. However, Achilles is a far superior athlete, so he easily covers the next 500 meters. During this time, the tortoise has managed to go another 250 meters. We can repeat the process for an infinite number of time slices while always finding the tortoise just a bit ahead of Achilles. Will Achilles ever catch up to the tortoise?

Clearly, we know that something is amiss with the story, as common sense tells us that the world doesn't work this way and that there exists some distance in which Achilles should be able to overcome the tortoise and pass it. But what is that distance and how long does it take Achilles to finally reach the tortoise? There is an algebraic solution to the problem, but this doesn't directly address the paradox of Achilles always being somewhat behind the tortoise when we break the race up into small time slices.

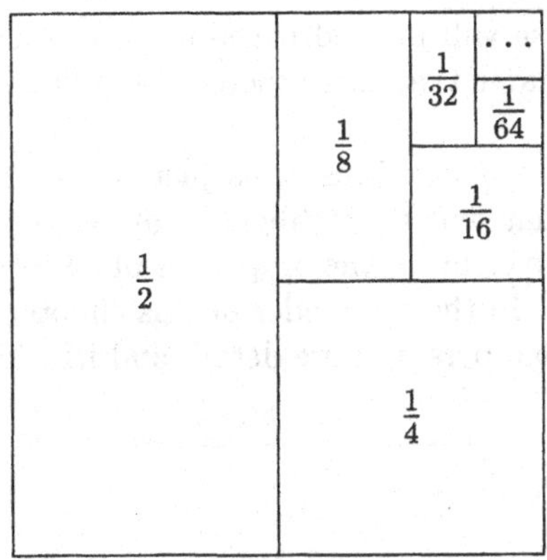

Figure 2.1 An infinite summation captured in a square

Let's add a little more information to the story and concentrate on the question of how long it will take Achilles to catch up to the tortoise. First, let's assume that Achilles can run 1000 meters in exactly one minute. After one minute, Achilles has traveled 1000 meters while the tortoise has covered 500. When Achilles travels the next 500 meters (and the tortoise another 250), one-half of a minute has passed. Similarly, each "time slice" that we are looking at will be exactly half the previous time.

Recall that it was earlier stated that we could look at an infinite number of time slices and always come to the conclusion that the tortoise was always slightly ahead of Achilles. However, just because there is an infinite number of time slices, it does not necessarily mean that the sum of all of the time slices (the total elapsed time) is also infinite. More specifically, what is the sum total of $1 + \frac{1}{2} + \frac{1}{4} + \frac{1}{8} + \cdots$?

Forget for the moment that the 1 appears in the sum and just concentrate on the fractions. Another way of writing this is:

$$\sum_{i=1}^{\infty} \frac{1}{2^i} = \frac{1}{2} + \frac{1}{4} + \frac{1}{8} + \cdots.$$

At any step in the infinite sum we can represent the current running total by the area of a divided box whose total area is 1. At each step, we divide the empty portion of the box in half, mark one side as used and leave the other half for the next step. As Figure 2.1 illustrates, if we continue the process for an infinite number of steps, we will eventually fill the box. Therefore, the sum total of all of the infinite time slices is really equal to two minutes ($1 + 1 =$ one minute for the infinite sum and the other minute that we originally ignored). Moreover, since we know that Achilles can run exactly 1000 meters a minute, we can conclude that Achilles and the tortoise will be tied if the track is 2000 meters in length. If the track is any length greater than 2000 meters, Achilles will win the race; any less, and Achilles will lose.

Zeno's paradox illustrates just one of the interesting aspects of numbers and infinity that will be highlighted in this chapter. To solve the paradox, we were required to examine the properties of an infinite summation of fractions (or rational numbers). In the remainder of this chapter, we will look at counting numbers, the rational numbers in more detail, and irrational numbers.

2.2 Counting Numbers

Consider the set of natural numbers: 1, 2, 3, ... We know that there is an infinite number of natural numbers. We can say the same thing about all of the even natural numbers. But are there more numbers than even numbers? Surprisingly, the size of the two sets is identical. The reason is that for every member in the set of natural numbers, there is a corresponding member in the set of even numbers. For example, we could construct what is known as a one-to-one mapping:

$$\begin{array}{cccccccc} 1 & 2 & 3 & 4 & 5 & 6 & \\ \updownarrow & \updownarrow & \updownarrow & \updownarrow & \updownarrow & \updownarrow & \cdots. \\ 2 & 4 & 6 & 8 & 10 & 12 & \end{array}$$

What about more complex sets, such as the set of all perfect cubes? Before answering this question, let's examine the first five perfect cubes in the context of the other natural numbers:

$$\boxed{1}\ 2\ 3\ 4\ 5\ 6\ 7\ \boxed{8}\ 9\ 10\ 11\ 12\ 13\ 14\ 15\ 16\ 17\ 18\ 19\ 20\ 21\ 22\ 23\ 24\ 25\ 26$$
$$\boxed{27}\ 28\ 29\ 30\ 31\ 32\ 33\ 34\ 35\ 36\ 37\ 38\ 39\ 40\ 41\ 42\ 43\ 44\ 45\ 46\ 47\ 48\ 49$$
$$50\ 51\ 52\ 53\ 54\ 55\ 56\ 57\ 58\ 59\ 60\ 61\ 62\ 63\ \boxed{64}\ 65\ 66\ 67\ 68\ 69\ 70\ 71\ 72$$
$$73\ 74\ 75\ 76\ 77\ 78\ 79\ 80\ 81\ 82\ 83\ 84\ 85\ 86\ 87\ 88\ 89\ 90\ 91\ 92\ 93\ 94\ 95$$
$$96\ 97\ 98\ 99\ 100\ 101\ 102\ 103\ 104\ 105\ 106\ 107\ 108\ 109\ 110\ 111\ 112\ 113$$
$$114\ 115\ 116\ 117\ 118\ 119\ 120\ 121\ 122\ 123\ 124\ \boxed{125}\ \cdots.$$

Since the space between successive perfect cubes grows dramatically and perfect cubes become less common as we move down the list, you may think that there are far more natural numbers than perfect cubes. This is wrong. There are two reasons why the number of perfect cubes is equal to the number of natural numbers. First, the function to produce perfect cubes is invertible. If I tell you that I am looking at perfect cubes and you give me an example, say 2197, with some effort I can respond by saying that your number is the thirteenth perfect cube. Also, this function yields a one-to-one mapping between its argument and its result, just like the mapping from natural numbers to even numbers. A more general picture of a one-to-one mapping looks like:

$$\begin{array}{cccccccc} 1 & 2 & 3 & 4 & 5 & 6 & & \\ \updownarrow & \updownarrow & \updownarrow & \updownarrow & \updownarrow & \updownarrow & \cdots, \\ \mathrm{f}(1) & \mathrm{f}(2) & \mathrm{f}(3) & \mathrm{f}(4) & \mathrm{f}(5) & \mathrm{f}(6) & \end{array}$$

where $f(x)$ is our mapping function. Depending on the circumstances, instead of talking about the natural numbers $\{1, 2, 3, \ldots\}$ it may be more appropriate for us to talk about integers $\{\ldots, -1, 0, 1, \ldots\}$ or the positive integers $\{0, 1, 2, \ldots\}$. It really doesn't matter which of these sets we are using, because all of them have same number of elements; that is, they all contain a *countably infinite* number of elements.

2.3 Rational Numbers

A rational number (or fraction) is a number that can be represented as the ratio of two natural numbers, such as a/b, with the understanding that the denominator, b, is never zero. One limiting aspect of the natural numbers is that for any two natural numbers, there is only a finite number of natural numbers between them. This is not so for the rational numbers. To convince yourself of this, you only need to take the average of any two different rational numbers. For example, given a_1/b_1 and a_2/b_2, we can compute the arithmetical mean or average as $(a_1b_2 + a_2b_1)/(2b_1b_2)$. Call this average a_3/b_3. We can repeat the process as long as we like by taking the average of a_1/b_1 and a_3/b_3, then a_1/b_1 and a_4/b_4, and so on.

Notice that there is no such thing as the smallest nonzero rational number, which implies that we simply cannot enumerate all of them by size. However, we can construct a simple procedure to enumerate all of the rationals based on another method. To do this, we will consider only rational numbers between 0 and 1 at first (excluding 0 and including 1), which implies that $a \leq b$. We can construct a triangular matrix that contains all of the rationals between 0 and 1 by having one row per denominator. In row b, there are exactly b columns, one for each value of a with $a \leq b$. The first few entries of the table look like this:

$$\begin{array}{cccccc} \frac{1}{1} & & & & & \\ \frac{1}{2} & \boxed{\frac{2}{2}} & & & & \\ \frac{1}{3} & \frac{2}{3} & \boxed{\frac{3}{3}} & & & \\ \frac{1}{4} & \boxed{\frac{2}{4}} & \frac{3}{4} & \boxed{\frac{4}{4}} & & \\ \frac{1}{5} & \frac{2}{5} & \frac{3}{5} & \frac{4}{5} & \boxed{\frac{5}{5}} & \\ \vdots & \vdots & \vdots & \vdots & \vdots & \ddots \end{array}$$

The boxed fractions are repeats and can be removed from the table so that all entries represent unique rational numbers. Now, if we read the table left-to-right and top-down (as one would read a book), all of the fractions between 0 and 1 will eventually be encountered. Thus, we could map each fraction between 0 and 1 to an odd natural number:

$$\begin{array}{cccccccccc} 1 & 3 & 5 & 7 & 9 & 11 & 13 & 15 & 17 & 19 \\ \updownarrow & \updownarrow & \updownarrow & \updownarrow & \updownarrow & \updownarrow & \updownarrow & \updownarrow & \updownarrow & \updownarrow \\ \frac{1}{1} & \frac{1}{2} & \frac{1}{3} & \frac{2}{3} & \frac{1}{4} & \frac{3}{4} & \frac{1}{5} & \frac{2}{5} & \frac{3}{5} & \frac{4}{5} \end{array} \cdots.$$

For rational numbers greater than 1, we know that $a > b$. By taking the reciprocal of such a fraction, b/a, we are left with a number that is strictly greater than 0 and less than 1. Therefore, by the same process that allowed us to map the small fractions to the odd numbers, we can map the large fractions to the even numbers.

This leads us to a startling conclusion: There are as many natural numbers as fractions! The most important point about our construction is that it is one-to-one and invertible. Specifically, if you wanted to play devil's advocate and claim that the mapping failed, you would have to produce two rational numbers that mapped to the same natural number or one rational number that mapped to no natural number. Based on our method of construction, we are guaranteed that this will never happen.

2.4 Irrational Numbers

Fractions are known as rational numbers because they can be expressed as the ratio of two natural numbers. Irrational numbers, such as π and $\sqrt{2}$, are numbers that cannot be represented as the ratio of two natural numbers. If we represent a number by its decimal expansion, we find that rational numbers have a finite or a periodic decimal expansion, while irrational numbers have an infinite decimal expansion that has no pattern. For example, the rational number $\frac{1}{3}$ has the decimal expansion $0.\bar{3}$, where the bar over the last digit signifies that the expansion repeats forever. Moreover, there are numbers such as $0.12345\overline{6789}$ that are also rational because the last four digits repeat. Whenever a number's decimal expansion falls into a pattern, it is always possible to convert the decimal expansion into a fraction.

Taking the analysis one step further, rational numbers can also be represented as a summation of fractions, such as $0.123 = \frac{1}{10} + \frac{2}{100} + \frac{3}{1000}$. What about the repeating fractions? It turns out that the repeating fractions require an infinite summation, but this is not a problem for us because the infinite series converges to a rational number. We saw this when we solved Zeno's paradox and computed that the footrace between Achilles and the tortoise would be tied two minutes into the race.

Infinite series of this type reveal a quirky aspect of rational numbers. Specifically, for any rational number we can construct multiple decimal expansions that

Is the Square Root of 2 Really Irrational?	**Digression 2.1**

Here is a great proof that $\sqrt{2}$ is irrational. It was first discovered by Pythagoras around the fifth century B.C. The technique is called a proof by contradiction and starts off with the assumption that $\sqrt{2}$ is actually rational. By making this assumption, we will be faced with an impossibility, which implies that $\sqrt{2}$ is in fact irrational.

Now if $\sqrt{2}$ is rational, then it is equal to some fraction, a/b. Let's take the square of the fraction that we know is equal to 2. We now have the equality $a^2/b^2 = 2$. Multiply each side by b^2 to get $a^2 = 2b^2$. Here comes the tricky part: We are going to take advantage of the fact that every natural number has a unique prime factorization. Taking the prime factorization of a and b, we know that the prime factorization of a^2 must have twice as many 2s as the factorization for a. The same thing applies to b^2 and b. Therefore, the prime factorizations of a^2 and b^2 must have an even number of 2s.

Now, looking at the equation $a^2 = 2b^2$, we know that the left side has an even number of 2s while the right side has an odd number of 2s. One side will have more than the other. We don't know which side, but we don't care. If we take the product of the smaller number of 2s and divide each side of $a^2 = 2b^2$ by that number, then one side will have at least one 2 in it, while the other will have none. Since 2 is the only even prime number and an odd number multiplied by an odd number always yields an odd result, we know that the side with the 2s must be an even number while the side with no 2 is an odd number. A contradiction! Therefore, it is impossible for $\sqrt{2}$ to be expressed as a fraction.

are clearly different but are numerically equivalent. As an example consider the equivalence of $1 = 0.\bar{9}$. It may seem counterintuitive to state that 1 and $0.\bar{9}$ are equal, but in fact they are because $\frac{9}{10} + \frac{9}{100} + \frac{9}{1000} + \cdots = 1$. This is not some subtle flaw in the properties of numbers, but an artifact of the different ways we can represent them.

Another way to represent a number is as a point on a number line. We are all familiar with the process of labeling a number line and placing a point on it to represent a particular value. This is easy enough for natural numbers and rationals, but where would you put a point on a number line for an irrational number? For example, suppose we want to put a point on a number line for the value of $\sqrt{2} = 1.41421356\cdots$. We could approximate $\sqrt{2}$ with three digits and place a point at 1.41 on the number line. However, we know that $\sqrt{2}$ is really a little bit to the right of 1.41, so we go one step further and put another point at 1.414. Once again our estimate is a bit short of the true location. It would seem that we could continue the process indefinitely, always failing to put a point on the correct location.

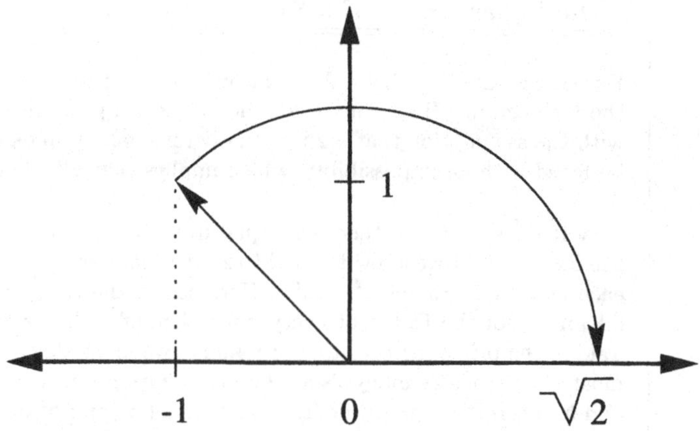

Figure 2.2 Isolating the square root of two on the number line

Does $\sqrt{2}$ really have a true location on the number line and can we find it? Our problem seems to be that $\sqrt{2}$ is always to the right of our best estimate, but we could approach the problem from another side, literally. Instead of using 1.41 as a first guess, we can use 1.42, which is just larger than $\sqrt{2}$. At the next step we use 1.415, and so on. Now we have $\sqrt{2}$ trapped. In fact, the infinite sequence of the $\sqrt{2}$ converges to a real location on the number line, just like the infinite series in Zeno's paradox. By approaching that point from each side, we can see that it can be isolated. Another method for isolating $\sqrt{2}$ is best illustrated with the diagram in Figure 2.2.

In Figure 2.2, I have constructed a triangle with two sides equal to 1 in length. We know that the third side must have a length equal to $\sqrt{1+1}$. Now take the arrow of length $\sqrt{2}$ and swing it around to the x-axis. Voila! We have found $\sqrt{2}$.

Up to this point, we found that natural numbers, integers, and fractions all contain the same infinite number of elements. Is there the same number of irrational numbers as well? Let's assume for the moment that there are. We will attempt to construct a one-to-one mapping, just as before, between the natural numbers and the irrational numbers to see what will happen. Below is a table with a natural number on the left side and some corresponding irrational number on the right side. Unfortunately, we cannot write out the full decimal expansion of the irrational numbers in the table, but this does not matter for our purposes. Moreover, instead of writing digits for the irrational numbers, we will use the notation x_{ij} to signify the jth digit of the irrational number that maps to i, and to keep things simple, we will worry only about irrational numbers between 0 and 1 so that each digit is to the right of the decimal point, as in $0.x_{i1}x_{i2}x_{i3}\cdots$.

$$\begin{array}{cccccccc}
1 & \leftrightarrow & \boxed{x_{11}} & x_{12} & x_{13} & x_{14} & x_{15} & \cdots \\
2 & \leftrightarrow & x_{21} & \boxed{x_{22}} & x_{23} & x_{24} & x_{25} & \cdots \\
3 & \leftrightarrow & x_{31} & x_{32} & \boxed{x_{33}} & x_{34} & x_{35} & \cdots \\
4 & \leftrightarrow & x_{41} & x_{42} & x_{43} & \boxed{x_{44}} & x_{45} & \cdots \\
5 & \leftrightarrow & x_{51} & x_{52} & x_{53} & x_{54} & \boxed{x_{55}} & \cdots \\
\vdots & & \vdots & \vdots & \vdots & \vdots & \vdots & \ddots
\end{array}$$

Boxes have been placed around the diagonal elements to highlight them. Now the important question is: Does this mapping work? Remarkably the mapping fails, but this is not a failure for us because we have found a deeper truth concerning the nature of irrational numbers. To see that the mapping fails, we must first agree that for it to work, there must be a place in the table for all of the irrational numbers. This seems reasonable, but consider an irrational number that is constructed as a sequence of digits that differ from the diagonal entries. If we represent this new number in the same way as the irrational numbers in our table, it will look like:

$$\text{NOT } x_{11} \quad \text{NOT } x_{22} \quad \text{NOT } x_{33} \quad \text{NOT } x_{44} \quad \text{NOT } x_{55} \quad \cdots .$$

If we try to find a place in our table for this irrational number, we are faced with the inevitable conclusion that our new number cannot exist in the table because it will always differ from each entry in the table by at least one digit. Specifically, if we assume it belongs in the table at, say, line 835, then by virtue of the way we constructed the number, the 835th digit must differ from the real entry at line 835.

We have just proved that the infinity of the irrational numbers is greater than the infinity of the natural numbers. In doing so, we followed in the footsteps of the great German mathematician Georg Cantor, who invented set theory and was the first to prove that not all infinities are equal. Since the size of the natural numbers is countably infinite, the size of all of the real numbers is properly referred to as *uncountably infinite*.

The next property of numbers that we will examine in this chapter concerns the density of the real number line. Let's start by considering only a mapping between the positive real numbers into a segment between 0 and 1. Including the negative real numbers or using a different segment is just as easy, but the examples will be clearer if we use this restriction. It turns out that any segment of finite length on the real number line is infinitely dense, in that you can squeeze all of the real numbers into it. As before, this is accomplished with a mapping function with a few special properties. The first property of our function is that it must be monotonically increasing. A monotone function is one that strictly increases or decreases but never both. This is a formal way of saying that the mapping function has no "humps." Readers familiar with calculus will recognize this property as a way of saying that the first derivative of a function is never 0. Further specifying that the function is increasing means that for any two arguments, a and b, if $a > b$,

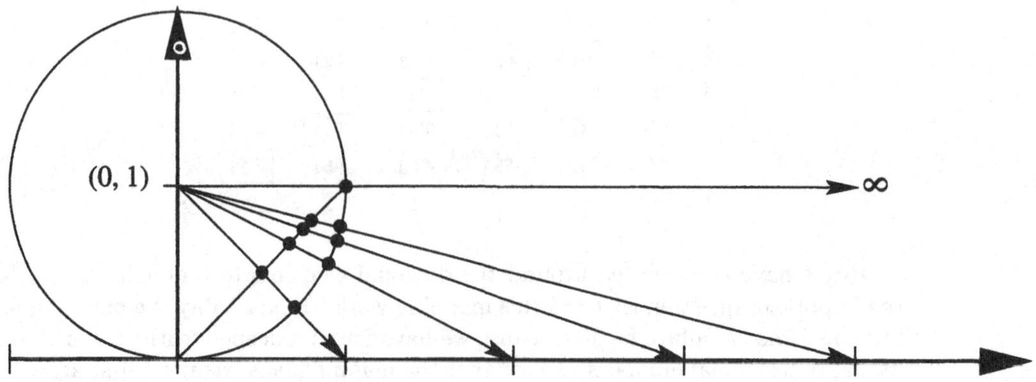

Figure 2.3 Mapping real numbers into a circle or a segment

then for the mapping function, $f(x)$, $f(a) > f(b)$. The second property is that the mapping function must asymptotically approach a constant value as the function argument approaches infinity. This means that if we increase the function argument, the function result will get larger, but each further increase will increase the function result by only a little bit more each time. The function result will get infinitely close to a constant value of our choice but never quite reach it. This is very similar in spirit to how an infinite series converges to a constant value.

Figure 2.3 demonstrates two mapping functions that meet our requirements. To see how they work, consider a vector starting at the coordinate (0, 1) and ending at some value on the number line. The number at the end of the vector is the one that we want to map into another value between 0 and 1. As the vector travels to its destination, it always passes through a fixed location on the unit circle centered at (0, 1). We can put a mark on the circle where the vector passes through. Notice that no matter how large the vector is, it will always hit somewhere in the bottom right quarter of the circle. Therefore, the x-coordinate of the marked points will always be between 0 and 1. In this way we have mapped all of the numbers on the number line to a corresponding point on the surface of the circle. Doing this type of mapping in higher dimensions is known as constructing a Riemann sphere.

Instead of mapping the vectors to a point on the surface of a circle, we can just as easily map them to a line segment that extends from (0, 0) to (1, 1). Figure 2.3 also shows this type of mapping, which is a bit easier to understand analytically. The line equation of the vector is $y = 1 - \frac{x}{c}$, where c is the number on the number line that we are mapping from. The line equation of the segment from (0, 0) to (1, 1) is simply $y = x$. By combining these two equations and solving for x, we end up with the equation $y = \frac{x}{x+1}$. Thus, if we plug any positive real value into the last equation, we will always get another number between 0 and 1. It is often tempting to try to imagine a size for infinity—but doing so is actually misleading. Using Figure 2.3 as a reference allows us to think of infinity as the direction, pointing due east.

Let's pause for a moment to consider what we have found so far. The natural numbers and integers occupy fixed locations on the number line at regular intervals. We know that there is the same number of rational numbers, but strangely enough there is a countably infinite number of rationals between any two points on the number line. We also isolated an irrational number on the number line, so we know that irrational numbers have a fixed place on the line as well. What is truly bizarre is that even though there is an infinite number of rational numbers between any two rational numbers on the number line, there are infinitely more irrational numbers than rational numbers in the same segment. Going back to the example of isolating $\sqrt{2}$ on the number line, there was a countably infinite number of rational number pairs that we could use to get increasingly closer to the real location of $\sqrt{2}$. Yet between any of those pairs of rational numbers there is an uncountably infinite number of irrational numbers. It is as if the points on the number line where the irrational numbers fall are like holes in which rational numbers are not. However, there are many, many more of these irrational holes than non-holes.

To fully appreciate how truly amazing rational and irrational numbers are, we will now use an irrational number as a sort of infinite memory. Because you are reading this book, I am going to assume that you have some general idea of how computers work. Specifically, you probably already know that computers store everything as one long sequence of zeros and ones. You also know that the number of natural numbers (or fractions) that you can store in your computer is determined solely by how much memory you have; that is, if you want to store twice as many numbers as you can now, you need to double your computer's memory. Therefore, no matter how many numbers you have, no matter how large the numbers are, as long as they are natural (or rational) and finite in size, there is some amount of memory that will do the job of storing the numbers.

Now, take all of your computer's memory and arrange it as one long line of zeros and ones: 0, 1, 1, 1, 0, 0, 0, 1, 1, 0, 1, ... Take this very long number and put a zero and a decimal point in front of it. We've just translated one huge number into a rational number between 0 and 1. By placing this single point at exactly the right spot on the number line, we can store an unlimited amount of information. Ah, if only it were so simple. In the real world, we simply don't have the precision required to put this method of storing memory into practice. We never will, either, but it's an interesting mental exercise to see that it can be done in theory in an idealized world. The point of this whole mental exercise is that in many ways an irrational number has as much "information" as an infinite number of natural numbers.

Figure 2.4 illustrates some of the properties that we have found so far about numbers. The set of all of the numbers on the number line is called the real numbers. The reals can be divided into rational numbers and irrational numbers. A proper

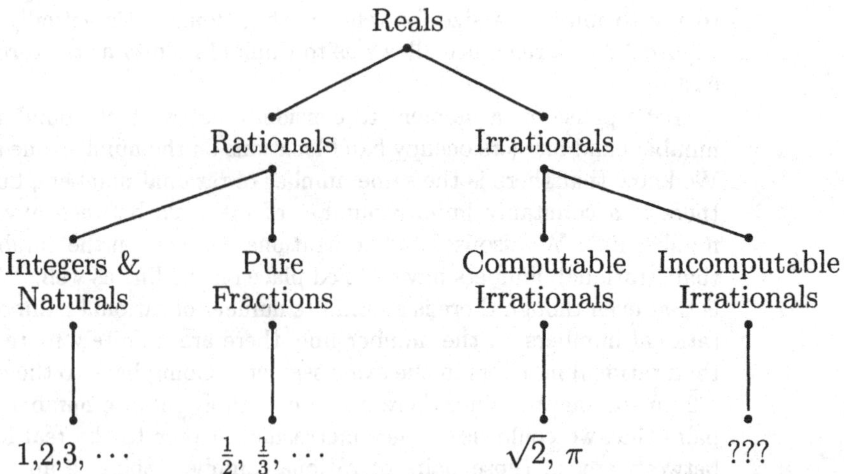

Figure 2.4 Subdivision of the real numbers

subset, A, of another subset, B, is a set such that all of the members of A are also members of B, but there exists some member of B that is not a member of A (for example, cars are a proper subset of vehicles). We can now say with certainty that the natural numbers are a proper subset of the rationals. Similarly, the irrationals have a proper subset known as the computable irrationals. You are already familiar with some computable irrational numbers, such as π and $\sqrt{2}$. In the next chapter we will define what it means to compute, which will give us some insight into what uncomputable irrational numbers look like.

2.5 Further Reading

Beckmann, P. (1977). *A history of π* (Fourth ed.). Boulder, Colo.: Golem Press.

Dauben, J. W. (1990). *Georg Cantor: His mathematics and philosophy of the infinite.* Princeton: Princeton University Press.

Ore, O. (1988). *Number theory and its history.* New York: Dover.

Rucker, R. (1995). *Infinity and the mind: The science and philosophy of the infinite.* Princeton: Princeton University Press.

Stewart, I. (1996). *From here to infinity.* Oxford: Oxford University Press.

3 Computability and Incomputability

Computer Science is no more about computers than astronomy is about telescopes.
— E. W. Dijkstra

To use: Apply shampoo to wet hair. Massage to lather, then rinse. Repeat.
— A typical hair-washing algorithm that fails to halt

But let your communication be Yea, yea; Nay, nay: for whatsoever is more than these cometh of evil.
— An early proposal for binary code, Matthew 5:37

FOR MOST PEOPLE, the notion of what is computable is closely related to what types of programs exist. A typical computer has an operating system that acts as an interface between the computer hardware and the software. Window systems that provide graphical user interfaces to other programs are at an even higher level of abstraction. A typical program that could operate in this environment is a word-processing program that allows the user to type in keystrokes and to perform mouse actions such as pointing, clicking, dragging, and using menus. Many things appear to be happening at once, but in fact each action by the user is processed by the computer program during a discrete time interval. When you type a key to insert text into your document, the program must update the graphical representation of your document by drawing the raw pixels that make up the letters. The program will usually have to update some internal representation of the text of your document as well. Similarly, when you use a mouse, the program translates the mouse clicks to a coordinate system and performs whatever action is required to make the graphical representation of your document look the way it is supposed to. Each action is carefully coordinated by the computer program, which can be a daunting task, considering the thousands of details that go into writing a program such as a word processor.

The example above illustrates an interactive session that a human could have with a program; however, there is no reason why the session would have to be interactive at all. As a thought experiment, imagine that we could record each keystroke and mouse action. The recording could be saved into a file that has strings[1] of the form `keystroke 'k'`, `mouse-down (113, 156)`, or `mouse-up (115, 234)`. It is always possible to take a program like a word processor and convert it into a similar program that processes a file that has the recorded actions. If one of those actions corresponded to pulling down a menu and selecting a "save file" option, then one form of the output of the program can be saved as well. Moreover, each graphical action taken by the word processor could be saved into another file with entries indicating which pixels were drawn and in what color. In this way it is possible to convert any program into a form that takes one long string as input and produces one long string as output.

As a historical footnote, in the early days of computers, both programs and input data had to be submitted to a computer via an antiquated device known as a punch-card reader. The output of the program could then be sent to a printer or some other device. Graphical user interfaces are a very convenient way of using a computer, but in no way does the user interface change what is fundamentally possible for a computer to compute. If a mad computer programmer had the desire to, there is no reason why he couldn't have simulated an entire interactive computer session back in the 1950s with punch cards and printer output.

Therefore, without losing any of the notion of what it means to compute, we can completely disregard the "bells and whistles" of modern computers and only concentrate on the gist of what happens inside of a computer. What is left is a picture not unlike the earliest computer mainframes that handled only punch cards as input. Why bother to do this? If we were to attempt to discuss the notion of computability in the context of user interfaces, sound cards, mice, and laser printers, there would be no clear way of reducing all of the detail into something that looks remotely mathematical. If we could not reduce what happens inside of computers into some mathematical formalism, there would be no way of proving or disproving the properties that computers have.

Scientists like to boil things down to the simplest terms possible, and it turns out that this picture of having a string of input and a string of output is still overly verbose for a theoretical computer scientist's tastes. Just as we were able to dispense with most of the details of how modern computers operate, so it is possible to dispense with the idea that programs have "strings" of input and output. It is possible (and also theoretically useful) to convert a program, input string, or output string into a single natural number.

---

[1] The term *string* will be used to denote any sequence of letters, numbers, or digits, or any other type of list.

3.1 Gödelization

Kurt Gödel, one of the greatest mathematicians of the twentieth century, literally shocked his contemporaries with some of his mathematical results. We will talk more about Gödel and his contributions to mathematics toward the end of this book part; however, in this section we will concentrate on the process for converting many numbers into one number that bears his name.

A *Gödelization* is a method for mapping many natural numbers into a single natural number. The details of how the mapping is performed are not very interesting, but the fact that it can be done is extremely important. Recall that the input or output to a program can be represented as some finite-length string. Also note that a program can be represented in the same way. Don't be bothered by the fact that one form of the input string may look like **keystroke 'k'** or some other nonnumerical form. We can always adopt some convention whereby we agree to represent actions such as **keystroke 'k'** by two natural numbers, one for the action, **keystroke**, and the other for the key that was pressed, **'k'**. It is always possible to perform some mapping such that any string is unambiguously coded into a sequence of integers. The interesting question is: How can many numbers be encoded into one?

The key to the whole process is the fact that every number has a unique prime factorization. If you pick any natural number, x, then there is exactly one sequence of prime numbers, $p_{x_1}, p_{x_2}, \ldots, p_{x_n}$, such that the product of the n prime numbers is equal to x. Now, let's go back to looking at a program's input, which we earlier agreed to think of as a sequence of numbers. If there are n numbers in the sequence, then let every number in the sequence be denoted by $x_1, x_2, \ldots, x_n$. To calculate the Gödel number of the input string, we use the first n prime numbers and calculate

$$\prod_{i=1}^{n} p_i^{x_i} = p_1^{x_1} p_2^{x_2} \cdots p_n^{x_n},$$

which forms a unique natural number. Granted, Gödel numbers will tend to be huge in size, but who cares? Given a Gödel number, we can reconstruct the original string by taking the prime factorization of the Gödel number. If there are thirteen 2s in the prime factorization of the Gödel number, then that means that the first number in the original string was 13. If there are eighty-seven 3s in the prime factorization, then the second number in the original string was 87. And if there is a single 5 in the prime factorization, then the third number was 1.

Gödelization adds another simplification to studying the nature of computation. Instead of worrying about programs with multiple input and output sequences we can now ignore most of the details and just concentrate on functions that take a single number as input and produce a single number as output. Even with this restriction, a computer program that operates in this manner is still doing all of

How Many Prime Numbers Exist?	**Digression 3.1**

Constructing a Gödel number from a string depends on there existing an infinite number of prime numbers. If there were only a finite number of prime numbers, say n of them, then it would be impossible to encode strings of length greater than n. Here is an extremely elegant proof discovered by Euclid around the third century B.C. that shows that there are an infinite number of primes.

If there are a finite number of prime numbers, then we could list all of them as $p_1, p_2, \ldots, p_n$, where p_n is the largest prime number. We will now construct a new number from these n prime numbers by taking the product of all n prime numbers and adding one

$$p' = \prod_{i=1}^{n} p_i + 1 = (p_1 p_2 \cdots p_n) + 1.$$

What does the prime factorization of p' look like? Before you answer, take note of the fact that none of the n prime numbers, $p_1, \ldots, p_n$, evenly divides p'. Try it and you will see that you always get a remainder of 1. But if no prime number evenly divides p', then one of two things must be true: Either p' is prime or it is not and there exists some other prime number greater than p_n that does evenly divide p'. We don't care which is the case, since either implies that there is another prime number greater than p_n. Therefore, there must be an infinite number of primes.

the "hard" part of computing. Therefore, without loss of generalization, when we speak of computation, we will sometimes refer to the computation as manipulating strings, numbers, or even bits. It really doesn't matter. What does matter is that the representation of a computer's input and output can always be converted from one form to another. We will simply use whatever form is most convenient at the time.

Another conclusion that can be reached from the ideas of this section is that there are as many programs as there are natural numbers, since we can Gödelize programs as well. This fact will be expanded on toward the end of this chapter. In the next section we will get into the details of what it means to compute by studying some models of computation.

3.2 Models of Computation

There is a subtle difference between computations and models of computation that we should examine. It is fair to think of a computation as a "method" for producing one number from another. Computer textbooks often speak of algorithms and instructions. If it makes you feel more comfortable with the subject, you can think of a computation, method, algorithm, or instruction as merely a recipe like one you would find in any cookbook. We are, after all, cooking here, but with numbers instead of food.

What is a model of computation? Generally speaking, a model of computation describes how to build recipes or, if you like, a recipe for recipes. Actually, computations describe how to map numbers to other numbers, and models of computation describe how to construct the mappings.

In the past century, many mathematicians have grappled with the problem of how to describe all of the infinitely many computations that are possible. The problem, put more concisely, is: What is the minimal set of rules that we can use to construct computations such that every possible computation can be realized by the rules? Many models of computation have been proposed in the past century. What follows is a brief description of some of the better-known ones. What they have in common is that each model of computation operates on numbers, strings, and symbols by manipulating them at discrete time steps. Moreover, each model has a well-defined "program," "input," and "output." If the presentation of the models is too formal for your tastes, feel free to skim the descriptions and jump ahead to the end of this section.

General Recursive Functions General recursive functions are constructed by composing a small number of rules together. The idea is that one can take a few simple functions and construct more complex functions by applying the following rules repeatedly. The rules will either specify a base general recursive function, in which case a name and an example are given, or a rule for composing a new general recursive function.

- **Zero:** The zero function returns zero for any argument, e.g., $Z(x) = 0$.
- **Successor:** The successor function adds one to its argument, e.g., $S(x) = x + 1$.
- **Projection:** The projection rule simply states that a general recursive function is allowed to return any one of its arguments as the result, e.g., $P_i(x_1, \cdots, x_n) = x_i$.
- **Composition:** The composition rule allows for a new function to be constructed as the composition of two or more functions. Thus, if $g(x)$ and $f(x)$ are general recursive functions, then so is $g(f(x))$.
- **Recursion:** General recursive functions can have recursive definitions. For example, if $g(x)$ and $h(x)$ are general recursive, then so is $f(x, y)$ defined as $f(x, 0) = g(x)$, for $y = 0$, and $f(x, y + 1) = f(h(x), y)$, for all other y.

- **Minimization:** A general recursive function can be expressed as the minimization of another general recursive function. For example, if $g(x, y)$ is general recursive, then so is the function $f(x) = \mu y[g(x, y) = 100]$, where μ is the minimization operator. We can interpret $f(x)$ as being "the smallest value of y such that $g(x, y) = 100$." Note that there may be no y that satisfies the constraint for the supplied x, in which case f is undefined for that x.

Notice that the definition of general recursive functions is closely coupled to natural numbers, in that the functions clearly operate on the natural numbers. If we wanted to construct a general recursive function to add two numbers, the definition would look like:

$$\begin{aligned} f(x, 0) &= P_1(x) = x \\ f(x, y+1) &= S(P_3(x, y, f(x, y))) = f(x, y) + 1. \end{aligned}$$

Here we can think of a "program" as being a general recursive function that is constructed, of the program's "input" as the natural number that we plug into the function, and of the program "output" as the natural number that we get as a result.

Turing Machines A Turing machine is a hypothetical device proposed by Alan Turing in 1936. The machine has a read/write head mounted to a tape of infinite length. The tape consists of an infinite number of discrete cells in which the Turing machine can read or write symbols. At every discrete point in time a Turing machine exists in one and only one state. The "program" for a Turing machine consists of a state transition table with entries that contain: the current state, the symbol underneath the head, the next state that the machine should enter, the new symbol that should be written, and the direction that the tape should move (left, right, or none). There is also a unique state known as the starting state and one or more halting states. When a Turing machine starts up, the "input" to the program consists of the symbols already written on the tape. At each time step, the Turing machine performs an action, determined by the current state and the symbol

State	Input	Action/Output	Next State
Start	⋆	get in cruise lane	cruise
Cruise	cruise lane clear	drive at cruise speed	cruise
Cruise	slow driver ahead	get in pass lane	pass
Pass	cruise lane clear	get in cruise lane	cruise
Pass	slow driver in cruise lane	accelerate	pass
⋆	desired exit ahead	exit highway	halt

Table 3.1 A driving "program" for a Turing machine

Alan Turing: A Mini-Biography **Digression 3.2**

Alan Turing was born in 1912. As one of the pioneers in the theory of computation, his importance to the field is staggering. He participated in many public debates concerning the future of computers and artificial intelligence, and as part of this activity he invented what is now popularly known as the *Turing test*, a method to determine if a computer has "intelligence." During World War II, Turing was part of a British research team that cracked the Germans' most secret encryption device. The success of the project allowed Winston Churchill to listen in on many of the Axis powers' most classified command decisions.

Alan Turing was also a homosexual. While filing a complaint to the police department about a burglary of his house, he implied that he had more than a casual relationship with a possible suspect. The police interrogated Turing regarding this, and he confessed to being a homosexual. Subsequently, he was forced to undergo hormone therapy that led to depression. In 1954, Turing was simultaneously experimenting with chemicals and making candied apples. In what may or may not have been suicide, he ate a poisoned apple and died (Hodges, 1983).

underneath the head. This action may involve writing a new symbol, moving the head, and/or moving into a new internal state. The Turing machine continues this process until one of the halting states is reached. The "output" of the program consists of the remaining symbols on the tape.

At first glance, Turing machines seem very alien, but in actuality most people are familiar with how they work on an intuitive level. Table 3.1 illustrates a sort of Turing machine algorithm (without reference to the tape) for driving on a highway. To simplify things, we will consider only four types of states while driving: entering the highway (the starting state), cruising at a steady speed, passing a slow driver, and exiting the highway. For passing and cruising, we consider two special cases: when we should maintain the current state and when we should switch to another state.

In the table the $\star$ character is a wild card, meaning that it matches any possibility for that entry. Thus, according to the table, whenever you see the desired exit, you should exit the highway and go into the halting state, regardless of what state you are currently in.

Lambda Calculus The λ-calculus is a model of computation proposed by Alonzo Church in 1941. In it, computations are defined in terms of λ-expressions that consist of either a symbol or a list of λ-expressions, or have the form:

$$(\lambda \textit{bound-variable}(\lambda\text{-expression})).\lambda\text{-expression}.$$

The last form describes a way of rewriting the leftmost λ-expression. The result is to take the leftmost λ-expression and replace every occurrence of the bound variable with the lambda expression on the right-hand side. For example $(\lambda x(fx)).a = (fa)$, since we replace every occurrence of x in (fx) by a.

In λ-calculus the "program" corresponds to the left-hand λ-expression, and the "input" is the right-hand λ-expression. The "output" corresponds to the λ-expression resulting from continuously expanding the input applied to the program. You may be inclined to think that expanding a λ-expression is a one-step process but, in fact, λ-expressions can consist of λ-expressions nested within more λ-expressions, which means that expanding a single λ-expression may take many steps. The λ-calculus is very similar to the programming language Lisp, which is discussed in further detail shortly.

General recursive functions, Turing machines, and λ-calculus are not the only formal models of computation, just the best known. There are actually several more. You probably noticed that each model was very different from the others. An interesting question at this time is: Are there any functions that can be computed by one model of computation but not by another? In 1941, Church proved that λ-calculus was capable of representing exactly the same functions as general recursive functions. Later Turing proved that Turing machines could compute exactly the same functions as λ-calculus, which proved that all three models of computation are equivalent. This is a truly remarkable result, considering how different the three models of computation are. In Church's 1941 paper he made a statement that is now known as the Church-Turing thesis: Any function that can be called *computable* can be computed by λ-calculus, a Turing machine, or a general recursive function.

Recall the point that was made about functions describing relationships between numbers and models of computation describing functions. Well, the Church-Turing thesis is yet another level more fundamental than a model of computation. As a statement about models of computation, it is not subject to proof in the usual sense; thus, it is impossible to prove that the thesis is correct. One could disprove it by coming up with a model of computation over discrete elements that could calculate things that one of the other models could not; however, this has not happened. The fact that every posed model of computation has always been exactly equivalent to (or weaker than) one of the others lends strong support to the Church-Turing thesis.

3.3 Lisp and Stutter

So far we have really discussed computation only in very broad terms. It would be nice to demonstrate exactly how one could compute some useful functions with one of the three mentioned models. As we shall see, there is a certain beauty in deriving higher mathematical functions from such primitive beginnings. To illustrate this point, we will now examine a simple computer language that is as powerful as the other models but is a bit more understandable. In the late 1950s John McCarthy created a computer language known as Lisp (which stands for list processing). Lisp was inspired by λ-calculus, but I like to think of it as a close cousin of general recursive functions as well. A testament to the elegance of Lisp is that it is one of the few “old” languages still in common use today.

Modern Lisp (Common Lisp) is a very rich language, with hundreds of defined functions, macros, and operators. What follows is a description of a subset of Lisp that I will refer to as Stutter.[2] Stutter is an interpreted language which means that all expressions are evaluated during the runtime of a program, unlike compilers, which translate modern computer languages into the native machine language of the computer or an intermediate language (as in the case of Java and its bytecode compilation). The heart of the Stutter interpreter is the read-eval-print loop, which does exactly what its name describes. More specifically, when using Stutter, the user is prompted by the ‘>’ prompt. After the user types in a Stutter expression and presses the “Enter” key, the computer evaluates the expression and prints the result, which brings us back to the “read” portion of the loop.

But what is a Stutter expression? In Stutter everything is either a *list* or an *atom*. An atom is simply a sequence of characters, such as `bob`, `xyz`, or `256`. There is nothing significant about any of these atoms, including `256` since the Stutter interpreter has no hardwired notion of what the value of 256 means to you and me. There are also four reserved punctuation characters that have special meaning: ‘(’, ‘)’, ‘’’, and ‘;’. Other than these four characters an atom can consist of any sequence of nonblank characters in any order. The parentheses are used to contain lists, and the quotation character is used to quote atoms and lists. The reason why the quotation character is necessary will be explained in the examples below. The semicolon is used as a comment delimiter, that is, any text in a single line of a Stutter program following a semicolon is ignored by the Stutter interpreter and serves only to add comments within a Stutter program.

A list can have any number of members of any type, including other lists. Function definitions in Stutter are also lists, which lends to the beauty of the language, since functions can operate on other functions. As a special case, the empty list is denoted as either `()` or `nil`, and can be considered both an atom and a list. A function call is yet another list of the form `(f a b c)`, which means that the named function, `f`, will be called with the supplied arguments, `a`, `b`, and `c`. We must also make a distinction between the name of an atom and the value of an atom. Because it is useful to store things in variables, we are allowed to treat each atom as a variable. In this case, we say that the atom and variable are “bound” to each other. Later we will see how one can extract the value of an atom, but for now note the distinction that an atom unevaluated is itself, while an atom evaluated results in its value.

[2]Motivated readers can consult the C source code to Stutter. All of the examples from this chapter were produced from the supplied Stutter interpreter.

In the examples that follow, we will see the input to the Stutter interpreter as the text immediately following the '>' prompt. The line immediately following the input is the Stutter interpreter's output. Sometimes the output will be omitted if it is not interesting. To start, let's examine how things look when quoted:

```
> 'testing
testing
> 'testing-1-2-3
testing-1-2-3
> '(this is one way of writing a string of text)
(this is one way of writing a string of text)
> '(here is a list (with a list and another (list)))
(here is a list (with a list and another (list)))
> this-is-an-unquoted-undefined-atom
Error: unbound atom "this-is-an-unquoted-undefined-atom"
```

In the last example, when we typed in the unquoted atom, the Stutter interpreter responded with an error message because the unquoted atom was not bound to any value. We can set the value of an atom with the `set` function. Because this is our first use of a Stutter function, a brief digression is in order. In general, all Stutter functions either are built-in primitives or are user-defined. We will see how to define a user-defined function a little later, but for now let's examine how a function call is evaluated. When the Stutter interpreter is asked to call a function such as `(f a b c)`, the Stutter interpreter will first evaluate the first element in the list, `f`, which must be bound to a function or an error will occur. If `f` is a user-defined function, then the Stutter interpreter will immediately evaluate the arguments, `a`, `b`, and `c`.

For built-in functions, things are a little more subtle. The built-in functions are either *value functions* or *special functions*. Value functions behave just like user-defined functions but are primitives in the Stutter language because there is no way of defining them as user functions. Some value functions that we will encounter later on are `car`, `cdr`, and `cons`. The `set` function is also a primitive value function. Special functions behave similarly to the other functions except that their arguments are not evaluated initially. This allows the special functions to evaluate arguments only if it is appropriate. For example, the quote, character `'` is really equivalent to the special function `quote`. Instead of using the single quote we could also type `(quote a)`, which evaluates to `a`—not the value of `a`. Later we will use another special function, `if`.

To use the `set` function, we supply it with two arguments. The first argument should evaluate to the atom that we want to bind a value to. The second argument is also evaluated, and the result is bound to the atom the first argument evaluated to. Most uses of `set` will look like `(set 'a b)`, with the first atom being quoted. Requiring the quote may seem like an unnecessary inconvenience, but it actually gives us some latitude in how we define things. Consider the examples:

```
> (set 'name 'call-me-Ishmael)
> name
call-me-Ishmael
> (set 'ten '10)
> ten
10
> (set ten '5-plus-5)  ;;; Change the value of '10 indirectly.
> ten
10
> 10
5-plus-5
```

Let's now look at how **car**, **cdr**, and **cons** work. All three functions are used to manipulate lists in some way. Computer science has had some strange effects on spoken language, and one such oddity is that Lisp programmers often say things like "the car of the list" or "the cdr of something." What they really mean in the first example is "the result of calling the car function with the given list as an argument." That's too much of a mouthful for my tastes, so you should not be confused when I use the programmer's verbal shortcut.

The `car` function always returns the first element in a list. If you try to take the `car` of something that is not a list, an error will occur. As a special case, the `car` of `nil` is also `nil`. Complementary to `car`, the `cdr` function returns the supplied list with everything but the first element. If you like, you can think of `cdr` as being synonymous with "everything but the car." Thus, the `cdr` of a list with a single element is `nil`, and as another special case the `cdr` of `nil` is also `nil`

The `cons` function is used to construct a new list from two arguments. The first argument will be the `car` of the result list and the second argument will be the `cdr` of the result. Thus, for any list `l` except `nil`, `(cons (car l) (cdr l))` is always equal to `l`. Here are some example uses of `car`, `cdr`, and `cons`.

```
> (car '((a b c) x y))
(a b c)
> (cdr '((a b c) x y))
(x y)
> (car (car '((a b c) x y)))
a
> (cdr (cdr '((a b c) x y)))
(y)
> (car (cdr (cdr (car '((a b c) x y)))))
c
> (cons 'a nil)
(a)
> (cons 'a '(b))
```

```
(a b)
> (cons '(a b c) '(x y))
((a b c) x y)
> (cons '(a b c) nil)
((a b c))
```

During the lifetime of a program, it is often necessary to ask questions. Stutter is no exception to this, so to facilitate this need, Stutter has a built-in special function known as `if`, which takes three arguments. The first argument is a condition. The `if` function evaluates the condition, and if it is true, then `if` will return the second argument evaluated but not evaluate the third argument at all. If the condition is false, then `if` will not evaluate the second argument but return the third argument evaluated instead. Any missing arguments are presumed to be `nil`. But what is "true" and "false" in Stutter? We will take "false" to be synonymous with `nil` and "true" to mean anything that is not `nil`. Because it useful to have a consistent name for the concept of "true," we will use `t` to mean just that. Moreover, `t` evaluates to itself because it is defined by `(set 't 't)`. Yet, in Stutter there is nothing special about the symbol `t`; it is just an atom like any other atom. By themselves, `if` expressions are not very interesting, but here are two that illustrate how they work:

```
> (if nil '(it was true) '(it was false))
(it was false)
> (if 'blah-blah-blah '(it was true) '(it was false))
(it was true)
```

In general, `if` statements usually take the form: `(if (condition-expression) (then-expression) (else-expression))`. The real power of an `if` statement is when the "then" or "else" portions of the statement contain even more expressions.

The last type of Stutter expression that will be highlighted is a special type of expression known as a *lambda expression*. Lambda expressions in Stutter are similar to λ-expressions in λ-calculus, in that they allow the user to define new functions. The symbol `lambda` is not a function per se, but a special atom. In general, a lambda expression will look like `(lambda (arg1 arg2) (function body ...))`. You should read the last expression as "This is a function with two arguments. When the function is called, the function body is evaluated, with the supplied arguments replacing the arguments that appear in the body."

That's all there is to Stutter. Nothing else. Your first reaction to Stutter may be that it is a rather weak programming language. For example, how would one go about adding numbers? The concept of numbers doesn't even appear in the language definition, let alone addition. Yet Stutter is as powerful as any other programming language. It is universal in that it can do anything that the other three models of computation can do (as well as your home computer[3]). How so? To

[3]Technically speaking, your home PC is weaker than any of the other models of computation because it has only finite memory.

illustrate this, we will reinvent the basic mathematical operations in Stutter. Doing so will also illustrate how to use lambda expressions.

To begin with, we need a representation for the numbers. For a start, let's define zero:

```
> (set '0 nil)
```

That's fine, but there is an infinite number of other numbers to deal with. Instead of giving a unique definition for each number, we will define what it means to be a number. More specifically, for every number there is always another number that is one greater than the first. In this spirit, let's define an increment function:

```
> (set '1+ (lambda (x) (cons t x)))
```

In English the `1+` function definition reads as "take the argument (which is presumably a list) and append the symbol `t` to the front of it." Now, if we wanted to, we could define other numbers:

```
> (set '1 (1+ 0))
> (set '2 (1+ 1))
> (set '3 (1+ 2))
  ...
> (set '10 (1+ 9))
```

But these definitions are not strictly necessary, since Stutter now understands that `'(t t t)` means the same thing as `(1+ (1+ (1+ 0)))`, which means the same thing as 3 does to us. This may seem like a cumbersome way of representing numbers, but not for Stutter.

It would also be useful to have a notion of "one less" than some number. The only difficulty is that all natural numbers are positive. Thus, the following decrement function will do just fine for positive numbers:

```
> (set '1- (lambda (x) (cdr x)))
```

Now that we have numbers, how do we do useful things with them? Let's start with addition:

```
> (set '+ (lambda (x y) (if y (1+ (+ x (1- y))) x)))
```

This definition is clearly recursive since it refers to itself. The definition in English reads "The sum of two numbers is defined as the first number if the second number is 0. If the second number is not 0 then the result is equal to 1 plus the sum of the first number and 1 less than the second number." In other words, if you ask Stutter to compute $(5 + 2)$, it will roughly carry out the expansion: $(5+2) = (1+(5+1)) = (1+(1+(5+0))) = 7$. Let's try it out:

```
> (+ 5 2)
(t t t t t t t)
> (+ 9 3)
(t t t t t t t t t t t t)
```

Multiplication and exponentiation are just as easy to define as addition since they have their own elegant recursive definitions:

```
> (set '* (lambda (x y) (if y (+ (* x (1- y)) x) 0)))
> (set '^ (lambda (x y) (if y (* x (^ x (1- y))) 1)))
```

With these definitions, we can now do some fancy calculating:

```
> (* 3 5)
(t t t t t t t t t t t t t t t)
> (^ 2 4) ;;;  2 raised to the 4th power.
(t t t t t t t t t t t t t t t t)
> (^ (+ 1 2) (* 2 2)) ;;; 3 raised to the 4th power.
(t t t t t t t t t t t t t t t t t t t t t t t t t t t
 t t t t t t t t t t t t t t t t t t t t t t t t t t t
 t t t t t t t t t t t t t t t t t t t t t t t t t t t)
```

Included with the Stutter source code are Stutter statements that define many more useful operations and predicates, such as subtraction, division, logarithm, an equality test, and greater than and less than. Moreover, if you are still troubled by the fact that numbers are represented by very long lists, there is a simple function that converts lists of the form `'(1 2 3)` into unary lists (which is the form that we have been using) and back. It is also possible to define a representation for floating-point numbers and to define more complex operations, such as the square root.

3.4 Equivalence and Time Complexity

Since all of the mentioned models of computation are equivalent, in that each of them can compute exactly what all of the others can compute, what can we say about the relative efficiency of each model? Is one type of model more efficient than another, in the sense that it can do exactly what another model can do but faster? There are some differences in speed between the different models, but not a significant amount. Why this is so is the topic of this section.

Computer science theory has a branch, known as *time complexity theory*, that deals with the question of how fast something can be computed. In each model of computation, the "computer" has to take some step-by-step actions. For example, in one time step the Turing machine reads the symbol underneath the head, writes

```
(+ 2 3)                                ;;; Expand   (+ 2 3)
  (1+ (+ 2 (1- 3)))                    ;;; Evaluate (1- 3)  -> 2
  (1+ (+ 2 2))                         ;;; Expand   (+ 2 2)
    (1+ (1+ (+ 2 (1- 2))))             ;;; Evaluate (1- 2)  -> 1
    (1+ (1+ (+ 2 1)))                  ;;; Expand   (+ 2 1)
      (1+ (1+ (1+ (+ 2 (1- 1)))))      ;;; Evaluate (1- 1)  -> 0
      (1+ (1+ (1+ (+ 2 0))))           ;;; Evaluate (+ 2 0) -> 2
      (1+ (1+ (1+ 2)))                 ;;; Evaluate (1+ 2)  -> 3
    (1+ (1+ 3))                        ;;; Evaluate (1+ 3)  -> 4
  (1+ 4)                               ;;; Evaluate (1+ 4)  -> 5
5
```

Table 3.2 Stutter execution path of `(+ 2 3)`

the appropriate new symbol, moves the tape left or right, and then makes a virtual jump to the next state. For a general recursive function, λ-calculus expression, or Stutter program there is also an iterative process taking place. You can imagine that each primitive or built-in function takes exactly one time step to execute, and that user-defined functions take as many time steps as the number of primitive functions they ultimately call upon. Modern digital computers also have a fetch-execute cycle that involves retrieving a machine language instruction from memory, decoding it, then executing it.

How do we measure the speed of a computer program? First of all, some programs will always take longer than others, given the same input. As an example, let's simulate how Stutter would add the numbers 2 and 3. Recall that addition was defined as `(lambda (x y) (if y (1+ (+ x (1- y))) x))`. Table 3.2 shows roughly what takes place to compute the final result by indenting each level of recursion. The listing is simplified somewhat, in that most of the details have been omitted of how, say, `(1- 3)` is evaluated, since it is not self-recursive and simply calls `cdr`. Moreover, instead of expanding each recursive function call into the full function body, I have expanded recursive function calls only into the portion of the body that is evaluated by the `if` expression. Looking closely at how the `+` function executes, there appear to be three types of steps. First of all, there are several expansions of the `+` function because it recursively refers to itself. Next, there are three `1+` calls and three `1-` calls. The fact that there are three of each of these calls is a consequence of 3 being the second argument. If 7 been the second argument, then there would have been seven calls to `1+` and `1-`. Likewise, the four expansions are a result of 3 being the second argument. Putting this all together, we find that the total number of steps for performing the operation `(+ a b)` is roughly $3b + 1$.

Obviously, the smart thing to do would be to make sure that the second argument is at least as small as the first. If we amended the + function so that this check is performed initially, then we would have the additional overhead of computing which is the smaller of the two arguments. The supplied Stutter code contains a Stutter definition for the relational operator <, which takes approximately the same number of steps as the smaller of the two arguments. Therefore, combining all of this into a "smart" + operation would yield a total number of steps roughly equal to $4x + 1$, where x is the smaller of the two arguments.

This is still not quite the answer that we are looking for, since we really don't want to estimate the time a function takes to execute on the basis of only one of its arguments. What we really need is a way of expressing the execution time as a function of the length of the input. In the case of the + function, the input length is equal to the length of the two list arguments. Therefore, let's agree to call x the sum of the length of the two arguments, a and b. As a worst case, let's also assume that a and b are really equal to one another. Why? If one of the two arguments was less than the other, then, since the + function executes in time proportional to its smallest argument, this would be faster than if a and b were really equal. With this assumption the smallest argument is equal to $\frac{x}{2}$. Therefore, the execution time of the + function, expressed in terms of the length of the input, is equal to $2x + 1$. This means that if you give the + function any two arguments, you can reasonably expect it to take about $2x + 1$ steps to compute the result.

However, we are not yet finished with simplifying the time measure. Time complexity analysis is one of the few mathematical disciplines in which one is supposed to take shortcuts. More specifically, the expression $2x + 1$ is just an affine linear function, and the 2 is simply a coefficient. Since we really want to know how well the + function scales when we give it really big numbers, the 2 doesn't tell us anything special, since one computer can easily be twice as fast as another. Moreover, if instead of $2x + 1$, the number of steps that a function takes was something more complicated, like $\frac{1}{2}x^4 - 2x^2 + 82x + 13$, under time complexity analysis we would simplify the whole expression down to x^4, which is the most significant term in the polynomial. The reason we are allowed to do this is not as superficial as I have made it seem, and is in fact mathematically sound. As an exercise you could compute $\frac{1}{2}x^4 - 2x^2 + 82x + 13$ divided by x^4 on a calculator with some very large values for x. As you increase the size of x, the ratio of the numbers will eventually approach a constant factor of $\frac{1}{2}$. We are allowed to simplify time complexity expressions in this manner because the ratio approaches a constant value. A computer scientist would express the x^4 time complexity measure with what is known as "big-Oh" notation, or $O(x^4)$, which is just a formal way of saying that a function or program takes about x^4 time steps to execute, given an input of length x.

Now back to the issue of how fast the + function is. Since we are now in agreement that the addition operation takes time proportional to x, we will denote this fact by saying that + has a time complexity of $O(x)$. Intuitively, this analysis makes sense,

```
(* 2 3)                                ;;; Expand   (* 2 3)
  (+ (* 2 (1- 3)) 2)                   ;;; Evaluate (1- 3)  -> 2
  (+ (* 2 2) 2)                        ;;; Expand   (* 2 2)
    (+ (+ (* 2 (1- 2)) 2) 2)           ;;; Evaluate (1- 2)  -> 1
    (+ (+ (* 2 1) 2) 2)                ;;; Expand   (* 2 1)
      (+ (+ (+ (* 2 (1- 1)) 2) 2) 2)   ;;; Evaluate (1- 1)  -> 0
      (+ (+ (+ (* 2 0) 2) 2) 2)        ;;; Evaluate (* 2 0) -> 0
      (+ (+ (+ 0 2) 2) 2)              ;;; Evaluate (+ 0 2) -> 2
    (+ (+ 2 2) 2)                      ;;; Evaluate (+ 2 2) -> 4
  (+ 4 2)                              ;;; Evaluate (+ 4 2) -> 6
6
```

Table 3.3 Stutter execution path of `(* 2 3)`.

since our smart + operation is very similar to the way you would "add" two piles of stones. You would take one stone from the smaller of the two piles and place it into the larger pile, repeating the process until the smaller pile was gone. If you doubled the size of your original pile of stones, then the whole task would take you twice as long as before. This is exactly what it means to have a time complexity of $O(x)$: If you multiply the input size by n, then the task will take roughly n times as long as before. Isn't it nice to see that mathematics agrees with intuition?

We are now going to take a quicker look at multiplication in Stutter. The execution of `*` is illustrated in Table 3.3. The multiplication listing is very similar to the listing for addition. Note, however, that we did not expand each of the `+` function calls. A quick look of the listing shows that to perform `(* a b)` requires $b+1$ expansions, b `1-` operations, and b `+` operations, with `a` always being the second argument to the `+` function. As before, the worst-case scenario for the `*` function is for `a` and `b` to be equal to one another. Thus, denoting the input length by x, we know that `a` and `b` are equal to $\frac{x}{2}$. A quick estimate of the running time reveals that the costliest portion of the function is the $\frac{x}{2}$ additions that we have to make with $\frac{x}{2}$ being the second argument. Since we are performing an $O(x)$ operation $\frac{x}{2}$ times with input length $\frac{x}{2}$, the time complexity of the `*` function is equal to $O(x^2)$, which means that if you double the size of the arguments to the `*` function, you can reasonably expect the function to take four times as long. Similarly, if you increased the size of the arguments by a factor of n, it would take n^2 times as long to compute the product. This means that in some ways multiplication is "harder" than addition, but you knew this already. Once again, mathematics confirms intuition.

We are now ready to go back to the question posed at the beginning of this section, "Which model of computation is more efficient than the others?" If you were hoping for a definitive answer, then I am afraid you are going to be disappointed, since some models of computation are ideally suited for certain problems that are difficult for other models. However, what is truly interesting is that no matter what the problem is and no matter what model you use to solve it, any of the other models can compute the same result in time proportional to some polynomial of what it took the first model to compute it. In other words, if it takes Stutter $O(f(x))$ time steps to compute some function, then in the worst case a Turing machine can do the same thing in $O(g(f(x)))$ time, where g is a polynomial function.

Polynomial functions always have the form

$$a_n x^n + a_{n-1} x^{n-1} + \cdots + a_2 x^2 + a_1 x + a_0,$$

where the a_i terms are coefficients and n is the largest power. Under time complexity analysis we would simplify the above function to $O(x^n)$. Computer scientists like functions that take polynomial time because of all the possible functions, polynomials are relatively well-behaved. On the other extreme, many well-known problems have no known solution that takes less than exponential time. To see the difference in how these functions can grow, you can take a moderate polynomial like x^4 and a small exponential function like 2^x. For small values of x (less than 16), the polynomial will be larger than the exponential. For slightly larger values of x, such as 20 or 30, the exponential will explode in size relative to the polynomial. Another redeeming feature of polynomials is that they are closed under composition. This means that if you take a polynomial of a polynomial, you will still have a polynomial. Therefore, if a problem can be solved in a "reasonable" amount of time under one model of computation, it can be solved in a "reasonable" amount of time with any of the other models. If the problem takes exponential time to solve, then it really isn't all that solvable to begin with, and taking a polynomial of an exponential makes it marginally worse. Thus, relatively speaking, all of the models of computation are roughly equivalent in speed. Nevertheless, if you try to use the Stutter exponentiation function, you'll be in for a long wait, so these facts should be taken with a grain of salt.

3.5 Universal Computation and Decision Problems

One of the nice things about Lisp and Stutter is that function definitions are also lists. This property not only is cosmetically appealing but also lends the languages a certain degree of power, in that functions can operate on function definitions very easily. For example, in Stutter (or Lisp) one could theoretically write a Stutter program with only about a hundred lines of code that is actually a Stutter interpreter running on top of the original Stutter interpreter. You may have seen commercial software that allows one type of computer to run software from another type. Such programs are known as emulators, and they are normally very complicated. Moreover, to write a program on a computer that emulates the computer that the program is running on is normally very difficult. But Stutter's simple and compact

- Input x and y.
- If $x = 0$, then output 0 and halt.
- If $y = 0$, then output 1 and halt.
- (We can assume that $x \geq 1$ and $y \geq 1$.)
- Set h to 1.
- Repeat until $x^y < h$ is true.
    - Set l to h.
    - Set h to $2 * h$.
- (We now know that x^y is between l and h.)
- Set m to $(h + l)/2$.
- Repeat until $x^y < m$ is false and $x^y < m + 1$ is true.
    - If $x^y < m$ is true, then set h to m.
    - If $x^y < m$ is false, then set l to m.
    - Set m to $(h + l)/2$.
- Output m.

Table 3.4 An algorithm that computes x^y from queries.

representation makes doing the same thing under Stutter relatively easy. However, having a universal computer emulate itself is always possible, no matter what the underlying model of computation is.

Recall that we were able to reduce any program's input into a single natural number via Gödelization. Using the same technique as before, it is possible to represent all of the Stutter primitive function names and punctuation characters as a list of integers. For example, we could represent **car**, **cdr**, **cons**, **if**, **lambda**, **quote**, **set**, '**)**', and '**(**' by the numbers 1 through 9. Any additional variables or atom names that we need for a program could be mapped into the numbers 10, 11, 12, and so on. Now that the program is represented as a list of natural numbers, one could code the entire program into a single Gödel number.

The important thing to realize is that any of our models of computation can convert a program representation into a Gödel number. Moreover, they also can invert the process to retrieve the original program. Combining the facts that computers can invert Gödel numbers and emulate themselves means that for any computational model there theoretically exists a very special program that takes two numbers as input and performs the following computation. The first number is interpreted as the Gödel number of a program, and the second number is interpreted as the Gödel number for the input that one would want to supply to the program represented by the first input number. This special program can emulate the Gödelized program on the Gödelized input as if the real program were being executed. Such a program is known as a universal computer, and I will use the notation $U(x, y)$ to mean that "the universal computer is executed with the Gödel number x of some program on the Gödel number y as input."

We are also used to thinking of programs as producing some sort of meaningful output. Yet it is possible to take any program and convert it to another program that performs a computation similar to that of the first but outputs only either a 1 or a 0. The new program is referred to as solving a *decision problem*. Using decision problems will provide us with another mathematical shortcut later on, but for now let's see what this idea really means.

Consider a program that takes two inputs, x and y (or a single Gödel number for the two inputs), and outputs x^y. We could use this program to write another program that takes three inputs, x, y, and z, and outputs a 1 if $x^y < z$ and 0 otherwise. Now suppose that you never really have access to the first program, and you are allowed to only use the second program. How would you find out what x^y really is? Table 3.4 gives an algorithm that computes x^y by querying the second program. The basic idea behind the algorithm is to perform what is known as a binary search. It works in two stages. In the first stage the algorithm figures out an upper bound for x^y by doubling an estimate until the estimate exceeds x^y. Since the previous estimate was less than x^y, we can assume that x^y must be between l (for low) and h (for high). In the second stage the algorithm computes a middle point, m, between l and h and checks to see which half of the range (l to h) x^y is in. The value of l or h is updated to reflect the in which half x^y was found, and the process is repeated until x^y is finally isolated.

How significant is the extra overhead in computing x^y in such a manner? Surprisingly, not very. As a worst case, exponentiation in Stutter takes $O(2^x)$ time (where x is the input length). However, the binary search performs the exponentiation operation only $\log_2(x)$ times in the worst case, which is actually better than a polynomial. Therefore, computing an exponent via a decision problem is just as "hard" as the original exponentiation program but not significantly harder.

In general, any program can be converted into a similar program that solves a decision problem, that is, set membership determination for some predetermined set. Moreover, using the decision program instead of the original program increases the original complexity only by an amount polynomial in the original running time. Why would you want to compute something in such an awkward manner? You wouldn't, but theoretically this gives us a simplification in how computers work that we will exploit in the next section.

3.6 Incomputability

Do there exist problems that are unsolvable by any computer? "Unsolvable" should be understood in the strictest sense of the word; that is, if all of the computers in the world worked in conjunction on one specific problem and they theoretically re-

Subsets	Natural Numbers 1	2	3	4	5	6	...
Even Numbers	no	yes	no	yes	no	yes	...
Odd Numbers	yes	no	yes	no	yes	no	...
Primes	no	yes	yes	no	yes	no	...
Squares	yes	no	no	yes	no	no	...
Powers of 2	yes	yes	no	yes	no	no	...
Multiples of 3	no	no	yes	no	no	yes	...
⋮	⋮	⋮	⋮	⋮	⋮	⋮	⋱
Diagonal Set	yes	yes	no	no	yes	no	...

Table 3.5 Listing out simple sets to derive a diagonal set.

quired a billion times the age of the universe to finally compute the correct answer, we would still consider such a problem "solvable." This definition may seem unreasonable, but the fact is that there are many problems that can't be solved even with such loose criteria.

Recall once again that every program can be reduced to another program that computes set membership. Some computable sets for sophisticated programs are very complex, but others should be familiar to all of us. Listed in Table 3.5 are some simple sets with the membership for a particular number being given in the entries.

Since the number of programs and computable sets is countable, we can enumerate all of the computable sets (or programs) in one long list, just as we did with the natural numbers in Chapter 2. Once again, the entries along the diagonal are boxed for emphasis. With the diagonal entries we can construct a diagonal set such that each member of that set is exactly opposite the entry in the main diagonal. Amazingly, the full infinite set represented by the complement of the diagonal is not computable because it differs by at least one entry from every computable set; thus no computer program could ever exist that could tell you for any natural number whether it was a member or not. Our diagonal set is a nice illustration and serves as an existence proof, but it really doesn't tell us what a truly impossible problem looks like.

Alan Turing was the first to demonstrate that there are many problems that are not computable. For the rest of this section, we will concentrate on a single noteworthy incomputable problem that Turing discovered. Suppose you had a program and some data that you wanted to run the program on. A reasonable question to ask is: Will the program ever halt with a solution? Let's assume that the program you want to check looks for the solution to a problem and halts only when it finds one. Therefore, the program may not ever stop if a solution doesn't exist (or if it is simply too dumb to find one). Wouldn't it be nice if there existed a special program that could tell us if another program would not halt? We could save a lot of time by seeing if the program we are really interested in would halt, and only then would we go to the next step of running it to find the solution. If such a program existed, programmers could use it to see if other programs had bugs in them that caused infinite loops. You could also use this special program on your home computer's operating system (which is just another program) to eliminate those annoying software crashes.

Let's assume that this special program exists. We will denote an instance of this program by the notation $M(x, y)$, where x is the Gödel number of the program that we wish to check and y is the Gödel number of the input that we want to feed to program x. Note that this is very similar to the universal computer that we constructed in the last section, but instead of producing the normal output of program x on y, it outputs

$$M(x,y) = \begin{cases} 1 \text{ if } U(x,y) \text{ halts} \\ 0 \text{ if } U(x,y) \text{ does not halt} \end{cases} .$$

If the program $M(x, y)$ exists, then we can easily construct another program, $M'(x)$, based on it that gives the output

$$M'(x) = \begin{cases} \text{runs forever in an infinite loop if } M(x,x) = 1 \\ \text{halts with any output if } M(x,x) = 0 \end{cases} .$$

Don't be bothered by the fact that we have purposely designed M' so that it can conceivably run forever (that is, diverge). Doing so is actually quite easy; for example, the Stutter function defined by `(set 'f (lambda () (f)))` will run forever if called. Since M' is just another program, it has its own unique Gödel number, which we will call m'. Let's see what happens if we try to run $M'(x)$ with an input of m'. What do you think will happen? Will it halt or run forever?

Let's assume for a moment that $M'(m')$ halts. If this is so, we know that $M(m', m') = 0$ must be true. This means that program m' with input m' runs forever, which contradicts our original assumption that $M'(m')$ halts. Similarly, assuming that $M'(m')$ runs forever, we can conclude that $M(m', m') = 1$, which further implies that program m' on input m' halts. Again, a contradiction! We are faced with contradictions no matter what assumption we make because the original program, $M(x, y)$, simply cannot exist since it pretends to solve an unsolvable problem.

Notice that the real difficulty in constructing a program similar to $M(x, y)$ is in determining when a program fails to halt. If a program will halt, then plugging the program and input into the universal computer will tell us this is the case because the universal computer will also halt. Determining if a program will not halt is impossible because you would have to wait forever to see that it did not halt.

One tantalizing facet of our proof above is that it relies on running the program M' on its own Gödel number, m'. Think about this: We are feeding a program itself as input. In other words, the program is examining itself and trying to perform some sort of self-analysis: Do I halt—or not? "Know thyself" seems to be an impossible command for a computer program. If a model of computation is so weak that it cannot ask questions about programs, then it will skirt the abyss, but at the cost of being too stupid to solve interesting problems. Once a model of computation has the ability to look within itself, it pays the price of not being able to halt under the right (or wrong) set of circumstances.

3.7 Number Sets Revisited

Let's put a few of the ideas from the last two sections together. Since every program has a unique Gödel number, let's think about what those numbers look like. Obviously they will be very large numbers. Moreover, not every natural number will represent a legal program; for example, we could compute a Gödel number for the character sequence `(xy))(z''()`, but such a string of characters does not represent a legal Stutter program because it violates the syntax of the language. However, syntax checking is not too difficult a problem, so it would be theoretically possible to write a program that takes a single natural number as input and decides if it represents a Gödelization of a legal program. With this program, we could write another program that also takes a single natural number, x, as input, but this time the new program will output the xth Gödel number that represents a legal Stutter program.

This new program maps the natural numbers to programs, just as we did in Chapter 2 with simpler sets. Since we now know how to do a one-to-one mapping of natural numbers to programs, consider the set of numbers that map to a program that halts. This set is known as the halting set and has the property that it is recursively enumerable (RE for short) but not computable.

A *recursive set* is a set of numbers such that some program can decide if a number is a member or not. Recursive sets obviously can be finite in size, since a program to decide set membership for a finite set can always be written as a simple lookup table. There are also recursive sets that are infinite in size, such as the set of even numbers, or primes, or the infinite set of numbers that represent the Gödelization of three numbers, x, y, and z, such that $x^y < z$ is true.

The really important attribute that recursive sets have is that a program can determine if a number is or is not a member. On the other hand, for strictly RE sets (i.e., a set that is RE but not recursive) a program can decide only if a number is a member of the set. If a number is not a member of an RE set, there is no general way of determining that this is the case.

Since for every strictly RE set there is a program that halts only if its input is a member of the RE set, there are as many RE sets as programs (and natural numbers); that is, there is a countably infinite number of RE sets. There is a close relationship between RE sets and the computable irrational numbers. Recall from Chapter 2 that two examples of irrational computable numbers are π and $\sqrt{2}$. These numbers are called "computable" because you can write a program that enumerates each digit, one after the other. All modern operating systems have the ability to multitask, which gives the impression that the computer is running many programs simultaneously. All of our formal models of computation are also capable of emulating an arbitrary number of "virtual" computers. With such a scheme, it is possible for a master program to spawn another virtual program that checks the set membership of one particular number. At a future time step, the master program can spawn another virtual program that checks a second potential member, and so on. If any of these virtual programs ever halts with the answer "yes, this element is a member of the RE set we are considering," then the master program can halt that particular virtual program. A virtual program may never halt with an answer of "no" but instead just keeps running forever. Thus, it is theoretically possible for one program to continuously spit out members of an RE set, which is why we say it is recursively enumerable. The master program will never halt, but there also will never be a last element that it gives a positive membership classification to. This master program is similar to a program that would continuously print out digits of π. The π program also will never halt (unless we explicitly tell it to halt at some future time), but always produce another digit, and another, and so on. The main difference between computable numbers and RE sets in this analogy is that we can't compute the nth member of an RE set the way we can compute the nth digit of π, but it is still interesting to see that both RE sets and computable numbers can, in a sense, be perfectly described by an algorithm.

Things get really strange when you start to think about sets that are not recursively enumerable, or "NOT-RE." To start, let's consider a set that is the complement of an RE set that is not recursive. The complement of a set consists of all numbers that are not in the original set. We will give the label "CO-RE" to sets that are constructed in this manner. The complement of the halting set is an example of a CO-RE set. We can think of CO-RE sets as being special cases of the more general NOT-RE set type.

Just as for RE sets, for a CO-RE set you could never write a program that would halt if and only if the input was a member of the CO-RE set. However, in many ways CO-RE sets are more pathological than RE sets because we cannot even determine in a general way if some number is a member. We can answer only the opposite question with any degree of reliability: Is this number not a member? This is reminiscent of trying to draw a picture only by filling in the background—we are not allowed to draw the foreground but can only infer things about it based on what we see in the background. I like to think of CO-RE sets as the "black holes" of recursive mathematics because of this property.

Yet, there are sets that are NOT-RE and also are not CO-RE. What could this possibly mean? Such a set defies algorithmic description, meaning that no

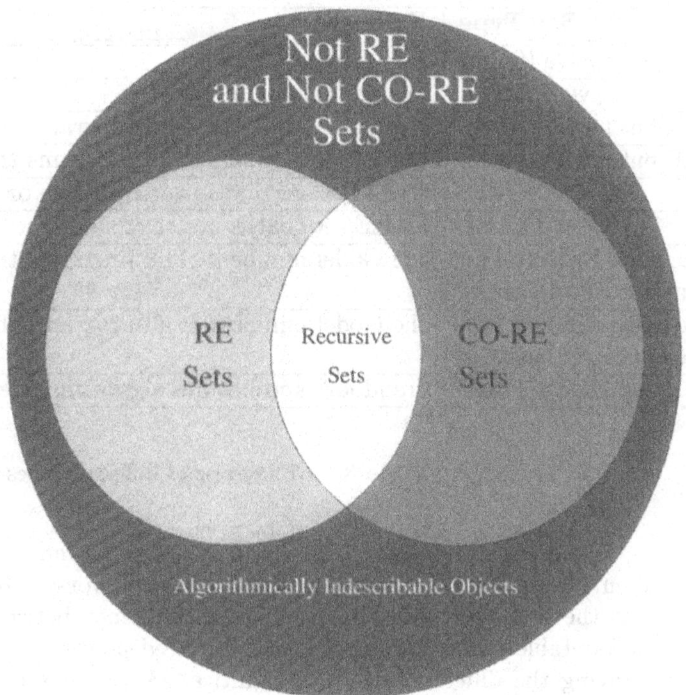

Figure 3.1 Subdivision of numbers and sets

program could tell you anything at all about a potential member with any certainty. The truly disturbing thing about such sets is that there is an uncountably infinite number of them—more than the recursive, RE, and CO-RE combined. These sets are analogous to the uncomputable irrational numbers. You can imagine that the digit expansion of an uncomputable irrational number is effectively random because there is no consistent relationship between any of the digits. (We will talk more about such random numbers in Chapter 9.)

Figure 3.1 gives a stylized representation of numbers and sets, and specific examples of these different set types are given in Table 3.6. Recursive sets are a special case because their complements are also recursive. Recursive sets are trivially RE as well. Sets that are not recursive but are RE are found in the large light-gray section on the left of Figure 3.1. The NOT-RE sets that are also CO-RE are in the darkest nonblack section. The black section contains the uncountably infinite NOT-RE sets that are "very" NOT-RE, in that their complements are also NOT-RE. You can view the lightest regions of the figure as denoting the most "knowable" sets. In the darker regions the sets under consideration become more and more "unknowable."

Set Type	Example
Recursive (finite)	1, 2, and 3
Recursive (infinite)	all even numbers
RE but not Recursive	the Gödel numbers of all programs that halt
CO-RE but not Recursive	the Gödel numbers of all programs that never halt
NOT-RE	a CO-RE set that is not recursive or a "random" set
NOT-CO-RE	an RE set that is not recursive or a "random" set
Recursive Subset of an RE but not Recursive Set	the Gödel numbers of all programs that provably halt
Recursive Subset of a CO-RE but not Recursive Set	the Gödel numbers of all programs that provably never halt
NOT-RE and NOT-CO-RE	"random" and beyond algorithmic description

Table 3.6 Examples of different types of sets

If you are still bothered by the fact that some infinities are larger than others, then I have some bad news for you: It gets worse. Recall that Georg Cantor was the first to realize that there is a difference between countable infinity and uncountable infinity. Cantor also discovered power sets, which is another way of deriving the differences in the infinities. A power set of another set, A, is the set of all subsets of A. For example, if $A = \{1, 2, 3\}$, then the power set of A is $\{\{\}, \{1\}, \{2\}, \{3\}, \{1, 2\}, \{1, 3\}, \{2, 3\}, \{1, 2, 3\}\}$. Notice that we include the original set and the empty set. If A has n members, then its power set will have 2^n members. The set of all natural numbers has a power set. There is also a power set of the power set of all of the natural numbers. The sizes, or cardinalities, of each successive power set are known as the transfinite numbers, with the size of the set of natural numbers being the first transfinite number. It is regarded as true but not provable that the second transfinite number is equal to the cardinality of the real numbers. What is really astounding is that there is an infinite number of transfinite numbers.

3.8 Further Reading

Abelson, H., Sussman, G. J., & Sussman, J. (1996). *Structure and interpretation of computer programs.* Cambridge, Mass.: MIT Press.

Dewdney, A. K. (1989). *The Turing omnibus: 61 excursions in computer science.* Rockville, Md.: Computer Science Press.

Gödel, K. (1986). On completeness and consistency. In S. Feferman, J. W. Dawson, Jr., S. C. Kleene, G. H. Moore, R. M. Solovay, & J. Van Heijenoort (Eds.), *Kurt Gödel: Collected works*, volume 1 (pp. 235–237). Oxford: Oxford University Press.

Goldstine, H. H. (1993). *The computer from Pascal to von Neumann.* Princeton: Princeton University Press.

Hodges, A. (1983). *Alan Turing: The enigma.* New York: Simon and Schuster.

Hopcroft, J. E. & Ullman, J. D. (1979). *Introduction to automata theory, languages, and computation.* Reading, Mass.: Addison-Wesley.

McCarthy, J. (1960). LISP 1 programmer's manual. Technical report, Computation Center and Research Laboratory of Electronics, MIT, Cambridge, Mass.

Minsky, M. (1972). *Computation: Finite and infinite machines.* London: Prentice-Hall.

Ribenboim, P. (1991). *The little book of big primes.* New York: Springer-Verlag.

Turing, A. M. (1936). On computable numbers, with an application to the Entscheidungsproblem. *Proc. London Math. Soc.*, 2(42): 230–265.

Turing, A. M. (1950). Can a machine think? *Mind*, 59(236): 433–460.

Wang, H. (1987). *Reflections on Kurt Gödel.* Cambridge, Mass.: MIT Press.

4 Postscript: Computation

All Cretans are liars.
— Epimenides, who was himself a Cretan

Trying to define yourself is like trying to bite your own teeth.
— Alan Watts

IN THE LAST chapter I hinted at a mathematical result due to Gödel[1] that shocked many of his contemporaries. To put Gödel's research in the proper context, we should probably take a look at what other researchers were doing in the early part of the twentieth century. Mathematicians such as Bertrand Russell, Alfred North Whitehead, and David Hilbert were expending a great deal of effort in trying to construct a mathematical formalism that was consistent in the sense that all mathematical statements could be safely classified as being true or false, and complete in the sense that all true statements could be proven true and all false statements could be proven false. This seemed at the time to be a reasonable goal; however, all attempts to show that mathematics could be made "complete" failed. Philosophically, if logic and arithmetic were inconsistent, then they would be almost useless as tools for inferring facts about the universe. Not only would profound things be difficult to analyze with a broken logic, but simple statements such as "$1 + 1 = 2$" would be in question. On the other hand, if logic and arithmetic were incomplete, then there would be mathematical truths that could never be identified as being true. Both possibilities hold little attraction for mathematicians; thus, Gödel's contemporaries were extremely shocked when Gödel proved that any sufficiently powerful mathematical formalism that is consistent must also be incomplete.

In this first postscript chapter we will examine Gödel's incompleteness in the context of Turing's result on incomputability and see how both results relate to an

[1] Unrelated to the contents of this chapter, but interesting nonetheless, Kurt Gödel, like Alan Turing, died under strange and ironic circumstances. In 1978 Gödel was working at Princeton University's Institute for Advanced Study. Quite simply, one of the century's greatest minds starved himself to death because he suspected that someone was trying to poison him (Wang, 1987).

inherent paradoxical quality found in any formalism, including language, hypothetical super-analog computers, and real physical systems. This unavoidable paradox has implications for any natural computational system, including all of the topics covered in Parts II-V.

4.1 Gödel's Incompleteness Result

Initially, Gödel set out to prove that first-order predicate calculus with arithmetic was complete. Predicate calculus has a very simple and compact form that makes it easy to use and analyze. In predicate calculus one is allowed to make statements about numbers with the basic arithmetic operations (the general recursive function rules from Chapter 3 would suffice), logical operations (AND, OR, and NOT), and the universal and existential quantifiers ("For all numbers x..." and "There exists a number x..."). Predicate calculus also has a few axioms and inference rules built into it to allow one to construct new mathematical statements from old ones.

Clearly, since predicate calculus with arithmetic only makes statements about numbers, each statement is either true or false, so let's agree for the moment that predicate calculus is consistent. Would it be possible to prove that predicate calculus is complete as well? What Gödel did was essentially construct a mathematical statement that almost (but not quite) read "This statement has no proof." This is a lot like Epimenides's assertion quoted in the beginning of this chapter, or the Liar's Paradox "This sentence is false." The difference between Gödel's statement and these more familiar paradoxes is that while the statement "This sentence is false" obviously leads to a paradox, Gödel's statement is undoubtedly true.

Let's examine Gödel's statement a bit more closely to see why it must be true. The first thing we must realize is that all statements in predicate calculus have a unique Gödel number. We will use the notation S_y to mean that S is a statement that can be coded by the Gödel number y. Also note that a formal proof (which is just a sequence of statements) can also be Gödelized, so let P_x mean that P is a proof with Gödel number x.

Verifying that a proof is correct can be broken down into a mechanical procedure where the proof checker simply verifies that each statement can be derived from some previous statement by the application of a known axiom or theorem. Thus, the notion that a proof exists can be mathematically formalized. In fact, it is possible to construct a very general predicate calculus statement, $\text{Proof}(x, y, z)$, which has three free variables and reads "P_x is a proof for the statement $S_y(z)$ that makes an assertion about the number z." With this last statement, we can formalize an assertion that a proof for something does not exist. We can also play with the free variables a bit to construct a statement that is in some ways self-referential: $\neg\exists x \text{Proof}(x, y, y)$. The $\neg$ symbol denotes logical negation and the $\exists$ symbol denotes the existential quantifier and reads as "there exists." Therefore, the statement $\neg\exists x\text{Proof}(x, y, y)$ reads "There does not exist any proof for the statement $S_y(y)$." Notice that $\neg\exists x\text{Proof}(x, y, y)$ asserts something about a statement that asserts something about its own Gödel number. Since $\neg\exists x\text{Proof}(x, y, y)$ is a formal statement, it has its own Gödel number, which we will denote by g. Finally, this brings us to the following statement:

Gödel's Statement: $\neg\exists x\text{Proof}(x, g, g)$

Is Gödel's statement true or false? If predicate calculus is consistent, then all statements, including Gödel's statement, must be one or the other. If predicate calculus is complete, then either Gödel's statement is provably true or its negation is. Gödel considered all of these issues and came up with the following remarkable theorem:

Gödel's Theorem: $\neg\exists x\text{Proof}(x, g, g)$ is a true statement in predicate calculus, but cannot be proven true in predicate calculus.

The proof for Gödel's Theorem is actually very simple. Suppose that the theorem was not true, and that there really existed a proof for $\neg\exists x\text{Proof}(x, g, g)$. If $\neg\exists x\text{Proof}(x, g, g)$ is provable, then it must also be a true statement (otherwise, predicate calculus would be inconsistent). If it is a true statement, then a proof for Gödel's statement cannot exist. But this is in direct contradiction with our starting assumption that the proof exists. Therefore, since it cannot be false, it must be true.

There is one more remaining little nuance of Gödel's Theorem that we will look at. Suppose a magical oracle tells you with absolute certainty that some formal statement, $\neg\exists x S(x)$, is neither provable nor disprovable. The oracle makes no claim as to the validity of the statement, only that you and I will never be able to prove it one way or the other. What can we deduce about the validity of $\neg\exists x S(x)$ based on what we now know? Assuming that $S(x)$ is a simple statement that contains no additional quantifiers, if $\neg\exists x S(x)$ is false, then $\exists x S(x)$ would be true. But if some x existed for which $S(x)$ is true, then the statement $\neg\exists x S(x)$ would be provably false. Therefore, as long as $S(x)$ has no additional quantifiers, statements of the form $\neg\exists x S(x)$ must always be true if they cannot be proved true or false.

4.2 Incompleteness versus Incomputability

While Turing's result on incomputability is concerned with the limitations of computers and Gödel's result is concerned with the limitation of mathematics, Turing's result is more general in that Gödel's result is a special case of it. This is because the notion of proof verification can be automated by a computer since any of the mathematical statements from the previous section can be implemented as programs. Therefore, asking the question "Is there a proof for a mathematical statement?" can always be reexpressed as "Does some program halt?"

Despite this fact, from a purely subjective and intuitive point of view, Gödel's theorem seems to be more profound because it is primarily concerned with the limitations of mathematics and, by implication, the limitations of mathematicians as well as other humans. On the other hand, some mathematicians, most notably Roger Penrose in his best-selling book *The Emperor's New Mind*, have taken Gödel's incompleteness result to be evidence that human minds do something that no computer could ever do. To paraphrase, the argument works something like this:

> Looking at Gödel's statement, we know that it must undoubtedly be true, since if it is false, we reach a contradiction. You and I, being humans, were able to "leap" out of the formal mathematics to see the validity of Gödel's statement. This ability to see beyond mathematics demonstrates that in some ways, human thought is not only non-algorithmic, but also intrinsically more powerful than algorithmic processes.

Many scientists, philosophers, and mathematicians have pointed out that there are at least two problems with Penrose's interpretation of Gödel's incompleteness result. First, while Gödel's incompleteness result certainly implies that there are true mathematical statements that cannot be proven true—with $\neg\exists x \text{Proof}(x, g, g)$ being just one example—it does not necessarily follow that a computer cannot "see" the validity of a Gödel statement with any less certainty than we could. Why? Because, within predicate calculus, neither you nor I (nor anyone else) would be able to prove a Gödel statement. "Seeing" truth is not the same as proving truth. Nevertheless, Gödel did prove that the Gödel statement was true, *but not in predicate calculus*. His proof was in a formal system of mathematics that was slightly more powerful than the system he started out with. Let's denote the original system, predicate calculus, by the symbol P, and the system in which Gödel proved his incompleteness result by the symbol P'. Is P' immune to Gödel's incompleteness? Surprisingly, P' is also incomplete. We can prove this by using another formal system, P'', which is also incomplete (but provably so in P'''), and so on.

The second problem with the argument is that Penrose assumes that humans are both complete and consistent. If humans were somehow immune to Gödel's incompleteness, then (as computational systems) we would have to be either inconsistent or so computationally weak that self-referential statements could not be expressed. Either of these results would imply that humans are, at least in some ways, weaker than computers. But even if humans are consistent, we aren't immune to Gödel's incompleteness. This is illustrated by the following humorous scenario, which I quote, with some minor editing, from Peter Grogono:[2]

> Imagine that we have an instrument with which we can examine Penrose's brain in great detail (a sort of souped-up interactive NMR scanner,

[2]From a posting on the USENET newsgroup `comp.ai.alife`, dated September 29, 1995.

> perhaps). After some investigation, we find a neuron, G, with the following property: G is usually dormant, but if we tell Penrose that G is dormant, G promptly fires. Then there is a true fact (G is dormant) that Penrose can never know because, whenever he knows it, it is false. Furthermore, we can know this because we are "outside the system."
>
> It is unlikely that a neuron with this property exists. It is very likely, however, that there are some aspects of Penrose's brain's behavior that he cannot know, because knowing them would render them false. Thus Penrose is not exempt from Gödel's theorem.

Furthermore, consider the sentence "Penrose cannot truthfully assert this statement." You and I can say this sentence without contradicting ourselves. But no matter how Penrose contorts himself, he cannot say the sentence without being inconsistent. Moreover, Penrose can "see" the validity of the statement, but he is helpless to express it truthfully, unlike us, because we are "outside" of the system that is Penrose.

4.3 Discrete versus Continuous

Another interesting line of thought that could possibly imply that the universe cannot be understood in terms of computational processes involves the notion that since the universe is obviously continuous, computers—which can represent only discrete entities by definition—are incapable of accurately representing what happens in the universe. If it turned out that the universe is in fact continuous, then it would seem very unlikely that computational processes tell the full story of how nature works.

To counter this, we must first examine the premise, namely, that the universe is obviously continuous. Counter to most people's intuition, it is not at all clear whether or not the universe is continuous. Our everyday experiences seem to indicate that the universe—at least on the macroscopic scale that we are used to—obeys the laws of continuous mathematics; however, physics at infinitesimal scales seems to indicate that the universe is spatially or temporally discrete. Moreover, there would certainly be a precedent for natural phenomena being discrete, since many subatomic particles are indivisible and represent a discrete amount of energy or mass.

Despite this fact, let's examine what it means to compute on a continuous level. Lenore Blum, Mike Shub, and Steven Smale have formulated a model of computation that operates over real numbers. This model of computation exists only in theory, and will never be physically realizable, since it depends on a perfect representation for real numbers (that is, storing an irrational number's infinite decimal expansion). Nevertheless, let's pretend for the moment that you could build a machine that corresponded to this formal model of computation over the real numbers.

The remarkable thing about such a device is that theoretically there exists a "program" for this machine that would be able to solve the Halting Problem for discrete computers. The way the program would work would be essentially to have the uncomputable real number that corresponded to the halting set as some constant in the program.

Does this mean that the Halting Problem would be solved if this device existed? Interestingly, if one continues the analysis of this model of computation (it is a bit too complicated to get into in this short chapter), it turns out that it has its own halting set. In other words, it would seem that there really is no such thing as a free lunch, since even this hypothetical computer has its own infinite set of problems that are incomputable.

The moral of the story is that Gödel's incompleteness result applies to all mathematical formalisms that are so complicated they can make statements about mathematics. Thus, no sufficiently complicated (or interesting) model of computation will ever be free of these basic limitations.

4.4 Incomputability versus Computability

Much of the confusion surrounding the issue if how closely nature can be approximated in a computational framework seems to revolve around the terms *computable* and *incomputable*. There are two shades of meaning for the terms that are often confused. In the formal sense, that is, how a computer scientist would use the words, the term computable / incomputable is used to indicate that a program will halt / will not halt, respectively. But in the weaker sense, people often use the two terms to mean something can (or cannot) be simulated for an arbitrary length of time. For example, given three objects—say a star, a planet, and a satellite—it has been proved that it is impossible, in the general case, to analytically determine the future position of the three objects.[3] So in the strict sense, the Three Body Problem is incomputable. But in the weaker sense of the words, it can be simulated on a computer with very good accuracy—enough to put a man on the moon, in fact.

This confusion has been used by some people to make a claim that physical systems do things that are intrinsically beyond the capabilities of computers. At the risk of picking on Penrose, I am once again going to use an example from his book. Penrose cites a theoretical "billiard-ball" computer, introduced by Edward Fredkin and Tommaso Toffoli (1982), that is capable of computation through a series of billiard-ball switches that operate on a principle similar to the way digital circuitry works in a computer. Fortunately for the purposes of this discussion, it is not really necessary for us to go into the details of how the billiard-ball computer actually

[3]This is the well-known Three Body Problem, proved unsolvable by Henri Poincaré, which forshadowed the importance of chaos.

works. We just need to appreciate that it is a deterministic system that behaves similarly to a real-world physical system. In fact, the billiard-ball computer is also capable of universal computation, which means that no digital computer could ever determine if the billiard-ball computer would "halt" for an arbitrary configuration. Does this mean that physical systems operate in a manner that is qualitatively more advanced than a computer?

Penrose is absolutely correct to point out that the billiard-ball computer is incomputable in the strong sense of the word. But it is "computable" in the weak sense of the word because we could simulate it to any degree of accuracy that we wished. If, for some initial configuration, the billiard-ball computer failed to "halt," then our own computer simulation of it would also fail to halt. But if it did reach some final state, so would the simulation of it.

Here is the point. Nature is so rich and complex in its behavior that computers are incapable of answering many questions about the future. The only way to come close is to simulate a natural system at the risk that a program may never halt. But this richness goes both ways. Computer programs exist that are so complex that their future cannot be predicted either by another computer or by a natural system. Nothing that we know about nature indicates that it stands a level above computational processes. Moreover, Turing's and Gödel's results are really a strength and not a weakness. How so? These sorts of paradoxes are possible only in systems that are strong enough to refer to themselves. Computers obviously fall into this category. But natural systems with a built-in form of parallelism and feedback have much of this same strength. In Parts II–V we will see how this computational paradox is really a sort of power, since all of the subjects that we will examine have a richness that is directly related to incomputability.

4.5 Further Reading

Casti, J. L. (1994). *Complexification: Explaining a paradoxical world through the science of surprise.* New York: HarperCollins.

Fredkin, E. & Toffoli, T. (1982). Conservative logic. *Int. J. Theor. Phys.*, 21(3–4): 219–253.

Gödel, K. (1965). On intuitionistic arithmetic and number theory. In M. Davis (Ed.), *The undecidable* (pp. 75–81). New York: Raven Press.

Gödel, K. (1986). On completeness and consistency. In S. Feferman, J. W. Dawson, Jr., S. C. Kleene, G. H. Moore, R. M. Solovay, & J. Van Heijenoort (Eds.), *Kurt Gödel: Collected works*, volume 1 (pp. 235–237). Oxford: Oxford University Press.

Hofstadter, D. R. (1979). *Gödel, Escher, Bach: An eternal golden braid.* New York: Basic Books.

Margolus, N. (1984). Physics-like models of computation. *Physica D*, 10(1–2): 81–95.

Penrose, R. (1989). *The emperor's new mind.* Oxford: Oxford University Press.

Wang, H. (1987). *Reflections on Kurt Gödel.* Cambridge, Mass.: MIT Press.

Whitehead, A. N. & Russell, B. (1910). *Principia mathematica.* Cambridge: Cambridge University Press.

II Fractals

Euclidean geometry can be extended to account for objects with a fractional dimension. Such objects, known as *fractals*, come very close to capturing the richness and variety of forms found in nature. Fractals possess structural self-similarity on multiple spatial scales, meaning that a piece of a fractal will often look like the whole. Related to this property is the fact that fractals are extremely compressible in the sense that an algorithm or recipe for the image is far simpler to store than the image itself. This is due to the recursive and/or iterative nature of the fractal algorithm. But since fractals are so closely tied to algorithms, some fractals have the same paradoxical properties as systems that can compute.

Chapter 5 introduces some of the basic ideas behind fractal geometry by considering some unusual geometric objects as well as some common stochastic processes found in nature. Chapter 6 focuses on L-systems, which are simple program fragments that can define plantlike and other fractals. Chapter 7 considers fractals that can be defined by linear algebra operators, and Chapter 8 focuses on two special types of nonlinear fractals. This part is concluded by Chapter 9, which examines how fractals can be seen as "nearly simple" objects by some candidate measures of complexity.

5 Self-Similarity and Fractal Geometry

So, Na'ralist observe, A Flea
Hath smaller fleas that on him prey,
And these have smaller fleas to bite 'em
And so proceed ad infinitum.
— Jonathan Swift

There is no "royal road" to geometry.
— Euclid to King Ptolemy I

God used beautiful mathematics in creating the world.
— Paul Dirac

MOST MAN-MADE objects are geometrically simple in that they resemble idealized forms such as points, lines, planes, cubes, circles, or spheres. Ever since Euclid invented geometry, people have been content with the idea that everyday objects can be classified as compositions of regular geometric shapes. Sometimes using simple geometry seems to work; for example, this book in your hand is roughly rectangular, and most people would rightly conclude that attempting to classify the shape by any other means would be silly. But what about natural objects such as a tree, a snowflake, or a mountain range? Do these objects easily fit into a simple geometric category? While it is clear that the idealized geometric shapes only grossly approximate these common natural structures, for some reason conventional wisdom has dictated that such objects are somehow exceptions to the rule; hence, as the reasoning goes, we should not be bothered by the fact that not everything can be described by simple lines and curves.

The term *fractal* was coined by Benoit Mandelbrot to differentiate pure geometric figures from other types of figures that defy such simple classification. Fractals have two interesting qualities that will be explored in this chapter. First, fractals are *self-similar* on multiple scales, in that a small portion of a fractal will often

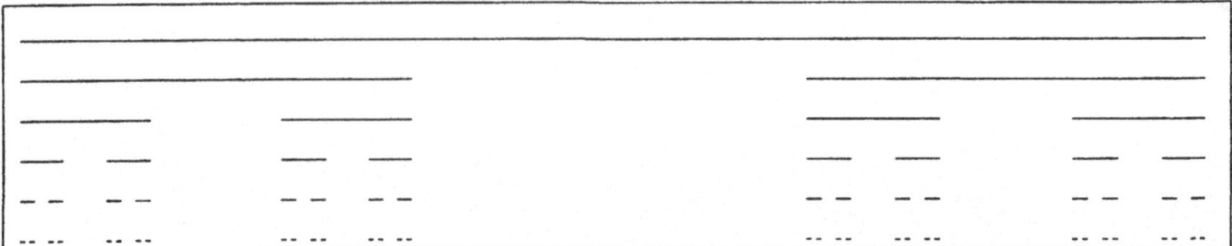

Figure 5.1 The first few steps in constructing the Cantor set

look similar to the whole object, much as a fern leaf looks very much like a fern tree. Second, fractals have a fractional dimension, as opposed to an integer dimension that idealized objects have. This characteristic means that a fractal with a dimension of 1.5 is in some way more than a line but less than a plane.

Because fractals are self-similar, all fractals have a built-in form of recursion. Sometimes the recursion is explicitly visible in how the fractal is constructed. Other times the recursion is a little more subtle and may be an artifact of an underlying fractal-building process that occurs on multiple spatial scales. The first type of fractal can typically be defined by a program-like specification, while the second type of fractal is usually related to a random or stochastic process. In this chapter, we will examine both types of fractals so as to better appreciate both the explicit and the implicit recursion they contain.

5.1 The Cantor Set

Interestingly, the earliest discovered fractals predate the modern computer; were introduced by mathematicians such as Georg Cantor, Helge von Koch, and Waclaw Sierpinski (among others); and were presented as mathematical monsters because of some nonintuitive properties they possess that we will be examining in this chapter. These properties will be easier to understand with some concrete examples; thus, we begin once again with Georg Cantor and the Cantor set.

To construct the Cantor set, we start with the line segment that exists on the interval $[0, 1]$. We then remove the middle third of the segment (leaving the end points) to form two new line segments that exist at $[0, \frac{1}{3}]$ and $[\frac{2}{3}, 1]$. Next, we repeat the process of removing the middle third of each of the two line segments from the previous step to get four smaller line segments. The process of removing the middle third of each remaining line segment continues forever. We obviously cannot do this an infinite number of times with pencil and paper, but, in theory, if we did, we would end up with a image not unlike the bottom line of Figure 5.1, which shows the first few steps in our construction.

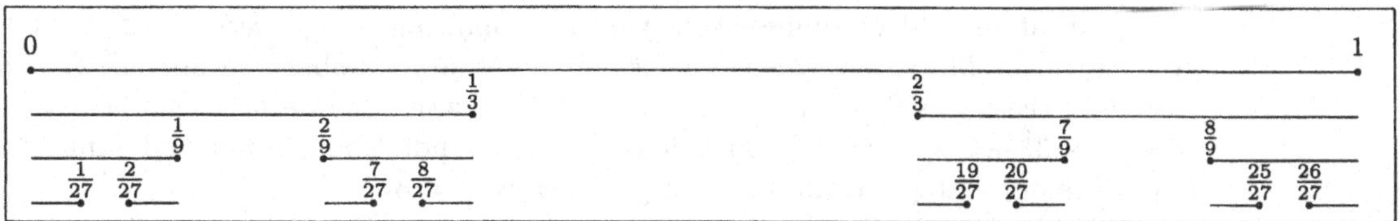

Figure 5.2 The Cantor set with points labeled

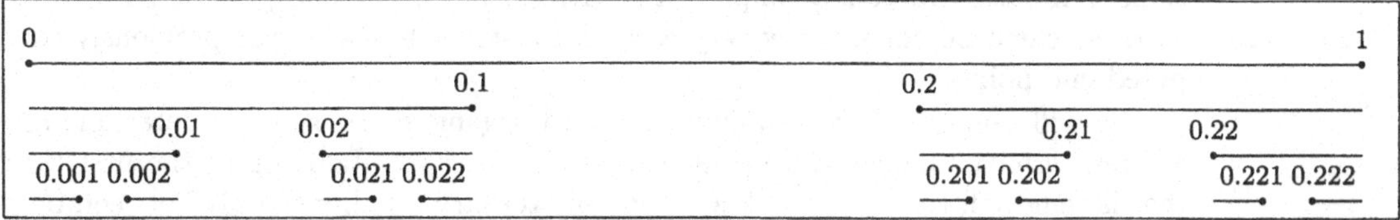

Figure 5.3 The Cantor set with points labeled in ternary notation

Let's pretend that we are able to construct the full Cantor set. What points will remain after an infinite number of steps? Whenever we remove the middle third from a line segment, we keep the old end points and the newly formed end points. Therefore, the end points that remain after any of the steps will always remain in the picture and we can safely conclude that they are members of the Cantor set. But are these the only points that are in the Cantor set?

Figure 5.2 once again illustrates the first few steps in constructing the Cantor set, but this time the newly formed end points from each step are labeled. Notice that we can enumerate the end points as they are discovered: 0, 1, $\frac{1}{3}$, $\frac{2}{3}$, $\frac{1}{9}$, $\frac{2}{9}$, $\frac{7}{9}$, $\frac{8}{9}$, $\frac{1}{27}$, $\frac{2}{27}$, $\frac{7}{27}$, $\frac{8}{27}$, $\frac{19}{27}$, ..., which means that we have discovered an algorithm that maps Cantor set end points to natural numbers. We can refine the list of end points by noting that each such point is the sum of perfect inverse powers of 3. This means that the end points can be efficiently represented by ternary numbers.[1]

The value of a decimal number, such as 123.456, is computed as

$$123.456 = 1 \times 10^2 + 2 \times 10^1 + 3 \times 10^0 + 4 \times 10^{-1} + 5 \times 10^{-2} + 6 \times 10^{-3}.$$

Since decimal numbers have a base-10 representation,[2] we are allowed to use only the digits from 0 to 9. A ternary or base-3 number is similar to a decimal number

[1]Readers familiar with binary numbers will be glad to know that ternary numbers are similar to binary numbers except that a base of 3 is used instead of 2.

[2]There is nothing magical about decimal or base-10 numbers. We find them comfortable to use because most of us have ten fingers to count on. Since computers are good at representing only "on" and "off" states, binary numbers are the most convenient representation for computers because they have only two "fingers" to count on. Moreover, it is fair to say that any base is just as "good" as any other, that is, base-10 is in no way intrinsically "better" than base-2 or base-3.

except that instead of representing values as multiples of powers of 10, we use powers of 3. Moreover, when writing out a ternary number, we are allowed to use only the digits 0, 1, and 2. Thus, one could write the decimal number 17 as $3^2 + 2 \times 3^1 + 2 \times 3^0 = 122$. Fractions in ternary notation are handled similarly; thus, the decimal $\frac{1}{3}$ is equal to ternary 0.1, since $\frac{1}{3} = 3^{-1}$.

Going back to the Cantor set, we can revise Figure 5.2 into the form of Figure 5.3, which uses ternary notation instead of decimal fractions.

Since the Cantor set is constructed by removing thirds, writing end points in ternary notation reveals a simpler numerical form for the end points. Notice that successive end points are now very easy to construct based on the previously computed end points.

We will now see if we can come up with a generalized rule for determining if a given ternary number is a member of the Cantor set. Looking at the first third that is removed, (0.1, 0.2), we know that any ternary number strictly between these two end points is not in the Cantor set. Recall from Chapter 2 that decimal 1.0 was equivalent to $0.\bar{9}$. In ternary notation we have the similar equivalence that 0.1 equals $0.0\bar{2}$. Therefore, any ternary number between $0.0\bar{2}$ and 0.2 is not in the Cantor set. What do these numbers look like? If you play with these two numbers for a while, one thing becomes clear: All numbers strictly between $0.0\bar{2}$ and 0.2 must have a 1 somewhere in the middle of the digit sequence.

Performing the same analysis on the end points $0.00\bar{2}$ and 0.02, or $0.20\bar{2}$ and 0.22, leads us to the same conclusion. Thus, the points of the Cantor set are exactly those points that can be written without any 1s. How many such points are there? Clearly, the number of end points in the Cantor set is countably infinite because we can enumerate them. Moreover, we can observe that all end points have the property that in ternary notation they end either with an infinite number of 2s or with an infinite number of 0s (as $0.2 = 0.2\bar{0}$). Of all of the ternary numbers that can be written without using a 1 the end points are in fact a small subset. There are many other points on the real number line that can be written without using the digit 1 but do not terminate with $\cdots\bar{2}$ or $\cdots\bar{0}$. One such example would be:

$$0.020022000222000022220000022222000000222222\cdots.$$

In fact, there is an uncountably infinite number of points in the Cantor set, which is to say there are as many points in the Cantor set as there are numbers in the real number line.

Suppose we wished to measure the width of all the points in the Cantor set. Mathematicians refer to this as the *measure* of a set. Let us refer to the step in the Cantor set construction by the number n, with the original starting line being step $n = 0$. At any step, n, we have 2^n candidate line segments, each of width $\frac{1}{3^n}$. Therefore, at any step the measure of the remaining line segments is $2^n \times \frac{1}{3^n} = \left(\frac{2}{3}\right)^n$. Thus, as n grows to infinity, the measure of the Cantor set diminishes to 0.

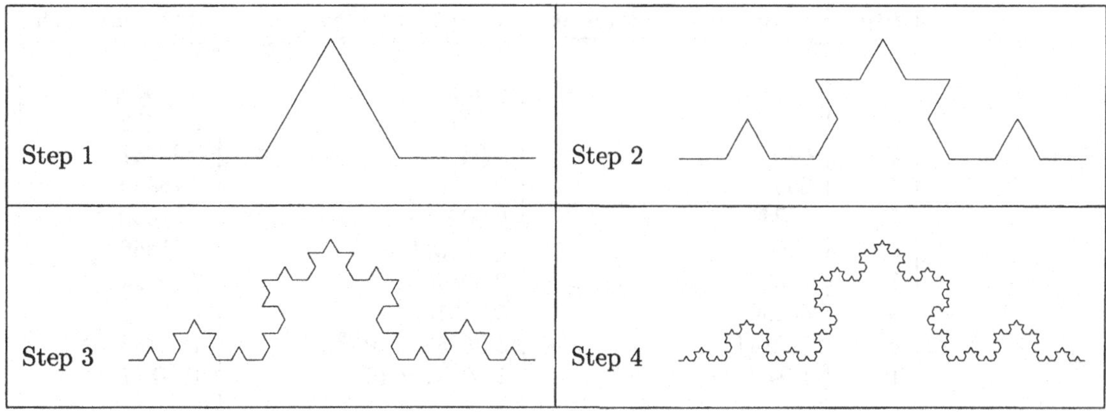

Figure 5.4 The first few steps in constructing the Koch curve

The fact that the Cantor set has as many points as the real number line but has zero measure was perplexing to most of Cantor's contemporaries, and this counter-intuitive property was inspiration for other mathematicians to discover many more mathematical monsters, some of which we will sample shortly.

5.2 The Koch Curve

The Koch curve was created by Helge von Koch as an example of a curve that has no tangent at any point. The first few steps in constructing the Koch curve are shown in Figure 5.4. The construction starts with a single straight line (which is not shown, and is understood to be unit length) and iteratively applies the following transformation: Take each line segment of the Koch curve from the previous step and remove the middle third. Replace the middle third with two new line segments, each with length equal to the removed part. The two new line segments are inserted into the curve such that had the removed piece been left in place, the three segments would form an equilateral triangle.

The method of construction is very easy to understand once Figure 5.4 is examined closely. If one could repeat the process forever, the final Koch curve would consist of no line segments at all but instead would have a corner coincident on every point in the curve. In other words, the curve consists entirely of corners. This is the gist of the earlier statement concerning the fact that the Koch curve has no tangent anywhere, and it is why many have characterized the Koch curve as a mathematical monster.

The Koch curve is obviously related to the Cantor set because they both rely on removing the middle third segment in their respective constructions. After applying

Step	Number of Segments	Length of a Segment	Total Length
0	1	1	1
1	4	0.333333	1.33333
2	16	0.111111	1.77778
3	64	0.037037	2.37037
4	256	0.0123457	3.16049
5	1024	0.00411523	4.21399
6	4096	0.00137174	5.61866
7	16384	0.000457247	7.49154
8	65536	0.000152416	9.98872
9	262144	5.08053×10^{-5}	13.3183
10	1.04858×10^{6}	1.69351×10^{-5}	17.7577
$\vdots$	$\vdots$	$\vdots$	$\vdots$
100	1.60694×10^{60}	1.94033×10^{-48}	3.11798×10^{12}

Table 5.1 The length of the Koch curve

an infinite number of steps in the Koch curve's construction, the points that remain on the original line segment are exactly the same points that are in the Cantor set after an infinite number of steps.

The most interesting facet of the Koch curve is found when one tries to compute its length. We can compute the length of the Koch curve at any step by noting that at step n, the curve consists of 4^n line segments, each with length $1/3^n$. The total length is therefore equal to $(4/3)^n$. A list of these values for some reasonably small step sizes is shown in Table 5.1.

Looking at the total length for step 100, we see the value 3.11798×10^{12}. Suppose that the length of the starting line segment was 1 inch and that we were somehow able to create a Koch curve that consisted of 100 steps. If we could grab the curve by the two end points and stretch it out so that it expanded to its full length, our 1 inch Koch curve would be long enough to wrap around the Earth at the equator nearly fourth thousand times! In fact, as the number of step goes to infinity, so does the total length of the Koch curve. The reason is that the growth rate of the Koch curve is exponential; thus, despite the fact that the length after a small number of steps is small, the rate of growth is such that with a moderate number of iterations, the resulting length is truly gargantuan.

5.3 The Peano Curve

Since we can obviously enclose the Koch curve in a box, all of this would seem to imply that in some ways (at least mathematically) it is possible to twist a line of infinite length within a finite area. In 1890 Giuseppe Peano introduced a type of

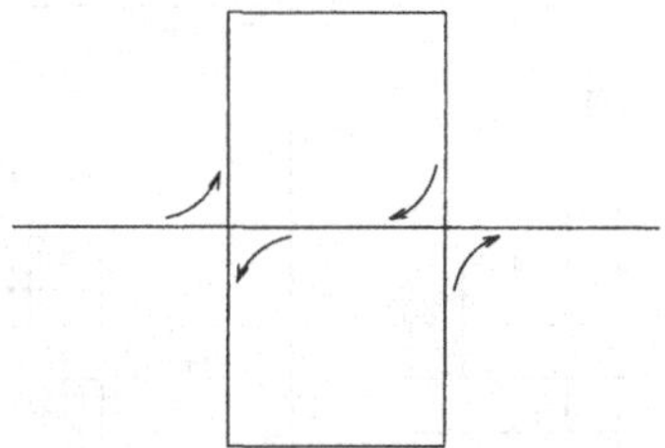

Figure 5.5 One step of the Peano curve

infinite-length curve that not only can fit within an enclosed area but can also fill it. Such curves are known as *space-filling curves* and were also studied by David Hilbert shortly after Peano.

Like the Cantor set and the Koch curve, the Peano curve starts with an initial line segment and is expanded iteratively with a simple rule. For each step in the construction we replace all line segments from the previous step with a curve consisting of nine smaller line segments. Each of the smaller line segments is one-third the length of the line segments from the previous step. There will also be eight 90 degree turns between each of the new smaller line segments. Figure 5.5 illustrates the curve that results from expanding one line segment. The arrows illustrate the path of the curve and reveal that there are two points where the corners touch.

Despite the intersections in the transformation, it is clear that one could draw the curve with pencil and paper without lifting the pencil off the paper. Also note that both end points of the curve after one transformation are in the same location as before the transformation. Thus, we are justified in calling the Peano curve a "curve," since one could draw the whole Peano curve that stopped at any finite step without lifting the pencil from the paper.

The later stages of the Peano curve are illustrated in Figure 5.6. As can be clearly seen, by step 4 we have come close to filling a square. Since each step in the construction replaces each line segment with nine new line segments that have a length one-third the previous size, the total length of the Peano curve is multiplied by a factor of 3 at each stage; thus, if the starting line segment had a length of 1, the step 4 Peano curve in Figure 5.6 has a length of 81.

5.4 Fractional Dimensions

Knowing what you know about the Cantor set, the Koch curve, and the Peano curve, how would you classify them in terms of dimension? Is the Peano curve just a very long line, and if it is, does it therefore merit a dimension of 1, just like any other line? What about the Cantor set? We know that it has zero measure. Does

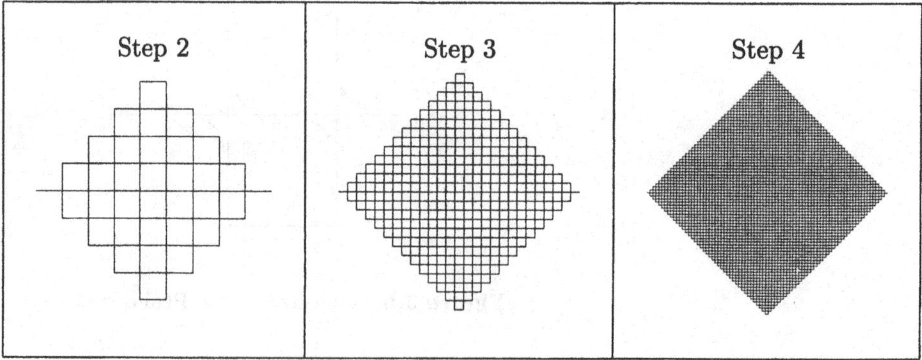

Figure 5.6 The second through fourth steps of the Peano curve

this imply that the Cantor set should be classified as having a dimension of 0? In the case of the Cantor set, we may be content to say that it is "point-like" because it has zero measure, but this seems to ignore the fact that the Cantor set also has an uncountably infinite number of points within it.

The difficulty in assigning a dimension to an object is not unique to the mathematical monsters from this chapter. In fact, a similar phenomenon was reported (posthumously) in 1961 by the English meteorologist Lewis Richardson when he attempted to measure the lengths of various coastlines. Richardson found that the apparent length of a coastline seemed to increase whenever the length of the measuring stick was reduced. For example, the difference between two maps, one with 10 miles scaled to 1 inch and the other with 1 mile scaled to 1 inch, is that the latter map simply shows much more detail than the former. Thus, to measure the length of a coastline at greater magnification than before, one would have to consider small inlets, streams, and peninsulas that may have been invisible on the coarser map. This phenomenon is partially illustrated in the sequence of images shown in Figure 5.7. When moving to even greater magnifications, the twists and turns of individual rocks and speckles of sand would affect the measurement as well. How, then, do we measure the length of a coastline? Are coastlines simply infinite in length?

Richardson found that when the logarithm of the length of the measuring unit was plotted against the logarithm of the total length of a coastline, the points tended to lie on a straight line. The slope of the resulting line in some ways measured the amount of "meandering" of the coastline. Mandelbrot (the father of fractals) found Richardson's work and realized that mathematical monsters could be classified in a similar manner. In this section, we will duplicate some of the analysis performed by Richardson and Mandelbrot to discover what it really means for something to have a fractional dimension.

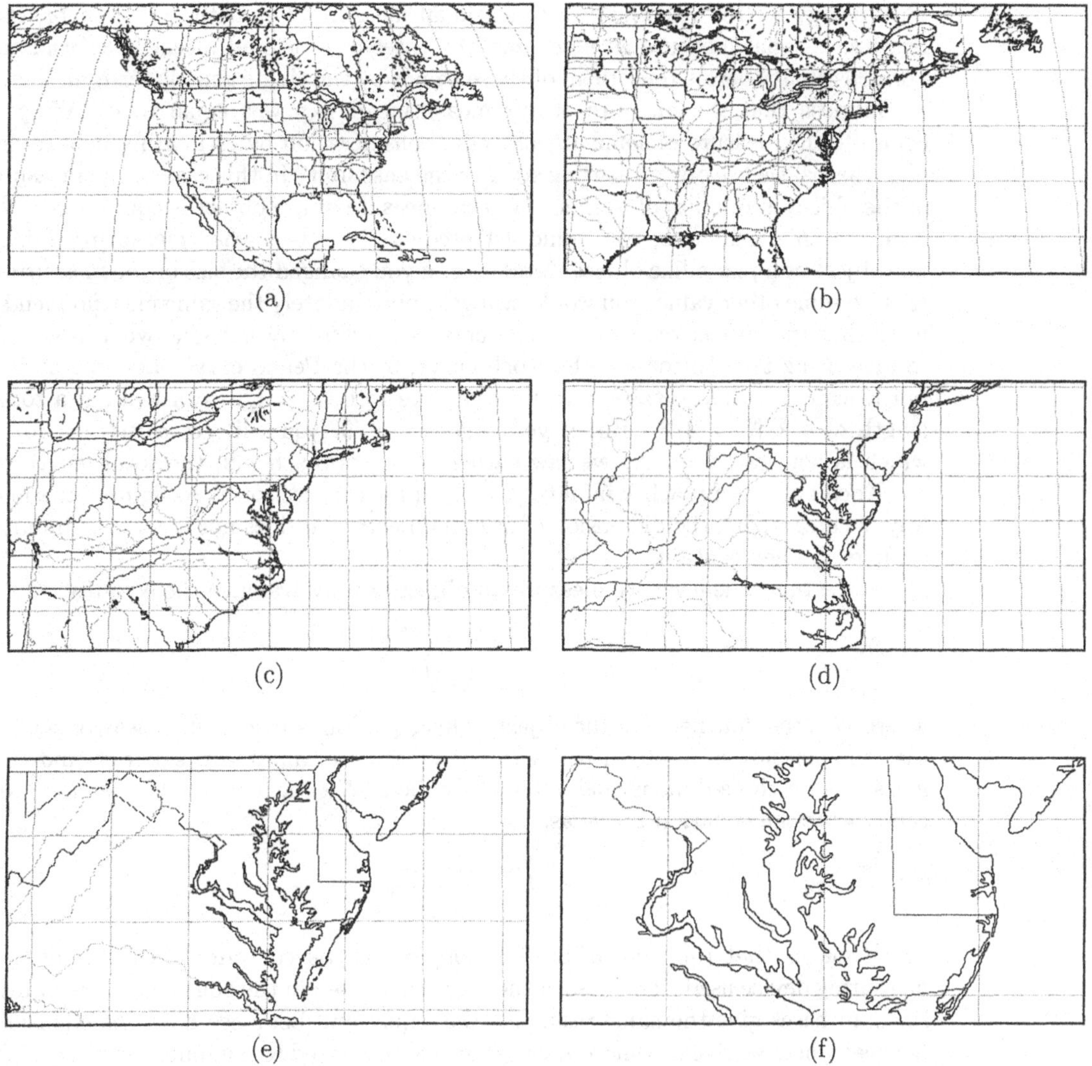

Figure 5.7 Maps of the United States. Each subsequent image enlarges a portion of the previous image by a factor of 2. The last image is of the Chesapeake Bay area off the coast of Maryland

Let us review some basic ideas from geometry that will help us in solving this dilemma. Suppose you had a measuring stick and an object to measure. In standard terminology we refer to the one-dimensional measure of something as *length*, the two-dimensional measure as *area*, and the three-dimensional measure as *volume*. For consistency, let us refer to all of those things by the single generic term *measure*.

Suppose that the measure of our measuring device was equal to a. We can compute the measure of some object under consideration by estimating it in terms of a, that is, we use our measuring stick as the base unit. In this case, if the measure of the object is N units of a, then the total measure of the object is equal to $a \times N$.

Using this technique, you would get predictable results when measuring a line-like object or a plane-like object. Moreover, if you changed the size of the measuring stick to some other value, you would still get approximately the same measurements. Note that this aspect of taking measurements is distinctly not true when it comes to measuring the Cantor set, the Koch curve, or the Peano curve. Looking at the full Koch curve, if you take your unit measure to be $a = 1/3$, you will get a total length of $a \times N = 4/3$. But if you take $a = 1/9$, you will get $a \times N = 16/9$, which is not the same. As we saw earlier, as a approaches 0, the total length of the Koch curve approaches infinity. Our goal for this section is to figure out some way of categorizing the dimension of fractal objects that does not ignore the infinite complexity they contain.

Notice that whenever we measure an object, we always have the equality

$$N = \left(\frac{1}{a}\right)^D,$$

where D is the dimension of the object. This equation is just another way of saying that the measure of a length is linear, the measure of an area is squared, and the measure of a three-dimensional volume is cubed. With a little bit of coercion[3] we can rewrite the equation above as:

$$D = \frac{\log N}{\log\left(\frac{1}{a}\right)},$$

which means that the dimension of an object can be computed in terms of the measuring device used. The base of the logarithms used in the equation is irrelevant, since all bases give the same result for this equation. Let's see how this equation behaves when we give it some known values. If we wanted to compute the dimension of the length of a line from the earlier example, we would always get something like $N = 10$ and $a = 1/10$, which gives us $D = \log 10/\log 10 = 1$. For the face of a wall we would have $D = \log 100/\log 10 = 2$. These results would seem to confirm the fact that our dimension-measuring equation makes some sense for "normal" objects. What about the mathematical monsters from the earlier portions of this chapter?

[3]The derivation is $N = \left(\frac{1}{a}\right)^D \Rightarrow \log N = \log\left(\frac{1}{a}\right)^D \Rightarrow \log N = D \log\left(\frac{1}{a}\right) \Rightarrow D = \frac{\log N}{\log\left(\frac{1}{a}\right)}$.

To construct the Cantor set, we started with a line segment on the interval [0, 1]. After the first step, we removed the middle third. Therefore, for this stage of the construction, let's use a value of 1/3 for a. Exactly two line segments of length $\frac{1}{3}$ remain after the first stage, which gives us a dimension of $\log 2/\log 3$. Since the measure of fractal objects seems to change drastically when we alter the length of the measuring stick, let's see what happens for smaller values of a.

Carrying out the same analysis for the next step in the construction of the Cantor set, we get four line segments with length 1/9. In general, at any stage n of the construction, if we take a to be $1/3^n$ we always get $D = \log 2^n/\log 3^n$. The n's always cancel each other out, which means that no matter how small we make our measuring stick, we always get the same result: $D = \log 2/\log 3 \simeq 0.63093$. Thus, we have somehow expanded on the notion that the Cantor set is something more than a point but less than a line: It is an object with a fractional dimension between 0 and 1.

For the Koch curve, if the value of a is $1/3^n$ (for stage n), then the total length at stage n is always equal to $4^n/3^n$. This yields a dimension of $\log 4/\log 3 \simeq 1.26186$, which means that the Koch curve is slightly more than a line but less than a plane.

The Peano curve has a subtle surprise for us. Once again using $a = 1/3^n$, we get a dimension of $\log 9/\log 3$ since each line segment is expanded into nine new line segments that are one-third the size of the original. However, $\log 9/\log 3 = 2$, which is an integer. This may seem like a strange result, but if we consider the fact that the Peano curve is a space-filling curve, then the result makes some sense after all. Thus, the Peano curve, constructed out to an infinite number of steps, has the same dimension as a plane.

5.5 Random Fractals in Nature and Brownian Motion

When we look at natural phenomena such as the roots of a tree, rivers, coastlines, and clouds, it is easy to see that not all of nature is adequately described by straight lines, curves, or even pure fractals. Most of the listed phenomena seem to have a stochastic or random aspect, leaving us to conclude that some of the analysis that we did in the last section may not necessarily apply to these types of phenomena. However, as we will see in this section, randomness and self-similarity are not mutually exclusive concepts.

A random walk is a path generated by a random process. One way to generate such a path would be to take a drunk person, blindfold him or her, spin the person around a few times, then let him or her go. Another, although less interesting, method for generating a random walk is to take the x and y coordinates of some object, and add to those values two random step sizes. The random steps sizes can be calculated such that they are always equal to either -1 or +1. The new location is the previous location plus the random steps. Repeat as often as you like, for as many steps as you wish.

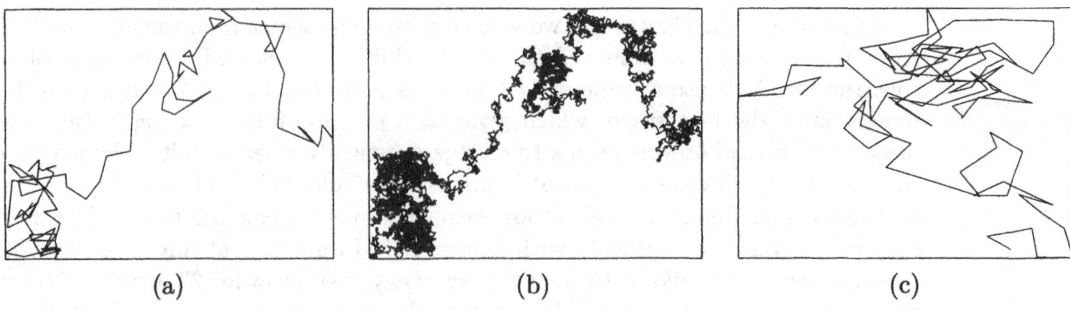

Figure 5.8 Random walks. (a) 100 big steps; (b) same as (a) except with 100 small steps between each big step; and (c) the first 100 small steps from (b)

Suppose that we are able to simulate the path of a drunkard's walk with a computer and the method mentioned above. Let's pretend that we can photograph our virtual drunkard at some shutter speed such that we are able to get about 100 photographs of the drunkard, in sequence. The leftmost image in Figure 5.8a shows what the path of our drunkard could look like under this experimental setup.

For comparison, let's suppose that the drunk really moves a great deal between each photograph, and that we are able to set up a second camera that can shoot pictures about 100 times faster than the first. The new path is illustrated by the middle image of Figure 5.8b, and shows considerably more detail than the original random walk.

Referring back to the first path, on the left of Figure 5.8a, let's now look at just the first step. With the second camera, the single step from the first random walk will have 100 sub-steps to it. The third image in Figure 5.8c shows this path, and has been enlarged for illustrative purposes.

Obviously, the first and third images of Figure 5.8 are not identical, but suppose you didn't know ahead of time which image corresponded to which sampling rate. Would you be able to say with certainty which image was a sub-path of the other? You probably could not solve this puzzle with any success better than a guess, since random processes in nature are often self-similar on varying temporal and spatial scales. The random walk described above is closely related to *Brownian motion*, which is found in the movement of particles in liquids, and *white noise*, which is often used to describe other things believed to be formed by random walk-like processes.

Another instance of white noise can be found in economic data. Figure 5.9 show the S&P 500 stock index for one year, five year, and ten year spans. There is clearly an upward trend to the time series, since the global economy has been steadily expanding since stocks have been traded. Once again, let's suppose that these time

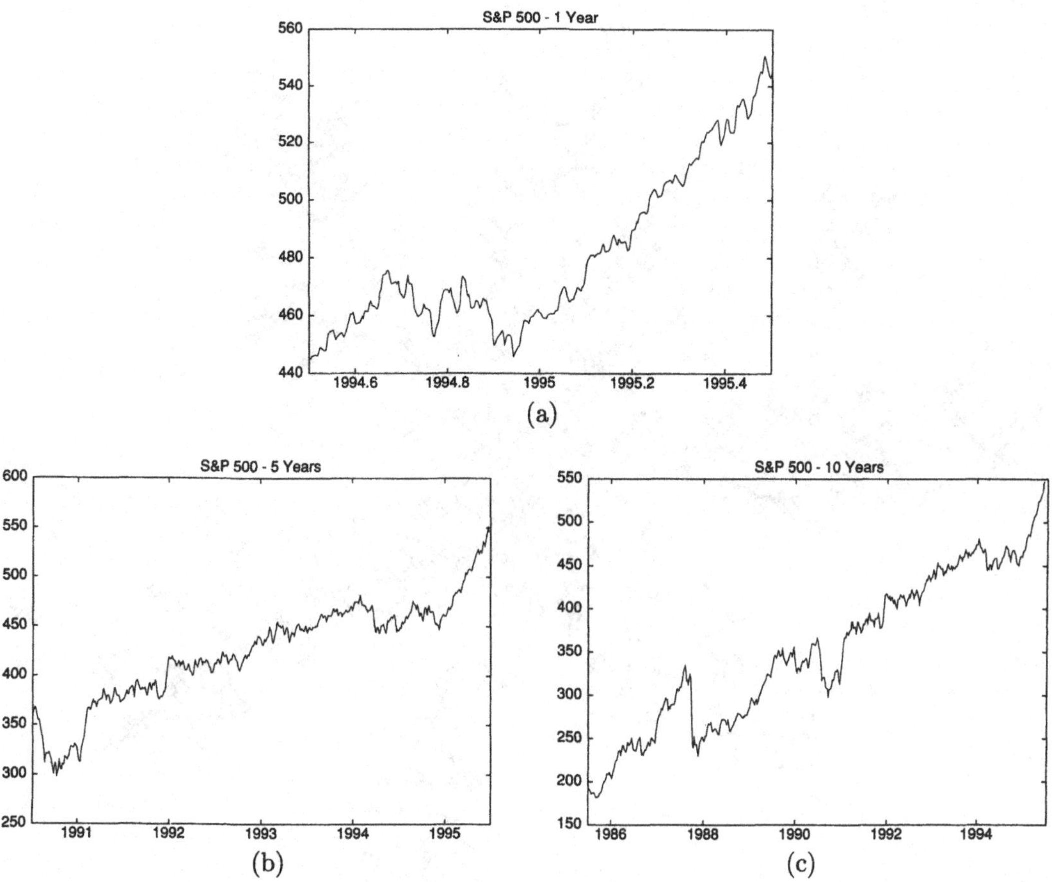

Figure 5.9 The S&P 500 stock index shown on various time scales. (a) one year, (b) five years, (c) ten years

series are not labeled. Can you identify which time series represented what time span? One might assume that since the market appears to increase over the long run, time series that do not show a strong upward trend are more likely to be taken from a short time span. However, professional stock traders have been known to mistake daily data for yearly or ten year data. Time series data is even more confusing after it has been detrended, that is, the general drift is removed. In fact, detrended financial data can pass many statistical tests for randomness, which implies that financial time series may not merely look random, but are actually generated from extremely complicated processes that contain similar events occurring on many

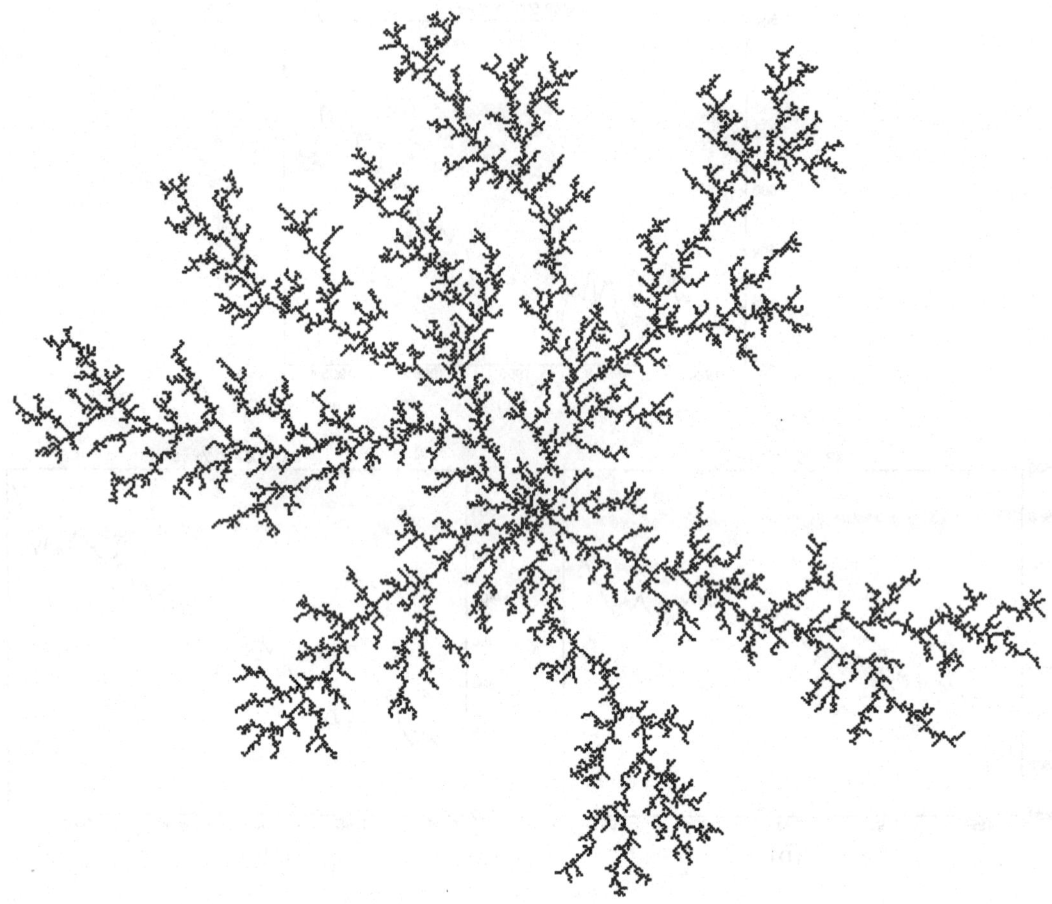

Figure 5.10 An example of growth from diffusion limited aggregation

scales. Thus, self-similarity from random-like processes can extend to the economic sector as well.

Related to Brownian motion is a process known as *diffusion limited aggregation*. Suppose there exists a medium in which many particles move via Brownian motion. Furthermore, imagine that each particle has the property that it continues to move as long as it never touches a stationary object. We can "seed" a growth process by placing a single fixed particle in the center of our mixture. Eventually, a moving particle will touch the fixed particle and will become fixed itself. As the process continues, more and more particles will stick to the growing structure, resulting

Figure 5.11 Fractal mountain generated by **xmountains** (an X Windows program written by Steven Booth)

in something that looks similar to Figure 5.10. Diffusion limited aggregation is found in crystal growth, coral reefs, and other natural systems. The self-similarity of the resulting structures always has a fractional dimension since diffusion limited aggregation is a process that occurs on multiple spatial scales.

A three-dimensional version of Brownian motion also yields a very good description of how mountains, streams, and coastlines look. Figure 5.11 shows a landscape that was generated with a relatively simple program called **xmountains**. The method used to generate the image is a bit too complex to describe in this book, but this does not diminish the fact that the image is very realistic.

A different type of random self-similarity can be found in clouds. Sometimes, clouds that are thousands of feet away look close enough to touch. But on the other hand, close clouds often appear to be very far away. All of this is due to self-similarity on multiple spatial scales.

5.6 Further Exploration

This section contains a brief overview on how to use **diffuse**, a program that simulates diffusion limited aggregation. The program starts with a single point seed located in the middle of the plot, that is fixed throughout the entire simulation, and several pixel-size floating particles (with the number determined by the **-num** option) that are placed randomly on the screen. At each time step, the particles will float about the screen in a random-walk pattern, each independent of one another. Any particle that moves adjacent to a fixed cell (such as the seed) will become fixed as well, resulting in a new floating particle being randomly regenerated to take the newly fixed particle's place. In this way, a stochastic fractal gradually grows on the screen.

Option Name	Option Type	Option Meaning
`-width`	INTEGER	width of the plot in pixels
`-height`	INTEGER	height of the plot in pixels
`-num`	INTEGER	number of floating particles
`-steps`	INTEGER	number of simulated steps
`-invis`	SWITCH	invisible particles?
`-seed`	INTEGER	random seed for initial state
`-inv`	SWITCH	invert colors?
`-xmag`	INTEGER	magnification factor for X Windows
`-term`	STRING	how to plot points

Table 5.2 Command-line options for `diffuse`

Table 5.2 lists the legal command-line options for `diffuse`. To vary the simulation between runs, you should use a different seed and try different values for the `-num` option. This program also has an option called `-invis` which only affects the output when the `-term` option is set to `x11`. When correctly used, the particles will be displayed only when they become fixed in location; thus, no floating particles will be displayed. This makes the simulation run much faster.

The next chapter will introduce another method of generating fractals that will enable you to produce the deterministic fractals illustrated earlier in this chapter.

5.7 Further Reading

Mandelbrot, B. (1983). *The fractal geometry of nature.* New York: W. H. Freeman.

Peitgen, H.-O., Jürgens, H., & Saupe, D. (1992). *Chaos and fractals.* New York: Springer-Verlag.

Schroeder, M. (1991). *Fractals, chaos, power laws.* New York: W. H. Freeman.

6 L-Systems and Fractal Growth

The development of an organism ... may be considered as the execution of a "developmental program" present in the fertilized egg. ... A central task of developmental biology is to discover the underlying algorithm from the course of development.
— Aristid Lindenmayer and Grzegorz Rozenberg

Nature uses as little as possible of anything.
— Johannes Kepler

FROM WHAT WE have seen in the last chapter, fractals seem to be very good at squeezing a great deal of length—perhaps infinite—into a small finite area. This property, which, for lack of a better term, we can think of as packing efficiency, is found in virtually every organism in nature. For example, a great deal of the work performed by the human body involves circulatory functions, which have the goal of moving something from one part of the body to another. This task, while simple to state, is in fact very complex and involves a delicate trade-off between conflicting goals. If we were to design a circulatory system from scratch, one requirement would be that our system should be capable of transmitting things from potentially any source to any destination. However, we would also want our circulatory system to have as small a volume as possible, since it is obviously not feasible to make an organism that consists entirely of plumbing. Nature solves the problem by building circulatory systems with fractal geometry that achieves both of the goals.

We encounter similar designs in many other types of natural systems, as shown in Figure 6.1: Wrinkled folds on the surface of the brain maximize surface area; the respiratory, lymphatic, and nervous systems all have a fractal treelike organization similar to the circulatory system; complicated fractal folding is found on the macroscopic level of the kidneys and also on the microscopic level of mitochondria.

Nature minimizes material requirements while maximizing functionality through the ubiquitous use of fractals. However, all of our examples have one very important aspect that, while obvious once seen, is easily overlooked: Fractals in biological systems must be grown.

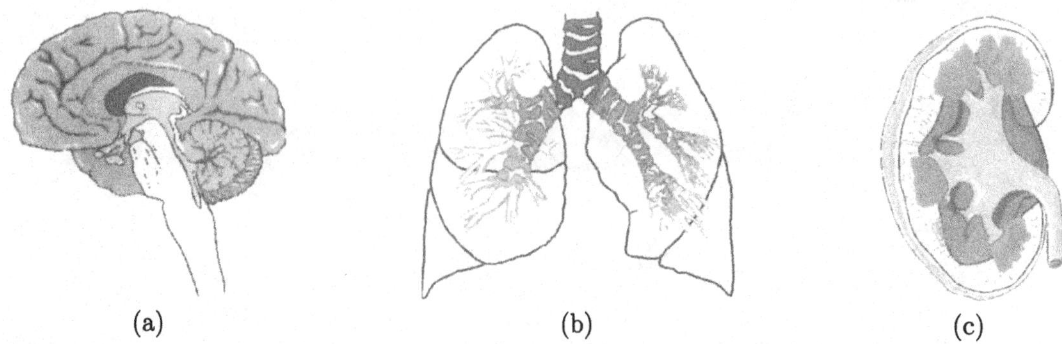

(a) (b) (c)

Figure 6.1 Naturally occurring fractals in the human body: (a) brain, (b) lungs, (c) kidney

Why is this important? When something is grown, the instructions for how the growth is to progress must be contained somewhere. In the case of biological systems, the programs for all cell growth are found in DNA, which contains instructions that are as digital as those found in computers. Toward the end of this book part we will examine a topic, known as *algorithmic complexity*, that will shed some light as to why it is important for biological systems to have efficiently encoded growth instructions.

In 1968, Aristid Lindenmayer, a biologist, invented a formalism that yields a mathematical description of plant growth known as an *L-system*. L-systems can be used to efficiently describe not only plant growth but also many types of mathematical monsters, including the examples from the last chapter. L-systems are also remarkably compact, which is especially impressive when one considers the infinite detail that can be found in fractals. We will use L-systems in this chapter to generate some familiar and not-so-familiar objects.

6.1 Production Systems

Since L-systems describe growth, an L-system consists of a special seed cell and a description of how new cell types can be generated from old cell types. The seed cell is known as an *axiom*, and for a particular L-system all growth starts from the same axiom. The descriptions of how to grow new cell types from old cell types are known as *production rules*. Consider the following L-system as an example:

$$\begin{array}{rl} \textbf{Axiom:} & B \\ \textbf{Rules:} & B \rightarrow F[-B]+B \\ & F \rightarrow FF \end{array}$$

Depth	Resulting String
0	B
1	$F[-B]+B$
2	$FF[-F[-B]+B]+F[-B]+B$
3	$FFFF[-FF[-F[-B]+B]+F[-B]+B]+FF[-F[-B]+B]+F[-B]+B$

Table 6.1 Simultaneous string substitutions in an L-system

You don't need to worry about what the symbols mean, since we are concerned, at this point, only with how to "grow" things with the L-system. The rules specify a simple rewriting scheme that involves taking the axiom and substituting as many of the symbols as we can, as specified by the rules. After performing the substitution on the axiom, we will have another string of symbols. We can apply the substitution rules on this result to get a third string of symbols, and so on. Using the L-system specified above yields the strings shown in Table 6.1.

The length of the string grows dramatically at each step, but what does the string mean? By itself, the string means absolutely nothing, but in the context of a device that can interpret each symbol as a simple instruction, the string can represent the building plan for a fractal structure. For example, one such interpreting device can be found in the cellular machinery of plants and animals. In algae (and almost all multicelled organisms) it is known that individual cells can specialize in how they reproduce. Figure 6.2 illustrates how a hypothetical algae strain could grow as specified by the production rules (and ignoring the brackets).

Initially, we start with a single B cell. At some future time the lone B cell could reproduce as specified by the $B \rightarrow F[-B]+B$ rule. Next, the resulting B cells and the single F cell could each divide again—producing the third generation—but notice that the F cell reproduced as specified by the $F \rightarrow FF$ rule.

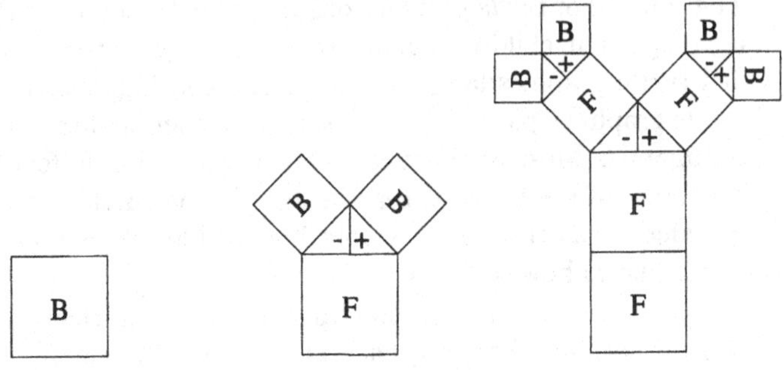

Figure 6.2 String substitution as cell division

Cmd.	Turtle Action
F	(Draw Forward) Move the turtle forward by a fixed length, drawing a line from the old position to the new position.
G	(Go Forward) Move the turtle forward by a fixed length, but do not draw a line.
+	Turn the turtle to the right by a fixed angle. If an integer precedes the "+" symbol, then the turtle effectively makes that number of right-hand turns.
−	Turn the turtle to the left by a fixed angle. If an integer precedes the "−" symbol, then the turtle effectively makes that number of left-hand turns.
[	Save the turtle's current position and angle for later use onto a stack of saved states.
]	Remove the last saved state from the stack and use it to restore the turtle's last saved position and angle.
|	Move the turtle forward by a length computed from the execution depth, drawing a line from the old position to the new.

Table 6.2 Turtle graphics commands

In this manner, it is easy to see that cell specialization combined with growth rules specific to each cell type can result in some interesting growth patterns. Next, we will look at another related method of interpreting the symbols produced by an L-system that can be used by a computer to produce simulated growth.

6.2 Turtle Graphics

The concept of *turtle graphics* originated with Seymour Papert as a simple computer language that children could use to draw graphical pictures. We will use a modified turtle graphics language to interpret strings generated from L-systems. Under turtle graphics, plotting is performed by a smart little turtle that can follow certain commands. Most of the commands involve simple forward movement or rotation. The state of the turtle is represented by the turtle's current (x, y) coordinates and the angle that the turtle is pointing. Table 6.2 lists all of the commands that the turtle knows how to follow.[1]

If the turtle receives a command that is not in the list, it will ignore the command and do nothing. Looking back at the last three strings generated by the example

[1]The "|" command is an advanced command that is not strictly required, but makes certain types of images easier to draw. See Section 6.3 for further details.

Figure 6.3 Three L-system stages

L-system, our turtle would produce the three images in Figure 6.3; they correspond to the images in Figure 6.2, from left to right.

For the images, the "+" and "−" commands rotate the turtle by 20 degrees. In general, we will be allowed to set this angle to anything that we wish. Since the first image corresponds to the string "$F[-B]+B$," the turtle draws a single line; however, it is worth noting that after drawing the figure, the turtle will be pointing 20 degrees to the right of the single line because of the last "+" command. The second image corresponds to the string "$FF[-F[-B]+B]+F[-B]+B$." The second image looks like a "Y" with the main segment double the length of the original because the first rule, $B \to F[-B]+B$, in effect orders the turtle to convert all Bs to "Y" branches, while the second rule, $F \to FF$, doubles the length of all interior stems. In the third image, all of the segments double in length once again and all exterior stems branch into two more stems.

Notice that the "[" command tells the turtle to remember where it currently is. When the matching "]" is encountered, the saved state is restored. Having this ability is not strictly necessary for many L-systems, but it does save us the trouble of having to construct additional rules to backtrack to some prior position and angle.

6.3 Further Exploration

This section contains a brief tutorial on how to use **lsys**, which is the program used to generate all of the images in this chapter. A list of the legal options can be found in Table 6.3. Many of the options are self-explanatory; however, the options that are specific to **lsys** will be discussed in greater detail.

The **-a0** option is used to specify the starting angle of the turtle. The option is given in degrees, where 0 degrees corresponds to pointing at 12 o'clock, and 90 degrees refers to 3 o'clock. The **-da** option specifies the number of degrees that the "+" and "−" commands will rotate the turtle.

The **-ds** option can be cleverly used to make the L-system produce images that are scale-invariant in the depth. If a "F," "G," or "|" command is processed at a depth of d, then the step size will be equal to δ^d, where δ is the value specified with **-ds**, which should always be less than or equal to one. By using this option

Option Name	Option Type	Option Meaning
`-width`	INTEGER	width of the plot in pixels
`-height`	INTEGER	height of the plot in pixels
`-border`	INTEGER	number of pixels in border
`-depth`	INTEGER	recursion depth of L-system
`-a0`	DOUBLE	initial angle
`-da`	DOUBLE	delta angle
`-ds`	DOUBLE	delta step size factor
`-unoise`	DOUBLE	amount of uniform noise to use
`-rule`	STRING	specify a production rule
`-axiom`	STRING	starting axiom
`-inv`	SWITCH	invert all colors?
`-xmag`	INTEGER	magnification factor for X Windows
`-term`	STRING	how to plot points

Table 6.3 The command-line options for `lsys`

in conjunction with the "|," you can more easily build fractals that are made of segments of different lengths. For example, Big-H in Figure 6.4 uses the rule $F \rightarrow |[+F][-F]$ and a step size of 0.65. Unlike the "F" and "G" commands, the "|" command is processed by the `lsys` program at every depth, not just the final depth, since the "|" command is never recursively expanded. The "|" command essentially means that the `lsys` program should draw a line whose length is computed by the current step size. With these options, the Big-H figure is drawn such that each branch is drawn 65 percent the size of the previously drawn branch. Controlling the ratio of subsequent branch sizes would be extremely difficult without this option.

The `-unoise` option specifies the amount of uniform noise to add to the angles for each L-system command that moves the turtle forward. This option can have the effect of making the images look more natural by adding unexpected twists and turns that could be found in real plant growth.

The `-rule` option is used to specify all of the rules for the computed L-system. For each rule that is required, you should use the pair "`-rule F=ABC`" to specify the rule. There can be no spaces in the rule, and the cases of the letters are ignored; thus "`-rule F=ABC`" is the same as "`-rule f=abc`." You may also need to enclose the rule strings with quotes to protect them from being interpreted by the command shell of your computer.

The best way to learn more about L-systems is to use `lsys` to generate your own L-systems. You could start by trying to reproduce the L-systems illustrated at the end of this chapter. The rules and delta angle are supplied for each figure. You may still need to figure out appropriate values for the options `-ds`, `-a0`, and

The Chomsky Hierarchy of Formal Languages **Digression 6.1**

In 1959 Noam Chomsky introduced four types of formal languages that form what is now known as the *Chomsky hierarchy* of formal languages. The language types can be classified by the types of productions that are permitted in their grammars. For each of the descriptions below, uppercase Roman letters will be used to represent nonterminal symbols that can be further expanded, lowercase Roman letters will be used to represent terminal symbols (which cannot be further expanded), and Greek letters will be used to represent an arbitrary string of terminal or nonterminal letters.

Regular: Regular grammars may consist only of rules in the form of $A \rightarrow b$ or $A \rightarrow bC$.

Context-Free: The context-free grammars may have rules of the form $A \rightarrow \alpha$, and are therefore unrestricted in the form that the right-hand side of production rules may take.

Context-Sensitive: Context-sensitive grammars may have rules of the form $\alpha A \beta \rightarrow \alpha\gamma\beta$, where γ is not the empty string.

Unrestricted: The unrestricted grammars are identical to the context-sensitive grammars except that γ may be the empty string.

The four grammar types generate exactly the same languages and sets that are recognized by finite-state machines, pushdown automata, linear bounded automata, and Turing machines, respectively. L-systems can be thought of as special types of context-free grammars that operate in parallel.

-depth. After mastering the L-systems in this chapter, you can go on to make your own. For your first attempt, try executing the command:

```
lsys -depth 3 -a0 90 -da 60 -rule "F=F-F++F-F"
```

which should produce the Koch curve from the last chapter. You can change the depth option to a larger number to make a more detailed picture.

Several more examples are given in Figures 6.4–6.11, which appear over the next few pages. These examples illustrate how some interesting structures can be generated with L-systems. Each L-system will be shown with three images: the first two are the first two interesting stages of the L-system and the last image is some later stage. Some of the rules may seem confusing at first glance; however, this should not stop you from aesthetically appreciating the figures.

Readers familiar with the C programming language may wish to look at the source code for `lsys`. With the exception of the low-level graphics routines and the command line parsing functions, the whole program, excluding comments, fits in about two full pages.

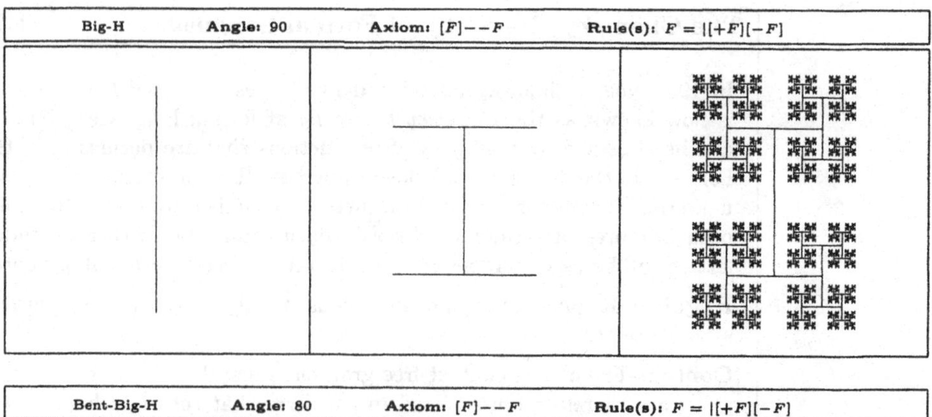

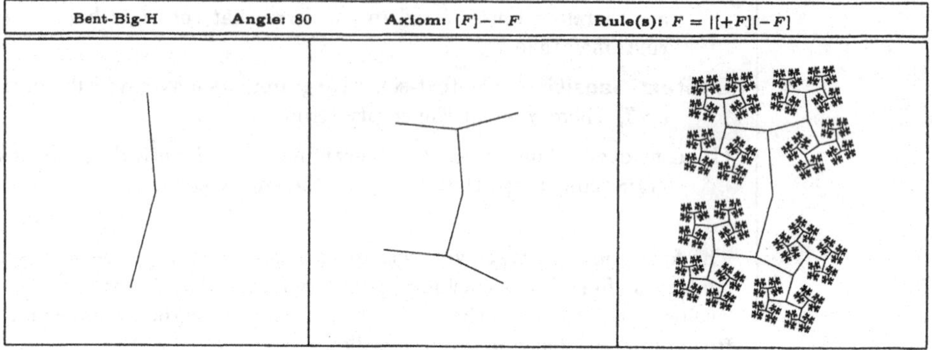

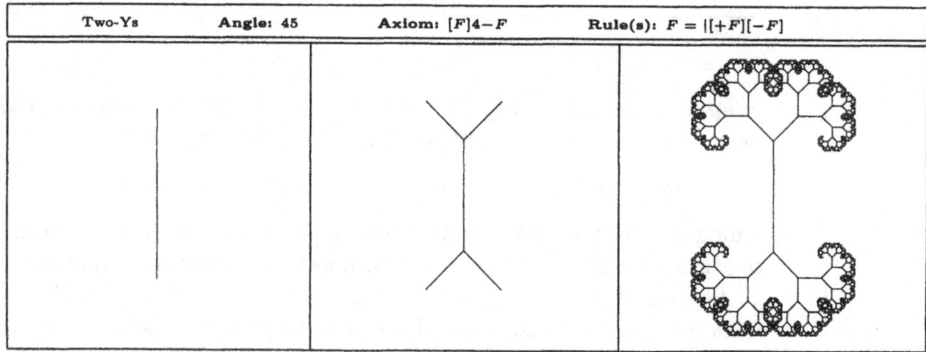

Figure 6.4 Simple branching fractals: Big-H and Bent-Big-H use the "|" command to draw consecutive segments lengths in a 20:13 ratio, which I found more pleasing to the eye than 2:1. The only difference between Big-H and Bent-Big-H is in the specified angle, which differs by 10 degrees. All of these figures efficiently divide the square plane into a network structure, as found in many biological systems.

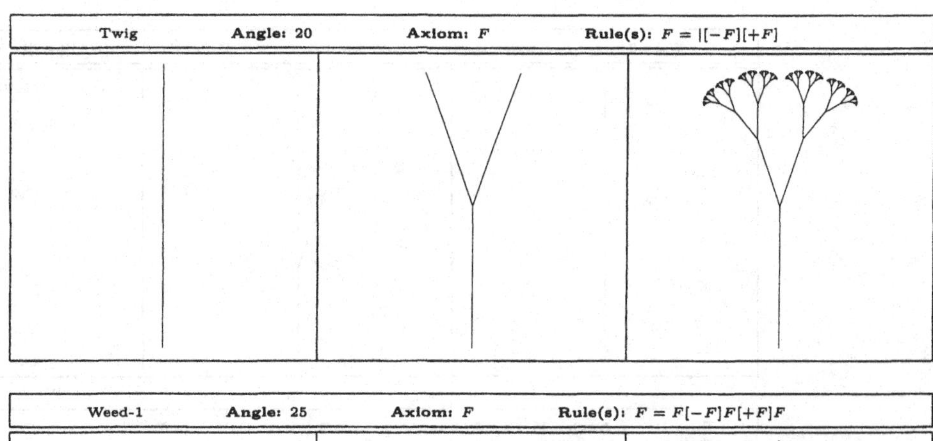

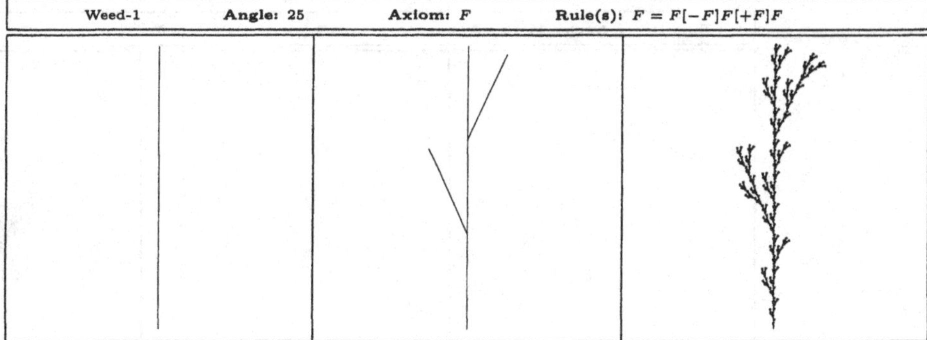

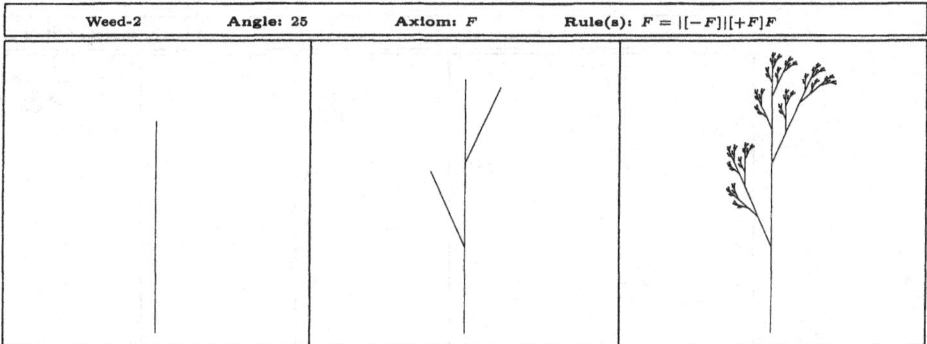

Figure 6.5 Plantlike fractals: With only a little bit of effort, one can change the turn angle, the ratio between consecutive segments, and the rules to produce a wide variety of weed-like and twig-like structures.

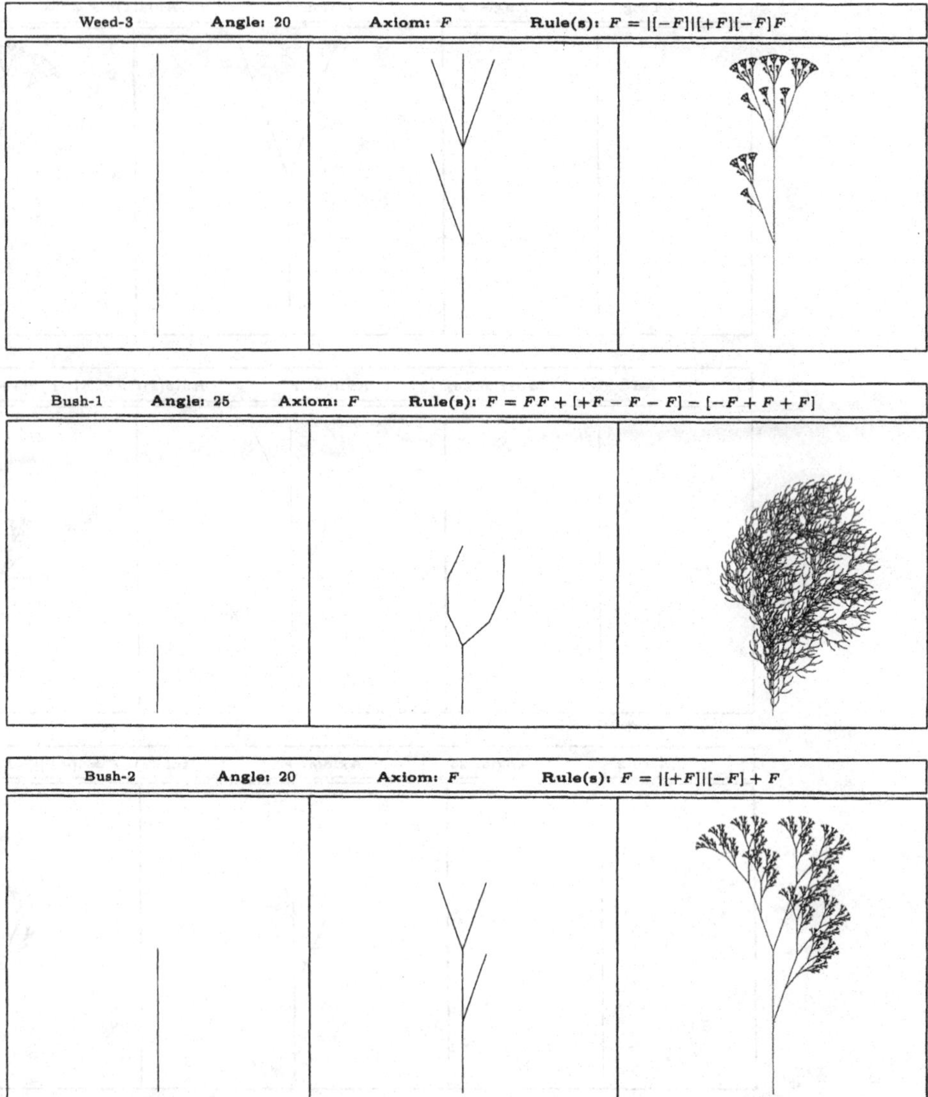

Figure 6.6 More plantlike fractals: The production rules are now a bit more complicated but yield even more realistic plant growth.

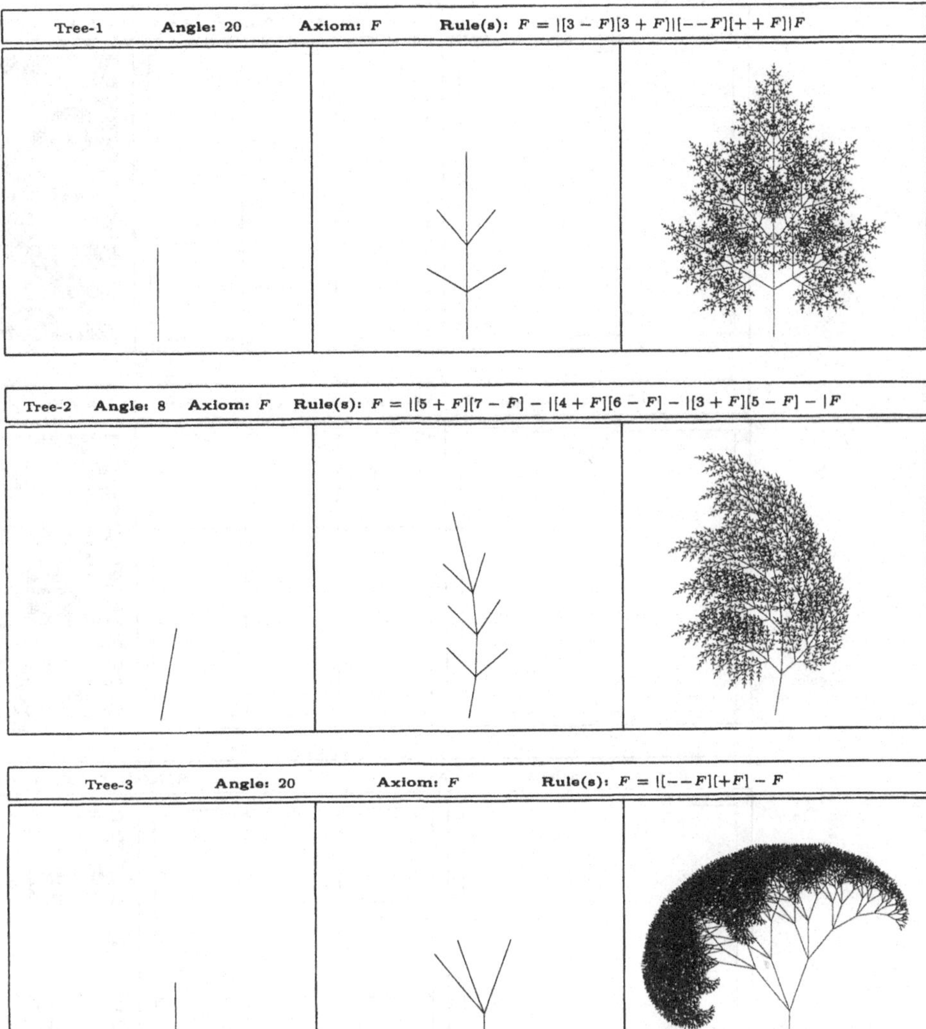

Figure 6.7 And yet more plantlike fractals: Tree-1 has an increased branching factor that creates a fuller image. Tree-2 illustrates how to use a small turning angle to make more realistic curves.

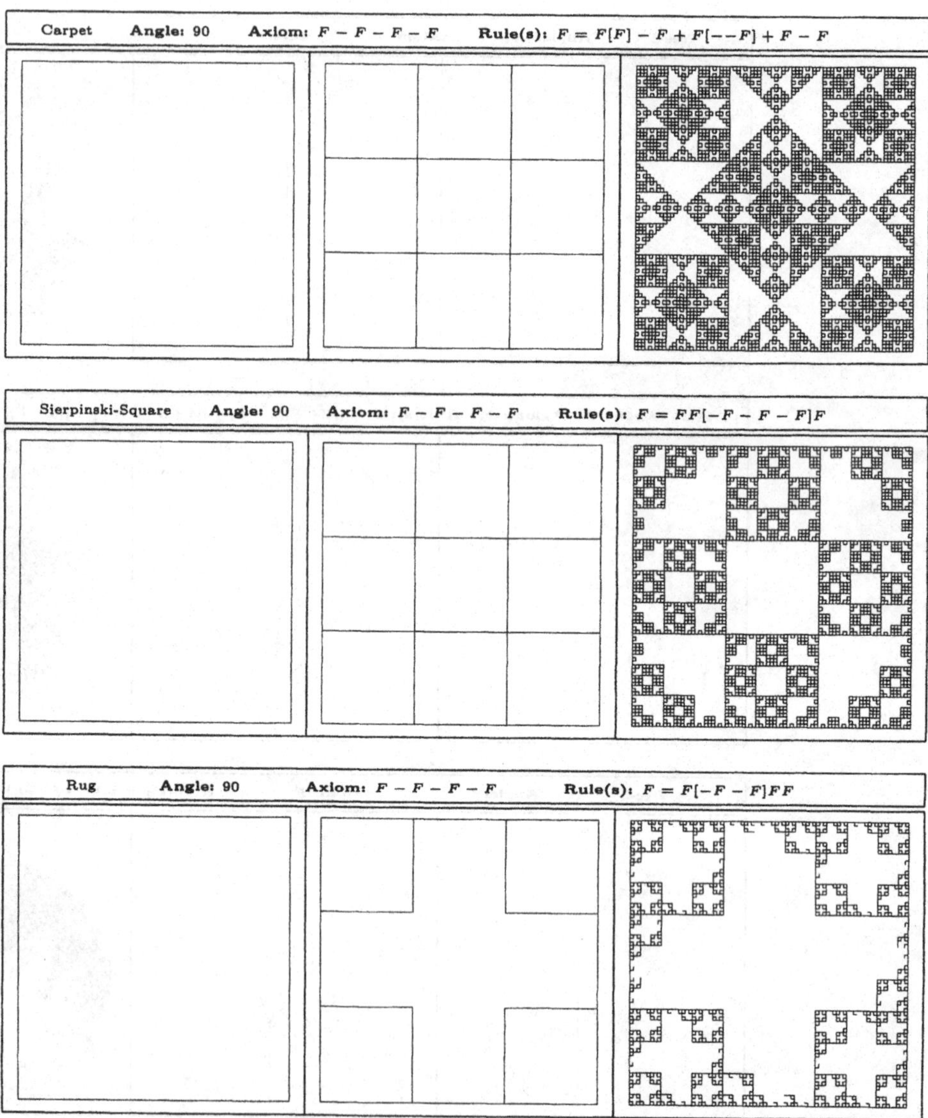

Figure 6.8 Mosaic fractals: It is interesting to see that Carpet and Sierpinski-Square are identical at the second expansion stage but diverge greatly later on. Many other interesting patterns of this type can be found with only a subtle change to a single rule.

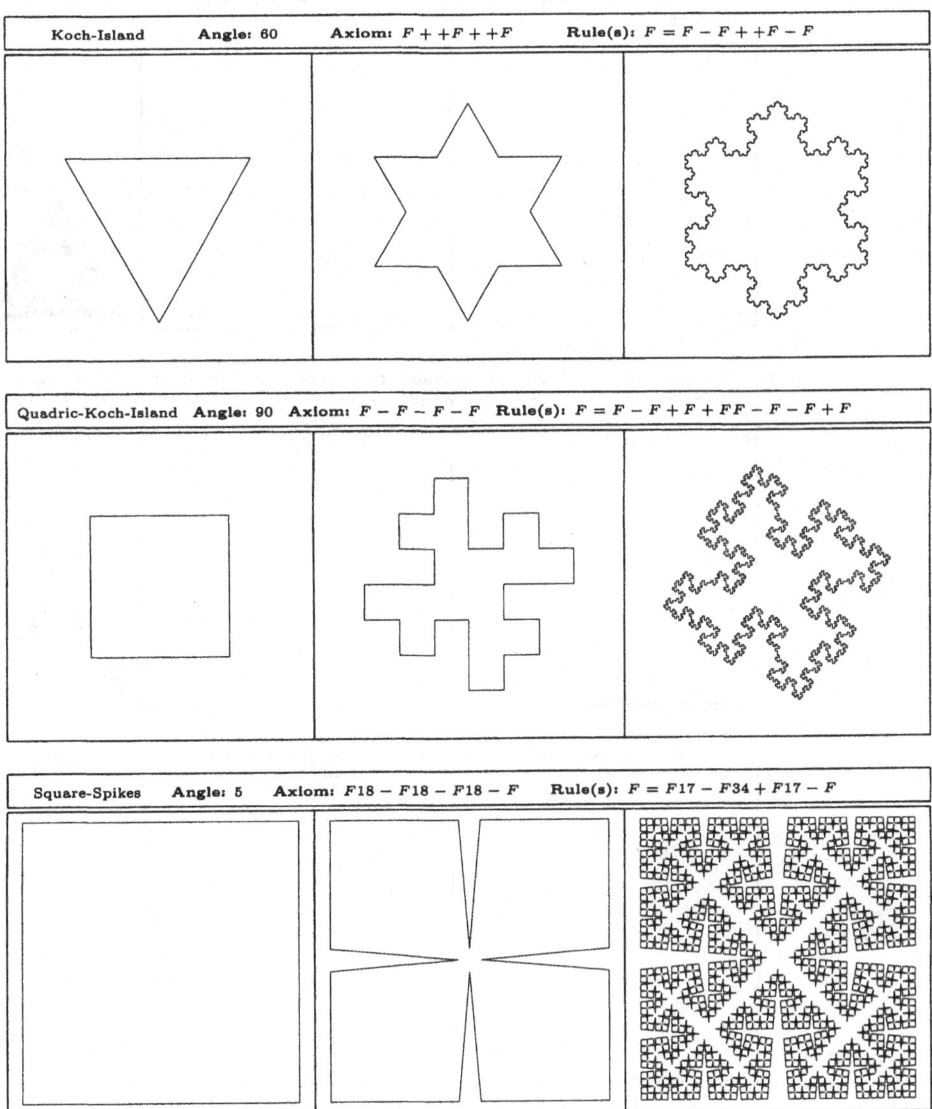

Figure 6.9 Fractals islands: The Koch-Island consists of three Koch curves from the last chapter pasted together. The Quadric-Koch-Island continues on a similar theme as the Koch-Island, but uses more turns with right angles. Square-Spikes is an example of how to effectively use the feature that turning commands can be preceded by an integer.

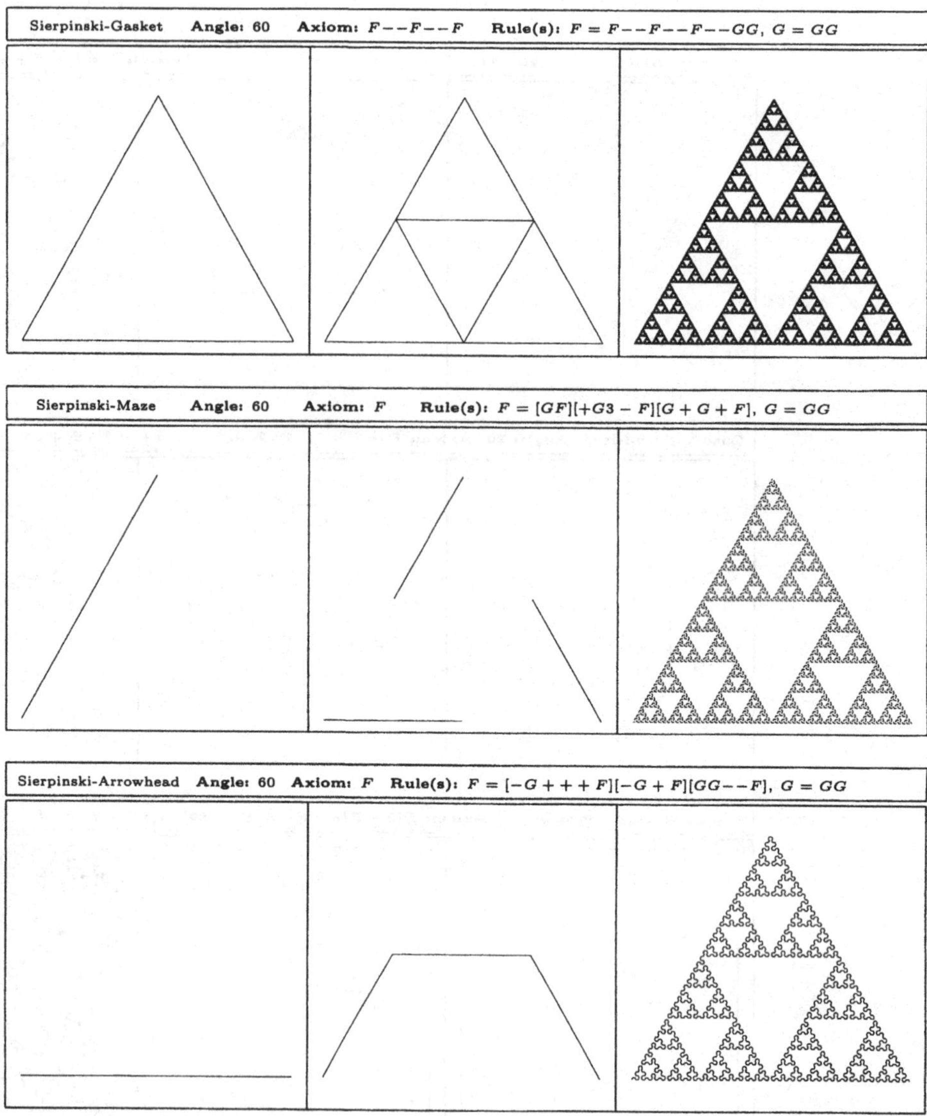

Figure 6.10 Sierpinski triangles: The Sierpinski-Gasket L-system rules convert each line segment into three new line segments that form a triangle. Unlike the other two L-systems, the Sierpinski-Maze is totally unconnected. The Sierpinski-Arrowhead is formed by one long and continuous curve. These three L-systems also illustrate how to use multiple rules. In this case we have expanded the "*G*" turtle graphics command so as to increase the distance between line segments.

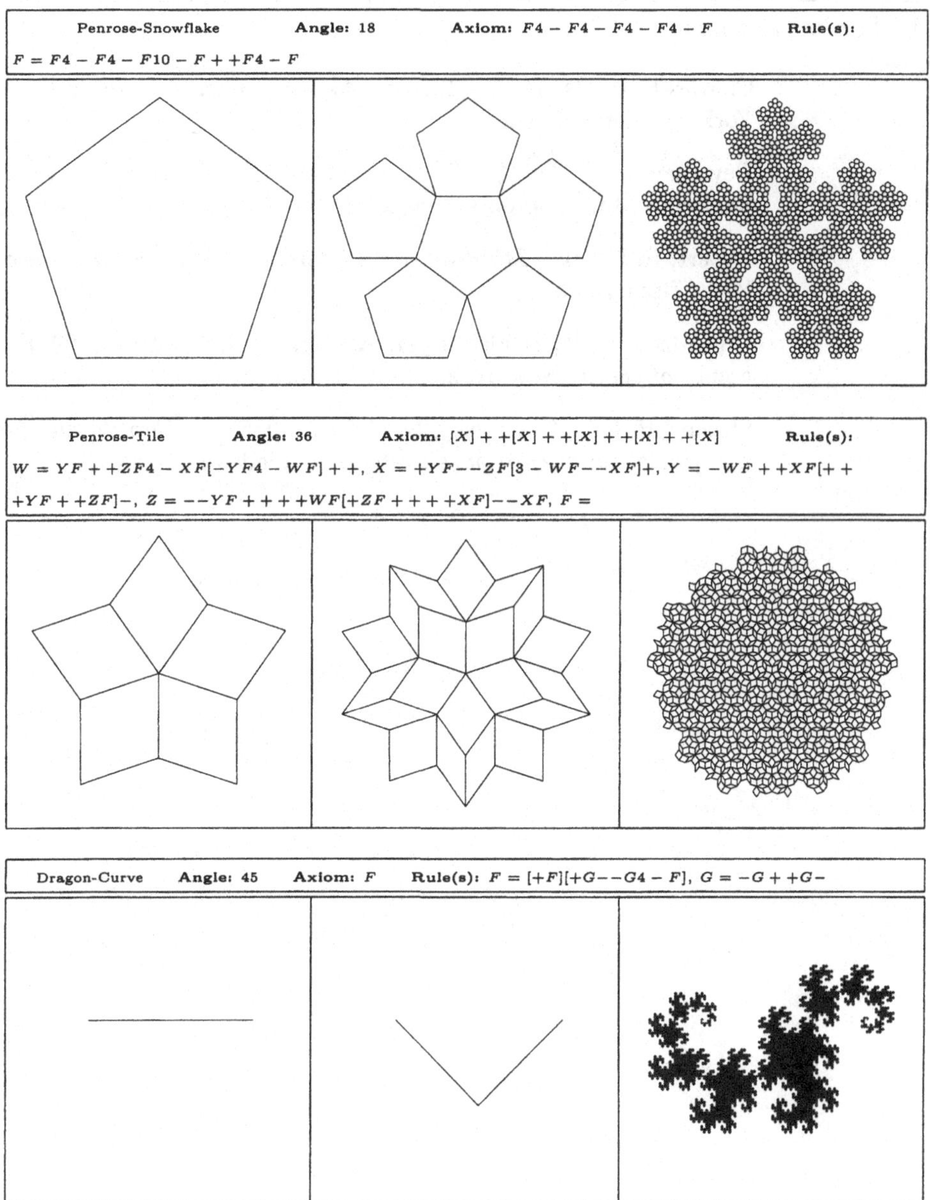

Figure 6.11 Fractal oddities: The first two L-systems form aperiodic tilings of the plane. The Dragon-Curve is one long and continuous curve with only right-angle turns. The rules for Penrose-Tile originated with the DOS program `fractint`.

6.4 Further Reading

Charles-Edwards, D. A. (1986). *Modelling plant growth and development.* New York: Academic Press.

Dewdney, A. K. (1989). *The Turing omnibus: 61 excursions in computer science.* Rockville, Md.: Computer Science Press.

Papert, S. (1980). *Mindstorms: Children, computers, and powerful ideas.* New York: Basic Books.

Prusinkiewicz, P., Lindenmayer, A., Hanan, J. S., et al. (1990). *The algorithmic beauty of plants.* New York: Springer-Verlag.

Stanley, H. E. & Ostrowsky, N. (Eds.). (1985). *On growth and form: Fractal and non fractal patterns in physics.* Kluwer Academic.

7 Affine Transformation Fractals

Fractal geometry will make you see everything differently. There is danger in reading further. You risk the loss of your childhood vision of clouds, forests, flowers, galaxies, leaves, feathers, rocks, mountains, torrents of water, carpets, bricks, and much else besides. Never again will your interpretation of these things be quite the same.
— Michael F. Barnsley

Clouds are not spheres, mountains are not cones, coastlines are not circles, and bark is not smooth, nor does lightning travel in a straight line.
— Benoit Mandelbrot

WHEN SOMEONE TRIES to describe a fractal-like object, one common description could be "It has a miniature version of itself embedded inside it, but the smaller version is slightly rotated," or something like that. In this chapter, we will study two techniques for producing fractals that have the very nice intuitive property that they can be described in terms of where and how some miniature versions of the object should be placed in order to construct the fractal object.

The trick is to come up with a way to describe how the miniature version of the whole should be placed. In general, there are four types of transformations that one could imagine as being useful: translation, scaling, reflection, and rotation. All four of these can be described by linear or affine linear operations. This is important for two reasons. First, affine linear transformations are mathematically simple, in that a single transformation can be described in terms of a *matrix* and *vector* multiplication or vector addition. Second, multiple linear transformations can be composed together to form a single composite linear transformation that does exactly what all of the original transformations did, but in a single step.

In this chapter, we will explore fractals defined by affine linear transformations to see how an intuitive form of self-similarity can be seen in a variety of shapes. We will begin this chapter with a brief review of linear algebra, which is followed by the two aforementioned techniques for building fractals, and finished by several examples.

7.1 A Review of Linear Algebra

Linear algebra is the branch of mathematics that deals with matrix and vector operations. Technically speaking, a matrix is a rectangular array of numbers such as

$$\begin{bmatrix} a & b \\ c & d \end{bmatrix} \text{ or } \begin{bmatrix} e \\ f \end{bmatrix}$$

where the terms a through f are understood to be real numbers. The number of rows and columns of a matrix specifies the dimension of the matrix; for example, our square matrix above is a (2×2) matrix, where the first 2 specifies that there are two rows and the second 2 specifies that there are two columns. Vectors can be thought of as special matrices that have either a single column or a single row. By convention, in most mathematical literature the unqualified "vector" term is used to signify a column vector (as opposed to a row vector), which is a vector with a single column. For convenience, I will sometimes write a column vector as $[x \ \ y]^T$, where the T superscript indicates that the vector has been transposed (flipped along its diagonal).

We can represent points on a plane with a (2×1) column vector, if we agree that the two numbers in the vector correspond to the x and y coordinates, respectively. Our goal for this section is to mathematically describe how translation, scaling, reflection, and rotation can be performed with linear algebra. For each of the descriptions listed below, you should imagine that we are transforming a simple image that can be described by a small number of points. For a more intuitive idea of how these translation can be described, consult Figure 7.1, which illustrates each transformation geometrically.

Translation If we wish to move a point on the plane along a straight line to some new location, then all that we need to do is to add the x and y offsets (which we will call Δx and Δy) to the original vector. Translation is really just a simple vector addition operation, and is mathematically described by:

$$\begin{bmatrix} x \\ y \end{bmatrix} + \begin{bmatrix} \Delta x \\ \Delta y \end{bmatrix} = \begin{bmatrix} x + \Delta x \\ y + \Delta y \end{bmatrix}.$$

Scaling The scaling of an image can be changed in such a way that the original image is stretched or squeezed into an area with a different width and height. If we wish to scale an image such that the vertical and horizontal scales are identical, then scalar-vector multiplication can be used to scale an image:

$$s \begin{bmatrix} x \\ y \end{bmatrix} = \begin{bmatrix} sx \\ sy \end{bmatrix}.$$

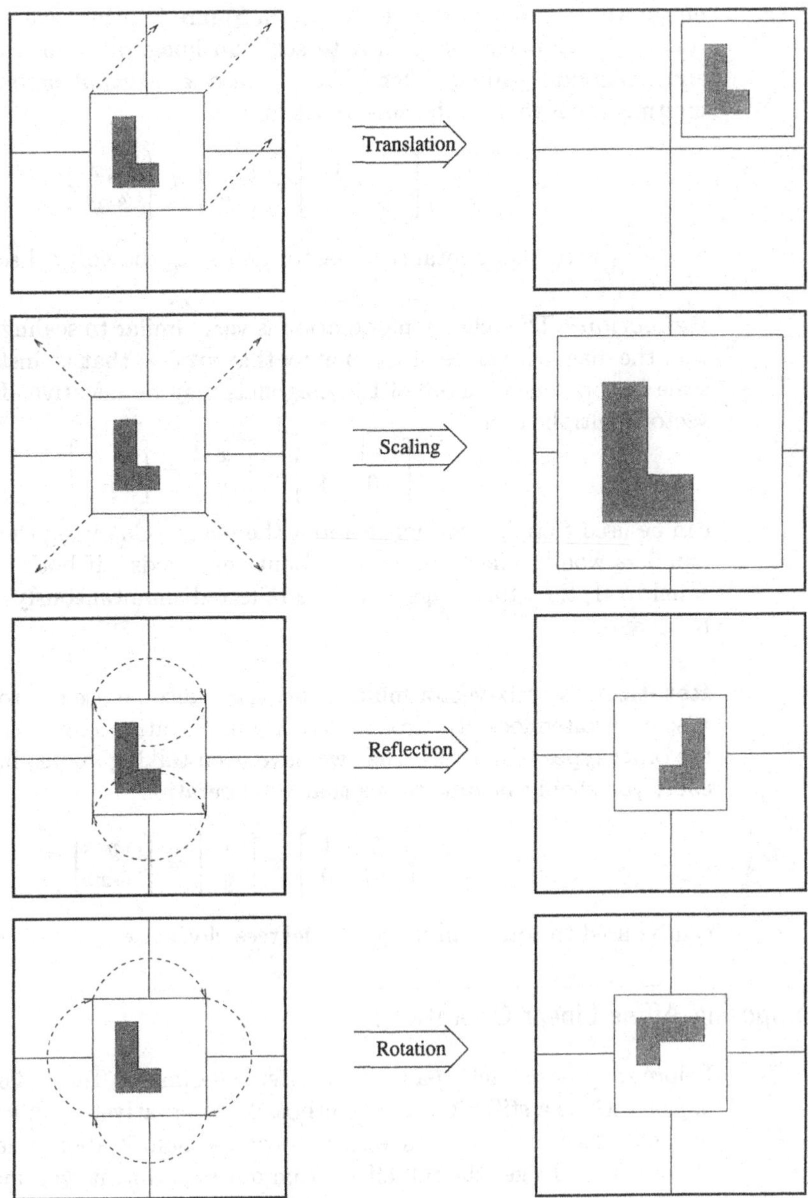

Figure 7.1 Geometric representation of affine linear transformations

If s is greater than 1, then the image will be enlarged. If s is less than 1, then the image will be reduced in size. Notice in Figure 7.1 that scaling is performed about the origin. Suppose we wished to scale an image in such a way that the vertical and horizontal scaling differ. We can use a *diagonal matrix* and matrix-vector multiplication to describe such a scaling:

$$\begin{bmatrix} s_h & 0 \\ 0 & s_v \end{bmatrix} \times \begin{bmatrix} x \\ y \end{bmatrix} = \begin{bmatrix} s_h x \\ s_v y \end{bmatrix},$$

where s_h is the horizontal scale factor and s_v is the vertical scale factor.

Reflection The reflection operation is very similar to scaling. The only difference is in the diagonal values of the matrix that we use, that is, instead of using positive scale factors, one or more of the diagonals may be negative. For example, matrix-vector multiplication

$$\begin{bmatrix} -1 & 0 \\ 0 & 1 \end{bmatrix} \times \begin{bmatrix} x \\ y \end{bmatrix} = \begin{bmatrix} -x \\ y \end{bmatrix}$$

can be used to reflect an image about the y-axis. Changing the signs of the nonzero numbers would reflect the image about the x-axis. If both diagonal entries were equal to -1, then the image would be reflected simultaneously about the x-axis and the y-axis.

Rotation Matrix-vector multiplication can also be used to rotate an image clockwise or counterclockwise around the origin. Rotation matrices are not as simple as the other types of matrices that we have been talking about, but with a little bit of effort you should be able to see that the operation

$$\begin{bmatrix} 0 & 1 \\ -1 & 0 \end{bmatrix} \times \begin{bmatrix} x \\ y \end{bmatrix} = \begin{bmatrix} y \\ -x \end{bmatrix}$$

can be used to rotate an image 90 degrees clockwise.

7.2 Composing Affine Linear Operations

Before we proceed, let's pause for a brief experiment. Take a flat, rigid, rectangular object such as a stiff piece of posterboard. Alternatively, you could use a thin book or even a sheet of paper. Take this object and hold it about one or two feet in front of your face. To get the full effect from our experiment, you may wish to close one eye to eliminate your depth perception

Now, with the object in hand, you can perform the four basic transformations on your object. Scaling can be achieved by moving the object closer or farther away. The reflection operation always spins the object about an axis such that the object moves depthwise.

Three-Dimensional Computer Graphics **Digression 7.1**

Computer imaging and visualization (including virtual reality) rely on mathematical techniques that are very similar to the affine linear operations explored in this chapter. In the medical field, magnetic resonance imaging (MRI) is often used to take a sort of three-dimensional picture of an internal portion of a human body. A computer stores an MRI as a set of three-dimensional points that have a special value to indicate the intensity of the point.

With modern computers, doctors can rotate, enlarge, and view slices of internal portions of the human body without making a single incision in the patient. The problem of manipulating the data so that doctors can view the internal portions with varying rotation and scale is solved in a two-step manner.

In the first step, the three-dimensional points are transformed similarly to the way we have been manipulating two-dimensional points, except that a (3×3) matrix and (3×1) vector are used instead. Applying the three-dimensional affine linear transformation to each point yields a new perspective to the original image. The second step in producing the final image is to convert the set of three-dimensional points into two-dimensional points that can be plotted on a computer monitor. This step is also achieved with matrix multiplication. Additionally, points can be sorted by depth to remove portions of the data that should be hidden from view.

You can compose the operations by doing them in sequence. Notice that it is possible to transform the object so that it appears as a parallelogram instead of a rectangle. In general, for any way that you can transform the object in your hand, there are a matrix and a vector that would mathematically translate a rectangle into the same orientation. In this section, we will see why this must be true.

If we want to translate a single point, $[x \;\; y]^T$, by any of the four basic types of operations, we can always represent the transformation as

$$\begin{bmatrix} a & b \\ c & d \end{bmatrix} \times \begin{bmatrix} x \\ y \end{bmatrix} + \begin{bmatrix} e \\ f \end{bmatrix} = \begin{bmatrix} ax + by + e \\ cx + dy + f \end{bmatrix},$$

with the appropriate choices for terms a through f. We can rewrite the operation above as a single matrix-vector multiplication operation if we expand the matrix and vector dimensions by 1. This gives us

$$\begin{bmatrix} a & b & e \\ c & d & f \\ 0 & 0 & 1 \end{bmatrix} \times \begin{bmatrix} x \\ y \\ 1 \end{bmatrix} = \begin{bmatrix} ax + by + e \\ cx + dy + f \\ 1 \end{bmatrix}.$$

Therefore, if you want to translate, scale, reflect, or rotate any point, there exists

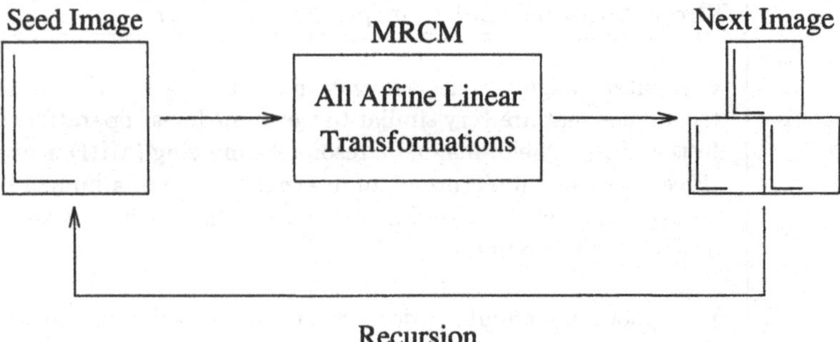

Figure 7.2 A schematic of the MRCM algorithm: The whole input image is simultaneously transformed by each of the affine linear rules.

some choice for the a through f terms in the (3×3) matrix that does the required job. Now, suppose you really wanted to perform many transformations in sequence. We can represent a sequence of operations as $\mathbf{C} \times (\mathbf{B} \times (\mathbf{A} \times \mathbf{p}))$, where $\mathbf{p}$ is the augmented point vector $[x \;\; y \;\; 1]^T$, $\mathbf{A}$ is the first (3×3) transformation matrix[1], $\mathbf{B}$ is the second, and $\mathbf{C}$ is the third. Under linear algebra, we are allowed to rewrite this last expression as $(\mathbf{C} \times (\mathbf{B} \times \mathbf{A})) \times \mathbf{p}$. The $(\mathbf{C} \times (\mathbf{B} \times \mathbf{A}))$ portion of the equation represents two matrix multiplications, and because multiplying any two $(n \times n)$ matrices together always results in a third $(n \times n)$ matrix, the whole expression can be simplified to something like $\mathbf{D} \times \mathbf{p}$ where $\mathbf{D} = (\mathbf{C} \times (\mathbf{B} \times \mathbf{A}))$. Moreover, the bottom row of $\mathbf{D}$ will always look like [001]; thus we can rewrite the resulting (3×3) matrix into a (2×2) matrix and a (2×1) vector.

This concludes the mathematical preliminaries. In the remainder of this chapter, we will look at two fractal construction techniques pioneered by Michael Barnsley. For both techniques, one or more matrices are used to represent affine linear transformations. These matrices can always be uniquely described by the six terms a through f.

7.3 The Multiple Reduction Copy Machine Algorithm

The Multiple Reduction Copy Machine (MRCM) algorithm gets its name from the fact that one could simulate certain instances of it with a real copy machine. The algorithm depends on there being two or more affine linear transformations defined. The algorithm is recursive, as is illustrated in Figure 7.2; however, let's concentrate on what happens in a single step.

[1]By convention, whenever an entire matrix or vector is denoted by a single variable, the letter is boldface. Moreover, matrices are usually named with uppercase letters and vectors are named with lowercase letters.

For our first example MRCM fractal, we have defined three affine linear transformations that are in reality just scale operations followed by a translation; that is, we are reducing the original image and then placing it somewhere else. The fractal that we want to produce will look something like the Sierpinski Gasket in Figure 6.10, which has a smaller version of the whole fractal embedded within the interior of the image at the three corners of the triangle. One could imagine that the image was created by a special copy machine that has three lenses instead of a single lens. Each lens automatically reduces whatever is being photocopied and offsets it by some fixed translation. If we feed this particular MRCM with a seed[2] image as input, the output will look something like the image in Figure 7.3.

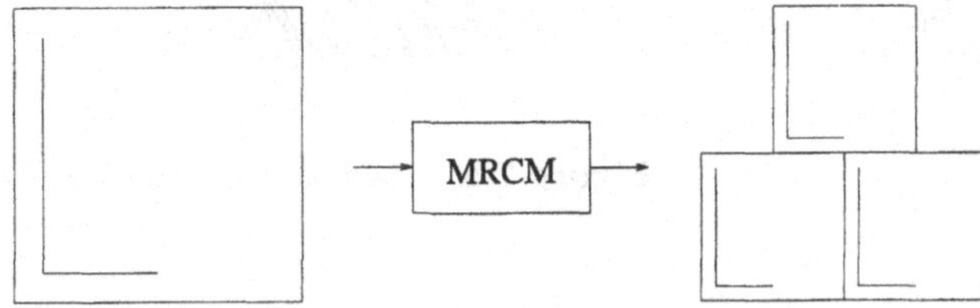

Figure 7.3 The first step of the MRCM algorithm

The resulting image shows exactly what the three affine linear transformations do: Each moves a smaller version of the image to the corner of a triangle. Suppose that, pleased with the resulting image, you wished to photocopy the output for posterity, but by mistake you used the MRCM instead of a normal copy machine. Figure 7.4 shows what would happen.

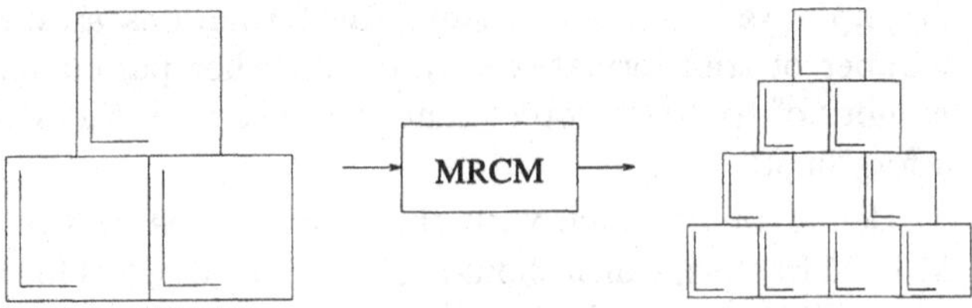

Figure 7.4 The second step of the MRCM algorithm

[2]In the examples that follow, I have used a seed image that looks like a box with an "L" in a corner. The "L" is there so that you can see how the transformations rotate and reflect the seed image. In general, the seed image could be anything we wished it to be: a picture of your house, or a picture of my cat, or a circle. It really doesn't matter, since each seed image gets smaller and smaller the more times we pass it through the MRCM.

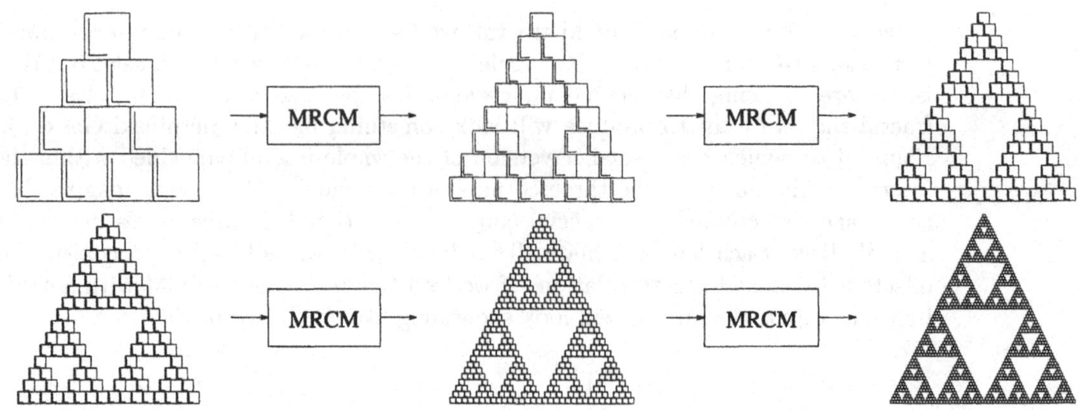

Figure 7.5 Many steps of the MRCM algorithm

Now, this is interesting. For each of the three small squares on the input image, the MRCM has placed a miniature version of the input image. Let's run the output image through the MRCM four more times, as shown in Figure 7.5, to see what happens.

As you can see, the last image is remarkably similar to the Sierpinski Gasket in the last chapter. To fully appreciate how the MRCM algorithm produces such interesting images, let's take a closer look at how it really works. This first example MRCM fractal requires three affine linear transformations to specify where the recursive portions of the image are located. Shortly, we will look at other MRCM fractals that require even more transformations, but for now, let's agree that in principle we can use as many transformations as we wish. We will refer to the number of transformations by n. Another parameter that we can control is the number of recursive copies that we make with the MRCM. Let's call this number d for "depth."

Before we continue with the analysis, see Figure 7.6; it shows another set of MRCM fractals, which should help you to get a feel for how the images are computed with a different set of rules. Here we have used five affine linear transformations, one for each corner of the snowflake. In both example MRCM fractals, the self-similarity of the whole fractal is explicitly defined by the transformations used; thus, in the images, the five small boxes after the first transformation tell us exactly where later images will be self-similar.

In general, with n transformations computed to a depth of d, the final image will have n^d smaller versions of the seed image embedded within it; thus, the last snowflake-like image has 625 miniature versions of the original seed image inside of it. Notice that in the final image the small "L" symbols in each box are not

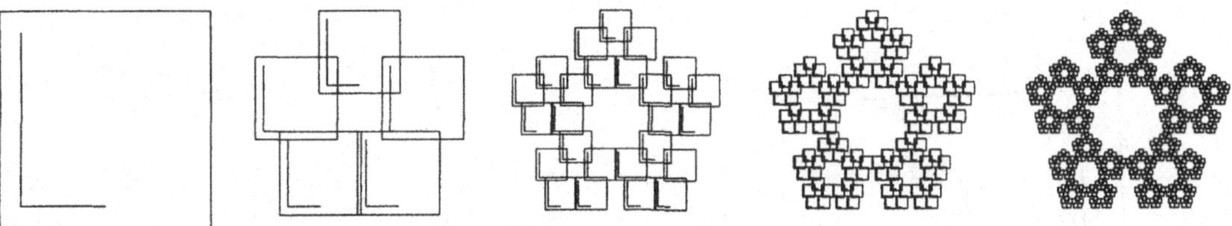

Figure 7.6 More MRCM images made with different rules

large enough to see. This is due to the fact that each of the three transformations squeezes the previous image into a smaller and smaller region. If we computed the MRCM fractal to an infinite depth, each of the smaller versions of the fractal would contract into a point. And as you can see, the greater the depth, the more interesting the final image. The only problem is that we can compute an image only to some finite depth. Moreover, because the final image will have n^d small seed images inside of it, as d grows larger, n^d becomes enormous.

This raises in an interesting dilemma: To get a very clear image, we must compute the MRCM fractals to a large depth; however, as the depth grows, the computational work required to compute the image grows exponentially. To make things worse, for some MRCM fractals, each additional pass through the MRCM reduces the building blocks of the image only by a small amount, that is, we really want the fractal to be constructed from very small versions of itself; however, if the affine linear mappings do not contract the areas of the input images by a large amount, it will take a very large depth to make an image that is composed only of very small versions of itself. This point is illustrated by the images in Figure 7.7, which are the first few stages of an MRCM for producing a fern.

The fern MRCM has four affine linear transformations in it, which can be seen in the second image. The first two are the two small ones that form the leaves. The third is the tiny line segment between the leaves that forms the stem. The fourth transformation is only slightly rescaled, and tilted a bit to the right. It essentially specifies that the top of a fern looks similar to the whole fern—just as the last seven feet of an enormous pine tree can look similar to the whole pine tree.

It is this fourth transformation that causes problems for the MRCM algorithm. Since the fourth transformation contracts the area by only a small amount at each pass, the final image of the fern is still composed of rather large boxes. We could get better results if we computed the MRCM to, say, a depth of 20; however, this would require more than 1 trillion recursive transformations to be computed.

It would be nice if there were some way to compute an MRCM fractal to an infinite depth. We can't really do this, but it turns out that there is a remarkably simple way to approximate what such an image would look like. The technique uses what is know as an Iterated Functional System (IFS), which we will examine next.

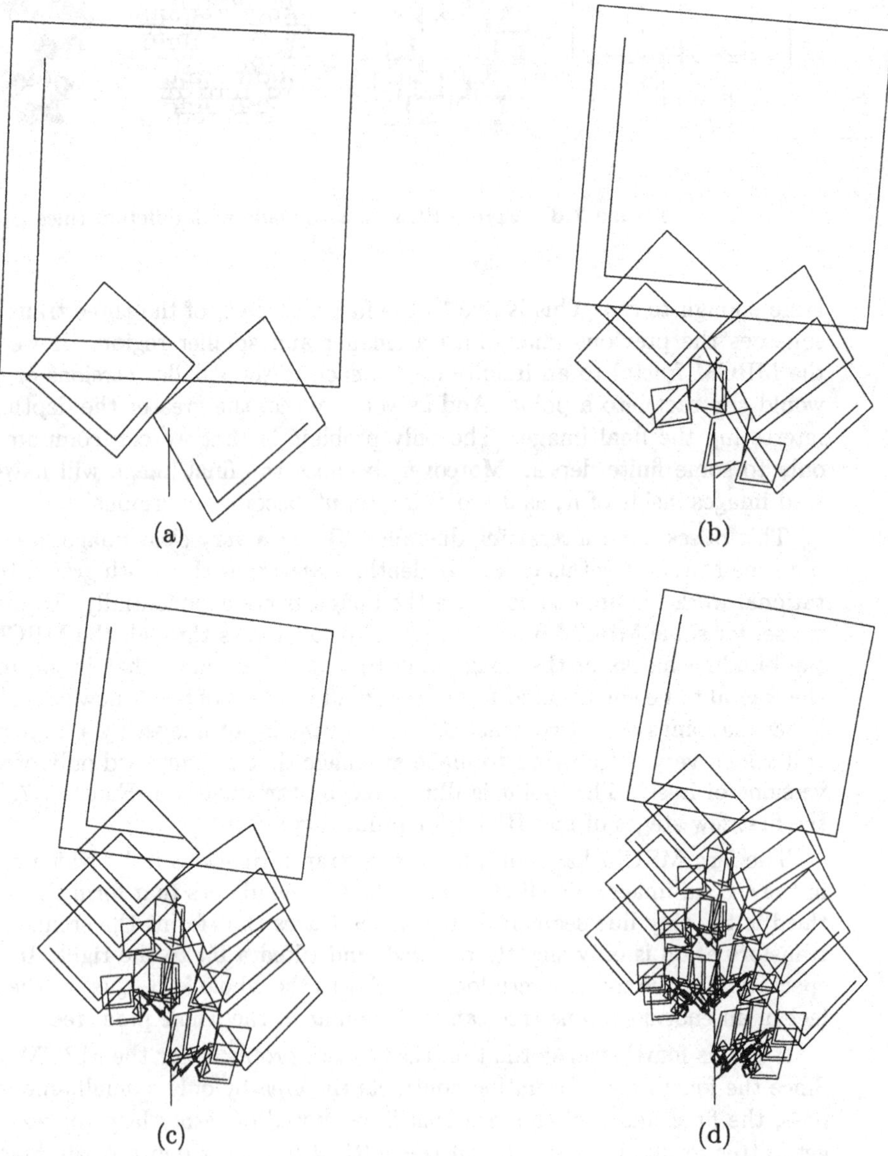

Figure 7.7 An MRCM Fern which illustrates how the MRCM algorithm can produce unsatisfactory results

7.4 Iterated Functional Systems

Before we take a close look at the IFS algorithm, let's pause to think about what an MRCM image would look like if it could be computed to an infinite depth. We will refer to such an image as an "idealized MRCM fractal." Here is a list of useful facts that we can deduce about what idealized MRCM fractals will look like:

Fact 1 An idealized MRCM fractal will be composed entirely of a set of points. We know this is true because each affine linear transformation reduces the size of the seed image. After an infinite number of steps the original seed image must reduce to a point.

Fact 2 For all of our affine linear transformations (which we will generically refer to as $L_i(p)$), if some point p is part of an idealized MRCM fractal, then, for all i, $L_i(p)$ must also be part of the idealized MRCM fractal. This is just another way of saying that an idealized MRCM fractal will have small copies of itself embedded inside of it.

Fact 3 It is possible for an affine linear transformation, $L_i(p)$, to have a unique inverse that we will refer to as $L_i^{-1}(p)$. If a transformation does not have an inverse, then the transformation must squeeze the input image into a line or point (like the third transformation for the fern, which would produce the stem).

Fact 4 If $L_i(p)$ has an inverse, then for all points within an idealized MRCM fractal, p, $L_i^{-1}(p)$ must also be part of the idealized MRCM fractal. This is just another way of saying the reverse of the second fact: An idealized MRCM fractal will look like the composition of a few smaller copies of itself.

Fact 5 Think of all of the points that are part of an idealized MRCM fractal. Now consider a point that is not part of this set. For all affine linear transformations, $L_i(p)$, if p is not part of the idealized MRCM fractal, then $L_i(p)$ will be closer to the idealized MRCM fractal than p is. This just states that if you want to make an intelligent guess for a point that is in an idealized MRCM fractal, $L_i(p)$ will always be a better choice than p.

Putting all of these facts together reveals a remarkable algorithm that was discovered by Michael Barnsley. The idea of the IFS algorithm is to pick a single random point from within a seed image. Next, we randomly pick one of the affine linear transformations for some fractal that we want to produce—it doesn't matter which one we choose, just as long as it is random. We transform the random point by the randomly chosen rule, which gives us a second point. We can then produce a third point by picking another one of the transformation rules randomly and applying the second point to it. If we repeat this process for a few thousand points, what do you think will happen?

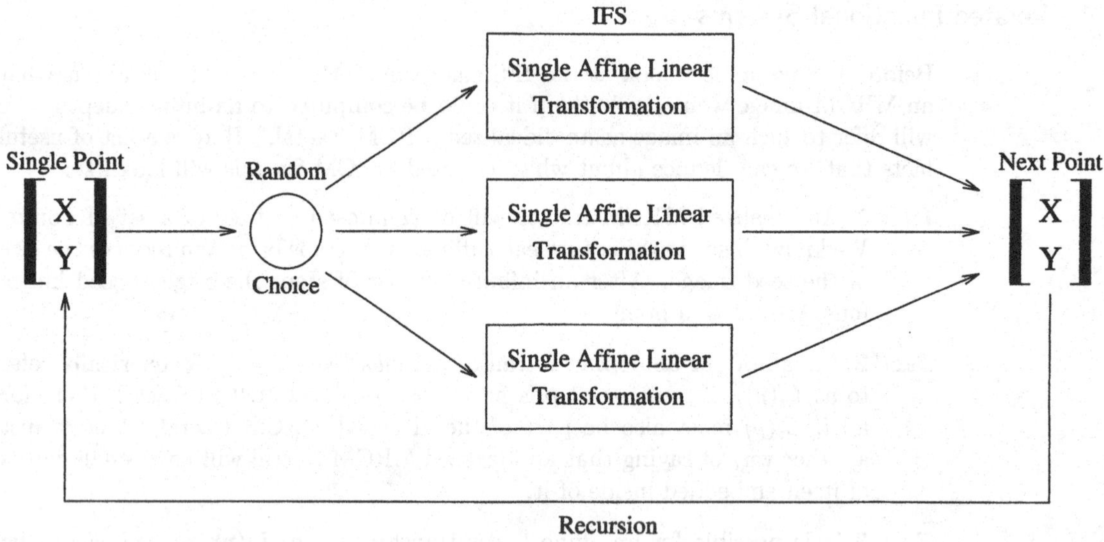

Figure 7.8 A schematic of the IFS algorithm: A single point is transformed by a single randomly chosen transformation.

First of all, we know that the first few points will probably not be very close to the idealized MRCM fractal. However, because of Fact 5 listed earlier, we know that each subsequent point will be closer to the real fractal. Knowing this ahead of time, we can agree to discard the first 100 or so iterates that we produce.

The remaining points will all be extremely close to the idealized MRCM fractal. In fact, they will usually be so close that as far as a computer is concerned, the iterates are on top of the real fractal (because of limited floating-point precision). The gist of the IFS algorithm is illustrated by Figure 7.8.

The last detail that we need to be concerned with is how the random choice is made among the possible affine linear transformations. If there are n transformations, then we could pick any of them with probability n^{-1}. The problem with this method lies in the fact that some transformations take up more space than others. Looking back at the four transformations for a fern, the rules for the leaves are much smaller than the rule for the body; thus, a smarter way for us to choose among the transformations is to randomly pick one with probability proportional to the area of the transformation.

The *determinant* of a matrix is a measure of the amount the matrix expands or contracts a vector that is multiplied by it. For our (2×2) matrices, the determinant is computed as $ad - bc$. If we take the sum of the absolute values of the determinants

Figure 7.9 A fern as computed by an IFS: Compare this with the MRCM ferns computed earlier.

of the transformation matrices, then divide each determinant by the sum, the results will correspond to the probabilities that we should use.

Care must be taken with special cases in which the determinant is equal to 0 (such as for the stem of the fern). If we agree to give every transformation at least some small chance of being chosen, say 1 percent, the IFS algorithm can usually produce excellent results.

Figure 7.9 shows the result of running the IFS algorithm on the affine linear rules for the fern. Obviously, the IFS approach yields a significant improvement in the quality of the image.

7.5 Further Exploration

All fractal images in this chapter were made with either `mrcm` or `ifs`, which you can use to explore the MRCM and IFS algorithms. The programs take a few simple command-line arguments that are listed in Table 7.1. Each transformation must be defined by six numbers that are expected to be found in the file specified by the `-infile` option. If the value of this option is a single dash, input is taken from the standard input.

Option Name	Option Type	Option Meaning
Options Common to Both Programs		
`-infile`	STRING	data input file
`-width`	INTEGER	width of the plot in pixels
`-height`	INTEGER	height of the plot in pixels
`-border`	INTEGER	number of pixels in border
`-inv`	SWITCH	invert colors?
`-xmag`	INTEGER	magnification factor for X Windows
`-term`	STRING	how to plot points
Options Only for `ifs`		
`-its`	INTEGER	number of iterations to plot
`-skip`	INTEGER	number of initial iterates to skip
Options Only for `mrcm`		
`-depth`	INTEGER	depth of recursive calls
`-bw`	INTEGER	width of the seed box
`-bh`	INTEGER	height of the seed box
`-L`	SWITCH	should an "L" be drawn in each box?

Table 7.1 The command-line options for `mrcm` and `ifs`

Most of the options are self-explanatory. For `mrcm` you should try to vary the depth of the recursive calls to generate different images. For `ifs`, you may wish to vary the number of iterations.

Figures 7.10 through 7.17 illustrate some of the possible fractals that one can generate with `mrcm` and `ifs`. The eight figures give the affine linear transformations in both numerical form and geometric form. As an exercise, you could try to reproduce some of these fractals on your own.

7.6 Further Reading

Barnsley, M. (1988). *Fractals everywhere.* New York: Academic Press.

Esbensen, B. J. & Davie, H. K. (1996). *Echoes for the Eye: Poems to celebrate patterns in nature.* New York: HarperCollins.

O'Rourke, J. (1994). *Computational geometry in C.* Cambridge: Cambridge University Press.

Strang, G. (1980). *Linear algebra and its applications.* San Diego: Harcourt Brace Jovanovich.

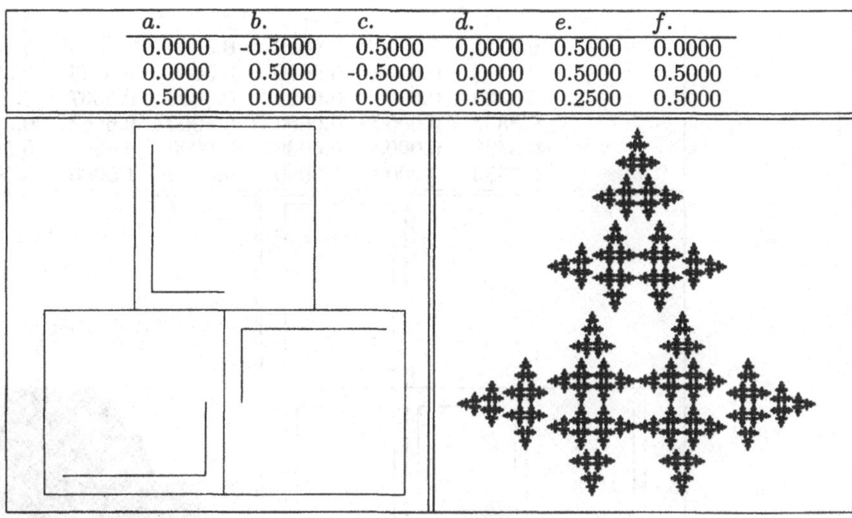

a.	*b.*	*c.*	*d.*	*e.*	*f.*
0.0000	-0.5000	0.5000	0.0000	0.5000	0.0000
0.0000	0.5000	-0.5000	0.0000	0.5000	0.5000
0.5000	0.0000	0.0000	0.5000	0.2500	0.5000

Figure 7.10 A crystallike structure

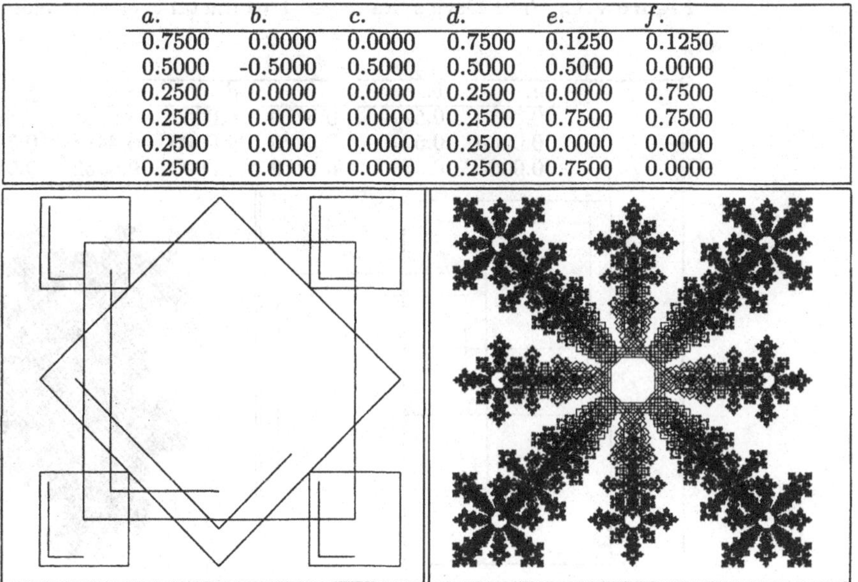

a.	*b.*	*c.*	*d.*	*e.*	*f.*
0.7500	0.0000	0.0000	0.7500	0.1250	0.1250
0.5000	-0.5000	0.5000	0.5000	0.5000	0.0000
0.2500	0.0000	0.0000	0.2500	0.0000	0.7500
0.2500	0.0000	0.0000	0.2500	0.7500	0.7500
0.2500	0.0000	0.0000	0.2500	0.0000	0.0000
0.2500	0.0000	0.0000	0.2500	0.7500	0.0000

Figure 7.11 Another snowflake-like fractal

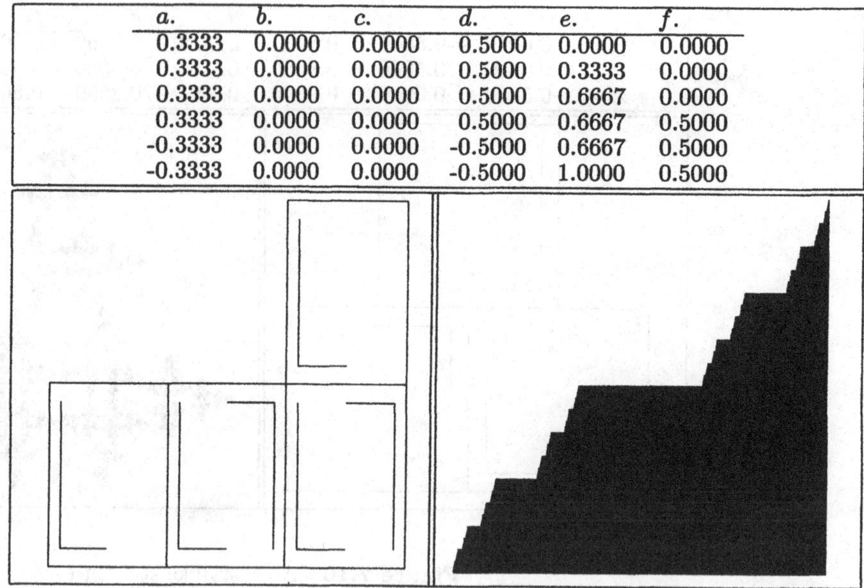

a.	b.	c.	d.	e.	f.
0.3333	0.0000	0.0000	0.5000	0.0000	0.0000
0.3333	0.0000	0.0000	0.5000	0.3333	0.0000
0.3333	0.0000	0.0000	0.5000	0.6667	0.0000
0.3333	0.0000	0.0000	0.5000	0.6667	0.5000
-0.3333	0.0000	0.0000	-0.5000	0.6667	0.5000
-0.3333	0.0000	0.0000	-0.5000	1.0000	0.5000

Figure 7.12 The Devil's Staircase: This fractal is closely related to Cantor's set.

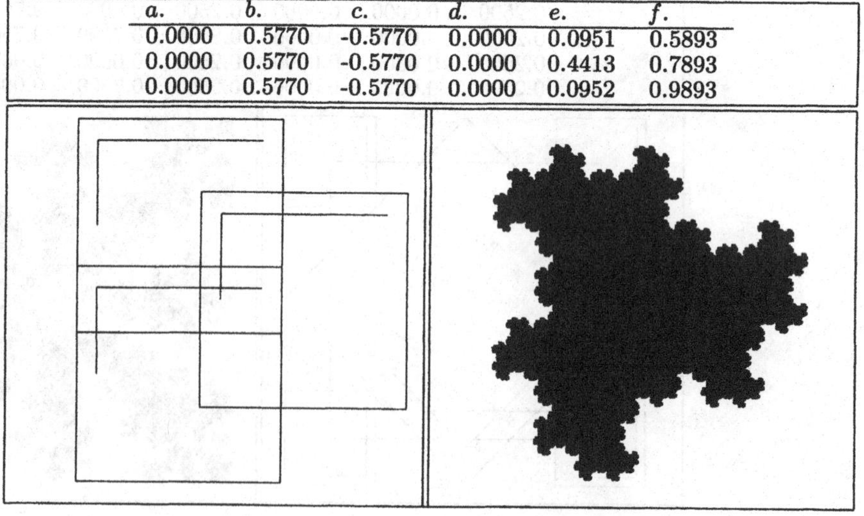

a.	b.	c.	d.	e.	f.
0.0000	0.5770	-0.5770	0.0000	0.0951	0.5893
0.0000	0.5770	-0.5770	0.0000	0.4413	0.7893
0.0000	0.5770	-0.5770	0.0000	0.0952	0.9893

Figure 7.13 A fractal island

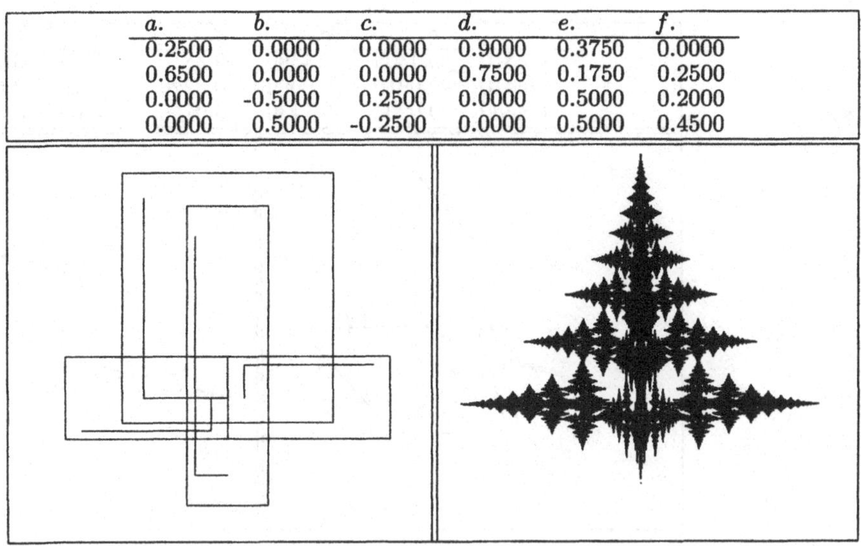

a.	b.	c.	d.	e.	f.
0.2500	0.0000	0.0000	0.9000	0.3750	0.0000
0.6500	0.0000	0.0000	0.7500	0.1750	0.2500
0.0000	-0.5000	0.2500	0.0000	0.5000	0.2000
0.0000	0.5000	-0.2500	0.0000	0.5000	0.4500

Figure 7.14 A pine tree

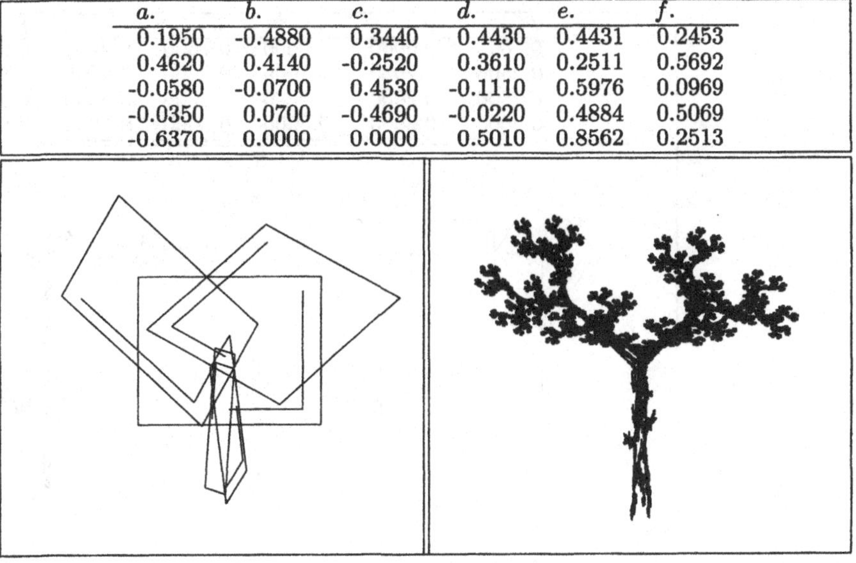

a.	b.	c.	d.	e.	f.
0.1950	-0.4880	0.3440	0.4430	0.4431	0.2453
0.4620	0.4140	-0.2520	0.3610	0.2511	0.5692
-0.0580	-0.0700	0.4530	-0.1110	0.5976	0.0969
-0.0350	0.0700	-0.4690	-0.0220	0.4884	0.5069
-0.6370	0.0000	0.0000	0.5010	0.8562	0.2513

Figure 7.15 Another tree

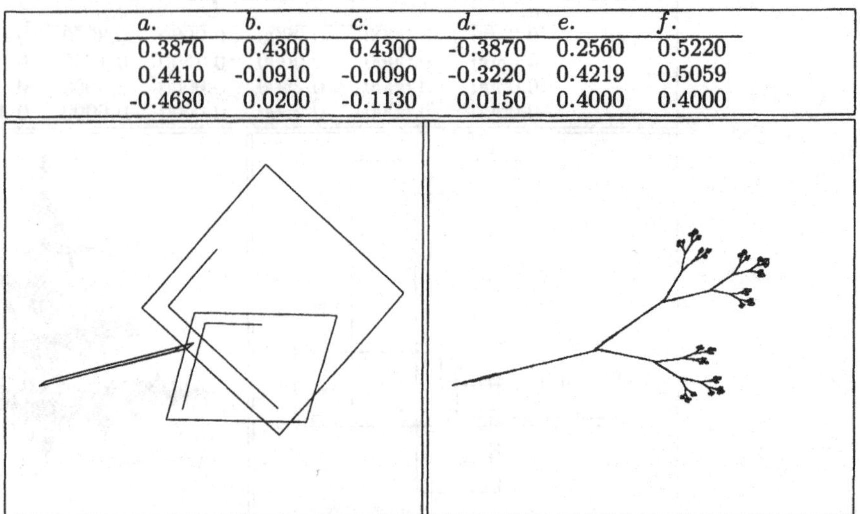

a.	b.	c.	d.	e.	f.
0.3870	0.4300	0.4300	-0.3870	0.2560	0.5220
0.4410	-0.0910	-0.0090	-0.3220	0.4219	0.5059
-0.4680	0.0200	-0.1130	0.0150	0.4000	0.4000

Figure 7.16 A twig

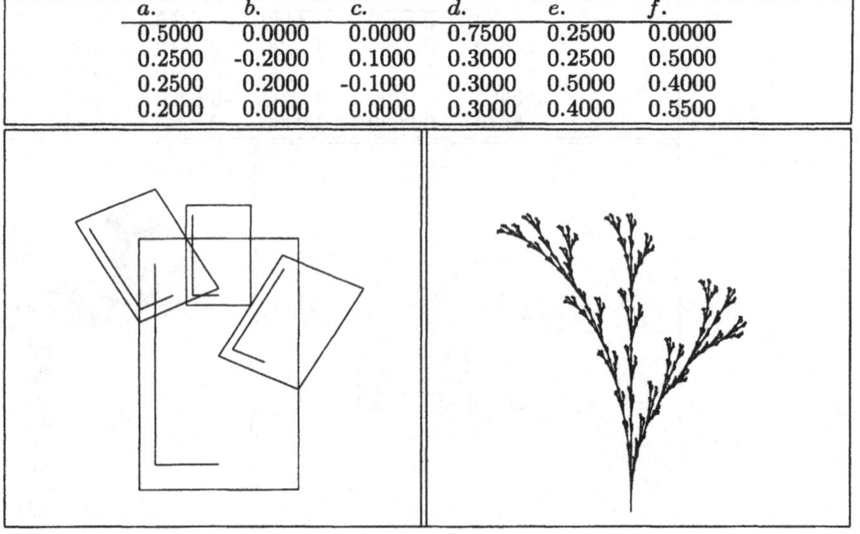

a.	b.	c.	d.	e.	f.
0.5000	0.0000	0.0000	0.7500	0.2500	0.0000
0.2500	-0.2000	0.1000	0.3000	0.2500	0.5000
0.2500	0.2000	-0.1000	0.3000	0.5000	0.4000
0.2000	0.0000	0.0000	0.3000	0.4000	0.5500

Figure 7.17 A weed

8 The Mandelbrot Set and Julia Sets

The universe is full of magical things patiently waiting for our wits to grow sharper.
— Eden Phillpots

Beauty is the first test; there is no permanent place in the world for ugly mathematics.
— G. H. Hardy

IN PART I of this book, we looked into the properties of sets of natural numbers. In Part II, we have been looking at some special sets of real numbers. In this chapter we will expand our scope to include sets of complex numbers. Natural number sets and real number sets are really two different types of beasts entirely, which is to say that mathematically they really shouldn't be compared with one another. Moreover, since it is possible to encode an infinite number of natural numbers into a single real number, an infinite set of real numbers introduces us to a whole new level of infinity.

Despite this hazard, there is an intuitive theme from Chapter 3 that will be continued in this chapter. Recall that at best we could only enumerate members of RE sets and that we could never be sure if something was not a member of an RE set in the general case. Similarly, if we consider a CO-RE set, then at best we can only enumerate numbers that are not members of the CO-RE set. This would seem to imply that any attempt to visualize what these sets look like would be doomed to failure. However, this is not necessarily the case, for in this chapter we are going to examine complex number sets that have this same sort of pathological quality but are subject to being approximated in the sense that taking an educated guess at the set membership of a complex number will still produce an enlightening image for us.

What all of this means will become clearer as we continue. But before we dive into the nonlinear fractals that are the subject of this chapter, we need to take a brief look at iterative dynamical systems. This will be followed by an introduction to complex numbers. Afterwards, we will examine the Mandelbrot and Julia sets, which are sets of complex numbers defined by iterative processes.

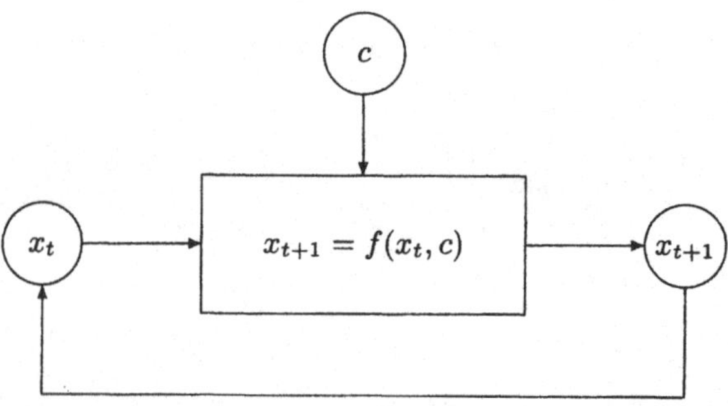

Figure 8.1 Recursion in iterative functions

8.1 Iterative Dynamical Systems

The focus of much of this chapter is a deceptively simple iterative process described by Figure 8.1. The process begins with a starting value for x_0 and a constant value for c. At the next time step we compute x_1 by plugging x_0 and c into $f(\cdot)$, then we compute x_2 with x_1 and c, and so on.

Notice that this is similar to how we recursively expanded the L-system strings in Chapter 6 and the affine transformations in Chapter 7. However, instead of using real valued numbers or vectors for the x terms and c, we will use complex numbers, which form a superset of the real numbers. The need for complex numbers in mathematics arises from the fact that the square root function has no real number solution for negative arguments. We know from basic algebra that if $x = \sqrt{y}$, then $x^2 = y$. But what number squared is equal to a negative number? Mathematicians solve this problem by defining a special *imaginary* number, i, as being equal to $\sqrt{-1}$. Algebraic consistency is maintained by allowing for the fact that $i^2 = -1$.

8.2 Complex Numbers

A complex number consists of the pair $(a + ib)$ where a and b are real numbers and a is known as the real part while ib is known as the imaginary part.[1] Complex numbers can be added and multiplied by the rules

$$\begin{aligned}(a+ib)+(c+id) &= (a+c)+i(b+d)\\(a+ib)\times(c+id) &= (ac-bd)+i(ad+bc).\end{aligned}$$

In the addition rule we simply add the real parts of the two operands to get the real part of the result and add the imaginary parts of the operands to get the imaginary

[1] Imaginary numbers are just as "real" as real numbers are. They are frequently used in physics and engineering to describe natural phenomena.

Iterative Methods for Computing Roots — Digression 8.1

It is not too difficult to imagine how a computer computes functions that involve addition, subtraction, multiplication, and division. In fact, the techniques used in computers to carry out the basic mathematical operations are not too different from how you and I compute them with pencil and paper. But how would you compute the cube root of a number? There is a surprisingly simple yet efficient technique for computing roots (square, cube, or whatever) that dates back to Newton and is known as *Newton's method* for finding the values in which an equation equals 0. We can use Newton's method for finding the cube root of 2 by noting that the equation $f(x) = x^3 - 2$ is equal to 0 only when $x = \pm 2^{\frac{1}{3}}$. To use Newton's method we iterate the equation

$$x_{t+1} = x_t - \frac{f(x)}{f'(x)} = x_t - \frac{x^3 - 2}{3x^2},$$

where $f(x)$ is defined as above and $f'(x)$ is the first derivative of $f(x)$ with respect to x. All that remains is for us to make an initial guess for x_0, which we will take as 1. The table below prints the first few iterates of Newton's method.

t	x_t	x_t^3
1	1.33333333333333333333	2.37037037037037037034
2	1.26388888888888888890	2.01895522548010973941
3	1.25993349344997696647	2.00005925932265425012
4	1.25992105001776977374	2.00000000058525861914
5	1.25992104989487316479	2.00000000000000000009

Notice how the number of accurate digits doubles after each iteration. This attribute, known as *quadratic convergence*, makes Newton's method a powerful technique for approximating many functions over the real numbers.

part. The multiplication rule is very similar to the way you would multiply two simple sums with the algebraic distributive rule, but notice that the $-bd$ portion comes from multiplying $ib \times id = -1 \times bd$; thus, it is possible to multiply two imaginary numbers and get a strictly real result.

Also notice that if we make the imaginary parts of two complex numbers equal to 0, then addition and multiplication will take on the standard form for real numbers. Thus, complex arithmetic encompasses all of what one could do with real numbers as well.[2] Since the real numbers can be placed on a line, it is often convenient to

[2]Incidentally, the cardinality of the set of complex numbers is the same as the cardinality of the real numbers. To see this, consider the complex number $(a+ib) = (a_1a_2a_3\cdots + i \times b_1b_2b_3\cdots)$ where the list is a decimal expansion. We can interleave the two decimal expansions as $a_1b_1a_2b_2a_3b_3\cdots$ to map a complex number into a real number.

```
• For each number, c, in a subset of the complex plane
    • Set x_0 = 0
    • For t = 1 to tmax
        • Compute x_t = x_t^2 + c
        • If |x_t| > 2, then break out of loop
    • If t < tmax, then color point c white
    • If t = tmax, then color point c black
```

Table 8.1 Pseudo-code to compute the M-set

think of the complex number as occupying a place on what is known as the complex plane. To locate the point $a + ib$ on the complex plane, we place the real part on the x-axis, and the imaginary part on the y-axis.

8.3 The Mandelbrot Set

Now that we know how to add and multiply complex numbers, we can go back to looking at the function $x_{t+1} = f(x_t, c)$, which we will take as having the form $x_{t+1} = x_t^2 + c$ with $x_0 = 0 + i0 = 0$. The question that we want to answer is: For some constant complex value of c, what will happen to x_t as we let t go to infinity? Let's look at a few special cases. When $c = 0$, all of the x_t values will always be equal to 0; thus it is possible for the x_t values to remain bounded in size as t gets very large. Similarly, if we set $c = i$, then $x_0 = 0$, $x_1 = i$, $x_2 = -1 + i$, $x_3 = -i$, $x_4 = -1 + i$, and $x_5 = -i$. Since $x_3 = x_5$, the sequence has fallen into a period-2 pattern, meaning that it oscillates between two values, $-i$ and $-1 + i$.

For other values of c, things are not so simple. When $c = 1 + i$, the sequence becomes 0, $1+i$, $1+i3$, $-7+i7$, $1-i97$, $-9407-i193$, $88454401+i3631103$, ..., and keeps growing in size. In such a case, we say that the sequence *diverges*. We really want to know what values of c will make the sequence diverge and what values of c will keep the sequence bounded. This is not such an easy question to answer. For example, we know that for $c = i$ the sequence remains bounded. However, if we slightly alter that choice for c to be equal to $0.01+i$, we get the sequence 0, $0.01+1$, $-0.9899 + i1.02$, ..., $111.001311 + i57.871075$, ..., which again grows unbounded. In general, if $a^2 + b^2$ is greater than 4 (where $x_t = a + ib$), then we can be sure that the sequence will diverge; however, there exists an infinite number of points on the complex plane that will hover around this threshold for quite a while and exceed it only after a large number of steps. Moreover, as should be clear from the last sequence that we looked at, for any two values of c that are close to each other, it is not at all clear if one can conclude that one sequence will be bounded or diverge based on how the other sequence behaved. Thus, the simple function $x_t^2 + c$ is more than deceptively simple—it is downright diabolical.

Benoit Mandelbrot was the first person to study the function $x_t^2 + c$ in great detail with a computer. To see just how pathological this iterative equation is, Mandelbrot wrote a simple program that performed the algorithm shown in Table 8.1.

In the algorithm, the expression $|x_t|$ denotes the length of the vector formed by the complex number x_t, which is computed as $|x_t| = |a + bi| = \sqrt{a^2 + b^2}$. As mentioned earlier, it is possible to prove that if the length of the complex number exceeds 2, then the sequence will grow to infinity. Since Mandelbrot was interested in the set of points that remained bounded, he knew that if one of his iterated complex numbers exceeded 2 in length, then it was not in his set. But how could he tell if a complex number was in his set, that is, how could he ever determine that a complex number would remain bounded after an infinite number of iterations? Mandelbrot was fairly certain that there was no general way of answering this question, so he made a simple compromise: If the iterate was still less than 2 in length after some predetermined number of iterations, then he would assume that it was in his set. Thus, in the algorithm he iterated the function $f(\cdot)$ only a total of $tmax$ times. The first image that Mandelbrot produced looked something like what is shown in Figure 8.2.

When one tries to visualize a set of natural, real, or complex numbers that has some mathematical property it is usually the case that one imagines the set to be somehow "cold" because it represents a mathematical truth. Yet, the Mandelbrot set (or M-set) is distinctly ... organic. Notice that it looks like an island with smaller islets along the perimeter and that it has tendrils extending from the edges. Mandelbrot's first reaction to seeing the M-set was that either a mistake had been made in performing the computations or the detail of the image was some sort of artifact of the way his computer produced the sequence of iterates.

Figure 8.2 The Mandelbrot set

Figure 8.3 The Mandelbrot Set: Moving from left to right and top to bottom each subsequent image shows the boxed region from the previous image in greater detail.

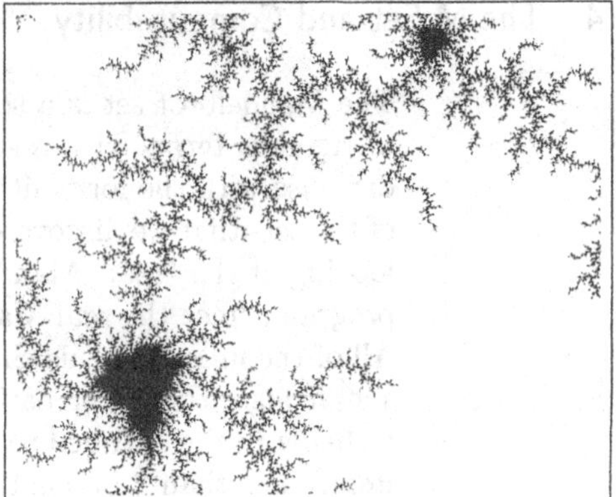

Figure 8.4 Another view of the Mandelbrot set: Zooming into the Mandelbrot set from another direction yields small but distorted versions of the whole set.

For further study Mandelbrot decided to enlarge portions of the image by considering only a smaller area but at a higher resolution. One possible outcome could have been that the M-set could have well-defined boundaries and, therefore, it would lose much of its detail under magnification. Figure 8.3 shows six images of the M-set at various magnifications. In the first image we see a global view of the M-set with the upper-left corner being at $-2.4 + i1.4$ and the lower-right corner at $1.34 - i1.4$. The small box in each of the first five images indicates what portion has been enlarged in the subsequent plot.

As you can see, as we zoom into the M-set, the detail does not diminish but instead becomes richer and more varied. The second image dives into the upper valley between the main body of the M-set and the largest islet. In the third image, we zoom into one of the buds that seem to have spiral-like filaments hanging off their tops. The fourth and fifth images illustrate the logarithmic nature of the spirals, and the sixth image shows that the "hairs" of the spirals are quite beautiful themselves. In the last picture, we have zoomed in by a factor of more than 12,000. In fact, we could zoom into the M-set forever, always finding more and more novel detail.

Yet zooming into certain areas of the M-set can lead to a feeling of déjà vu, as illustrated in Figure 8.4. The first plot once again shows the whole view of the M-set but has a box on one of the little buds on the perimeter of the largest islet to indicate where the next image comes from. When we enlarge the little bud, we find that it has what look like rivers extending from the main body. Zooming into one of the streams reveals several miniature versions of the M-set, yet each miniature version is a subtle distortion of the original.

8.4 The M-Set and Computability

The Mandelbrot set is a set of complex numbers; thus, it is not really comparable in rigorous terms with a set of natural numbers. However, in this section we will dispense with the formality so that we can compare the Mandelbrot set with some of the sets that we discovered in Chapter 3. Also note that we haven't actually been looking at the "real" Mandelbrot set but only an approximation as computed by a program, since the real Mandelbrot set is defined as the points that never diverge. All of the images in this chapter were computed by a program that is similar to the simple algorithm given earlier in the chapter; thus, each point that we have labeled as being in the Mandelbrot set (the black points) was really only found to have an iterate less than 2 in length after a fixed number of iterations.

The really important question is: How do we know that some point that we labeled as being in the Mandelbrot set really is? Looking back at any of the figures that contain the whole of the M-set, we can subdivide the image into a few subsets. The largest, kidney-shaped portion of the M-set is known as a cardioid (which

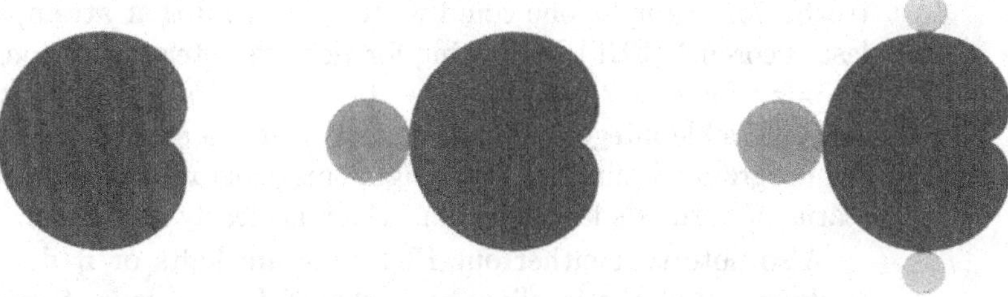

Figure 8.5 Progressively more complex M-set subsets

means "heart-shaped") and can be described by the parametric equations

$$\begin{aligned} x &= \frac{1}{4}(2\cos t - \cos 2t) \\ y &= \frac{1}{4}(2\sin t - \sin 2t) \end{aligned}$$

where t takes the values from 0 to 2π. Thus, if we wanted to draw a very rough sketch of the M-set, we could check to see if a point is within the cardioid defined by the equations above. It would also be possible to have another equation for the largest circle just to the left of the cardioid and two more equations for the smaller circles just above and below the cardioid. Figure 8.5 shows three stages in making successively more accurate rough sketches of the M-set.

Our rough sketches are not too bad for a start. Looking closely at some of the more complete images, we can see that there are many smaller circles that surround the perimeter at fairly regular intervals. We could also include these smaller circles in our next rough sketch to make it more complete. However, no matter how hard we try, there is always going to be something missing from our rough sketch.

Does all of this sound familiar? It should. Looking back at the complement of the halting set, we can "draw" a similar rough sketch of a CO-RE set by enumerating some well-known members, such as the Stutter function that always diverges `(set 'f (lambda () (f)))` or a Stutter function that attempts to take the `car` of the result of a divergent recursive function call `(set 'f (lambda () (car (f))))`, and so on. We could list an infinite number of these obvious members of a CO-RE set because we've figured an algorithm to enumerate a recursive *subset* of the CO-RE set.

What members will we fail to enumerate? Restating the question: For what members of a CO-RE set is there no clear method of enumerating the members? In many ways the members of a CO-RE set that are impossible to decide are the ones that are near a threshold or border. Programs that we can consider as being on the "edge" of halting are never trivial and usually encompass some deep mathematical truth. For example, one could write a program that attempts to disprove Fermat's last theorem[3] (FLT) by looking for positive integer solutions to the equation $x^n + y^n = z^n$ for $n > 2$. We could write this program so that it exhaustively searches every possible integer combination, so that if a solution to the equation exists then the program will find it. Deciding if this program halts is equivalent to proving the status of Fermat's last theorem, which is clearly nontrivial.

Also note that either our FLT program halts or it does not. This statement is obvious, but the implication is that if FLT is true, then another program that mindlessly outputs "Your FLT program will not halt" correctly decides halting set membership for the FLT program. If, on the other hand, FLT is false, then another program that mindlessly outputs "Your FLT program will halt with a counterexample" will correctly decide halting set membership. We don't know which program is correct, but we do know that one of them does output the correct result. Thus, deciding halting set membership for the FLT program alone is not impossible, since one of the two stupid programs above does the trick. What is impossible is to write a program that can decide if *any* program halts; not just one, or a finite number, or even a recursive subset of the halting set, but *any* program.

Turning our attention back to the M-set, on the perimeter we can see many fuzzy details. At one level of resolution our program may have placed a black dot to indicate that the point is in the M-set. But if one expands this point and magnifies the surrounding areas (as done in some of our images), our single plain point has turned into a forest of detail. Is the point in the M-set or not? If you stay sufficiently near the edge, you can repeatedly magnify the M-set to find an infinite amount of detail, but if you play it safe and stay either within the main cardioid or completely outside the circle of radius 2, then you can decide definitively if a point is in the M-set or not. Again, just as with the CO-RE sets, the difficulty in deciding membership comes when we attempt to live on the edge. This is where all of the beauty is found as well.

8.5 The M-Set as the Master Julia Set

To compute the M-set, we iterated $x_{t+1} = x_t^2 + c$ with $x_0 = 0$ to see if c was in the M-set or not. Let's make a subtle change in this procedure and consider a related family of sets known as Julia sets. We say "family" because instead of computing one image, we will use a single equation that can be used to produce an infinite number of images that are closely related to the M-set. The iterative equation that we will use will still be $x_{t+1} = x_t^2 + c$; however, instead of using c to denote the complex number that we are deciding membership for, we will keep c constant and

[3] During the writing of this book, Andrew Wiles of Princeton University succeeded in proving Fermat's last theorem.

- Set c to some constant complex value.
- For each number, x_0, in a subset of the complex plane
    - For $t = 1$ to $tmax$
        - Compute $x_t = x_t^2 + c$
        - If $|x_t| > 2$, then break out of loop
    - If $t < tmax$, then color point c white
    - If $t = tmax$, then color point c black

Table 8.2 Pseudo-code to compute J-sets

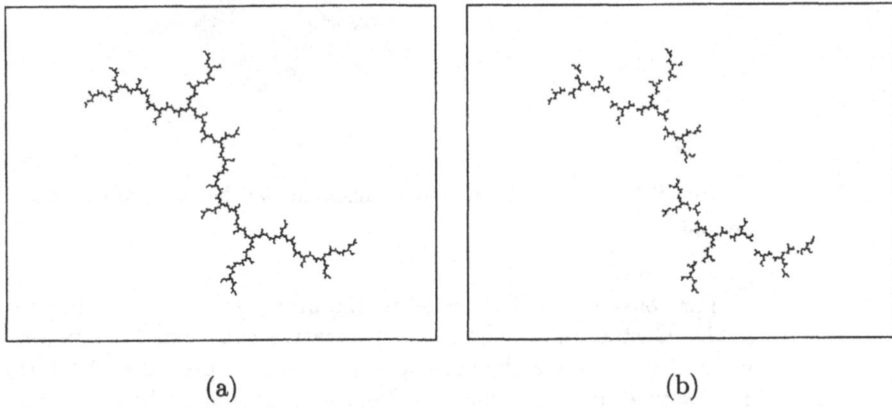

(a) (b)

Figure 8.6 Two Julia sets: (a) $c = i$, (b) $c = 0.01 + i$

set x_0 equal to the point on the complex plane that we wish to check. Our new Julia set algorithm will look something like the algorithm in Table 8.2.

Figure 8.6 shows two Julia sets for two different values of c. For the image on the left, we used $c = i$, which we know is inside the M-set because it led to a period-2 pattern. On the right, we used $c = 0.01 + i$, which we know is outside of the M-set because it diverges. There are several interesting facts about these two images. First, each image contains at least some sort of symmetry about a diagonal, in that one half of the image looks like the mirror image of the other. Next, each image is somewhat self-similar, since the portions of the Julia sets look like smaller versions of the whole. However, the most important fact about the two images is that they differ in that the left image is connected while the right image is composed of a "dust" and is not connected.

Figure 8.7 The Julia set that corresponds to the midpoint of the sixth image in Figure 8.3

For convenience, let's refer to the Julia set corresponding to some choice of c as J_c. Gaston Julia, who studied iterative equations long before computers could be used to calculate the corresponding images, proved in 1918 that if the equation $x_{t+1} = x_t^2 + c$ diverges, then the Julia set J_c would be dust-like and unconnected, but if the iterates stayed bounded, then J_c would be connected. Putting this together with our knowledge of how the M-set is computed, we see that the M-set consists of exactly those points for which J_c is connected. Thus, we can think of the M-set as a table of contents for all Julia sets. Ask the question "Is some J_c connected?" and the answer is "Is c in the M-set?" Mandelbrot himself knew of Julia's work, and his motivation for discovering the M-set was to visualize which Julia sets were connected or unconnected.

Yet, there is more to the M-set then just that. For example, look at the sixth image in Figure 8.3. The Julia set that is computed with c being equal to the midpoint of that portion of the M-set is shown in Figure 8.7. Notice how the Julia set has the same sort of motif as the portion of the M-set it is derived from. This similarity is no coincidence, as is illustrated in the next few pages. Figure 8.8 contains a global view of the M-set with various regions of the perimeter boxed and labeled. In Figure 8.9 the boxed regions of the M-set are enlarged and the Julia set that corresponds to the center point of the box is shown alongside the enlargement of the M-set.

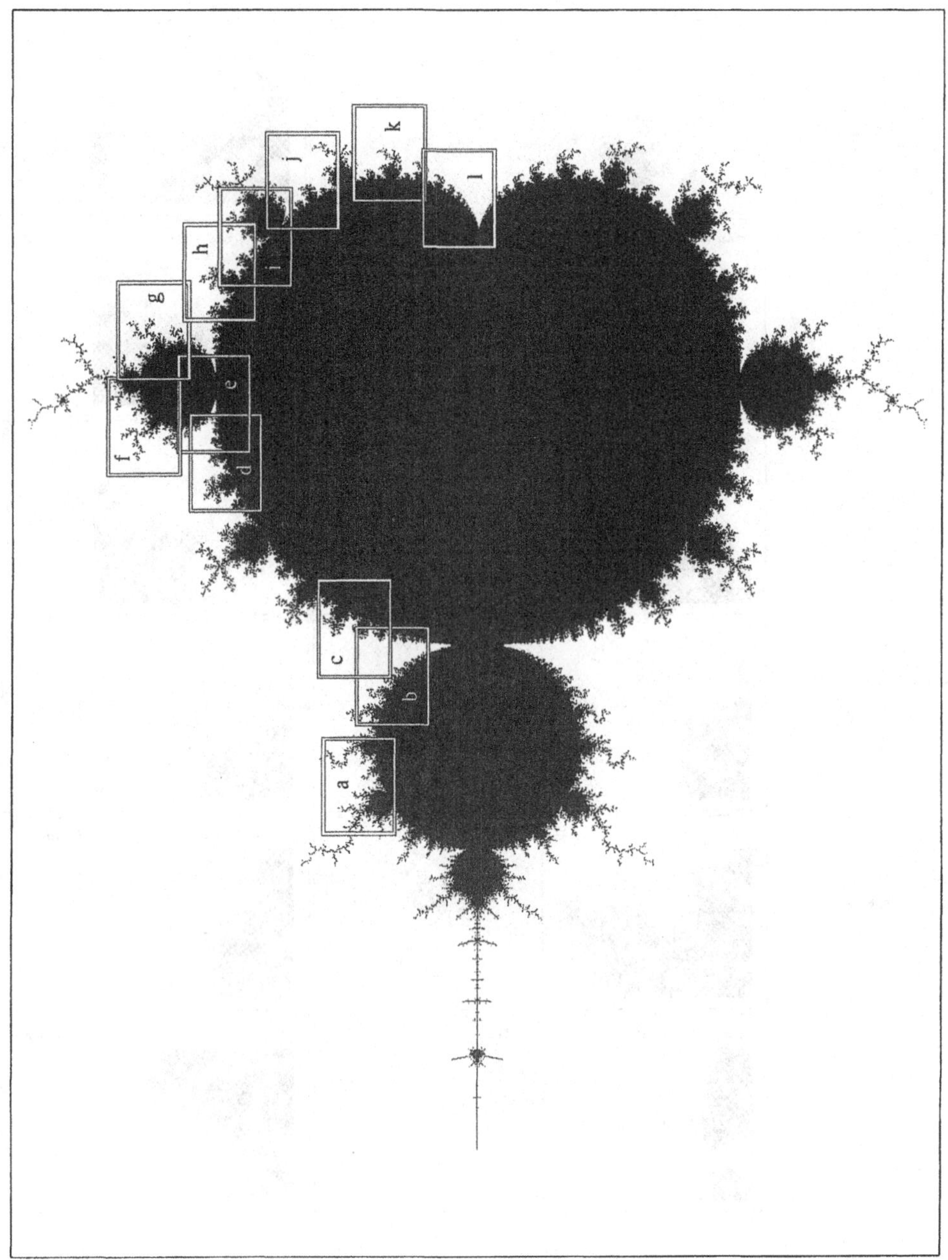

Figure 8.8 A map to the M-set images in Figure 8.9

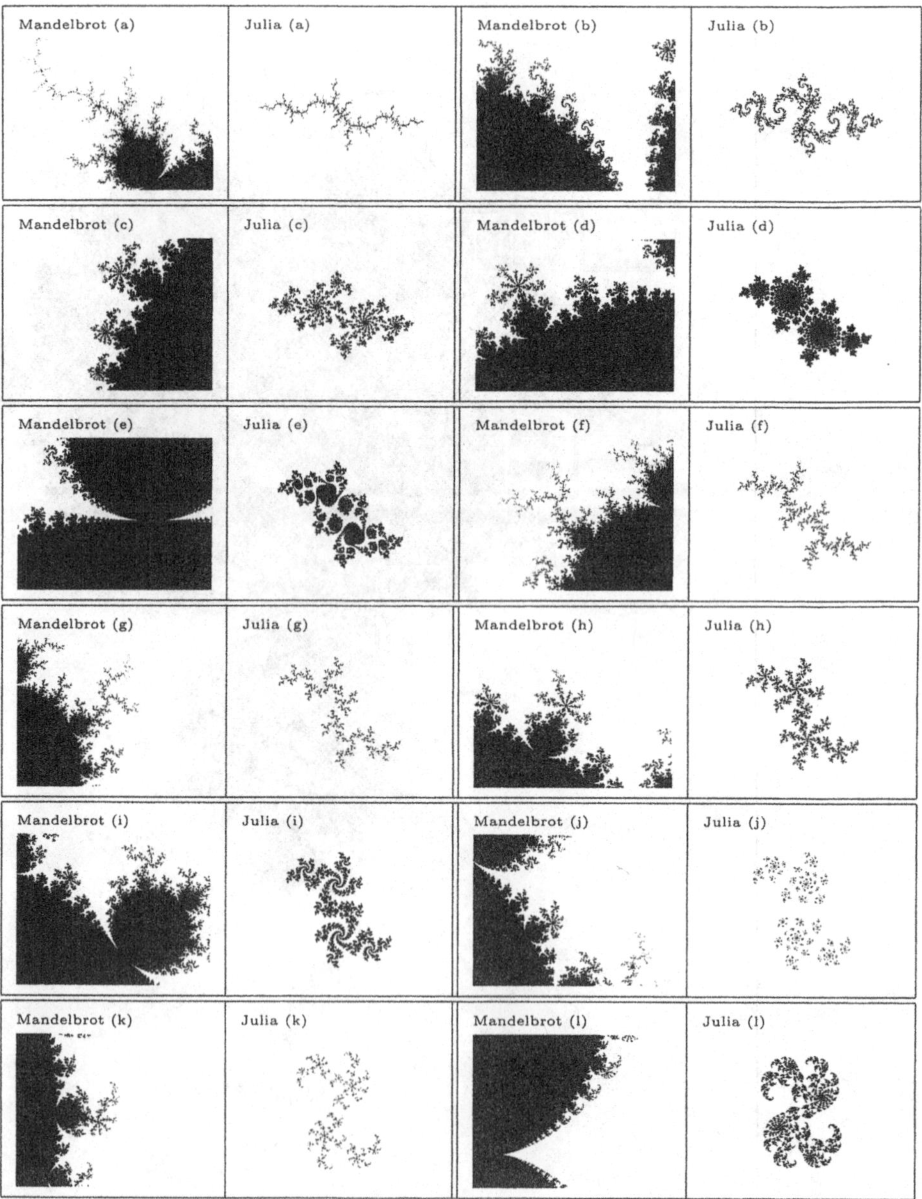

Figure 8.9 Enlargements of the M-set with the Julia set that corresponds to the centerpoint of the M-set image

Some of the Julia sets from Figure 8.9 are connected and others are unconnected. A simple litmus test of the connectedness is to see if the center point of the M-set image is black or not. Sometimes this fact will be clear, but not always. The tendrils that extend away from the perimeter of the M-set have a very distinctive pattern, and in general the corresponding Julia sets comply with the motif of the portion of the M-set they are derived from.

8.6 Other Mysteries of the M-Set

In 1991 David Boll made a fascinating discovery regarding the M-set and the constant π. Boll was trying to confirm that the "neck" of the M-set at $c = -\frac{3}{4} + 0i$ (where the largest circle on the left meets the main cardioid) is actually 0 in thickness. Boll set his program to test values of c in the form $-\frac{3}{4} + \epsilon i$, where ϵ is some small number. He constructed a table of values for ϵ and the number of iterations it took for the iterates to diverge. A partial list of the values he computed is shown below.

ϵ	**Iterations**
0.1	33
0.01	315
0.001	3143
0.0001	31417
0.00001	314160
0.000001	3141593
0.0000001	31415928

Do the values in the right column look familiar? In Boll's words, "What the hell is π doing here?" Multiplying ϵ and the corresponding number of iterations gives an approximation of π that is within $\pm\epsilon$. Notice that nowhere in the M-set algorithm does the number π appear. Instead, the value "emerges" as a higher-order pattern on its own. It is not at all clear whether or not someone could have predicted that the M-set contains the value of π without numerically exploring the M-set in great detail. Other locations of the M-set may yield similar surprises, and not all of them have been explained.

8.7 Further Exploration

As you can see, the M-set and Julia sets come in a rich variety of forms; from dendritic spikes to snowflake dusts. The images in this chapter only scratch the surface of all of the infinite Julia sets that can be found. For further study, the reader can use the programs `mandel` and `julia` to find new and unexplored regions of the M-set and the Julia sets.

Option Name	Option Type	Option Meaning
`-width`	INTEGER	width of the plot in pixels
`-height`	INTEGER	height of the plot in pixels
`-levels`	INTEGER	number of plot (gray) levels
`-maxit`	INTEGER	maximum number of iterations
`-bail`	DOUBLE	value of $\|x\|$ to end iteration
`-ulx`	DOUBLE	upper-left corner x-coordinate
`-uly`	DOUBLE	upper-left corner y-coordinate
`-lly`	DOUBLE	lower-left corner y-coordinate
`-box`	INTEGER	line width for a box
`-bulx`	DOUBLE	box's upper-left x-coordinate
`-buly`	DOUBLE	box's upper-left y-coordinate
`-blly`	DOUBLE	box's lower-left y-coordinate
`-idiv`	INTEGER	iteration divisor
`-rev`	SWITCH	reverse all colors but first?
`-inv`	SWITCH	invert all colors?
`-xmag`	INTEGER	magnification factor for X Windows
`-term`	STRING	how to plot points
Options Only for `julia`		
`-cr`	DOUBLE	real component of c
`-ci`	DOUBLE	imaginary component of c

Table 8.3 The command-line options for `mandel` and `julia`

Both `mandel` and `julia` take nearly identical command-line options. The only difference between them is that `julia` accepts two extra options that will be explained later. Thus, this brief tutorial will mostly concentrate on the features common to both programs. A full list of options is contained in Table 8.3.

The width and height of the plots that you create can be set with the `-width` and `-height` options. The values that you can use for these options may depend on the plotting device used. All of the images in this chapter were produced with only two levels of gray-scale (black and white), so that the images could be printed easily. However, if you run `mandel` or `julia` with a plotting device that can accept many levels of shading (such as X Windows, Linux SVGA, or the PGM file format, as determined by the `-term` option), then you may wish to set the number of gray-levels to some other value with the `-levels` option.

The maximum number of iterations to be used is controlled with the `-maxit` option. All points that never exceed the magnitude specified by `-bail` within the maximum number of iterations will be represented by gray points as determined by these options.

If you wish to zoom into different areas, then the `-ulx`, `-uly`, and `-lly` options can be used to determine the upper-left and lower-left corners of the viewing area. Notice that only the y-coordinate is specified for the lower-left corner. We don't need to specify the x-coordinate, since this is already determined by the `-ulx` option. Similarly, the rightmost edge of the image is predetermined by these options.

The `-bulx`, `-buly`, and `-blly` options specify corners of a box in a way similar to the options above. However, the corners determined by these options are used to draw a box with a width determined by the `-box` option. If the width is set to 0, then no box is drawn. These options are useful if you wish to highlight a subset of the image that you will later zoom into.

With the `-idiv` option you can divide the gray-scale map used for the image into several different bands. The effect is difficult to explain; however, with a little bit of trial and error you should be able to see exactly what the option does. The `-rev` option can be used to invert all of the gray-scale colors except black. Again, this option is best explored and not explained.

For computing Julia set images, recall that there is a unique Julia set for each value of the c parameter. The value of c used for a particular Julia set can be fixed with the `-cr` and `-ci` options, which set the real and imaginary components of c, respectively.

8.8 Further Reading

Hirst, B. & Mandelbrot, B. (1995). *Fractal landscapes from the real world.* New York: Distributed Art Publishers.

Mandelbrot, B. (1983). *The fractal geometry of nature.* New York: W. H. Freeman.

Peitgen, H.-O., Jürgens, H., & Saupe, D. (1992). *Chaos and fractals.* New York: Springer-Verlag.

Pickover, C. A. (1991). *Computers, pattern, chaos and beauty: Graphics from an unseen world.* New York: St. Martin's Press.

9 Postscript: Fractals

It is indeed a surprising and fortunate fact that nature can be expressed by relatively low-order mathematical functions.
— Rudolf Carnap

Everything you've learned in school as "obvious" becomes less and less obvious as you begin to study the universe. For example, there are no solids in the universe. There's not even a suggestion of a solid. There are no absolute continuums. There are no surfaces. There are no straight lines.
— R. Buckminster Fuller

Mathematics is the science of patterns.
— Lynn Arthur Steen

COMPUTER PROGRAMS HAVE a dual identity that is an artifact of a trade-off between time and space. From one viewpoint, and in the static sense, a stored computer program can be thought of as a compact recipe for distinguishing between numbers that do and do not belong to some specific set. From the opposite viewpoint, and in the dynamic sense, a running program is a flowing process that enumerates members of a set, one after another. This difference can be appreciated with the example set that can be described by "all prime numbers that are one less than a perfect power of 2" or enumerated as the infinite set of numbers that starts out {3, 7, 31, 127, 8191, 131071, 524287, ...}. While the verbal description is a perfect representation of the infinite set in that it contains a sufficient amount of information to enable one to enumerate an arbitrary number of members, it would still take an infinite amount of computational time to perform the task. Hence, while the verbal description is finite in length but requires infinite time to "unwind," the enumerated set requires infinite space to store it but exists independently of time.

Fractals, both deterministic and stochastic, derive from special types of programs that exhibit this same duality. Natural fractals—such as branching and folding structures found in biological systems and the random patterns in mountain ranges and river basins—are often structurally elaborate to such a degree that they are difficult to describe with classical geometry. Yet, in many cases, a fractal structure will have a simple underlying functional cause. For biological systems this cause is usually related to parallel growth processes and the need to optimize conflicting goals, such as surface area and building material usage, while stochastic fractals often result from a single parallel process that occurs on multiple spatial scales, such as erosion. Thus, the structural recursion of a fractal will always be related to a functional recursion that takes place in the creation of the natural fractal.

In this second postscript chapter we will see how fractals relate to many of the computational issues discussed in Part I. In particular, we will see how some of the stochastic and deterministic fractals that we examined in this part can be viewed as canonical examples of "almost simple" things under two very different but reasonable definitions of simplicity. Examining simplicity in this way will give us insight into what it means for something to be truly complex.

9.1 Algorithmic Regularity as Simplicity

Our first attempt at a definition for "simplicity" is related to the idea that things that can be compressed are simpler than things that cannot. This has relevance to scientific methodology because a scientist's principal job is to give explanations for phenomena that are simpler than the phenomena they describe. For example, the number of chemicals and chemical reactions is so staggeringly large that without any knowledge of atomic structure, chemistry looks a lot like magic. But with an understanding of atomic structure and how atoms bind to each other, it becomes possible not only to understand individual reactions but also to conceive of new chemical compounds that have never existed before. In this case, a scientific model of atomic structure has been used to compress much of the complexity of chemistry. Thus, compression can be thought of as a way of building models to explain more complex things.

The formal study of how things can be algorithmically compressed is known as Algorithmic Complexity (AC).[1] AC is a relatively new field that was independently pioneered by Ray Solomonoff, Andrei Kolmogorov, and Gregory Chaitin.[2] To better appreciate AC, recall from Chapter 3 that the time complexity of an algorithm is a bound on the amount of time that it takes to compute a function for some particular input length. Similarly, the space complexity is used to characterize the amount of computer memory that an algorithm will need at any time during its execution.

[1] The topic of AC goes by a number of different names but is often referred as "Kolmogorov Complexity" in academic circles. I am using "Algorithmic Complexity" instead, since this name seems to better indicate what the topic is about to the uninitiated.

[2] Amazingly, Chaitin was just fifteen years old when he started working on defining AC. He published his first results at the age of nineteen.

AC Measure

Low Information Content	High Information Content
High Compressibility	Low Compressibility
Orderly	Random

Figure 9.1 AC in terms of information, compressibility, and randomness

Like time complexity, space complexity is given as a function of the length of the input.

AC differs from these other two complexity measures in that it is not always concerned with how long it takes to compute a function or how much memory is required, just as long as both are finite. Instead, in AC the central issue is the required length of a program to produce a set of numbers or symbols. As an example similar to but simpler than the one found in the opening of this chapter, suppose you were interested in the first n even natural numbers. One way of storing this information would be to sequentially list each number that you wanted to remember: 0, 2, 4, 6, 8, ..., $(2n - 2)$. For large values of n a more efficient storage technique would be to store a program fragment that could reproduce the desired set of numbers:

```
for(i = 0; i < n; i++) printf("%d\n", i * 2);
```

The one constraint that we place on programs of this nature is that they must take no input, that is, we require that all of the information needed to reproduce the set must be in the program itself; thus, in the C program fragment above, we would really need to replace the variable, n, by the hard-coded limit of the number of even numbers in our set. How much information is in a consecutive sequence of even numbers? After replacing n with the limit, the length of the program will always grow proportionally to $O(\log n)$, since n can be represented by a character sequence of length $\log n + 1$ and everything else in the program is independent of n. This means that if you used the values 10, 100, 1000, ..., 1,000,000 for n, you could compress the set of numbers down to a length of approximately 2, 3, 4, ..., 7, respectively (plus the extra three-dozen or so characters required for the rest of the code fragment), which is a remarkable compression rate. Going back to the earlier discussion on time and space, AC tells us exactly how much one can be traded for another, that is, if you can't actually store a large set of numbers in a computer's memory, then AC tells us that a portion of the space in memory can be replaced with computational time if we are willing to make the sacrifice that the set would have to be reconstructed on the fly.

Thus, AC formalizes what it means for a set of numbers to be compressible and incompressible. Data that are redundant or that can be more easily described than enumerated—like the set of even numbers—contain relatively little information; therefore, one can compress sets like this into something of a smaller size. Data that have no clear pattern and defy algorithmic description are incompressible. This notion of incompressibility yields a nice description of what it means for data to be random. If there is no discernible relationship between numbers in a set, then they are most likely statistically independent of each other and are therefore random. Figure 9.1 illustrates all of these characteristics in terms of AC.[3]

9.2 Stochastic Irregularity as Simplicity

One failing of AC is that it defies intuition to a certain extent; after all, most people would not necessarily associate randomness with complexity. In fact, some forms of randomness can be considered simple, since a collection of purely random events can often be statistically characterized very concisely. Complementary to this, moderately "simple" things from an AC point of view often have complicated statistical descriptions. This would seem to imply that AC and statistical complexity are somewhat incompatible. To get at the heart of what it really means for something to be "simple," we will consider how many random things can be compactly described.

As we saw in Chapter 5, a fair coin toss can be used to generate a type of random walk by letting the outcome of two coin tosses be mapped to the four compass directions. We can simplify a random walk considerably by constraining the moves to only the left and right directions, thus limiting the walker to a one-dimensional line instead of a two-dimensional plane. This process can be conceptually simplified even further by noting that the position of a random walker relative to its origin will always be equal to a sum of random numbers such that each random number is either -1 or +1. Hence, by mapping heads to +1 and tails to -1, a random walk of n steps can be simulated by taking the sum of n ± 1 random numbers.

For large values of n—say, on the order of thousands or more—what will typical sums of ± 1 random numbers look like? Clearly, if we are using a fair coin toss, on average there will be as many heads as tails, which means that a random walker will stay relatively close to the origin. For a random walker to be significantly to the left or right, there must be a skewed number of heads or tails in the coin tosses, which, while possible, is very improbable.

[3] Regarding the topic of compression and AC, an informal contest took place on the USENET newsgroup `comp.lang.c` to see who could come up with the shortest program that produced the song "1 little, 2 little, 3 little Indians ..." complete with the final line "... 10 little Indian boys." The whole song has 133 text characters in it. Using the compression program **gzip**, it is possible to compress this down to 83 bytes. However, one entry consisted of a cryptic program that contained a mere 78 characters that faithfully reproduces the whole song. Interestingly, attempting to compress the 78 byte program with **gzip** yields a file that is 109 bytes in size. Since the "compressed" file is larger than the original file, the file is incompressible as far as **gzip** is concerned.

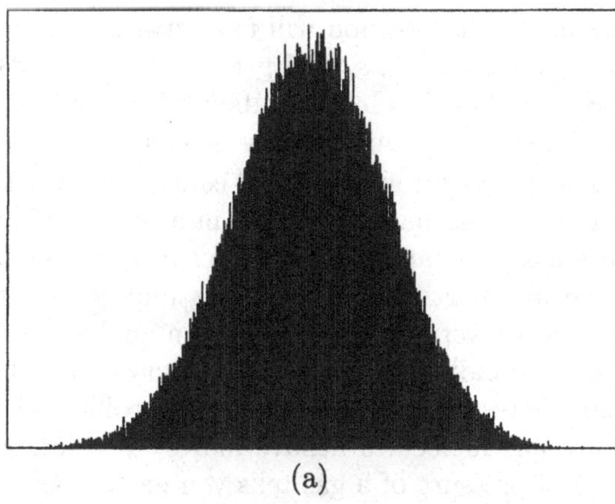
(a)

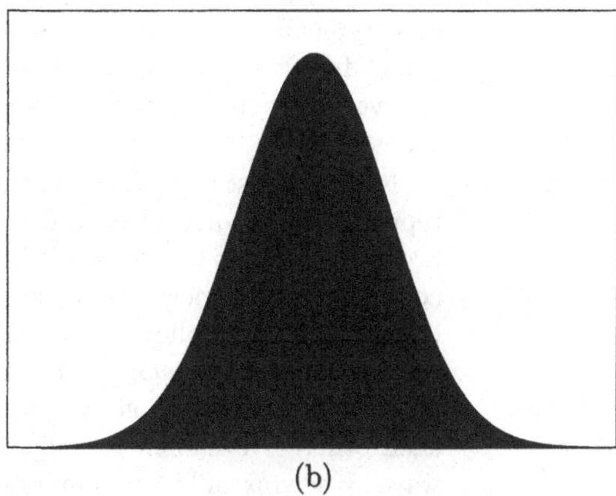
(b)

Figure 9.2 Gaussian distributions (a) from random coin tosses and (b) from the equation $(1/\sigma\sqrt{2\pi})\exp(-(x-\mu)^2/2\sigma^2)$

If we were to generate several million random walks, each walk consisting of thousands of steps, we could take note of the final resting position of the random walkers and plot a histogram of these positions. Figure 9.2a shows such a histogram, with the center of the plot representing a final position of 0 (meaning that the left and right moves canceled out). As can be seen, the plot is very close to a true normal bellcurve, otherwise known as a Gaussian distribution. Figure 9.2b shows the smooth curve plotted from the actual Gaussian function. Clearly, the two graphs are very similar. Had we increased the number of walks and the lengths of the walks, the two curves would have approached each other to the point that they would be visibly indistinguishable.

The curves graphically show how likely it is for a particular outcome to occur with the random walker. The most likely case is that the random walker will end up at or near the starting point. Slightly less likely, but still very possible, is that the walker will end up just to the left or just to the right. As the final distance from the origin increases, the probability that the random walker will end up at that distance diminishes. To end up at one of the absolute extremes requires that a thousand coin tosses come up with a thousand heads or a thousand tails in a row, which is for all practical purposes impossible.

Gaussian curves like those shown in Figure 9.2 have many useful statistical properties. First and foremost, they are unimodal, meaning that they have a single peak, so that knowing where the center of the distribution is located tells you a great deal about every point in the distribution. Second, Gaussian distributions also have a well-defined standard deviation, which is the average amount that all of the points deviate from the center of the distribution. With a standard deviation of s, typically 68 percent of all points in the distribution will fall between $-s$ and $+s$. A full 95 percent of the points will be between $\pm 2s$, 99.7 percent between $\pm 3s$, and very close to 100 percent between $\pm 4s$. This is why after 1000 coin tosses, you are very likely to have hit 50 percent heads plus or minus a few percent.

Knowing just the mean and the standard deviation, one could come very close to reproducing the actual data from a normal distribution. Hence, in a way, random processes are also compressible because many instances can be described by a small collection of numbers. So even though any particular coin toss is unpredictable, the properties of collections of coin tosses are very predictable. As an analogy, it is impossible to keep track of the trajectories of individual molecules in a closed volume of air, since there are simply too many ways that gas molecules can collide with each other. Nevertheless, collections of gas molecules behave in very predictable ways. Knowing only the temperature and pressure of a gas tells you enough about the whole ensemble of molecules that you can effectively ignore what the individual molecules are doing. Notice that the properties of temperature and pressure cannot be attributed to a single gas molecule but only to collections of molecules. Similarly, the mean and standard deviation of a normal random process make sense only for collections of random events. Yet these two numbers manage to get to the essence of what is important about a particular normal distribution.

9.3 Effective Complexity

We now have at our disposal two very different definitions of what it can mean for something to be simple. Both seem reasonable but are somewhat in conflict with one another. For instance, if we think of the random bit sequences generated for a random walk, we know from the results in Section 9.1 that it would be very difficult to get a computer program to duplicate such a sequence. Any program that succeeds would probably have to store the random sequence explicitly, because random strings cannot be compressed. However, if we have a coin at our disposal, even though we cannot reproduce a specific random sequence, we can still duplicate an infinite number of random strings that would have the same statistical properties as the candidate sequence that we wished to reproduce. Complementary to this, regular sequences of strings or sets (the very sorts of things that a computer would be able to compress) would be nearly impossible to reproduce with a coin toss. Thus, a coin toss is good at doing the exact sorts of things that a computer is bad at, and vice versa.

How, then, do we describe what it really means for something to be complex? Simply stating that "complexity is the opposite of simplicity" seems to violate at least one of our two definitions of simplicity. Nevertheless, a number of scientists, most notably James Crutchfield, Charles Bennet, Murray Gell-Mann, and David Wolpert and William Macready, have been working on this problem, producing

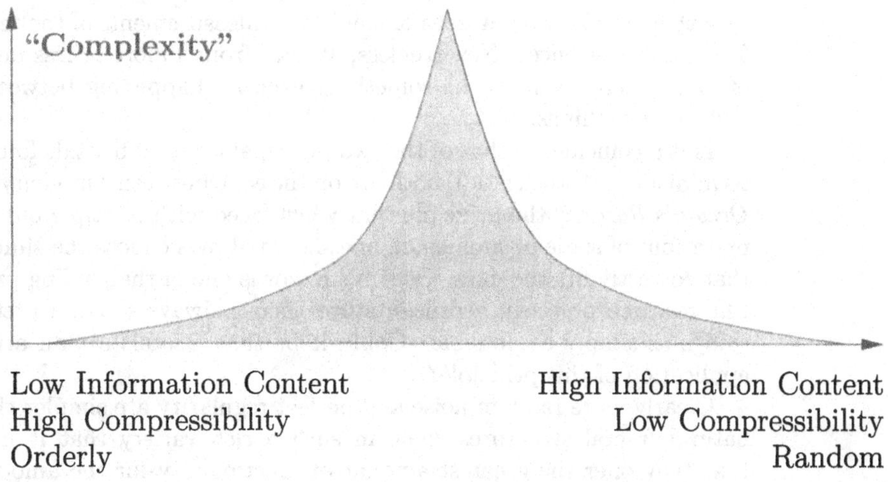

Figure 9.3 Complexity in terms of information, compressibility, and randomness

several candidate measures of "effective complexity." Most of the proposed measures differ from each other but share at least one important characteristic, in that strictly regular things as well as strictly irregular things are "simple," while things that are neither regular nor irregular are "complex." Figure 9.3 illustrates how information, compressibility, and randomness relate to any of these useful notions of complexity.

On one extreme we have the pure regularity found in Euclidean objects. Deterministic fractals, while not simple, have compact algorithmic descriptions but elaborate structures. Fractals fail to be strictly simple because even though they are defined by short programs, these programs must be made to run forever in order to completely express the infinite self-similarity that they contain.

On the other extreme of Figure 9.3 is pure noise. Brownian motion is slightly more complex than pure noise because Brownian processes must have "memory," in that every random injection is always made relative to the previous state; thus, a random walker's position is not just a random location but the sum of an infinite number of random steps. Hence, fractals, both deterministic and stochastic, while not simple, seem to be on the edge of being complex. They can be compactly described but can be realized only by "programs" that never halt. At the very peak of complexity, we would hope to find things such as the human brain, but this is just speculation on my part.

To be sure, the jury is still out as to how the word "complexity" should be defined. Moreover, it is not even clear to many people that there can exist a catchall definition or measure that adequately captures any reasonable intuitive notion of what it means for something to be complex. This is especially true when we consider that there are literally dozens of conflicting measurements of the term "complexity" found in the sciences. Nevertheless, at least from a more or less philosophical point of view, there seems to be something exciting happening between orderly things and random things.

Is it a coincidence that of the two principal types of fractals found in nature (deterministic and stochastic), both are on the edge between simplicity and complexity? *Occam's Razor* is the principle that when faced with multiple but equivalent interpretations of some phenomenon, one should always choose the simplest explanation that correctly fits the data. Occam's Razor is one of the guiding principles of scientific research precisely because nature almost always shows a preference for doing things as simply as possible. Could it be that fractals are an artifact of nature's application of this principle?

Clearly, pure random noise and perfect regularity are simpler than fractals. But natural fractal structures come in such a rich variety that it may very well be that they offer the greatest amount of functionality for the amount of underlying complexity consumed. This idea, that truly complex things occur at a transition point between two extremes, is a theme that will recur many more times throughout book.

9.4 Further Reading

Chaitin, G. J. (1997). *The limits of mathematics: A course on information theory & limits of formal reasoning.* Singapore: Springer-Verlag.

Cowan, G., Pines, D., & Meltzer, D. (Eds.). (1994). *Complexity: Metaphors, models, and reality,* volume XIX of *Santa Fe Institute Studies in the Sciences of Complexity.* Reading, Mass.: Addison-Wesley.

Dewdney, A. K. (1993). *200 percent of nothing: An eye-opening tour through the twists and turns of math abuse and innumeracy.* New York: John Wiley & Sons.

Gell-Mann, M. (1995). *The quark and the jaguar: Adventures in the simple and the complex.* New York: W. H. Freeman.

Gonick, L. & Smith, W. (1993). *The cartoon guide to statistics.* New York: HarperCollins.

Stinson, D. R. (1995). *Cryptography: Theory and practice.* Boca Raton: CRC Press.

Wassermann, G. D. (1997). *From Occam's Razor to the roots of consciousness: 20 essays on philosophy, philosophy of science and philosophy of mind.* Avebury.

III Chaos

Simple motion is rare in nature. It is more common to find highly complicated nonlinear motion due to *chaos*. Chaotic systems can easily be mistaken for randomness despite the fact that they are always deterministic. Part of the confusion is due to the fact that the future of chaotic systems can be predicted only on very short-term time scales. Chaotic systems possess a form of functional self-similarity that shows itself in fractal strange attractors. This fractal functionality, combined with chaotic unpredictability, is reminiscent of the uncertainty found in computing systems.

Chapter 10 introduces the key components of chaotic systems and highlights the properties common to all such systems. Chapter 11 contains a sampling of fractal *strange attractors* that are generated from chaotic systems. Chapter 12 considers a type of chaos found in producer-consumer systems, and compares and contrasts two very different types of modeling methods. Chapter 13 shows how some of the properties of chaotic systems can be exploited for the purpose of controlling them. Finally, Chapter 14 compares and contrasts chaos to randomness and incomputability.

10 Nonlinear Dynamics in Simple Maps

Chaos is the score upon which reality is written.
— Henry Miller

... it may happen that small differences in the initial conditions produce very great ones in the final phenomena.
— Henri Poincaré

Prediction is difficult, especially of the future.
— Mark Twain (also attributed to Niels Bohr)

IN THE PREVIOUS book part we saw how natural physical structures could be described in terms of fractal geometry. In this book part we will be concerned with the related topic of *chaos* in *nonlinear dynamical systems*. A dynamical system can be loosely defined as anything that has motion, such as swinging pendulums, bouncing balls, robot arms, reactions in a chemical process, water flowing in a stream, or an airplane in flight. For each of these examples there are two important aspects that must be considered. First, we need to determine what it is about a dynamical system that changes over time. In the case of the pendulum, both position and velocity vary over time, so we would be concerned with the "motion" of both of these states of the pendulum. A less obvious example is found in a chemical reaction, where the "motion" can be found in the ratio of reactants to reagents, or perhaps in some physical aspect of the chemicals, such as temperature or viscosity. The second aspect of a dynamical system that we must be concerned with is in the collection of rules that determine how a dynamical system changes over time. Usually, scientists have a mathematical model of how a real dynamical system works. The model will typically have equations that may be parameterized by time and the previous states of the system. Sometimes these equations can be used to get an estimate of what the future state of a dynamical system will be. In

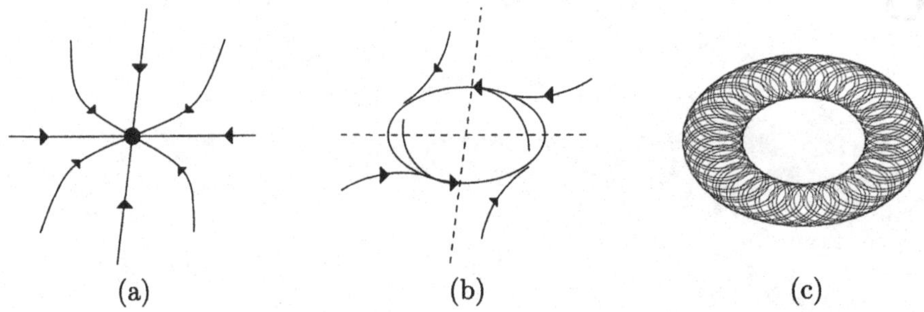

Figure 10.1 Different types of motion: (a) fixed point, (b) limit cycle (c) quasiperiodic

this spirit, let's agree that the "motion" of a dynamical system is dependent on how the state of the system changes over time. Moreover, there must exist a set of rules that governs how a dynamical system in some state evolves to another state. We may not know what the rules are, but if a dynamical system is deterministic, a set of rules for the time evolution of the system exists independently of our knowledge of it.

There are many different types of motion that can be exhibited by a dynamical system. The simplest is *fixed point* behavior, which can be seen in a pendulum when friction and gravity bring the system to a halt. Most fixed points can be likened to a ball placed on top of a hill, which rolls downward until at some point the ball sits on a flat spot and has no momentum to carry it further.

The next simplest type of motion is known as a *limit cycle* or *periodic* motion, which involves movement that repeats itself over and over. A lone planet orbiting a star in an elliptical orbit is an example of a limit cycle. Some limit cycles are more complicated than others. For example, a child on a swing drives the motion of the swing by periodically rocking in beat with the natural frequency of the swing, much like an idealized pendulum. Now, if the child rhythmically swings one leg at a higher frequency, the motion of that leg will cause the motion of his or her body to subtly wobble back and forth. If it is timed accurately, the child may be able to coerce the motion into behavior that is more complicated than that of the planet, with his or her body moving back and forth along the main axis of the swing, and perpendicularly left to right in step with the leg.

A slightly more complicated form of motion is found in *quasiperiodic* systems, which are similar to periodic systems except that they never quite repeat themselves. For example, the moon orbits Earth, which orbits the sun, which, in turn, orbits the galactic center, and so on. In order for the combined motion of the moon and Earth to be truly periodic, they must at some future point return to some previously occupied state. But in order for that to happen, all of the individual motions must resonate, which means that there must exist a length of time that will evenly divide all of the frequencies. Figure 10.1c shows quasiperiodic motion as consisting of two independent circular motions that fail to repeat due to a lack of resonance.

Up until the last thirty years or so, almost every scientist believed that everything in the universe fell into either fixed point, periodic, or quasiperiodic behavior. The belief in a clockwork universe, as exemplified by the mathematician Pierre-Simon de Laplace[1], held that, in principle, if one had an accurate measure of the state of the universe and knew all of the laws that govern the motion of everything, then one would be able to predict the future with near perfect accuracy. We now know that this is not true, since science was mistaken in its assumption that everything is either a fixed point or a limit cycle. Chaotic systems are not just exceptions to the norm but are, in fact, more prevalent than anyone could imagine. Chaos is everywhere: in the turbulence of water and air, in the wobble of planets as they follow complicated orbits, in global weather patterns, in the human brain's electrochemical activity, and even in the motion of a child on a swing. In all of these cases the complicated motion produced by chaos prohibits predicting the future in the long term. On the other hand, phenomena that were once thought to be purely random are now known to be chaotic. The good news in this case is that chaotic systems admit prediction in the short term.

Chaos is related to the other topics of this book in many ways. The pathological nature of the incomputable functions from Part I is very similar to the unpredictability of chaotic systems. The motion of chaotic systems can be described by fractal geometry. There is also a hypothesis known as "computation on the edge of chaos" that will be relevant in the next book part when we study complex systems.

In this chapter we will be primarily concerned with getting an intuitive feel for how chaos works in a simple, discrete time, iterative system. The nice thing about the examples that we will be looking at is that the richness, diversity, and beauty of chaos are exhibited by a deceptively simple dynamical system.

10.1 The Logistic Map

The logistic map (also known as the "quadratic map" or the "Feigenbaum map") is a simple population growth model that is defined by the iterative equation[2]

$$x_{t+1} = 4rx_t(1 - x_t),$$

where r is a parameter that can be set to reflect the reproduction rate of the population. The legal values of x_t (as well as x_{t+1}) range between 0 and 1 inclusively.

[1]Laplace claimed that "given for one instant an intelligence which could comprehend all the forces by which nature is animated and the respective positions of the beings which compose it ... nothing would be uncertain, and the future as the past would be present to its eyes."

[2]In many scientific writings the logistic map is given as $x_{t+1} = rx_t(1 - x_t)$, with r ranging from 0 to 4. I have deliberately added the 4 in my presentation so that r can range from 0 to 1.

If x_t equals 0, then we can interpret the population as being extinct. If x_t equals 1, then the system is overpopulated (with imminent extinction at the next time step). All other values between 0 and 1 represent intermediate population levels.

The value of r is also allowed to vary between 0 and 1. If r is 0, then nothing reproduces in the population. If r is equal to 1, then the members of the population are reproducing at the maximum rate. Over the course of this section, we will look at several different values of r. Since the logistic map is so simple, you may wish to use a calculator while reading this chapter, so as to simulate population growth yourself.

To use the logistic map, we must choose a constant value for r and an initial population, x_0. From x_0 we can compute x_1, then x_2, and so on. Intuitively, we can assign a useful interpretation to the individual terms of the dynamical system. We can think of $4rx_t$ as being positive feedback in the sense that as x_t grows in size, so does the value of $4rx_t$, which is akin to saying that a population size is partially determined by the product of the previous size and the rate at which members reproduce. The $(1 - x_t)$ portion of the equation can be thought of as negative feedback, since increasing x_t will decrease $(1 - x_t)$; thus, $(1 - x_t)$ can be thought of as population decline due to overpopulation and scarce resources.

What we would like to know is, for some value of r, what happens to the long-term behavior of the system as t goes to infinity. Let's consider some special cases. Suppose that r is less than or equal to $\frac{1}{4}$. In this case the time evolution is described by $\alpha x_t(1-x_t)$, with α, x_t, and $(1-x_t)$ all between 0 and 1. Since the population at the next time step is the product of three numbers between 0 and 1, the population at the next time step must always be smaller than what it is at the current time step. Thus, no matter what initial value we choose for x_t, if $r \leq \frac{1}{4}$, then the population is doomed to extinction.

Suppose that r is greater than $\frac{1}{4}$ but less than $\frac{3}{4}$. In this case the long-term behavior of the logistic map is to fall into a fixed point. Figure 10.2 illustrates this graphically. The graph on the left shows the values of x_t plotted over time for 100 steps. The graph on the right shows the *state space* of the dynamical system (also referred to as the *phase space*) that plots x_t versus x_{t+1} to illustrate how the next iterate depends on the current value. The parabola in the graph is a plot of $x_{t+1} = 4rx_t(1 - x_t)$ with $r = \frac{7}{10}$. At any time step, we can geometrically determine the value of the next iterate by taking the current value of x_t, drawing a line at that value from the identity line to where it intersects the parabola, and then making a 90 degree turn toward the identity line again. In this way, the time evolution of the logistic map can be seen to be attracted to the fixed point. Moreover, it doesn't matter what initial value we pick for x_0, since any choice between 0 and 1 will cause the system to converge into the same fixed point.

If we set r greater than $\frac{7}{10}$ but less than $\frac{3}{4}$, then the value of the attracting fixed point will increase as we make r larger. Intuitively, this makes sense since one would expect a stable population to increase in size if the reproduction rate increases. All

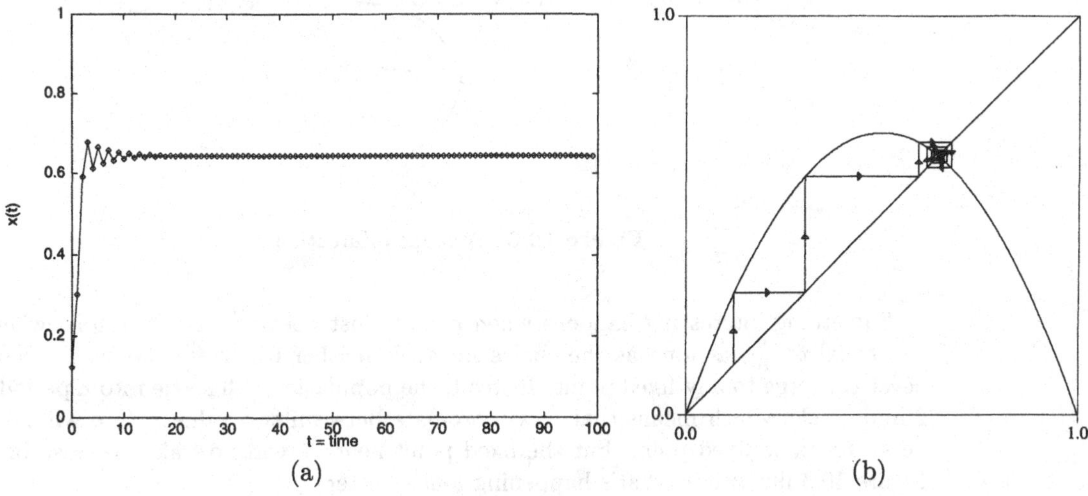

Figure 10.2 Logistic map with $r = \frac{7}{10}$: (a) The time series quickly stabilizes to a fixed point. (b) The state space of the same system shows how subsequent steps of the system get pulled into the fixed point.

fixed points, regardless of the value of r, can be found by seeing where the state space plot of x_t versus x_{t+1} intersects the identity line. With $\frac{1}{4} < r \leq \frac{3}{4}$ the parabola will always intersect the identity line at two points: the *stable fixed point*, which attracts all nonzero points, and 0 which is an *unstable fixed point*. The first fixed point is stable because if you randomly perturb the system away from the fixed point, the system will quickly converge back to the attracting fixed point again. Zero is an unstable fixed point because any perturbation will cause the system to leave that infinitesimal region forever. If you like, you can think of a stable fixed point as being similar to a ball at the bottom of a crater, valley, or depression. If you softly kick the ball, it will move just a bit, then stop. If your depression is shaped like a perfect bowl, then the ball will come to rest at the same location it started from. An unstable fixed point is like a ball perfectly balanced on the peak of a mountain. The slightest nudge will cause the ball to move away from the fixed point, never to return. We can squeeze one more useful notion out of this metaphor. Considering the stable fixed point once again, notice that there is an area defined by the perimeter of the depression. If you drop the ball anywhere within the perimeter, the ball will fall to the bottom of the depression. If the ball is dropped outside of the perimeter, the ball will go elsewhere. This area within the perimeter is sometimes referred to as the *basin of attraction*. An unstable fixed point has a basin of attraction that has 0 volume and area.

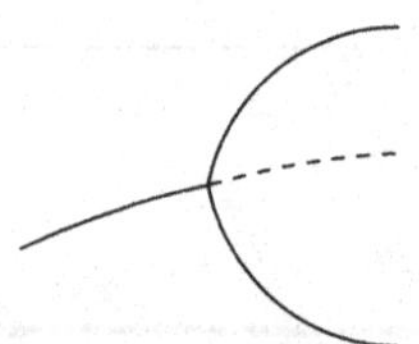

Figure 10.3 A single bifurcation

Something interesting happens when r is set just above $\frac{3}{4}$. For example, when r is equal to $\frac{8}{10}$, as long as the choice for x_0 is neither 0 nor $\frac{22}{32}$, the system will never converge to any fixed point. Instead, the population will settle into a period-2 limit cycle, which means that it will oscillate between two values. Zero will still be an unstable fixed point, but the fixed point near $\frac{22}{32}$ will now also be unstable. Figure 10.3 illustrates what's happening much better.

The leftmost portion of the drawing illustrates how the location of the fixed point gradually increases as we increase the value of r; however, at a critical value, the path will split in two. The two solid lines on the right illustrate how the location of the period-2 limit cycle changes as the value of r is increased. The dashed line shows how the once stable fixed point continues to exist, but in a form that is unstable. Thus, solid lines denote stable paths, and dashed lines denote unstable paths. Figure 10.4 illustrates the period-2 limit cycle in a form that is similar to Figure 10.2. Notice that the state space diagram now clearly shows how the state of the system oscillates between two values.

10.2 Stability and Instability

For one-dimensional maps like the logistic map, there is a very simple method to determine if a fixed point or limit cycle is stable or unstable. The idea behind the technique is to examine the local behavior of the map in the vicinity of a fixed point or limit cycle. For notational purposes, let's refer to the mapping function as $f(x)$, that is, $f(x) = 4rx(1-x)$ for the logistic map. The first derivative of $f(x)$, which is equal to $f'(x) = 4r(1-2x)$, tells us how steeply sloped the function is in the vicinity of x. Now, suppose there exists a fixed point, which we will call x_F, and that we would like to know whether the fixed point is stable or unstable. If we look at the derivative of $f(x)$ evaluated at x_F, then the following possibilities may characterize the behavior of $f(x)$ at x_F:

$$
\begin{array}{rcll}
|f'(x_F)| & < & 1 & \text{attracting and stable} \\
f'(x_F) & = & 0 & \text{super-stable} \\
|f'(x_F)| & > & 1 & \text{repelling and unstable} \\
|f'(x_F)| & = & 1 & \text{neutral}
\end{array}
$$

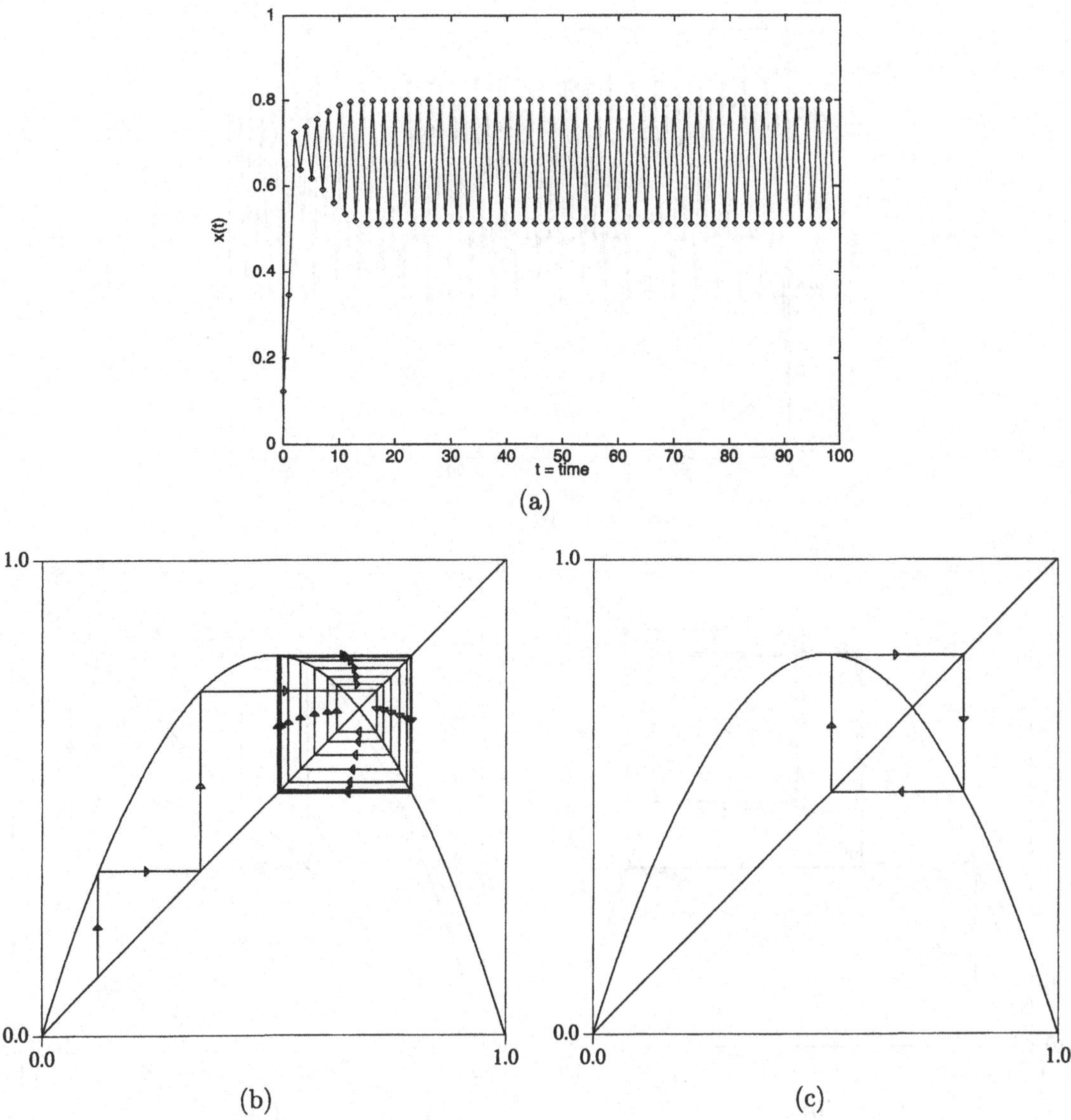

Figure 10.4 Logistic map with $r = \frac{8}{10}$: (a) The time series quickly stabilizes to a period-2 limit cycle. (b) The state space of the same system shows how subsequent steps of the system get pulled into the limit cycle. (c) The state space of the same system but with only the converged values for x_t plotted, so as to clearly show the limit cycle's location.

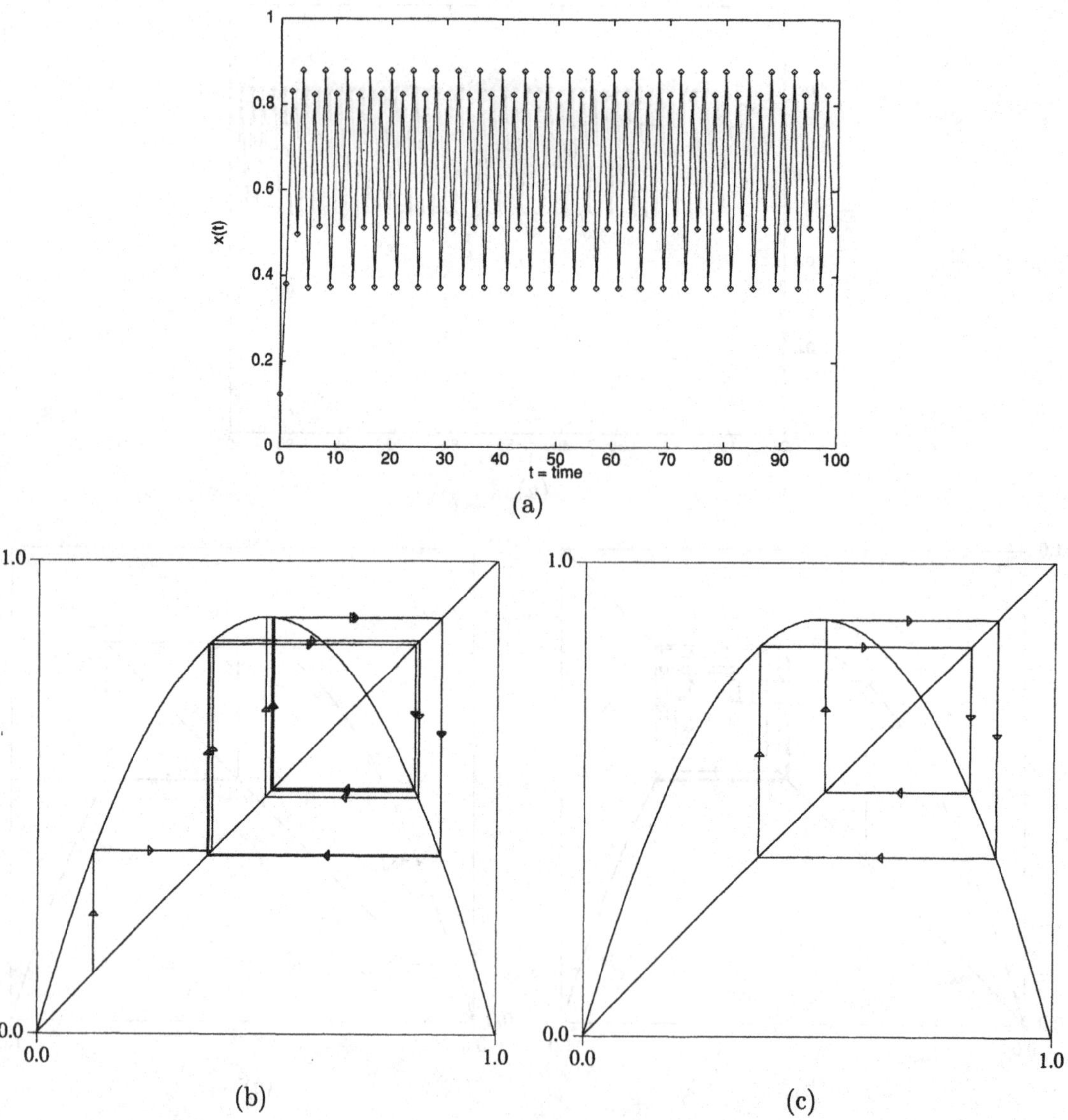

Figure 10.5 Logistic map with $r = \frac{88}{100}$: (a) The time series quickly stabilizes to a period-4 limit cycle. (b) The state space of the same system. (c) The state space of the same system but with only the converged values for x_t plotted.

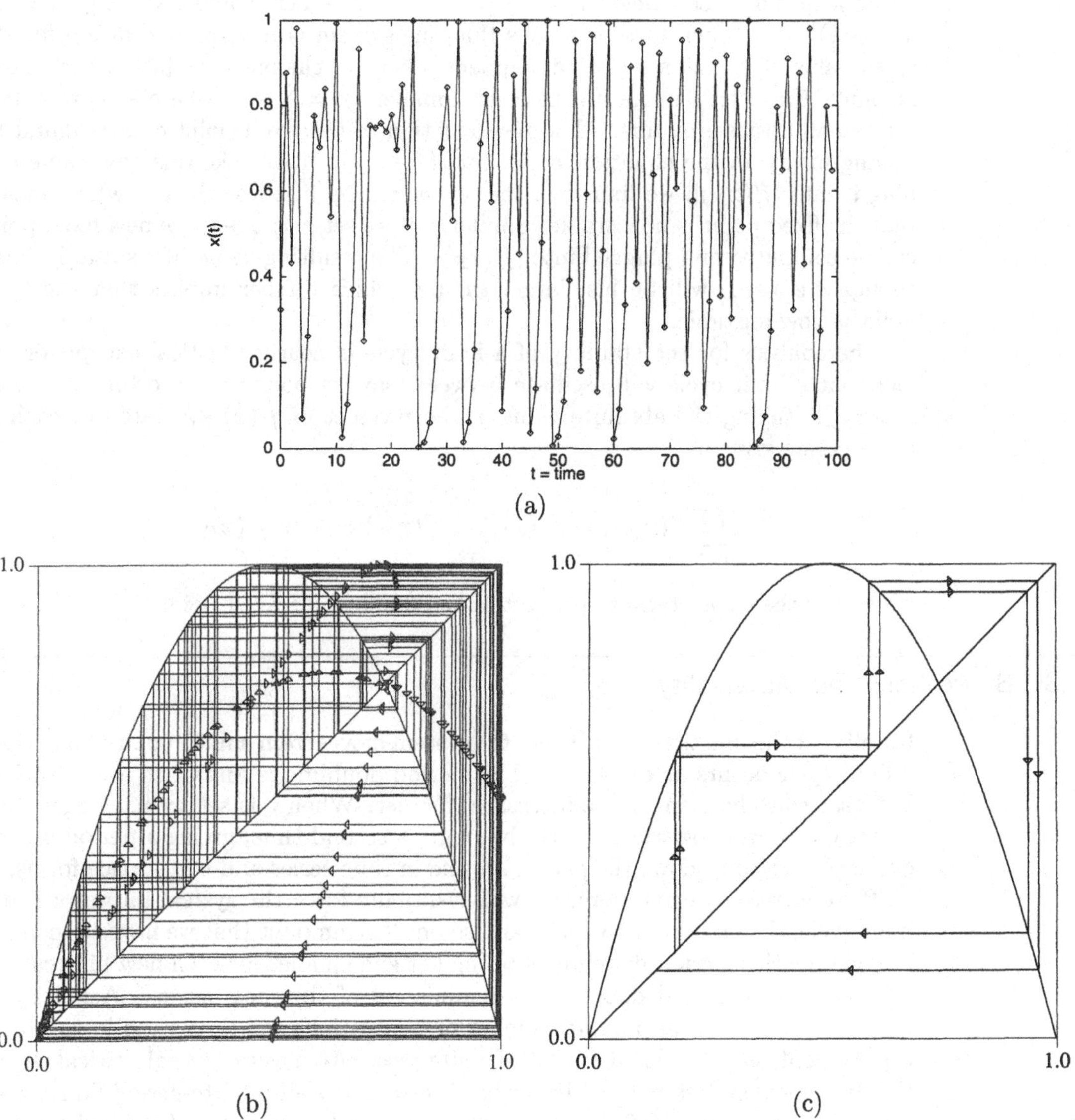

Figure 10.6 Logistic map with $r = 1$: (a) The time series is chaotic and has the appearance of noise. (b) The state space of the same system, which illustrates how the system's trajectory visits every local region. (c) The state space of the same system with only four steps plotted, so as to show how small differences turn into larger differences.

As a specific case, consider $r = \frac{3}{4}$ and $x_F = \frac{2}{3}$, which would give us $|f'(x_F)| = |3(1 - \frac{4}{3})| = 1$, which further means that the system is neutral at that x_F for the given value of r. Let's see what happens when we change r by just a very small amount. First, let's make r a little bit smaller: $r = \frac{3}{4} - \epsilon$, where ϵ represents a very small positive number. The new location of the fixed point can be found by solving for x_F in the equation $x_F = 4rx_F(1 - x_F)$. If we take this new value and plug it into $|f'(x_F)|$, we find that the result will be just less than 1, which means that the fixed point is now stable. Similarly, if we set r to $\frac{3}{4} + \epsilon$, the new fixed point can be computed and plugged into $|f'(x_F)|$. The resulting value (if a suitably small enough ϵ is used) will be just larger than 1, which further implies that the fixed point is now unstable.

The analysis for the stability of a limit cycle is nearly identical except for the fact that a limit cycle will oscillate between, say, m points in an orbit: x_{F_1}, x_{F_2}, $\cdots$, x_{F_m}. Taking the absolute value of the product of $f'(x)$ evaluated at each of these points gives us

$$\left| \prod_{i=1}^{m} f'(x_{F_i}) \right| = |f'(x_{F_1}) \times f'(x_{F_2}) \times \cdots \times f'(x_{F_m})|,$$

which has the same stability properties listed above for fixed points.

10.3 Bifurcations and Universality

Recall that the junction point where the system moves from a fixed point to a period-2 limit cycle occurs at exactly $\frac{3}{4}$. This period doubling is known as a *bifurcation*. Let's see what happens as we increase r further. When r is set to just larger than $(1 + \sqrt{6}) \div 4$, the logistic map will bifurcate a second time, giving a period-4 limit cycle. Figure 10.5 shows the period-4 cycle in time-series and state-space forms.

If we increase r even more, we will eventually force the system into a period-8 limit cycle, then a period-16 cycle, and so on. The amount that we have to increase r to get another period doubling gets smaller and smaller for each new bifurcation. This cascade of period doublings is reminiscent of the race between Achilles and the tortoise, in that an infinite number of bifurcations (or time steps in the race) can be confined to a local region of finite size. At a very special critical value, the dynamical system will fall into what is essentially an infinite-period limit cycle. This is chaos. Figure 10.6 shows the time series and state space of the logistic map for $r = 1$, which is in the chaotic regime.

Figure 10.7 illustrates the transition from order to chaos with two bifurcation diagrams. The x-axis represents a value for r, and the y-axis shows the period of the limit cycle. Notice that the diagram clearly shows how each period doubling spans a shorter amount of space than the previous doubling. Eventually the period doublings converge to what looks like an infinite-period attractor. Notice also that

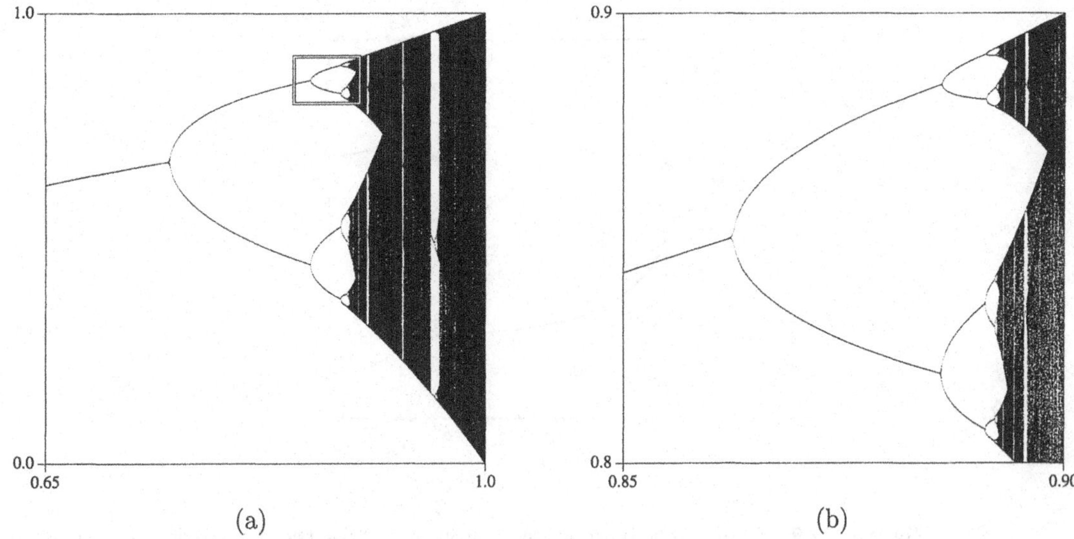

Figure 10.7 Bifurcation diagrams for the logistic map: (a) This image has values of r such that fixed points, limit cycles, and chaos are all visible. (b) This image shows the detail of the boxed section of (a).

the two images are very self-similar in that we could enlarge a portion of Figure 10.7b to get another self-similar section, and so on.

Bifurcations of this sort are seen in many different types of phenomena. What is truly astonishing is that for a very broad class of bump-like functions, such as the logistic map, the cascade of bifurcations behaves in accordance with a universal number known as the *Feigenbaum constant*. For notational convenience let's refer to the value of r at which the logistic map bifurcates into a period-2^n limit cycle as a_n, that is, $a_1 = \frac{3}{4}$. Thus, we would know that for $a_{k-1} < r \leq a_k$ the logistic map would have a stable period-2^k limit cycle. Mitchell Feigenbaum considered the properties of the series of numbers generated by

$$d_k = \frac{a_k - a_{k-1}}{a_{k+1} - a_k},$$

for $k \geq 2$. In the equation above, the numerator and denominator represent the distance between successive bifurcation points, as is shown in Figure 10.8. Therefore, the whole expression, being the ratio of the two distances, quantifies how fast the next bifurcation occurs relative to the previous one. Feigenbaum showed that $d_\infty = 4.669202\cdots$, not just for the logistic map but for all one-dimensional maps that have a single hump. Thus, every chaotic system that falls into this class bifurcates at the same rate.

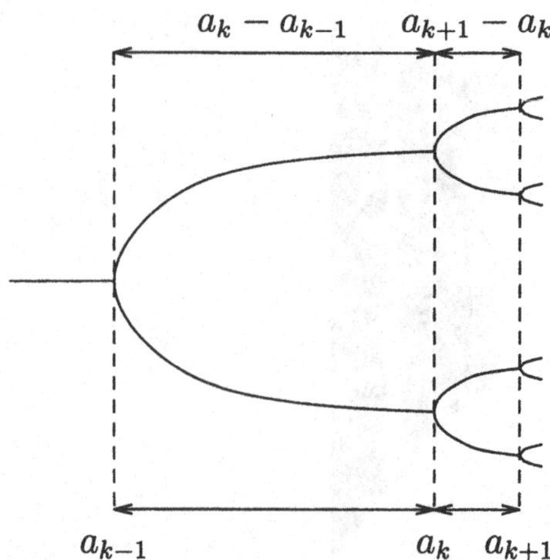

Figure 10.8 Detail of a bifurcation diagram to show the source of the Feigenbaum constant

By itself, this is an amazing result, yet it turns out that there is a very practical application for this knowledge. Suppose you are interested in a chaotic process that has a single tunable parameter like r for the logistic map. By empirically noting where the first few bifurcations occur, it is possible to get an accurate estimate for a_∞, which is the point where the system becomes chaotic. Thus, it is possible to estimate when a system will become chaotic before it ever happens.

10.4 Prediction, Layered Pastry, and Information Loss

One of the most important differences between chaotic processes and truly stochastic processes is that the future behavior of a chaotic system can be predicted in the short term, while stochastic processes can be characterized only statistically. For example, in a fair coin toss, knowing the results from earlier coin tosses does absolutely nothing for you if you are trying to predict what the next coin toss will yield. The best you could do, in terms of being able to predict the future, would be to generalize over an entire history, for instance, we could safely say that about half of our future coin tosses will result in heads; however, we are powerless to make any accurate assertions about any particular random event, such as the very next coin toss. Chaotic processes, on the other hand, can be predicted, since chaos always has hidden order within it. For many chaotic processes, the order becomes apparent when one looks at state space plots, as was done earlier. In contrast to chaos, plotting x_t against x_{t+1} for a stochastic process will reveal no hidden structure whatsoever.

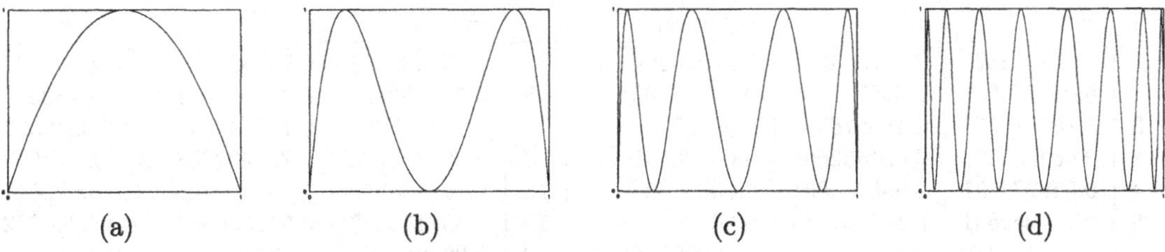

Figure 10.9 Functional mappings with $r = 1$: (a) $f^1(x)$, (b) $f^2(x)$, (c) $f^3(x)$, (d) $f^4(x)$

The flipside of this is that long-term prediction of a chaotic process becomes more difficult the farther into the future we try to predict. To predict one time step into the future, we would need to have an idea of what $f(x)$ looked like. If we wanted to predict two time steps into the future, we would have to examine $f(x)$ recursively applied to itself as $f(f(x))$. For the general case, let's agree that $f^m(x)$ denotes the mapping function of $f(x)$ recursively applied to itself a total of m times. Figure 10.9 illustrates how the mapping functions become more and more complicated as we increase the number of time steps into the future that we are looking at.

The pathological nature of chaos can be better appreciated with an analogy. Suppose you are a pastry chef who wants to make a pastry crust that has many layers in it. One way to accomplish this would be to stretch out your dough, fold one half over the other, and then repeat as often as needed. Notice that each step doubles the number of layers. It turns out that the motion of a chaotic system is very similar to the way we would form the pastry crust. For the logistic map, the $4rx$ portion of the function "stretches" out the input surface, while the $-4rx^2$ term "cuts" and "folds" the input. In this way, two grains of sugar that were originally close to one another in the pastry dough would gradually move away from one another, becoming decorrelated from one another as time went on. The sensitivity of chaotic systems is a result of these mixing actions.

Looking again at Figure 10.9, we can see that $f^m(x)$ has 2^{m-1} "humps" in it, which is similar to the way our pastry has an exponential number of layers. We will now see how all of this relates to a firm theoretical limitation on how far into the future one can predict. To make the analysis a bit simpler, let's assume that you only need to distinguish x_t values that are greater than or equal to $\frac{1}{2}$ from those that are less than $\frac{1}{2}$. In other words, if you are predicting m time steps into the future and I supply you with a value for x_t, your prediction scheme should return 1 bit of information: either "Yes, $x_{t+m} \leq \frac{1}{2}$" or "No, $x_{t+m} > \frac{1}{2}$."

To represent the starting value of x_t, we must ultimately encode the information in binary form. First, consider the case of $m = 1$. To determine if x_{t+1} is greater than (or less than) $\frac{1}{2}$, we essentially need to partition the input space into at least

t	x_t^a	x_t^b	$\lvert x_t^a - x_t^b \rvert$
0	0.987654321	0.987654320	0.000000001
1	0.048773053	0.048773057	0.000000004
2	0.185576969	0.185576983	0.000000014
3	0.604552629	0.604552665	0.000000035
4	0.956274991	0.956274961	0.000000030
5	0.167252531	0.167252639	0.000000108
6	0.557116488	0.557116776	0.000000288
7	0.986950827	0.986950696	0.000000132
8	0.051515568	0.051516080	0.000000512
9	0.195446856	0.195448694	0.000001839
10	0.628989529	0.628994009	0.000004480
11	0.933446806	0.933442183	0.000004623
12	0.248495467	0.248511497	0.000016030
13	0.746981880	0.747014131	0.000032252

t	x_t^a	x_t^b	$\lvert x_t^a - x_t^b \rvert$
14	0.755999804	0.755936076	0.000063729
15	0.737856401	0.737986901	0.000130500
16	0.773697331	0.773448940	0.000248390
17	0.700359085	0.700902708	0.000543623
18	0.839424949	0.838552408	0.000872541
19	0.539162817	0.541529069	0.002366252
20	0.993865095	0.993101346	0.000763749
21	0.024389072	0.027404252	0.003015180
22	0.095176980	0.106613035	0.011436055
23	0.344473289	0.380986782	0.036513494
24	0.903245768	0.943343416	0.040097648
25	0.349571401	0.213786462	0.135784940
26	0.909484947	0.672327242	0.237157705
27	0.329288313	0.881213286	0.551924973

Table 10.1 Exponentially divergence: With two slightly different starting positions, two chaotic trajectories will exponentially diverge from one another.

three sections: the middle section, where the hump is greater than $\frac{1}{2}$, and the left and right extremes, where the function descends below $\frac{1}{2}$. For arbitrary values of m, we need to partition the input space into $2^m + 1$ sections. Consequently, we need at least $m + 1$ bits of accuracy to encode the initial value for x_t. If our floating-point representation for numbers uses any number of bits less than $m + 1$, then the accuracy of the predictions can be no better than a random guess. The situation is such that in a very real way, we lose 1 bit of information for each time step into the future that we try to predict.

To put all of this in perspective, the most advanced computers today use 128 bits for floating-point numbers. So even though the logistic map is an extremely simple system, modern computers can make only marginally accurate predictions for less than 128 time steps into the future. You may be thinking that a clever programmer could work around this by using more bits for the floating-point numbers. However, since a computer's memory is finite in size, there will always be a value m for which all computers are helpless to predict what x_{t+m} looks like.

The problem gets even worse when we consider two other factors. First, for all of this section we have been assuming that our initial measurement of x_t was accurate. In the real world there is always some sort of measurement error. Any error, even something unbelievably infinitesimal, will grow at an exponential rate, breaking any prediction scheme we can think of. The second factor relates to some of the discussion from Chapter 2. More specifically, what happens when the state falls on an irrational number? Since there are infinitely many more irrational than rational numbers, any encoding scheme that attempts to represent all numbers by rational numbers must have—by definition—at least some error in the storage technique.

We will now demonstrate all of this with an experiment that you can perform on a simple calculator. We are going to compute two chaotic trajectories of the logistic map for $r = 1$. One trajectory, which we will label x_t^a, will have an initial value of $x_0^a = 0.987654321$. The second trajectory will be labeled x_t^b, and use an initial value of $x_0^b = 0.987654320$. Therefore, the two starting positions differ only by about 1 part in a billion, which would be regarded as an amazingly accurate measurement in the real world.

To represent a decimal number requires about three bits of information per decimal place. Since our numbers have nine digits, there is a total of approximately twenty-seven bits of information per number. Therefore, let's see what happens to the two trajectories after twenty-seven time steps. For the first few steps the error seems quite tolerable. In fact, the two trajectories are very similar for about the first twenty steps. It is not until the very last step that x_t^a and x_t^b fall on different sides of the $\frac{1}{2}$ divider; however, from this point on, the two trajectories will have no correlation with each other at all, since, as can be seen in Table 10.1, the error roughly doubles in size for each additional time step.

10.5 The Shadowing Lemma

There are a few troubling facts about the results from the last section. As touched on briefly before, since computers can represent only digital quantities and approximate real numbers with finite precision, any computer simulation of a chaotic system is doomed to degrade increasingly the farther into the future one tries to predict. Another facet of this problem involves the fact that if we simulate a chaotic system in a computer, at some point in the future the simulated system must start to repeat itself because of the finite precision available. In other words, computers cannot really generate aperiodic trajectories, but only limit cycles with, admittedly, very long periods.

How, then, do we know if computer simulations of chaos are valid in the sense that they yield true characterizations of real chaos? Worse still, is it possible that "chaos" is nothing more than a computer artifact that results from trying to represent a stochastic world with digital numbers? The *shadowing lemma* is a remarkable result that has an answer to these questions, at least for certain types of chaotic systems.

Figure 10.10 contains two graphs that illustrate the shadowing lemma in action. The graph on the left shows an exact trajectory (from a chaotic system) plotted alongside a simulated one. For the reasons outlined earlier, the two trajectories inevitably drift apart.

The graph on the right of Figure 10.10 shows the same computed trajectory as in the first graph, but this time a *shadow trajectory* is plotted alongside it. For

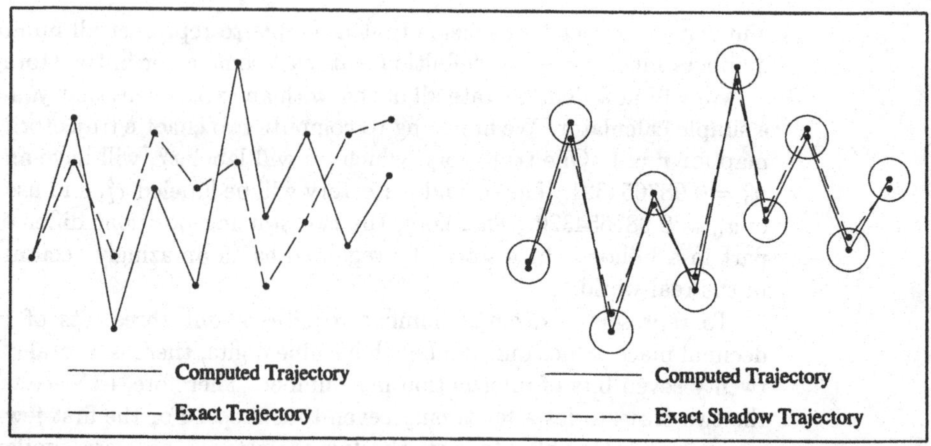

Figure 10.10 Shadow trajectories: On the left, the computed trajectory deviates from the exact (real) trajectory because of accumulated errors. On the right is a shadow of the computed trajectory that is arbitrarily close to the computed trajectory.

any computed trajectory, the shadowing lemma posits the existence of a shadow trajectory that follows arbitrarily close to the computed trajectory. In other words, the shadowing lemma tells us that a computer simulation of chaos does, in fact, provide an accurate picture of the motion in a chaotic system.

As an example of what the shadowing lemma means, consider the problem of weather forecasting. We know that all weather forecasts are doomed to be inaccurate in the long term. However, if we look at a weather simulation as it evolves over time, it is quite possible that the simulation captures all of the richness and complexity of the real weather system as it could happen.

10.6 Characteristics of Chaos

In this section we will summarize the characteristics of chaos that are common to all chaotic systems. Most of the issues that we will discuss in this section simply summarize material from the earlier portions of the chapter. The other topics that we will discuss will serve as motivation for the latter chapters in this part.

The goal of this section is to provide a working definition of chaos. This task is somewhat difficult in that many scientists do not agree on a single definition of chaos. Nevertheless, the characteristics listed in this section should go a long way toward showing you what chaos looks like. Also, keep in mind that these characteristics are necessary but not sufficient, that is, all chaotic systems will have all of these characteristics, but just because a dynamical system possesses one of these attributes does not make it chaotic.

Deterministic Chaotic systems are completely deterministic and not random. Given a previous history of a chaotic system, the future of the system will be completely determined; however, this does not mean that we can compute what the future looks like.

Related to this distinction between chaotic and random processes are the topological properties of their respective state spaces. The motion of a random process is, by definition, uncorrelated with the previous states of the system. As such, if you looked at the state space of a random process, you would see only a "blob-like" structure with no order whatsoever. Complementary to this, for all chaotic systems there is always a way of showing structure in the system's state space. We may need to look at a higher-dimensional state space in order to see this structure, but the structure is there, nevertheless.

Sensitive Chaotic systems are extremely sensitive to initial conditions, since any perturbation, no matter how minute, will forever alter the future of a chaotic system. This fact has sometimes been referred to as the "butterfly effect," which comes from Edward Lorenz's story of how a butterfly flapping its wings can alter global weather patterns. In his book *Chance and Chaos*, David Ruelle gives an even better example of sensitivity to initial conditions, which I will paraphrase here. Suppose that by some miracle the attractive effect of a single electron located at the limit of the known universe could be suspended momentarily. How long do you think it would take for this slight perturbation to change the future on a macroscopic scale? Since the motion of air causes individual molecules to collide with one another, it would be interesting to know how long it would take for these collisions to be altered. Amazingly, after only about fifty collisions the molecules in Earth's atmosphere will have collided in a different manner than they would have originally. If we wait another minute or two, the motion in a turbulent portion of the atmosphere will be altered at the macroscopic level. And, if we wait another week or month, the motion of the entire weather system will be measurably altered.

Thus, the next time you hear your local weather forecaster tell you what next week's weather will look like, you can recognize it for the nonsense it is. But this is not to say that all prediction is hopeless, since chaotic systems can be predicted over the short-term with a fair amount of accuracy. Another facet of the sensitivity of chaotic systems is that in many ways chaotic systems are more susceptible to control. You can look at it this way: Since any perturbation causes an exponential divergence in the state space trajectory of a chaotic system, with a minute alteration to the system we could profoundly alter the system's future behavior.

Ergodic Chaotic motion is ergodic, which means that the state space trajectory of a chaotic system will always return to the local region of a previous point in the trajectory. For example, we can define a local region of interest by a single point in a state space and a distance measure. Every point in the state space that is within the specified distance from the point will be considered to be in the local region of the point. If a system is ergodic, then no matter how small we make the local region, as long as it's nonzero, we are guaranteed that the system will eventually return to this local region. Using the weather as an example, ergodicity means that it is very likely that someday in the future you will experience weather almost—but not exactly—identical to today's weather.

Embedded Chaotic attractors are embedded with an infinite number of unstable periodic orbits. Looking back at Figure 10.9, recall that the function $f^m(x)$ got more and more complicated as we increased m. For any of the plots in Figure 10.9, it is easy to see that the identity line, $y = x$, will intersect $f^m(x)$ at multiple locations. For all points, x_p, where $f^m(x)$ intersects the identity line, x_p will be part of a period-2^{m-1} unstable limit cycle. Since we can do this for any positive value of m, it follows that there must be an infinite number of limit cycles embedded within the chaotic attractor.

Over the next four chapters we will examine these and other properties of chaotic systems. Chapter 11 will introduce us to chaos in multidimensional systems, strange attractors, as well as some important tools of the trade for visualizing chaos. In Chapter 12 we will examine a form of chaos that is commonly found in chemistry, biology, ecology, and economics. In Chapter 13 we will take a closer look at how chaos can be exploited to control the future. Finally, in Chapter 14, we will see how incomputability, randomness, and chaos can be seen as multiple facets of a single phenomenon.

10.7 Further Exploration

There are four programs that I used to generate all of the computed figures in this chapter. In this section, I will briefly describe how to use these programs. The command-line options for all of the programs are summarized in Table 10.2. As with just about every other program listed in this book, most of the programs for this chapter use the `-term` option to specify how images are plotted.

Another option that is common to all of the programs for this chapter is the `-func` option, which can be used to specify what one-dimensional map to use. The logistic map is the default map to use. Other possibilities include the tent map, the sine map, and the Gaussian map.

The first program that you should try is `gen1d`, which will generate a one-dimensional time series. You may wish to use the `-x0` option to specify the initial point, and the `-r` option to specify the value of r to use.

The next program is `phase1d`, which can be used to generate state space plots. As with `gen1d`, the `-points` option can be used to specify the number of points

Option Name	Option Type	Option Meaning
Options Common to All Featured Programs		
`-points`	INTEGER	number of points to plot
`-skip`	INTEGER	number of points to skip
`-aux`	INTEGER	value for auxiliary map parameter
`-x0`	INTEGER	initial value, x_0
`-func`	STRING	which map function to use
Options Only for `gen1d`, `phase1d`, and `phase1d2`		
`-r`	INTEGER	value for r
Options Only for `phase1d`, `phase1d2`, and `bifur1d`		
`-width`	INTEGER	width of the plot in pixels
`-height`	INTEGER	height of the plot in pixels
`-inv`	SWITCH	invert colors?
`-xmag`	INTEGER	magnification factor for X Windows
`-term`	STRING	how to plot points
Options Only for `bifur1d`		
`-rmin`	INTEGER	smallest value for r
`-rmax`	INTEGER	largest value for r
`-factor`	INTEGER	multiplicative factor for iterates
`-ymin`	INTEGER	smallest value for y-range
`-ymax`	INTEGER	largest value for y-range
`-box`	INTEGER	line width for a box
`-brmin`	INTEGER	smallest r-value for the box
`-brmax`	INTEGER	largest r-value for the box
`-bymin`	INTEGER	smallest value for box y-range
`-bymax`	INTEGER	largest value for box y-range

Table 10.2 The command-line options for `gen1d`, `phase1d`, `phase1d2` and `bifur1d`

in the series. You may also change the initial value with `-x0`. You can skip the first few initial points with the `-skip` option. This is useful if you only want to see where a map will converge to, and not how it got there.

The program `phase1d2` is identical to `phase1d` except that you may use the `-dx` option to specify where a second trajectory will start relative to the first trajectory. This is useful if you want to see how rapidly two nearby points will diverge.

The last program for this chapter is `bifur1d`, which you can use to plot bifurcation diagrams. You need to supply values with `-rmin` and `-rmax` to specify the first and final values of r to be contained in the bifurcation plot. Similarly, you can change the y-ranges with `-ymin` and `-ymax`. If you wish to use this program to generate a PostScript image, generating a `PGM` file and converting it to PostScript with `pnmtops` or `xv` is far more efficient.

Since the source code for all of the programs in this chapter includes the file `maps1d.c`, to extend the capabilities of all of the programs, you only need to modify `maps1d.c`. Contained in this file are the function definitions for the various one-dimensional maps that you can use. The file is documented with an example of how to add your own functions.

10.8 Further Reading

Gleick, J. (1987). *Chaos.* New York: Viking.

Ruelle, D. (1993). *Chance and chaos.* Princeton: Princeton University Press.

Stewart, I. (1990). *Does God play dice?: The mathematics of chaos.* Oxford: Blackwell.

11 Strange Attractors

There is no excellent beauty that hath not some strangeness in the proportions.
— Francis Bacon

I am strangely attracted to you.
— Cole Porter

IN THIS CHAPTER we will examine three well-known chaotic dynamical systems, with the major difference between the systems in this chapter and the logistic map from the previous chapter being that all of the systems in this chapter are multidimensional because the state of the systems can be characterized only by multiple variables instead of a single state variable. Because the dynamical systems under consideration have a larger state space dimension, our state space plots will typically be plotted in two or even three dimensions. The rewarding part of all of this is that the state space plots in this chapter will have a fractal dimension, and therefore a bit of visual appeal.

Our main approach in this chapter will be one of intuitive exploration. We will look at the mathematics of the chaotic systems only to the extent that you should be able to duplicate any of the computed figures that appear in this chapter. If you are less inclined to dive into the mathematics, feel free to skip the details, but do follow along for the remainder of the chapter, which will be largely devoted to illustrating how the characteristics of chaos from the last chapter universally apply to the systems in this chapter.

The state space plots also illustrate what are known as *strange attractors*. The "attractor" portion of the term comes from the fact that the chaotic system gets attracted into a very specific and well-defined behavior, just the way the state space plots of limit cycle or fixed point systems show where the final system behavior will tend toward if given enough time. As for the "strange" portion of the term, you will just have to take my word for the moment that the adjective is quite appropriate. We'll see why shortly.

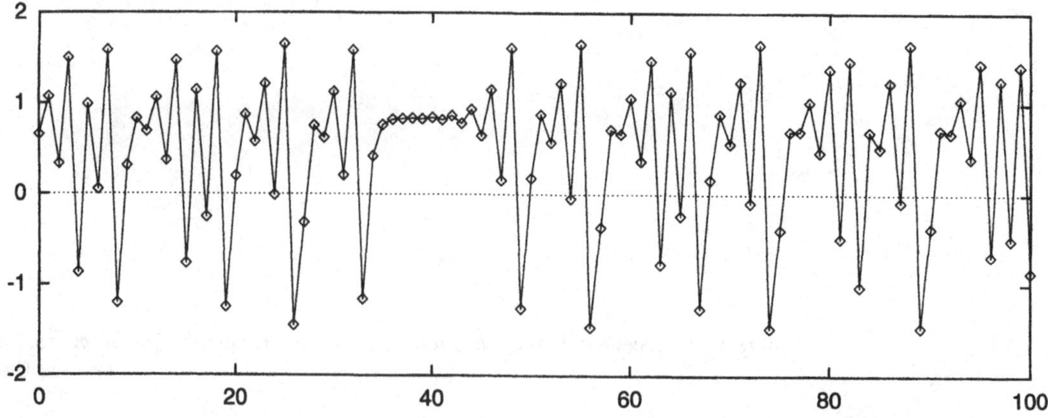

Figure 11.1 The Hénon map for $a = 1.29$ and $b = 0.3$

The three dynamical systems in this chapter, together, are fairly representative of many low-dimensional chaotic systems because each has a mathematical description that is common to a broad class of dynamical systems. For instance, the first chaotic system that we will see, the Hénon map, is a system of difference equations that evolves in discrete time steps much like the logistic map from the last chapter. After that, we will see the Lorenz attractor, which is described by a system of ordinary differential equations and is, therefore, continuous in time. Finally, we will see the Mackey-Glass system, which is described by a single delay-differential equation that combines discrete and continuous dynamics into one form.

11.1 The Hénon Attractor

The Hénon map was discovered by Michel Hénon, who was investigating the properties of two-dimensional functions that have the same characteristics as more complicated systems. The Hénon map is a discrete two-dimensional map defined by the equations

$$\begin{aligned} x_{t+1} &= a - x_t^2 + by_t \\ y_{t+1} &= x_t, \end{aligned}$$

where a and b are constant parameters that determine whether the system is chaotic or not. A common setting for the parameters is $a = 1.29$ and $b = 0.3$, which gives the Hénon system chaotic dynamics. To compute the time evolution of the Hénon system, we begin with two initial values, x_0 and y_0, that can be chosen randomly so as to give a unique starting location. Virtually any value between -1 and 1 is a safe starting place for both x_0 and y_0. With the initial values determined, we can compute the next values, x_1 and y_1, and so on.

Figure 11.1 shows x_t plotted against t for 100 points. The time series is extremely erratic because the system is in a chaotic regime; however, near $t = 40$ there appears to be momentary stability. This brief period of stability is due to an embedded unstable fixed point that is contained within the chaotic attractor. We can analytically find the location of the fixed point by setting x_{t+1}, x_t, and y_t to the same value, say x_F, which gives the quadratic equation $-x_F^2 + (b-1)x_F + a = 0$. Solving for x_F yields

$$x_F = \frac{1}{2}\left(b - 1 + \sqrt{(b-1)^2 + 4a}\right) = 0.838486\cdots.$$

If you look at the value of the Hénon time series near $t = 40$, you will see that it is very close to the analytical fixed point. Since the fixed point is unstable, the system eventually diverges from it. What is happening is very similar to what would happen if you tried to balance a pencil on its point; you may get it to sort of hover in place for a fraction of a second, but the tiniest of nudges will knock the pencil over.

Figure 11.2 shows the state space[1] of the Hénon map with y_t plotted against x_t. Each subsequent state space plot enlarges the boxed section from the previous image. This is a strange attractor. Since the state of the Hénon map consists of two variables, plotting the long-term values of y_t against x_t illustrates the type of behavior that evolves when the system is iterated for many steps. Zooming into the attractor reveals more and more detail, which is just as we would expect a fractal to behave. In theory, we could zoom into the attractor forever, never finding an end to the detail. This fractal nature is the essence of the "strangeness" of a strange attractor.

Like the logistic map, the Hénon map goes through a cascade of period doublings when either a or b is varied. Figure 11.3 shows the bifurcation diagram for the Hénon map for the specified values of a and b. As with the logistic map, many period doublings are visible at this scale. It would also be possible to zoom into regions of the bifurcation diagram to discover self-similar areas. Near the right-hand side of the bifurcation diagram a period-7 limit cycle emerges from within the chaos, only to go through further period doublings and move back into chaos.

Looking at the Hénon map in the chaotic regime and considering the fractal nature of the state space plot, we become faced with the following questions: Why does the Hénon map converge to this particular, irregularly shaped, fractal attractor? Why not some other shape? What, exactly, does the attractor represent? To answer these question in an intuitive manner, we will perform an experiment that will reveal some clues for us. Since the state space diagram that we've plotted is

[1] It may very well be more intuitive to plot x_t versus y_t. Nevertheless, I have swapped the variables for purely esthetic reasons.

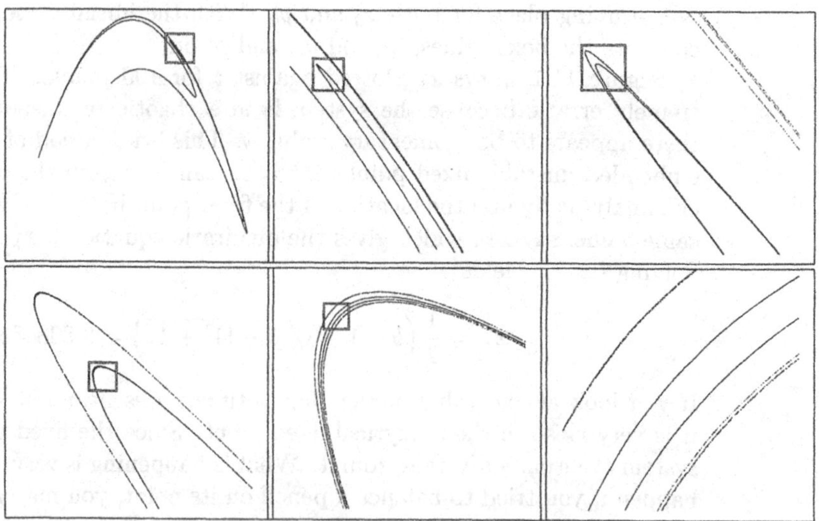

Figure 11.2 The Hénon attractor viewed from many scales

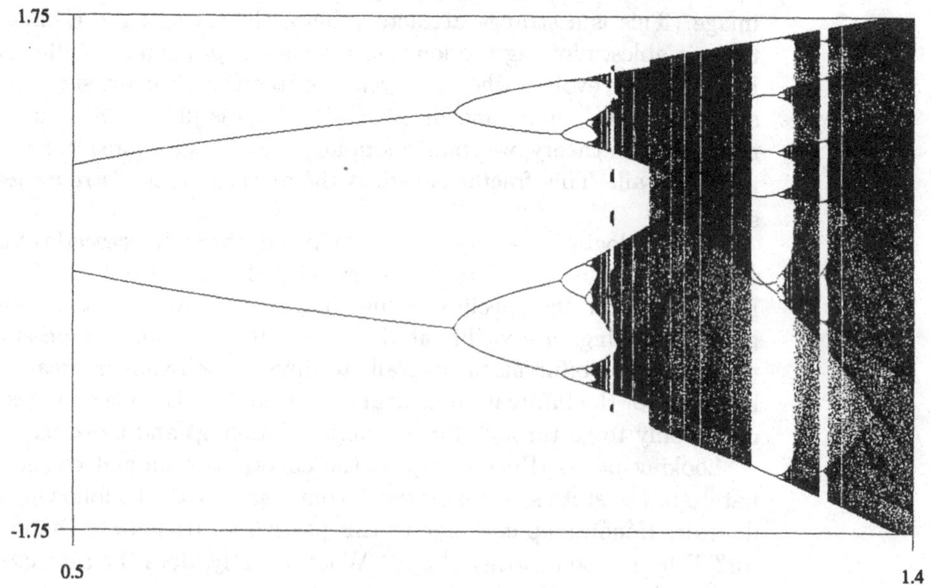

Figure 11.3 A bifurcation diagram of the Hénon map for a varying from 0.5 to 1.4, and b set to 0.3

really just a very fine grid, suppose we place a square at the center of the state space. This square will itself be a small grid of points. Now, for each point in the square, transform the current point into a new point by passing it through the Hénon map's equations. If we do the same transformation for each point, and then plot all of the new points, we can see how the Hénon map "warps" the original square into another shape. Similarly, we can take the new shape and transform the whole thing by the same process again, and so on.

Figure 11.4 shows the first five transformations for warping a square via the Hénon map. Notice how at each stage we can clearly see the stretching and folding operations, as discussed in the previous chapter when we made an analogy between making pastry and making chaos. Moreover, the stretching and folding have the effect of spreading the original square all over the state space of the system. Had we used a smaller square, it would have taken a few more steps to get a figure that looks like the real attractor; yet, no matter how small we make the initial square, the stretching and folding operations will eventually cause the square to converge to the same attractor.

Another interesting fact revealed by this experiment is that the Hénon attractor consists of exactly those points that, when transformed by the Hénon map's equations, stay on the attractor. In other words, the Hénon attractor is invariant in the Hénon map's equations. Recall from Chapter 7 that an affine transformation fractal has the property that for any point on the fractal, the transformed point is also on the fractal. We can see this same property in the Hénon attractor.

The last property of the Hénon map that we will examine involves the short-term and long-term predictability of the system. Suppose that we wanted to see what the relationship was between previous states and future states of the Hénon map. Ignoring the y_t term for the moment, if we look at state pairs in the form of (x_t, x_{t+m}), then the complexity of the resulting plot in some ways tells us how related the future points are to the previous points. For the case of $m = 1$, we get the familiar state space plot that we saw earlier, since $y_{t+1} = x_t$. Looking at any of the previous plots for this case, we can see that if we were supplied with some value of x_t, we could make a fairly accurate guess of x_{t+1} by looking only at the state space plot (and not cheating by using the formulas). The only problem that we would have in this prediction scheme is that for some x_t value, it is possible for there to be multiple valid values of x_{t+1}; thus, when faced with this ambiguity, we would have to guess one of the possible values. Also note that if we had y_t in addition to x_t, then the ambiguity would be removed and we could make an extremely accurate guess for x_{t+1}.

For larger values of m, plotting out the "delayed" state space plot reveals a form that is inevitably more complicated because each iteration of the Hénon map stretches and folds the attractor even more. Figure 11.5 shows the delayed state space plots for various values of m. In the final plot, with m equal to 100, we see that the state space has become, for all practical purposes, uncorrelated with itself.

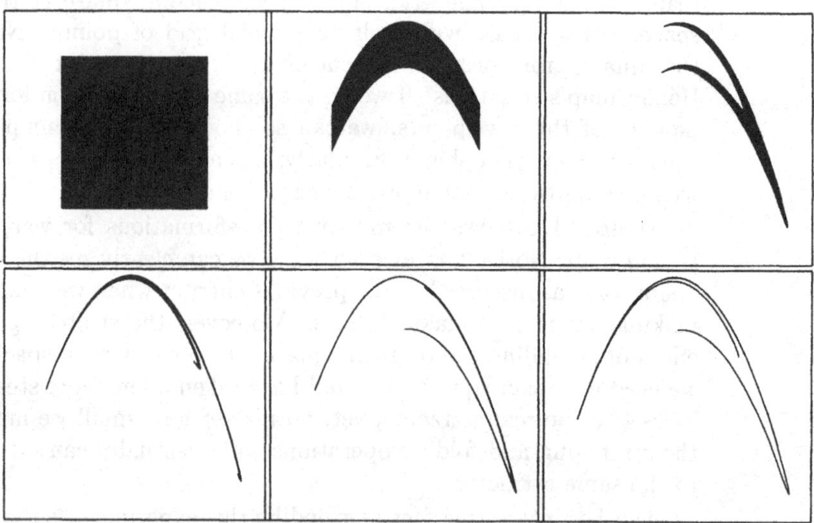

Figure 11.4 Recursively warping the points of a square by the Hénon transformation, for 0 through 5 steps

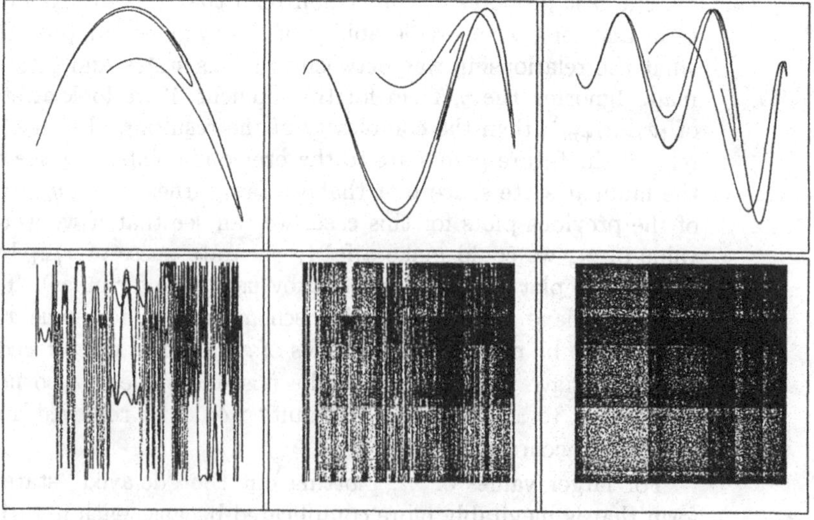

Figure 11.5 Plotting x_t versus x_{t+m} with m equal to 1, 2, 3, 10, 20, and 100

In fact, the data from the last plot could pass most tests for randomness, even though they are derived from a deterministic process. This property of the Hénon attractor is very similar to the way the logistic map, when recursively composed with itself, forms an extremely complicated function surface with an exponential number of humps.

In Chapter 13, we will dissect the Hénon attractor in even greater detail to show an amazing technique for controlling chaos.

11.2 A Brief Introduction to Calculus

Portions of the remainder of this chapter depend on the reader's possessing a basic understanding of calculus. This section gives a brief but sufficient introduction to the topic, but is by no means a substitute for an advanced textbook. Readers already familiar with calculus may wish to proceed to the next section.

Calculus was invented by Isaac Newton around 1666 and then invented a second time by Gottfried Wilhelm Leibniz about ten years later.[2] Calculus is most useful for describing how physical systems behave over time. The canonical example is of a cannonball being fired in the air, which always travels in a parabolic arc.

Figure 11.6 shows three graphs that relate various attributes of the cannonball to time. The top graph shows how the height of the ball changes over time, while the second and third graphs describe the velocity and acceleration. Calculus provides an elegant technique for converting information about one of these attributes into information about another attribute using two basic operations: *integration* and *differentiation*. Both operations can be calculated analytically or numerically. An analytical calculation is an exact transformation of one equation into another that yields a perfectly accurate result, while a numerical calculation is an estimate of the analytical result that is prone to having errors. Analytical solutions are always preferred over numerical, but often analytical solutions are unknown or impossible. The analytical version of the differentiation operation is relatively easy to perform, but the numerical version is very error-prone. On the other hand, integration is extremely hard to perform analytically but fairly easy to do numerically.

To make the example of the cannonball more concrete, suppose the height of the cannonball is described by the function $h(t)$. The velocity at some point in time can then be approximated by the difference equation $(h(t + \Delta t) - h(t))/\Delta t$, which estimates the slope of the function near a specific point in time. (This is, in fact, the numerical version of differentiation.) The accuracy of the estimate is determined by the size of the time increment, Δt, with smaller values, in general, providing

[2]Newton was a rather secretive fellow who did his best to keep much of calculus a secret. Only when people started crediting Leibniz with its invention did Newton step forward. A bitter feud ensued that lasted decades and consumed much of Newton's energies.

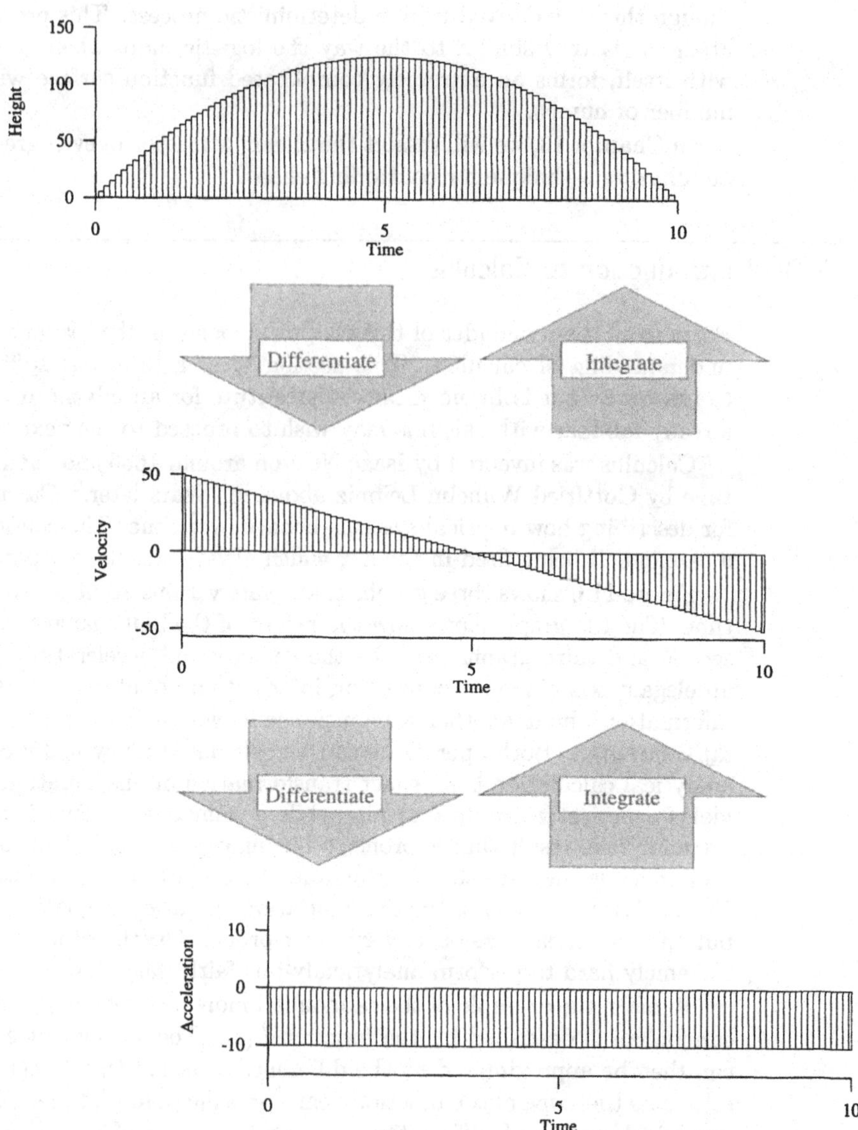

Figure 11.6 The two basic operations of calculus: differentiation and integration. Figure adapted from (Stewart, 1995).

The Oldest Profession	**Digression 11.1**

A doctor, an architect, and a computer scientist were arguing about whose profession was the oldest. In the course of their arguments, they got all the way back to the Garden of Eden, whereupon the doctor said, "The medical profession is clearly the oldest, because Eve was made from Adam's rib, as the story goes, and that was a simply incredible surgical feat."

The architect did not agree. He said, "But if you look at the Garden itself, in the beginning there was chaos and void, and out of that, the Garden and the world were created. So God must have been an architect."

The computer scientist, who had listened to all of this said, "Yes, but where do you think the chaos came from?"

— From `fortune`

more accurate estimates. Ideally, we would like to make Δt equal to 0, but doing so causes a problem because we cannot properly divide something by 0. The analytical version of differentiation allows you compute the slope of a function at a point as if you were allowed to set Δt to 0. The details of how it works are not too important for our purposes; suffice it to say that with analytical differentiation, one can easily take a function that describes the height of a cannonball and convert it into another function that describes the velocity, which, in turn, can be differentiated again to yield a function that describes the cannonball's acceleration.

Integration is the reverse of differentiation. With integration, you can take a function that describes a cannonball's speed and convert it into a function that describes its height. The process of numerical integration is very similar to iterating a discrete time equation. In general, to integrate some quantity, say h for height, we would need to know how the height changes over time. We represent this information by a *differential equation*,[3] which, in the case of our cannonball, is $dh/dt = 50 - 10t$ (this is also the function that is plotted in the middle graph of Figure 11.6). We also need to know the starting condition, h_0, that is, the initial height. Given the initial position, and the way a cannonball moves in time, we can now approximate the successive positions of the cannonball by iterating the equation

$$h_{t+1} = h_t + \Delta t \frac{dh}{dt},$$

[3]While the differential equation that follows is true to calculus, it is a slight simplification, in that real physical issues such as Earth's actual gravitational pull on a ball, are ignored.

which is known as *Euler's method* for numerical integration, and uses the time increment, Δt, which plays a role similar to the one it did in differentiation. This method is the simplest technique for performing numerical integration, but it is also the least accurate and is, therefore, rarely used for serious calculations. However, it is sufficient for our purposes, and it also provides a good intuitive feel for how integration really works.

Differential equations describe how forces act on an object. With a differential equation and a method of integration, physicists will often attempt to predict the future position or motion of an object. If an analytical solution to a differential equation is known in advance (as with the parabola for the cannonball), then the future of an object can be perfectly determined with a single equation. If, however, no analytical solution exists (as with most configurations of three gravitational bodies—the Three Body Problem), then a physicist must be content to solve the problem numerically, which amounts to approximating the very near future, using that approximation to guess at the next time step, and so on.

The beauty of physics is that simple differential equations can produce astonishingly complicated behavior. It was Newton's most profound discovery that the forces that describe objects in motion are much simpler than the motions themselves.

11.3 The Lorenz Attractor

Consider a closed chamber of air that has a heat source at the bottom. Since the air at the bottom of our chamber is closer to the heat source, the lower the air, the hotter it gets. As gas heats up, it expands, becomes lighter, tends to float toward the top of the chamber, and gradually cools as it moves away from the heat source. Now, if the temperature difference between the gas at the top and the bottom of the chamber is small, the hot air will gradually rise to the top in a somewhat predictable manner. However, if we increase the temperature of the heat source, resulting in a temperature difference that is more pronounced, then the rising hot air and falling cooler air will form a circulating flow known as convection. Convection is seen in atmospheric activity when the sun warms a layer of air closer to the surface of Earth, resulting in a similar circular flow.

In 1962, Edward Lorenz was studying a simplified model of convection flow. His system contained three state variables to represent various physical quantities. For Lorenz's computer model of the system, he could plug arbitrary values into the equations, let them iterate for a while, and then stop the simulation. Thus, Lorenz was essentially playing with a very simple "toy" weather system in a computer, with Lorenz being in the godlike position of having the ability to alter the weather on a whim.

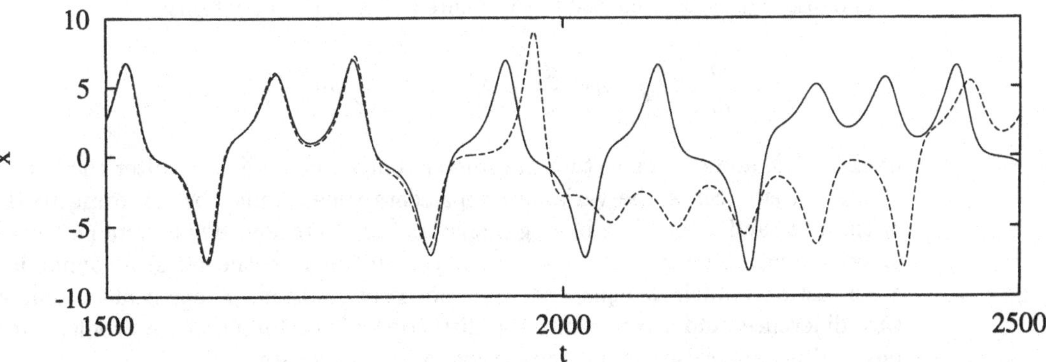

Figure 11.7 Two time evolutions of x with an infinitesimal initial difference

While running a particularly interesting simulation of his system, Lorenz had to stop the system prematurely. Later, Lorenz wanted to resume the simulation a little bit before where he had let it stop; thus, with printout in hand, he entered in the last known values of the three state variables and continued the simulation. To Lorenz's surprise, the simulation continued as it had before, but with a slight deviation in how the state variables changed over time. Small differences become large differences, and in short time the system was nowhere near where it had been before. Figure 11.7 shows how an infinitesimal difference in initial conditions can cause two trajectories to diverge.

Having read the last chapter, you already know why the system deviated over time. However, in 1962 everyone "knew" that all dynamical systems ultimately fall into predictable patterns. The fact that Lorenz's system had a measly three variables just added to the confusion: If something this simple could be so pathological, what about more complex dynamical systems? Eventually, Lorenz retraced his steps to determine the source of his computer "glitch." As it happened, Lorenz's printout of the state variables displayed the numbers only to a fixed number of digits. In reality, the computer stored the numbers with slightly more precision then what was displayed in the printout. So, when Lorenz reentered the values of the state variables, he essentially truncated the last few digits. However, keep in mind that the error introduced by truncating the numbers was really only on the order of one part in a thousand or so.

Lorenz wrote up his experience for a journal article, but unfortunately for the rest of us, it took about a decade or so for his discovery to become known in the physics and mathematics communities. In the remainder of this section we will look at the Lorenz system in greater detail.

The Lorenz system consists of the three differential equations:

$$\frac{dx}{dt} = ay - ax, \quad \frac{dy}{dt} = bx - y - zx, \text{ and } \frac{dz}{dt} = xy - cz.$$

Each of a, b, and c is a constant parameter that we can adjust to alter the behavior of the system. Since the variable t represents time, it may be tempting to think of the x, y, and z terms as having a spatial interpretation. This assumption is not quite correct. The x, y, and z terms actually refer to the physical dynamics of a convection model: x represents the convective motion, y represents a temperature difference, and z represents the distortion of the temperature profile, but the physical interpretation is not important for our purposes.

Figure 11.8 shows a typical time evolution of the three variables with a, b, and c fixed to 5, 15, and 1, respectively. By varying the three parameters, we could force the system into a cascade of bifurcations, as we did with the logistic and Hénon maps. The Lorenz system also possesses sensitivity to initial conditions; as Lorenz himself found out, any slight change exponentially grows in size over time. Not so visible, but present nevertheless, are periodic cycles embedded in the dynamics of the system, which also happens to be ergodic. Looking at the three graphs in the figure, if you were to draw a vertical line straight through all three, it would intersect each trajectory at exactly one point. Imagine that we could slide the vertical line to the right, thus taking a brief snapshot in time of the evolution of the system. By interpreting each of the state variables as a coordinate in space, the time evolution of the three variables can be represented by a one-dimensional trajectory flowing through a three-dimensional space.

This plotting technique is demonstrated in Figures 11.9 and 11.10, which show different views of the Lorenz strange attractor. The important thing to keep in mind is that the resulting plots do not represent the spatial attributes of the air flow, only the physical parameters that were mentioned earlier. Nevertheless, the plots are wonderfully beautiful. Similar to the Hénon attractor, the Lorenz attractor has a fractal dimension, and one could view this property by zooming into smaller and smaller regions of the attractor. Since the Lorenz attractor looks vaguely like a butterfly, it would be interesting to see how regular the flow of the attractor is as it weaves from one "wing" to the other. Sometimes the flow will move from one wing to the other, then back to the first. Other times it may move around one wing for a large number of loops, then quickly jump to the other wing, and so on. It has been conjectured, but not proved, that for any finite sequence of integers that are not too large, say 7, 3, 12, 4, ..., there exists a trajectory on the Lorenz attractor that loops around one half of the attractor for the first number of times, switches to the other half for the second number of loops, and so on. If you watch the flow of the attractor on a computer screen, you can easily see some very complicated patterns emerge.

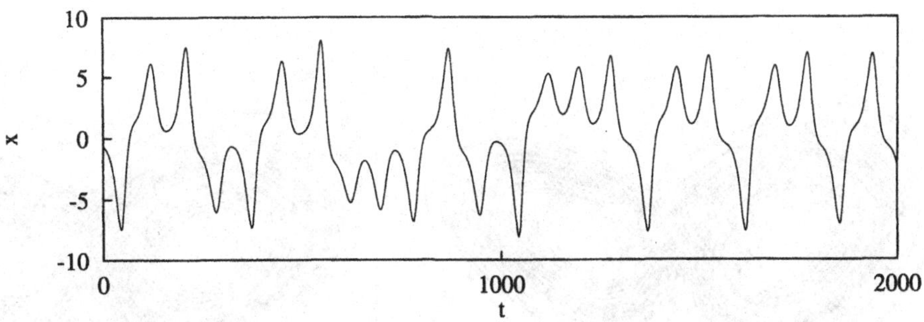

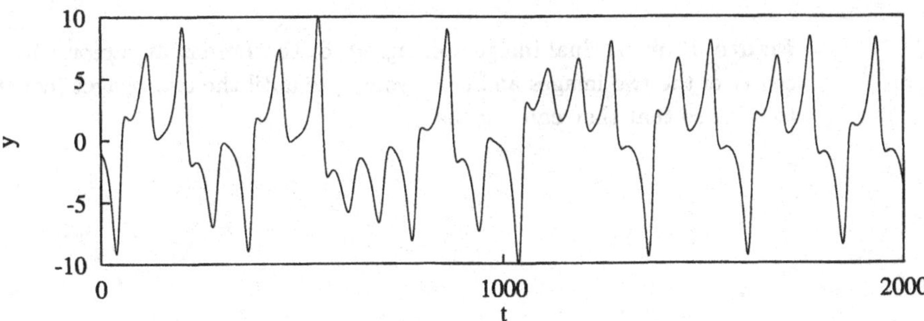

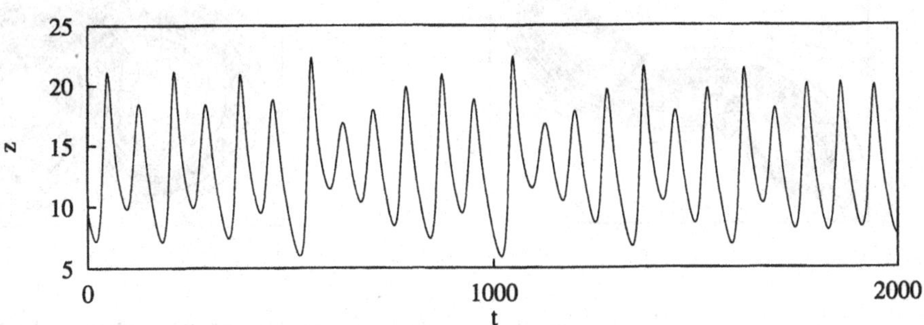

Figure 11.8 The time evolution of x, y, and z from the Lorenz system

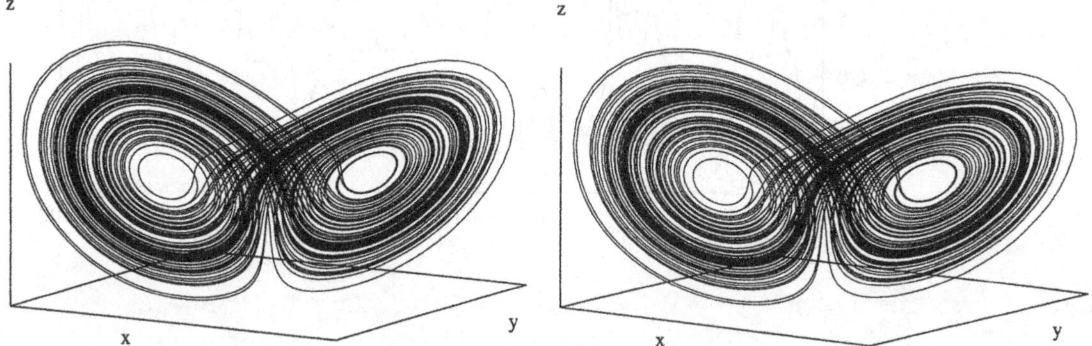

Figure 11.9 A dual-image stereogram of the Lorenz attractor: To view, stare at the center of the two images and cross your eyes until the two images merge. Allow your eyes to relax so that they can refocus.

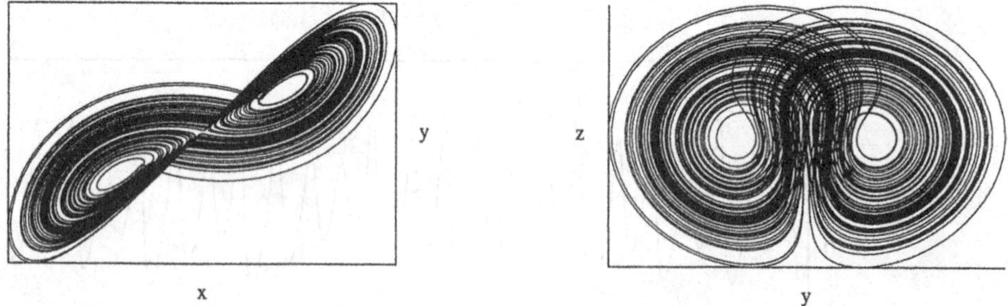

Figure 11.10 Two more views of the Lorenz strange attractor from different angles

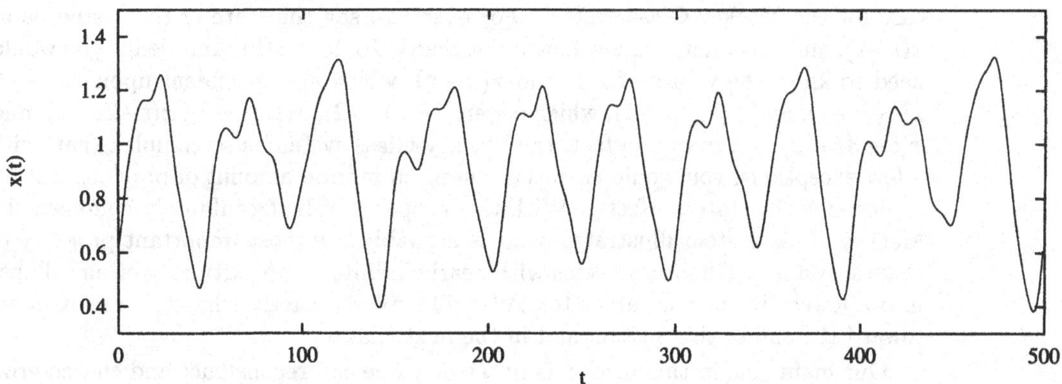

Figure 11.11 The time evolution of x from the Mackey-Glass system

11.4 The Mackey-Glass System

Recall that the Hénon and Lorenz systems had two and three variables that changed over time, respectively. The last chaotic system that we will look at in this chapter has only a single time-varying variable; however, this last system turns out to be many times more complex than both the Hénon and Lorenz systems.

The Mackey-Glass system consists of a single delay-differential equation that was originally used as a model of white blood cell production:

$$\frac{dx}{dt} = \frac{ax(t-\tau)}{1 + x^{10}(t-\tau)} - bx(t),$$

where a and b are typically fixed at 0.2 and 0.1, and τ is a special parameter that we can use to alter how pathological the resulting time series is. Since this is a delay-differential equation, to compute the corresponding time series, we need to numerically integrate the equation to simulate a continuous stream of data, but we must also maintain a history of values because of the delay term, $x(t-\tau)$, that appears in the equation. For now, we will use a τ of 17, which makes the system chaotic. Making τ smaller could force the system into fixed point or limit cycle behavior, and increasing the size of τ would make the system even more chaotic. Figure 11.11 shows 500 time steps from the Mackey-Glass system.

The $x(t-\tau)$ terms mean that we should use the value of x from τ time steps in the past. This is the "delay" portion of the delay-differential equation, and it is the reason why the Mackey-Glass system is so chaotic. For instance, in the Hénon and Lorenz systems, for every possible state of the system there is exactly one history of previous states that can account for the current state. This is not the case for the Mackey-Glass system. For example, say the state of the system is at $x(t+1)$, and you want to know how it got there. To divine this knowledge you would need to know the values of $x(t)$ and $x(t-\tau)$, which are dependent upon $x(t-1)$, $x(t-\tau-1)$, and $x(t-2\tau-1)$, which depend on $x(t-2)$, $x(t-\tau-2)$, $x(t-2\tau-2)$, and $x(t-3\tau-2)$ and so on. In fact, the Mackey-Glass system is so complex that, with a few exceptions, you would essentially need an infinite amount of previous history to describe the state perfectly. With this property of being infinitely complex, the Mackey-Glass system illustrates what is arguably the most important property of chaotic systems: Chaotic systems with nearly infinite complexity may often collapse into a lower-dimensional attractor. We will explore exactly what this means more toward the end of this section and in the next chapter.

Our main goal in this section is to see how one can reconstruct and characterize the behavior of a dynamical system that operates via an unknown process. This is the classic "black box" problem, in which you can observe some measurement change over time, but you are not sure which laws determine how the measurement changes, or even what the measurement means. In other words, you do not have a differential, difference, or delay-differential equation at your disposal that perfectly describes your system. All you have are data, and lots of them. To make matters worse, in many "black box" systems, one can observe just a single time-varying quantity, but it may be known in advance that there are many other time-varying quantities that you cannot measure. How, then, do you go about trying to recover the dynamics of the system? Is it even possible to do so as the problem has been described?

This question is especially relevant to the problem of time-series forecasting. As a specific example, no one really understands how the stock market works. If you did, you'd be rich. Nevertheless, we should appreciate the fact that the stock market is a function not only obvious of things, like trade deficits, the budget deficit, the prime rate, and so on, but also of many things that we can't measure simply because we don't know any better. Is it possible to characterize the dynamics of the system by considering only a single time-dependent variable? For the stock market example, the question boils down to whether or not a long history of the S&P 500 is sufficient information to predict the future of the S&P 500.

For deterministic processes (and the stock market may or may not be among them) there is a marvelous tool known as delayed coordinate *embedding*, which was rigorously formulated as a mathematical theorem by Floris Takens. In a nutshell, the embedding theorem tells us that if the dimension of the underlying attractor of the system fits in a D-dimensional space, then a history of length $2D+1$ can be used to reconstruct the attractor. In other words, at each time, t, we can examine $x(t)$, $x(t-\Delta)$, ..., $x(t-2D\Delta)$ to reconstruct the underlying system dynamics. Note that Takens's theorem doesn't tell us anything about how to pick Δ, which specifies the spacing of our samples, but simply postulates that for some Δ the embedding will work.

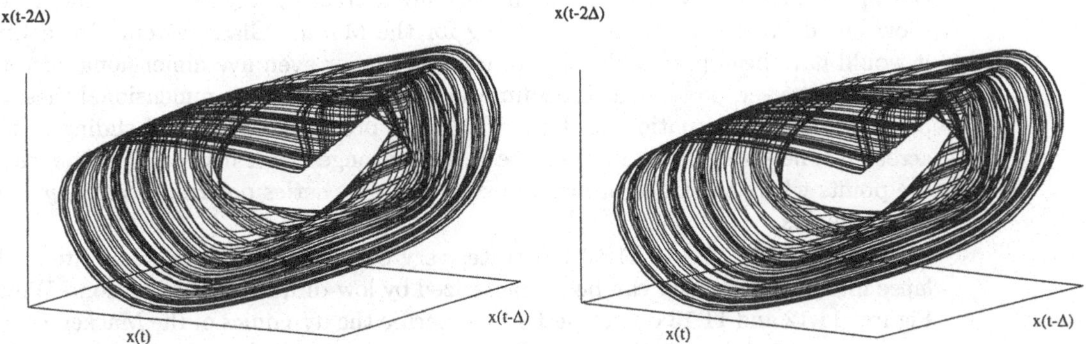

Figure 11.12 A dual-image stereogram of the a three-dimensional embedding of the Mackey-Glass system. Here Δ is set to 6. To view, stare at the center of the two images and cross your eyes until the two images merge. Allow your eyes to relax so that they can refocus.

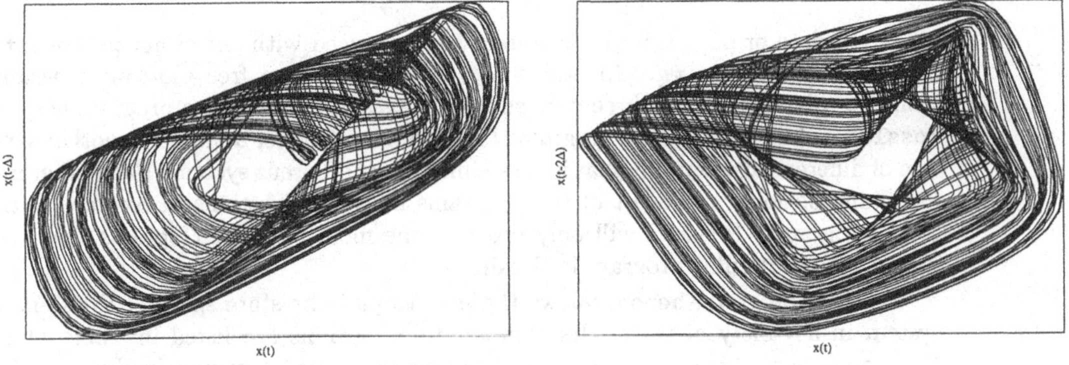

Figure 11.13 Two dimensional embeddings of the Mackey-Glass system, with Δ set to 6

If we apply this tool to the Mackey-Glass system, Takens's theorem essentially tells us that a bigger history is better, but for some finite choice of $2D + 1$, we can approximately reconstruct the underlying attractor. Figures 11.12 and 11.13 show our delayed coordinate embedding for the Mackey-Glass system. In reality, it would have been preferable to have used a four- or even five-dimensional history window; however, plotting a three-dimensional space on a two-dimensional sheet of paper strains the situation as it is. Using our previous example of sliding a line across a time series, if we were to use a three-pronged fork instead of a line, then the points where the three prongs intersect the time series determine the x, y, and z coordinates.

As Figures 11.12 and 11.13 illustrate, very complicated systems can often collapse into behaviors that can be characterized by low-dimensional attractors. While Figures 11.12 and 11.13 do not perfectly describe the dynamics of the Mackey-Glass system, we can tell that they provide a large amount of information regarding the system's dynamics because of the amount of structure in the state space plots. Had there been no information in the embedding, the state space plot would have looked random. Instead, we have structure. In the next chapter we will look at a class of dynamical systems that are related to many processes found in chemistry, economics, and biology. The amazing thing about this class is that most of these systems have a near infinite number of degrees of freedom (that is, they are very, very complicated), yet their behaviors still collapse into a very low-dimensional attractor.

11.5 Further Exploration

All of the data or images in this chapter were produced with one of **henon**, **henbif**, **henwarp**, **lorenz**, or **mg**. In addition, the excellent and free plotting program **gnuplot** was used for the three-dimensional images. There is also a program named **rossler** included with these programs that plots the Rossler attractor, another system of differential equations that is very similar to the Lorenz system. Each program has many options, and most of the programs have some options in common with other programs. Hence, I will only describe the most important options that are unique to a particular program in detail.

The first program, **henon**, allows the user to plot the state space of the Hénon system in a variety of ways. Its command-line options are listed in Table 11.1. With no options, **henon** will produce a plot similar to the first plot in Figure 11.2. To zoom in on a specific region of the attractor, as done later in Figure 11.2, use the **-ulx**, **-uly**, and **-lly** options. The **-delay** option can be used to plot delayed versions of the state space, as was done in Figure 11.5. Finally, the **-data** switch will force the program to generate raw data points from system, which is useful if you wish to make a time-series plot, as done in Figure 11.1.

Option Name	Option Type	Option Meaning
-width	INTEGER	width of the plot in pixels
-height	INTEGER	height of the plot in pixels
-skip	INTEGER	number of initial points to skip
-swap	SWITCH	swap the x and y axis?
-points	INTEGER	number of points to plot
-delay	INTEGER	time steps to delay for
-A	DOUBLE	value of the A parameter
-B	DOUBLE	value of the B parameter
-ulx	DOUBLE	upper-left corner x-coordinate
-uly	DOUBLE	upper-left corner y-coordinate
-lly	DOUBLE	lower-left corner y-coordinate
-box	INTEGER	line width for a box
-bulx	DOUBLE	box's upper-left x-coordinate
-buly	DOUBLE	box's upper-left y-coordinate
-blly	DOUBLE	box's lower-left y-coordinate
-data	SWITCH	don't plot but print points
-inv	SWITCH	invert all colors?
-xmag	INTEGER	magnification factor for X Windows
-term	STRING	how to plot points

Table 11.1 Command-line options for `henon`

The next program, `henbif`, takes the command-line options summarized in Table 11.2 and can be used to make bifurcation diagrams of the Hénon system like the one in Figure 11.3. The diagrams can have either parameter varying (a or b), by using the `-ab` switch. The range of the varied parameter is set by using `-abmin` and `-abmax`. To zoom in on the specific region of a bifurcation diagram, you will also need to use `-ymin` and `-ymax`.

Table 11.3 lists the command-line options for `henwarp`, a program that warps a square via the Hénon system equations (as done in Figure 11.4). The square is understood to be centered at the origin. The length of each edge of the square is determined by the `-len` option, which has a value that is understood to be in pixels; thus, this value should be less than both the width and the height of the plot. The program will transform every pixel in the square by the Hénon system equations a number of times specified by the `-count` option.

Table 11.4 lists the options for `lorenz` and `rossler`, which are identical except for the underlying dynamical systems that each uses. The programs will plot any state variable against any other variable or any delayed state variable. The exact form of the plot is determined by the values supplied to the `-xp` and `-yp` options.

Option Name	Option Type	Option Meaning
-width	INTEGER	width of the plot in pixels
-height	INTEGER	height of the plot in pixels
-skip	INTEGER	number of initial points to skip
-abmin	DOUBLE	smallest value for A (or B)
-abmax	DOUBLE	largest value for A (or B)
-ab	SWITCH	if TRUE plot for A; B otherwise
-A	DOUBLE	value of the A parameter
-B	DOUBLE	value of the B parameter
-factor	DOUBLE	multiplicative factor for iterates
-ymin	DOUBLE	smallest value for y range
-ymax	DOUBLE	largest value for y range
-box	INTEGER	line width for a box
-brmin	DOUBLE	smallest r-value for the box
-brmax	DOUBLE	largest r-value for the box
-bymin	DOUBLE	smallest value for box y range
-bymax	DOUBLE	largest value for box y range
-inv	SWITCH	invert all colors?
-xmag	INTEGER	magnification factor for X Windows
-term	STRING	how to plot points

Table 11.2 Command-line options for **henbif**

Option Name	Option Type	Option Meaning
-width	INTEGER	width of the plot in pixels
-height	INTEGER	height of the plot in pixels
-swap	SWITCH	swap the x and y axis
-len	INTEGER	length of edge of square
-count	INTEGER	number of transformations
-A	DOUBLE	value of the A parameter
-B	DOUBLE	value of the B parameter
-ulx	DOUBLE	upper-left corner x-coordinate
-uly	DOUBLE	upper-left corner y-coordinate
-lly	DOUBLE	lower-left corner y-coordinate
-inv	SWITCH	invert all colors?
-xmag	INTEGER	magnification factor for X Windows
-term	STRING	how to plot points

Table 11.3 Command-line options for **henwarp**

Option Name	Option Type	Option Meaning
-width	INTEGER	width of the plot in pixels
-height	INTEGER	height of the plot in pixels
-skip	INTEGER	number of initial points to skip
-points	INTEGER	number of points to plot
-A	DOUBLE	value of the A parameter
-B	DOUBLE	value of the B parameter
-C	DOUBLE	value of the C parameter
-delta	INTEGER	time delay term
-dt	DOUBLE	time step
-x0	DOUBLE	initial X value
-y0	DOUBLE	initial Y value
-z0	DOUBLE	initial Z value
-data	SWITCH	don't plot but print points
-xp	STRING	x-coordinate for plot
-yp	STRING	y-coordinate for plot
-factor	DOUBLE	auto-scale expansion factor
-inv	SWITCH	invert all colors?
-xmag	INTEGER	magnification factor for X Windows
-term	STRING	how to plot points

Table 11.4 Command-line options for `lorenz` and `rossler`

Both of these command-line options must take a value that is from one of the strings: `x(t)`, `y(t)`, `z(t)`, `x(t-delta)`, `y(t-delta)`, or `z(t-delta)`.[4] For example, the command:

```
lorenz -xp "x(t)" -yp "z(t)"
```

will plot the state space of $x(t)$ versus $z(t)$, and the command:

```
lorenz -xp "y(t)" -yp "y(t-delta)"
```

will plot $y(t)$ versus $y(t-\Delta)$, a delayed coordinate embedding for the Lorenz system, with Δ being determined by the `-delta` option.

The plotting ranges for these programs are automatically determined by the programs by examining the scales of the initially skipped points. If your plots appear to be off-centered, you may need to increase the number of skipped points with the `-skip` option. Moreover, the `-factor` option can be used to increase or decrease the amount of border placed around the plots. To generate raw data, the `-data` switch should be set.

[4]On UNIX systems, you may need to enclose the strings in double quotes to prevent your command shell from interpreting the parentheses as special characters.

Option Name	Option Type	Option Meaning
-width	INTEGER	width of the plot in pixels
-height	INTEGER	height of the plot in pixels
-skip	INTEGER	number of initial points to skip
-points	INTEGER	number of points to plot
-delta	INTEGER	time steps to delay for
-tau	INTEGER	value of the Tau parameter
-A	DOUBLE	value of the A parameter
-B	DOUBLE	value of the B parameter
-dt	DOUBLE	time step size
-x0	DOUBLE	initial X value
-factor	DOUBLE	auto-scale expansion factor
-data	SWITCH	don't plot but print points
-inv	SWITCH	invert all colors?
-xmag	INTEGER	magnification factor for X Windows
-term	STRING	how to plot points

Table 11.5 Command-line options for **mg**

Finally, Table 11.5 lists all of the options for **mg**, which have identical or similar meaning as the options listed for **lorenz** and **rossler**. The only command-line option unique to **mg** is the **-tau** option, which has meaning as described in the previous section.

11.6 Further Reading

Benhabib, J. (Ed.). (1992). *Cycles and chaos in economic equilibrium.* Princeton: Princeton University Press.

Hall, N. (Ed.). (1991). *Exploring chaos: A guide to the new science of disorder.* New York: W. W. Norton & Co.

Peitgen, H.-O., Jürgens, H., & Saupe, D. (1992). *Chaos and fractals.* New York: Springer-Verlag.

Stewart, I. (1995). *Nature's numbers: The unreal reality of mathematical imagination.* New York: Basic Books.

Strogatz, S. (1994). *Nonlinear dynamics and chaos.* New York: Addison Wesley.

12 Producer-Consumer Dynamics

Big whorls have little whorls,
Which feed on their velocity;
And little whorls have lesser whorls,
And so on to viscosity.
— L. F. Richardson

Chaos often breeds life when order breeds habit.
— Henry Brooks Adams

Nature itself, even in chaos, cannot proceed except in an orderly and regular manner.
— Immanuel Kant

HAVING SEEN SOME of the main characteristics of chaos as well as a fair sample of the mathematical techniques used to describe them, we are now ready to see a form of chaos that is strongly motivated by real-world natural systems.

In this chapter, we will examine systems that consist of producers and consumers interacting in cooperative and competitive ways. The canonical example is of an ecosystem that consists of multiple species. We will use two distinctly different techniques for modeling the populations of the species. The first technique is to model each species as a simple function of the other species. This method makes no distinction between individuals in a population, in that they are all considered one and the same. Moreover, by reducing a whole species to a single number we are obviously ignoring a great deal of information that one could find in real organisms, such as location, age, health, and other characteristics one would normally associate with an individual. Nevertheless, we will see that a mere three equations (for three species) are sufficient to produce chaotic dynamics.

The second method we will use is to model each individual of a population separately and then simulate the behavior of the entire system by simulating each individual simultaneously. This technique is exactly the opposite of the first, in that instead of three equations, we essentially must consider thousands at once.

The remarkable conclusion of the comparison is that both techniques yield similar results. This is a double-edged result. On the one hand, we have a mathematically simple system producing behavior that is so complex that it defies long-term prediction. On the other hand, we have a mathematically complex system that by all accounts should be nearly random in its behavior, yet it eventually settles down into behavior that can be described by approximately three variables. Hence, we have simplicity yielding complexity and complexity yielding simplicity. In the next section, by way of introduction, we will explore some of the general characteristics of producer-consumer interactions that make this result possible.

12.1 Producer-Consumer Interactions

Living things, almost by definition, must be capable of an endless variety of behavior in order to adapt to an infinite number of scenarios. Failure to adapt usually means death, which implies that every adaptive system must possess a form of fluidity. An organism's metabolism is just one method by which creatures can alter their internal chemistry to deal with external pressures. At the most basic level, one can think of metabolic-like adaptation as a feedback process in which internal changes in an organism are made in direct response to external changes in the environment. Lower the temperature, and mammals will start to produce more heat. Flash a bright light or emit a loud blast, and internal mechanisms in the eyes or ears will dampen the input to lower the potential for sensory overload.

Ecosystems and economies also possess a metabolic-like thermostat that aids in adapting population levels to environments. Overpopulation spreads resources thinly and can encourage famine, causing populations to plummet. Underpopulation makes individuals resource rich and also adds some difficulty for predators of the thinned population, which enables the thinned population to grow. Even Adam Smith's invisible hand, which is the force that Smith credited with adjusting a market's output to meet the market's needs, can be viewed as yet another example of how nature is replete with a form of built-in feedback that keeps things moving smoothly.

All of the preceding examples describe stabilizing processes that encourage systems to find a happy equilibrium. Presumably, if resources and competitors were kept constant, animal population levels would stabilize to constant levels. For mammalian metabolism, it usually turns out that animals can maintain a relatively constant internal temperature precisely because minute adjustments of their internal temperature have very little effect on the immediate environment. As everyone knows, the exception to this rule is when you place many people in a small space. Given enough time, many bodies will increase the temperature in a small environment, causing people to pant and sweat in order to cool themselves.

The lesson here is that stabilization is easy when the state of an environment is mostly independent of the state of an individual. If you couple the two states, you get feedback, which makes each state recursively dependent on the other. Looking back at the case of animal population levels, predator-prey systems are tightly coupled in that it is impossible to change one state (say the prey's population level) without affecting another state. In fact, if we look at each individual—be it molecule, animal, species, or company—as a consumer and producer, that is, something that has a functional-like input and output, then the interconnectedness of the world becomes much more obvious. Chemical reactions consume reactants and produce reagents. Animals eat plants and other animals and produce heat, waste, or another meal. Businesses purchase products from other companies, consume natural resources, and produce products and services. And populations prey on one another and may compete for many other resources. Everything is connected to everything else in an endless web of interactions so that a small ripple in one location can conceivably be transformed into a tidal wave elsewhere.

In the remainder of this chapter, we will examine predator-prey systems that illustrate the complexity induced by feedback in similar systems.

12.2 Predator-Prey Systems

The simplest type of predator-prey system consists of just two species with one preying on the other. An example of this sort of system would be sharks and small fish. During World War I, fishermen refrained from fishing for small plankton-eating fish, which initially had the effect of increasing the population. However, the increased small-fish population made for a well-fed shark population, which encouraged the shark population to increase. As the sharks' numbers grew, they began to eat more of the small-fish, eventually depleting the small fish population to the point that the shark population could no longer sustain itself. With the sharks dying off from starvation, the small fish were once again able to increase their numbers, leading back to a situation much like where we started.

The above scenario is applicable to many other types of animals (foxes and rabbits are frequently used as examples) but is very idealized, in that it assumes that the small fish (or rabbits) are preyed upon only by a single species, which is almost certainly never the case, considering the amount of hunting done by humans and the ubiquity of parasites.

Nevertheless, in the early part of this century Vito Volterra and Alfred J. Lotka independently noticed the cyclic nature of population dynamics and set out to describe the phenomenon mathematically. The Lotka-Volterra system consists of two differential equations, one for each species. In its simplest form the two equations are usually presented as

$$\frac{dF}{dt} = F(a - bS) \quad \text{and} \quad \frac{dS}{dt} = S(cF - d),$$

where F represents the small-fish population and S represents the shark population.

Don't worry, we are going to go over each of the terms in detail so as to explain exactly what they mean. First of all, notice that each equation contains both an F term and an S term, which illustrates the coupled nature of the small fish and sharks. The four other terms, a, b, c, d, are parameters that reflect certain properties of the small fish and sharks. By convention, all four parameters are understood always to be greater than or equal to 0.

The parameter a can be thought of as representing the reproduction rate of the small fish. Ignoring b for the moment and simplifying the first equation to $dF/dt = Fa$, we can see that the change in the small-fish population is always positive and proportional to the current population, meaning that in the absence of predators, the small fish will always increase exponentially in numbers.[1]

The second parameter, b, is proportional to the number of small fish that a shark can eat. Expanding dF/dt reveals the term $-bFS$. We can think of the product FS as representing the chance that a random shark will encounter a random small fish, since the product obviously increases with any increase in either F or S. Putting the whole thing back together again, the equation $dF/dt = F(a - bS)$ means that the small-fish population will grow exponentially in the absence of sharks, but will decrease by an amount proportional to the chance that a shark and a small fish bump into each other.

As for the second equation, the parameter c can be thought of as the amount of "energy" that a small fish supplies a shark when the shark eats it. If c is big, then cSF will also be large and positive, which means that the shark population will increase by an amount proportional to the chance that shark and small fish encounter one another. If c is small, then the shark population will increase more slowly than it would otherwise.

The final parameter, d, represents the death rate of the sharks. If F is 0, meaning that there are no more small fish, then the shark population will decay exponentially. Putting the second equation back together, we can see that the shark population can increase only proportionally to the number of small fish, but that the sharks are also simultaneously faced with decay due to the constant death rate.

With any set of choices for a, b, c, and d, this simplest version of the Lotka-Volterra system will always contain a fixed point that is located at $F = d/c$ and $S = a/b$, since $dF/dt = dS/dt = 0$ at these values. However, the system will also have an infinite number of limit cycles that appear to orbit around the embedded fixed point. Perturbing either population away from the orbit will force the system into a different limit cycle. This is illustrated by Figure 12.1 which shows four such limit cycles.

---

[1]It is clearly unreasonable for there to be no limit on the population of fish, given the finite size of the oceans, but for our purposes we can ignore this problem. However, for those curious, a more realistic modification to the equation is to include a logistic term that punishes a large small-fish population, i.e., $dF/dt = F(a - bS - eF)$. With no sharks, the small-fish population will reach equilibrium when $a = eF$, thus keeping a cap on the population.

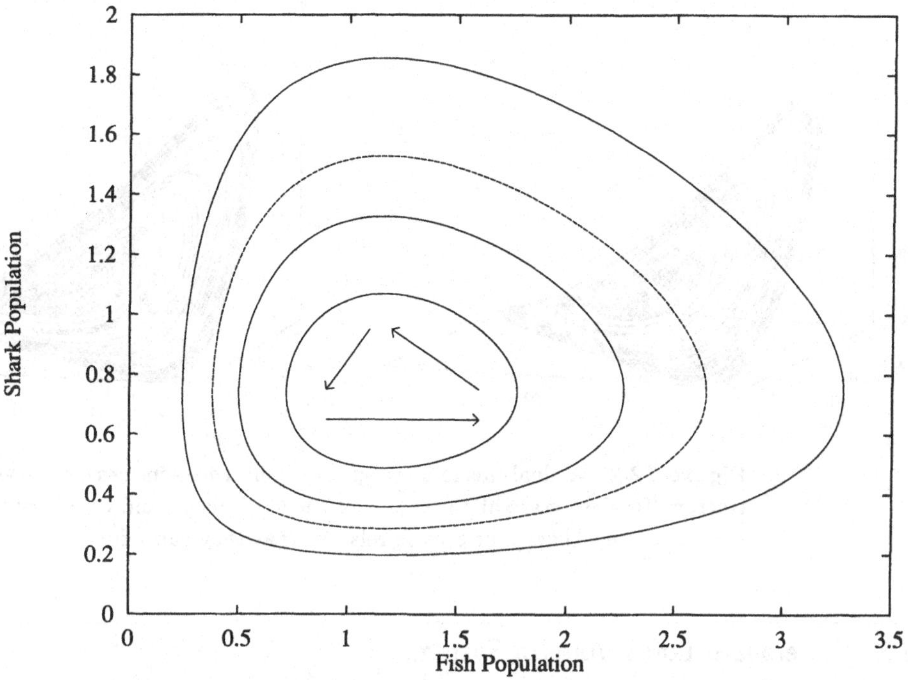

Figure 12.1 A simple Lotka-Volterra attractor which shows four (out of an infinite number of possible) limit cycles. The value of the four paramters are equal to 3.029850, 4.094132, 1.967217, and 2.295942, which yields a fixed point at 1.1671, 0.740047.

In any event, the fact that the fixed point location is given by $F = d/c$ and $S = a/b$ reveals a couple of surprises in terms of how the system behaves under certain parameter changes. For example, suppose you were responsible for managing a small ecosystem similar to the shark and small-fish system, and that you wished to increase the population level of small fish. You may be inclined to increase the reproduction rate (supposing you have the aquatic equivalent of the mythical Spanish fly); however, doing so would increase only the number of sharks, and have no affect on the number of small fish. To increase the number of small fish, you would have to increase the death rate of the sharks or decrease the nutritional value of the small fish, which may seem very counterintuitive.

All of this goes to show that even the simplest models of population dynamics reveal the delicate balance that exists in almost all ecological systems. In the next section, we are going to look at a generalized version of the Lotka-Volterra system that can be used to model the interaction among an arbitrary number of species.

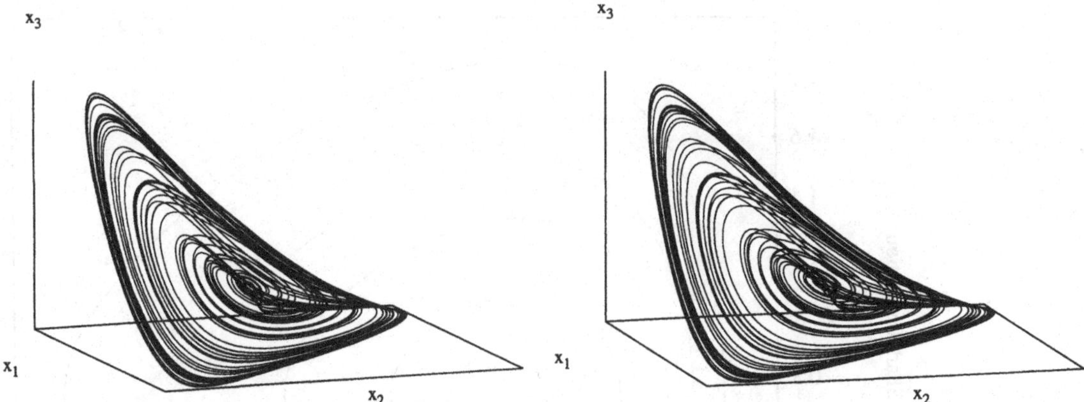

Figure 12.2 A dual-image stereogram of the three-species Lotka-Volterra chaotic attractor: To view, stare at the center of the two images and cross your eyes until the two images merge. Allow your eyes to relax so that they can refocus.

12.3 Generalized Lotka-Volterra Systems

In this section, we will consider three-species predator-prey systems so that we can see chaos in motion. If you think about how continuous dynamical systems work, with a point in an n-dimensional space representing the complete state of the system, then it should be clear that continuous chaos (as opposed to the discrete chaos found in the logistic or Hénon maps) requires three dimensions to flow through. Here is why. Suppose you had only two dimensions for the state space. For something to be chaotic, it not only must never repeat itself, but it also must return to a state that is very similar to a state that it has been at before. Since we are talking about continuous systems, we can represent the motion of the system by drawing a very long line on a sheet of paper. If you scribble long enough on some paper, it should become apparent that there is no way to meet these two constraints in only two dimensions because we are not allowed to intersect the line with itself; doing so would be to return to an old state, that is, to repeat. Hence, to have chaos, we really need to be able to "jump" over lines in a third dimension. This is why continuous chaos can exist only in three- or more dimensions.

With this in mind, we are now going to transform the previous Lotka-Volterra system into another form that is more powerful and can account for more species. There are many ways to do this, and many scientists have done so with their own unique twists. However, I am going to use a model discovered by A. Arneodo, P. Coullet, and C. Tresser. To start, we can write the whole system of ordinary differential equations for an n-species predator-prey system as

$$\frac{dx_i}{dt} = x_i \sum_{j=1}^{n} A_{ij}(1 - x_j),$$

where x_i represents the ith species and A_{ij} represents the effect that species j has on species i and plays the same role that the parameters in the last section did. Representing the A_{ij} terms as a matrix, we can list all of the parameters as

$$\mathbf{A} = \begin{bmatrix} A_{11} & A_{12} & A_{13} \\ A_{21} & A_{22} & A_{23} \\ A_{31} & A_{32} & A_{33} \end{bmatrix} = \begin{bmatrix} 0.5 & 0.5 & 0.1 \\ -0.5 & -0.1 & 0.1 \\ \alpha & 0.1 & 0.1 \end{bmatrix}.$$

The values listed in the matrix above were found by Arneodo, Coullet, and Tresser to have chaotic dynamics. Notice that the whole system is now parameterized by a single variable, α, which we can set to make the system behave in any number of ways. Setting α to 1.5 forces the system into chaotic behavior. The attractor at this value is shown in Figure 12.2. The time evolution of the three species is shown in Figure 12.3.

By using α as a knob, we can see how the generalized Lotka-Volterra system can display a wide variety of behavior. This is illustrated more concretely in Figure 12.4, which shows the attractor plotted for five different values of α. In Figure 12.4a, α has been set to 0.75, which gives the system a stable fixed point attractor. As you can see, the system spirals into the fixed point, eventually dampening out completely. In Figure 12.4b, α is set to 1.2, which puts the system into simple periodic behavior. There are versions of the two-species Lotka-Volterra system that can show this type of behavior, but they are more complicated than the system from the last section.

In Figure 12.4c, α is set to 1.32, which shows us the first period doubling. The state-space portrait of the system shows a twist in the loop that was not there when it was a simple periodic orbit. Increasing α to 1.387 gives us a stable period-4 attractor (Figure 12.4d), which looks much like the twisted version of the period-2 system. The cascade of period doublings continues. By the time α gets to 1.5, the system is wildly chaotic (Figure 12.4e).

12.4 Individual-Based Ecology

The Lotka-Volterra model takes a sort of species-eye view of the world by ignoring variations in individuals and assuming that all members of a species are either identical or similar enough that differences can be safely ignored. In this chapter, we will use a modeling technique that is relatively new to the discipline of ecology. The technique depends on a type of computing machine known as a *cellular automaton*, which happens to be the focus of Chapter 15, and is individual-based in that it

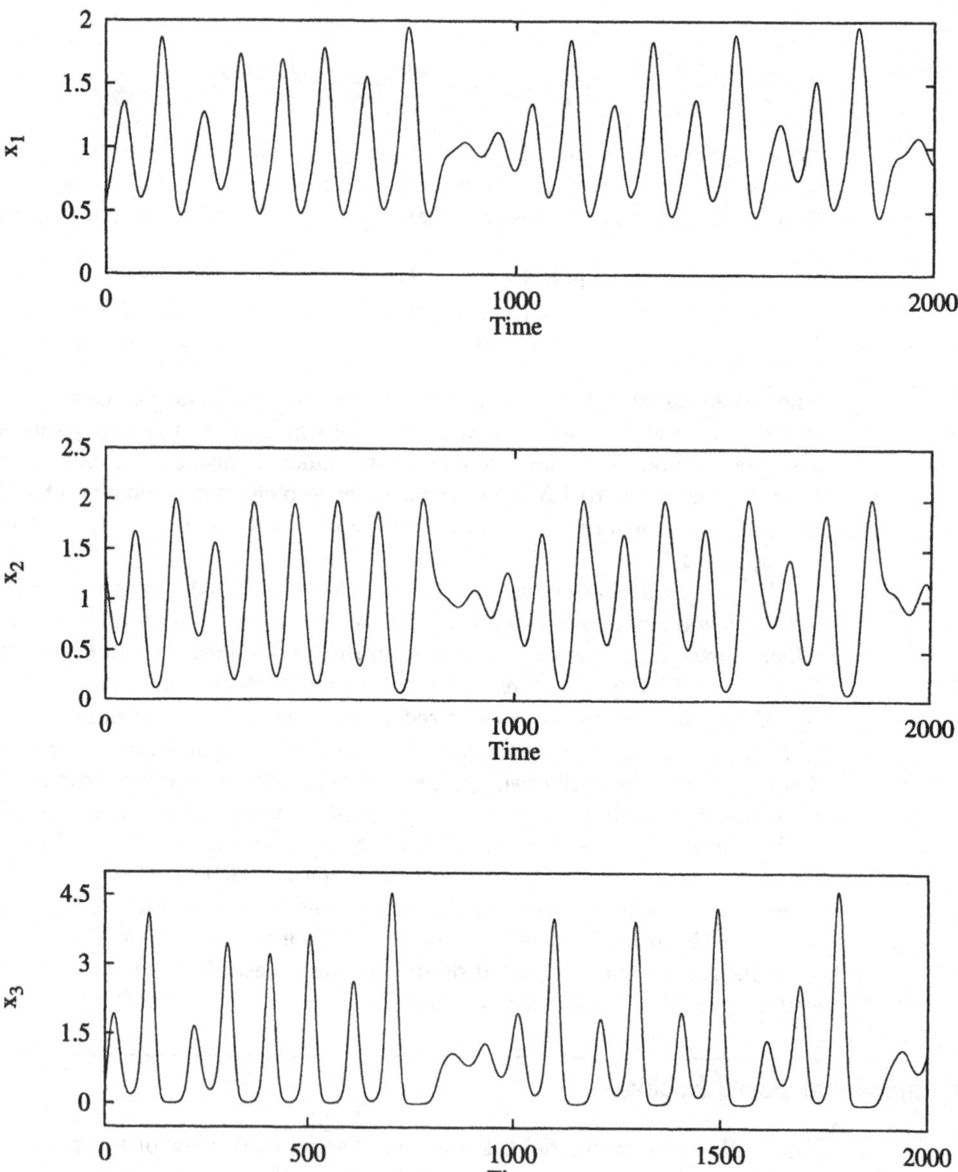

Figure 12.3 Population levels for the three-species Lotka-Volterra system

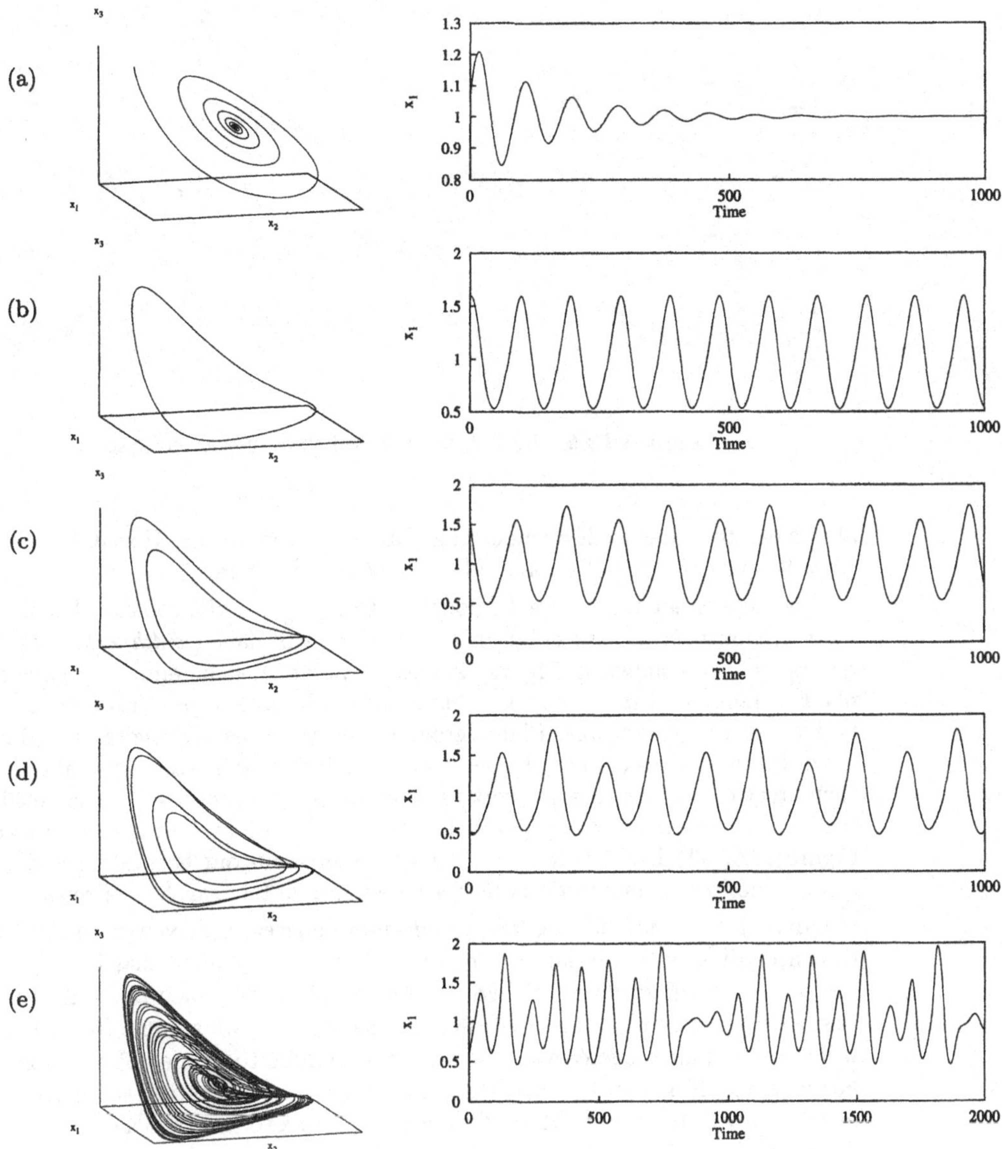

Figure 12.4 Period doublings in a three-species Lotka-Volterra system: phase space is on the left and x_1 is plotted on the right. (a) spiral fixed point, (b) simple periodic orbit, (c) period-2 orbit, (d) period-4 orbit, (e) chaos

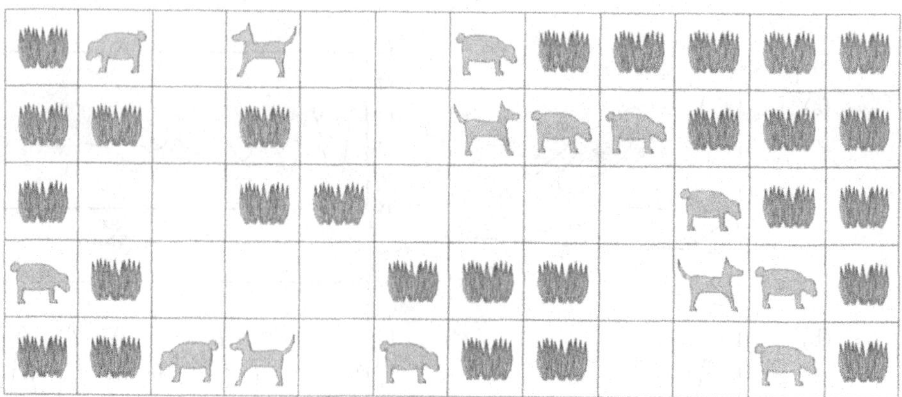

Figure 12.5 An individual-based three-species ecosystem

allows one to model each member of a population separately. Hence, in this section we will consider more of an animal-eye view of the world.

The ecosystem that we will model in this section will consist of a finite grid with a definite width and height and, therefore, will have (*width* × *height*) discrete points on it. As shown in Figure 12.5, every point must be empty or have a single plant or animal on it. In our ecosystem there are three types of creatures: plants, herbivores, and carnivores. Plants grow in empty spaces, herbivores eat plants and move through space, and carnivores eat herbivores and also move about. Since each creature consumes some sort of resource that is produced by something else (the plant "consumes" an empty space to grow), you may find it helpful to consult Figure 12.6, which illustrates the flow of resources in our ecosystem and lists the types of actions or interactions that are responsible for transfers of resources.

Given a grid that has creatures and empty spaces, the system will evolve over time according to the update algorithm in Table 12.1. Notice that the algorithm is not completely deterministic; there are several places in which randomness is used. Besides using a random update order for the animals, we assume that the animals will make a random choice when presented with more than one option for an action. For instance, if a herbivore has three plants as near neighbors, the herbivore may move to any of the three plants. Similarly, a carnivore will take a step in a random direction if there are no herbivores in its vicinity. Hence, the individual-based model combines deterministic and random processes, much like the way things appear to work in the real world.

Another form of complexity in the individual-based model is in the sheer size of its state space. Recall that the state of the three-species Lotka-Volterra system could be described by three real numbers. Since the system was chaotic, we would

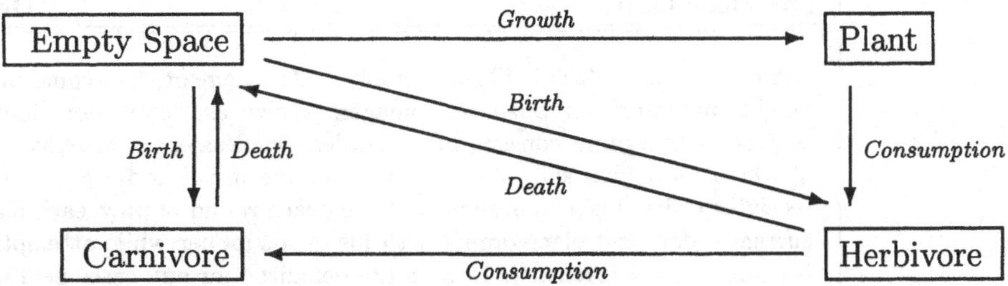

Figure 12.6 Flow of resources in the three-species individual-based ecosystem

- For every time step:
  - For every empty cell, e:
    - If e has three or more neighbors that are plants, then e will become a plant at the next time step (assuming it isn't trampled by a herbivore or carnivore).
  - For every herbivore, h (in random order):
    - Decrease energy reserves of h by a fixed amount.
    - If h has no more energy, then h dies and becomes an empty space.
    - Else, if there is a plant next to h, then h moves on top of the plant, eats it, and gains the plant's energy.
      - If h has sufficient energy reserves, then it will spawn a baby herbivore on the space that it just exited.
    - Else, h will move into a randomly selected empty space, if one exists, that is next to h's current location.
  - For every carnivore, c (in random order):
    - Decrease energy reserves of c by a fixed amount.
    - If c has no more energy, then c dies and becomes an empty space.
    - Else, if there is a herbivore next to c, then c moves on top of the herbivore, eats it, and gains the herbivore's energy.
      - If c has sufficient energy reserves, then it will spawn a baby carnivore on the space that it just exited.
    - Else, c will move into a randomly selected empty space that is next to c's current location. If there are no empty spaces, then c will move through plants.

Table 12.1 Update algorithm for individual-based ecological model

The Beer Game **Digression 12.1**

John Sterman, of MIT's Sloan School of Management, has come up with a sort of "flight simulator" for business managers known as "The Beer Game." A team of players in the game consists of a retailer, wholesaler, distributor, and brewer, all of whom must pass sales orders down the line in the order listed, with the retailer receiving orders from a consumer. During each round of play, each player must fill all current orders and place orders with his own supplier while attempting to minimize back orders and inventory. Players are penalized for any cases held in inventory and any back orders. The goal of a team is to minimize the collective penalties.

In one scenario, Sterman fixed the customer's orders to four cases of beer per week for the first four weeks. Starting at the fifth week, the customer orders eight cases per week, and continues with this amount for the rest of the game.

One would think that the four players would be quickly able to coordinate their ordering habits and that they would rapidly settle down into regular buy-and-sell orders of eight cases each. Instead, order sizes fluctuate to a surprising degree. At one point in the game it is common to see players ordering forty cases of beer despite the fact that the consumer never orders more than eight cases. Nonlinearity due to delays in information flow, coupled with feedback, makes a "trivial" economic model nearly pathological. Real-world systems, with their added complexity, are therefore much more susceptible to chaotic dynamics.

essentially need infinite precision to perfectly capture the state. But in practice, most people are still comfortable with the idea of simulating the Lotka-Volterra system on a computer with three floating-point numbers.[2] Given the density of the real numbers (as discussed in Chapter 2), you may be more impressed with the volume (and density) of the Lotka-Volterra system's state space, but the state space of the individual-based ecosystem is in some ways more impressive than that of the continuous system. Here is why. On my computer, three floating-point numbers require just less than 200 bits of storage, which means that the state of the three-species Lotka-Volterra system takes about 200 bits to approximate. The individual-based ecosystem requires $2 \times \textit{width} \times \textit{height}$ bits[3]; hence, a tiny 10×10 ecosystem needs the same number of bits that the Lotka-Volterra system required for an approximation. If we increase the dimensions to something more realistic, say 100×100 or even 1000×1000, the memory requirements grow dramatically. In fact, the number of legal states for the individual-based ecosystem easily approaches astronomically obscene numbers, such as the number of electrons in the universe.

[2]That is, the computer's fixed-precision approximation of a real number.

[3]We need two bits for each cell to encode the four possible states.

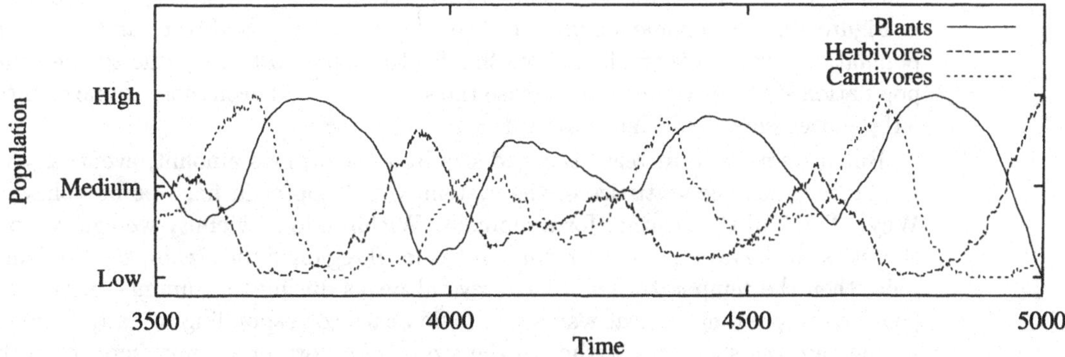

Figure 12.7 Population levels for all creatures, normalized for comparison

In short, the Lotka-Volterra system uses three real numbers for its state, but it is still confined to a three-dimensional space. The state space of the individual-based ecosystem can easily require thousands of dimensions, especially when we also factor more information into the simulation, such as the energy level of a creature or the direction a creature is moving. Moreover, it would be fairly straightforward to turn the discrete dynamics of the model into one consisting of continuous dynamics, so that a creature's position, health, and direction are all represented by real numbers instead of discrete numbers. The point is that since the individual-based model consists of many subunits, it is far more complicated than the simpler Lotka-Volterra systems. All of this may make you wonder how "well-behaved" the individual-based ecosystem will be when simulated. Will it seethe like a boiling pot of water, rapidly changing states, with little correlation between successive states? Or will the simulation fall into more mundane behavior that is more typical of trivial dynamical systems that exhibit fixed-point behavior?

Figure 12.7 shows the populations of the three species over 1500 time steps for a simulation on a 100 × 100 grid. The population levels have been normalized so that they can be plotted on a single chart because, on an average basis, one would expect the number of plants to be far greater than the number of herbivores, which, in turn, is greater than the number of carnivores. What we see is that a peak in the plant population is typically followed by a peak in the herbivore population, which is then followed by a peak in the carnivore population. The carnivores eat up the herbivores, making room for the plants to grow again, thus repeating the cycle.

A grid with dimensions of 100 × 100 is, perhaps, a bit unrealistic in that it is very small in comparison with the size of natural ecosystems; but it is pleasing, nonetheless, to see that the resulting cyclic behavior is not unlike the patterns found in the Lotka-Volterra system. In any event, the population values plotted in Figure 12.7 show some simulation artifacts, in that the herbivore and carnivore population levels have small random-like fluctuations most likely due to the small population sizes. If we were to increase the size of the grid even more, some of these jerky movements would be smoothed out.

But if we were to increase the grid size by an enormous amount, eventually we would find that the statistics of the system would approach fixed-point behavior. Why? Think of the weather for a moment. Within a local vicinity we can compile statistics on the average temperature. If the local region is the size of, say, Philadelphia, then the temperature will have several peaks during the summer, with large peaks corresponding to heat waves and little peaks corresponding to daily highs. If we increase the size even further to the size of the northern hemisphere, then the localized peaks from the heat waves and daily highs will average out some more, giving a smooth, sinusoidal appearance. Finally, if we make our "local" region the size of the entire planet, then the average temperature as a function of time will approach something close to a constant function because the seasons in the northern hemisphere are exactly the opposite of the seasons in the southern. Something like this also happens as one changes the size of a measured region in an individual-based ecosystem.

For example, if we look at a single grid point, the population level for that single point will be either 0 or 1. The exact value depends on the random movements of creatures close to the point of interest. Hence, predicting the future of a single grid point is impossible because it breaks down to predicting the outcome of a coin toss. On the other extreme, if we simulate an ecosystem on a one-billion square grid, local fluctuations in different regions will start to average out just the way local weather differences will average out on a global scale. So at the two extremes we have tiny ecosystems yielding randomness and enormous ecosystems yielding static behavior. Somewhere in between an enormous grid and a tiny one, population dynamics becomes more interesting.

David Rand and his collaborators performed a series of numerical experiments that showed much the same, but in a far more rigorous manner. They, too, studied a three-species predator-prey ecosystem that was modeled as a system of individuals, but they also varied the size of the grid and came up with a technique for determining which sampling size would reveal interesting properties. To be clear, larger grid sizes always result in more realistic simulations; what Rand and company did was to vary the size of a subset of the grid in which they computed their statistics. After finding an interesting sample size, they proceeded to generate population data for a sampled window at the right size. With this data, they were able to construct a four-dimensional attractor that was capable of predicting the system's behavior with 94 percent accuracy. This means that the dynamics of the system essentially collapse onto a lower-dimensional space, meaning that some of the simpler predator-prey models, like the Lotka-Volterra system, may not be so far-fetched after all.

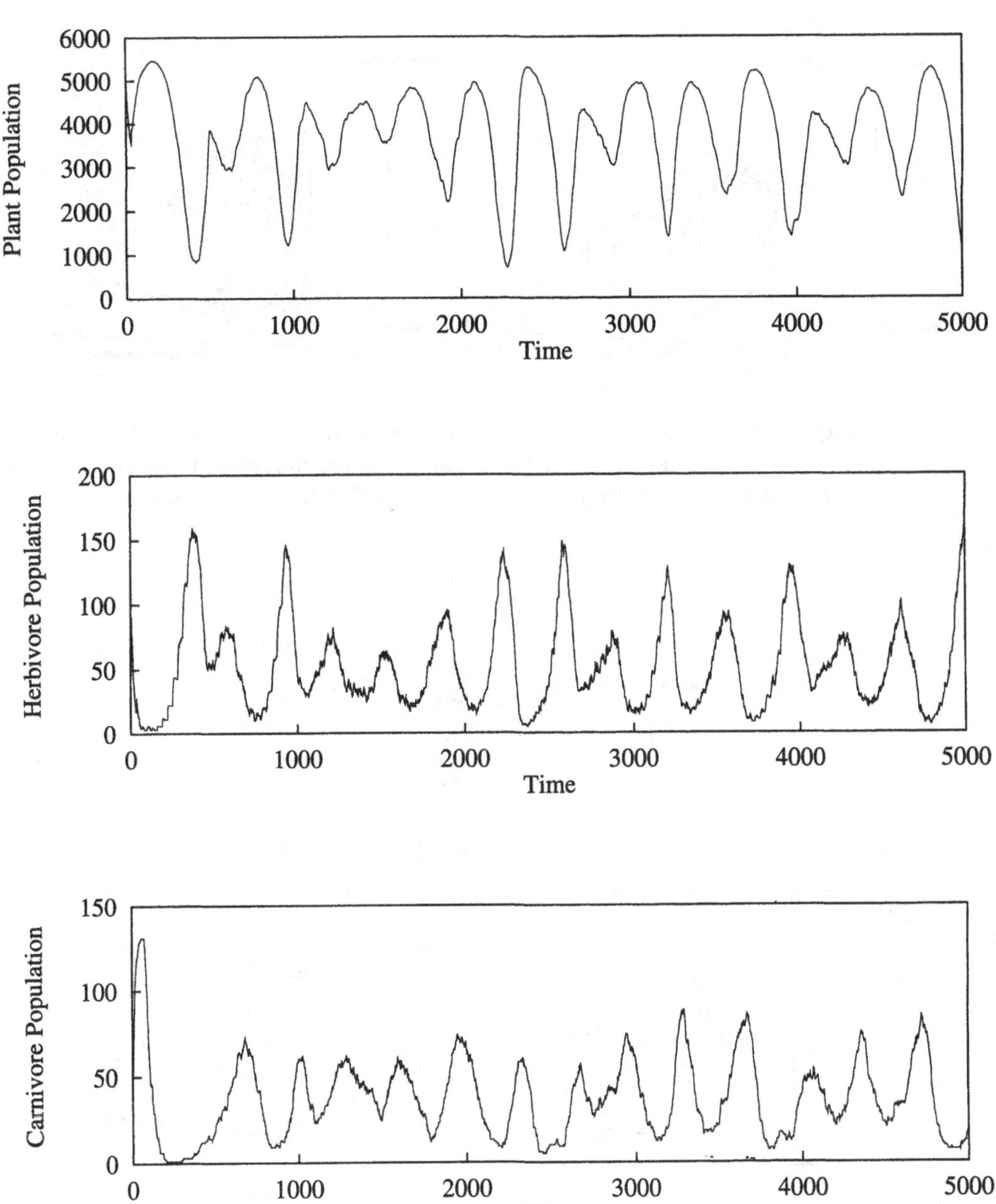

Figure 12.8 Population levels for the individual-based predator-prey system

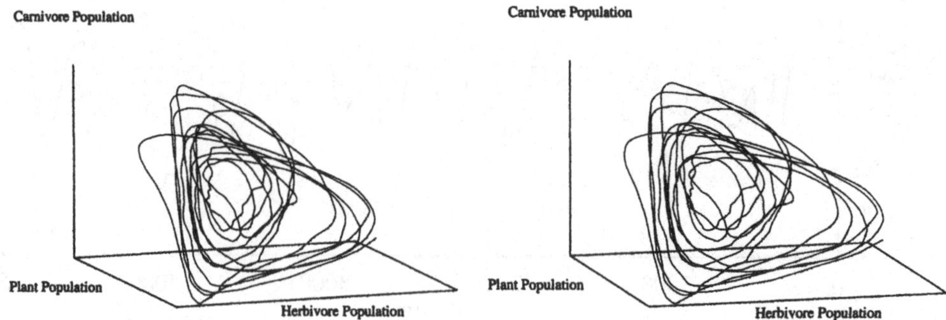

Figure 12.9 A dual-image stereogram of the attractor of the individual-based predator-prey system: To view, stare at the center of the two images and cross your eyes until the two images merge. Allow your eyes to relax so that they can refocus.

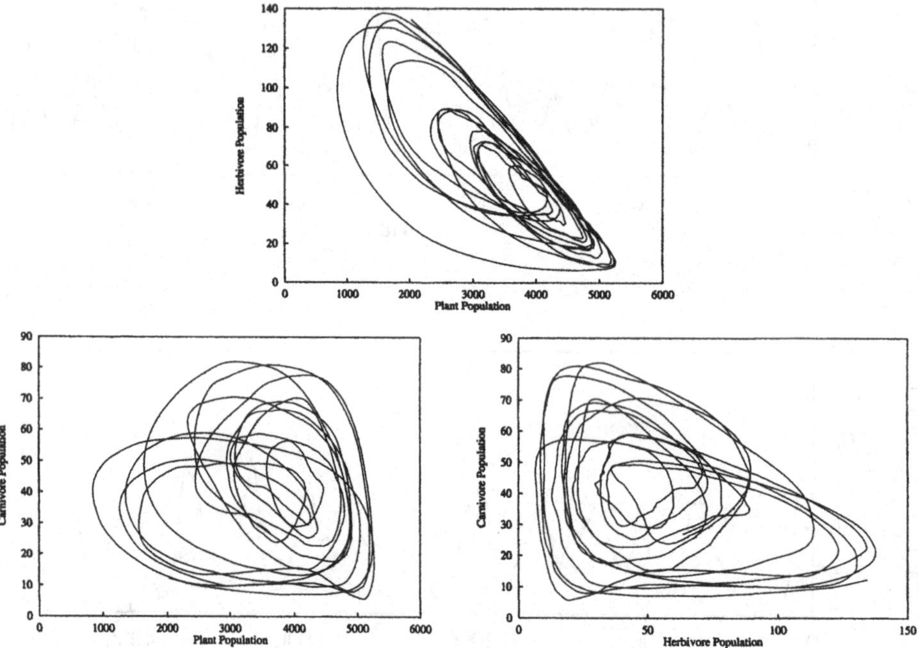

Figure 12.10 Population phase portraits for the individual-based predator-prey system

Figure 12.8 shows the population levels of the three species over 5000 time steps, while Figures 12.9 and 12.10 show the same data plotted in a three-dimensional space. While the data don't perfectly collapse into a three-dimensional space, there is still a great deal of structure in the images. The state-space plots are neither random (i.e., a scattered mess) nor simple (i.e., a single point). Instead, there is structure with some order mixed with disorder.

12.5 Unifying Themes

In any situation in which many simple units interact in a love-hate, give-take, or cooperate-compete manner, it is possible that differential equations like those found in the generalized Lotka-Volterra system can account for many of the underlying dynamical properties. We have, here, a clear case in which radically different phenomena can be described with similar mathematical tools precisely because producer-consumer-type interactions are so common even in different areas such as chemistry, biology, and the social sciences.

We have also seen how chaos is not randomness but is, in fact, order masquerading as disorder. Pathologically complex systems, consisting of thousands or even trillions of units, can often collapse into patterns that are describable by a mere handful of equations. The interesting thing is that there appears to be a tendency for systems of all sizes to approach chaos from two different directions, in the form of small and simple systems that produce surprisingly complex motion, and enormously complex systems with dynamics that ultimately break down into something simpler.

Parallel to this last point, there is an ironic twist to be found in the comparison of how the complexity of rules and motions changes when viewed on different scales. Individuals can be described by simple rules. Table 12.1 is an example of an algorithm that completely describes how every individual in an ecosystem is to behave from one time step to another. Nevertheless, we are helpless to predict the motion of a species or an ecosystem in the long run because the composite motion is far more complex then the individual motions. This is even the case in completely deterministic systems and is not due solely to the partial randomness in the algorithm from Table 12.1. So it would appear that this is a case of the composition being more complex than the totality of the components.

But if we look at the statistics of our individual-based ecosystem, things seem to get more complex as we narrow our view. On a very large scale, famine in one region is balanced by a growth spurt in another, yielding near constant statistics over very large spatial scales. Complementary to this, if we look at a single point on a grid, its statistics are far more complex precisely because we are ignoring the rest of the world. So it is possible—depending on your viewpoint—for the components to be more complicated than the composition.

Option Name	Option Type	Option Meaning
-seed	INTEGER	seed for random parameters
-points	INTEGER	number of points to produce
-f0	DOUBLE	initial fish population
-s0	DOUBLE	initial shark population
-a	DOUBLE	fish growth rate
-b	DOUBLE	shark consumption rate
-c	DOUBLE	fish nutritional value
-d	DOUBLE	shark death rate
-dt	DOUBLE	time step increment

Table 12.2 Command-line options for `lotka`

In the end, viewing things from either the microscopic or the macroscopic viewpoint fails to capture what it is about these systems that is most interesting. For at the intermediate scales we find that the order and disorder—or perhaps the computability and incomputability—balance out to produce a pattern of behavior that is far more interesting than either of the extremes.

12.6 Further Exploration

All of the plots in this chapter where made with **lotka**, **predprey**, or **gsw**. The first program, **lotka**, numerically integrates the two-species Lotka-Volterra system with a second-order Euler's method. The program is very simple and its command-line options, listed in Table 12.2, work exactly as explained in Section 12.2. Since this program will only produce data as output (and no graphics), it is primarily useful as an example of how to numerically integrate ordinary differential equations. You may wish to use the source code of **lotka** as a template for writing similar programs that use other differential equations.

The time-series and state-space plots of the generalized Lotka-Volterra system were produced from data generated with **predprey**. The options for the program are summarized in Table 12.3, and most their usages should be clear from the description in the table and from the text in this chapter. The system parameter, α, is set with the **-alpha** option. Similar to some of the programs from Chapter 11, the specifics of **predprey**'s graphical output can be controlled with the **-xp**, **-yp**, and **-delta** options. The **-xp** and **-yp** options determine what time varying variables are used as the x- and y-coordinates of the plots and must take a value that is from one of the strings: **x(t)**, **y(t)**, **z(t)**, **x(t-delta)**, **y(t-delta)**, or **z(t-delta)**.[4]

[4]On UNIX systems, you may need to enclose the strings in double quotes to prevent your command shell from interpreting the parentheses as special characters.

Option Name	Option Type	Option Meaning
`-width`	INTEGER	width of the plot in pixels
`-height`	INTEGER	height of the plot in pixels
`-skip`	INTEGER	number of initial points to skip
`-points`	INTEGER	number of points to plot
`-alpha`	DOUBLE	value of the alpha parameter
`-delta`	INTEGER	time delay term
`-dt`	DOUBLE	time step
`-x0`	DOUBLE	initial X value
`-y0`	DOUBLE	initial Y value
`-z0`	DOUBLE	initial Z value
`-data`	SWITCH	don't plot but print points
`-xp`	STRING	x-coordinate for plot
`-yp`	STRING	y-coordinate for plot
`-factor`	DOUBLE	auto-scale expansion factor
`-inv`	SWITCH	invert all colors?
`-xmag`	INTEGER	magnification factor for X Windows
`-term`	STRING	how to plot points

Table 12.3 Command-line options for `predprey`

For example, the command:

```
predprey -xp "x(t)" -yp "z(t)"
```

will plot the state space of $x(t)$ versus $z(t)$, and the command:

```
predprey -xp "y(t)" -yp "y(t-delta)"
```

will plot $y(t)$ versus $y(t-\Delta)$, a delayed coordinate embedding for the system, with Δ being determined by the `-delta` option. Thus, the program will plot any state variable against any other variable or any delayed state variable.

Table 12.4 summarizes the options for `gsw` (which is short for grass, sheep, wolf), the program used to produce the data for the individual-based models. Although it was not demonstrated in this chapter, `gsw` can also produce plots that represent each creature by a single colored point. A single plot for a single time step is not very informative (which is why I didn't include any in this chapter), but viewing them in succession, you can witness the rise and fall of each of the species much like a movie. The `-width` and `-height` options are used to specify the spatial size of your ecosystem and, hence, the size of your plot.

Together, the `-plants`, `-herbs`, and `-carns` options determine the initial population sizes of the species. A new plant will grow in an empty space only if the

Option Name	Option Type	Option Meaning
`-width`	INTEGER	width of the plot in pixels
`-height`	INTEGER	height of the plot in pixels
`-steps`	INTEGER	number of simulated steps
`-seed`	INTEGER	random seed for initial state
`-plants`	INTEGER	initial number of plants
`-herbs`	INTEGER	initial number of herbivores
`-carns`	INTEGER	initial number of carnivores
`-pmin`	INTEGER	min. plants to grow new plant
`-pmax`	INTEGER	max. plants to grow new plant
`-Ep`	INTEGER	energy of plant
`-Eh`	INTEGER	energy of herbivore
`-Ec`	INTEGER	energy of carnivore
`-Ch`	INTEGER	step energy cost for herbivores
`-Cc`	INTEGER	step energy cost for carnivores
`-Pt`	INTEGER	number of steps to grow plant
`-samp`	INTEGER	size of subsample statistaics
`-stats`	SWITCH	show statistics?
`-pfreq`	INTEGER	plot frequency
`-noext`	SWITCH	prevent extinction?
`-inv`	SWITCH	invert colors?
`-xmag`	INTEGER	magnification for X Windows
`-term`	STRING	how to plot points

Table 12.4 Command-line options for `gsw`

space has a number of plant neighbors that is inclusively between the values specified by `-pmin` and `-pmax`. The `-Ep`, `-Eh`, `-Ec`, `-Ch`, and `-Cc` options determine how much energy animals gain and lose each time step and each time they eat another creature. And with `-Pt` you can make it so that plants need many steps in order to regrow.

For the collected statistics, the population of each species is printed out at each time step. With the `-samp` option you can change the behavior of the program so that instead of printing out the total population, it will only count creatures within the square defined by the upper-left corner of the grid and the point located at n points down and to the right from the upper-left corner, where n is the value given with the `-samp` option.

If you want to cheat and make it impossible for the animals to die out completely, make sure that the `-noext` switch is set. All other options should be self-explanatory.

12.7 Further Reading

Capra, F. (1996). *The web of life: A new scientific understanding of living systems.* New York: Doubleday.

Casti, J. L. (1994). *Complexification: Explaining a paradoxical world through the science of surprise.* New York: HarperCollins.

Dewdney, A. K. (1984). Computer Recreations: Sharks and fish wage an ecological war on the toroidal planet wa-tor. *Sci. Am.*, 251(6): 14–22.

Kuang, Y. (1993). *Delay differential equations with applications in population dynamics.* New York: Academic Press.

Rand, D. A. & Wilson, H. (1995). Using spatio-temporal chaos and intermediate-scale determinism to quantify spatially-extended ecosystems. *Proc. R. Soc. Lond. B*, 259(1355): 111–117.

Sterman, J. D. (1984). Instructions for running the beer distribution game. Technical Report D-3679, System Dynamics Group, MIT, Cambridge, Mass.

Tu, P. N. V. (1992). *Dynamical systems: An introduction with applications in economics and biology.* Berlin: Springer-Verlag.

13 Controlling Chaos

It turns out that an eerie type of chaos can lurk just behind a facade of order—and yet, deep inside the chaos lurks an even eerier type of order.
— Douglas Hofstadter

Amid the turmoil and tumult of battle, there may be seeming disorder and yet no real disorder at all.
— Sun Tzu

All stable processes we shall predict. All unstable processes we shall control.
— John von Neumann

IN THIS CHAPTER, we will put together several key points from the last three chapters to show how chaotic dynamical systems can be more easily controlled than nonchaotic systems of comparable complexity. The basic technique, due to Edward Ott, Celso Grebogi, and James Yorke, turns out to be relatively simple to implement. However, the formal derivation of the technique can be a bit difficult to comprehend. Nevertheless, one goal of this chapter is to present the material in bite-sized, easily digestible parts.

The implications for the existence of a method to control chaos are extremely exciting. Some possible applications include smart pacemakers, epileptic seizure inhibitors, intelligent control strategies for adjusting the global economy, and (who knows?) even weather control. It may be decades (if at all) until the last two examples are realized, simply because they involve global systems that are extremely complex. On the other hand, the first two examples are currently the subject of much research, and products for such devices are either already available or will be in the near future.

Throughout this chapter, please keep in mind the following aspects of how chaotic systems work. Each item listed below makes the control problem a little bit easier than it would normally be. Taken together, all of these issues make controlling chaos a more tractable problem.

- *Bang for the buck.* Since chaotic systems are extremely sensitive, a very small perturbation can cause a large difference in a system's future behavior. Thus, with only minute adjustments to a system, we can trick a chaotic system into more desirable behavior.

- *Preselected goals.* Typically, one would like to see a chaotic system converted into either fixed-point or limit-cycle behavior. Since every chaotic attractor has an infinite number of limit cycles embedded within it, a choice for the desired behavior may already be identified for us.

- *What goes around comes around.* Since we have a preselected goal for the desired system behavior, and since we wish to use only small perturbations, how can we be sure that the chaotic system will get close to the desired behavior? The answer lies in the ergodic nature of chaotic systems. Ergodicity means that with a finite amount of patience, we can get as close to the goal behavior as we want, if we just wait long enough.

Over the next few pages, we will examine four "bite-sized chunks" that are needed to explain the derivation of this strategy to control chaos. In order of presentation, we will look at Taylor expansions, vector calculus, vector inner and outer products, and eigensystems.

13.1 Taylor Expansions

Suppose you want to approximate a complicated function by a simpler function, and furthermore that you care if your approximation is accurate only within a small portion of the complicated function's range. In other words, if $f(x)$ is the complicated function, and a is the point at which we want our approximation to be accurate, then we couldn't care less how accurate the approximation is for x far from a. With these ground rules in place, a good approximation can be found in a *Taylor expansion*. The first-order Taylor expansion of $f(x)$ is written as:

$$\hat{f}(x) = f(a) + (x - a)f'(a).$$

Let's examine each term in detail. The little "hat" above the function name, that is, $\hat{f}(x)$, means that we are attempting an approximation of $f(x)$. Next, we have the term $f(a)$, which is just the value of the complicated function at the point, a. The $(x - a)$ term gives us an idea of how far x is from a, and also whether x is to the left or right of a. Finally, $f'(a)$ is the first derivative or slope of $f(x)$ at a.

Putting everything together, here is how a Taylor expansion works. If x happens to be equal to a, then $\hat{f}(x)$ will be equal to $f(x)$; thus, for this one example, the approximation is perfect. Suppose, instead, that x is a little to the right of a and, therefore, just a bit larger than a. In this case, $(x-a)$ will be a small positive number that, when multiplied by the slope of the function, $f'(a)$, tells us approximately how

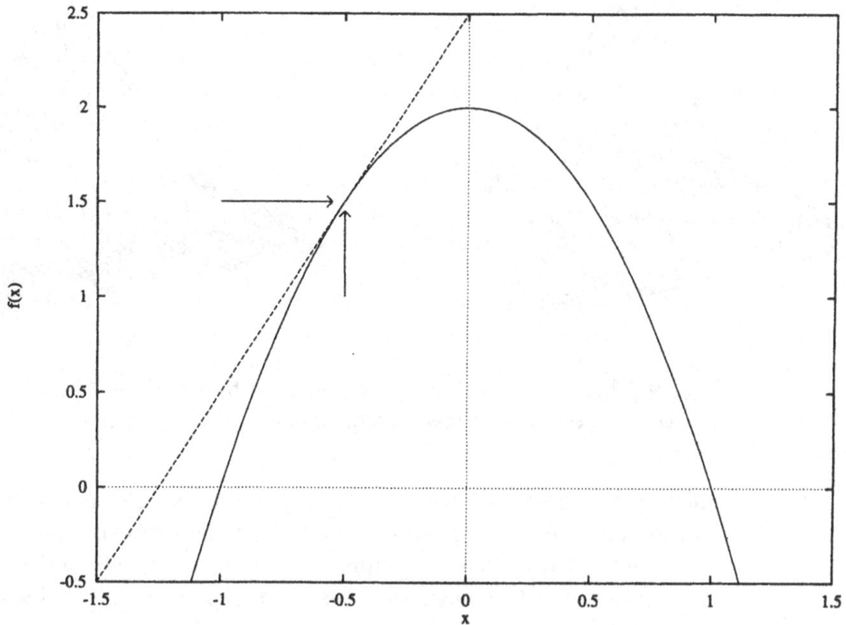

Figure 13.1 An example of a Taylor expansion: The function, $f(x) = -2x^2 + 2$, is plotted alongside the Taylor expansion constructed at the point $x = \frac{1}{2}$, $\hat{f}(x) = \frac{5}{2} + 2x$.

far $f(x)$ is from $f(a)$. If x is just smaller than a, then $(x-a)$ will be a small negative number. The Taylor expansion works similarly for the case of x being a little bit to the left of a. Figure 13.1 contains an example Taylor expansion illustrating these facts much better.

In a nutshell, the Taylor expansion of a function is accurate only near the point it was constructed about, because the Taylor expansion is a simple linear[1] function drawn such that it passes through the point $(a, f(a))$ and has the same slope as $f(a)$.

13.2 Vector Calculus

What most people think of as a *function* is usually more properly referred to as a *scalar function*, where the *scalar* portion of the name indicates that the function takes a single scalar argument and returns a single scalar result. For many ap-

[1]You can also construct more complicated Taylor expansions that include polynomial terms that are multiplied by the higher derivatives of $f(x)$. However, for our needs, the first-order Taylor expansion is sufficient.

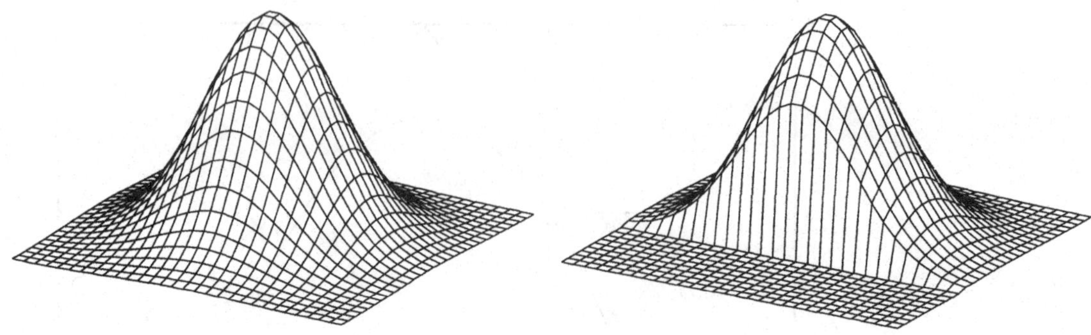

Figure 13.2 A vector function represented by a surface: Taking a slice parallel to one axis through the surface reveals a one-dimensional function.

plications, scalar functions aren't quite good enough because the application may require functions that take many arguments and return many results.

Since the Hénon map is a function of two arguments and returns two results, it maps nicely into this notation. Just to make things clear, let's agree to write the "next state" function of the Hénon map as

$$\mathbf{f}(x_t, y_t) = \begin{bmatrix} a - x_t^2 + by_t \\ x_t \end{bmatrix}.$$

We boldface $\mathbf{f}(x_t, y_t)$ to denote the fact that $\mathbf{f}$ returns a vector result. We also could have written the function with a single boldface argument, that is, $\mathbf{f}(\mathbf{x})$, to indicate that the argument is a vector as well. However, having a boldface $\mathbf{x}$ could lead to some confusion, since the $\mathbf{x}$ term is quite a different animal than x_t. Anyway, vector functions are really equivalent to listing multiple scalar functions (as we did in the last chapter), but it is important to recognize the distinction that a vector function explicitly groups the equations together so as to state "these things belong with each other."

Putting all of this together, what do you think the derivative of a vector function looks like? We know that the derivative of a scalar function tells us about the slope of the function. Well, the derivative of a vector function reveals the same information, but in a slightly more complicated manner. Breaking up the Hénon map into two scalar equations that take two arguments, it would be possible to plot the function responses as a surface where the x- and y-coordinates specify values of x_t and y_t, and the height of the plot, the z-coordinate, is the function result (i.e., x_{t+1} or y_{t+1}).

Here comes the tricky part. Imagine that our three-dimensional plot looks something like a hill (it really doesn't matter what form we imagine it to take, as long that we agree that it is three-dimensional), as shown in Figure 13.2. With the x-

axis running left-to-right, and the y-axis running forward-and-backward, suppose an earthmover is used to cut a long slice across the hill such that the slice is parallel to the x-axis and at a right angle to the y-axis. The newly created edge of the slice is just like a scalar function that was constructed from the vector function by holding the y argument constant and letting x vary. We can now define a *partial derivative* as a special function that tells us about the slope of one of the function arguments, but is possibly parameterized in the other function argument.

In the case of the Hénon map, there is a total of four partial derivatives that we can compute because there are two arguments and two results. To compute a partial derivative of a result with respect to one of the arguments (say x_t), we pretend that all of the other arguments (in this case y_t) are simply constants. In this way, we can now go on to compute the four partial derivatives of the Hénon map as:

$$\frac{\partial x_{t+1}}{\partial x_t} = -2x_t, \frac{\partial x_{t+1}}{\partial y_t} = b, \frac{\partial y_{t+1}}{\partial x_t} = 1, \frac{\partial y_{t+1}}{\partial y_t} = 0.$$

The little curly character, ∂, should be read as a d but specifically indicates that the derivatives are partial derivatives. The partial derivatives of a system reveal exactly how the state space variables evolve relative to each other. For example, since $\partial y_{t+1}/\partial x_t = 1$ and $\partial y_{t+1}/\partial y_t = 0$, we can determine that the value of y_{t+1} closely depends on the value of x_t but is completely independent of y_t.

The four partial derivatives above can obviously be written as a single (2×2) matrix. This is a special matrix known as a *Jacobian matrix*. The Jacobian matrix of a vector function tells us how each result of the vector function slopes relative to varying each argument. Since we have extended the definition of a derivative for vector functions, we can construct a Taylor expansion for vector functions as well.

13.3 Inner and Outer Vector Product

Given a pair of vectors, it is often useful to have some sort of measure to indicate how similar or dissimilar the vectors are. The inner product (or dot product) of two vectors is one such measure that happens to have a nice geometric interpretation. As a specific example, consider the two vectors, $\mathbf{x}$ and $\mathbf{y}$. The inner product of the two $(n \times 1)$ column vectors can be written in many ways:

$$\mathbf{x}^T\mathbf{y} = \mathbf{x} \cdot \mathbf{y} = \sum_{i=1}^{n} x_i y_i = x_1 y_1 + \cdots + x_n y_n.$$

The first written form of the inner product indicates that the inner product can be computed by performing matrix multiplication on a $(1 \times n)$ row vector and an $(n \times 1)$ column vector. In this chapter, I will mostly use the first form, $\mathbf{x}^T\mathbf{y}$, for reasons that will be explained at the end of this section.

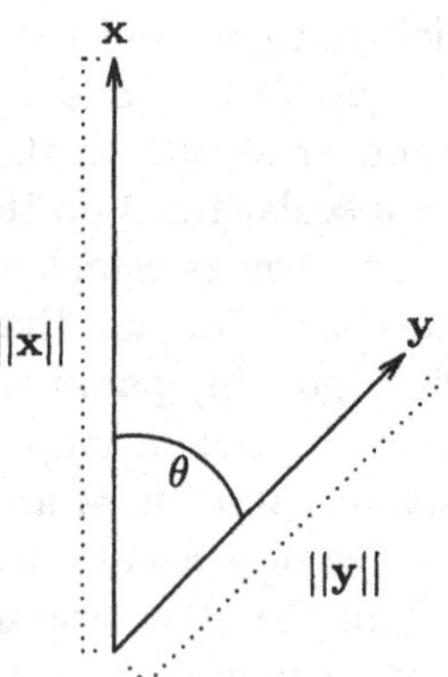

Figure 13.3 The inner product of two vectors as a function of their lengths and the angle between them

As for the geometric interpretation, let $||\mathbf{x}||$ and $||\mathbf{y}||$ denote the length of $\mathbf{x}$ and $\mathbf{y}$, respectively. Also, let the angle between the two vectors be denoted by θ, as shown in Figure 13.3. We can now express the inner product as

$$\mathbf{x}^T\mathbf{y} = ||\mathbf{x}||||\mathbf{y}||\cos\theta.$$

Here comes the neat part. By doing a little bit of algebraic manipulation, we can rewrite the last equation as

$$\frac{\mathbf{x}^T}{||\mathbf{x}||}\frac{\mathbf{y}}{||\mathbf{y}||} = \cos\theta.$$

Why is this neat? The normalized vector $\mathbf{x}/||\mathbf{x}||$ is a vector that has the same direction as $\mathbf{x}$, but has length of exactly 1 (assuming that $||\mathbf{x}||$ is not 0). We can say the same thing about the relationship between $\mathbf{y}/||\mathbf{y}||$ and $\mathbf{y}$ as well. Therefore, the inner product of two unit-length vectors is exactly equal to the cosine of the angle between them. Thus, if the two unit vectors are parallel (i.e., θ is 0), then the inner product of the two vectors is equal to 1. Likewise, if the two vectors are orthogonal (i.e., θ is 90 degrees), then the inner product of the two vectors will be 0.

Since an inner product converts two vectors into a scalar, is there some way to transform two vectors into a matrix? The outer product is complementary to the inner product in that it does exactly that. Like the inner product, the outer product can be written in many ways:

$$\mathbf{x}\mathbf{y}^T = \mathbf{x} \times \mathbf{y} = \begin{bmatrix} x_1y_1 & \cdots & x_1y_n \\ \vdots & & \vdots \\ x_ny_1 & \cdots & x_ny_n \end{bmatrix}.$$

The outer product also has a geometric interpretation, but it is nontrivial to visualize.

A good reason to write the inner and outer products as $\mathbf{x}^T\mathbf{y}$ and $\mathbf{x}\mathbf{y}^T$ is that if you have to mix multiple operations together, the rules for manipulating the expressions are more explicit. By way of example, if we were to perform an outer product (to get a matrix) and we wanted to multiply the result by a third vector, $(\mathbf{x}\mathbf{y}^T)\mathbf{y}$, we could reorder the operations as $\mathbf{x}(\mathbf{y}^T\mathbf{y})$, thus simplifying the computation.

13.4 Eigenvectors, Eigenvalues, and Basis

The final advanced topic that we will review involves what are known as *eigenvectors* and *eigenvalues*. Imagine a scalar function, $f(x)$, plotted in some manner. Furthermore, suppose that the identity function, $y = x$, is plotted on the same surface as the original function. For all points, x, where the identity function intersects the first function, we have the property that $f(x) = x$. A similar property exists for vector functions as well.

Let $\mathbf{A}$ represent an $(n \times n)$ matrix and $\mathbf{x}$ represent an $(n \times 1)$ column vector. Matrix-vector multiplication of $\mathbf{A}$ times $\mathbf{x}$ is computed as

$$\mathbf{A}\mathbf{x} = \begin{bmatrix} A_{11}x_1 + \cdots + A_{1n}x_n \\ \vdots \\ A_{n1}x_1 + \cdots + A_{nn}x_n \end{bmatrix}.$$

Notice that multiplying $\mathbf{A}$ times $\mathbf{x}$ results in another $(n \times 1)$ column vector; thus, one way to think of an $(n \times n)$ matrix is as a function that maps vectors to vectors. It so happens that for some matrices there can exist as many as n unique special vectors, $\mathbf{e}_1, \ldots, \mathbf{e}_n$, that have the property $\mathbf{A}\mathbf{e}_i = \lambda_i \mathbf{e}_i$. The term $\mathbf{e}_i$ denotes the ith eigenvector of $\mathbf{A}$, and λ_i denotes the ith eigenvalue of $\mathbf{A}$. In many ways, eigenvectors are a lot like the points of a scalar function that map to themselves. By convention, eigenvectors are understood to have unit length, which means that the inner product and length of the vector equal 1.

A good example of how to visualize what an eigenvector looks like comes from Gilbert Strang, author of *Linear Algebra and Its Applications*. Imagine the rotation of Earth. Using the techniques of Chapter 7, we could describe the rotation in terms of a (3×3) matrix that maps surface coordinates to their future location. The poles of Earth are eigenvectors because their direction is always unchanged under Earth's rotation. Furthermore, the eigenvalues of the poles are equal to 1 because the length stays the same.

If an eigenvector has an associated eigenvalue that is less than 1, then all vectors that lie in the same direction as this eigenvector will shrink when multiplied to the matrix. Similarly, for eigenvalues greater than 1, a matrix will expand a vector through multiplication. In this way, eigenvectors and eigenvalues can be seen as descriptions of how a matrix will expand and contract vectors when the vectors are multiplied by it. This observation really gets to the heart of our earlier observation that all chaotic systems stretch and fold state spaces. By understanding eigenvectors, we can understand how chaos works a little better.

Eigenvectors also have a very useful property that we are going to exploit in the next section. In a nutshell, eigenvectors form a *basis* in an n-dimensional space, which means that for any n-dimensional vector, $\mathbf{x}$, it is possible to rewrite $\mathbf{x}$ as a linear combination of the n n-dimensional eigenvectors:

$$\mathbf{x} = a_1\mathbf{e}_i + \cdots + a_n\mathbf{e}_n,$$

for some choice of a_1 through a_n. As an example, the simplest basis of a three-dimensional space consists of the unit vectors, which can be combined as

$$a_1 \begin{bmatrix} 1 \\ 0 \\ 0 \end{bmatrix} + a_2 \begin{bmatrix} 0 \\ 1 \\ 0 \end{bmatrix} + a_3 \begin{bmatrix} 0 \\ 0 \\ 1 \end{bmatrix} = \begin{bmatrix} a_1 \\ a_2 \\ a_3 \end{bmatrix},$$

to form any three-dimensional vector. In any event, let's assume that for an $(n \times n)$ matrix, $\mathbf{A}$, you found n unique eigenvectors, $\mathbf{e}_1, \ldots, \mathbf{e}_n$. If you were to rewrite an $(n \times 1)$ column vector, $\mathbf{x}$, as a linear combination of the eigenvectors, performing the operation $\mathbf{Ax}$ becomes much simpler:

$$\begin{aligned} \mathbf{Ax} &= \mathbf{A}(a_1\mathbf{e}_i + \cdots + a_n\mathbf{e}_n) \\ &= a_1\mathbf{Ae}_1 + \cdots + a_n\mathbf{Ae}_n \\ &= a_1\lambda_1\mathbf{e}_1 + \cdots + a_n\lambda_n\mathbf{e}_n. \end{aligned}$$

Thus, instead of having to perform the matrix-vector multiplication the "hard" way, we can transform the operation into one that requires only scalar multiplication and vector addition.

Related to this property, for every set of vectors that forms a basis in an n-dimensional space, there exist n more vectors, $\mathbf{g}_1$, …, $\mathbf{g}_n$, that have the two properties that for all i, the inner product $\mathbf{g}_i^T\mathbf{e}_i = 1$, and for all $i \neq j$, $\mathbf{g}_i^T\mathbf{e}_j = 0$. This new set of vectors is said to be a *contravariant basis*. For the example of $[1\,0\,0]^T$, $[0\,1\,0]^T$, and $[0\,0\,1]^T$, the same three vectors form their own contravariant basis, but for a more complicated set of vectors the contravariant basis will almost surely be different from the original basis. With a set of eigenvectors and a contravariant basis, it is possible to rewrite the original matrix in terms of the two sets of vectors. To demonstrate that this is possible, we will once again perform an example matrix-vector multiplication, but this time we will rewrite $\mathbf{A}$ in terms of the contravariant basis and the eigenvectors, to get the same result as before. First, let's rewrite $\mathbf{x}$:

$$\mathbf{Ax} = \mathbf{A}(a_1\mathbf{e}_1 + \cdots + a_n\mathbf{e}_n).$$

Term	Meaning
$\mathbf{x}_t$	the state at time t
p_t	the control parameter, equal to $\mathbf{k}^T(\mathbf{x}_t - \mathbf{x}_F)$
$\mathbf{k}$	the control vector
$\mathbf{f}(\mathbf{x}_t, p_t)$	the chaotic dynamical system
$\mathbf{A}$	the derivative (Jacobian matrix) of $\mathbf{f}(\mathbf{x}_t, p_t)$ with respect to $\mathbf{x}_t$
$\mathbf{b}$	the partial derivative of $\mathbf{f}(\mathbf{x}_t, p_t)$ with respect to p_t
$\mathbf{e}_s, \mathbf{e}_u$	the stable and unstable eigenvectors of $\mathbf{A}$
λ_s, λ_u	the stable and unstable eigenvalues of $\mathbf{A}$ with $\lambda_s < 1 < \lambda_u$
$\mathbf{g}_s, \mathbf{g}_u$	contravariant basis vectors with $\mathbf{g}_s^T\mathbf{e}_s = \mathbf{g}_u^T\mathbf{e}_u = 1$ and $\mathbf{g}_s^T\mathbf{e}_u = \mathbf{g}_u^T\mathbf{e}_s = 0$

Table 13.1 A lexicon of the terms used in Section 13.5

Now we need to rewrite $\mathbf{A}$:

$$\mathbf{A}\mathbf{x} = (\lambda_1\mathbf{e}_1\mathbf{g}_1^T + \cdots + \lambda_n\mathbf{e}_n\mathbf{g}_n^T)(a_1\mathbf{e}_1 + \cdots + a_n\mathbf{e}_n).$$

Since $\mathbf{g}_i^T\mathbf{e}_j = 0$ and $\mathbf{g}_i^T\mathbf{e}_i = 1$, for $i \neq j$, most of the cross terms can be discarded to get the familiar expression

$$\mathbf{A}\mathbf{x} = a_1\lambda_1\mathbf{e}_1 + \cdots + a_n\lambda_n\mathbf{e}_n,$$

which is the same result that we calculated earlier. The notion of an eigensystem may seem a bit complicated; however, through the use of eigenvectors and eigenvalues, many mathematical problems that are extremely difficult can be transformed into a simpler version by taking advantage of the properties listed in this section.

13.5 OGY Control

We are now finally ready to discuss the control strategy introduced by Ott, Grebogi, and Yorke. We will derive the OGY control law for a generic two-dimensional chaotic system. The derivation may seem complicated; however, other than the four topics that we discussed in the earlier sections, the only math that we need to derive the control law is algebra. Nevertheless, you should consult Table 13.1 when needed, which lists the mathematical terms used throughout this section.

Let the chaotic system that we want to control be described by $\mathbf{x}_{t+1} = \mathbf{f}(\mathbf{x}_t, p_t)$, where $\mathbf{x}_t$ is the current state, $\mathbf{x}_{t+1}$ is the next state, and p_t is a scalar control parameter, sort of like a knob, that we can set to any value we want within a small range. Since this is a two-dimensional system, all of the vector terms are (2×1) column vectors. The system, $\mathbf{f}$, may be an iterated map, or it may represent a delayed coordinate embedding. We don't care which, since in many ways discrete maps and delayed coordinate embeddings of continuous systems are equivalent.

Controlling Cardiac Chaos **Digression 13.1**

One of the more exciting areas in which chaos theory is being used is in the control of cardiac chaos. In 1992 Alan Garfinkel, Mark Spano, William Ditto, and James Weiss (GSDW) performed a remarkable experiment with a piece of rabbit ventricle. GSDW first placed the heart tissue in a solution with a small amount of drug capable of inducing arrhythmia in the heart tissue. Initially the heart tissue beat at a regular interval; however, in short order the tissue began to beat in a period-2 pattern, then a period-4, and eventually it fell into a totally aperiodic pattern.

If the heart tissue was behaving normally, then the interbeat interval would be approximately constant. GSDW decided to look at a state-space plot of the interval at time t versus time $t+1$. Through numerical calculations, they were able to determine that the viewed state space had both a stable direction and an unstable direction.

The control strategy used by GSDW was the following modified version of the OGY control law. Given an interbeat interval, I_t, attempt to select the next interbeat interval, I_{t+1}, such that the pair (I_t, I_{t+1}) is as close to the stable location of the state space as possible. Then, with a small electrical pulse, induce a premature beat to correspond with the interval I_{t+1}. Notice that this control strategy is unidirectional, in that a premature beat can be induced but it is not possible to prolong a beat. In any event, GSDW were able to coerce the heart tissue back into periodic behavior, with only small control forces.

By definition, $\mathbf{f}(\mathbf{x}_t, p_t)$ must have at least one fixed point embedded within its chaotic attractor, which we will denote by $\mathbf{x}_F$. Let's agree that our real goal is to tune p_t so as to force the chaotic system into $\mathbf{x}_F$. What we really need is a simplified model of the dynamics of $\mathbf{f}(\mathbf{x}_t, p_t)$ when $\mathbf{x}_t$ is near $\mathbf{x}_F$. Therefore, we need to compute the Taylor expansion of $\mathbf{f}(\mathbf{x}_t, p_t)$ about the point $\mathbf{x}_F$:

$$\begin{aligned} \mathbf{x}_{t+1} &\approx \mathbf{f}(\mathbf{x}_F, 0) + \mathbf{A}(\mathbf{x}_t - \mathbf{x}_F) + \mathbf{b}p_t \\ &\approx \mathbf{x}_F + \mathbf{A}(\mathbf{x}_t - \mathbf{x}_F) + \mathbf{b}p_t. \end{aligned}$$

Here, $\mathbf{A}$ is the Jacobian matrix of $\mathbf{f}$ and $\mathbf{b}$ is the partial derivative of $\mathbf{f}$ with respect to p_t, both evaluated at the fixed point. Let's now assume that we want p_t to be a linear function of $(\mathbf{x}_t - \mathbf{x}_F)$, that is, $p_t = \mathbf{k}^T(\mathbf{x}_t - \mathbf{x}_F)$; thus, $\mathbf{k}$ defines the control law that we will use. It is now helpful to rewrite the Taylor expansion above as

$$\begin{aligned} \mathbf{x}_{t+1} &\approx \mathbf{x}_F + \mathbf{A}(\mathbf{x}_t - \mathbf{x}_F) + \mathbf{b}\mathbf{k}^T(\mathbf{x}_t - \mathbf{x}_F) \\ \mathbf{x}_{t+1} - \mathbf{x}_F &\approx (\mathbf{A} + \mathbf{b}\mathbf{k}^T)(\mathbf{x}_t - \mathbf{x}_F). \end{aligned}$$

This may look like a mess, but the problem of choosing a good $\mathbf{k}$ can now be more easily discussed. Looking at the equation above, our real goal is to make

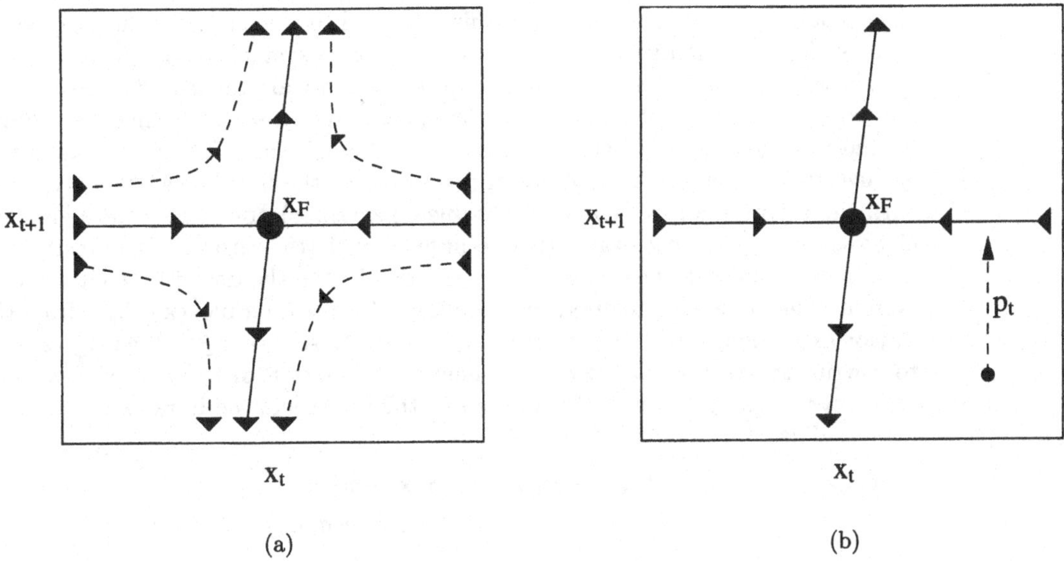

Figure 13.4 An embedded unstable fixed point: (a) the stable and unstable eigenvectors shown simultaneously attracting and repelling state trajectories (b) at time t, we influence $\mathbf{x}_{t+1}$ with a choice of p_t that moves the point defined by $(\mathbf{x}_t, \mathbf{x}_{t+1})$ closer to the stable path

$(\mathbf{x}_{t+1} - \mathbf{x}_F)$ as small a vector as possible, since we want the next state, $\mathbf{x}_{t+1}$, to be equal to the fixed point, $\mathbf{x}_F$. Let's rewrite the last equation yet another time by making the substitutions $\mathbf{C} = \mathbf{A} + \mathbf{b}\mathbf{k}^T$ and $\mathbf{d}_t = \mathbf{x}_t - \mathbf{x}_F$, to get $\mathbf{d}_{t+1} = \mathbf{C}\mathbf{d}_t$. Since our goal is for $\mathbf{d}_{t+1}$ to be as small as possible, suppose that $\mathbf{d}_t$ is equal to one of the eigenvectors of $\mathbf{C}$, thus giving $\lambda_i \mathbf{e}_i = \mathbf{C}\mathbf{e}_i$. If the eigenvalue, λ_i, is smaller than 1, then iterating $\mathbf{d}_{t+1} = \mathbf{C}\mathbf{d}_t$ will force $\mathbf{d}_{t+1}$ to go to 0. If λ_i is greater than 1, then iterating $\mathbf{d}_{t+1} = \mathbf{C}\mathbf{d}_t$ will force the system to explode in size.

We are now ready to reveal the secret to OGY's control technique: For all chaotic systems, and for any embedded fixed point, the Jacobian matrix evaluated at a fixed point, $\mathbf{A}$, must have at least one eigenvalue greater than 1 and one eigenvalue less than 1. Why? The unstable fixed point can be likened to Figure 13.4a, which shows two hypothetical eigenvectors, one leading toward the fixed point and the other leading away. Let's imagine that instead of having one direction that is repelling and the other that is attracting, both are attracting. If this were the case, then the fixed point would, in fact, be stable and attracting and this would not be a chaotic attractor, but a simple fixed point attractor. Similarly, if the fixed point were repelling in every direction, then the fixed point would not be embedded within the chaotic attractor. Also note that this is related to the discussion in Chapter 10 on how chaotic dynamical systems stretch and fold a system's state space.

We will now see how this fact can be mathematically exploited. Recall that any vector can be rewritten as a linear combination of a set of eigenvectors. Since we have already agreed that $\mathbf{x}_t$ is a (2×1) column vector, let's refer to the two eigenvectors of the Jacobian, $\mathbf{A}$, as $\mathbf{e}_s$ and $\mathbf{e}_u$, with the first being the eigenvector with the eigenvalue less than 1 (the *s*table eigenvector) and the second being the eigenvector with the eigenvalue that is larger than 1 (the *u*nstable eigenvector).

When p_t equals 0, the system $\mathbf{f}(\mathbf{x}_t, p_t)$ is identical to the uncontrolled dynamical system. Therefore, let's temporarily drop the subexpression $\mathbf{bk}^T(\mathbf{x}_t - \mathbf{x}_F)$ from the Taylor expansion, to get the iteration $\mathbf{x}_{t+1} - \mathbf{x}_F \approx \mathbf{A}(\mathbf{x}_t - \mathbf{x}_F)$. Finally, we need to rewrite the vector $(\mathbf{x}_t - \mathbf{x}_F)$ as a linear combination of the two eigenvectors: $(\mathbf{x}_t - \mathbf{x}_F) = (a_s\mathbf{e}_s + a_u\mathbf{e}_u)$. Putting all of this together, the iterates can now be expressed as

$$\begin{aligned}(\mathbf{x}_{t+1} - \mathbf{x}_F) &= \mathbf{A}(\mathbf{x}_t - \mathbf{x}_F) \\ &= \mathbf{A}(a_s\mathbf{e}_s + a_u\mathbf{e}_u) \\ &= a_s\lambda_s\mathbf{e}_s + a_u\lambda_u\mathbf{e}_u,\end{aligned}$$

with the λ terms being the stable and unstable eigenvalues. What does all of this mean? Suppose that we could magically make $a_u\lambda_u\mathbf{e}_u$ go away. In this case, the iterates will tend toward 0 because λ_s is less than 1; thus, an effective control strategy could consist entirely of doing our best to make $(\mathbf{x}_t - \mathbf{x}_F)$ as similar to $\mathbf{e}_s$ and as dissimilar to $\mathbf{e}_u$ as possible.

To do this, we have to pull one more mathematical trick so as to define exactly what we mean by "similar" and "dissimilar." Let $\mathbf{g}_s$ and $\mathbf{g}_u$ form a contravariant basis of $\mathbf{e}_s$ and $\mathbf{e}_u$ such that $\mathbf{g}_s^T\mathbf{e}_s = \mathbf{g}_u^T\mathbf{e}_u = 1$ and $\mathbf{g}_s^T\mathbf{e}_u = \mathbf{g}_u^T\mathbf{e}_s = 0$. If $(\mathbf{x}_t - \mathbf{x}_F)$ is dissimilar to $\mathbf{e}_u$, then $\mathbf{g}_u^T(\mathbf{x}_t - \mathbf{x}_F)$ will be close to 0. Therefore, our goal will be to choose $\mathbf{k}$ such that the next iterate is closer to $\mathbf{e}_s$ than it was before.

To compute a good choice for $\mathbf{k}$, we need to go back to the equation

$$\mathbf{x}_{t+1} - \mathbf{x}_F \approx (\mathbf{A} + \mathbf{bk}^T)(\mathbf{x}_t - \mathbf{x}_F).$$

Let's now specify that we want $\mathbf{g}_u^T(\mathbf{x}_{t+1} - \mathbf{x}_F)$ to be equal to 0 (making the next iterate dissimilar to $\mathbf{e}_u$), which gives us

$$\mathbf{g}_u^T(\mathbf{A} + \mathbf{bk}^T)(\mathbf{x}_t - \mathbf{x}_F) = 0.$$

Rewriting the Jacobian as $\mathbf{A} = \lambda_s\mathbf{e}_s\mathbf{g}_s^T + \lambda_u\mathbf{e}_u\mathbf{g}_u^T$ and combining this with the last equation allows us to simplify the expression as follows:

$$\begin{aligned}\mathbf{g}_u^T(\mathbf{A} + \mathbf{bk}^T)(\mathbf{x}_t - \mathbf{x}_F) &= 0 \\ &\vdots \\ \mathbf{k} &= -\frac{\lambda_u\mathbf{g}_u}{\mathbf{g}_u^T\mathbf{b}}.\end{aligned}$$

Therefore, by using this choice of $\mathbf{k}$, we could, in theory, coerce a two-dimensional chaotic system into its fixed point. Figure 13.4b shows how this choice of $\mathbf{k}$ will force the state of the chaotic system on to the path defined by the stable eigenvector, thus coercing the system into a state that is more likely to naturally fall into the fixed point on the next time step. In the next section, we will turn theory into practice by using this last equation to control the Hénon map.

13.6 Controlling the Hénon Map

The main purpose of this section is to explain the results of controlling the Hénon map with the OGY control law. Secondary to this task is the description of the low-level details of how to compute the control law, $\mathbf{k}$. If you have no intention of ever duplicating the numerical experiments in this chapter, please feel free to skip the remaining mathematical digressions. Nevertheless, a full description of how to apply the OGY technique to the Hénon map is given, specifically for those who wish to duplicate the work within this section.

With that disclaimer in mind, recall that the dynamics of the Hénon map are described by

$$\mathbf{f}(x_t, y_t) = \begin{bmatrix} a - x_t^2 + by_t \\ x_t \end{bmatrix},$$

and that the unstable fixed point is located at

$$x_F = \frac{1}{2}\left(b - 1 + \sqrt{(b-1)^2 + 4a}\right) = 0.838486\cdots.$$

In order to use the OGY control technique, we must know the values of λ_u, $\mathbf{g}_u$, and $\mathbf{b}$, which, in turn, requires that we compute $\mathbf{A}$ (the Jacobian matrix), $\mathbf{e}_u$, $\mathbf{e}_s$, and λ_s. We already computed $\mathbf{A}$ earlier in this chapter, and $\mathbf{b}$ is simple to compute:

$$\mathbf{A} = \begin{bmatrix} -2x_t & b \\ 1 & 0 \end{bmatrix} \quad \text{and} \quad \mathbf{b} = \begin{bmatrix} 1 \\ 0 \end{bmatrix}.$$

The remaining terms can be solved for by exploiting the properties of the eigenvectors. First, by using the fact that $\mathbf{A}\mathbf{e}_u = \lambda_u \mathbf{e}_u$ and $\mathbf{A}\mathbf{e}_s = \lambda_s \mathbf{e}_s$, we can compute λ_u as $-x_F - \sqrt{x_F^2 + B}$ and λ_s as $x_F - \sqrt{x_F^2 + B}$. With the eigenvalues now being known and using the fact that the eigenvector must be unit length, we can compute the eigenvectors as

$$\mathbf{e}_u = (\lambda_u^2 + 1)^{-\frac{1}{2}} \begin{bmatrix} \lambda_u \\ 1 \end{bmatrix} \quad \text{and} \quad \mathbf{e}_s = (\lambda_s^2 + 1)^{-\frac{1}{2}} \begin{bmatrix} \lambda_s \\ 1 \end{bmatrix}.$$

Last, we compute the unstable contravariant basis vector, which requires that we reference specific components of the other vectors; thus, let the notation e_{u1} denote

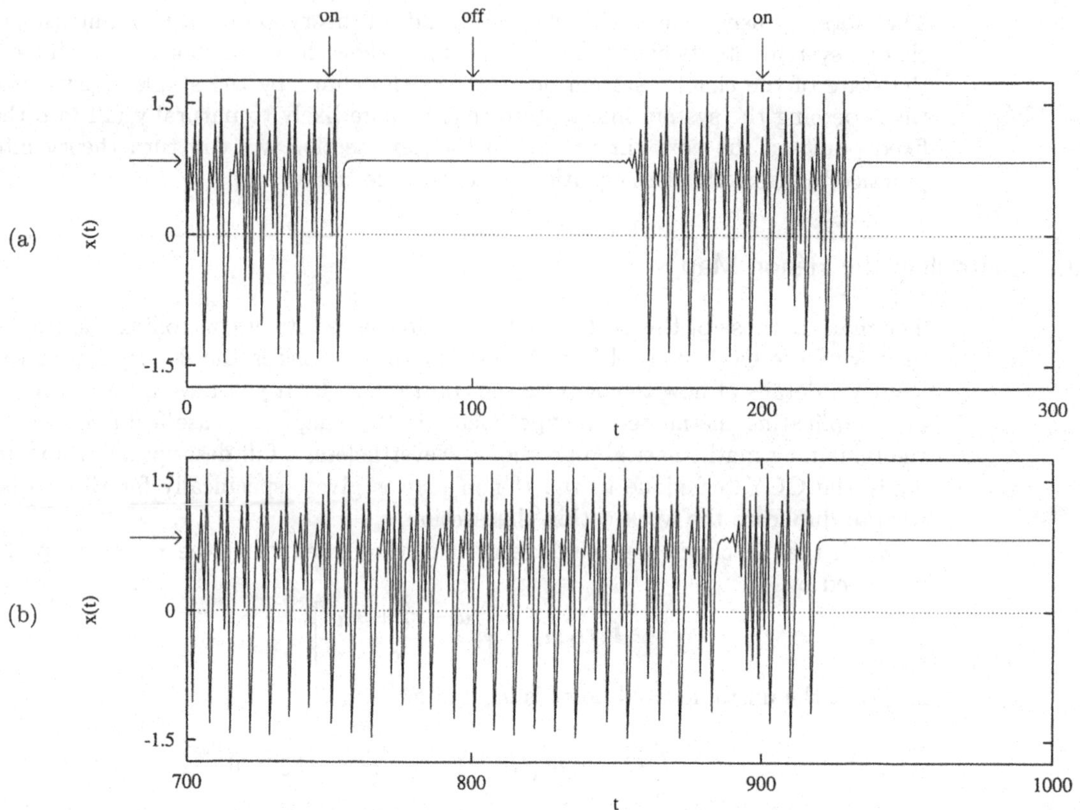

Figure 13.5 Controlling the Hénon map with p^* equal to (a) 0.2 and (b) 0.01

the first element of $\mathbf{e}_u$, and let's agree to use similar notation for the other vectors, as needed. We can then express the unstable contravariant basis vector as

$$\mathbf{g}_u = \begin{bmatrix} (e_{u1} - e_{s1}e_{u2}/e_{s2})^{-1} \\ -g_{u1}e_{s1}/e_{s2} \end{bmatrix}.$$

With this last vector, we can now use the equation $\mathbf{k} = -\lambda_u \mathbf{g}_u / \mathbf{g}_u^T \mathbf{b}$ to derive the control law.

This ends the mathematical presentations for this chapter. The remaining task in this section is to describe the experimental constraints. You may recall that one of our initially stated goals was to find a control law that would work with only small perturbations. Therefore, let's adopt the following rule: If the absolute value

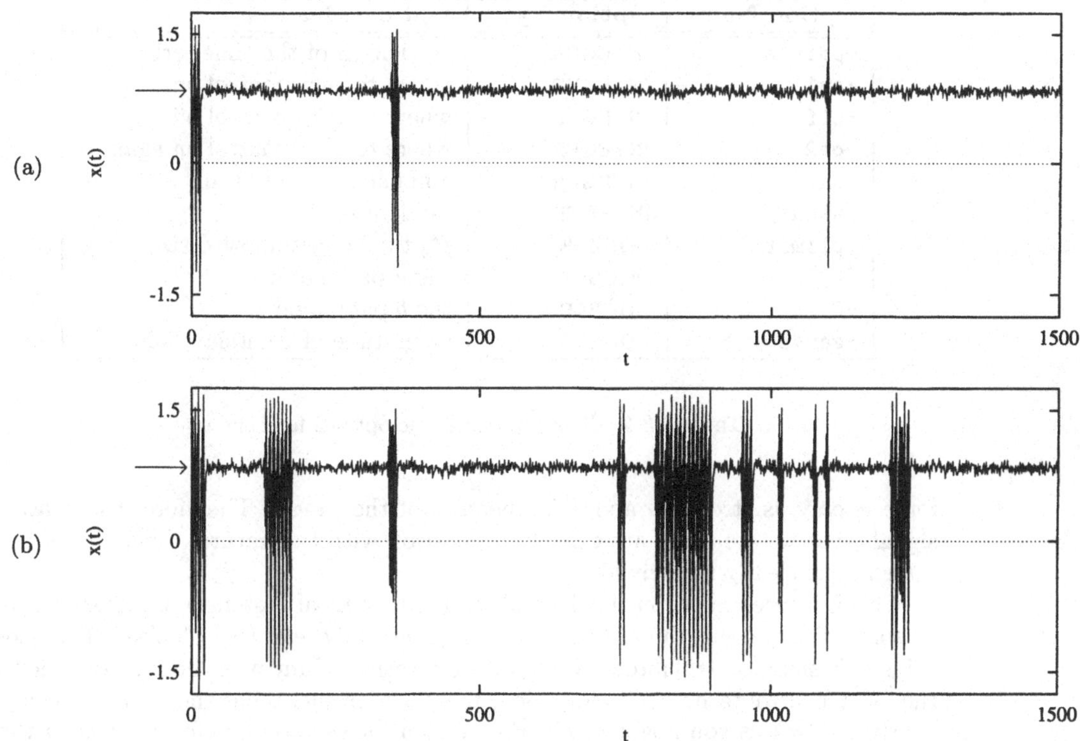

Figure 13.6 Controlling the Hénon map in the presence of noise (δ equal to (a) 0.035 and (b) 0.04, p^* equal to 0.2)

of p_t is ever larger than some small positive constant, p^*, we will use a p_t of 0. We can restate this rule mathematically as

$$p_t = \begin{cases} 0 & \text{if} \, |\mathbf{k}^T(\mathbf{x}_t - \mathbf{x}_F)| \geq p^* \\ \mathbf{k}^T(\mathbf{x}_t - \mathbf{x}_F) & \text{otherwise} \end{cases} .$$

Figure 13.5 shows two plots for controlling the Hénon map with p^* equal to 0.2 and 0.01, respectively. In the first plot, the control signal is turned on and off at multiple locations so as to illustrate how long it takes to establish control and how long it takes for the uncontrolled Hénon map to diverge away from the fixed point. In the second plot, we attempt to control the system at all times, but show only the last 300 time steps of a 1000-step run. With p^* equal to 0.2, we are allowed to influence the trajectory of the Hénon map by an amount that is approximately equal to 10 percent of the range of the system. With p^* equal to 0.01, our control

Option Name	Option Type	Option Meaning
`-points`	INTEGER	the length of the time series
`-on1`	INTEGER	where to turn control on
`-off`	INTEGER	where to turn control off
`-on2`	INTEGER	where to turn control on again
`-skip`	INTEGER	amount to skip initially
`-seed`	INTEGER	random seed
`-plimit`	DOUBLE	p^*, the largest allowed size for p_t
`-A`	DOUBLE	the a parameter
`-B`	DOUBLE	the b parameter
`-gauss`	DOUBLE	magnitude of Gaussian noise

Table 13.2 The command-line options for **hencon**

force is only as strong as about 0.5 percent of the range. Therefore, the control signals that we are using are tiny in comparison with the natural dynamics of the system, but clearly not trivial.

This is a nice result, but in the real world, dynamical systems are influenced by all sorts of extraneous things that engineers generically refer to as "noise." If we are using only small control forces, wouldn't the presence of any noise be catastrophic to the OGY control technique? Noise does present a problem, but the situation is not nearly as bleak as you might think. Figure 13.6 shows two plots for controlling the Hénon map in the presence of noise, with p^* set to 0.2 for both plots. The amount of noise is controlled by a single parameter, δ, that is multiplied by the output of a Gaussian random number generator that has zero mean and unit variance. For the first plot, we have set δ equal to 0.035, and in the second plot δ is set to 0.04. In both cases, the magnitude of the noise is smaller than the magnitude of the control force, but it is certainly not so small as to be insignificant. Nevertheless, the OGY control law does a pretty fair job of suppressing the chaos.

13.7 Further Exploration

You can perform some control experiments yourself with the **hencon** program. The command-line arguments are listed in Table 13.2. You will probably want to use the **-gauss** and **-plimit** options to change the magnitude of the noise and the allowed size of the control force. With the **-on1**, **-on2**, and **-off** options you can select two points to turn the control on, and one place to turn control off. The values of these options must obey the relationship 0 ≤ **on1** ≤ **off** ≤ **on2** ≤ **points**. If you want to have control on at all times, simply set **on1**, **off**, and **on2** all to 0.

13.8 Further Reading

Doyle, J. C., Francis, B. A., & Tannenbaum, A. R. (1992). *Feedback control theory.* New York: MacMillan.

Garfinkel, A., Spano, M. L., & Ditto, W. L. (1992). Controlling cardiac chaos. *Science*, 257(5074): 1230.

Ott, E., Grebogi, C., & Yorke, J. A. (1990). Controlling chaos. *Phys. Rev. Lett.*, 64(11): 1196–1199.

Ott, E., Sauer, T., & Yorke, J. A. (1994). *Coping with chaos.* New York: Wiley.

Strang, G. (1980). *Linear algebra and its applications.* San Diego: Harcourt Brace Jovanovich.

Vanecek, A. & Celikovsky, S. (1996). *Control systems: From linear analysis to synthesis of chaos.* New York: Prentice-Hall.

Wiener, N. (1948). *Cybernetics, or control and communication in the animal and the machine.* New York: John Wiley.

14 Postscript: Chaos

Order is not sufficient. What is required, is something much more complex. It is order entering upon novelty; so that the massiveness of order does not degenerate into mere repetition; and so that the novelty is always reflected upon a background of system.
— Alfred North Whitehead

Nothing in Nature is random. ... A thing appears random only through the incompleteness of our knowledge.
— Benedict Spinoza

God has put a secret art into the forces of Nature so as to enable it to fashion itself out of chaos into a perfect world system.
— Immanuel Kant

PRIOR TO THE discovery of chaos, determinism and randomness were believed to be mutually exclusive principles. Today, we know that this is not the case. The uncertainty introduced by chaos is disturbing enough that scientists and philosophers have had to rethink what it means for something to be random. In the strictest sense of the word, randomness is used to describe events that appear to be nondeterministic; for example, quantum-level events appear to fall into this category. Yet chaos introduces a type of phenomenon that is effectively random even though it is deterministic.

In one sense, we have a form of randomness due to the intricate folding of the state space of a system that occurs over time. This is the same property that makes long-term prediction of chaos impossible because of the inevitable magnification of measurement errors. This is certainly an interesting form of uncertainty, but it does not tell the whole story. In another sense, chaotic systems are close cousins to systems that can compute. In some cases, it is possible to cast a chaotic system into a type of computing system. Doing so reveals how the random-like uncertainty due to chaos is closely related to the uncertainty due to incomputability.

The point that we will make is that chaos is actually a little more pathological than you would think. Not only does chaos introduce uncertainty from a practical point of view, but chaotic systems that can compute possess all of the incomputable properties of traditional models of computation. So not only is long-term prediction impossible with imperfect knowledge, but prediction may be hopeless even with perfect knowledge of a system's initial conditions.

In this third postscript, we will compare and contrast chaos, randomness, and incomputability. Surprisingly, there are many different connections between the three different topics that imply that all can be viewed as being different incarnations of the others.

14.1 Chaos and Randomness

The logistic map from Chapter 10 is an elegant example of chaos precisely because it is so simple. There exists a related one-dimensional map known as the "tent map" that can be transformed to and from the logistic map in such a way that the two maps can be clearly seen to be mathematically equivalent. This is a useful exercise because it is easy to show that the tent map yields behavior that is effectively equivalent to a coin toss. Hence, by moving from the logistic map, to the tent map, to a coin toss, we can more clearly see how chaos is related to randomness.

For the purposes of this discussion, let the logistic map (with r fixed at 1) be written as $L(x) = 4x(1-x)$. The tent map, $T(x)$, is defined as $2x$ for $0 \le x < \frac{1}{2}$ and $2(1-x)$ for $\frac{1}{2} \le x \le 1$; thus, the tent map forms a simple tent-like structure that has a peak at $\frac{1}{2}$. Since the logistic map is a smooth parabola while the tent map is piecewise linear with a discontinuous bend in the middle, it is not at all obvious at first glance how the two maps can be equivalent. However, there exists a relatively simple transformation function, $f(x)$, that has an inverse, $f^{-1}(x)$, and yields the two identities $L(x) = f^{-1}(T(f(x)))$ and $T(x) = f(L(f^{-1}(x)))$. Hence, the logistic map can be perfectly expressed in a form that is equal to the tent map, and vice versa.[1] In other words, even if you never knew the mathematical form of the logistic map, for any starting condition, x_0, you could compute any x_t by using only $T(x)$, $f(x)$, and $f^{-1}(x)$, and never making reference to $L(x)$. This also means that whatever we discover about one map applies directly to the other because they are equivalent.

To see how the tent map behaves over long stretches of time, we could compute successive iterates for the tent map just as we did for the logistic map in Chapter 10, but it turns out that there is an easier way of understanding what long-term iterates the tent map will produce for a particular starting condition. The technique requires us to rewrite input values in the tent map in binary form.[2] For example, assuming

[1] The transformation is $f(x) = \frac{2}{\pi}\sin^{-1}(\sqrt{x})$ with $f^{-1}(x) = \sin^2(\frac{\pi}{2}x)$.

[2] Section 5.1 on page 62 explains how fractions can be rewritten in other bases.

that the inputs are always between 0 and 1, we can rewrite any value for x as $0.b_1b_2b_3\cdots$ where b_i is the ith binary digit in the binary expansion. We will now see how $T(x)$ transforms such a number.

To compute $T(x)$, we need to know if x is less than $\frac{1}{2}$, which is easy to check for in binary notation. If x is less than $\frac{1}{2}$, then b_1 in the expansion will always be equal to 0. If b_1 is equal to 1, then x must be at least as large as $\frac{1}{2}$.

Now let's assume that x is larger than $\frac{1}{2}$. Since we now know what b_1 is, we can rewrite x as $0.1b_2b_3\cdots$. We now need to compute $2(1-x)$. Let's handle the subtraction first. Binary subtraction works just like decimal subtraction except that our task is further simplified by the fact that we are subtracting from 1 which can be written in binary form as $0.1111\cdots$, where the 1s continue forever. This means that $(1-x)$ will be equal to $0.0\bar{b}_2\bar{b}_3\cdots$, where $\bar{b}_i$ is equal to the complement of b_i. As for the multiplication portion of $2(1-x)$, multiplying a binary number by 2 is very similar to multiplying a decimal number by 10. All that is necessary is for us to move the decimal point one position to the right. Thus, for x larger than $\frac{1}{2}$, $T(0.b_1b_2b_3\ldots)$ is equal to $0.\bar{b}_2\bar{b}_3\cdots$. The final effect is to turn all 1s in the binary expansion to 0s, to turn all 0s into 1s, and to throw away the most significant bit in x. For x less than $\frac{1}{2}$, $T(0.b_1b_2b_3\cdots) = 0.b_2b_3\cdots$ because we only need to multiply x by 2.

All of this may seem like superfluous detail, but we can now examine what many successive iterates of $T(x)$ will look like. Suppose that we started out with an initial value for x_0 chosen at an arbitrary location. There are three interesting cases for x_0 that will determine what the long-term behavior of the tent map will look like:

- x_0 is a rational number that can be written in a finite binary decimal expansion, such as, $0.5322265625 = \frac{1}{2} + \frac{1}{32} + \frac{1}{1024} = 0.1000100001$.

- x_0 is a rational number that can be written as an infinite but repeating binary expansion, such as, $0.333251953125\cdots = 0.0101010101\cdots$.

- x_0 is an irrational number that can be written only as an infinite binary expansion that never repeats, such as, $\frac{\pi}{10} = 0.01010000011011\cdots$.

For the first case, we know that successive iterates of the tent map will eventually go to 0 because the leftmost bit will always be removed at each iteration. Eventually, there will be only 0 bits remaining. Consequently, initial conditions that can be described by rational numbers with finite binary expansions will always end up at 0. If x_0 is such a number for the tent map, then $f^{-1}(x_0)$ will converge to 0 when iteratively applied to the logistic map.

In the second case, the repeating periodic cycle in the binary expansion will result in periodic behavior in the tent map. Similarly, $f^{-1}(x_0)$ applied to the logistic map will result in the system converging to an embedded limit cycle.

For the final case, with x_0 being specified by an infinite non-repeating binary expansion, the tent map will never repeat. It will consume a single bit of x_0 at each iteration, but since x_0 has an infinite number of non-repeating bits, it will always be in a different location. The value of $f^{-1}(x_0)$ will yield the same behavior for the logistic map.

In a nutshell, this means that all irrational numbers will result in chaotic behavior if they are used as initial conditions for the logistic map or the tent map. Rational numbers give periodic or fixed point behavior. From the discussion in Chapter 2, we know that rational numbers actually are grossly outnumbered by irrational numbers. So if you were to pick a random number from a uniform distribution between 0 and 1, you would almost be guaranteed to pick an irrational number.

The tent map can be turned into something that resembles a series of coin tosses by means of a simple convention. Suppose we wished to have access to an infinite number of random bits. We use an irrational starting place for the tent map, x_0, and compute x_1. If x_1 is less than $\frac{1}{2}$, then we call the result heads; otherwise, we call it tails. To perform another coin toss, we calculate x_2 and use the same criterion. The resulting sequence of heads and tails, for almost all initial starting conditions, will be indistinguishable from true randomness. And since the logistic map can be trivially transformed into the tent map and back, the long-term behavior of the logistic map is effectively random as well.

14.2 Randomness and Incomputability

In the previous postscript, we briefly looked at algorithmic complexity (AC) as it applies to a notion of "real" or effective complexity. To rehash the idea, the complexity of an object—be it a real number, a set of natural numbers, or a binary string—can be defined as the length of the shortest program that can reproduce the object. Under AC, incompressible objects are said to be random. In this context, consider the set of real numbers between 0 and 1. Every number in this range can be described by a potentially infinite sequence of binary digits that corresponds to the number's binary expansion. Rational numbers will have a binary expansion that either is finite in length or has a pattern that repeats. But note that some irrational numbers, such as $\frac{\pi}{10}$, can also be compactly expressed as a program. Thus, both rational and irrational numbers may be compressible.

But we also know from Chapters 2 and 3 that there are many more real numbers than there are rational numbers. Moreover, computable numbers such as π are also in the minority because each computable irrational number corresponds to a specific program; and since there is only a countable number of such programs, there is only a countable number of computable numbers.

Putting all of this together, randomness, incomputability, and chaos are intertwined in how and why uncertainty becomes manifest in mathematics. If the initial state for the tent or logistic map is a computable number, then another program exists that characterizes any possible future state of these systems for that initial condition—even if it is irrational. But if the initial state of the system cannot be described algorithmically, then the future of these systems becomes indescribable as well. The question "Does the tent map fall into deep chaos?" can be restated as "Can a computer program describe the initial state?"

While these are interesting observations, Gregory Chaitin has added yet another twist to these ideas that casts even greater doubt on our ability to characterize things found in nature. To see where all of this is going, consider the number described by the phrase "the smallest number that cannot be expressed in fewer than thirteen words." The number described by this phrase doesn't exist because the phrase we used to describe it has only twelve words. So if it existed, then it, in fact, could be described by fewer than thirteen words; thus, its very description prohibits its existence. This sentence, known as the Berry Paradox, bears some resemblance to one of the paradoxes from the first postscript in Chapter 4, that is, "This sentence has no proof." Chaitin has described a form of uncertainty that exploits the ideas in the Berry Paradox but also turns out to be a more general version of Turing's and Gödel's incomputability and incompleteness results.

Chaitin's result hinges on the idea that although there are more random (i.e., algorithmically indescribable) numbers than nonrandom numbers, we cannot necessarily tell the random numbers from the nonrandom numbers. For every program that can find and compress patterns in data, there are always going to be strings of data that cannot be compressed even though the strings may be compressible. This is the case because programs are incapable of recognizing patterns that are more complex than the programs.

Put another way, suppose we had a program that looked for the simplest string of numbers that could not be computed by any program of length n. This program has its own length, which we can call n'. If n is less than n', then this program will identify a string that has complexity greater than n but less than n'. However, this program is incapable of producing a string that is more complex than n' because doing so would produce a contradiction: n cannot simultaneously be greater than and less than n'.

In a very strong sense, Chaitin's result is also a statement about the ability of humanity to describe nature. Science as a whole has the goal of providing simple explanations for complex phenomena. Specifically, scientists strive to explain patterns by natural laws that are simpler than the observations. To do this, a scientist will often look for patterns and try to mold old explanations into new ones that fit the new data. However, this process of building explanations is another incarnation of the more general process of algorithmic compression. If an observation for a natural phenomenon is more complex than the algorithmic complexity of our identification procedure, then it is impossible to explain the data by anything more compact than the data themselves.

14.3 Incomputability and Chaos

In the first postscript I briefly mentioned a billiard-ball computer introduced by Edward Fredkin and Tommaso Toffoli. This computer is capable of universal computation because it can emulate the rudiments of digital circuitry through a series of switches modeled after the interactions of billiard balls. In addition to Fredkin and Toffoli's billiard-ball computer, several other types of continuous dynamical systems have been shown to possess the ability to perform universal computation.

Hava Siegelmann and Eduardo Sontag proved that a recurrent artificial neural network (with an infinitely precise irrational synaptic weight) could be made to simulate a Turing machine. Shift maps were shown to be universal computers by Pascal Koiran, Michel Cosnard, and Max Garzon, and by Christopher Moore (who also studied billiard-ball-like models of computation). The interesting thing about all of these models is that whenever a dynamical system is shown to be capable of universal computation, the dynamical system possesses, at least in part, chaotic dynamics. This duality of chaos and computability is primarily a result of the recursive nature of dynamical systems and computing devices. For all of these models of computation, if one were to write a "program" that attempted to answer an incomputable question, such as the Halting Problem, running the resulting program would place all of these systems into a potentially chaotic state. If these chaotic computers happen to halt, then the dynamics for the starting conditions correspond to the attractor of a fixed point. But if the chaotic computer never halts for such a question, then the system has fallen into a chaotic attractor.

Yet the relationship between computation and chaos goes deeper than this. As the examples above partially illustrate, many reasonable questions that one would like to ask about dynamical systems are often undecidable, in the strict sense, from the theory of computation. For example, it is, in general, not possible to definitively say that data come from a chaotic or nonchaotic source. Posing this question for a chaotic computer is akin to solving the Halting Problem. It is not even possible to determine if the state of a chaotic system will ever fall into a specific region of state space. If portions of a state space are known to eventually fall into a fixed point, then knowing this fact is equivalent to solving the Halting Problem. The reason for all of this uncertainty is related to the fact that symbolic mathematics (which can be used to formalize the questions listed above) cannot always make definitive statements about things that exist on a continuum.

Take, for example, the Three Body Problem, mentioned in the first postscript. The Three Body Problem, simply stated, is, given the initial position and velocities of three isolated bodies in space, find a set of equations that perfectly describes the future positions and velocities of the objects. With this equation, you would plug in the length of time into the future that you desired to know about, and the position and velocities of the bodies would have some analytical values based only on the initial conditions and the length of time. Henri Poincaré showed that a general solution to the problem does not exist.

The motion of the bodies can be described by differential equations. The changes in the positions and velocities can be approximated by numerically integrating the differential equations. The integral of the differential equations, which is used to denote the analytical solution to the future values of positions and velocities, cannot be expressed in a closed form. In other words, as most students of calculus eventually find out, integration (or solving an integral) is very hard. Not only is it a difficult task to find the right answer, but it may turn out that no answer exists. Symbolic mathematics, like integral calculus, is a language that can be only as powerful as its alphabet. The alphabet of calculus, being symbolic, is equivalent to the alphabet of the natural numbers. Hence, there are many things that can occur in continuous mathematics that cannot be described by symbolic mathematics precisely because there are more objects in the continuum than there are objects in the symbolic world. In the end, we simply do not have the language to pull it off.

Chaos, then, has properties that are reminiscent of randomness and incomputability. Under some special cases, chaos can be seen to be effectively equivalent to stochastic randomness. For other special cases, chaos is equivalent to the deterministic actions of a computer. The dividing line between the two types of phenomena is the same division that separates the computable function from the incomputable functions.

14.4 Further Reading

Blum, L., Shub, M., & Smale, S. (1988). On a theory of computation over the real numbers; NP completeness, recursive functions and universal machines (extended abstract). In *29th annual symposium on foundations of computer science*, (pp. 387–397)., White Plains, N.Y. IEEE.

Chaitin, G. J. (1997). *The limits of mathematics: A course on information theory & limits of formal reasoning.* Singapore: Springer-Verlag.

Crutchfield, J. P. & Young, K. (1989). Computation at the onset of chaos. In W. Zurek (Ed.), *Complexity, entropy and the physics of information.* Reading, Mass.: Addison-Wesley.

Margolus, N. (1984). Physics-like models of computation. *Physica D*, 10(1–2): 81–95.

Ruelle, D. (1993). *Chance and chaos.* Princeton: Princeton University Press.

IV Complex Systems

Complex systems are things that consist of many similar and simple parts. Often the underlying behavior of any of the parts is easily understood, while the behavior of the system as a whole defies simple explanation. Part of the reason why complex systems can behave in such complicated ways is that some general forms are known to be capable of universal computation. This double-edged result also implies that the future of complex systems cannot be predicted in the general case. By changing the type and form of interactions that exist among the parts of a complex system, the type of global behavior can be varied such that the complex system as a whole can be globally goal-seeking while only local information is passed around by the parts. This means that a collective form of computation can take place without an explicit global algorithm.

Chapter 15 introduces a simple and nearly canonical form of a complex system, known as a *cellular automaton*. Chapter 16 shows how collective systems composed of individual *agents* can demonstrate *self-organized* behavior. Chapter 17 reveals how mixtures of competition and cooperation can produce many different and interesting types of behavior that are seen in nature. Chapter 18 illustrates how a collective form of computation can be performed by feedback *neural networks* with fixed synapses. Finally, Chapter 19 examines how the global form and function of composite objects can be influenced by the parts of the system and the types of interactions permitted.

15 Cellular Automata

If patterns of ones and zeros were "like" patterns of human lives and death, if everything about an individual could be represented in a computer record by a long string of ones and zeros, then what kind of creature would be represented by a long string of lives and deaths?
— Thomas Pynchon

The chess-board is the world; the pieces are the phenomena of the universe; the rules of the game are what we call the laws of Nature.
— T. H. Huxley

WHEREAS CHAOS IS the science of how simple things produce complex behavior, *complexity* is the study of how complex collections of simple units produce a wide variety of behavior. Continuing with the discussion from Chapter 1 on emergent phenomena, examples of complex systems include autocatalytic chemical sets (which may explain the origins of life); cellular regulation through gene excitation and inhibition; multicellular animals; collective "super-organisms" such as ant colonies, bee hives, flocks of birds, schools of fish, and oceanic reefs; and larger collections of organisms such as ecosystems, economies, and societies. Don't be distracted by the fact that I have called each of these complex systems a collection of "simple" things. To be sure, there is nothing simple about a single cell, or about a stock trader, for that matter. The important point is that even if we limit the types of interactions that can occur among agents (thus "simplifying" the essence of what an agent is, relative to its environment), extremely rich and complex behavior can still result.

Also note that the phenomena listed above occur on many different levels—from the molecular level of autocatalytic sets all the way up to the global level of the world economy. In this book part we will be able to sample only a small subset of the many types of complex systems that can be found. Nevertheless, the primary goal of this book part is to provide you with enough detail concerning the nature of complex systems that you will be able to identify and appreciate these same qualities in phenomena that we do not examine explicitly. In this first chapter on

$\Longleftarrow$ Space $\Longrightarrow$

$\Uparrow$ Time $\Downarrow$	$c_{i-r}(t-1)$	$\cdots$	$c_{i-1}(t-1)$	$c_i(t-1)$	$c_{i+1}(t-1)$	$\cdots$	$c_{i+r}(t-1)$
				$c_i(t)$			

Figure 15.1 The neighborhood of a one-dimensional cellular automaton

complex systems, we will examine a type of computing machine known as a cellular automaton (commonly abbreviated as CA), which is a dynamical system that is discrete in both space and time. Our goal here will be to convey a sense of breadth in the types of behavior that can be seen—from simple fixed-point dynamics, to periodic limit cycles, all the way to chaos. In between order and chaos lies a special region sometimes called the "edge of chaos," where true computation may be possible.

The formalism for cellular automata was invented by John von Neumann (with some suggestive help from his close friend Stanislaw Ulam) in the 1940s as a framework in which to study the process of reproduction. Von Neumann was interested in the essence of reproduction and not in any particular implementation of the process. Thus, he purposely abstracted away all of the details of, say, how animals reproduce, and instead concentrated on the simplest mathematical framework that would allow information to reproduce. As with most of his life's work, von Neumann was decades ahead of just about everyone else. Others continued to study CA after von Neumann's premature death from cancer in 1957, but it would be more than a decade before cellular automata attracted widespread attention in the scientific community.

The first type of cellular automaton that we will examine in this chapter is one-dimensional, remarkably simple to describe but capable of all of the types of behavior listed earlier. Afterward, we will look at Conway's Game of Life, a two-dimensional cellular automaton that is capable of emulating any Turing machine, and is therefore capable of universal computation. We will conclude this chapter with a summary of natural phenomena that can be modeled by cellular automata.

15.1 One-Dimensional CA

Imagine a linear grid that extends to the left and right. The grid consists of cells that may be in only one of a finite number of states, k. At each time step, the next state of a cell is computed as a function of its neighbors local in space. We will denote the radius of a cell's relevant neighborhood by r. In Figure 15.1 the $2r$ cells that fall to the immediate left and right of the center cell, i, are shown to form a neighborhood that consists of a total of $2r+1$ cells. We will denote the state of cell

$c_{i-1}(t)$	$c_i(t)$	$c_{i+1}(t)$	$c_i(t+1)$
0	0	0	0
0	0	1	1
0	1	0	1
0	1	1	1
1	0	0	1
1	0	1	1
1	1	0	1
1	1	1	0

Table 15.1 One possible rule table for a one-dimensional CA with $r = 1$ and $k = 2$

i at time t by $c_i(t)$. The index of the cell indicates the position of the cell in the linear grid such that cell $i - 1$ is just to the left of cell i.

The nice thing about one-dimensional CAs is that a lengthy chunk of a CA's history can be characterized on a two-dimensional grid. Moving to the left or right of the grid corresponds to moving in space, while moving up and down on the grid corresponds to looking at a cell's history in time. By convention, we will agree that time flows in a downward direction; thus, the cell immediately below another cell represents the next state.

Considering Figure 15.1 once again, the only cells that are shown are those that have a direct effect on the future state of $c_i(t)$. As a concrete example, imagine that the number of states, k, is equal to 2 and that the radius, r, is equal to 1. Furthermore, let the states be denoted by either a 0 or a 1. We can characterize a deterministic set of rules for a CA's next-state function by a simple lookup table, as shown in Table 15.1.

Table 15.1 essentially defines a *finite-state automaton*. To determine the next state of a cell, we look at the table entry that contains the cell's current state and the state of its two immediate neighbors. Notice that the left three columns of Table 15.1 contain all permutations for a CA with cells with two states and a neighborhood that consists of three cells. It would be possible to have an entirely different rule table for different cells, but even when each cell is constrained to obey the same single rule table, exceptionally interesting behavior can arise. Figure 15.2, below, shows an alternative representation of the CA rules in Table 15.1 that may be a bit more intuitive to understand. In the figure you can see how the state of three cells maps to the next state of the center cell in the neighborhood.

In general, for a CA with a neighborhood size of $2r+1$ and with each cell having the ability to take k possible states, a rule table that completely specifies the next-state function of a cell must have k^{2r+1} entries in it. Thus, for this example with $k = 2$ and $r = 1$, there are $2^3 = 8$ entries in the rule table.

For the last column of Table 15.1, which contains the next-state values for $c_i(t)$, we could have filled in the values with anything we wanted. Since there are eight rows in the table, there are 256 different rule tables that could have been used, which doesn't seem like such a large number, all things considered. However, if we take $k = 10$ and $r = 2$, which intuitively seem like small numbers, then a rule table for this CA would have to have 10^5, or 100,000, entries. The number of legal rule tables will therefore be $10^{100,000}$. To put this number in perspective, there are only about 10^{80} molecules in the universe; thus it is fair to say that there exist a mind-boggling number of CA rule tables that we will never be able to examine simply because there are not enough time and computational resources available in the whole universe to do so.

Table 15.1 is still, perhaps, overly verbose, in that the rule table can be easily compressed if we adopt just one more convention. To see this fact, note that another way of stating the rules in Table 15.1 is the following: If all of the cells in a neighborhood are on or all of the cells in a neighborhood are off, then the next state is off; otherwise, the next state will be on. Taking the sum of the states of the cells in a particular neighborhood, it can be seen that our CA yields a 1 if, and only if, the sum is equal to 1 or 2. Looking once again at Figure 15.2, it is easy to see that this particular interpretation of our rule table is correct; only the two configurations with homogeneous states map to a new state that is off.

If we simplify the set of possible rules such that we consider only the sum of the states in a neighborhood, then our rule tables will dramatically shrink in size and our rules will be invariant in the ordering of the cells. (This means that if we randomly shuffle the cells within a neighborhood, the next state will still be the same, since we are looking only at the sum of the states.) Regarding the size of the rule table, with a radius of r and with k states, we must have $(k-1)(2r+1)+1$ entries (instead of k^{2r+1}) in a rule table to account for each possible sum total. However, even with this simplification, using the example that was used before with $r = 2$ and $k = 10$, there are still 9^{46} unique CA rule tables, which is nothing to sneeze at.

In this section and the sections that follow, we will examine many different CA rule sets. I will never use more than ten states; thus we can safely denote each state by the numbers 0 through 9. Also, since the rule table needs to be only $k(2r+1)$ in length, we can represent the entire rule table by one long decimal number with

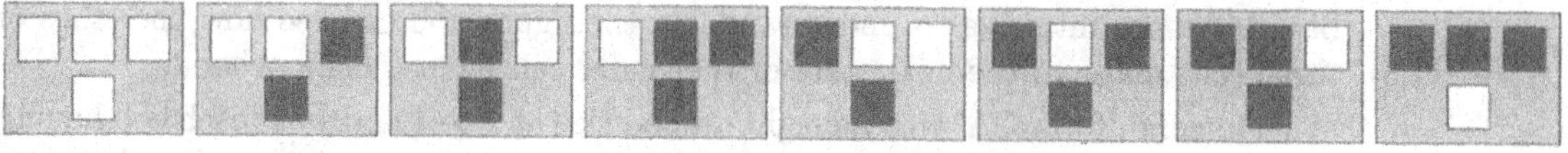

Figure 15.2 A graphical representation of the rules in Table 15.1

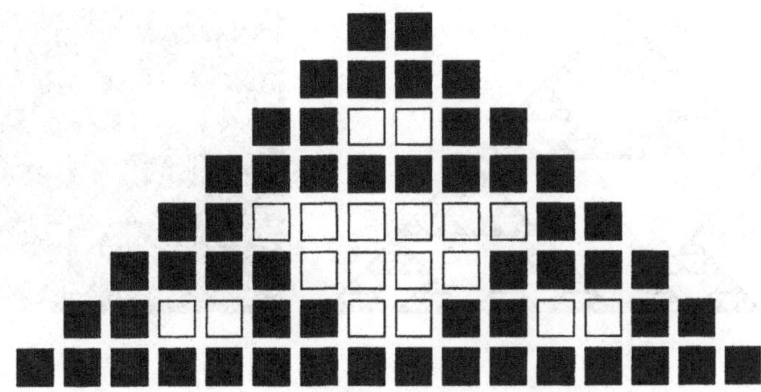

Figure 15.3 The first few steps from simulating the time evolution of Table 15.1

$k(2r+1)$ digits. Rewriting the rule table from Table 15.1 in this manner gives us the string "0110" which obviously is much more compact.

Let's now simulate the first few steps of the time evolution of the cellular automaton specified by the rules in Table 15.1 and Figure 15.2. Using an initial state of "11" as a seed, Figure 15.3 shows the results of running our CA for a few time steps. After one time step the initial seed of "11" doubles in size to form "1111." At the second time step, the two center cells are now victims of overcrowded conditions in that they and their two respective neighbors are on; thus, their next state is to turn off. At this point, you should be able to confirm that each subsequent step in the figure is correct. To further aid in your understanding of how CAs work, you may want to simulate with pencil and paper the same rules from Table 15.1 but with a different starting conditions.

Running a CA on pencil and paper is fine for CAs that are small in area and duration; however, to look at more elaborate CAs we will ultimately need to simulate the time evolution on a computer. Therefore, we will briefly go over some conventions that I have used in the CA software written for this chapter. To completely specify how we are to simulate a particular CA, we need to agree on a size (or width) for the linear array of cells, and the number of time steps (or height) that the CA is to be run. For the height, our choice is limited to a finite number; however, for the width, there are several different ways that we could implement things. The simplest choice for implementing the width would be just to pick a size and leave it at that. The problem with this is that the cells on the two edges may have only half the number of neighbors that the other cells have. One could imagine allowing the array width to grow as new cells are needed, with the assumption that newly added cells are in the off state prior to being added (which is sort of what we did in the Figure 15.3), but this presents another set of problems from an implementation point of view. A common convention—and one that we will use

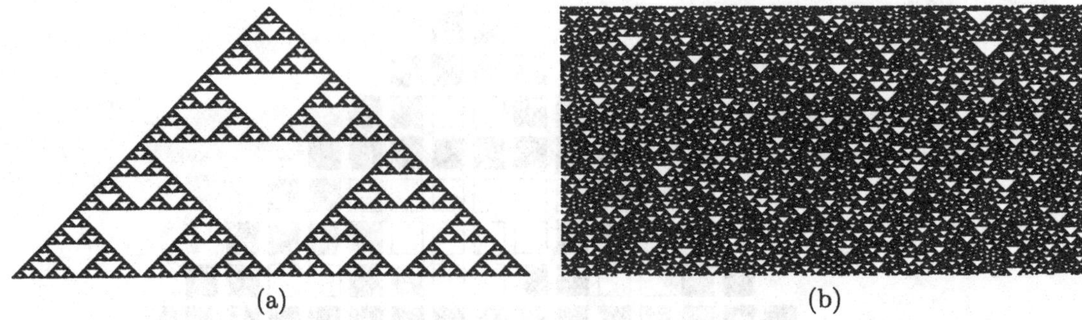

(a) (b)

Figure 15.4 Two time evolution histories for the CA described by Table 15.1: (a) the initial state consists of all zeros except for the two center cells being on (b) a random initial state is used

almost without exception—is to allow cells on one edge to be the neighbors of the cells on the opposite edge, thus forming a ring of cells. This is a nice solution to the problem, since it allows each cell to have the same number of neighbors, and can be implemented on a grid with a predetermined area.

The final thing that we need to specify is the initial state of all the cells in the ring. Two common strategies are to use either a random assignment of states to cells or to start almost all of the cells in the off state and allow a few cells to be on so as to form an initial seed (as in Figure 15.3). Figure 15.4 shows both of these techniques for the CA described by Table 15.1, with a grid width of 512 and 256 time steps shown. The plot on the left is an extension of Figure 15.3, which you may wish to compare with the Sierpinski triangles from Figure 6.10 on page 90. The plot on the right shows the results of running the same CA rule table with a random initial condition.

15.2 Wolfram's CA Classification

In the 1980s Stephen Wolfram almost single-handedly resurrected cellular automata research, giving the subject a firm mathematical analysis that rivaled any other contribution to CA research at the time. Wolfram is a physicist by training, and most of his work on cellular automata is far too detailed to adequately describe in this book; however, I will describe the gist of one aspect of Wolfram's contributions to the subject of CA. During the 1980s, Wolfram's research was primarily concerned with one-dimensional CAs, as described in the last section. One of his contributions was to establish four different CA classes. Before we take a close look Wolfram's classification scheme, let's briefly review the theoretical limits of the types of patterns that can be generated from one-dimensional CAs.

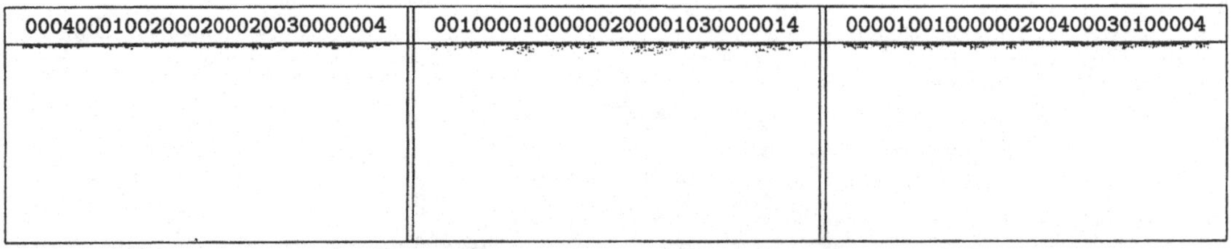

00040001002000200020030000004 | 00100001000000200001030000014 | 00001001000000200400030100004

Figure 15.5 Examples of Wolfram's Class I

With a ring consisting of n cells and k possible cell states, there are at most k^n unique configurations of a row of cells. For all but trivial cases this number will be extremely large—easily more than the number of electrons in the universe—but finite. Even though the legal state space of the CA as a whole is enormous, the fact that it is finite implies that for any one-dimensional CA with a finite state space, if we were to run it long enough, the CA would eventually have to repeat itself. Don't be too impressed by this fact, since we could say the same thing about your home computer as well.

With that disclaimer said, we are now ready to examine Wolfram's classification scheme, which consists of four classes:

- *Class I.* CAs in the first class always evolve to a homogeneous arrangement, with every cell being in the same state, never to change again.
- *Class II.* CAs in the second class form periodic structures that endlessly cycle through a fixed number of states.
- *Class III.* CAs in the third class form "aperiodic," random-like patterns that are a lot like the static white noise on a bad television channel.
- *Class IV.* CAs in the fourth class form complex patterns with localized structure that move through space in time. The patterns must eventually become homogeneous, like Class I, or periodic, like Class II.

Figures 15.5, 15.6, 15.7, and 15.8 show examples of the four classes. In each figure, the long number strings on the top of the plots denote the rule table used. You can plug the rule string into the program **ca**, which I used for all of these figures, as described at the end of this chapter.

There are some interesting analogies that we can make between the behavior of CAs and the topics covered in the rest of this book. Class I CAs are very much like trivial programs that halt after only a few execution steps. Class I CAs are also similar to dynamical systems that fall into a fixed point attractor, discussed in Chapter 10. In either case, the behavior of the system is simple and not very interesting, but serves as an example of one extremity of the range of CA behavior.

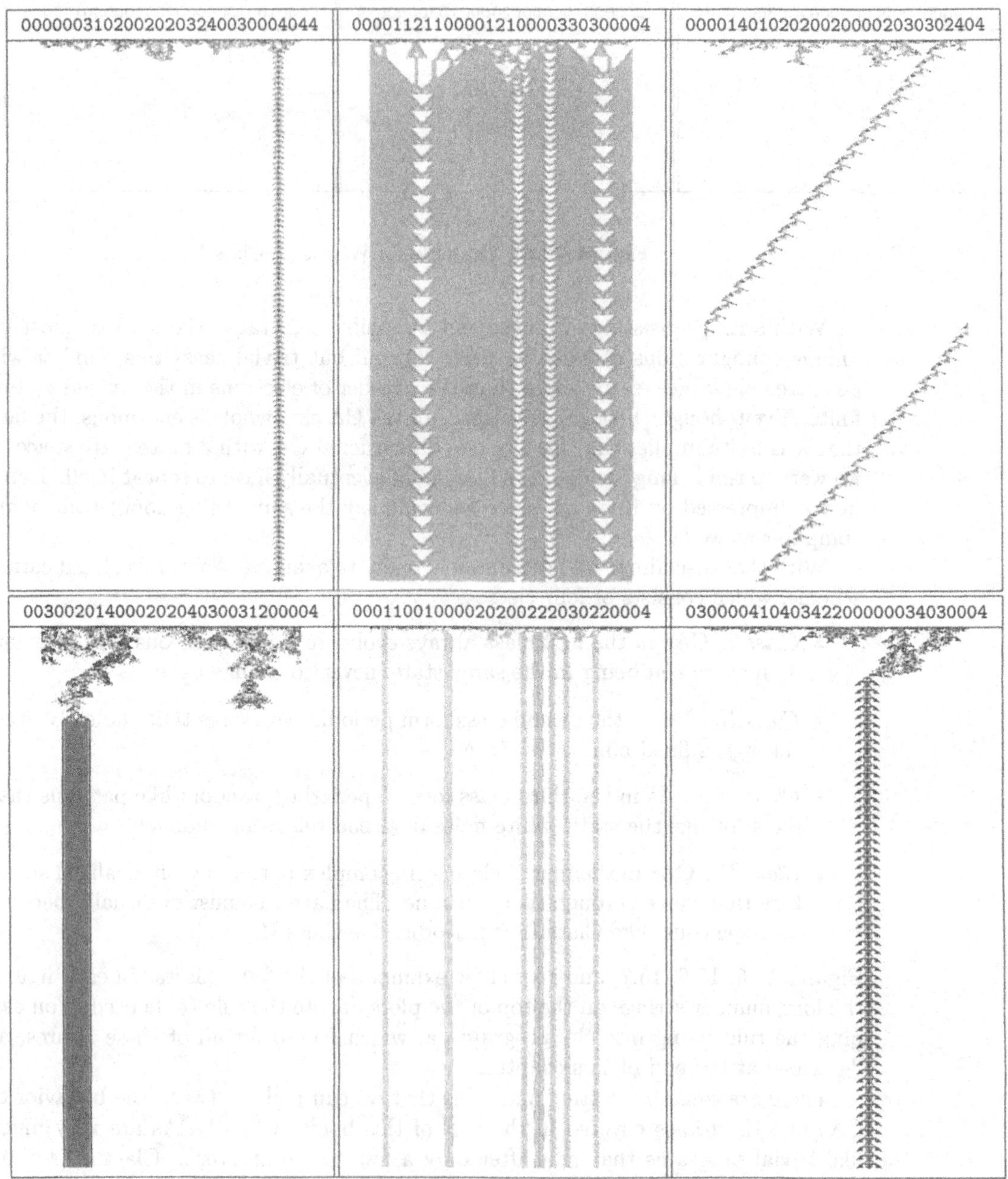

Figure 15.6 Examples of Wolfram's Class II

```
while(TRUE) {
  for(i = 0; i < 10; i++)
    print("%d\n", i);
}
```

```
i = 0;
while(TRUE) {
  print("%d\n", i);
  i = i + 1;
}
```

(a) (b)

Table 15.2 Two program fragments that are similar to Class II CAs and dynamical systems: (a) simple periodic CA and fixed point dynamical systems (b) unbounded periodic CA and quasiperiodic dynamical systems

Class II CAs are repetitive and bear some resemblance to programs that execute in an infinite loop, or dynamical systems that fall into limit cycles. In Figure 15.6 there are really two distinct types of Class II CAs. The first, second, and fourth through sixth plots in the figure illustrate what I would call "simple periodicity," in that their behaviors can be adequately captured in the finite-sized space. The third plot in the figure differs from the other five in that it continuously wraps around the CA space. It is periodic because we have limited the amount of space in which it can travel to a ring. If we allowed for an infinite amount of space, then the floating structure would fly away forever, never to return to any previous state but always similar to some previous state. I'll refer to this type of Class II CA behavior as "unbounded periodicity." The difference between simple and unbounded periodicity can be better appreciated when compared with program types. Consider the two C program fragments in Table 15.2, which are both designed to fall into an infinite loop.

The program fragment on the left of Table 15.2 will spit out the digits 0 through 9 and then repeat the sequence forever. This program fragment is not unlike the simple periodic Class II CA because the program cycles through a fixed number of states and does so even with a finite amount of memory. The program fragment on the right of Table 15.2 is similar to the unbounded periodic. If a program like this were run on a machine with infinite memory (some theoretical device like a Turing machine), then the program would never repeat and never halt, but forever enumerate the natural numbers. In reality, computers have finite memory, and on a real computer this program fragment would repeat forever, but at a certain point—determined by the precision of the computer's representation of numbers—the program will start to repeat itself when the maximal integer for the computer is reached and then overflows back to 0.

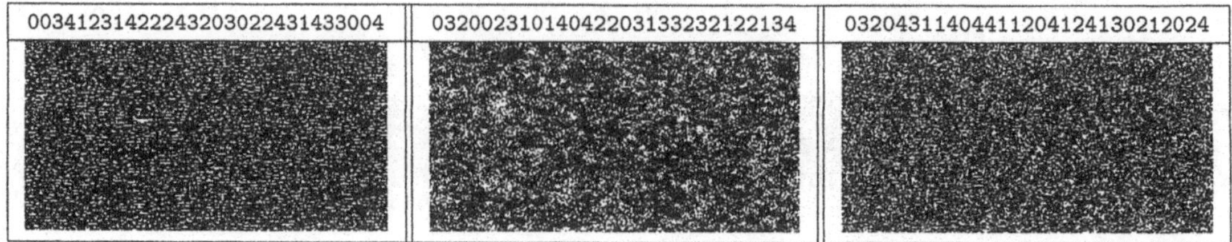

Figure 15.7 Examples of Wolfram's Class III

In the first case we have a pure form of periodicity that is independent of the memory constraints of the underlying computer. If your computer has finite memory or if your cellular automaton operates on a ring of finite space, then you will still get periodicity. In the second case we have periodicity that is a result of the finite nature of the universe. If we could magically create a real Turing machine that had an infinite tape or a CA with an infinite space, then the second type of behavior would no longer be periodic. It is only when space is finite that this second type of periodicity emerges. These two types of periodicities are also analogous to simple periodicity and quasiperiodicity in continuous dynamical systems, since the latter's ability to never strictly repeat itself depends on the density of the real number line.

We next consider Class III CAs, as shown in Figure 15.7. Like Class I, Class III is boring, but for opposite reasons. Whereas Class I CAs fall into boring static configurations, Class III CAs are so random-like that there is little visual appeal to be found in them. Wolfram and others compare Class III to chaotic dynamical systems, which is an interesting comparison for many reasons. First, given a finite space of "reasonable" size, Class III CAs are almost guaranteed to never repeat themselves, and even when the do they can have extremely long cycles. Class III CAs also show sensitivity to initial conditions: If you alter the starting state by just flipping a couple of cells, the resulting behavior will be radically different from what would have emerged otherwise. Finally, Class III CAs are very likely to have embedded limit cycles of short duration; with the right starting state you could force such a system into regular behavior similar to Class II CAs, but like embedded limit cycles in chaotic attractors, the limit cycles will probably be unstable, in that any slight perturbation will force the system back into chaotic behavior.

Drawing a comparison between programs and CAs, Class III is very similar to the types of programs that are pseudo-random number generators. Given an initial seed, a pseudo-random number generator can produce sequences that are so uncorrelated that they easily pass most tests for randomness. With a slightly different starting seed, a pseudo-random number generator will produce a dramatically different sequence, just the way the initial configuration of a Class III CA is sensitive to slight variations.

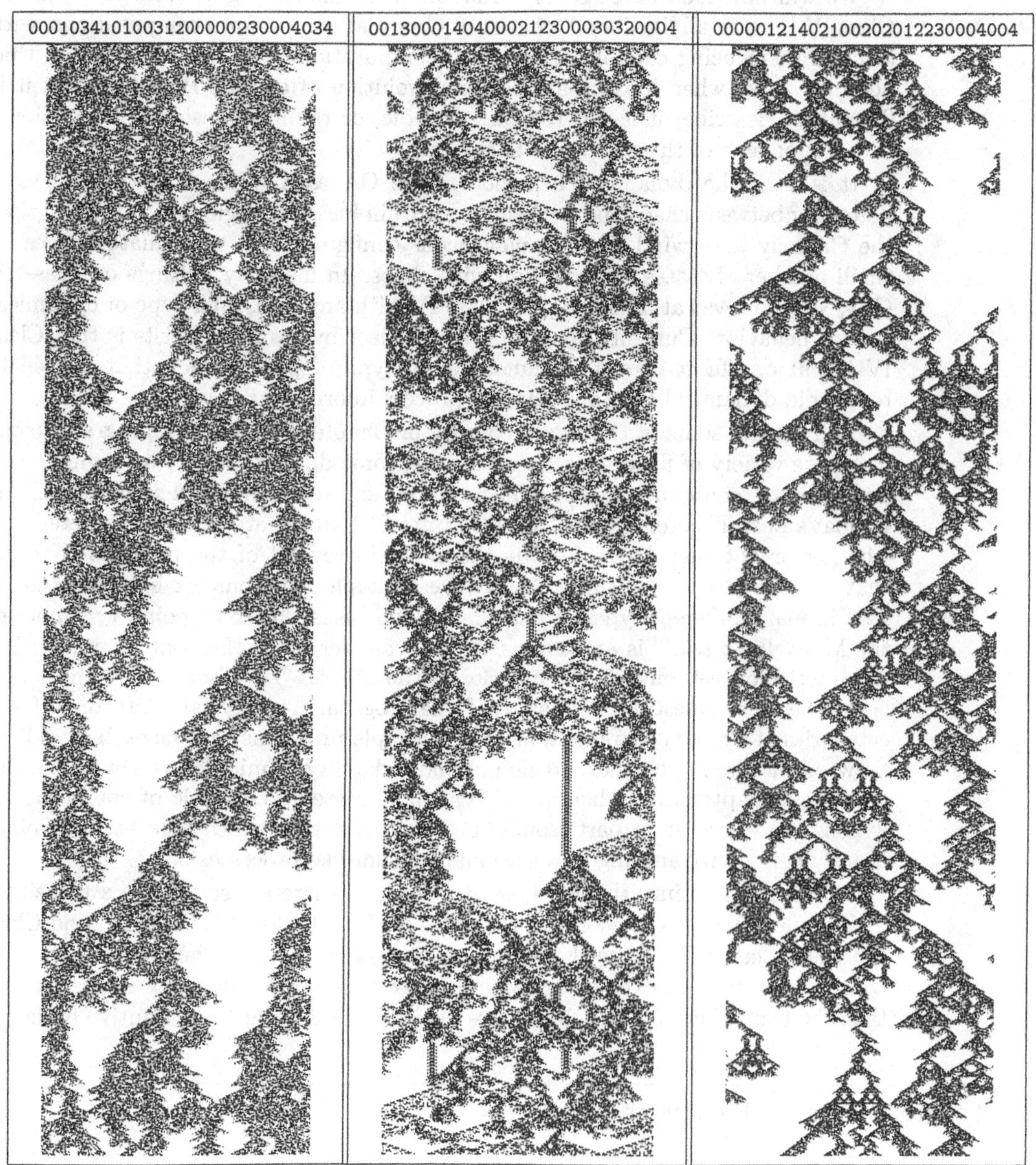

Figure 15.8 Examples of Wolfram's Class IV

We will now look at Class IV CAs, the most interesting of Wolfram's classes. Class IV CAs, in all likelihood, consist of CAs that can perform computations, with some of them being capable of universal computation. The first observation that one may make when looking at the time evolution of a Class IV CA is that it is difficult to describe; it is not regular, periodic, or random. Instead, it contains a little bit of each of these types of behavior.

It is as if the dynamical behavior of the CA as a whole is hovering near a boundary between chaos and periodicity. Within localized regions of space and time the CA may have windows of homogeneous configurations, or oscillate between a small number of states, or even boil with chaos. In his early writings on Class IV CAs, Wolfram was at a loss to pair Class IV with any particular type of dynamical system behavior. Current thought on the subject by many scientists is that Class IV is but one facet of a more fundamental type of phenomenon that is seen in real-world dynamical systems that can process information.

To reiterate some of the topics covered in Chapter 3, computer programs come in a wide variety of flavors: some never halt; some do halt, but with varying space and memory requirements; and some programs express such complex ideas (e.g., "Is Fermat's Last Theorem true?" from Chapter 8) that we are at a loss to determine whether or not they halt. I made the claim in several of the previous chapters that there is a sort of dividing line between simple and complex behavior that is seen in many different types of phenomena and ideas. "Is some point a member of the Mandelbrot set?" is an easy question to answer when the point is well within the interior or well outside the exterior of the M-set. "Does some program halt?" is another easy question to answer, if the program trivially falls into one of the categories of simple programs that halt or simple programs that never halt; but in between the two regions lies a region of undecidability. Similarly, we saw in the last postscript chapter that whenever a dynamical system is capable of computation, it possesses, at least in part, something akin to chaos (which falls between plain orderly periodicity and high-dimensional random-like processes).

In short, on an intuitive level, we can see how there appears to be a transition in CA rule space that proceeds in the order of Class I, Class II, Class IV, and Class III; thus, Class IV is somewhere between the other classes. The question that we will examine in the next section is how do we view a CA rule space in such a way that the transition between the classes is visible on a more than intuitive basis.

15.3 Langton's Lambda Parameter

Chris Langton, one of the earliest evangelists of the artificial life movement, greatly contributed to the study of cellular automata with a parameterization scheme that allows the relationship between Wolfram's classes to be more plainly seen. Like Wolfram, Langton ran thousands of CA simulations and cataloged the rules that yielded the types of dynamics described in the last section. Langton knew of Wolfram's classes, but was really interested in finding a sort of virtual knob that he could turn to coerce the behavior of a CA from one class to another. If Class IV is truly between Class II and Class III, then there must be some way of mapping CA rules into scalar numbers that show the same relationship.

The first step that Langton took was to define a quiescent state, which we can think of as the state that we define as being inactive or off. Next, Langton considered all of the rules that defined the mapping from one neighborhood configuration into another. Some of these rules will map a cell into the quiescent state and others will map into the other states. We can split these two rule types into two distinct sets, with the union of the sets being all of the rules. Recall that the total number of entries in the rule table is equal to k^{2r+1}. For simplicity, let's refer to this number as N. Letting the number of rules that map to the quiescent state be n_q, we can define a special parameter as the fraction of all the rules that map to a non-quiescent state:

$$\lambda = \frac{N - n_q}{N}.$$

Computing λ for the CA rules from the earlier examples requires a little bit of work because our compact representation for the rule tables is not uniformly distributed in the rule space. For example, with a neighborhood size of three ($r = 1$) and two states ($k = 2$), one table that we used was "0110," which means that neighborhood sums of 1 and 2 map to the on state, and everything else maps to off. There is exactly one way for a CA of this type to have a neighborhood sum of 0 or 3 ("000" or "111"), but three different ways for a neighborhood sum of 1 or 2 ("001," "010," "100," and "110," "101," "011"). Therefore, the rules for a sum of 1 or 2 should be weighted to reflect this fact when we compute λ. Table 15.1 shows exactly how we have to break down the rule space to correctly compute λ. Since two rules map to off and the others map to on, we get $\lambda = (8 - 2)/8 = \frac{3}{4}$ for this example.

But exactly what does λ tell us? Looking at some particular values, a λ of exactly 0 means that all rules map to the quiescent state; with λ equal to exactly 1, all rules map to non-quiescent states; and with λ equal to $1 - \frac{1}{k}$, statistically speaking, all states will be represented equally in the rule table. Therefore, $\lambda = 0$ represents the most homogeneous rule table and $\lambda = 1 - \frac{1}{k}$ represents the most heterogeneous rule tables.

Mapping a whole rule table into a single scalar number is a little bit dangerous, in that one should be wary about concluding too much based on only a single example. For one particular rule table the value of λ may not be too informative, but if we look at several CA rule tables with similar λ values, then in a statistical sense we may be able to see some interesting trends.

We will now consider the values of λ for the examples from Wolfram's four CA classes. Since all of these CAs have five states, in theory the interesting values of

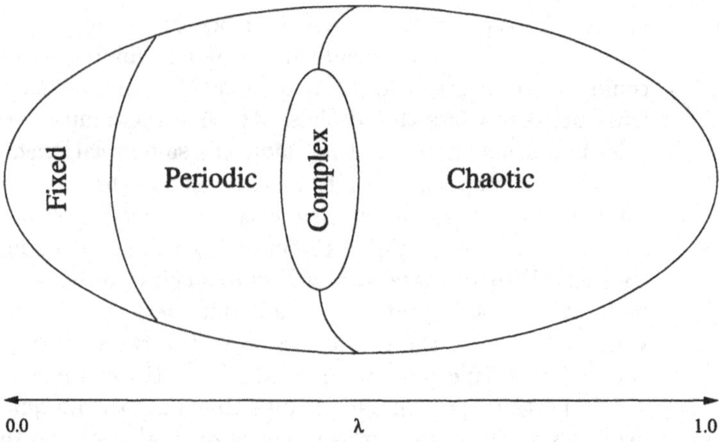

Figure 15.9 Langton's schematic representation of CA rule space characterized by the λ parameter

λ should be between 0.0 and 0.8. For the fixed point-like Class I, the three values of λ are 0.266880, 0.188749, and 0.229069, with an average of 0.22823267. These values are all on the low end of the spectrum, and not surprisingly they have simple behavior because they are near the extreme of $\lambda = 0$.

For the periodic Class II, the λ values are equal to 0.522330, 0.432013, 0.326822, 0.441331, 0.430848, and 0.483174, with an average of 0.43941967. In general, these values are near the middle of the range, where we would expect things to be interesting. To be fair, when selecting the examples for Class II, I was biased against very simple periodic CAs because I wanted the examples to have rich behavior; thus, for periodic CAs, my class II examples are somewhat complex.

For the random-like Class III, the λ values are equal to 0.821146, 0.787008, and 0.841306, with an average of 0.8164867. Notice that these are all near the extremity of $\lambda = 0.8$, where the rule space is the most heterogeneous. Therefore, it is not too surprising that all of these CA are random-like.

Finally, for the complex Class IV, the three values of λ are 0.430669, 0.514982, 0.559872, with an average of 0.501841, which agrees with our intuition that complex CAs reside somewhere between the periodic and the random regions of rule space.

Figure 15.9 shows a schematic representation of Langton's view of CA rule space. At the two extremes we find fixed point and chaotic behavior. In between the two extremes are periodic dynamics and truly complex behavior that resides in a special region near the center. Langton has compared these different regions to the different states of matter. Fixed points are like crystals in that they are for the most part static and orderly. Chaotic dynamics are similar to gases, which can be described only statistically. Periodic behavior is similar to a non-crystal solid, and complexity is like a liquid that is close to both the solid and the gaseous states. In this way, we can once again view complexity and computation as existing on the edge of chaos and simplicity.

While Langton's λ parameter can sometimes be used to roughly characterize the type of behavior that one could expect from a particular CA, it has at least three weaknesses that should be noted. First, it is possible for a CA rule set to have a high λ-value and still produce very simple behavior. This can happen if most of the rules map to the same non-quiescent state, in which case the CA will tend to fall into fixed point behavior dominated by this one state. Thus, care must be taken in picking the state that we call quiescent. Second, since a CA can conceivably perform universal computation, if we think of a CA rule set as a "program" and an initial configuration as "input" to this program, then we know that λ may be very uninformative, in that sophisticated programs can demonstrate a wide variety of behaviors. Last, even if the λ parameter is modified to account for the initial state, it is impossible to have a method for computing λ such that it always reveals what the long-term behavior of the CA would look like. We know that this is impossible because if such a method for calculating λ existed, then we could use this method to distinguish between CAs that halt and never halt, which is identical to solving the Halting Problem. The moral of the story is that determining the complexity of a CA or a program is an extremely complex subject that is itself intractable in the general case.

15.4 Conway's Game of Life

In the late 1960s, John Conway was motivated to extend von Neumann's work as described earlier. Von Neumann had succeeded in describing a self-reproducing cellular automaton, but the machine itself was enormous and took approximately 150 pages to describe. Conway wanted to refine the description of a cellular automaton to the simplest one that could support universal computation. Conway's cellular automaton had only two states, on and off, and had a very simple set of rules for determining what the next state of the system would be. He christened his creation "The Game of Life" because of the binary (live or dead) state of the cells and the lifelike rules that were used. Since Life is a two-dimensional cellular automaton, it can be simulated with checkers on a checkerboard, which helped Conway and his students to find many patterns that encouraged their belief that Life could support universal computation. In 1970 Martin Gardner described Conway's work in his *Scientific American* column. Gardner's article inspired many people around the world to experiment with Conway's rules, which eventually led to the final pieces of how the Game of Life could support universal computation in what was surely a globally collaborative effort.

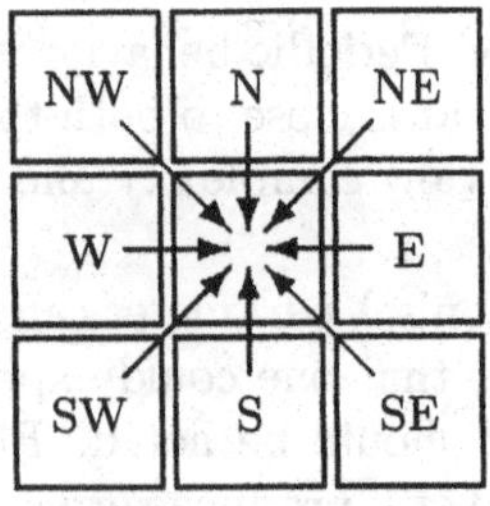

Figure 15.10 The neighborhood of Conway's Game of Life

As with the one-dimensional CA, the next state of a cell in Life is a function of the states of the cell's nearest neighbors. The only neighbors that we consider are the eight cells that form the immediate perimeter of a cell, which we can label by the directions N, S, E, W, NE, NW, SE, and SW, as shown in Figure 15.10. The rules for the time evolution of Life are quite simple:

- If a live cell has less than two neighbors, then it dies (loneliness).
- If a live cell has more than three neighbors, then it dies (overcrowding).
- If an empty cell has three live neighbors, then it comes to life (reproduction).
- Otherwise (exactly two live neighbors), a cell stays as is (stasis).

Notice that the rules contain the most basic properties of how real-world creatures interact with the basic constraints on population density and the conditions for "reproduction."

One could start a grid with a random initial configuration and watch how the system evolves in time; in fact, there are screen savers available for virtually every computer that do just this. In this section we will be able to observe only a very small portion of the types of behavior that are possible in Life. Instead, the goal of this section is to illustrate how Life, being in Langton's critical area, is capable of universal computation. We will not be able to give a full and rigorous proof that Life is a universal computer, but we will at least see how computations can be carried out in principle.

To start, we will examine three simple classes of objects that can be found in Life. Our first class consists of simple static objects that do not change over time as long as nothing interferes with them. Figure 15.11 shows some examples of static objects in Life. In each configuration, every cell is such that if it is filled, then it has two or three live neighbors, and if a cell is empty, then it has less than two or greater than three neighbors; thus, if a cell is alive or dead, it will always remain so. Having the ability to form static objects is important from a computational point

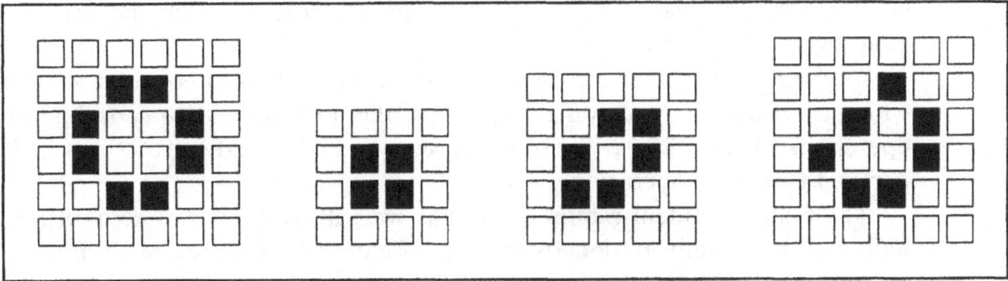

Figure 15.11 Examples of static objects in Conway's Game of Life

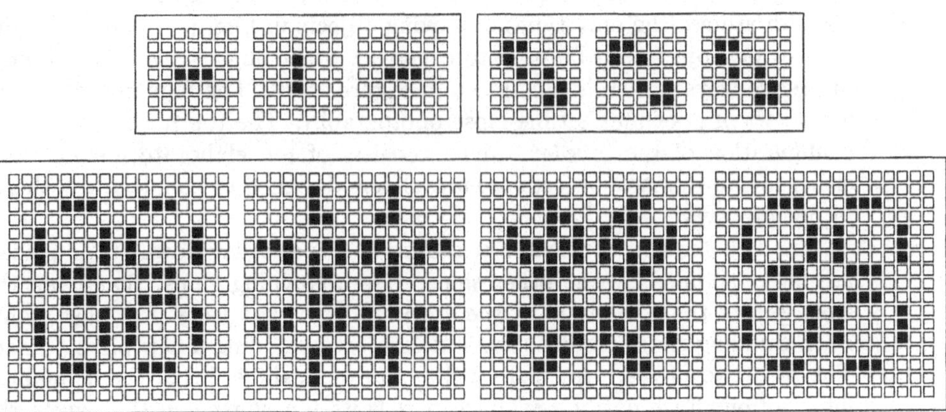

Figure 15.12 Examples of simple periodic objects in Conway's Game of Life

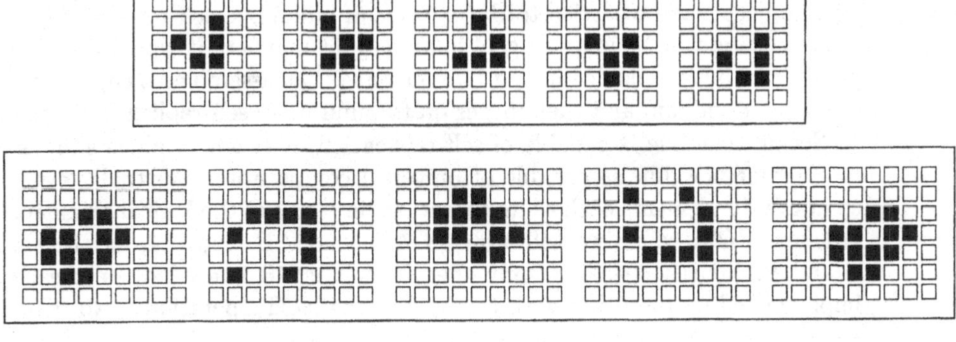

Figure 15.13 Examples of moving objects in Conway's Game of Life

of view because fixed objects—being persistent in time—allow for a basic type of memory.

Another requirement for computation is the ability to count in some manner, which is needed to synchronize events parallel in time and to coordinate iterative operations. Figure 15.12 illustrates three types of periodic structures in Life that perform this basic operation.

The final functional requirement that we will consider is a computing device's ability to move information to and fro. Figure 15.13 shows two types of moving objects. The first moving object is sometimes referred to as a *glider* and moves one diagonal space in four time steps. The second object is sometimes called a *fish* and moves two horizontal (or vertical) squares in four time steps. Both gliders and fish can be rotated to make them travel in any of the eight possible directions. Gliders and fish are not the only types of moving objects in Life, just two of the simplest.

Moving objects can be used to construct other objects by having them collide in precise ways, which is illustrated in Figure 15.14. The four images in the figure are a sort of poor man's time-lapse photography. The top image shows the initial configuration of the *breeder*, which consists of ten elaborate moving ships that either lay down static objects or emit gliders designed to collide with other objects in precise ways.[1]

The two ships in the center of the front row each lay down static pieces which are later modified by the other ships. The remaining ships, that flank the trail, emit gliders that collide with the static objects that were previously laid down. Each colliding glider modifies the static object by adding a new piece of machinery. The final two pieces, provided by the outermost ships, bring the assembled parts into motion. Each newly assembled part is itself a *glider gun* that emits gliders at regular intervals. In the last portion of Figure 15.14, the screen is now filled with glider guns; the breeder continues on its infinite journey, building more and more glider guns, which build more and more gliders.

The process of recursively assembling pieces to make larger and more complicated objects can be carried to the extreme of building a self-reproducing machine, thus realizing von Neumann's goal in an elegant manner. It would theoretically be possible to build a device in the Life universe that assembles a copy of itself, sets the copy in motion, and then moves on to build more self-replicating machines.

Seeing that Life is capable of self-replication, it is now a much simpler matter to consider how Life is capable of universal computation. Virtually every digital computer implements each of its operations in terms of the logical primitives AND, OR, and NOT, which we will write as $A \wedge B$, $A \vee B$, and $\neg A$, for the arguments A and B. Strictly speaking, only one of AND or OR is needed, since each can be implemented by the other with the help of the NOT operation.[2] No matter what

---

[1] The pattern for the breeder is distributed with the marvelous Life implementation `xlife`.

[2] In general we can rewrite each operation as $A \wedge B = \neg(\neg A \vee \neg B)$ and $A \vee B = \neg(\neg A \wedge \neg B)$. Try these out to see that it really works.

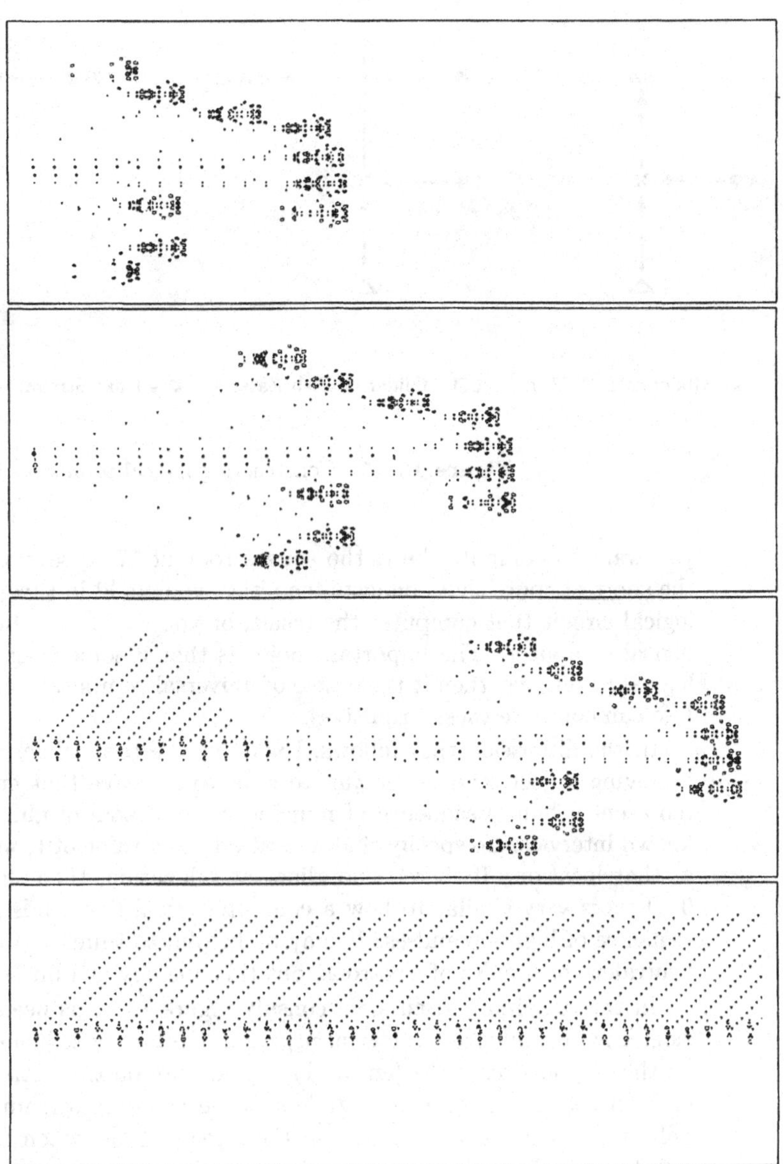

Figure 15.14 Examples of a breeder in Conway's Game of Life

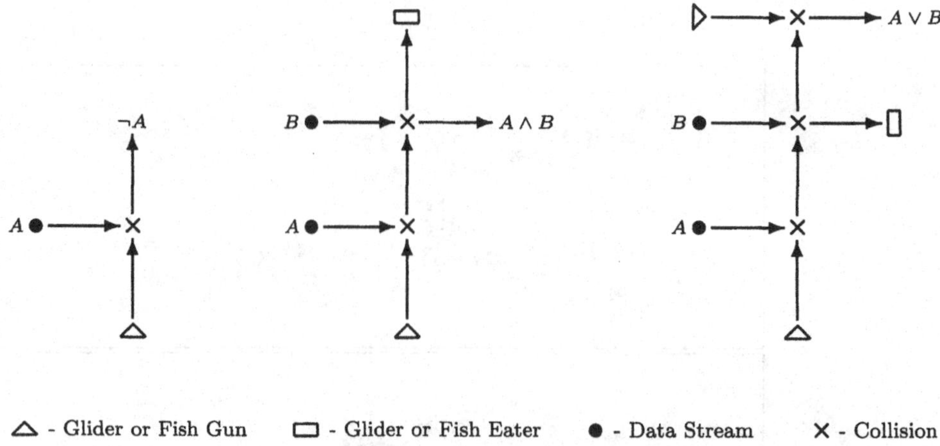

Figure 15.15 Constructing logical primitives in Life

you want to compute, be it the square root of 17 to seventeen decimal places or the shortest route that connects ten cities, you could in theory build one enormous logical circuit that computes the result, or you could even build a general-purpose digital computer. The important point is that if something can provide the basic logical primitives, then it is capable of universal computation. We will now see how Life can compute these primitives.

In the discussion that follows, I will use the term *glider* to generically refer to a moving object, and *glider gun* to refer to a device that emits a glider. We can represent a binary sequence of numbers by a stream of gliders that are spaced at known intervals. To specify that a location has a value of 1, we simply place a glider at that location. If there is no glider at a location, then the value of the digit is 0. This is very similar to how a computer serial line sends a stream of data as a sequence of high-low pulses. It may be helpful to think of a glider stream as being equivalent to a pulse of electrons, but this analogy is a bit strained.

In the remaining discussion, consult Figure 15.15 as needed. We will first consider how to compute the logical negation of a binary sequence, which is illustrated on the left portion of the figure. The glider gun on the bottom of the NOT circuit emits a continuous stream of gliders, while the data stream source emits a glider only when there is a value of 1 in the stream; thus, when the current bit of A is a 0, there will be a hole for the glider coming from the glider gun to fly through, But when the current bit is a 1, the hole is filled with another glider, forcing a collision that annihilates both gliders. The gliders from the glider gun that survive the encounter correspond exactly to the empty locations in A, yielding the logical negation of A as the output.

We can build on the NOT circuit to form an AND gate, as shown in the middle portion of the figure. Consider the collision that occurs just to the right of B, which has the stream $\neg A$ coming in from the bottom. We want there to be a glider arriving at $A \wedge B$ only when both A and B are 1. If A is 1, then there must be a hole for B to fly through. But if A is 0, the $\neg A$ glider will collide with B (if B is not a 0, that is). The glider eater at the top of the circuit is there only to destroy the extraneous gliders.

The right portion of Figure 15.15 shows how an OR circuit can be built from part of the AND circuit. The output of the AND that goes to the glider eater is equal to $\neg A \wedge \neg B$, since gliders from $\neg A$ survive only if $\neg B$ is true to provide a hole. Negating this stream one more time with another glider collision yields $A \vee B$, which completes the circuit. As before, the extraneous stream is destroyed by a glider eater.

To fully realize a digital computer implementation built on top of Life, we would have to solve some other problems, such as synchronization issues and memory requirements, but a computer science theorist would say that those are only boring details, in that we have already solved the key problems in principle.

15.5 Natural CA-like Phenomena

Perhaps the most interesting aspect of cellular automata, and of complex systems in general, is that they describe phenomena that occur on radically different time and space scales. This is in sharp contrast to the two "sexiest" branches of physics, quantum mechanics and relativity, which deal with phenomena on only the most extreme scales, the absurdly tiny and the outrageously enormous. Complexity in the form of complex systems is a universal and ubiquitous phenomenon that is found in the very small, the very large, and everywhere in between. In the chapters that follow, we will sample complex systems that reside on varying time and space scales. In the remainder of this section, we will briefly look at some real-world examples with the purpose of conveying the breadth that is found in complexity.

Statistical Mechanical Systems Prior to the advent of supercomputers finding a home in the physics communities, scientists usually had to be content with purely statistical descriptions of low-level stochastic systems. But now that powerful computers are readily available to all scientists, it is possible for the theorist to experiment and the experimentalist to theorize by actually programming the laws of physics into a computer model so as to simulate the millions of interactions that occur on the elementary level of atoms and molecules. For example, a lattice-gas automaton is a model of how gas or plasma interacts in a local space. The beauty of this model is that a lattice-gas CA uses only local interactions, in that each molecule "cares" about only its nearest neighbors, and nothing else. With such a

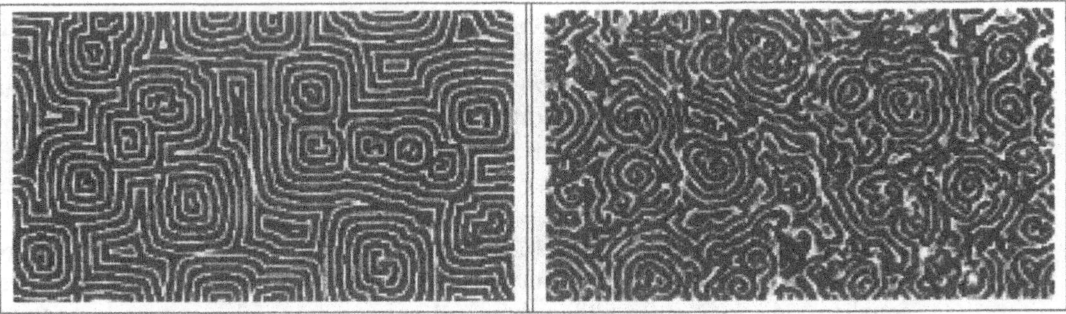

Figure 15.16 Two runs from the program **hp**, which emulates the hodgepodge machine

simulation, a scientist can control the "temperature" of the system to observe how the collective behavior changes. Similarly, other statistical systems, such as models of ferromagnetism and the process of annealing metals, can be simulated in a similar manner.

Autocatalytic Chemical Sets Of relevance to the origin of life, an autocatalytic chemical set is a collection of chemicals that is self-catalyzing and therefore capable of highly nonlinear dynamics. For example, suppose that two chemical reactants, A and B, could in theory combine to form the reagent C, but only on a very slow time scale. A catalyst, which we'll call D, is a chemical that can increase the rate of a reaction by orders of magnitude; thus, in the presence of D, A and B will produce C at a very rapid rate. Things get interesting when C catalyzes yet another reaction (say one consisting of D and A), to produce a catalyst for another reaction, and so on.

Since each molecule in the chemical soup can interact only with other molecules that are located near the first molecule, local interactions, combined with a parallel evolution of the simultaneously occurring chemical reactions, yield remarkably accurate pictures of how these systems self-organize.

Martin Gerhardt and Heike Schuster have created a CA rule known as the hodgepodge machine that does a remarkable job of capturing the types of behavior seen in chemical systems such as the Belousov-Zhabotinsky reaction. Figure 15.16 illustrates two runs from **hp**, a program that implements the hodgepodge machine. The spiral-like patterns are seen in many biochemical reactions.

Gene Regulation Similar to the last example, a single gene product can inhibit or encourage the activation of another gene. In this way, one gene can activate another, which activates a third, and so on. Through this regulation process, cells that have identical DNA can perform many different types of tasks via specialization. Yet, one prominent difference between the process of gene regulation and an autocatalytic chemical set is that genes are not inhibited by space in terms of affecting other genes. Despite this fact, biological systems are remarkably stable systems that are capable of functioning in a wide variety of environments.

Why this is so has been explained, at least partially, by Stuart Kauffman, who pioneered the use of random Boolean networks as models of biological processes. Kauffman wired a large collection of cells together with randomly selected Boolean functions. A random Boolean network is exactly equivalent to having a cellular automaton with an inhomogeneous rule table that allows cells to have different rules for each cell (unlike the CA that we played with in this chapter, which had cells that all had the same rule table). With such a random collection of rules, one would think that the random networks would display only chaotic-like behavior; however, with some minor constraints on the amount of connectivity in his networks, Kauffman found that the networks would often stabilize to low-order periodic behavior, which is a seemingly counterintuitive result. Kauffman has referred to this phenomenon as "order for free."

But this is not the whole story. The real beauty in Kauffman's work was that he was able to correlate the behavior of the random Boolean networks with a number of properties found in biological systems. For example, Kauffman was able to accurately predict the number of cell types in a species, given the number of genes that the species possessed, by considering only the behavior of a Boolean network.

Multicellular Organisms The first multicelled organism in all likelihood was the result of several single-cell organisms pooling resources and abilities so as to become more proficient at the task of survival. At some point, joined but genetically dissimilar cells merged their DNA and developed a mechanism for cell specialization through gene regulation. By doing this, organisms could begin to build more complex types of creatures with fully developed digestive, circulatory, nervous, respiratory, and other systems.

Colonies and "Super-Organisms" The combination of parallelism, specialization, and local interactions with limited autonomy has been exploited by many species in the insect world, such as ants, termites, bees, and wasps. Specialization at this level is exemplified by the presence of different castes. One incorrect view of how such collectives work is that the queen rules the nest, which couldn't be further from the truth. An equally acceptable explanation is that the queen is held captive by the sterile castes, being nothing but a machine for producing offspring. Neither view is quite correct, since the relationship between all of the castes is at least partly mutually exploitative and cooperative. Regardless of the control hierarchy (or lack thereof), insect colonies are able to produce remarkable results that go well beyond the scope of any individual insect or caste.

Flocks and Herds Clearly, flocking structures are related to there being safety in numbers; however, there are many open questions about flocking that deal with the level at which safety is "optimized" by a flock. When birds of a flock travel, they will in general tend to travel in the direction the rest of the flock is moving. But simultaneously, birds probably solve two other subproblems associated with this task. First, they prefer to be an optimal distance from their nearest neighbor, since they don't want to be too close or too distant from the other birds. But second, birds will often attempt to fly in the middle of a flock so as to minimize their exposure to predators.

Similar behavior is observed in fish and herd animals as well. From a hindsight point of view, it is not surprising that animals prefer that their neighbors be eaten instead of themselves. Nevertheless, the local goal optimization by a collection of autonomous agents yields a globally effective solution, that is, there is safety in numbers because the average exposure of a cluster of animals is less than that of individuals moving in isolation.

Ecosystems As we saw in Chapter 12, isolated ecosystems often display a rich variety of population dynamics. A warm summer can trigger plant growth, which increases the population of a grazing species, which feeds a predator population, which will then diminish the food source for the predators, and so forth. Within a consistent environment, an ecosystem can reach a stable point; however, perturbations to the system in the form of weather changes and the introduction of new species can affect the short- and long-term dynamics of an ecosystem.

It is also worth noting that differing environments promote varying amounts of genetic diversity (e.g., rain forests versus deserts). Complexity may help to explain how we can promote ecological stability without sacrificing genetic diversity.

Economies and Society Economic systems depend on both competition and cooperation. Without competition, a centrally controlled economy is doomed to certain failure due to stagnation. Complementary to this, purely self-serving business units in an anarchical economic system fail to compete with a collection of business units that cooperate on a limited scale. Again, there seems to be a happy middle ground with an ideal mixture of cooperation and competition. An even more fascinating aspect to this is that the combination of competition and cooperation can spontaneously form because of the increased yield in efficiency.

Scientists specializing in complexity theory have used these notions to partially explain the rise and fall of religions, countries, and cultural ideas.

We could continue this list with such odd phenomena as collapsing sandpiles and seashells (as shown in Figure 15.17), but I think the point has been made that complex systems occur on nearly every level of observation. This first chapter on complex systems has been largely devoted to presenting the theoretical background,

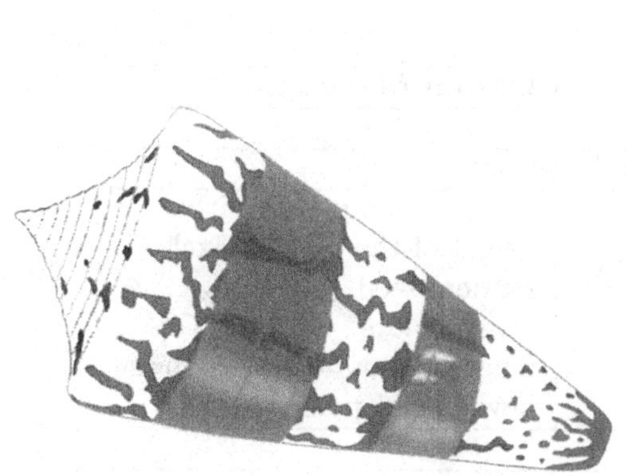
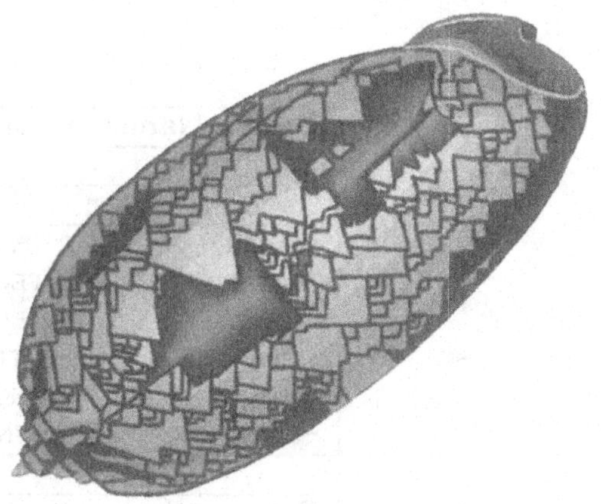

Figure 15.17 Seashells and CA: The process by which seashells are created has been likened to a one-dimensional CA

providing an introductory feel for the breadth of the phenomena, and examining low-level cases of complex systems. Over the next few chapters in this book part, we will examine complex systems that occur on larger scales. In Chapter 16 we will look at collectives composed of autonomous agents, such as flocking birds and ant colonies. In Chapter 17 we will examine competition and cooperation in the iterated Prisoner's Dilemma. And in Chapter 18, we will see how analog systems not unlike the other complex systems in this book part can solve problems from classical computer science.

15.6 Further Exploration

This section contains a brief tutorial on how to use `ca`, which is the program used to generate most of the images in this chapter; `life`, which implements Conway's Game of Life; and `hp`, a program that implements the hodgepodge machine, as briefly discussed in the last section. A list of program options can be found in Table 15.3. Many of the options are self-explanatory or are common to many of the other programs in this book; however, options specific to `ca`, `life`, or `hp` will be discussed in greater detail.

The most important thing to remember when using `ca` is that you must always use either `-rules` or `-lambda` but not both. The `-rules` option will allow you to specify the rule of your choice. The rules should be specified by a string of integers. Any of the rules listed with the figures will work. You can also use `-lambda` to specify a random rule that has a λ-value close to the specified value. Note, however, that

Option Name	Option Type	Option Meaning
Options Common to all Three Programs		
`-width`	INTEGER	width of the plot in pixels
`-height`	INTEGER	height of the plot in pixels
`-seed`	INTEGER	random seed
`-inv`	SWITCH	invert colors?
`-xmag`	INTEGER	magnification for X windows
`-term`	STRING	how to plot points
Options only for `ca`		
`-states`	INTEGER	number of CA states
`-radius`	INTEGER	radius of CA neighborhood
`-wrap`	SWITCH	use a wraparound space?
`-rules`	STRING	CA rules to use (< 0 is random)
`-init`	STRING	starting state (< 0 is random)
`-lambda`	DOUBLE	lambda-value for rules
`-sq`	SWITCH	enforce strong quiescence?
`-bin`	SWITCH	binary colors?
Options Only for `life`		
`-extra`	INTEGER	number of extra border pixels
`-wrap`	SWITCH	wraparound world?
`-infile`	STRING	initial configuration file
Options Only for `hp`		
`-freq`	INTEGER	plot frequency
`-diag`	SWITCH	diagonal cells are neighbors?
`-wrap`	SWITCH	use a wraparound space?
`-steps`	INTEGER	number of simulated steps
`-states`	INTEGER	number of cell states
`-g`	DOUBLE	infection progression rate
`-k1`	DOUBLE	first weighting parameter
`-k2`	DOUBLE	second weighting parameter

Table 15.3 Command-line options for `ca`, `life`, and `hp`

the `-lambda` option is really only a suggestion, since not every λ-value between 0 and 1 can be represented by every CA, but the program will do its best to get a value that is close. When you use `-lambda`, the randomly generated rule and the actual λ will be displayed. Similarly, if you specify your own rule, its λ-value will be displayed.

The `-init` option allows you to specify an initial configuration, which should be a string of integer digits. Regardless of the length of the configuration that is specified, the program will attempt to center the initial string in the middle of the CA space, filling every other cell with the quiescent state. If a negative integer is supplied as the initial string, then a random initial state will be used.

The `-sq` option is turned on by default; thus, using it turns off strong quiescence. Strong quiescence ensures that if each cell in a configuration has the same state, then the next state of the center cell will be the same. Having strong quiescence turned off is in general not a good idea, since your CA will tend to be very chaotic.

Finally, the `-bin` option can be used to force the display to be strictly binary, with the quiescent state mapping to one color (say black) and every other state mapping to the other (white).

Using the `life` program is very simple. The `-infile` option is used to specify an initial configuration for the the program, which should be in the Portable Bit Map (PBM) file format. The source code for `life` comes with several example files. Since the width and height can be determined by the initial configuration, the `-width` and `-height` options are used by the program only if they are bigger than the dimensions of the pattern in the initial configuration. Similarly, the `-extra` option can be used to pad the initial configuration with the specified number of extra cells running around the perimeter of the pattern. This is useful if your `life` simulation needs extra "working space" to move about in. Finally, the `-wrap` option determines if the `life` CA space wraps around from one edge to another. The `life` program is interesting in that it demonstrates how to write such a simulation with a small amount of code; however, there are many Game of Life simulations freely available (such as `xlife`) that are much more sophisticated and have many more features.

As for `hp`, the first four options unique to it are not very critical. The normal mode of `hp` is to plot out each and every state at every time step. If you are simulating a large hodgepodge machine, you may wish to use `-freq` n to specify that only every nth time step is plotted. If the `-diag` switch is used, then the neighborhood of a cell will consist of the eight nearest neighbors; otherwise, only the nondiagonal neighbors are officially part of the neighborhood. With the `-wrap` switch you can make cells on an edge be the neighbors of cells on the opposite edge. Since `hp` is supposed to emulate chemical reactions, it may be more realistic to have this switch off.

The last four options are crucial in that they specify the dynamics of the hodgepodge machine. The number of possible states that a cell may have is specified by the `-states` option. Let the possible cell states be denoted by the integers 0 through n. A cell in state 0 is said to be "healthy," while a cell in state n is said to be "ill." Anything in between is considered "infected." Within a given cell's neighborhood, let the number of infected neighbors be denoted by N_{inf} and the number of ill cells be denoted by N_{ill}. Moreover, let S be the sum of the states of a cell's neighbors and its own state. With the parameters k_1, k_2, and g, as specified by the options `-k1`, `-k2`, and `g`, we update a cell based on the following rules:[3]

- If a cell is healthy, then its next state is equal to $\lfloor N_{\text{inf}}/k_1 \rfloor + \lfloor N_{\text{ill}}/k_2 \rfloor$.
- If a cell is infected, then its next state is equal to $\lfloor S/(N_{\text{inf}} + 1) + g \rfloor$, with the understanding that if the update equation yields a next-state value greater than n, then we replace it with n.
- If a cell is ill, then at the next time step its state is 0.

The combination of k_1, k_2, and g specifies how fast infections spread. With a suitable choice of parameters, one can produce reactions that are relatively stable, periodic, or complex.

15.7 Further Reading

Berlekamp, E., Conway, J. H., & Guy, R. (1982). *Winning ways for your mathematical plays.* London: Academic Press.

Dewdney, A. K. (August 1988). The hodgepodge machine makes waves. *Sci. Am.*, 225(8): 104–107.

Fowler, D. R., Meinhardt, H., & Prusinkiewicz, P. (1992). Modeling seashells. *Comp. Graphics*, 26(2): 379–387.

Gardner, M. (October 1970). Mathematical Games: The fantastic combinations of John Conway's new solitaire game 'Life'. *Sci. Am.*, 223(4): 120–123.

Li, W., Packard, N., & Langton, C. G. (1990). Transition phenomena in CA rule space. *Physica D*, 45(1–3): 77–94.

MacRae, N. (1992). *John von Neumann: The scientific genius who pioneered the modern computer, game theory, nuclear deterrence, and much more.* New York: Pantheon Books.

Meinhardt, H. (1995). *The algorithmic beauty of sea shells.* New York: Springer.

[3] The expression $\lfloor x \rfloor$ denotes the floor operator which rounds down its argument to the greatest integer less than x.

Poundstone, W. (1985). *The recursive universe.* New York: William Morrow.

von Neumann, J. (1966). *Theory of self-reproducing automata.* Urbana: University of Illinois Press.

Wolfram, S. (1984a). Cellular automata as models of complexity. *Nature*, 311(4): 419–424.

Wolfram, S. (1984b). Universality and complexity in cellular automata. *Physica D*, 10(1–2): 1–35.

Wolfram, S. (1994). *Cellular automata and complexity.* Reading, Mass.: Addison-Wesley.

16 Autonomous Agents and Self-Organization

Some primal termite knocked on wood.
And tasted it, and found it good.
And that is why your Cousin May
Fell through the parlor floor today.
— Ogden Nash

Go to the ant, thou sluggard; consider her ways, and be wise.
— Proverbs 6:6

... and the thousands of fishes moved as a huge beast, piercing the water. They appear united, inexorably bound by common fate. How comes this unity?
— Anonymous

LOOSELY SPEAKING, AN *autonomous agent* is a unit that interacts with its environment (which probably consists of other agents) but acts independently from all other agents in that it does not take commands from some seen or unseen leader, nor does an agent have some idea of a global plan that it should be following. In other words, an agent simply does its own thing. With this definition, we will explore how multiple agents can seemingly perform tasks that appear to follow a global plan. The process by which autonomous agents interact in such a way as to create global order is known as *self-organization*, and is seen in many different types of phenomena: chemical soups, gene regulation systems, super-organisms, animal collectives, and economic systems, to name a few.

In this chapter we will explore three examples that are inspired by the real-world animal kingdom: termites, ants, and birds. In each case, the model of animal behavior that we will be exploring only grossly approximates the respective real-world counterpart. Nevertheless, it is surprising to see that simplified models are still capable of astonishingly complex behavior.

There are two main themes to this chapter. The first theme is what Stuart Kauffman calls "order for free," or the fact that complex systems seem to tend toward orderly behavior. The second theme is that even when agents obey simple or even stupid rules, it is not always possible to predict the future behavior of such a system.

16.1 Termites

In many animal species, large collections of creatures cooperatively build structures that appear to have some sort of planning behind them. In the case of beavers, it is almost as if a foreman beaver is busily consulting blueprints and directing the placement of individual sticks to construct a dam. Clearly this is not the case, but exactly how does such order arise in such a directionless scheme?

Beavers are relatively intelligent creatures, so to make the question more interesting, let us consider a collection of agents that are so individually simple that they primarily wander around randomly. Mitchel Resnick has studied a wide variety of systems that consist entirely of very primitive agents. One noteworthy example of Resnick's creatures is a theoretical termite that follows the following simple rule:

- Wander around aimlessly, via a random walk, until the termite bumps into a wood chip.
- If the termite is carrying a wood chip, it drops the chips and continues to wander.
- If the termite is not carrying a wood chip, it picks up the one that it bumped into and continues to wander.

Clearly, Resnick's rule is about as simple a plan as possible. There is no room for intelligence in this scheme at all, and it seems highly unlikely that one or more termites following this rule could produce anything more meaningful than just a random mess. Or could they?

Figure 16.1 shows six stages from simulating a simple rule set with a small number of termites. In the initial configuration the termites' universe consists of a square grid that has wood chips randomly distributed throughout the entire space. As with nearly every other CA-like simulation in this book, the square grid wraps around, in that the points on an edge are considered to be the neighbors of points on the opposite edge. Almost immediately after beginning the simulation, the termites are moving chips into small clusters. As time goes on, the clusters become larger and more defined.

Hundreds of thousands of time steps have elapsed by the time we get to the sixth and final plot, but at this point the wood chips are in a fairly well defined collection. This is obviously a suboptimal method for collecting wood chips, and

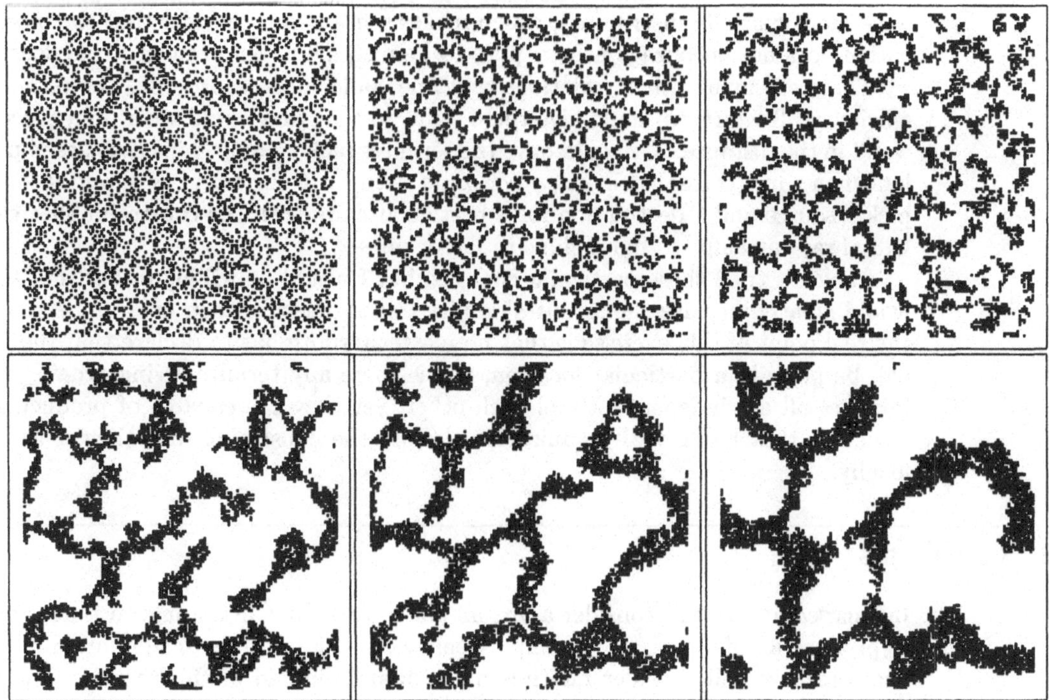

Figure 16.1 Termites randomly placing wood chips according to a simple rule produce order

it is extremely frustrating to watch the process, because after a while the termites will at times mindlessly ferry chips back and forth. However, the very fact that as time increases, so does the order of the system is a remarkable result.

There are several simple changes that we could make in the simulation to get different results. For example, instead of performing a strict random walk, Resnick had his termites make a random left or right turn and then take a step (instead of just taking a random step in any direction), which prevents the termites from wasting time by moving forward, then backward. In addition to this, Resnick made sure that after dropping or picking up a piece of wood, the termites would always make a 180 degree turn, which reduces the chance that a termite will pick up a piece, then immediately drop it. With these changes, Resnick's termites almost always collected the wood chips into a single large pile.

For the images displayed in Figure 16.1, I modified the termites so that after dropping a wood chip, they would randomly jump to an unoccupied place on the grid. As shown in the figure, this change resulted in clusters that, while connected, were more spatially distributed, which makes sense if you consider that the modification does not encourage nearby piles to be merged, as the standard rule does.

There are many other variations that one could make to improve the termites' efficiency. To start, we could give them sight, so that they could see a juicy piece of wood in the distance. We could have the termites pick up only chips that are in piles less than some threshold in size. We could even have the termites simultaneously pick a source and a destination for a particular chip, with the constraint that they will always attempt to move chips to larger piles.

I haven't tried these particular changes, but I would be willing to bet that they would greatly increase the termites' ability to self-organize their environment. But the real point of this exercise is that no master termite has to declare that the pile will be place in a particular location, nor is there any termite giving orders. The termites all act independently of each other, yet they are capable of producing a structure that has global organization despite the constraint that they must act locally.

16.2 Virtual Ants

In this section we will consider a virtual ant created by Chris Langton that is able to produce a different type of complex behavior. It is possible to simulate multiple ants—and we will consider multiple ants toward the end of this section—but for the purposes of this introduction we need to consider only a single ant. Like the termites, our ant is located on a grid that wraps around from edge to edge. At each time step, the ant is always facing in one of four directions: north, south, east, or west. All of the points on the grid are painted either black or white. At each time step, the ant acts according to the following simple rule set:

- The ant takes a step forward.
- If the ant is now standing on a white point, then it paints the point black and turns 90 degrees to the right.
- Otherwise, if the ant is standing on a black point, then it paints it white and turns 90 degrees to the left.

Figure 16.2 illustrates eight steps that an ant would take starting from an initially blank grid. One difference between Langton's virtual ants and the cellular automata in the last chapter is that for almost all of the CAs we considered, it was possible for the CA configuration to fall into a state that had the property that it could have been achieved from multiple previous configurations, which is to say that the CAs are *time irreversible*. This is clearly true since, in the case of Class I CAs, for example, a CA could fall into a configuration consisting of all dead cells. How did the CA get there? Unless we know the CA's whole time history, we can only

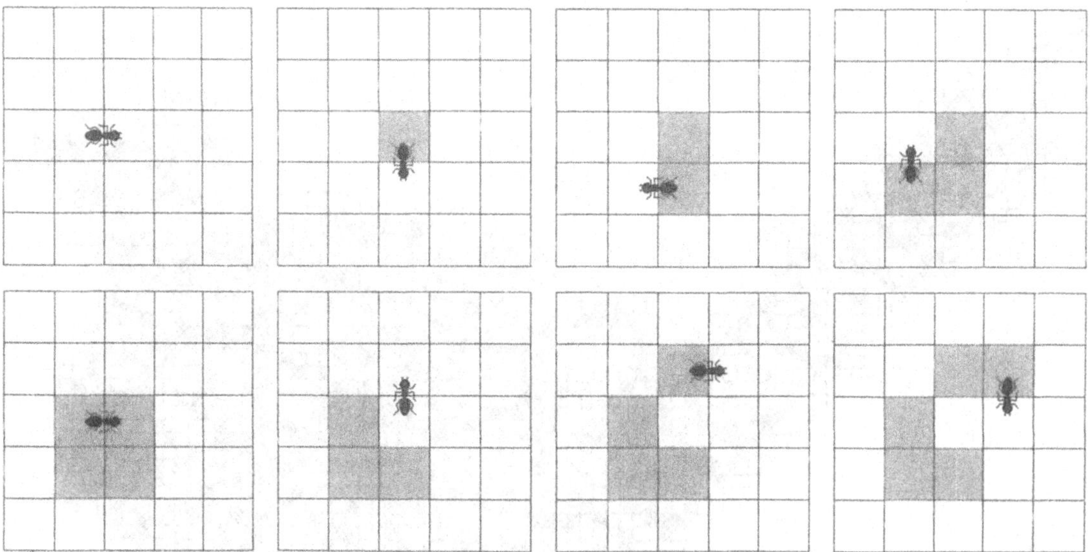

Figure 16.2 Eight steps of Langton's virtual ant, starting from an initially blank grid

rarely answer this question, because it could have evolved to its present form from multiple places in the state space.

This is interestingly not the case for Langton's virtual ants. Looking at any of the eight stages shown in Figure 16.2, we can always "unwind" the simulation in time because the rules for Langton's ant are *time reversible*. If the ant is standing on a black cell, then we know that at the previous time step the cell was white and that the ant just made a 90 degree turn to the right. In fact, not only is the ant's entire future determined, but so is its past. This would seem to imply that Langton's ants, while obviously simple in the parsimony of the rule set, are also simple over a global spatial and temporal scale.

We will see shortly that this conclusion is not true, since time reversibility does not necessarily imply global simplicity. To get a feel for why this is so, we only need to notice that the ant is hopelessly recursive in its prior actions. Look again at Figure 16.2; the ant quickly starts to interact with grid locations that it has been at in the past, which means that the ant's future state and future behavior are a function of all its past actions. Thus, if we were to randomly flip the color of a cell at some point in the past, the ant's entire future could be dramatically altered. Thus, in a way, Langton's ants possess a form of sensitivity to initial conditions.

But does this mean that an ant will always behave in a way that appears random in the long term? Not necessarily. If we continue to simulate the ant from

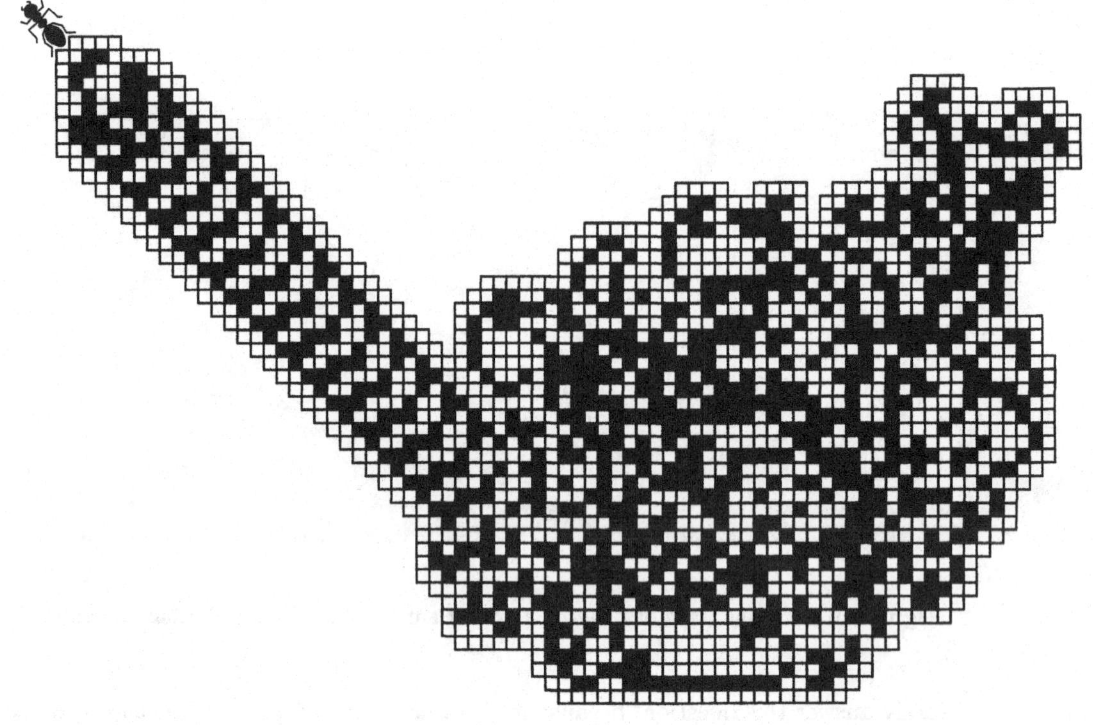

Figure 16.3 A virtual ant building a highway

Figure 16.2 for another 10,000 time steps or so, the ant will indeed form a chaotic-looking mess that has little or no structure. But after another 250 or more steps, the ant will start to build what James Propp, who discovered this phenomenon, calls a highway.

Figure 16.3 shows an ant highway created from an initially blank configuration. The highway in this case extends along the north-west direction, but an ant can build a highway that flows in any of the four diagonal directions. If the ant's universe consists of an infinite cell space that is initially blank, then the ant will happily build the highway forever. In our toroidal wraparound universe the highway must eventually intersect a place in the ant's grid space where the ant has been before. Such a "bump in the road" will usually force the ant back into a chaotic-like behavior, but it will often spontaneously start to build another highway, and so on. In all of the simulations that I have personally run with a single ant, given enough time, the ant's universe would always converge to a random-like mess. Eventually,

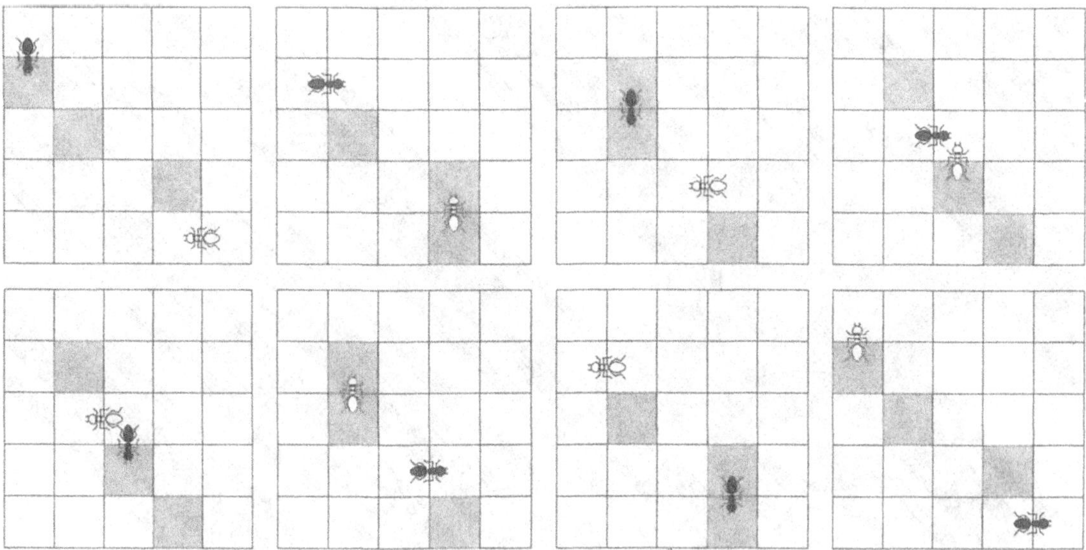

Figure 16.4 Two virtual ants reversing one another's work

the ant must fall into some sort of cyclic pattern, given the finite (but large) number of states that the ant and the grid can be in, but I suspect that such periodic cycles are, almost without exception, profoundly long in length and duration.

But what happens if we let more than one ant move in a single cell space, thus allowing them to interact? Because of the reversible nature of the ants' rules, two virtual ants can collide with one another in such a way that each starts to undo the other's work. Figure 16.4 shows such a situation. Notice that in the last step, the configuration of the grid is the same as in the first step, but now the ants have exchanged positions and they point in opposite directions. The situation displayed in Figure 16.4 depends on the black ant being updated before the white ant. Hence, between the fourth and fifth steps the black ant lands on a white cell, turns it black, then turns right, which allows the white ant to turn the black cell back to white, and then turn left. The collision shown in Figure 16.4 is not especially interesting; however, if two ants are allowed to move around for a while before they intersect one another, then during the remainder of the simulation they will often go into a stage of unbuilding highways and removing random-like patterns, thus cleaning up the cell space.

Two or more ants can also exploit a type of synergy by cooperating in the construction of extremely elaborate highways. Figure 16.5 illustrates such a highway that was built by two ants. During this particular simulation, the two ants suddenly

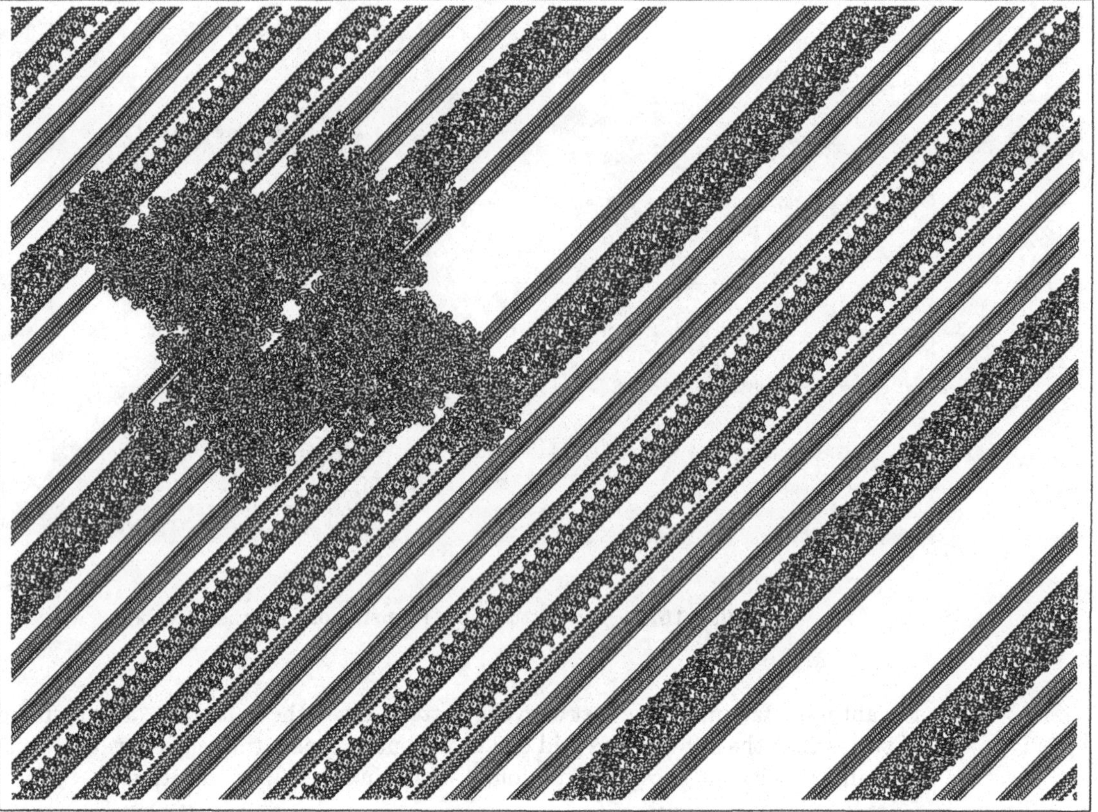

Figure 16.5 Two virtual ants can build more complex structures than a single ant acting alone

collided in the manner shown in Figure 16.4, which forced them to completely undo all of their work to bring the cell space back into an empty configuration! But then, since the ants had swapped initial positions and were facing in the opposite directions of how their counterpart started out, they went on to build yet another highway system. Eventually they collided once again, undid all of the second highway system, and proceeded to rebuild the first. Thus, for this particular simulation, the ants oscillated through a very elaborate cyclic pattern.

When three or more ants are allowed to roam about in the same space, even more interesting things can occur. Consider the case of three ants. Suppose that at some point two of the ants intersect in such a way that they start reversing the each other's work. Everything proceeds as you would expect, except for the fact

Can One Ant Ever Reverse Itself? Digression 16.1

Two ants can collide so that they start to reverse each other. But can one ant intersect its own path and start reversing that path? Let's assume that we are even allowed to help the ant by placing an object in the cell space that acts as a sort of mirror, so that any ant hitting it in a precise manner will eventually get turned around and start reversing its own path.

To prove that such an object cannot exist, we only need to take note that for each cell in the space, an ant can enter a cell only either vertically or horizontally, but not both. Also, if a cell is entered vertically, then the ant must exit horizontally. The vertical cells will spatially alternate with the horizontal cells, sort of like the red and black squares of a checkerboard.

Now, suppose that our magic ant mirror exists and that the ant first hits it by moving into it from the left. Let's refer to this first cell of the mirror as cell X. In order for the ant to reverse itself, it must eventually return to cell X from the top or the bottom, because it must make a right-angle turn and return along the path it came from. But to do this, cell X would have to have the property that it can be entered vertically and horizontally, which cannot be true. Therefore, a single ant cannot reverse itself.

E. G. D. Cohen and X. P. Kong used a similar technique to prove that an ant's trajectory cannot be contained in a finite area with a finite configuration.

that the third ant may be running around and causing minor havoc in the work of the other two ants. As a result, the two reversed ants will hit a cell that the third ant has more recently visited, thus halting their reversed progress. Consequently, it is common to see highways being built, then only partially unbuilt.

Besides changing the number of virtual ants in a cell space, we could vary the simulation in other ways. Probably the simplest (besides changing the number of ants) is to start the cell space with an initial configuration that is not empty. A more elaborate variation has been independently proposed by Greg Turk, Leonid Bunimovich, and S. E. Troubetzkoy that involves a generalization of Langton's ants into a form where the cells can have n states instead of just two. With n states we can represent an ant's behavior by an n-bit rule string: if an ant lands on a cell in state i, then if the $(i+1)$th bit of the string is 1, the ant turns right; otherwise it turns left. Also, when an ant leaves the cell that was in state i, it changes the cell to state $i+1$, or to 0 if the cell was in state $n-1$. With this generalization, Langton's virtual ant is represented by the rule string "10."

Some scientists have analytically studied the properties of these generalized virtual ants and obtained some interesting results. One obvious result is that any generalized virtual ant with a rule string that consists of all 0s or all 1s will never do anything more interesting than travel around in a little square. A not so obvious result is due to E. G. D. Cohen and X. P. Kong (see the digression box for a similar result); it states that any virtual ant defined by a rule string that has at least one 0 and one 1 cannot be contained in a finite-sized box, that is, it will always escape any boundary that you try to place around it.

Highway-building, as a property of virtual ants, is found in many other types of ants besides Langton's. Some examples of generalized virtual ants will behave chaoticly for hundreds of thousands of steps and only then spontaneously break into highway-building behavior. For other examples, no one knows if they will ever build highways because chaotic patterns persist even after hundreds of millions of time steps.

Ian Stewart (1994) has made an interesting observation regarding our lack of knowledge about the long-term behavior of some of these virtual ants. To paraphrase, for any of these ants we know their Theory of Everything, in that all of the "physical" laws that govern the ant's universe are simple and known to us. We also know the initial configuration of the ant's universe. Yet we are helpless to answer a simple question: Does the ant ever build a highway? Putting this all in perspective, if physicists ever uncover a Theory of Everything for our universe, and even if we deduce the initial state of the universe, we may still be helpless to deduce the long-term behavior of our own universe. Thus, as Stewart has said, the Theory of Everything in this case predicts everything but explains nothing.

It may be that a highway-building proof exists for these ants. We don't know at this point. But as we saw in the last chapter, other cellular automata that are only moderately more complicated than these virtual ants are known to be capable of universal computation, and it is therefore known to be impossible to prove many things about their long-term behaviors.

16.3 Flocks, Herds, and Schools

In the previous sections we saw how simple agents acting in isolation could display self-organizational properties despite their simplistic behavioral limitations. In the case of termites, adding more agents to the simulation did no harm, in that self-organization persisted even when multiple termites were acting as if they were alone; however, two termites were incapable of producing a qualitatively different type of behavior than a single termite. For the virtual ants, we briefly saw how two or more ants could create structures that no single ant could create. In this section we will take these ideas to an extreme by witnessing a type of agent that always produces uninteresting behavior by itself, but displays a stunning variety of behaviors when interacting with many similar agents. Specifically, in this section, we will examine a model of how collections of animals, such as flocks, herds, and schools, move about

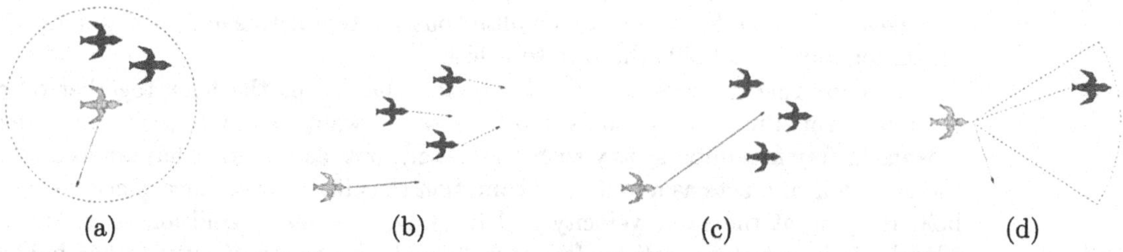

Figure 16.6 Four boid rules: (a) avoid flying too close to others; (b) copy near neighbors; (c) move towards center of perceived neighbors; (d) attempt to maintain clear view.

in a space in a way that appears to be orchestrated.

In the late 1980s, Craig Reynolds created a model of animal motion, named *boids*, that he used to simulate the motion of a flock of birds. Reynolds's approach was to make each boid in the flock an independent agent that attempts to follow a simple set of rules so as to independently optimize various goals. This approach is radically different from a more explicit technique that scripts the motion of each individual boid, since none of the boids—and not even the programmer—have any idea where the boids will eventually fly off to.

The goals that the boids try to achieve are very simple and are for the most part intuitive. The following list of rules explains these goals and the simplest technique that a boid can exploit to achieve each goal:

- **Avoidance.** Move away from boids that are too close, so as to reduce the chance of in-air collisions.

- **Copy.** Fly in the general direction that the flock is moving by averaging the other boids' velocities and directions.

- **Center.** Minimize exposure to the flock's exterior by moving toward the perceived center of the flock.

- **View.** Move laterally away from any boid that blocks the view.

Reynolds used only the first three goals; the fourth is my own creation that I added for no better reason than that it seemed like a good idea. We will see how the boids behave with and without the fourth rule later on. All of the rules are geometrically illustrated in Figure 16.6, which should be helpful in the discussion that follows.

The avoidance rule is probably the most fundamental, since it is the one rule that every boid can never completely ignore. In this spirit we consider the avoidance rule absolute, in that the copy and center rules are inactivated for any offending boid that invades another boid's personal space. This is an important heuristic because it makes little sense for a boid to simultaneously attempt to avoid, and to copy or center on, any other boids that are too close.

The copy rule enforces a form of cohesion that keeps the flock together over the long term. Presumably, boids in a flock would want to stay together for many reasons (safety in numbers, stay with mate, etc.), but, as Reynolds has pointed out, the copy rule also acts as a first approximation to collision avoidance, since if every boid is flying at the same velocity and heading, the risk of collisions is reduced. Clearly, it is not very realistic for every boid to be aware of every other boid's velocity and heading. So, to make things more realistic, we allow the boids to have only a fixed viewing angle from which they can "see" other boids. Additionally, their "vision" is further limited by enforcing the constraint that they can see only a finite distance.

The center rule is a very greedy method for boids to watch out for themselves at the expense of their neighbors. Since almost every type of locomotion group found in nature has a natural enemy in the form of a predator, it is to any individual agent's advantage to stay away from the edge of a flock, herd, pack, or school. After all, it is far better from an evolutionary point of view for an agent's neighbor to become a predator's meal than for itself to be the meal.[1] We place the same visual constraints on the center rule as we did for the copy rule, except for the fact that we allow the boids to use a different viewing radius for the purpose of averaging neighbors' positions. Thus, conceptually a boid can try to maintain the same heading and velocity as every other boid that it sees within a hundred yards or so, but it attempts to stay in the center only of a smaller group within 100 feet, for example. Notice that while the copy rule depends on the other boids' headings and speeds, the center rule depends only on the other boids' positions.

As mentioned earlier, the view rule is my own addition. While the rule seems biologically plausible to me, the only fieldwork I have done on the subject is to watch geese from my backyard, so you should take it with the grain of salt it deserves. I added this last rule because the only way I could ever coerce Reynolds's boids into a "V" formation was to partially blind them with an unrealistic viewing angle. The view rule works by moving the boid in a direction perpendicular to the vector that joins the first boid and the boid that is interfering with its sight. Since there are two such perpendicular paths, the boid always chooses the direction that is closer to its original heading. This has the side affect that the view rule will never encourage a boid to slow down, which is probably not very realistic, but it still seems to have the desired effect. We also allow the boids to vary what they consider to be visual interference by having a parameter that defines a narrow region by an angle and distance.

[1] If this sounds a bit Machiavellian, consider the case of penguins jumping into water. If some penguins are safely in the water, then another penguin can safely assume that there aren't any predators around. But which penguin jumps in first if no penguins are already in the water? The characteristic of sacrificing one's self should be quickly removed from the gene pool, so how do penguins resolve the problem? Simple. They often try to push each other in first (Dawkins, 1976).

Since we have defined the different types of goals that a boid will attempt to achieve, we now need to consider how a boid will combine all of these urges into a single action. Since each rule specifies a suggested direction in which to fly, we take a weighted average of the four directions to yield a single new direction. It is also not realistic to give the boids the ability to instantaneously change direction, so we include a sort of momentum factor that makes the boid partially continue along its previous path. Mathematically, this looks like

$$\mathbf{v}_{\mathrm{new}} = \mu \mathbf{v}_{\mathrm{old}} + (1-\mu)(w_{\mathrm{avoid}}\mathbf{v}_{\mathrm{avoid}} + w_{\mathrm{copy}}\mathbf{v}_{\mathrm{copy}} + w_{\mathrm{center}}\mathbf{v}_{\mathrm{center}} + w_{\mathrm{view}}\mathbf{v}_{\mathrm{view}}),$$

where all of the $\mathbf{v}$ terms are velocity vectors, all of the w terms are weighting factors, and μ is the momentum term. With the new composite velocity vector, we can add it to the old position to get the new position:

$$\mathbf{p}_{\mathrm{new}} = \mathbf{p}_{\mathrm{old}} + \tau \mathbf{v}_{\mathrm{new}},$$

where the $\mathbf{p}$ terms are positional vectors and τ specifies a step size or time increment.

The weights for the rules can be varied to your liking, but I preferred something along the lines of

$$w_{\mathrm{avoid}} > w_{\mathrm{view}} > w_{\mathrm{center}} > w_{\mathrm{copy}},$$

which seems like a reasonable relationship between the four weights if we consider collision avoidance to be the most important rule for survival, and copying the least important. Moreover, the ordering seems to make sense temporally, in that when a boid needs to avoid an obstacle, it must act instantly, while staying with the rest of the flock is more of a long-term goal. But this is just my spin on things.

Putting all of this together, we can now look at some examples of boids in motion. Figures 16.7 and 16.8 show two examples of boids in flight with the view rule disabled. In the first example we can see how a disorganized collection of boids will coalesce into a single flock. The figure really doesn't do the process justice because what you can't see in the figure are things like the boids jostling each other to get into the center of the flock, or how an isolated boid will all of a sudden spot a flock in the distance and zip across the screen to join the others.

Watching the boids in flight is a fascinating exercise. I would be embarrassed to tell you just how long I played with the simulation in the process of writing this chapter. You should try the simulation yourself.

Figure 16.8 shows another example of what happens when you change the "physics" of the boids' universe in a strange manner. As you can see, the boids quickly form into two swarm-like structures with the boids orbiting each other in a cyclic manner. After a while, the smaller swarm on the left starts moving in an ever more eccentric manner because the boids in it periodically catch a glimpse of the larger swarm. Eventually, the smaller swarm becomes unstable and the boids leave it for the larger swarm. To coerce the boids into this type of behavior, I gave

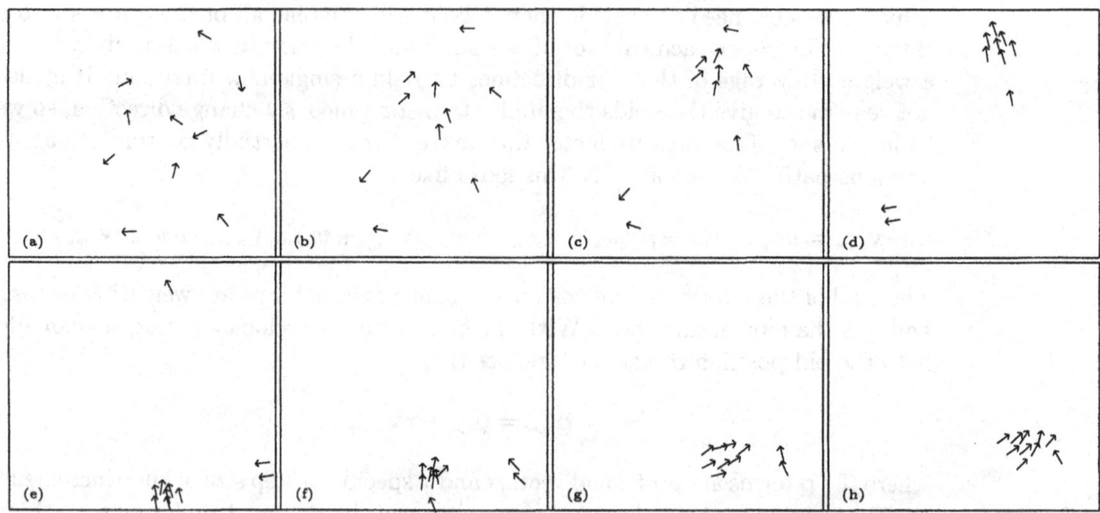

Figure 16.7 A collection of boids self-organize to form a flock

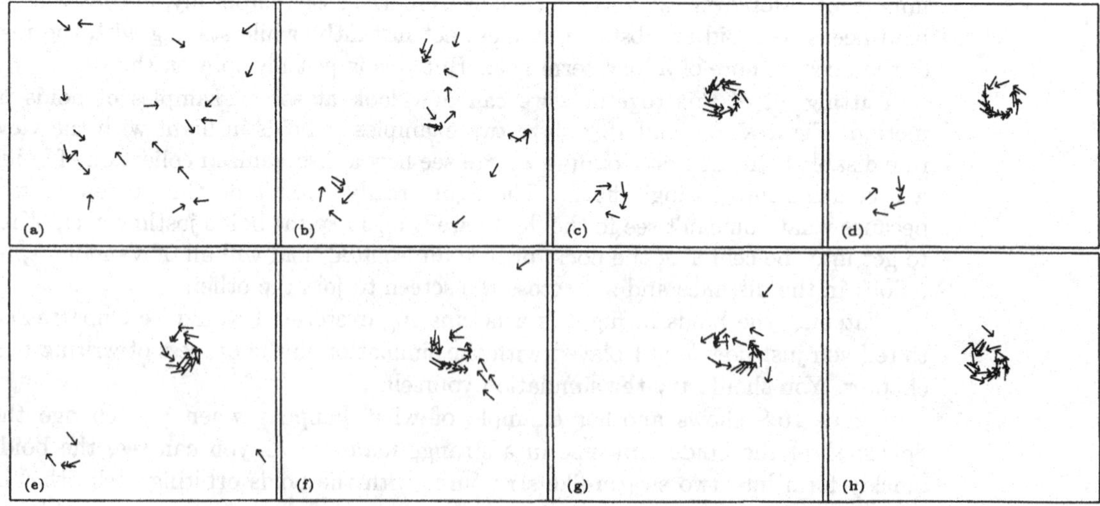

Figure 16.8 Changing the physics of the boids' universe allows for boid cycles.

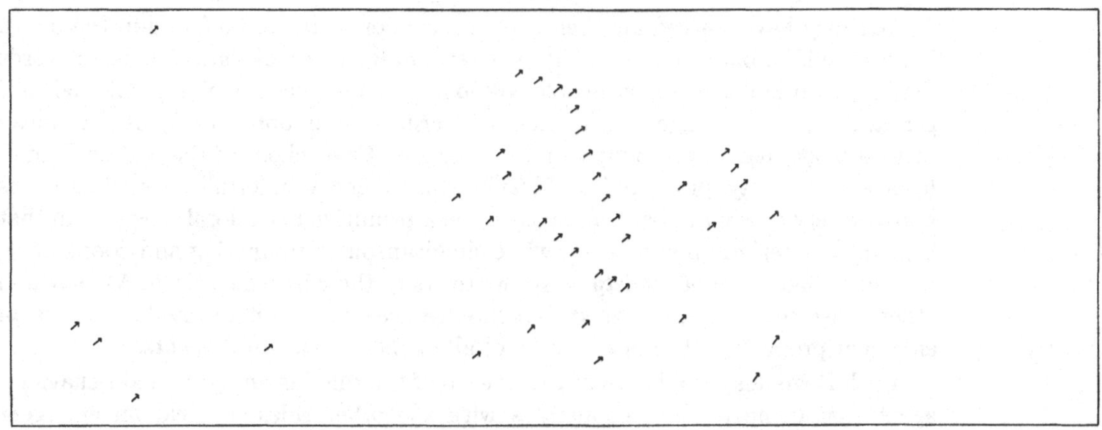

Figure 16.9 Activating the fourth boid rule promotes more realistic flocks

the center and avoidance rules large weights, turned off the view rule, and reduced the copy rule to a very small weight.

So far, all of these examples have been interesting, but the boids seem to behave more like fish or gnats than birds. This is where the view rule comes into play. Figure 16.9 shows the result of simulating the boids with all four rules activated. As you can see, the largest cluster of boids is actually in a "V" formation, which pleases me to no end. During the simulation, the boids can be seen to jostle each other as before, but now when one boid swerves in front of another, so as to cut it off, the offended boid will swerve to clear its line of sight. This action frequently results in a chain reaction that is reminiscent of traffic congestion.

16.4 Unifying Themes

In this chapter we have seen, firsthand, Kauffman's "order for free" concept in the way Resnick's randomly acting termites and Reynolds's boids self-organize to form clusters and flocks. In each case, the agents were able to form a global structure that seemed to require some oversight. But in both cases all agents were concerned only about their own goals, which makes the resulting organization almost a happy side effect. Langton's ant again demonstrated how deceptively simple agents can be pathologically complicated and also revealed how multiple agents can synergize to create structures that no single agent could build. Since the individual agents of all of our collectives were recursive in their and their neighbors' actions, and since each of the collectives consisted of many similar units acting in parallel, once again recursion and multiplicity reveal themselves as background themes.

You may have noticed another level of recursion that can be found in the boids. Let me explain; but first a warning. The term *agent* is one of those wonderful words that are so useful that many people will look at some phenomenon, point their finger, and say, "It's an agent." As such, the term is often ambiguously used to mean many things, and I am about to reuse it again. One school of the artificial intelligence community, pioneered by Marvin Minsky and wonderfully described in his book *Society of Mind*, posits an agent to be a primitive behavioral mechanism that attempts to perform a simple act while simultaneously competing and cooperating with other agents. The *society* of agents refers to the whole collection. Minsky and others have convincingly argued that intelligence—even human intelligence—is an emergent property of the interactions of all of these behavioral agents.

With Reynolds's boids, we can view each of the rules as an individual behavioral agent that competes and cooperates with the other rules to yield an emergent property that looks a lot like bird intelligence. Thus, the boids, as agents, are further composed of behavioral agents, which gives us another depth of recursion in how emergence and self-organization can come about. Minsky's book contains examples of how a human's behavioral agents can be composed of subagents, which can be composed of subsubagents, and so on. At the lowest level, the most primitive agents perform almost ridiculously simple tasks that no one would refer to as intelligent. But as one progresses to higher levels, the emergent composite behavior appears more and more complex, eventually hitting on something that is "intelligent."

But this idea is not reductionism. Reductionism claims that the whole can be understood as the sum of the parts. In every case that we have seen, the whole has revealed itself to be a surprise in that it is decidedly more than the sum of the parts. At all levels of nature, recursion and multiplicity of agents promote emergence and self-organization to yield an almost unexplainable form of complexity.

16.5 Further Exploration

All of the computer-generated figures in this chapter were made with **termites**, **vants**, and **boids**. Table 16.1 gives a brief summary of the options for all three programs. The options that are common to all three programs are listed first, and most of them have the same meaning as when they were used in the programs detailed earlier in this book. Probably the most important option for all of the programs is **-num**, which simply allows you to set the number of agents to use in a simulation.

For the **termites**, there is only one other possible option, **-dense**, which is used to determine the density of the wood chips at the start of the simulation. You should give the option a value between 0 and 1.

Similarly, **vants** has the same option, but in this case some random pixels are randomly set at the beginning of the simulation, which has the effect of thwarting

Option Name	Option Type	Option Meaning
Options Common to All Three Programs		
`-width`	INTEGER	width of the plot in pixels
`-height`	INTEGER	height of the plot in pixels
`-num`	INTEGER	number of agents to use
`-steps`	INTEGER	number of simulated steps
`-seed`	INTEGER	random seed
`-inv`	SWITCH	invert colors?
`-xmag`	INTEGER	magnification for X windows
`-term`	STRING	how to plot points
Options Only for `termites`		
`-dense`	DOUBLE	density of chips at start
Options Only for `vants`		
`-rule`	STRING	rule string
`-dense`	DOUBLE	density of random crud
Options Only for `boids`		
`-angle`	DOUBLE	number of viewing degrees
`-vangle`	DOUBLE	view avoidance angle
`-rcopy`	DOUBLE	radius for copy vector
`-rcent`	DOUBLE	radius for centroid vector
`-rvoid`	DOUBLE	radius for avoidance vector
`-rview`	DOUBLE	radius for view avoidance vector
`-wcopy`	DOUBLE	weight for copy vector
`-wcent`	DOUBLE	weight for centroid vector
`-wvoid`	DOUBLE	weight for avoidance vector
`-wview`	DOUBLE	weight for view avoidance vector
`-wrand`	DOUBLE	weight for random vector
`-dt`	DOUBLE	time-step increment
`-ddt`	DOUBLE	momentum term
`-minv`	DOUBLE	minimum velocity
`-len`	INTEGER	length of birds in pixels
`-psdump`	SWITCH	dump PostScript at the very end?

Table 16.1 Command-line options for `termites`, `vants`, and `boids`

orderly behavior in the virtual ants. The `-rule` option can be used to run a generalized virtual ant, and requires a value that is a string of any length that consists of only 0s and 1s.

The `boids` program has many options, but most of them should be familiar by now. There are four options used to specify the radius in which the four boid rules are active, and four corresponding weighting factors. The `-angle` option is used to specify the number of viewing degrees that the boids possess. The boids can see only other boids that fall within a cone of the specified number of degrees in front of them. The `-vangle` option has a similar meaning, but is used only for the view rule. The `-dt` and `-ddt` options specify time increment and momentum factors, and `-minv` is used to specify the minimum speed that the boids can fly.

For display purposes, `-len` can be used to specify the length of the boids in pixels. And finally, `-psdump` is used to tell the program to emit a PostScript image of the boids at the end of the simulation.

A boid is displayed as a flying arrow. The head of the arrow defines an arc that swings from the left edge, to the front, and then to the right edge of the head. This arc is the same as the viewing angle; thus, if you set the viewing angle to something large, say 320 degrees, then the head will make a very sharp point. With a viewing angle of 180 degrees, the head will be a flat line.

16.6 Further Reading

Dawkins, R. (1976). *The selfish gene.* Oxford: Oxford University Press.

Holldobler, B. & Wilson, E. O. (1990). *The ants.* Cambridge, Mass.: Belknap Press of Harvard University Press.

Langton, C. (1986). Studying artificial life with cellular automata. *Physica D*, 22(1–3): 120–149.

Langton, C. G. (Ed.). (1989). *Artificial Life*, volume 6 of *Santa Fe Institute studies in the sciences of complexity*, Reading, Mass. Addison-Wesley.

Langton, C. G., Taylor, C., Farmer, J. D., & Rasmussen, S. (Eds.). (1992). *Artificial Life II*, volume 10 of *Santa Fe Institute studies in the sciences of complexity*, Reading, Mass. Addison-Wesley.

Levy, S. (1992). *Artificial life: A report from the frontier where computers meet biology.* New York: Vintage Books.

Minsky, M. (1987). *The society of mind.* London: Heinemann.

Resnick, M. (1994). *Turtles, termites, and traffic jams: Explorations in massively parallel microworlds.* Cambridge, Mass.: Bradford Books/MIT Press.

Reynolds, C. W. (1987). Flocks, herds, and schools: A distributed behavioral model. *Comp. Graph.*, 21(4): 25–34.

Shaw, E. (1962). The schooling of fishes. *Sci. Am.*, 206: 128–138.

Stewart, I. (July 1994). Mathematical Recreations: The ultimate anty-particles. *Sci. Am.*, 271(1): 104–107.

Wilson, E. O. (1971). *The insect societies.* Cambridge, Mass.: Belknap Press of Harvard University Press.

17 Competition and Cooperation

Do onto others as you would have them do onto you.
— Luke 6:31

Eye for eye, tooth for tooth, hand for hand, foot for foot.
— Deuteronomy 19:21

Morality is the herd-instinct in the individual.
— Friedrich Nietzsche

ALMOST ALL TRADE—whether occurring in a stock market or in a bartering economy—depends on the simple fact that both traders believe that they are better off for making the trade. This fact includes favors as well. The simple principle of "You scratch my back, I'll scratch yours," as a behavioral guide, seems to be universally practiced by organelles, cells, plants and animals of all types, businesses, societies, and even nations.

Consider symbiosis as an example. Lichen, as an organism, is hard to classify because it consists of bacteria and algae living in complete harmony. Many animals, including humans, coexist with symbiotic bacteria that assist in digestion. The higher animals are better off for the trade because it would be impossible for them to digest certain types of food otherwise. Similarly, bacteria get a quick and easy meal out of the exchange, leaving both parties better off for the partnership. Cooperation among members of the same and even differing species also yields some striking examples. Slime molds demonstrate that conditional cooperation makes for a fuzzy boundary between single-celled and multicelled animals. During times of plenty, individual slime mold cells will fend for themselves; but when food is scarce, many slime mold cells will coalesce into a strange, multicellular creature that can crawl and even grow a stalk that emits spores. The higher animals provide more familiar examples. Some ant species are completely devoted to the task of defending a host plant from other animals. Mammals regularly groom one another, or form hunting packs. Specially adapted birds and fish clean other animals—even fierce predators such as sharks and crocodiles—without fear of being harmed in the process.

Cooperation persists despite the fact that all living things are in a state of perpetual competition. For any of the examples listed above, it would be interesting to consider what would happen if one of the participants "cheated." In the case of the symbiotes, cheating is not always a viable option because the successes of the symbiotes are often too closely intertwined. For example, there exist several ant species that defend plants from other predators. In return, the ants get a comfortable home with a built-in food supply. If the ants suddenly decided to no longer defend the plant from other animals, then the ants' nice home would quickly cease to exist. However, the case of species that clean predators presents us with a sort of paradox in that it is not at all clear why crocodiles do not occasionally eat the birds that clean them. Would this not give them an edge over other crocodiles that are more restrained? And if so, shouldn't we expect "cheaters" to benefit in the long run?

Darwin's theory of evolution, with it's emphasis on "survival of the fittest," seems to be at a loss to explain the emergence of mutual cooperation or "survival of the nicest." In this chapter, we will forgo the question of how cooperation can evolve in a competitive environment (it will be postponed until Chapter 20) and will instead examine several prerequisites for the evolvability of cooperation. Specifically, we will see exactly why cooperation is so robust and why cooperation is stable in the sense that acts of cheating do not pay off in the long run. To do this, we will follow in the footsteps of Robert Axelrod, a political scientist, who used game theory to study how cooperation among selfish agents can be not only a viable strategy but a profitable one as well. The implications of this result are quite remarkable: Some forms of ethical behavior may be not only morally correct but pragmatic as well.

17.1 Game Theory and Zero-Sum Games

The theory of games was created and formalized by John von Neumann and Oskar Morgenstern as a model of how thoughtful, rational, and potentially deceitful players with opposing interests will interact with each other. Under game theory, games such as chess and checkers are not "interesting" because for any board position there technically exists a "correct" or "best" move for a player to make, which leaves no room for real deceit. Moreover, chess and checkers are zero-sum games in that any gain made by a player yields an equal amount of loss for his opponent. We can therefore think of chess and checkers as transparent because given enough raw computing power, an opponent's move will always be perfectly determined.

An example of an "interesting" game for von Neumann and Morgenstern is poker. Poker is interesting not just because there is hidden information, but also because a player's best strategy depends equally on the strategies employed by the other players. For instance, suppose a poker player based decisions on nothing other than probability theory. Such a player would consider the cards in her hand, any other visible cards, and the amount of money at stake, then compute an expected return for each possible action. Now, if this probability-using poker player bet an unusually large amount of money on a particular hand, every other player in the game would immediately know the relative strength of her cards, which is to say that probability theory alone is a bad strategy for poker. Good poker players will exaggerate, deceive, simulate irrationality, and attempt to confuse the other players. In other words, good poker players must inject a fair amount of pseudo-randomness into their strategies, employ subtle psychological mind games, and know something about probabilities in order to be effective players.

But because poker depends on knowing both probabilities and people, games in which players know everything except what the other players are going to do are especially interesting because they get to the essence of the "mind game" part of poker that makes it fun to play. The canonical example of such a game, and one that is familiar to most people, is a method used by parents to solve disputes between two children. Suppose there is a cake that two children want. Not only are the children reluctant to share with one another, but neither trusts the other to fairly take the first slice of cake. The mother of the children solves the problem by allowing one child to slice the cake and the other child to choose either of the two pieces. Since the first child can be certain that his sibling is going to take the larger piece,, the child will have no choice but to slice the cake into two equal pieces. Any attempt by the first child to slice the cake into unequal pieces to his benefit can only result in a suboptimal solution for him. The cake-slicing problem shows a nearly perfect example of the type of solution that game theory attempts to provide. We will shortly see how solutions to other games capture the same spirit as the solution to the cake-slicing problem.

The primary goal of game theory is to provide a player with the best possible *strategy* for a particular game. In game theory, the term "strategy" refers not just to an overall plan but to a complete set of rules or an algorithm that prescribes exactly what a player should do in every possible situation and at any point in the game. By "best" I mean the strategy that yields the highest possible reward for a player. Sometimes a strategy will be as simple as "slice the cake as evenly as possible," but strategies may also possess a dose of pseudo-randomness as well.

To see an example of the latter type of strategy, consider a game between two players in which each player has a penny that he can place on a table. At each step in the game, the players can place their pennies with either side facing up; however, neither player knows ahead of time what the other player is going to do. After revealing their pennies to each other, if both pennies are **heads** or both are **tails**, then player A (the first player, if you wish) gets to keep both pennies; but if

		Player B's move	
		heads	**tails**
Player	**heads**	1, -1	-1, 1
A's move	**tails**	-1, 1	1, -1

Table 17.1 Payoff matrix for an even, zero-sum, matching-pennies game: Payoffs are listed as A's payoff, B's payoff.

the pennies have different sides showing, then player B gets to keep both pennies. The rules for the game can be more succinctly described by a *payoff matrix*, which is shown in Table 17.1. In the matrix, the entries describe each player's net payoff; hence, if each player plays **heads**, then player A wins one cent and player B loses one cent.

With the underlying assumption that each player never knows what the other player is going to do, game theory tells us that the best strategy for any player is to randomly pick **heads** or **tails** with equal probability. This is known as a *mixed strategy* because it prescribes that in the absence of information, a player should mix things up by being random. It may seem strange that the best strategy is to act randomly; in fact, one may be tempted to try to predict what the other player is going to do; but if this is possible, then the second player could just as well attempt similar predictions, leading to an infinite cycle of players trying to outsmart one another. This illustrates the futility of trying to be too clever in this particular situation.

The key to the solution of this game is threefold. First, we must assume that each player knows exactly what the other knows and that each will always act in his own self-interest. Second, any actions that are not random could be predicted, and therefore exploited by another player. Third, the best random mixed strategy will play **heads** and **tails** in a ratio that seeks a sort of middle ground like the one in the cake-slicing problem, that is, no one "won" the cake-slicing problem, in that the best solution was to avoid losing by doing something suboptimal or stupid.

We will now dive into the mathematical details of the solution. We need only some basic algebra to appreciate the mathematics; but if you find yourself lost in the details, it should be helpful to know that the math simply states that the matching-pennies game is a lot like the cake-slicing problem.

To start, let's get some notation out of the way. We will refer to the probability that player A will play **heads** as $P_A(\textbf{heads})$. Similarly, $P_B(\textbf{heads})$ is equal to the same probability for player B. We could also define similar terms for the probability that a player will play **tails**, but they are not really necessary because $P_A(\textbf{tails}) = (1 - P_A(\textbf{heads}))$ and $P_B(\textbf{tails}) = (1 - P_B(\textbf{heads}))$. We are now going to write down a mathematical expression that describes the expected score

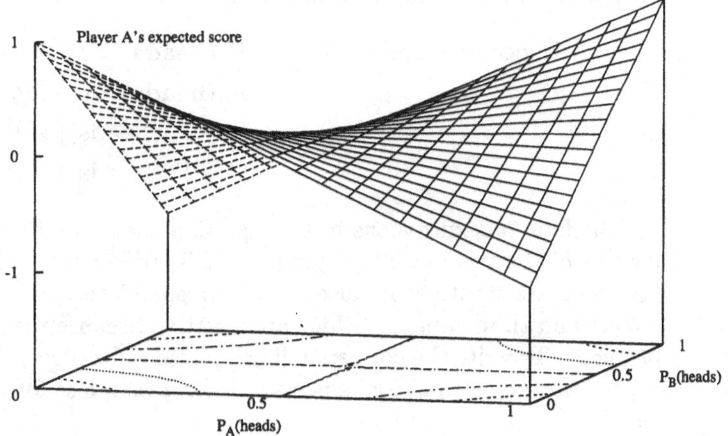

Figure 17.1 Plotting player A's expected score as a function of P_A(**heads**) and P_B(**heads**) results in a surface with a quarter-twist

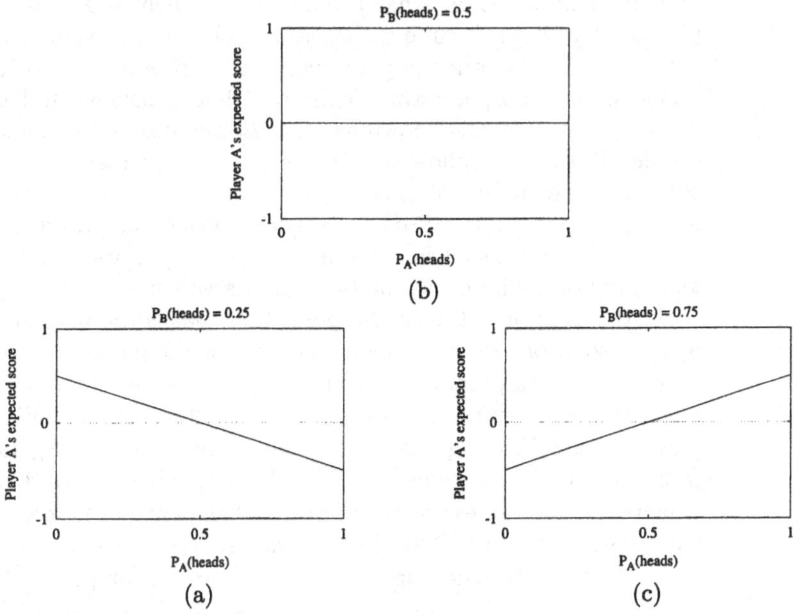

Figure 17.2 Cross sections of the surface from Figure 17.1 with P_B(**heads**) fixed at (a) $\frac{1}{4}$, (b) $\frac{1}{2}$, and (c) $\frac{3}{4}$

for player A, given the two probabilities described above:

$$\begin{aligned}\text{Expected score for } A \quad = \quad & P_A(\textbf{heads}) \times P_B(\textbf{heads}) - \\ & P_A(\textbf{heads}) \times (1 - P_B(\textbf{heads})) - \\ & (1 - P_A(\textbf{heads})) \times P_B(\textbf{heads}) + \\ & (1 - P_A(\textbf{heads})) \times (1 - P_B(\textbf{heads})).\end{aligned}$$

The four subexpressions in the equation correspond to the four possible combinations of the two players playing either **heads** or **tails**. The first and last subexpressions are positive because they correspond to a win for player A, while the second and third subexpressions are negative because they correspond to a loss for player A. To write the corresponding equations for player B, we would only need to negate the whole equation, since a win for B is a loss for A (this being a zero-sum game).

With this equation, we can compute the effectiveness of a mixed strategy that player A could use against strategies employed by player B. Since the equation has only two free variables, we can also draw a surface plot of the function, which is shown in Figure 17.1. The surface plot has some interesting properties that are a little difficult to see on a flat page, so it may help you to imagine that the surface plot is a flat sheet of rubber that you are holding in your hands, one edge in your left hand and the other in your right hand. If you were to twist the two edges in opposite directions, you would end up with a surface not unlike that of Figure 17.1. This type of surface is known as a *saddle* because it topologically resembles a real saddle. To see this, follow the line defined by $P_A(\textbf{heads}) = P_B(\textbf{heads})$. The cross section of the surface at this line is valley-shaped. As you follow the line defined by $P_A(\textbf{heads}) = (1 - P_B(\textbf{heads}))$, the surface has a cross section with a peak. Therefore, the surface has a saddle point directly in its center that is simultaneously at the top of a hill and at the bottom of a valley.

In this case, it is the saddle point that makes the matching-pennies game have a single solution. How so? Let's suppose for the moment that player B is going to play **heads** with probability $\frac{1}{4}$. Figure 17.2a shows the cross section of the saddle along the line defined by $P_B(\textbf{heads}) = \frac{1}{4}$. The graph in Figure 17.2a shows that player A can tilt the game in his favor by playing with $P_A(\textbf{heads})$ very small. In fact, if player B always uses $P_B(\textbf{heads}) = \frac{1}{4}$, then player A can always play **tails**, which gives him an expected profit of a half-cent per game. Moreover, if player B fixes $P_B(\textbf{heads})$ to be less than $\frac{1}{2}$, then player A can always exploit the situation to his favor. The same argument can be made for player B using a large value for $P_B(\textbf{heads})$ (whose cross section is shown in Figure 17.2c). For player B to fix $P_B(\textbf{heads})$ to a large or a small value is similar in spirit to a child who cuts a cake unequally. Any difference in any direction can be exploited by the other player. The only solution that enables no exploitation whatsoever is for both players to play **heads** and **tails** with equal probability. Figure 17.2b shows the cross section of the

		Player B's move	
		heads	**tails**
Player A's move	**heads**	HH, -HH	HT, -HT
	tails	TH, -TH	TT, -TT

Table 17.2 Payoff matrices for a generalized, zero-sum matching-pennies game: Payoffs are listed as A's payoff, B's payoff.

saddle at $P_B(\textbf{heads}) = \frac{1}{2}$, which is merely a flat line. The flat line indicates that player B has done the best one can hope for by simply eliminating the opportunity for player A to win. But Player A has the same information as player B, so we can expect both players to use the same analysis.

The preceding arguments were illustrative for an evenly matched game, but they were really only an introduction to a more general result. For any two-player finite game—even games that are skewed to be in the favor of one player—there exists at least one point that corresponds to two stable strategies for the players. By "stable" I mean that neither player could do better with any other strategy. This saddle point is known as a *Nash equilibrium*, named after its discoverer, John Nash.

Looking at Table 17.2, which contains a generalized version of the matching-pennies game, we can rewrite the expected score for player A as

$$
\begin{aligned}
E(A) \quad = \quad & HH \times P_A(\textbf{heads}) \times P_B(\textbf{heads}) + \\
& HT \times P_A(\textbf{heads}) \times (1 - P_B(\textbf{heads})) + \\
& TH \times (1 - P_A(\textbf{heads})) \times P_B(\textbf{heads}) + \\
& TT \times (1 - P_A(\textbf{heads})) \times (1 - P_B(\textbf{heads})),
\end{aligned}
$$

where the HH, HT, TH, and TT terms correspond to the four possible payoffs for player A, and the notation $E(A)$ stands for the expected earnings of player A. This equation will always have at least one Nash equilibrium, which means that a "best" strategy can be computed by looking for flat spots in the surface plot. (Such spots, mathematically speaking, will have a zero gradient.)

The remarkable fact about these solutions is that they will employ randomness in such a way that they cannot be outsmarted—neither in theory nor in practice—by a person or a computer. With such a powerful result, many game theorists have had the hope of modeling many other types of conflicts as multiplayer games. Some of these attempts have been very fruitful. It is also fair to say that game theory has resulted in a powerful way of looking at conflict in all conceivable areas, from economics, to politics, and even to biology. But it is game theory's failures that are even more telling.

17.2 Nonzero-Sum Games and Dilemmas

When we started this chapter, I began with the argument that cooperation in nature is more common than one would expect given the winner-take-all emphasis of Darwin's natural selection. In the last section, we were able to look at a toy game that had little resemblance to real-life scenarios but helped to explain the ideas behind game theory. In the matching-pennies game, there was no room for cooperation because the game was zero-sum; however, in this section we will look at games that are nonzero-sum, leaving open the possibility of cooperation among players. Moreover, nonzero-sum games permit win-win and lose-lose outcomes, which adds a nice dose of realism to the examples.

As a real-world example, consider a basic social dilemma. In most workplaces people share a communal coffee maker with the implicit (or sometimes explicit) rule that if you take the last cup of coffee from the pot, then you should make the next pot. Nevertheless, some people can't resist the temptation to take the last cup without making a new pot, thus leaving a thin layer of sludge for the next coffee drinker. Are such people sociopaths?[1] Or are such people merely exploitative because they can get away with it? The dilemma in this situation lies in the conflict: Be a good colleague, or a caffeine junky?

While this situation serves as an example of a social dilemma, it is a little too vague to be studied by game theory, primarily because there are an indefinite number of players playing for an indefinite length of time. Nevertheless, for the remainder of this section, we will use the communal coffee scenario as a metaphor because of its familiarity, and with the understanding that the games we will formally consider will only have two players who play for a single round. Thus, there is no chance of retribution or punishment in any of the games, in that a player will never encounter an opponent again. The goal of any player will always be to maximize her payoff and not to live up to some moral standard. These are games, after all, and players play to win. Hence, the communal coffee scenario does not meet these requirements, since colleagues can in some way punish each other for antisocial behavior, but it will still be useful as a basic example of the components of a dilemma.

With those caveats aside, we can now consider some formal properties of games that result in dilemmas. The usual meaning of a dilemma is summed up by the phrase "damned if you do, damned if you don't." For the purpose of this section I am going to use a slightly different definition that boils down to the notion that no matter what choice a player makes there exists the possibility that a player may feel regret after a single round of play. Also, by "regret" I do not mean that a player feels morally regretful, but that given the possibility, a player would act differently.[2]

---

[1] Okay, maybe I should switch to decaf.

[2] The literature on game theory often contains a similar notion of regret; however, my use of the word also includes the idea that a player has a sense of irony. This will make more sense when we look at why the Prisoner's Dilemma can be considered a dilemma.

		Player B's move	
		cooperate	**defect**
Player A's move	**cooperate**	(CC, CC) Reward for mutual cooperation	(CD, DC) Sucker's payoff, and Temptation to defect
	defect	(DC, CD) Temptation to defect, and Sucker's payoff	(DD, DD) Punishment for mutual defection

Table 17.3 Payoffs for a generic two-player dilemma: Payoffs are listed in parentheses as (A's payoff, B's payoff).

In order to see what sorts of dilemmas are possible, consider Table 17.3, which shows a payoff matrix for a two-player game in which there are four possible payoffs. In this game, each player must take one of two actions, cooperate or defect; and, as with the matching-pennies game, neither player knows ahead of time what the other player is going to do. For this section we will denote the payoffs as CC, CD, DC, and DD, which correspond to the four possible combinations of cooperation and defection. Each of the four possible payoffs could have a numerical value assigned to it; however, instead of assigning numbers to the specific entries, we will enforce an ordering on the payoffs that merely states which payoffs are preferable when compared with the others. Using the communal coffee scenario as an example, a reasonable ordering of the payoffs could be:

1. You get to drink all the coffee you want without ever brewing a pot (DC).
2. You get to drink coffee while making your fair share for others (CC).
3. You get to drink coffee but everyone else exploits you (CD).
4. No one makes coffees, so no one can drink coffee (DD).

This ordering simply encodes the idea that you like to drink coffee, but you would rather not have to make it yourself. It is also just one of many orderings that are possible for a two-player game of this type. With four different payoffs, there are exactly twenty-four different orderings. Of these twenty-four, most of the games have a trivial solution; for instance, when $CC > CD > DC > DD$, there is no dilemma because both you and your opponent always do better when either or both of you cooperate. In order for a dilemma to exist, players must have a possible reason for both cooperating and defecting. In this spirit, we will describe some conditions on the ordering that must be true in order for a dilemma to occur.

This first two conditions assume that you take one course of action, and then specify what you would prefer your opponent's action to be:

- $(CC > CD)$ This condition simply states that if you cooperate, then you will benefit more if the other player also cooperates, for instance, you would prefer that all players periodically make a fresh pot of coffee instead of just your being the only one who makes coffee.
- $(DC > DD)$ This condition means that if you defect, you get an additional bonus if the other player cooperates, for example, it is better for you to get your coffee through the other player's efforts than to have no coffee at all.

Together, in a nutshell, the first two constraints state that no matter what you do, you prefer that the other player cooperates.

The next two constraints explain things from a reversed point of view: They assume that the other player will take some course of action and then specify an ordering that is determined by your action. However, it is not necessary that both of these conditions be true, only that one or the other is:

- $(DC > CC)$ This condition states that if the other player cooperates, then you are better off defecting, for instance, if someone else makes a pot of coffee, then enjoy the java.
- $(DD > CD)$ This condition states that if the other player defects, then you are better off defecting. For the communal coffee scenario, this condition is not met, but $(DC > CC)$ is true, which still gives us a dilemma. We will see another dilemma that meets this requirement shortly.

The third and fourth rules together motivate players to defect. So considering all four conditions together, they express the idea that each player wants the other to cooperate, but both are tempted to defect. I am going to add a fifth condition of $(CC > DD)$, which simply states that mutual cooperation is preferred to mutual defection.[3] Putting all of this together, we can logically express the conditions for a game to be a dilemma as:

$$(CC > CD) \wedge (DC > DD) \wedge ((DC > CC) \vee (DD > CD)) \wedge (CC > DD),$$

where $\wedge$ represents the logical AND operation and $\vee$ represents the logical OR operation. (You may want to consult this logical statement later on to convince yourself that it in fact does describe the dilemmas that we will be considering shortly.) Of the twenty-four possible two-player games, this leaves only three games that can be properly referred to as dilemmas. Each has been thoroughly studied

[3] Actually, there is a game known as Deadlock that has $(DD > CC)$ and is sometimes considered a dilemma by game theorists. In Deadlock, players really have no incentive to cooperate; hence, it really isn't much of a dilemma.

by game theorists and has a common name: Chicken, Stag Hunt, and Prisoner's Dilemma. We will examine each dilemma in detail, saving the Prisoner's Dilemma for last, since for our purposes it is the most important of the three dilemmas.

Chicken ($DC > CC > CD > DD$) The prototypical version of the Chicken Dilemma, featured in films such as *Rebel Without a Cause*, works as follows. Two confused and maladjusted teenagers face each other in separate cars that are initially placed on opposite ends of a straight road. At an agreed-upon starting time, both players accelerate their cars, heading on a collision course. If one player unilaterally swerves his car to avoid a collision (i.e., cooperate), he is labeled a "chicken," while his opponent can make a claim to studliness. If both players swerve, then neither player wins or loses much in the way of reputation. But if both players stay their course (i.e., defect), then they die, which is clearly the worst possible outcome.

The Chicken Dilemma superficially has nothing in common with our communal coffee scenario, but the ordering of the payoffs is identical in the two. Other variants of the game can be found wherever social status can be achieved through dominance: playgrounds, animal pecking orders, and international politics (e.g., the Cuban missile crisis).

Regret in the Chicken Dilemma has two potential sources. If both you and your opponent cooperate, then you would have been better off defecting. On the other hand, if both players defect, you would have been better off cooperating. Thus, "damned if you do, damned if you don't" is an accurate description of the Chicken Dilemma. Note that the optimal move for any player is to do exactly what the other player doesn't do.

Stag Hunt ($CC > DC > DD > CD$) Stag Hunt is normally explained as a game in which players must choose to hunt either stag or hare. Since most people are not frequent stag hunters (and since most people don't use words like "stag" and "hare"), I have an alternative version of the Stag Hunt Dilemma that should be a little more familiar to most.[4] My version of the Stag Hunt Dilemma is actually a real dilemma that I personally contend with about once a week in the summer. Suppose you play in a softball league with several colleagues. When everyone shows up for a game, your team usually does well; but when only a few of the key players show up, your team will typically get slaughtered. You like to play softball, and you especially like to win, but losing takes its toll on your competitive spirit. What do I do? Typically I play.

[4]In the original version, you and another are hunting stag, which means that each player must guard one end of a trail so as to trap the stag in the middle. Prior to catching the stag, both you and your partner will each come across a hare. If either of you goes after the hare, then the stag will get away, but the one who defects will have the hare to eat. Both players would rather eat stag, but both are tempted to defect because the other may do so.

Regret in the Stag Hunt Dilemma is different than it was in Chicken, since any player's optimal move is to do the same thing that the other players do. If others play, so should you. If others don't play, you shouldn't either. Hence, our situation is exactly the opposite of the one we had in Chicken.

Prisoner's Dilemma ($DC > CC > DD > CD$) In the Prisoner's Dilemma, you and a partner in crime have been arrested for a crime that you are actually guilty of, but the prosecutor has too little evidence to win a conviction. You and your partner are being interrogated separately, but you have a good idea that he is being squeezed in a manner that is similar to your own predicament. Here is the situation: If both of you keep your mouths shut (i.e., you cooperate with each other), then both of you will get away with the crime. If one of you turns state's evidence (defect), then the other will be put in prison while the defector gets to live a life of luxury on the state payroll as a protected witness. If both of you confess and turn state's evidence (defect), then both of you will go to prison, but with a reduced sentence.

What do you do? The diabolical twist in the Prisoner's Dilemma is that no matter what your opponent (or partner) does, you are better off defecting. In fact, according to game theory, Prisoner's Dilemma isn't much of a dilemma because it has the clear-cut solution that you should always defect. The perversity of this situation is that if we are to assume that both players have this knowledge, then they will both defect, resulting in an outcome that is far worse than if they had both cooperated! Thus, the common good is subverted by individual rationality.

The Prisoner's Dilemma is reminiscent of economic trade wars. Every nation wants other countries to lower trade barriers, but no nations want to lower all of their own because they believe they have industries that need to be protected (especially interesting cases of this are Japan's near refusal to import rice, and France's strict conditions for the importation of movies). Regret in the Prisoner's dilemma comes from an appreciation of irony.

The Prisoner's Dilemma, as a game, was discovered by Melvin Dresher and Merrill Flood in 1950 while they were working at the RAND Corporation. Robert Axelrod has termed the Prisoner's Dilemma the *E. coli* of social psychology, since it nicely encompasses the most basic features of social conflict. Axelrod's statement is especially justified because Chicken and Stag Hunt (as well as Deadlock, mentioned earlier in this chapter in footnote 3) can be seen as slight variations of the Prisoner's Dilemma. For instance, if we take the ordering from the Prisoner's Dilemma, $DC > CC > DD > CD$, and swap the first two payoffs, we end up with Stag Hunt. Similarly, swapping the last two payoffs turns the Prisoner's Dilemma into Chicken. (Likewise, swapping the middle two payoffs retrieves Deadlock.) Hence, the Prisoner's Dilemma acts as a prototypical dilemma from which all of the others are derived.

You may have a bit of skepticism at this point regarding the relevance of the Prisoner's Dilemma to real-world scenarios; after all, game theory states that rational players should always defect when faced with the Prisoner's Dilemma. Clearly, the Prisoner's Dilemma is lacking some crucial quality that real-world situations have, but what is it? In the next section, we will see how simply allowing players to play the Prisoner's Dilemma for an indeterminate number of rounds allows "nice" strategies to be successful.

17.3 Iterated Prisoner's Dilemma

The iterated Prisoner's Dilemma, or IPD for short, is identical to the original version of the game except for the fact that players play for many rounds instead of a single round. Moreover, players have complete knowledge of their own and their competitor's previous moves; thus, one can make decisions based upon whether or not one's opponent has been cooperative or not. As we shall see, iteration makes all the difference.

In 1980, Robert Axelrod solicited entries for a round-robin tournament in which programs would play the IPD for 200 rounds. In order to keep score so as to determine a winner, Axelrod assigned numerical values[5] to each of the four possible outcomes: five points for the "temptation" payoff ($DC = 5$), three points for mutual cooperation ($CC = 3$), one point as punishment for mutual defection ($DD = 1$), and no points as the sucker's payoff ($CD = 0$). Since each program played every other program as well as a copy of itself, the winner was the program that earned the most points. Some of the participants in the study included game theorists, social scientists, mathematicians, and computer scientists; thus, the submitted programs came from a learned crowd that understood a thing or two about game theory and social conflict. As to the actual programs, there were many different types. Some of the programs could be described as nice, greedy, sophisticated, simple, stupid, or even devious. The surprising outcome of this tournament is that the simplest and shortest of all of the programs won. But before we examine the winner, let's take a look at some simple but unrealistic strategies:

- *Always Defect ("**ALL-D**").* This is perhaps the safest strategy, in that it is impossible to win against it. Moreover, it is impossible to exploit **ALL-D** because it will never leave itself open to attack. **ALL-D** has the added strength that it can endlessly exploit strategies that are endlessly forgiving, yielding the highest possible payoff, but will suffer when playing against itself or unforgiving strategies.

[5]Any numerical values assigned to the payoffs of the Prisoner's Dilemma should obey the relationship $(DC + CD) < (2 \times CC)$. Otherwise, in the IPD, players could take turns being the "sucker" for a total return greater than that from mutual cooperation.

	ALL-C	RAND	ALL-D	Average
ALL-C	3.0	1.5	0.0	1.5
RAND	4.0	2.0	0.5	$2.1\bar{6}\bar{6}$
ALL-D	5.0	3.0	1.0	3.0

Table 17.4 The expected score of the column-one strategy when played against the row-one strategy

- *Always Cooperate ("ALL-C").* This strategy, being the exact opposite of **ALL-D**, does well when it plays itself or other "nice" strategies, but is endlessly exploited by the likes of **ALL-D**.
- *Randomly Cooperate or Defect ("RAND").* By randomly switching between cooperation and defection, **RAND** achieves a sort of middle ground when compared with the other two strategies, since it is more resistant to the exploitation of **ALL-D**, can occasionally exploit **ALL-C**, and does fairly well when played against itself.

Table 17.4 describes how each of the three basic strategies would fare when played in a simple round-robin tournament. As can be seen, not only does **ALL-D** do best, but its average score is equal to the best score that **ALL-C** can ever achieve, which seems to imply that **ALL-D** may still be a pretty good approach after all. The problem with **ALL-D**, however, is that if every creature in a population practiced a strategy that amounted to **ALL-D**, then the population as a whole would have a very low fitness because every individual in the population would be constantly in a state of struggle. By comparison, a population that consisted entirely of **ALL-C** would have a relatively high fitness because everyone would be cooperating. Hence, **ALL-D** optimizes local fitness at the expense of global fitness while **ALL-C** optimizes global fitness at the expense of local fitness. Both strategies are bad for exactly opposite reasons. **RAND**, being a sort of stochastic merging of **ALL-C** and **ALL-D**, yields a compromise that most would find unsatisfying for a variety of reasons. How, then, should individuals and entire populations behave so that local and global fitness are both given a chance to flourish?

The major weakness with all of these simple strategies is that they lack the most basic notion of memory, in that they do what they do regardless of what has previously occurred. What is obviously missing is that strategies may depend on both players' previous actions. Enter Anatol Rapoport and his entry in the tournament, "Tit-for-Tat," or **TFT**. Of the fourteen programs submitted to Axelrod's tournament, Rapoport's was the shortest, a mere four lines of code. The principle behind **TFT** is amazingly simple but universally recognizable: Be nice at first, but punish any defections. In other words, **TFT** will offer to cooperate in the first round of any game of IPD, then it will do exactly what its opponent did in the previous round.

Hence, **TFT** is indistinguishable from **ALL-C** when played against **ALL-C**, and when played against **ALL-D**, **TFT** will get suckered on the first round but will reciprocate with defection for the remainder of the game. **TFT** also seems to nicely combine the two notions from the biblical quotes that appear in the beginning of this chapter.

TFT won the first round of Axelrod's tournament by being cooperative but resistant to exploitation. Encouraged by these results, Axelrod held a second round that drew many more entries (sixty-two) from six different countries. The participants now included hobbyists as well as academics. Yet, the most significant difference between the first and second rounds of the tournament was that in the second round all participants knew that **TFT** was the winner, and could therefore use the findings and analysis from the first round to better their chance of winning. Once again Anatol Rapoport entered **TFT**, and once again **TFT** won. This is especially impressive when you consider that all participants in the second round were motivated to specifically beat **TFT** . In the next section, we will look at some of Axelrod's analysis, which indicates why **TFT** is such a strong strategy.

17.4 Stable Strategies and Other Considerations

Despite **TFT**'s victories in both of Axelrod's tournament rounds, it is important to realize that there is no such thing as a "best" strategy for IPD. If most of your opponents consist of nice, **ALL-C**-like strategies, then it pays to be selfish; but if most of your opponents have a retaliatory streak in them, then it's better to keep your greed in check. **TFT**'s strength lies in the fact that it works in a wide variety of settings. Axelrod thoroughly analyzed the results from his tournament and was able to generalize what characteristics make strategies successful:

- *Don't be envious.* The most amazing fact about **TFT**'s victory is that **TFT** can never beat another strategy. At best, it can only tie. **TFT** seeks win-win situations because it doesn't get greedy for higher payoffs.

- *Be nice.* In the second round of Axelrod's tournament, some attempted to emulate **TFT** except that they would try to sneak in an occasional defection in order increase their net payoff. "Niceness," that is, never being the first to defect, was the single best predictor of success. "Mean" strategies almost always did more poorly than the nice strategies.

- *Reciprocate.* **TFT** elicits cooperation because it punishes defection and rewards cooperation. In fact, on a basic level, **TFT** is forgiving because it will resume cooperation if an opponent does so.

- *Don't be too clever.* Part of the elegance of **TFT** is that it is perfectly transparent. Once you know what **TFT**'s strategy is, it is fairly clear that there is no way to beat it. Other, more complicated strategies may attempt to

> be more sophisticated, but after a while, "sophistication" can look a lot like randomness. Moreover, complicated strategies can be endlessly subjected to feedback conditions because, if they are successful, they will most likely encounter strategies with a similar underlying algorithm.

As stated before, there is no such thing as a best strategy, and **TFT** has some known problems. Some have claimed that **TFT** is too eager to punish. In fact, a strategy known as "Tit-for-Two-Tats," which waits for two defections before administering punishment, would have won the first tournament round but did relatively poorly in the second round. Nevertheless, "Tit-for-Two-Tats" does better than **TFT** in a noisy environment. For example, if by mistake a defection occurs between two strategies using **TFT**, the two players will endlessly echo the error, each alternating between cooperation and defection. But "Tit-for-Two-Tats," being more forgiving, will shrug off an erroneous defection. Nevertheless, "Tit-for-Two-Tats" can be exploited by "Joss," a strategy that behaves like **TFT** but will defect randomly 10 percent of the time.

An example of a less forgiving **TFT**-like strategy is "Friedman," which starts off with cooperation but will forever defect after the first defection by an opponent. Of all the "nice" strategies, "Friedman" did the worst because of its unforgiving nature. Yet "Friedman" has the affect of making "Joss" a very impractical strategy, since one defection is enough to trigger an all-out war with "Friedman."

The moral of all of this is that you can never know what your environment will look like; thus, on a certain level, it is advantageous to be a generalist. Moreover, regardless of the system or substrate (economies, ecosystems, or computers), it is a fair bet that successful strategies will be emulated by others, which means that hypocrisy is an especially bad thing. In fact, we can almost conclude that any successful strategy must, by definition, be able to get along with itself. But this raises an interesting question: What qualities must a strategy have in order to plausibly be found in nature?

Axelrod and William Hamilton considered this question from a biological perspective and came up with three basic requirements. First, a strategy must be initially viable. Clearly, simple strategies such as **ALL-D** and **ALL-C** qualify because it is easy to imagine that a genetic program for such behavior can exist. **TFT**, being only slightly more complicated, has the same benefit of simplicity. Moreover, from a programming point of view, **TFT** requires the underlying "computer" to remember only a single bit of information, that is, you are currently in either a cooperative relationship or an uncooperative one. The simplest animals can and do practice this sort of behavior, even if it is in the form of "fight or flight" or "fight or ignore."

Successful strategies must also be robust, in that they can exist in a wide variety of environments. Both "mean" and "nice" strategies do well only when surrounded almost exclusively by nice strategies. In a varied environment, both of the extreme strategies will do poorly. But **TFT** is able to cope with almost any environment.

Finally, successful strategies must be resistant to invasions from mutated strategies. This characteristic is similar to the notion of an *evolutionary stable strategy* (ESS), a term that John Maynard Smith used in the 1960s when he used game theory to describe evolutionary systems. An ESS is almost identical to a Nash equilibrium from game theory, in that an ESS is in a Nash equilibrium with itself. What all of this means is that stable strategies can fight off invaders. A population of **ALL-D** is in one sense the most stable strategy because no single mutation could survive in such a kill-or-be-killed environment. Any deviation from **ALL-D** will be punished. Therefore, **ALL-D** is an ESS. An example of a very unrobust strategy is **ALL-C**, which can be successfully invaded by any other strategy. **TFT** can be stable, but is ironically susceptible to being invaded by **ALL-C**, which can exist in a mostly **TFT** population of protectors.

17.5 Ecological and Spatial Worlds

We have seen how the success of a strategy closely depends on the environment in which it exists. In this section we will examine how the reverse process can take place, that is, how a successful strategy can affect its environment. The study of the relationships and interactions that occur between organisms and environments is the science of *ecology*. Throughout this section we will consider the iterative Prisoner's Dilemma as seen through the eyes of an ecologist. Doing so is interesting for many reasons, one of which, as Axelrod has pointed out, is that ecological simulations of the iterated Prisoner's Dilemma yield insights into what future rounds of IPD tournaments would look like. More specifically, the second round of Axelrod's tournament reflected the failures and successes of the first round, in that the greater a strategy's score, the more likely it was to be emulated in a later round by other participants. Similarly, successful organisms in an ecosystem will increase their numbers and, therefore, change their environment.

The ecological model that we will use is identical to one used by Axelrod and is very simple mathematically. We assume that the ecosystem can support only a fixed number of "organisms" and that the population of each strategy is some fractional part of the whole ecosystem. For convenience, let the proportional populations of the strategies be represented by numbers between 0 and 1 so that the sum of the proportional populations of all strategies is equal to 1. With this representation, the populations reflect the probability that a randomly selected member of the ecosystem will obey a particular strategy. Also note that a population proportion of 0 means that a strategy is extinct and that a population proportion of 1 means that the environment is completely saturated with a particular strategy.

The dynamics of our ecological model can be mathematically described in terms of two time-varying quantities that we recompute at each time step, and a special lookup table that can be precomputed once for the whole simulation. The two

Cooperation and Defection in Nature **Digression 17.1**

While there are many examples of interspecies cooperation in nature, there are also some related examples of "defections" that illustrate some of the game-theoretic aspects of biology. One particular case of cooperation and defection can be found in fish.

A wrasse is a small fish that earns a living eating parasites off larger fish. The larger fish not only refrain from eating wrasse, but they also have been known to wait at an established station for the privilege of being cleaned. Normally this transaction proceeds with little surprise; the wrasse gets a meal and the larger fish gets cleaned.

Things are complicated, however, by another small fish, called a blenny, that not only looks like a wrasse but has adapted to mimic one as well. The blenny will approach a larger fish as if it is going to clean it, but instead it will take a bite of the larger fish's tail fin. Thus, nature has a form of defection that is much more subtle than the usual predator-prey type of competition. Moreover, the blenny is partially a victim of its own success, since if its population ever significantly exceeds the wrasse's, it will be more difficult for it to dupe the larger fish (Wickler, 1968).

time-varying quantities are the proportional populations and the scores, which we will denote by $P_i(t)$ and $S_i(t)$ where the i subscript denotes strategy i and t denotes the time step. The lookup table, $R_{ij}(t)$, stores the relative score that strategy i would win when played against strategy j. The numbers in the lookup table are computed in a manner similar to the way we calculated the values in Table 17.4, except that in this case we have to consider the number of rounds[6] that the IPD will be played in a given time step. Also notice that I have given the lookup table a time index to indicate that the simulation I wrote for this chapter recomputes the table at each time step for reasons that will be explained shortly.

The proportional population of a strategy at the next time step is updated by the equation

$$P_i(t+1) = \frac{P_i(t) \times S_i(t)}{\sum_{j=1}^{n} P_j(t) \times S_j(t)},$$

where n represents the total number of strategies in the ecosystem. The numerator of the update equation reflects the fact that the next population level is proportional to the current population times the score. Hence, the greater the current population or the greater the current score, the greater the next population level. The

[6] A single ecological simulation consists of many time steps. In each time step, we play many rounds of the Prisoner's Dilemma. This should clarify any remaining ambiguity in how "rounds" and "steps" are used in the discussion.

denominator of the equation is a normalization term that enforces the constraint that the sum of all of the proportional populations must be equal to 1. A strategy's score at a given time step is computed by the equation

$$S_i(t) = \sum_{k=1}^{n} P_k(t) \times R_{ik}(t),$$

which expresses the idea that the total score is equal to a weighted sum of how the strategy performs against all of the other strategies. In this case, we are weighting the total by the population levels of the strategies; thus, the greater the population of a particular opponent, the more the score against that opponent will count.

The only remaining things we must specify are the payoff matrix, the number of rounds for each step, and the initial populations. For our first example of how an ecosystem can change over time, we will have **ALL-C**, **ALL-D**, **RAND**, and **TFT** fight it out. We will use the same payoff matrix that Axelrod used ($DC = 5$, $CC = 3$, $DD = 1$, and $CD = 0$) and have each time step consist of 200 rounds. At the very first time step we will set **ALL-C** to occupy 60 percent of the population, **RAND** to 20 percent, and **ALL-D** and **TFT** to 10 percent each.

Figure 17.3a shows the population levels of the four strategies over fifty time steps. Right from the start, **ALL-C** suffers by being exploited by **ALL-D** and **RAND**, which both see an initial boost in their populations, while **TFT** initially suffers. Around the time that **ALL-D** takes the lead, **RAND** starts to drop off because it can't really compete with **ALL-D** in such a hostile environment. With the further decay of **RAND**, **TFT** makes slow but sure increases in its numbers. By cutting down on **ALL-C** and then **RAND**, **ALL-D** has carved a niche for itself, but has inadvertently made room for **TFT** to grow as well. In fact, **TFT** cannot grow without a little bit of help from the mean strategies, since, as pointed out before, it can never really beat another strategy in terms of outscoring it in a single pairing. All that **TFT** can really do is perform well in a wide variety of environments. By step 15, **ALL-D** has reached its peak and can grow no more because **TFT** now has a strong enough presence that it can start to cut down on **ALL-D**. Near step 20, **TFT** passes **ALL-D** and then proceeds to squash it out of existence.

The numbers for the initial population levels were deliberately chosen so as to make this particular simulation more interesting. This is not to say that there is anything like a "typical" ecological IPD simulation, but that it is not very common to see so many swings in the population levels so early in the simulation before the system settles down into fixed-point behavior. The next two simulations will be used to illustrate several other points. First, we will see how uniform starting conditions can result in population levels in which multiple strategies can coexist. This will also give us an opportunity to see a new strategy, "Pavlov" or **PAV**, that has several interesting properties.

(a)

(b)

(c)

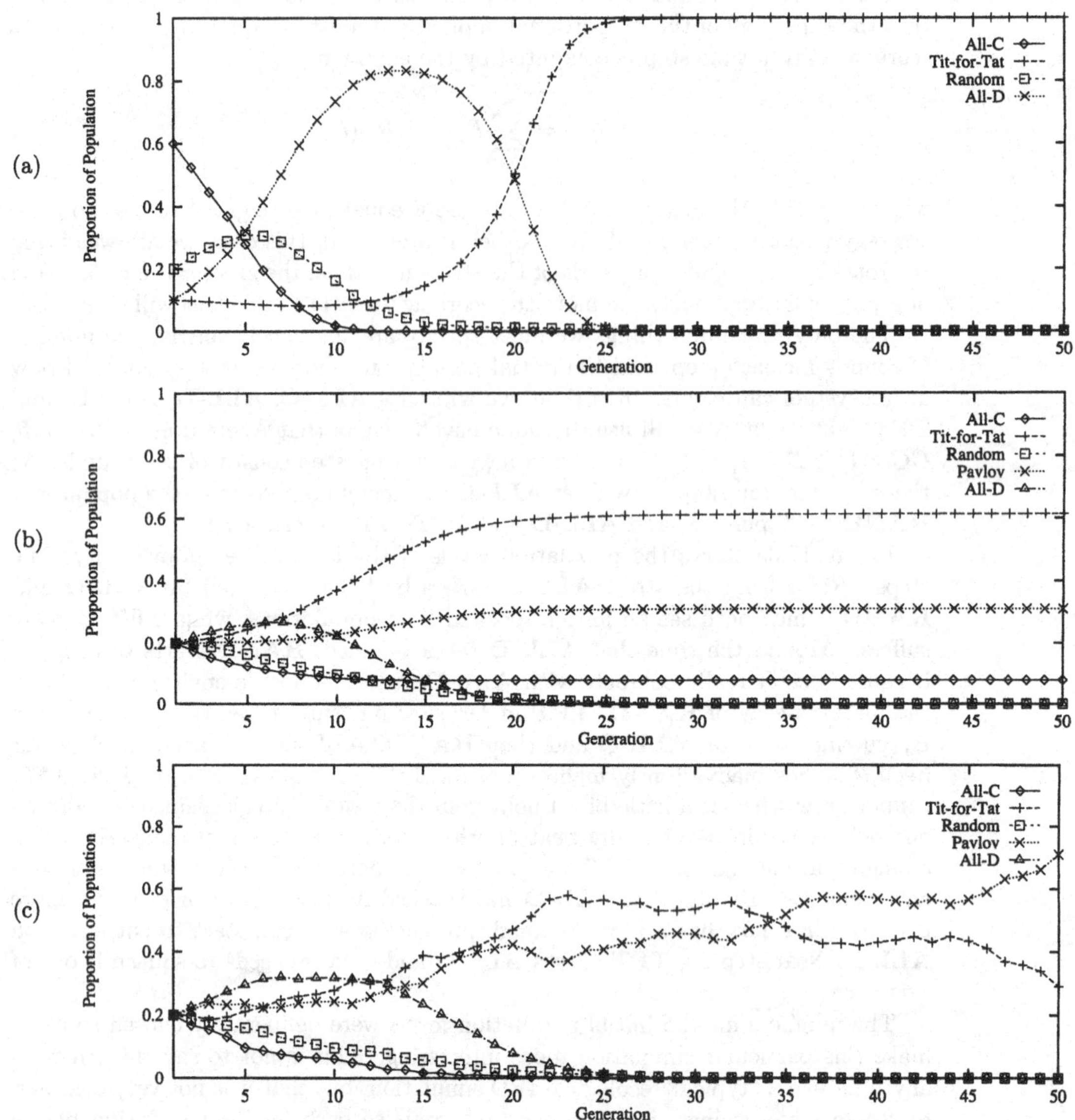

Figure 17.3 Population simulations of the ecological version of the iterated Prisoner's Dilemma: (a) an idealized version that illustrates the rise of **TFT**; (b) a noise-free simulation with **TFT** winning; (c) with 0.5 percent noise **PAV** wins

PAV is based on a simple "win-stay, lose-shift" principle that is reminiscent of Pavlovian learning. **PAV** starts off by cooperating but will change strategies whenever it is punished by a defection. If **PAV** plays against **ALL-D**, it will endlessly oscillate between cooperation and defection because it is continuously punished, which is slightly preferable to the beating that **ALL-C** receives under similar circumstances. What makes **PAV** interesting is that it seems to work better in a noisy environment than **TFT** does.

Figure 17.3b shows an ecological simulation of all five strategies with each having an initial population proportion of 20 percent. As before, **ALL-D** has an initial growth spurt, but this time it lasts less than five time steps because the population as a whole started off with 60 percent of the strategies being nice. In the end, the three nice strategies wipe out the mean strategies, with the final ranking reflecting the fact that **TFT** deals with defectors more sternly than does **PAV**, which in turn is less tolerant of defection than **ALL-C**. But Figure 17.3b is a very unrealistic simulation primarily because in the real world mistakes happen.

Consider what would happen if there was a slim chance that a transaction between two strategies could be botched by a random fluctuation. If this happened between two **TFT** players, then they would endlessly exchange cooperation followed by defection, like two drunks trading punches long after they know what they are fighting over. On the other hand, if this happened between two **PAV** players that were formerly cooperating, then the offended **PAV** player would "correct" the other player and eventually both would switch back to cooperation. Hence, **PAV** has a primitive sort of error correction built into it. But **PAV** can also exploit **ALL-C** in a noisy environment because it will continue with defection as soon as it "realizes" that it can get away with it. (Referring back to the earlier discussion on the update equations for the ecological simulations, I allowed $R_{ij}(t)$ to be computed on the fly so that noise could be easily thrown in.)

Since **PAV** can tolerate noise while **TFT** cannot, and since **PAV** can exploit **ALL-C** in a noisy environment, it stands to reason that **PAV** may have a huge advantage over **TFT** in the presence of even a small amount of noise. Martin Nowak and Karl Sigmund found this to be the case when they performed their own IPD simulations. Figure 17.3c shows the results from a simulation with exactly the same conditions as Figure 17.3b, but now there is a 0.5 percent chance that a transaction will be randomly corrupted by noise. The result is that **PAV** exploits **ALL-C** almost right from the start. Later on, **TFT** gets into trouble because it echoes mistakes back and forth. In the end, **PAV** has the greatest numbers.

Assuming that ecosystem members will interact with each other with frequency that is directly proportional to population levels is a lot like assuming that every one in a city will talk with every one person in equal proportions. In reality, people, animals, businesses, and countries are spatially divided so that it is most convenient to interact with immediate neighbors. In fact, in the absence of communication, there may be no interaction at all among distant neighbors.

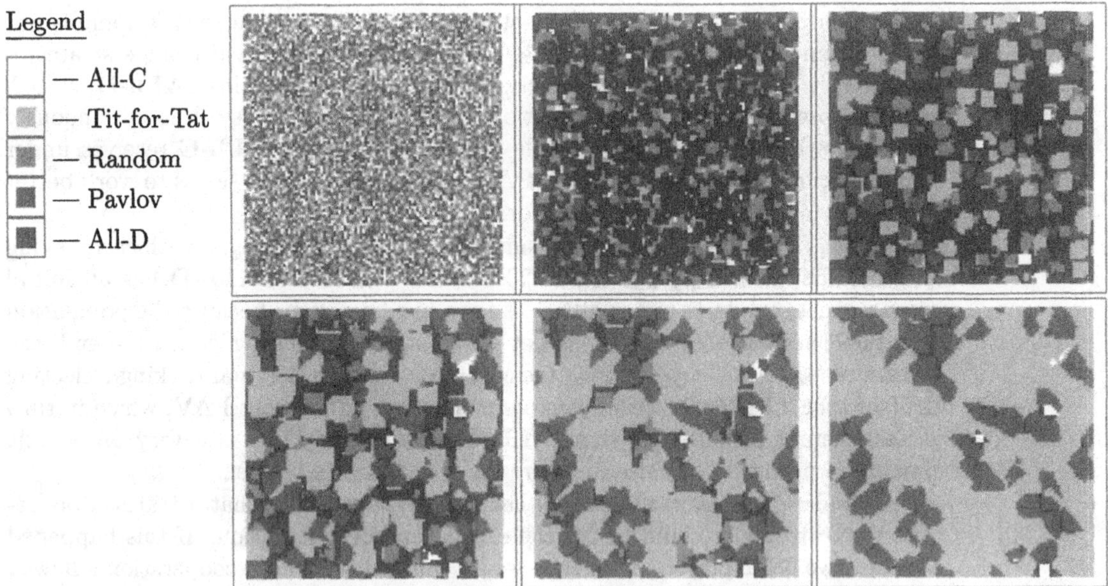

Figure 17.4 Competition in the spatial iterated Prisoner's Dilemma without noise

The spatial version of the IPD accounts for this by holding IPD contests only between immediate neighbors in a toroidal grid. At each time step, each cell will compete with its eight immediate neighbors and compute an overall score for itself. A cell will then adopt the strategy used by the neighbor with the highest score (ties always favor the current strategy).

Figure 17.4 shows six snapshots from a (100 × 100) grid over a few dozen time steps. Initially, the grid is randomly populated by the five strategies. After the first few time steps, **ALL-D** gains an advantage over the others, but is then partially displaced by the nicer players and **RAND** . It may be surprising that these strategies can push back **ALL-D**, but they do well in a spatial but hostile environment because a cluster of nice cells will partially cooperate with each other, while a cluster of **ALL-D** cells will be very unhealthy due to internal defections. Eventually, the three nice strategies start to take over the territory formerly owned by **RAND**. In the end, **RAND** is completely wiped out, leaving **TFT** in control of most of the space, **ALL-C** and **PAV** in small clusters, and **ALL-D** barely surviving on the borders. In the final snapshot, almost all the **ALL-D** cells reside in thin areas that border larger clusters of **ALL-C**, **TFT**, and **PAV** cells. This is due to the fact that **ALL-D** is an excellent parasite but can remain healthy only with a host.

For the simulation results shown in Figure 17.4, no noise was used. Had we used noise, the results would have been better for **PAV**, but that really wasn't the point of introducing the spatial IPD. The spatial version illustrates how a small cluster of cooperating agents can prosper in a hostile environment and how parasitic agents can exist only in limited numbers. Others have used the spatial version with specially contrived initial conditions to generate interesting patterns, which is a neat thing to do but really yields no insight into competition and cooperation because such patterns are almost always artifacts of the simulation techniques used.

17.6 Final Thoughts

None of this chapter is to suggest that anything in nature employs a pure **TFT** or **PAV** strategy, but it is remarkable, nonetheless, that techniques similar to these strategies have been found in so many different domains. Axelrod and others have shown that a "live and let live" strategy similar to **TFT** was used by both German and Allied forces in trench warfare during World War I. Many examples from politics, economics, and sociology abound: trade barriers, face-saving diplomacy, kindness to strangers, and so on.

The key to cooperation being a winning strategy is iteration. If there is no chance that two parties will ever meet again, then defection is a better action from a game-theoretic point of view. Even biological systems obey this principle to a certain extent, in that some organisms are specially adapted to detect when future interactions are not likely to occur. Even your own gut bacteria will start to attack you if your stomach lining is perforated.

Yet, the most important point in all of this is that unilateral, mindless cooperation and defection are both bad strategies. The stability, robustness, and resistance of a strategy depend on a special mixture of cooperation and defection.

17.7 Further Exploration

Those who wish to duplicate the results in this chapter can use `eipd` and `sipd` for the ecological and spatial versions of the IPD, respectively. Table 17.5 lists the options for `eipd` and `sipd`. The programs have many options, but most of the options have very simple usages. In each program, the initial population options that begin with `-I` take an additional argument that specifies the initial population number for the specified strategy. The argument supplied to this option can be any positive number and the total of each population need not add up to 1, since the program will automatically renormalize the population numbers for you. The `-rcp` option is used to specify how likely **RAND** is to cooperate. Setting this option to 0 or 1 allows you to force **RAND** to behave like **ALL-D** or **ALL-C**, or anywhere in between.

The `sipd` program has a few more options that are listed at the bottom of Table 17.5. The `-width` and `-height` options are used to set the size of the grid

Option Name	Option Type	Option Meaning
Options Common to **eipd** and **sipd**		
-seed	INTEGER	random seed
-steps	INTEGER	number of steps to simulate
-rounds	INTEGER	number of rounds per step
-CC	DOUBLE	reward payoff
-CD	DOUBLE	sucker's payoff
-DC	DOUBLE	temptation payoff
-DD	DOUBLE	punish payoff
-Iallc	DOUBLE	initial population for All-C rule
-Itft	DOUBLE	initial population for TFT rule
-Irand	DOUBLE	initial population for Random rule
-Ipav	DOUBLE	initial population for Pavlov rule
-Ialld	DOUBLE	initial population for All-D rule
-rcp	DOUBLE	probability of cooperation for RAND
-noise	DOUBLE	probability of noise
Options only for **sipd**		
-width	INTEGER	width of world
-height	INTEGER	height of world
-mute	DOUBLE	probability of mutation
-stats	SWITCH	print statistics?
-inv	SWITCH	invert colors?
-xmag	INTEGER	magnification for X windows
-term	STRING	how to plot points

Table 17.5 Command-line options for **eipd** and **sipd**

that the game is played out on. With a probability specified by **-mute**, a cell can have its strategy mutate into another strategy. This is useful if you wish to see under what conditions homogeneous strategy clusters can be invaded by other strategies. Finally, with the **-stat** option set, the program will print out population and fitness statistics for each strategy at each time step.

17.8 Further Reading

Axelrod, R. (1984). *The evolution of cooperation.* New York: Basic Books.

Axelrod, R. & Hamilton, W. D. (1981). The evolution of cooperation. *Science*, 211(4489): 1390–1396.

Maynard Smith, J. (1982). *Evolution and the theory of games.* Cambridge: Cambridge University Press.

Nowak, M. & Sigmund, K. (1993). A strategy of win-stay, lose-shift that outperforms Tit-for-Tat in the Prisoner's Dilemma game. *Nature*, 364(6432): 56–58.

Nowak, M. A. & May, R. M. (1992). Evolutionary games and spatial chaos. *Nature*, 359(6398): 826–829.

Poundstone, W. (1992). *Prisoner's Dilemma.* New York: Doubleday.

von Neumann, J. & Morgenstern, O. (1944). *Theory of games and economic behavior.* Princeton: Princeton University Press.

Wickler, W. (1968). *Mimicry in plants and animals.* New York: World University Library.

18 Natural and Analog Computation

A technique succeeds in mathematical physics, not by a clever trick, or a happy accident, but because it expresses some aspect of a physical truth.
— O. G. Sutton

What is important is that complex systems, richly cross-connected internally, have complex behaviours, and that these behaviours can be goal-seeking in complex patterns.
— W. Ross Ashby

I see the world in very fluid, contradictory, emerging, interconnected terms, and with that kind of circuitry I just don't feel the need to say what is going to happen or will not happen.
— Jerry Brown

SOAP BUBBLES, THE mechanism behind associative memory, and approximate solutions to combinatorial optimization problems all share a common trait. Let's start with soap bubbles. With some soap, water, a small circular wand, and a good gust of breath, you can create a large number of bubbles, limited only by the endurance of your diaphragm and the volume of your lungs. Now, in your mind's eye, slow down the process of how a single bubble is made. It starts with a thin film of soap-water stretched across the circular opening of the wand. You exhale a sufficient amount of air to force the film to expand outward. As the film expands, it envelops more and more of the air that you exhale, taking on an oval-like shape. Eventually, a combination of air pressure and surface tension forces the end of the expanding film near the wand to contract. The film collapses into a point and the bubble breaks away.

Here is the interesting part. When the bubble is first formed, it is not in the shape of a sphere. Instead, the bubble may contain imperfections, making it elongated along one or more directions. With an elastic snap, the bubble wobbles back and forth, expanding and contracting along different directions, to finally coalesce into a near perfect sphere. But why does the bubble seem to "want" to be in a sphere?

Why doesn't it look like a cube, pyramid, or football? Like a rubber band, a film of soap-water can be stretched but, given the option, rubber bands and soap films will always "prefer" to be in an unstretched state. Moreover, within the interior of a soap bubble there is a constant volume of air. Putting these two facts together, we see that the soap bubble has two conflicting goals that it must come to terms with before it can reach a "relaxed" state: It "wants" to minimize its surface area so as to minimize the amount that it is stretched while simultaneously maintaining a constant volume. Among the countless number of shapes that one could imagine a bubble taking, there is exactly one form that minimizes surface area while preserving volume, and that shape is a perfect sphere.

Flash back to your first course in physics and to some of the dynamical system ideas from Part III. If energy is the potential for change, then placing a ball on the top of a hill results in a system in a high energy state; that is, if we slightly perturb the ball, it will roll down the hill, resulting in a low-energy system. Similarly, a soap bubble in any shape other than a sphere is in a high energy state. As the bubble changes from non-sphere to sphere shape, it may overshoot the desired goal and temporarily move in the wrong direction, just as a rolling ball can be carried beyond the low point of a valley to momentarily move uphill. Balls can temporarily move uphill as long as they have sufficient momentum to do so. Momentum is responsible for the wavy motion that a bubble experiences as well.

The total amount of energy in either of these two systems is the sum of the potential energy—the height of the ball or the "unsphereness" of the bubble—and the kinetic energy, that is, the momentum of the moving portions of the systems. With this definition of total energy, a dissipative system will always move from a state of higher energy into a state of lower energy, and it will never go uphill. The energy doesn't just disappear, however. Instead, it is transformed and moved outside of the system, usually as friction but ultimately as heat. So when we say that the bubble "wants" to be in the shape of a sphere and that it "prefers" to be unstretched, we are really saying that all systems tend toward low energy states as time goes by. The energy low point for the system is the "relaxed" state.

But what has any of this to do with associative memory and combinatorial optimization problems? The lowly bubble and the mundane ball both turn out to be useful metaphors for distributed dynamical systems that can compute interesting things. Recall that the bubble "wanted" to minimize its surface area. Surface area is not a property of soap-water molecules, but of an entire soap film. Yet each molecule in a soap solution interacts only with a relatively small number of neighboring molecules. Hence, a global property—surface area—is minimized by only local interactions. Similarly, global properties such as the collection of neural activations that compose a distributed memory or the solution to an optimization problem may emerge from only local interactions.

In the remainder of this chapter we will examine artificial neural networks with fixed synapses that can act as associative memories and find approximate solutions

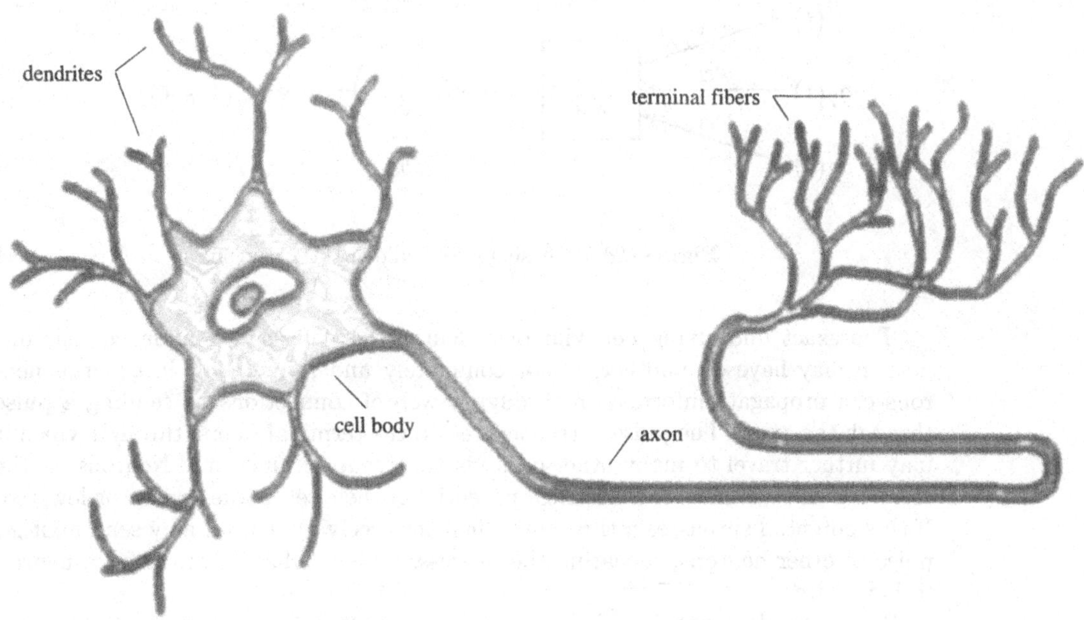

Figure 18.1 A "typical" neuron with major components identified

to combinatorial optimization problems. In each case, we will be able to use a formula to set the synaptic strength of the neural networks; hence, learning, that is, the process of adaptively changing synaptic strength based on experience, will not be covered in this chapter. After looking at the neural network models we will once again turn our attention to energy surfaces to see how all of these things are similar.

18.1 Artificial Neural Networks

There are many different types of *neurons*, but a typical example has a *cell body*, many *dendrites*, and a single *axon* that ends with a bundle of *terminal fibers*. The network of dendrites provides a large collection of connection points from which other neurons can interface, while the axon branches out and may form a few thousand *synapses* with other neurons. The receiving end of a synapse may be found on a dendrite or the cell body itself. You may find Figure 18.1 helpful; it shows a rough sketch of a neuron that is not drawn anywhere near realistic proportions because the axon on a real neuron is often enormous in length relative to the rest of the cell structure.

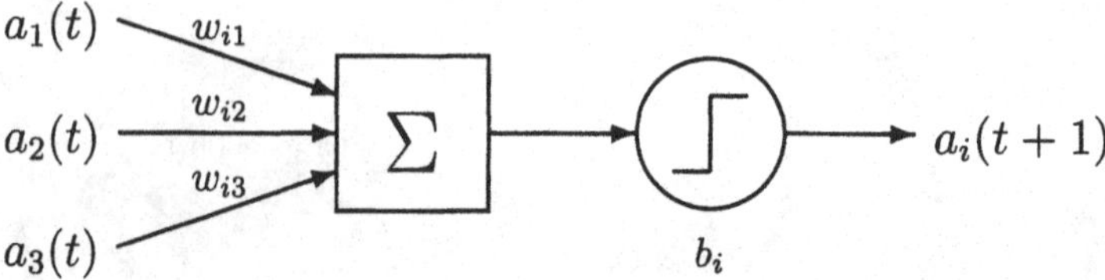

Figure 18.2 A single McCulloch-Pitts neuron

The exact underlying behavior of a neuron, as well as the influence that one neuron may have on another, is not completely understood but, in general, neurons can propagate information through a web of connections by sending a pulse through the axon. The pulse is transmitted to the terminal fibers, through which it may further travel to many other cells via the synaptic junctions. Neurons on the receiving end will have the electrical potential of their cell bodies raised or lowered. If this potential surpasses a threshold, then the receiving neuron may send another pulse to other neurons, repeating the process. This is what it means for a neuron to have "fired."

Since a single neuron can be connected to thousands of other neurons, the nervous system as a whole operates in an endlessly recursive manner, with one neuron stimulating many others that, in turn, may propagate activity that culminates in a feedback loop to the original neuron. With this high degree of interconnectivity and feedback, the normal state of the human brain is aperiodicity. In fact, epileptic seizures are known to be associated with regularity and periodicity in the brain's electrical activity. Healthy brains are chaotic.

We will consider a much more simplified view of how neurons work and limit the connectivity of a neural network to a form that explicitly makes chaotic behavior impossible. Even with the simplified neurons and connections, we will see that interesting computations are still possible.

One early neural model was proposed by W. S. McCulloch and W. Pitts in the early 1940s. Figure 18.2 contains a simplified drawing of a McCulloch-Pitts neuron, and a summary of all of the terms is given in Table 18.1. The idea behind the model is that a neuron's state or *activation*, $a_i(t)$, at time t, is a function of a weighted sum of all of the incoming signals:

$$a_i(t+1) = \Theta\left(\sum_{j=1}^{n} w_{ij} \times a_j(t) - b_i\right),$$

where $\Theta(x)$ is the unit step function that is equal to 1 if $x > 0$ and 0 otherwise, w_{ij} represents the synaptic strength of the connection from neuron j to neuron i, and b_i is the threshold that neuron i's net input must exceed before it can itself

Term	Meaning
$a_i(t)$	activation value of neuron i at time t
w_{ij}	strength of synapse connecting neuron j to neuron i
b_i	threshold that neuron i's net input must exceed in order to fire
$\Theta(x)$	unit step function: 1 if $x \geq 0$, 0 if $x < 0$
sgn(x)	sign function: 1 if $x \geq 0$, -1 if $x < 0$
h_i	net input, $\sum_j w_{ij}a_j(t)$, into neuron i

Table 18.1 Summary of terms used in the McCulloch-Pitts neural model

fire. Thus, a single McCulloch-Pitts neuron computes the answer to a simple logical question: Is the weighted sum of incoming signals greater than the threshold b_i? If the answer is "yes," then the neuron fires with an activation of 1; otherwise the neuron's activation is 0. The real power of the McCulloch-Pitts neuron is in the nonlinear activation function $\Theta(x)$, which permits the neuron to compute many different binary functions. We will explore the full power of a single neuron in Chapter 22.

When a neuron is quiescent, that is, its activation is 0, it cannot send signals to any of the neurons that it is connected to. Because of this, it is sometimes convenient to rewrite the state activation rule into another form where an activation is either +1 or -1, and -1 represents the "off" state. We can rewrite the update rule as

$$a_i(t+1) = \text{sgn}\left(\sum_{j=1}^{n} w_{ij} \times a_j(t) - b_i\right),$$

where sgn(x), the sign function, is 1 if $x > 0$ and -1 otherwise, and the $a_i(t)$ terms are now understood to take values of either -1 or 1. With a neuron state-activation rule expressed in this form, it is easier to represent the notion that some collection of neurons should always have the same activation value. For example, if many neurons are connected and all have weights equal to 1, and all neurons but one are in the off state, then the net input into the rogue neuron will be largely negative, forcing this neuron to get in line with the others. This modification to the rule is really just a mathematical convenience for two reasons. First, for any collection of (-1,1) neurons, there exists a setting of weights and threshold terms for (0,1) neurons that gives the exact same behavior. The two representations are in fact equivalent. Second, the new representation is not very biologically plausible, since real neurons cannot inhibit other real neurons in this precise manner.

The final thing that we need to consider is how to update the activation values at a given time step. There are several different ways of going about this, and each has advantages and disadvantages. The two main methods are *synchronous* updating and *asynchronous* updating. In synchronous updating, one simultaneously computes the next activation value for each neuron. The advantage here is that the method is completely deterministic but unrealistic in that it requires all neurons to obey a fixed clock. In asynchronous updating, one randomly picks a neuron and updates it. This method is slightly more realistic, but one must take care that individual neurons don't go too long without being updated because of some strange statistical burp.

With a fixed set of connections and thresholds as specified by the w_{ij} and b_i terms, the activation of the neurons will start with an initial value at time 0, and change from one time step to another. In this chapter, all of our choices of the weights and thresholds will result in a system that converges to a fixed point. Hence, at some final time T, the system that consists of all activation values will be in a state such that applying the update rules for any more time steps will result in the same set of activations.

Artificial neural networks of this sort, which have a collection of neurons that can potentially be wired to any other neuron in the system, are generically referred to as *feedback neural networks*. Researchers in this area have generalized the dynamical properties of the McCulloch-Pitts neurons to yield either more realistic or more powerful systems. There has also been considerable work that has provided more insight into the computational properties of the simpler neurons. Over the next three sections we will examine some of these key extensions and experiments. The big idea in each case is that the final converged state of a neural network can represent the answer to a question, thus performing a sort of analog computation.

18.2 Associative Memory and Hebbian Learning

With but rare exceptions, whenever people refer to memory in the context of computers, they are referring to memory that is referenced by location. What this means is that if you want a particular datum, you have to know where it exists. This is true even for the case of named objects, such as files or program variables. A name is really nothing more than convenient shorthand for the datum's actual location, since compilers and operating systems essentially maintain a giant list that maps names to locations, thus doing the tedious work for us.

Human memory bears little resemblance to this. To see why, answer this question: What 1960s rock band with four members was named after an insect and started the "British invasion?" Almost anyone old enough to remember the death of John Lennon could answer this instantly. The point of the exercise is that we accessed this particular memory by content and not by name, which in a way is exactly backward from the way one would reference computer memory. More specifically, instead of starting out with the name "The Beatles," we started out with some trivial facts (1960s, four members, insect, British) and ended up with the name. Humans are extremely adept at doing tricks of this sort, while computers usually must resort to something akin to brute force in order to do the same task.

Content-addressable memory of this sort is usually referred to as *associative memory*, but the underlying process is so common to intelligent systems and is found in so many different areas of cognition that the name really doesn't do the process justice. We, as humans, have several different but related cognitive processes that operate on this basic principle. We can consciously exercise one type of associative cognitive process by recalling memories from partial information, as we did with the Beatles or by playing a word association game. Face recognition is a similar process but occurs in a different portion of the brain that seems to be specially designed for the task. And even basic behavioral conditioning demonstrates a similar type of binding between two separate stimuli.

In 1949, Donald Hebb proposed a simple rule to account for such associative processes that now goes by the name of *Hebbian learning*. Hebb proposed that synaptic strength between two mutually connected neurons, adjusted in a manner proportional to the correlation between the two neurons, would account for associations. Simply stated, if two neurons fired at the same time, then the synaptic connections between them would be strengthened.

Looking back to the McCulloch-Pitts neuron with (0,1) activation levels, Hebb's rule simply states that if neurons i and j are on at the same time, then w_{ij} should be a positive value so as to reinforce the pairing of the two neurons. With the modified (-1,1) neurons, we can extend the original intention of Hebb's rule into a form that also specifies that two neurons that should be off at the same time should also have a positive w_{ij} term. Also note that two neurons with different activation values should have a negative weight connecting them. Thus, with the (-1,1) neurons we get slightly more expressive power at the expense of biological plausibility.

Now, suppose that we wanted to store a memory in such a way that it could be recalled from only partial information. We represent the memory as a vector of variables, denoted by x_i, that take either -1 or 1 values. You can assign an arbitrary meaning to each particular x_i value; for instance, in the case of face recognition x_1 could mean "big nose," x_2 could mean "brown eyes," and so on. We now use as many neurons as there are x_i terms, and set the weights according to

$$w_{ij} = \frac{1}{n} x_i x_j,$$

where n is the number of neurons in the system. For the time being we are going to ignore the b_i terms. Now, for the case of recalling a single memory, the update rule becomes

$$a_i(t+1) = \text{sgn}\left(\frac{1}{n}\sum_{j=1}^{n} x_i x_j a_j(t)\right).$$

Starting with values of $a_i(0)$ that are close to x_i, we want the system to converge to a state such that a_i equals x_i for all i. This will be true if the net input, $\frac{1}{n}\sum_{j=1}^{n} x_i x_j a_j(t)$, equals x_i. Setting $a_i(t)$ to x_i, we get

$$\frac{1}{n}\sum_{j=1}^{n} x_i x_j x_j = \frac{1}{n}\sum_{j=1}^{n} x_i = x_i.$$

Thus, the system is stable in the sense that when presented with the stored memory, it stays in the same configuration. But if less than half of the $a_i(0)$ terms are incorrect, the net input for neuron i will still have the same sign as x_i, meaning that it will eventually converge to the stored pattern even if given incomplete information.

One pattern is fine, but what we really want is an associative memory that can recall one pattern from many possible stored values. This is almost as easy, since we just need to compute the same weights as before, but for all of the stored patterns, and then add them up. Hence, if we have p patterns to store, the weights should be set to

$$w_{ij} = \frac{1}{n}\sum_{k=1}^{p} x_i^k x_j^k,$$

with x_i^k denoting the ith component of the kth pattern.

In the next section we are going to apply these ideas to the problem of recalling a stored letter of the alphabet from a corrupted initial seed. The idea will be that our neural network will have stored a few bitmap letter images in its memory, that we can give it noisy or partial information to start off with, and that it will still be able to correctly reconstruct the stored pattern from the partial information. In the remainder of this section I am going to go over a few more mathematical details that are essential to the program used to do the experiments. You, however, should consider the remainder of this section optional. Keep reading if you want more details. But if not, you can skip or skim to the next section without too much loss.

All of the preceding analysis for storing multiple patterns holds only if all of the patterns that we store are drawn from a random sample. When this is the case, the pattern and all of the individual components of each pattern are independent of each other. To see this more clearly, consider the full update equation with connection weights set to recall multiple patterns. If we set the $a_j(t)$ terms to be equal to one particular stored pattern, say x_j^l with $1 \le l \le p$, we want the next state of the network to be equal to the x_j^l terms. If it were any other way, then our network would fail to recall a stored pattern even with perfect information, so this is a sort of minimal requirement that we must place on the network as a whole. Fortunately, to analyze this condition, we do not need to look at the whole update equation; we only need to make sure that the net input for each neuron i, that is, everything inside of the $\mathrm{sgn}(x)$ function that we will abbreviate as h_i, has the same sign as x_i^l.

This net input is equal to

$$h_i = \frac{1}{n}\sum_{j=1}^{n}\sum_{k=1}^{p} x_i^k x_j^k x_j^l.$$

We can now break up the innermost summation into two parts: one that contains the terms for pattern l and another that contains everything but pattern l:

$$h_i = \frac{1}{n}\sum_{j=1}^{n}\left(x_i^l x_j^l + \sum_{k\neq l}^{p} x_i^k x_j^k\right) x_j^l = \frac{1}{n}\left(\sum_{j=1}^{n} x_i^l x_j^l x_j^l + \sum_{k\neq l}^{p} x_i^k x_j^k x_j^l\right).$$

Since $x_j^l x_j^l$ is always equal to 1, the whole thing finally simplifies down to

$$h_i = x_i^l + \frac{1}{n}\sum_{j=1}^{n}\sum_{k\neq l}^{p} x_i^k x_j^k x_j^l,$$

which finally gets down to the root of the problem. You see, if the terms inside of the summations are uncorrelated, then they will cancel each other out, meaning that the net input will in fact be very close to x_i^l. If you draw all of the patterns from a random sample, then this is almost always the case. But if the patterns have some structure to them, or even some spatial consistency, then we have a problem.

For example, if in the last equation we consistently find that $x_i^k = x_j^k$ for certain values of i and j, then this means that within every pattern there are many portions that are identical. This is an issue in the next section, where we will be trying to store bitmap images of letters. The images will always have a white border around them that corresponds to many neurons that are always off. Similarly, when $x_j^k = x_j^l$ is true for many pairs of patterns, it means that multiple patterns will always have one or more neurons that consistently have the same value such as the neuron that corresponds to the upper-leftmost bit in the bitmap which is always off.

Think of it this way: Associative memory works by finding similarities between a seed pattern and some stored pattern. But it is the differences among the stored patterns that account for the network's ability to finally converge to a single pattern as the answer. If there is too much regularity within a single pattern or in one location of all of the patterns, then this information biases the computation. It's a case of having too much of a good thing.

This particular problem, as well as other difficulties with associative memory, can be appreciated with another example from face recognition. Once again, suppose we stored several features that describe people's faces, but now we have many mostly useless features that have very little discriminatory power because they are so broad and general that they apply to almost everyone. Features of this sort could be "is between one foot and eight feet tall," "does not have a square head," and

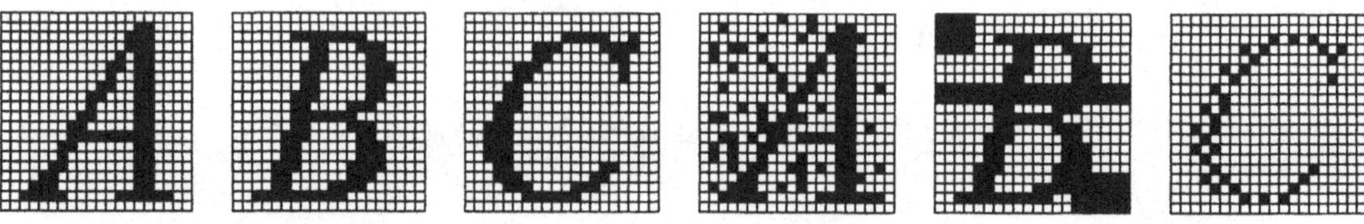

Figure 18.3 Bitmapped images of letters from the alphabet: The first three are clean version that are used as patterns to be stored. The last three are used as seed images that the associative memory must use to recall one of the first three.

"does not have a monstrous nose." Once again, these features are like the borders around bitmap images of letters, since in nearly all cases they cannot be used to differentiate stored patterns. Now, suppose you wanted to store several typical types of faces into your memory plus your uncle Philbert's face, which happens to have an enormous nose that could be described as "monstrous." Since all of the useless features are negatively correlated with Philbert's huge nose, when you attempt to recall Philbert's face from partial or even complete information, these useless features are going to combine in such a way as to suppress the neuron that signifies that Philbert has a monstrous nose. The result is that the associative memory will probably converge to a spurious memory that only resembles Philbert's features. If this happened in real associative memories, then we would be incapable of remembering extremely rare events, despite their novelty.

We can partially correct for this problem by employing the b_i terms, which we have been ignoring up until this point. One solution is to set

$$b_i = -\frac{1}{2}\sum_j w_{ij} = -\frac{1}{2n}\sum_j\sum_k x_i^k x_j^k.$$

To see the difference that this new term has, you could once again consider the case of storing and retrieving a single pattern. The effect is to make it easier for the neuron to fire because it factors in the "biasness" that all of the other neurons have on the one neuron that represents the odd feature.

18.3 Recalling Letters

Using the methods described in the last section for computing the values of the w_{ij} and b_i terms, we will now see an actual example of how an associative memory can recall stored patterns from partial or incorrect information. Figure 18.3 shows clean and corrupted versions of the letters A, B, and C. Each letter is described by a 20×20 grid of bits with black portions representing the "on" or +1 state and white bits representing the "off" or -1 state. Our neural network will have 400 neurons,

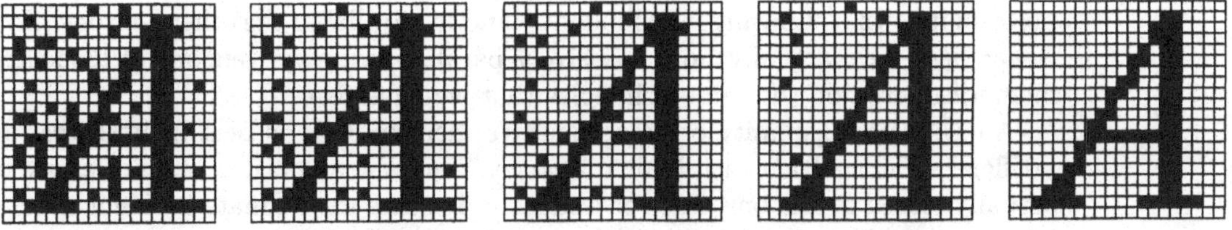

Figure 18.4 Recalling the letter A from a damaged seed image

one for each bit. How we map neurons to bits in the image doesn't really matter as long as we are consistent. For instance, we could simply agree that the upper-leftmost bit in the image is represented by neuron 1 and that the bottom-rightmost bit corresponds to neuron 400.

We will store the three clean versions of the letters as the memories in the neural network. The weights are set according to the Hebbian rule and the thresholds are set as described at the end of the previous section.

To test the ability of the neural network associative memory, we set the initial activations of the neurons to correspond to one of the corrupted versions of the letters. In Figure 18.4, I have done this for the letter A. The neurons were updated asynchronously, which makes the recall process a little more interesting to watch. As seen in the images, the network slowly starts to correct the erroneous portions of the image, eventually settling on the clean version of the letter. The process would work similarly for the corrupted versions of B and C as well.

The result is a process not unlike what happens in biological associative memories. Starting with incomplete and fuzzy information, the network can settle on something based on the similarity the seed pattern has to a stored memory. However, this particular example is somewhat contrived and not without some faults. For instance, there are many more weights in this network than there is information in the stored patterns, which means that this particular network is grossly inefficient memory-wise. One way of trimming the number of weights would be to remove any weights that were smaller than a certain threshold. There are also methods for merging weights and removing the redundancy of the stored patterns. The point is that there are real applications of artificial associative memories that are efficient with memory, but may not be as illustrative as this example of recalling letters.

The most interesting things about the artificial associative memory are the traits that it shares with real biological systems. First, while simulating this on a single processor computer is relatively slow, the mathematics behind the simulation is such that the whole system can be implemented as a collection of very simple parallel computers. If you imagine each artificial neuron to be a simple computer that looks at its net input and fires according to the update rule, then each neuron can perform its own computing independently and in parallel to the other neurons. Some researchers have actually built massively parallel hardware versions of associative memories based on the same principles that we have seen.

Another useful quality of an associative memory that is seen in both real and artificial versions deals with fault tolerance. Since the associative memories are not actually stored in any one place or weight, if by some unfortunate accident a weight is destroyed, the network still stands a good chance of recalling the correct pattern. In the process of preparing this chapter I destroyed up to 65 percent of the weights without adversely affecting the network's performance.

Finally, all associative memories are prone to recalling spurious memories that are unlike any one stored pattern but are, instead, a sort of composite of many of the stored patterns. This can happen if an associative memory is forced to store too many patterns or if the patterns themselves have a representation (like the letters of the alphabet) that is not conducive to being stored in this manner.

All of these points relate to the dynamical properties of the neurons. In the next section we will consider a more generalized neural model that is able to perform more interesting computational tasks. In Section 18.5 we will see how associative memories, cost optimization, and soap bubbles relate to each other from a dynamical system point of view.

18.4 Hopfield Networks and Cost Optimization

We now consider a more generalized type of neuron that makes up what is commonly referred to as a *Hopfield neural network*, although similar models of neural dynamics have been proposed by others. John Hopfield and his collaborator David Tank used mathematical tools from physics to yield some important insights into how neural networks change over time. We will briefly examine these results in the next section, but here we will concentrate on the model itself and on the types of computations that it can perform.

Recall that a McCulloch-Pitts neuron has a discrete state and changes in discrete time steps. The artificial neurons in this section take a continuous state and evolve continuously over time. Thus, the model itself has more biological plausibility than the McCulloch-Pitts model, but it is still far simpler than a real neuron. A main feature of the continuous version is that it possesses an internal continuous state that continuously varies over time. The external state, which is the information that other neurons can "see," is a simple function of the internal state. Like the McCulloch-Pitts neurons, the change in the internal state is a function of the signals that are received from other neurons.

The time evolution of the neurons is described by the equation

$$\frac{dU_i}{dt} = \sum_{j=1}^{n} T_{ij} V_j + I_i - \frac{U_i}{\tau},$$

Term	Meaning
U_i	internal state of neuron i
V_i	external activation or visible state of neuron i
T_{ij}	strength of synapse connecting neuron j to neuron i
I_i	external input injected into neuron i
$g(x)$	sigmoidal activation function: $1/(1+\exp(-x))$
τ	inverse decay term for internal state

Table 18.2 Summary of terms used in the Hopfield neural model

where U_i is the internal state. T_{ij} represents the strength of the connection from neuron j to neuron i, V_j represents the external activation or visible state of neuron j, I_i is an external input that is injected into neuron i, and τ is a fixed parameter that determines how much the internal state decays if not excited by other neurons or the external input. A summary of all of the terms is found in Table 18.2. This differential equation specifies how U_i changes over time. We can approximate this as a discrete system by the equation

$$U_i(t+1) = U_i(t) + \Delta t \left(\sum_{j=1}^{n} T_{ij} V_j(t) + I_i - \frac{U_i(t)}{\tau} \right),$$

where $U_i(t)$ and $V_j(t)$ are now annotated with a time index, and Δt is the simulation time-step increment. All other variables that are not annotated with a time variable are fixed for all time. Hence, T_{ij}, I_i, and τ are all chosen at the beginning of a simulation and left unchanged.

The activation function of the neuron is denoted by $g(x)$, which is known as a *sigmoid* function because it is S-shaped. The relationship between $U_i(t)$ and $V_i(t)$ is simply

$$V_i(t) = g(U_i(t)) = \frac{1}{1+\exp(-U_i(t))}.$$

Figure 18.5 shows a graph of $g(x)$. Notice that the sigmoid function is very similar to a step function in that it thresholds the input into one of two extremes, but differs from the step function in that it is continuous.

A Hopfield network typically starts out in a random state with the $U_i(0)$ terms chosen to be small random variables near 0. The weights and external inputs can be set in such a way as to solve a problem. Hopfield and Tank showed that if the weights are symmetric, meaning that $T_{ij} = T_{ji}$, then the network will always converge to state in which all $V_i(t)$ terms are equal to either 0 or 1. It is the final values of the $V_i(t)$ terms that represent a solution to a problem.

But what problem types can you solve with a Hopfield network? In the mid-1980s, Hopfield and Tank (and many other researchers) applied this network to a

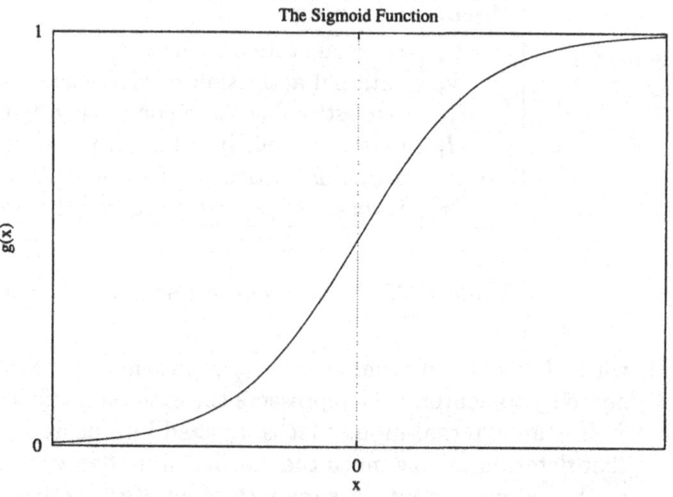

Figure 18.5 The sigmoid activation function, $g(x)$

number of combinatorial cost-optimization problems. Such problems are very easy to express but may have an optimal solution that is very hard to find. The example that we will consider is the task assignment problem, which Tank and Hopfield used as an example in their *Scientific American* article. We will use the exact same problem instance that they considered, but many of the details in my presentation will be different.

In the task assignment problem, one has n tasks that must be accomplished by using only n workers. Each worker has his own efficiency or cost for performing particular tasks; thus, for example, worker i may be better than worker j at task k. Our goal is to minimize the total cost for accomplishing all tasks or, stated another way, to maximize the throughput of all of the workers. We are also constrained in that each worker must perform one and only one task, and each task must be accomplished by exactly one worker.

As a specific example, suppose we had to shelve books in a library, using graduate students as workers. We have six book subjects that must be shelved and six students to do the work. Each student knows the subject areas to varying degrees, and the more familiar a student is with a subject, the faster he or she can shelve the books in the proper location. The data that define a particular problem instance can be summarized in a 6×6 table, as seen in Figure 18.6. The numbers indicate the number of books on a particular subject that a particular student can shelve in one minute. Here, we see that Karen is at her best with chemistry books, and Sam is the fastest at shelving poetry books.

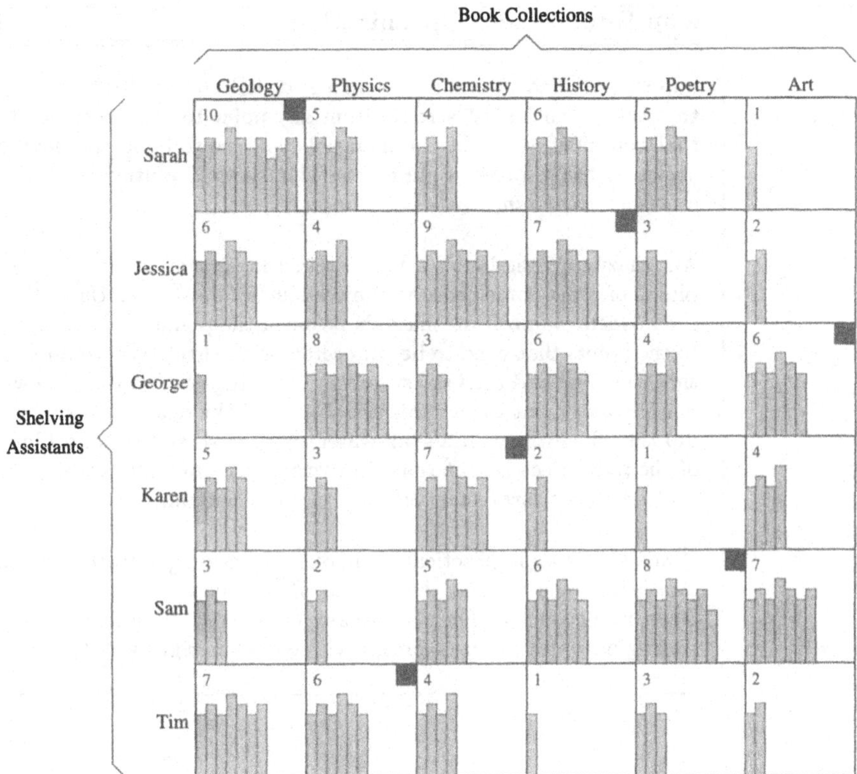

Figure 18.6 The task assignment problem: Black squares in the entries denotes the optimal assignment with a total shelving rate of 44.

At first glance, this seems like a simple problem. But notice that a brute force technique for this instance would have to consider 6! = 720 different possible assignments of students to subjects. This may be feasible for small problem sizes, but in the general case the factorial explosion in size makes brute force infeasible.

The trick to solving this problem with a Hopfield network is to interpret each square of the table in Figure 18.6 as a hypothesis for a partial solution. For instance, the upper-leftmost square represents the hypothesis that a solution should include Sarah shelving geology books. A feasible (but not necessarily efficient) solution to the problem will always be in the form of a permutation matrix, which means that each column and each row in the table will have a single element that is "on" to represent which person does which task. The optimal solution shown is a valid permutation matrix because there is only one marked square for each column and each row.

Soap Bubbles and Optimization **Digression 18.1**

Suppose you had several points on a grid that you needed to connect in a network such that there would exist a route from any point to any other point. Let's also assume that you must minimize the materials you use to build the network, be it wire, fiber optics, or other forms of plumbing. The optimal solution to this problem is known as a *Steiner minimum tree*.

An amazing method for finding a Steiner minimum tree involves only soap, water, two planes of glass, some rods, and miscellaneous hardware. Using the two glass planes as a sandwich, we position the rods between the planes so that they correspond exactly to the points that need to be connected on the grid. We would also need to make sure that the glass and rods are suitably bound together so that the whole apparatus does not fall apart; but I leave this as a detail for the reader's imagination. We would then dip the whole thing in a soap-water solution so that a soap film formed between all of the rods. Because the soap film "wants" to minimize its surface area, the film will coalesce into a form that represents a Steiner minimum tree.

While this is an impractical technique for very complicated problems, it still demonstrates how nature and the laws of physics can work together in order to solve interesting problems. There are many other types of phenomena that can be seen as solving optimization problems, if viewed in the right way (Isenberg, 1978).

Looking at each square as a separate hypothesis for a partial solution, we can see that every square is in competition with all other squares that reside in the same column and row. Thus, the hypothesis that George shelves chemistry books is in direct conflict with any other hypothesis that has anyone else working on chemistry books or George working on any other subject. If a square, or hypothesis, is not in the same column or row as another hypothesis, then those two hypotheses are not in conflict and may, in fact, reach a sort of cooperative arrangement. We will represent each of these partial hypotheses as a single neuron and wire the neural network in such a way that the competitive and cooperative relationships are left intact.

But how does this relate to setting the weights and external inputs? There is a very handy rule for setting these terms, discovered by Edward Page and Gene Tagliarini, known as the k-out-of-n rule, that offers one solution to the problem. The k-out-of-n rule states that if you have a collection of n Hopfield neurons that you want to converge to a configuration with exactly k on and $(n-k)$ off, then you should set each T_{ij} term to -2 if i is not equal to j (0 if i equals j) and set all I_i terms to $(2k-1)$.

Each column and row in Figure 18.6 represents a separate cluster in which we want exactly one out of six neurons to be on. Because each neuron is in two clusters

  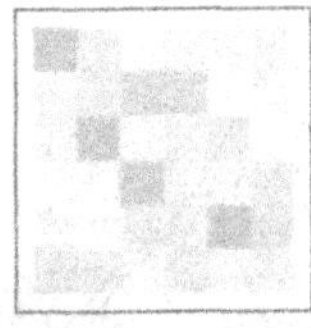 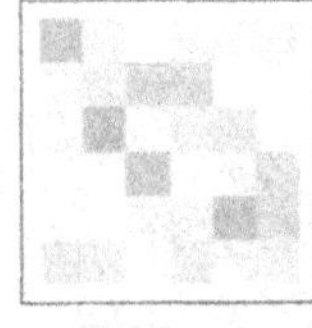 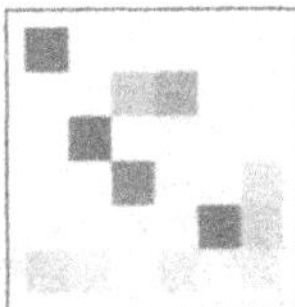 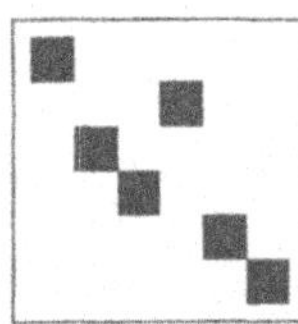

Figure 18.7 Computing a neural solution to the task assignment problem: This particular solution yields a total rate of 42, which is just less than the optimal solution.

(one for the column and one for the row), we need to use an external input for each neuron centered on $2(2k-1)=2$. Also, for any two different neurons, i and j, if they are in the same column or the same row, then T_{ij} should be set to -2, since they are in a k-out-of-n rule cluster.

With those settings, the neural network will converge to a solution that represents a feasible solution, but not necessarily a good one. I used the word "centered" in describing the external inputs of size 2 because, in fact, we need to bias the inputs proportional to the rate at which a student can shelve books. Thus, the neuron representing that Sarah should shelve geology books will receive the largest external input, while the neuron representing that Tim should shelve history books will receive one of the smallest external inputs. But over all, the average of all the external inputs will be 2. We will simply skew the inputs to reflect the skills of the students at the specific tasks. If you look back at the update equation for the Hopfield neurons, you will see that the larger the external input into the neuron, the larger the positive change for the neuron; thus, this method biases the neurons that have the best chance of contributing to a good overall solution.

Putting this all together, we start the network in a random initial state with each neuron being close to 0.5 in value so as to represent the initial idea that we are uncertain as to how the assignments should be made. The randomness is necessary so that ties can be broken, that is, with a constant initialization it is possible for the neurons to be stuck in a configuration that represents no solution. After that, we just let nature run its course.

Figure 18.7 shows a snapshot of a Hopfield neural network programmed for this particular problem. The leftmost image shows the random initial state, with the gray squares representing neural output values close to 0.5. In the heat of competition, the squares start to lighten in color, meaning that the neural outputs are now closer to 0. Shortly thereafter, a few of the "stronger" neurons, which have higher external inputs, start to grow in strength, which is illustrated by the darkening squares in the third and fourth images. By the fifth image several of the squares have dominated their competition, leaving all column or row competitors near a 0 state. This makes room for weaker neurons that do not directly compete with the stronger neurons to gain a foothold. Finally, in the sixth image, the system converges to state that represents a solution with a total shelving rate of 42.

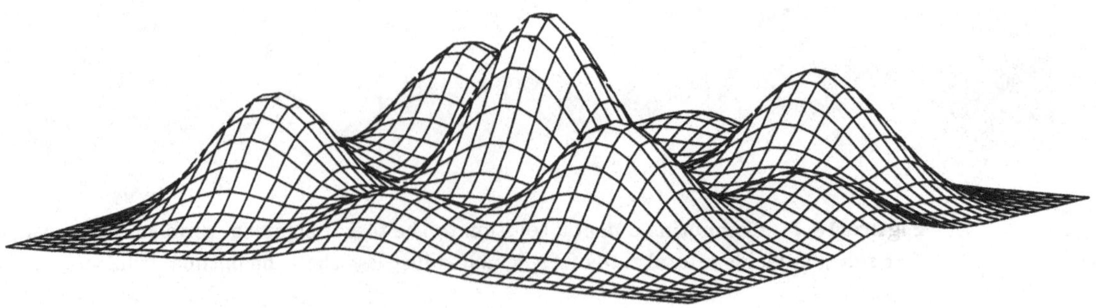

Figure 18.8 The energy of a system: Representing the state of the system by a ball on the energy surface, the system is constrained such that the ball (or state) must always move downhill, toward a minimum.

18.5 Unifying Themes

Hopfield and Tank's most important contribution to the field of neural computation was to show that there exists an energy function that describes the dynamical properties of both the McCulloch-Pitts and Hopfield models when the networks have symmetric weights and no self-connections. Energy functions are a tool from physics used to analyze and describe other, more traditional dynamical systems. At each time step the state of a network is always constrained to move to a point of lower energy. Figure 18.8 gives a representation for a two-dimensional system. If we imagine that the state at any particular time is a point on the surface, then the network as a dynamical system moves to a state like a ball rolling down the hill. Eventually, the ball (and network) reach a minimum. If the network has been wired appropriately, then the minimum can represent the solution to a problem.

Hence, we are finally coming full circle to see why soap bubbles, associative memories, and approximate solutions to combinatorial optimization problems are similar to each other. For the associative memory, the final converged state would, hopefully, correspond to a stored memory. And for the Hopfield network, the minima represented solutions to an optimization problem. One fact that we can glean from all of this is that energy surfaces will almost always have local minima. A minimum that is lower than all others is referred to as a *global minimum*. For the task assignment problem, the global minimum corresponds to the best solution possible. But as we saw, the network converged to a solution that was just suboptimal. This minimum is referred to as a *local minimum* because it is minimal only within a local area.

In any event, all three phenomena represent systems in which global properties are optimized with only local interactions. For the soap bubble, surface area is a

Option Name	Option Type	Option Meaning
`-pfile`	STRING	file with pattern to store
`-tfile`	STRING	file with test pattern
`-local`	INTEGER	locality of permitted weights
`-cut`	DOUBLE	cutoff size for weights
`-pprob`	DOUBLE	probability of random pruning
`-seed`	INTEGER	random seed for initial state
`-steps`	INTEGER	number of time steps
`-inv`	SWITCH	invert colors?
`-xmag`	INTEGER	magnification for X windows
`-term`	STRING	how to plot points

Table 18.3 Command-line options for `assoc`

property of the bubble as a whole and not of any one particular molecule. Likewise, for the neural networks, the converged memory or task assignment solution is something that has meaning only in the context of all of the neurons. By itself, each neuron is just a single piece of the equation. So it is with some satisfaction that we see how these global properties can emerge from only local interactions.

18.6 Further Exploration

All of the results in this chapter can be reproduced by the reader with two programs, `assoc` and `hopfield`. The command-line options for `assoc` are summarized in Table 18.3. This program can take multiple `-pfile` options to specify the files that contain the patterns to be stored. The files must be in the text version of the Portable Bit Map (PBM) file format. The dimensions of the PBM files must all agree in size. Use `-tfile` to specify the pattern to use as the initial state of the associative memory. For experimental purposes, you can use `-local`, `-cut`, or `-pprob` to remove or zero out portions of the weight matrix. The `-local` option will only allow weights that connect neurons which are near one another, "near" meaning that two neurons are in the neighborhood of the specified size. The `-cut` option will remove any weights that are smaller in magnitude than the specified value. The `-pprob` option will only allow the specified percentage of weights to remain intact; all other are randomly removed.

The command-line options for `hopfield` are shown in Table 18.4. The `-specs` option is used to specify a file that describes the task assignment costs. The file is in plain text and contains the number of tasks followed by the costs. The parameters of the Hopfield network can be modified with the corresponding program option. The `-gain` option is an extra multiplicative constant on the sigmoidal function that

Option Name	Option Type	Option Meaning
`-specs`	STRING	problem specification file
`-dt`	DOUBLE	time step increment
`-tau`	DOUBLE	decay term
`-gain`	DOUBLE	sigmoidal gain
`-scale`	DOUBLE	scaling for inputs
`-seed`	INTEGER	random seed for initial state
`-steps`	INTEGER	number of time steps
`-gray`	INTEGER	number of gray levels
`-inv`	SWITCH	invert colors?
`-xmag`	INTEGER	magnification for X windows
`-term`	STRING	how to plot points

Table 18.4 Command-line options for **`hopfield`**

makes the slope steeper for values greater than 1, and gentler for values less than 1. The **`-scale`** option is used to set how wide a spread the largest and smallest external inputs will have. Too large a value for this option can result in networks that converge on infeasible solutions. The **`-gray`** option is used to select the number of gray levels for plotting the activation level of the neurons. You will not need to use this option unless you are plotting on an unusual plotting device.

18.7 Further Reading

Dewdney, A. K. (1989). *The Turing omnibus: 61 excursions in computer science.* Rockville, Md.: Computer Science Press.

Isenberg, C. (1978). *The science of soap films and soap bubbles.* Avon, U.K.: Tiero.

March, R. H. (1995). *Physics for poets.* New York: McGraw-Hill.

McCulloch, W. S. & Pitts, W. (1943). A logical calculus of the idea immanent in nervous activity. *Bull. Math. Biophys.*, 5: 115–133.

Nilsson, N. J. (1965). *Learning machines: Foundations of trainable pattern classifying systems.* New York: McGraw-Hill.

Tank, D. W. & Hopfield, J. J. (December 1987). Collective computation in neuronlike circuits. *Sci. Am.*, 257(6): 104–114.

19 Postscript: Complex Systems

If this seems complex, the reason is because Tao is both simple and complex. It is complex when we try to understand it, and simple when we allow ourselves to experience it.
— Stanley Rosenthal

I want to stay as close to the edge as I can without going over. Out on the edge you see all kinds of things you can't see from the center.
— Kurt Vonnegut, Jr.

Life is pleasant. Death is peaceful. It's the transition that's troublesome.
— Isaac Asimov

HAVING SAMPLED A few types of complex systems that are reminiscent of many natural phenomena, it is interesting to note that they possess so many deep similarities that persist despite having obvious differences. For example, the complex systems that we simulated included insect colonies, flocking groups, greedy game players, ecosystems, and statically wired neural networks. Clearly, the natural phenomena that these systems resemble exist on very different spatial and temporal scales. Moreover, the components of these systems also have varying amounts of sophistication: from single cells all the way up to relatively smart animals. However, each of the complex systems has a global behavioral pattern that depends directly on how closely and precisely the components are "wired" together. Systems with few constraints can interact in wild ways and produce chaotic-like global patterns. Systems that are tightly constrained fall into persistent static patterns. In between are systems that exhibit global patterns that are more complicated than either of the extremes.

In this fourth postscript, we will examine the boundary between the two operational extremes found in complex systems and see how this boundary is found in many different types of phenomena. We will first reexamine Stuart Kauffman's work on random Boolean networks (first discussed in Chapter 15) and see how the global behavior of systems that consist of many simple parallel units is determined by the number of interactions that are permitted between the components.

Afterward, we will see that difficult problems from computer science often exhibit this same type of transition. The implication is that sophisticated behavior in natural complex systems may be closely related to the complexity of pure computation.

In the final section we will consider Per Bak's sandpile model of self-organized criticality. Bak has used this model to illustrate how complex systems can naturally fall into a critical region in which both stability and fluidity are partially allowed. Moreover, at this region of criticality, the line between local and global events becomes blurred, since small local perturbations can often lead to an avalanche of activity that has a global effect.

19.1 Phase Transitions in Networks

Stuart Kauffman, a theoretical biologist by training, began his study of random Boolean networks in the 1960s to better understand gene regulation and cell differentiation. A random Boolean network consists of several nodes, say N, that are connected in a very random way. At each time step, the state of each node in the network is updated as a function of its inputs. All nodes are updated simultaneously so that the entire state of the network changes in a single step. If the number of incoming connections per node is equal to K, then such a network is referred to as an NK network. And since these are Boolean networks, each node may be in one of two binary states: on or off, 0 or 1. With K incoming connections, a single node can receive 2^K different sets of signals. For example, with K equal to 2, there are exactly four possibilities: (0, 0), (0, 1), (1, 0), and (1, 1). A node's next-state function is a Boolean function that is used to match the incoming state into a next state for the node. If this Boolean function is, say, the AND function, then the node would map the incoming signal of (1, 1) to a next state of 1 and all other incoming signals to 0. With K connections, there are potentially 2^{2^K} different Boolean functions that could be used per node.

The interesting thing about Boolean networks is that they are general enough that they can be made to look like many different types of things. As a special case, any cellular automaton can be mapped into a specific Boolean network. For example, to build Conway's Game of Life into a Boolean network, we could arrange the nodes into a two-dimensional grid, connect each node with its eight nearest neighbors, and uniformly select the Boolean function that implements the rules of the Game of Life. With other modifications, it would be possible to implement a variation of each of the simulated topics from this book part into a Boolean network: Chris Langton's virtual ants, Mitchell Resnick's termites, a discrete version of Craig Reynolds's boids, a spatial version of the iterated Prisoner's Dilemma, and even a discrete Hopfield neural network. The point is that Boolean networks are extremely versatile. Consequently, any discoveries made concerning generalized Boolean networks can conceivably be applicable to a wide variety of phenomena.

But generality can also be a drawback, since even small values of K and N yield an astronomical number of ways to wire such a network; hence, it may be difficult to say—let alone prove—anything interesting about such a general structure. Whenever mathematicians are faced with a mathematical construct that exists in such a high-dimensional space, one of the first lines of attack is to try to characterize random instances of the object. By itself, a single random instance does not reveal very much, but looking at a large number of random instances can often reveal how things behave in a general case. This was the approach that Kauffman took.[1]

There are three sources of randomness in Kauffman's networks. First, the entire collection of N nodes can be initialized to one of 2^N starting states, which is a staggering number even for small values for N. Next, we can also vary how the network is connected. With K connections per node, there is ample room for randomness here. On the one extreme, with K equal to 1, each node can be potentially connected to any node, giving a total of N^2 different wiring configurations. On the extreme of K equal to N, every node must be connected to every other node (including itself), yielding exactly one wiring configuration. Values of K between 1 and N will yield an even greater number of possible configurations. The final source of randomness in the Boolean network resides in the choice of Boolean functions that are used. Since each node can use one of 2^{2^K} different Boolean functions, there are $N2^{2^K}$ different choices that could be made.

This seems complicated because it is. With K set to 2—a relatively small value for K that happens to have some very interesting properties—there are $2^N \times N^3 \times 16N$ different ways to initialize the network. Also note that for natural systems N will be extremely large because it represents the number of connected units in the network, for instance, genes in a string of DNA.

The key to randomly sampling something in an informative way is to parameterize the choices. Kauffman did this by choosing only random samples with prespecified values for N and K. In this way, he was able to see how random networks with specific values behaved over time. By performing many numerical experiments, it is possible to vary both N and K in a structured way so that trends can be identified.

Most of Kauffman's interests regarding NK networks were concerned with the long-term behavior of the networks. Since the state of a network can be one of 2^N values, every NK network must eventually fall into a previous state. But it is not at all obvious how long typical limit cycles will be. Some of the specific questions

[1]Kauffman did his first numerical experiments back in the days when computers were programmed with a stack of punch cards that usually had to be ordered in a very precise manner. Omitting or misplacing a single card would often yield disastrous results for the programmer. But at that time computers rarely had built-in routines for generating pseudo-random numbers. In order to randomly initialize his networks, Kauffman actually had to shuffle some of his cards, which would confuse onlookers to no end.

that Kauffman asked and answered include the following:

- On average, how many independent limit cycles will an NK network have?
- What is the average length of a limit cycle?
- How stable will limit cycles be if the state is perturbed? What if the structure is slightly altered by changing a Boolean function or a connection?
- How do all of these answers vary as a function of K?

The first two questions are obviously related, since if there is only a single limit cycle, then it either must pass through all 2^N states or all nonmember states must lead to the cycle; but if there are many limit cycles, then they must all be shorter than 2^N in length. Because 2^N is such an enormous number, if the average limit-cycle length is anywhere close to the maximum, then the length would be effectively infinite since it would be impossible to pass such a network through a single complete limit cycle using all of the resources of the universe for the entire age of the universe.

The third question is related to the first two questions. It is possible that some states may not belong to any limit cycle but may only lead to a limit cycle. If this limit cycle is perturbed to one of these nearby states, then the network will happily fall back into the original limit cycle. Stable limit cycles in Boolean networks are very similar to the attractors in continuous dynamical systems that have large basins of attraction. In both types of systems, an unstable limit cycle can be broken by the smallest perturbation while a stable system can withstand small nudges.

With all of these issues in mind, we can now look at some of Kauffman's findings. Networks with K set to 1 are mostly uninteresting. By chance, an isolated cluster of nodes can form a feedback loop that will almost always lock into a fixed state. Each of these clusters will be very stable because any perturbation can propagate to other portions of the network through only a single connection; thus, networks of this type are very similar to fixed point dynamical systems.

On the other extreme, for values of K equal to N, random Boolean networks yield tremendously complicated patterns, often with periodicities that are effectively infinite in length. The average length of the limit cycles will be close to $\sqrt{2^N}$, which is still exceptionally large. However, because the lengths of the limit cycles are so long, only a relatively small number of these cycles can exist within the finite state space of the network. Kauffman has found that on average there will be N/e distinct limit cycles in a $K = N$ network (with e being the well-known constant $2.718281\cdots$). These networks are extremely sensitive to perturbations; altering a single bit in the network's state will propagate changes throughout the entire network. For this reason, Kauffman describes these networks as chaotic.

Thus, we have static behavior on one extreme and chaos on another. In between the two regions, with K equal to 2, the order and chaos seem to balance out. Interestingly, the expected number of distinct limit cycles and the average length are both approximately equal to $\sqrt{N}$ when K is 2. Networks of this type will remain stable if slightly perturbed, but can be pushed to different portions of the state space if perturbed significantly. Collectively, $K = 2$ networks develop a frozen core of inactive nodes that resist most major changes, but will have islands of active sites that permeate most of the network.

More recently, Kauffman and others have extended these results for NK networks to a significant degree. Many of the findings listed here apply to networks with an average of K connections (instead of exactly K). It has also been shown that if biased Boolean functions are used (i.e., functions that are much more likely to return, say, a 1) instead of random Boolean functions, then the order associated with K at 2 can be found in networks with larger values of K.

Kauffman has made the following connection between Boolean networks and gene regulation. A single cell may consist of many tens of thousands of genes. Some genes regulate other genes, that is, when one becomes active, it will activate or inhibit other genes. In this way, the gene activity in a single cell closely resembles the activity in a Boolean network. If genes were so closely tied together that they forced the cell to enter into a chaotic pattern, then the cell would stand little chance of survival because the global behavior would be so irregular that it would have to be suboptimal. On the other extreme, if genes were too loosely coupled with each other, then a cell would be incapable of changing. But if genes were coupled at a critical level, then the right mixture of change and stasis could be achieved. Kauffman hypothesized that cell differentiation is related to this property and that what is different between two cell types, say a neuron and a blood cell, is the specific limit-cycle attractor that each is in. This would explain how one genetic sequence could contain several different "programs" for cell activity. A great deal of experimental evidence seems to support this hypothesis, since the number of specialized cell types for many species with, say, N genes is empirically very close to $\sqrt{N}$, as Kauffman's model predicts.

There are also similarities between Kauffman's results with NK networks, Chris Langton's λ parameter, and Stephen Wolfram's cellular automata classes. On a much more subtle level, the behavior of NK networks resembles many of the other topics covered in this book part: Boids are coordinated only through a mixture of attractive and repelling forces; Tit-for-Tat is successful precisely because it is both forgiving and vigilant; and Hopfield networks can solve problems only by combining inhibition and excitation in a very balanced manner.

We have seen that both static and overly dynamic processes are not very interesting. Complexity seems to be a delicate mixture of the two. From an information-processing point of view, things that behave chaotically can change rapidly but have little ability to store information from one time step to the next. After all, it is impossible to retain a static piece of information if an entire network changes at every time step. On the other hand, static networks can retain information but are incapable of processing it in a meaningful way. Successful information-processing depends on the ability to both store and manipulate information.

19.2 Phase Transitions in Computation

In the previous section, we have seen that to a certain degree, complex systems not only can be thought of as program-like entities but also may have interesting behavior that is related to computational sophistication. In this section we will look at a class of computer problems that has a similar quality; these problems are simple to solve when they are overconstrained or underconstrained, but are very difficult to solve in between. Thus, while in the last section we saw that sophisticated natural computational systems reside at a critical location, in this section we will see the related fact that difficult-to-solve problems reside at a similar critical point. This is important because naturally computing systems can often be seen to be solving a type of optimization problem (even if it is just to stay alive). If problems are naturally more difficult at a critical location, then we should expect nature—both organic and inorganic—to follow suit in the sort of computations that are performed.

We begin with a discussion of how computer scientists classify computer problems. One of the simplest groups is those that belong to the class P, which stands for "polynomial." Examples of problems in P are number sorting and matrix multiplication. For both of these problems, if the length of the input is of size n (e.g., you have n numbers to sort or two $(n \times n)$ matrices to multiply), then there exists an algorithm that computes the desired solution in time that is polynomial in n.[2] Computer scientists like polynomial time algorithms because they are very fast.

Another class of problems consists of those in NP, which stands for nondeterministic polynomial. Any problem that is in NP has the property that a guess for the solution can be verified in polynomial time. For example, the well-known Traveling Salesman Problem (TSP)—which is the problem of finding a tour through n cities that visits each city once, starts and finishes at the same city, and is smaller in length than some specified number, l—is a member of NP because if I allege that some particular path is less than l in length, you can verify that it is or is not by just adding up n numbers and checking that the tour meets the other constraints. Clearly, any problem that is in P is also in NP. In fact, problems in P are the simplest problems in NP.

A very special class of problems is known as *NP-complete*. Problems that are NP-complete are the most difficult problems in NP. TSP is such a problem. All problems that are NP-complete are such that any problem in NP can be polynomially transformed into any other NP-complete problem. This means that if you have a fast algorithm for solving an NP-complete problem, then that algorithm can be used to rapidly solve any problem in NP.

There is a big caveat for the last sentence, since there are no known algorithms that can rapidly solve any problem that is NP-complete. Some readers may have heard of a famous computer science question that is stated as "Does $P = NP$?"[3]

[2] See Section 3.4 on page 36 for an introduction to computational time complexity.

[3] A bad computer science joke answers the question "Yes. Set N equal to 1."

In everyday language, this question asks if there exists a fast way to solve challenging computer problems. If the answer is "yes," then this magical algorithm could be used to solve many problems that are currently intractable. Most computer scientists think that the answer to the $P = NP$ question is "no," but this doesn't stop most computer science graduate students from making at least one honest stab at finding the holy grail of algorithms. However, in reality NP-complete problems are so difficult that the best known algorithms that can solve any instance have a worst-case run time that is exponential. To add insult to injury, virtually every NP-complete problem represents a very practical real-world problem that many people would pay good money to solve.

As a result of this, most people have had to be content with only approximate solutions to NP-complete problems. For the TSP, this would mean that instead of finding the *best* tour through the cities, an algorithm would merely find a *good* tour. Also note that specific instances of a problem can be simplified by being overconstrained or underconstrained. In the TSP, if there are only two roads leading into and out of each city, then there can be only one possible ordering of the cities that completes the tour, so any solution will also be the best solution. However, in most cases, finding even a good approximate solution is often a challenging task.

Now that we know about NP-complete problems, we can look at another important example from this class, known as the *graph-coloring* problem. Given n countries and a number, c, the problem is to find a "coloring" for the map such that it uses no more than c colors and leaves no two bordering countries with the same color. If such a coloring cannot be done, then any algorithm for this problem should report that this is the case.

We can represent a map as a collection of nodes such that every country is itself represented by a single node and connections between any pair of nodes corresponds to a shared border between the two countries. Notice that such a graph looks a lot like a network except that the connections between the nodes are undirected. The degree of connectivity of a map has strong implications for how solvable a particular instance of this problem is. For example, if the graph has only a small number of connections, then there are few shared borders on the map. (Perhaps the map has many islands.) In this case, it is easy to find a solution to the problem. On another extreme, some maps may have a great many connections. In this case, it may be easy to find a cluster of $(c+1)$ nodes that are all mutually connected. This cluster of nodes presents proof that a valid coloring does not exist. For both of these cases, underconstraining or overconstraining the problem makes it easier to solve.

As you have probably guessed by now, with an intermediate number of connections in the graph, problem instances become much more difficult to solve and may often need an exhaustive search in order to come up with an answer. To make a crude analogy, finding the solution to an underconstrained problem is like playing solitaire with a heavily stacked deck—you are almost guaranteed to win; likewise, a random coloring of a highly underconstrained graph-coloring problem is likely to work. Continuing with the analogy, working on an overconstrained problem is similar to playing solitaire with an incomplete deck: By simply counting the cards, you can verify that you can never win. This is similar to overconstrained problems because they often provably lack a solution.

If a single card is missing from a deck, then you may not notice without a careful counting. With half of the deck missing, you are guaranteed to know right from the start that a solitaire game cannot be won. Similarly, one extra card does not assure victory, but having duplicates of every card comes very close to a guaranteed win. The constraints of an NP-complete problem are very similar to this. At the critical point (i.e., having a full deck), predicting whether a solution exists or not (i.e., can a hand of solitaire be won?) becomes most difficult.

Problems of this type are said to be critically constrained. Characterizing problem difficulty by a constraint parameter has been performed on several other NP-complete problems, including the *satisfiability problem* (which is the most fundamental member of the NP-complete class). Not only are many of these problems critically constrained in this manner, but some empirical evidence suggests that most real-world problem instances fall within the critically constrained region.

19.3 Phase Transitions and Criticality

In the first section we saw that the behavior of a complex system can be characterized by a phase transition in which the most interesting behavior lies on the border between order and chaos. In the second section we saw that pure computer science problems undergo a similar phase transition according to the degree of constraint, found in the problem instances. In this final section, we will consider *self-organized criticality*, a theory that suggests that many natural systems are naturally attracted to a critical state.

The canonical example of a critically self-organized system is a sandpile. Given a box of sand, we could gently sprinkle individual grains of sand into the center of the sandpile. As time goes on, the pile will grow in size by increasing in height and expanding outward. Sometimes adding a single grain of sand will have very little effect on the whole sandpile, that is, it lands on the top and just sits there. Other times, a single grain of sand can nudge other grains that start a small avalanche that moves quite a bit of material. This happens because the sandpile was at a critical state: If left alone, it would have remained at its previous state, but a slight perturbation causes a significant shift. After an avalanche, the sandpile is slightly more stable then it was before because the instability has been transferred and distributed to other regions of the sandpile. However, if one continues to slowly add sand to the pile, its dynamics will hover about this critical point, approaching instability, slightly toppling over, then approaching it once again. This is why the critical state is said to be self-organized; it naturally approaches an organized state without any design.

Sandpile models (as well as percolation networks) exhibit avalanches of many different sizes. Small avalanches are very common, but on rare occasions large avalanches are possible. The size and frequency of the avalanches seem to obey a power law relationship, with the smallest events being the most frequent and the largest events the least frequent. Sandpile models appear to apply to a wide variety of phenomena: earthquakes, species extinction, galaxy formation, and even stock market activity. In every case, the complex systems appear to "prefer" to be at the critical value.

For example, a sandpile that is analogous to a completely randomly connected NK network is like a ridiculously balanced pile with all of the grains stacked one on top of the other. Nudging a grain anywhere in this pile will topple the entire structure because it is so unstable and, therefore, infinitely sensitive. Similarly, a pile that is completely spread out and flat cannot be changed by moving any of the grains. The system is perfectly stable and resembles a $K = 1$ network.

This relates to what is perhaps the most interesting aspect of critically self-organized systems. Systems of this type often appear to transcend our usual notions of how information flows in and out of the different spatial levels of a complex system. One extreme view is that the collective subsumes and controls the component. Under this top-down viewpoint, the components of a system are forever subservient to the larger whole: Traders are at the mercy of the economy, neurons serve the higher-level brain components, and ants selflessly serve the colony. Under this worldview it is the dog that wags the tail.

The bottom-up extreme seems to imply that the tail wags the dog. Instead of the components being moved by the collective, the components exert a greater degree of influence on the whole. In this worldview we find that the stock market is manipulated by traders, our thoughts are at the mercy of our neurons, and the colony serves the needs of the ants.

Clearly, there is something wrong with both ways of looking at the world, since information and influence travel in both directions. Self-organized criticality introduces an elegant compromise to this schism. While the current stability of the sandpile determines how much a newly added grain of sand can alter the pile, the grain of sand can potentially have either no effect or a tremendous effect. The amount of influence is determined by the current state, but the next state is determined by the grain of sand.

In summary, complex systems exhibit a wide variety of behavior that depends on the degree of interaction among the components. The amount of local interaction largely determines the types of global interactions that are possible. The most interesting types of behavior are found at a phase transition between two extremes. These critical values are related to a complex system's ability to process information. Moreover, natural systems seem to be poised on the edge of this critical point.

19.4 Further Reading

Bak, P. (1996). *How nature works: The science of self-organized criticality.* New York: Springer-Verlag.

Bak, P. & Chen, K. (January 1991). Self-organized criticality. *Sci. Am.*, 264(1).

Garey, M. R. & Johnson, D. S. (1979). *Computers and intractability: A guide to the theory of NP-completeness.* New York: W. H. Freeman.

Hogg, T., Huberman, B. A., & Williams, C. P. (1996). Phase transitions and the search problem. *Art. Intell.*, 81(1–2): 1–15.

Kauffman, S. (August 1991). Antichaos and adaptation. *Sci. Am.*, 265(2): 64–70.

Kauffman, S. (1995). *At home in the universe: The search for laws of self-organization and complexity.* Oxford: Oxford University Press.

Kauffman, S. A. (1993). *Origins of order: Self-organization and selection in evolution.* Oxford: Oxford University Press.

V Adaptation

In the most general sense, *adaptation* is a feedback process in which external changes in an environment are mirrored by compensatory internal changes in an adaptive system. In the simplest case, an adaptive system may act in a regulatory manner, like a thermostat, so as to maintain some property of the environment at a constant level. An interesting type of adaptation is found in complex systems in which the interactions among the subunits are allowed to change. This process is very similar to a self-modifying program, since the actions of the adaptive unit can affect the environment, which, in turn, feeds information back to the adaptive system. Thus, adaptation can be seen as a computation of the most complex form that emerges through the multiplicity and recursion of simple subunits.

This final book part contains examples of adaptation that resemble naturally occurring forms of adaptation. Chapter 20 concentrates on *genetic algorithms* as methods for solving many different types of problems. Chapter 21 considers *classifier systems*, which contain a form of adaptation similar to what is found in social systems and immune systems. Chapter 22 shows how artificial *neural networks* can be used to classify patterns and to learn arbitrary functions. Finally, Chapter 23 considers how models, the phenomena they model, and search methods are all interconnected in a computation-like form of self-reference.

20 Genetics and Evolution

Natural selection is a mechanism for generating an exceedingly high degree of improbability.
— Sir Ronald Fisher

The goal of science is to build better mousetraps.
The goal of nature is to build better mice.
— Anonymous

A hen is only an egg's way of making another egg.
— Samuel Butler

Anyone familiar with the breeding of animals knows that offspring resemble parents. It doesn't take a scientist to reach this conclusion. In fact, given the agrarian culture and economics of centuries past, the average person living close to a farm a thousand years ago may have been more aware of inheritable traits than the average person today. In any event, Charles Darwin's mental leap from simple heredity to evolution and natural selection stands alone as the greatest scientific achievement in all of biology and is arguably the most important contribution to all of science. To paraphrase Richard Dawkins, never have so many natural phenomena been explained by so few facts. The predictive and explanatory power of evolution and natural selection has shed light on every facet of biology, from the microscopic scale of how bacteria quickly adapt and become resistant to new drugs all the way up to the macroscopic scale of the distribution and interrelatedness of whole species.

To be sure, there are many details behind evolution that are still a mystery. One current area of debate concerns the unit of selection. A related question concerns what the exact definition of an organism should be. While there are many areas in biology that abound in controversy, this is not to say that evolution as a theory is in any way tentative. The empirical evidence in support of evolution and natural selection is as rich and complete as for any theory. Our knowledge of evolution is like a mountain viewed from a distance: We may not be able to discern every little peak, bump, or pebble, but the outline of the mountain is so clear and distinct that we have virtually no doubt as to the mountain's existence.

The strength of evolution is further reinforced by advances in computers and mathematics made in the last few decades. In this chapter we will see how methods of adaptation that are strongly motivated by biological evolution can be exploited to evolve computer solutions to interesting problems. In so doing, we will see how computer science and biology have benefited from advances in both fields.

20.1 Biological Adaptation

The property of adaptation, from an evolutionary point of view, is often described by the equation **adaptation = variation + heredity + selection**. This distillation of ideas, known as *neo-Darwinism*, differs from strict Darwinism by explicitly making reference to a method of heredity. Breaking the equation down into basic terms reveals some interesting connections between adaptation and the fundamental computational issues highlighted earlier. For example, variation, which refers to how individuals in a population can differ from each other, is crucial to the neo-Darwinist view since evolution operates on no single individual but on entire species. Variations, by definition, can be expressed only in terms of multiple individuals; thus, parallelism and spatial multiplicity are essential ingredients in the algorithm of evolution. Similarly, heredity can be seen as a form of temporal persistence. When children inherit traits from their parents in discrete chunks of information, the traits can be seen to be iteratively passed down a time line. Thus, we have both parallelism and iteration as fundamental pieces of the biological equation for adaptation.

Now if we lived in a world of infinite resources where every organism was guaranteed an opportunity to reproduce, then that would be the end of the story; you and I would not be here since evolution would never have occurred in our world. So it is perhaps ironic that we are indebted to the finiteness of the universe. With limitations on available resources, reproduction is far from a sure thing since more organisms will exist than can reproduce. This brings us to the often misunderstood term "survival of the fittest." This phrase has been criticized as being a tautology since it is really equivalent to "survival of the survivors," a nearly meaningless phrase. The problem here seems to be with the word "fittest," which is usually associated with physical characteristics independent of the ability to reproduce. But by "survival of the fittest" we really mean "survival of the reproducers" and nothing more. As Richard Dawkins is fond of saying, you and I can proudly make the claim that every one of our ancestors—without exception—survived long enough to reproduce. This may be an obvious statement, but if we consider the number of organisms that did not survive long enough to reproduce, and consider the exponential number of descendants that could have been, then we can be seen as members of a truly exclusive club.

Our ancestors may have been strong, fast, clever, or even sexy, and "survival of the fittest" seems to refer to some of these traits, but in truth these admirable traits are secondary. What really counts in natural selection is an organism's ability to reproduce, and nothing else. If strength, speed, intelligence, and desirability happen to increase an organism's chances of reproducing, then these traits do indeed correspond to being "fit," but only in the context of reproduction. In fact, "fitness" can often be associated with a trait that is maladaptive in the sense that the trait may actually decrease the functionality of an organism. An example of this can be found in the peacock's gaudy tail feathers, which can hardly do anything but decrease a peacock's ability in the daily business of survival, but are selective for survival solely because peahens find them "sexy," in that they are indicators of a peacock's overall health and fitness.

Adaptation, natural selection, and evolution are indeed very strange things. This is especially apparent when one factors in how organisms can have a recurrent relationship with their environments. The concept *coevolution* refers to how two species can mutually adapt to one another in such a way as to have a circular relationship, with one species' influence on another ultimately returning to the first species in a feedback loop. We see this in the coevolution of predator and prey species, such as lions and gazelles. As lions became better hunters over the past several millions of years, they exerted selective pressure on the gazelles that they preyed upon, which had the effect of increasing the speed and elusiveness of future gazelles. This in turn made it harder for the lions to get a meal, turning them into victims of their own success. This phenomenon is often characterized as a biological arms race.

An even more elaborate and illustrative example is found in the coevolution of bats and moths. Bats use a form of sonar, known as echolocation, to locate moths to eat. To accomplish this, bats emit very high-frequency sounds that bounce off moths and other insects, giving them an estimate of the prey's relative location. The process is actually far more complicated than one would think, since the bat-emitted sounds are often thousands of times more powerful than the returning echoes; hence, bats have evolved a technique to filter out the most powerful sounds so that they can concentrate on the faint return signals. By itself, this form of navigation and target identification is an extremely impressive and creative feat of evolution. But moths have coevolved a defense in the form of a soft covering on their bodies and wings that absorbs the bat chirps. Bats, in turn, have evolved new chirp frequencies that can be used to identify moths' fuzzy coating. In response, the moths have enhanced their stealth technology and, furthermore, have come up with a jamming technique that involves emitting their own sounds to jam the bats' return signals. This is often coordinated with elaborate evasive maneuvers. As if that were not enough, bats have evolved an elaborate flight pattern that can overwhelm a moth's senses, and also periodically turn off their echolocation, making the jamming technique less affective. And so the arms race continues (Wesson, 1991).

The point is that every species partially molds its own environment, which makes the boundary between the selector and the selected somewhat indistinct. Hence, in many ways, Earth as whole may be best understood and appreciated as one enormous complex adaptive system.

20.2 Heredity as Motivation for Simulated Evolution

Just as biological systems have evolved to a fantastically creative degree, so the fundamental equations of biological adaptation can be used to evolve algorithms and solutions to problems within the confines of the computer. In the 1960s, a handful of scientists from different disciplines used ideas gleaned from natural selection and applied them to computational tasks. There are several variations on these ideas, but all of them share a biological motivation. We will briefly examine a broad sampling of all of these techniques in a later portion of this chapter so as to distinguish one from the other, but for now we will examine the ideas of the person most closely associated with simulated evolution.

In the 1960s, John Holland championed the idea of a *genetic algorithm*, but it wasn't until the late 1980s that the idea reached critical mass in academic circles. More than any other technique for simulated evolution, the genetic algorithm (GA) approach most closely simulates real biological evolution as it maps programs and data into DNA-like structures that express some sort of notion of "fitness." The DNA-like structures exist in populations whose members can mate, cross over, and mutate, thus sharing fitness-increasing traits similar to those of real populations of species found in nature.

Recall that the neo-Darwinist view of biological adaptation differs from Darwin's original formulation in that it includes a method of heredity. Darwin himself knew that his theory was incomplete, and it wasn't until the work of Gregor Mendel, an Austrian monk and amateur botanist, was rediscovered at the turn of the twentieth century that biologists had the beginnings for a theory of heredity. Mendel independently performed his studies shortly after Darwin's work was published. His careful experimentation on pea plants showed that traits are inherited in discrete chunks of information. The most telling example of this, and the example that refutes the idea that traits are blended or merged, involves traits that one can imagine ranging on a continuous scale but are in reality found only in either/or quantities. For example, the height of a pea plant may be influence by both inherited traits and the environment in which it grows. Thus, pea plants can be short, tall, or anything in between. But in a controlled environment that was a consistent and uniform for all plants, Mendel found that his plants would be either tall or short. Now if one were to mate a tall plant to a short plant, conventional wisdom at that time would suggest that offspring would be of medium height. Such a result would have added support to the view that traits are merged.[1] Mendel found that offspring from the paired tall and short plants would in fact be either tall or short, not medium. He also found that populations of plants bred in a similar manner had characteristics that obeyed very simple statistics.

In the 1950s, Mendelian genetics was further solidified by work in molecular biology, the discovery of nucleic acid, and the understanding of how DNA triplets code amino acids that form proteins, the building blocks for everything from digestive acids to skin, bone, eyes, brains, and blood. The DNA in an organism consists of extremely long, chains of chemical bases. In higher organisms, these chains are organized into chromosomes, but this is an irrelevant detail for our purposes. There are four chemical bases in DNA, denoted by A, C, G, and T. Each base has a complement that it pairs up with (A with T and C with G), which means that every sequence of bases has a "mirror" version, for instance, "CATTAG" complements "GTAATC" and vice versa. Thus, the famed double helix of DNA consists of two long, intertwining strings of these letters. The crucial part of all of this is that the language of nature is a discrete alphabet. The fact that it consists of four letters is important to molecular biology, but from a computational point of view we only need to recognize that the alphabet is fixed and agreed upon ahead of time.

With the GA approach to problem-solving, we represent candidate solutions of problems by a string of fixed length similar to the way organisms store directions for maintenance and building instructions inside cells. Our strings may consist of any alphabet that we wish, and in the simplest case we can restrict the strings to the binary symbols, 0 and 1. The most important thing concerning the representation for the candidate solutions is that there should be a clear one-to-one method for mapping the strings into a more useful form. For example, a string of 0s and 1s could represent a floating-point number that is near the maximum of some function that we wish to maximize, or it could represent a solution to an optimization problem, or it could even express a strategy for playing the iterated Prisoner's Dilemma. We will see examples of all of these types of encodings later, but for now you should recognize that just as long as there exists some invertible method for translating the strings into the information that we really want, it is possible to apply a GA to a problem.

20.3 Details of a Genetic Algorithm

A basic genetic algorithm is shown in Table 20.1. The algorithm is very simple, with the heart of it contained in the innermost loop, which references the processes of selection, mating, and mutation. In this section we will examine the details of the algorithm in Table 20.1 with emphasis on the three aforementioned processes.

[1]Note that this would be necessary but not sufficient evidence for a "merged trait" hypothesis, since it is often the case that one physically realized trait may correspond to many inherited factors that are related to each other.

- Initialize the population, P
- Repeat for some length of time:
  - Create an empty population, P'
  - Repeat until P' is full:
    - Select two individuals from P based on some fitness criterion
    - Optionally mate, and replace with the offspring
    - Optionally mutate the individuals
    - Add the two individuals to P'
  - Let P now be equal to P'

Table 20.1 A simplified genetic algorithm

For our first GA example, suppose we wished to evolve a string into a specific English phrase. You and I are "outside" the GA, so we can choose whatever phrase we wish. The GA, however, does not know what the string is. It is only allowed to make guesses, and for each guess it receives one piece of information in the form of the "fitness" of the string. How we define the fitness of the string is crucial to how the GA will work, because our method of selection must be based solely on this quantity. Ultimately, we want the selection process to somehow embody the idea of "survival of the fittest." Therefore, we will go into fitness measures with a fair amount of detail. Afterward, we can come back to the process of selection.

For the case of breeding text strings, it is natural to define fitness to be the percentage of correct letters in the guess. This fitness measure is fine for short phrases, but is problematic for long phrases because as we increase the length of the target phrase, the fitness difference between two phrases that differ by one correct letter becomes vanishingly small. To overcome this problem, we will define three different types of fitness measures, with the latter two being a function of the earlier fitness function. More concretely, our "raw fitness" will be the percentage of letters that are correct:

$$f^{\text{raw}} = \frac{\text{Number of Correct Letters}}{\text{Length of Target String}}.$$

Next, we would like the notion of fitness to somehow be invariant in the length of the target string. This is not always possible for all problems, but for our simple phrase-guessing problem it suffices to define the following "scaled fitness" measure:

$$f^{\text{scale}} = 2^{f^{\text{raw}}}.$$

This measure has the nice property that given two strings, where one string has one more correct letter than the other, the string closer to the target will be more fit by a constant factor as the other string. This is true regardless of the length of the target.[2]

The final step is to normalize the fitness measure from the last step so that decisions concerning selection can be made regardless of the magnitude of the raw and scaled fitness measures. We do this by summing up all of the scaled fitness scores for every member of a population and dividing by the total to compute a "normalized fitness:"

$$f_i^{\mathrm{norm}} = \frac{f_i^{\mathrm{scale}}}{\sum_{j=i}^{n} f_j^{\mathrm{scale}}},$$

where i and j are indices that range over all the members of the population.

Now that we have defined normalized fitness, we can finally talk about selection. There are several ways that one could imagine going about this. As a first approximation, we could simply allow the fittest 50 percent of the population to reproduce. This is an easy method, but it has the downside that it doesn't permit very much exploration in the DNA search space. After all, unfit individuals may still have some novel genes to contribute to the gene pool, so we don't want to throw away genetic diversity too hastily. A better method is to use the normalized fitness scores as a sort of roulette wheel. For example, suppose that we had four individuals in the population with normalized fitness scores of 0.1, 0.2, 0.3, and 0.4. Notice that these numbers conveniently sum to exactly 1, which is a result of the normalization step. Now take a roulette wheel with ten numbers on it such that spinning the wheel will randomly give you a number from 1 to 10. If the wheel comes up with the number 1, then the individual with fitness 0.1 wins. But if 2 or 3 comes up, then the individual with fitness 0.2 wins. Similarly, 4, 5, or 6 is a win for the 0.3 fit individual, and everything else is a win for the 0.4 fit individual. In this way, each individual can expect to win in the roulette with probability equal to its fitness. Every individual has a chance of winning, that is, being selected, just as in nature.

With the above scheme, we can now randomly select individuals to reproduce for the next generation. The next step in the GA is to optionally mate selected individuals. By "optionally" I mean that either we allow both parents to live in the next generation unchanged or we mate the two parents to get two offspring that live in the next generation. Taking either action could be a good thing to do, depending on some special circumstances, so we allow for either possibility by flipping a biased coin to randomly make the decision. "Mating" can mean several things, but in the simplest case we perform an operation that is similar to a real-world occurrence called *crossover*. When two strings are crossed, the result is two new strings, each of which contains part of the genetic material of the parents.

---

[2] One warning: Exponential scaling is applicable only to simple GA problems like this first example. In more realistic situations, a linear rescaling is more appropriate. Also, we could use another exponentiation base besides 2, say x, to express the idea that one more correct letter equates with being x times more fit.

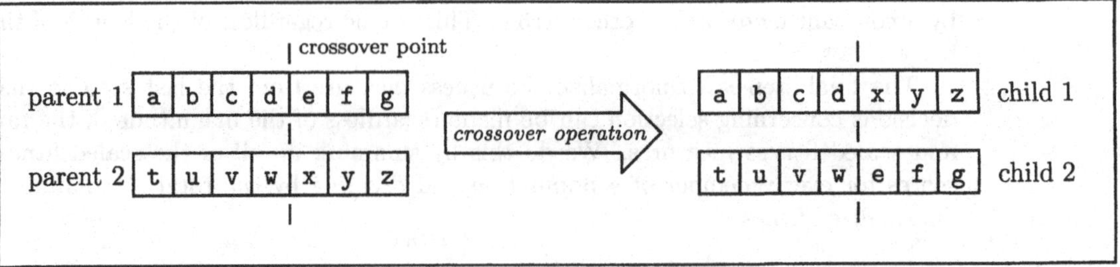

Figure 20.1 The crossover operation in action

Figure 20.1 illustrates the basic idea. First, a random crossover point is chosen. At that point in both strings the genetic material from the left side of one parent is spliced to the material from the right side of other parent. A second child is produced by swapping and pairing the other sides. In this way, portions of the genetic material from two fit individuals can be merged so as to potentially produce even more viable offspring. It is certain that crossover can result in less fit individuals, but this is usually a minor setback that lasts only a single generation, since the potential rewards for merging healthy parents far outweigh the downside.

The final thing that we need to consider from the GA in Table 20.1 is the mutation operator. Once again, we do not want to always apply mutation to every member of the population, so we randomly make the decision with a very biased coin toss on a letter-by-letter basis. Thus, it is possible for some individuals to have multiple portions of their DNA mutated. But if the mutation rate is small, then most members of the population will have zero mutations applied to them. Mutation allows for entirely new genetic material to enter the population, which can yield tremendous rewards if the mutation is favorable; however, it is usually the case that mutations are detrimental, so it makes sense to allow mutation only on a very infrequent basis.

Putting all of this together, we can now see how a GA can find an English phrase through evolution. The target string for the illustrated results is the nonsensical phrase "furious green ideas sweat profusely," which has a length of thirty-five characters. Before examining the GA solution, let's briefly examine the mathematical properties of searching for a string of this length. We have restricted the alphabet to the twenty-six lowercase letters and a space, for a total of twenty-seven characters. The number of possible strings of length 35 with twenty-seven characters is a staggering 27^{35}, equal to

$$125{,}236{,}737{,}537{,}878{,}753{,}441{,}860{,}054{,}533{,}045{,}969{,}266{,}612{,}127{,}846{,}243.$$

To put this number in perspective, assuming that there are 2^{80} electrons in the universe, and that the universe is around 10 billion years old, then each electron

Time	Average Fitness	Best Fitness	Best String
0	0.035314	0.200000	"pjrmrubynrksxiidwctxfodkodjjzfunpk "
1	0.070000	0.257143	"pjrmrubynrksxiidnybvswcqo piisyexdt"
⋮	⋮	⋮	⋮
25	0.708686	0.771429	"qurmous gresn idnasvsweqt prifuseky"
26	0.724286	0.800000	"qurmous green idnasvsweqt prifuseky"
⋮	⋮	⋮	⋮
36	0.806514	0.914286	"uurious green idnas sweqt profusely"
37	0.820857	0.914286	"qurmous green ideas sweqt profusely"
⋮	⋮	⋮	⋮
41	0.895943	0.942857	"uurious green idnas sweat profusely"
42	0.908457	0.971429	"qurious green ideas sweat profusely"
⋮	⋮	⋮	⋮
45	0.927714	0.971429	"qurious green ideas sweat profusely"
46	0.936800	1.000000	"furious green ideas sweat profusely"

Table 20.2 Evolving the text string "furious green ideas sweat profusely" from an initially random pool of strings: Fitness scores shown are for the raw fitness.

would have to make over 300 million guesses per second for the entire age of the universe before a correct guess was likely to be made. Hence, to put it mildly, a pure random search is not very feasible.

To solve this problem with a GA, I used a population of 500 strings, a crossover rate of 75 percent, and a mutation rate of 1 percent. The results are shown in Table 20.2. As can be seen, the GA finds the target string in forty-six generations. The best strings in the population make innovations that result in small jumps in the best fitness score, while the rest of the population benefits a few generations later as the healthy genes move through the population. We could have used a much smaller population size, which would have resulted in the GA taking more generations to solve. It would also have been likely that the GA could take a step backward, with the best and average scores temporarily dropping. A similar effect could be achieved by modifying the crossover and mutation rates as well. In any event, as the problem difficulty increases, so must the required population size and number of generations increase.

The real reason why a GA is able to solve this problem is that GAs can perform massively parallel searches. Each member of a population represents a hypothesis for the target string. Strings with equal fitness may, in fact, consist of completely different letters. This means that crossing such a pair could result in a drastic improvement in the average fitness. Moreover, many such partial solutions can be searched for simultaneously.

While this example is illustrative in the sense that you should now be able to appreciate how the selection, crossover, and mutation operations can be used to locate very specific and improbable strings, more common problems are not as trivially solved. One reason why the string-finding problem is so easy to solve is that each individual character has a clear ideal value, that is, the correct value for the target. This means that if a character is good for one member of the population, then it is good for every member of the population. In the real world, both biological and technological, fitness is usually a function of many things that are conditionally beneficial or harmful, depending on the context in which it exists. In other words, one gene may be helpful when paired with some genes but detrimental when paired with others. In the next section we will examine several other problem types that can be solved with a GA approach. In each case, the merit of any particular bit, letter, or number will be dependent on the state of the other characters in the genome of the individual. We will see that GA solutions can still yield interesting results even in the more challenging problem domains.

20.4 A Sampling of GA Encodings

In this section we will consider a continuous multidimensional function optimization problem, a combinatorial optimization problem, and the iterated Prisoner's Dilemma as candidate problems for solving with a genetic algorithm approach. By now, most of these problem types should be familiar to you, so the emphasis here will be on the relevance of these examples to real-world needs and on the techniques used to encode the problems into a form that a GA can use. The specific examples that we will consider are not necessarily more difficult than the string-finding problem that we saw in the last section, but the classes from which these new examples come as a whole are more challenging.

Function Optimization In a function optimization problem one typically has a real-world process that behaves as a function of some parameters. In this situation you would usually have an analytical model of the physical process to work with. The goal is to find parameter settings that maximize or minimize some quantity. This sounds easy—after all, if you had a model, then you would only need to plot out the function that you wished to maximize at several different parameter settings and pick the best one. This, alas, usually is not possible for many practical reasons. In real-world scenarios the target function may be parameterized by hundreds or even thousands of values, making a human-operated brute-force search infeasible. A large collection of real world problems that fall into this category includes finding optimal operating points for chemical plants, such as wastewater treatment, and for material

Figure 20.2 A two-dimensional function to maximize

production facilities, and in optimizing the design of parts and machines with certain known goals, such as minimizing drag in an airplane design. Quite often, one already has a fair-to-good solution to the problem in advance. Nevertheless, optimizing a huge industrial process by a fraction of a percent can yield tremendous time, financial, and ecological savings. So finding even a slim improvement to an existing solution is a worthy goal.

If we wish to maximize a quantity, then this function easily maps into our scheme of using a fitness function. We may need to rescale the function in order to enhance the searching abilities of the GA, but this is a detail that is very problem-specific. To encode a candidate solution into a form that a GA can use, we represent all of the parameters in one long binary string with a fixed number of bits for each parameter. The number of bits used will depend on the level of accuracy needed. Usually the parameters will have a known range of valid values, such as, *min* through *max*. By using n bits we can represent an integer range from 0 to $2^n - 1$. It is then a simple procedure to linearly rescale the integer into a valid floating-point number for the given parameter. Hence, if we had p parameters to search for, then an $n \times p$ bit string could be used to represent an individual of the population.

Figure 20.2 shows a two-dimensional surface that we will use as an example function to maximize. (This surface appeared in Figure 18.8 on page 324.) The function is a summation of nine Gaussian functions spaced out on a 3×3 grid. The center maximum is our goal. This image should give you an idea of why this is a challenging problem, since interesting functions almost always have many suboptimal local maxima. It so happens that this function is maximal at (0.0, 0.0), which is in the exact center of the plot, but our GA doesn't know this. Using ten bits for each number (thus, twenty for the whole string) and a population of 100, the GA comes up with a very good guess after only twenty-five generations or so. But by the seventy-fifth generation, the GA finds the optimal solution, which corresponds to the bit string "10000000001000000000." Due to our encoding, this string represents two binary numbers, "1000000000" and "1000000000." The method used to map binary numbers into floating-point numbers is

$$8 \times \text{integer}(\mathit{string})/2^{10} - 4,$$

where integer(*string*) represents the integer value of the binary substring. This illustrates an important point. The binary value just less than "1000000000" is "0111111111," which means that two substrings that are nearly identical in fitness may have exactly opposite bit string representations. Crossing such substrings will always result in inferior offspring despite the fact that either substring in isolation would be a good choice. Because of this, it is likely that one substring will come to completely dominate the other, since the two cannot safely coexist. Metaphorically speaking, it is like two phenotypically similar but genetically different animal species fighting for a single ecological niche. As soon as one species gains a firm foothold, the other can be wiped out. Such is the way of nature.

Combinatorial Optimization The first combinatorial optimization problem we encountered was the task assignment problem in Chapter 18 (pages 320–323). We will use a GA on the exact same problem described on those pages, so you may wish to review the task assignment problem before continuing. Many combinatorial optimization problems are characterized by the fact that a valid (but not necessarily good) solution is specified as a permutation of the first n integers. For example, with a size of 6, a valid solution to the task assignment problem can consist of any permutation of the numbers 1 through 6, with the numbers specifying which worker performs which task. For the example problem instance from Figure 18.6 (page 321), the best solution of 44 corresponds to the permutation 1, 4, 6, 3, 5, and 2. Also, any sequence of n integers that does not contain each integer from 1 to n exactly once does not map to a valid solution; hence, the representation of our strings for the GA is limited by this fact, since we do not want members of the population to map to invalid solutions.

The constraints on our string representation will also affect how we apply the mutation and crossover operations. For mutation, we cannot randomly change a character in a string, since this could result in a string that corresponds to a completely infeasible solution. Instead, we can randomly pick two positions in the string and swap the entries. This preserves the constraint that each integer must appear in a valid string but also provides a random mix that can potentially yield improvements to a solution. The idea is illustrated at the top of Figure 20.3. We also need to modify the crossover operation, since if we were to cross two strings in a manner similar to the way we did in the earlier problems, invalid strings could result. The fix to this problem is to once again randomly pick one crossover point in one of the strings. But now we look at the character. The bottom of Figure 20.3 shows this with the character "4" being picked from the first parent. Now if the two parents are sufficiently different, when we scan the second parent for the occurrence of "4"

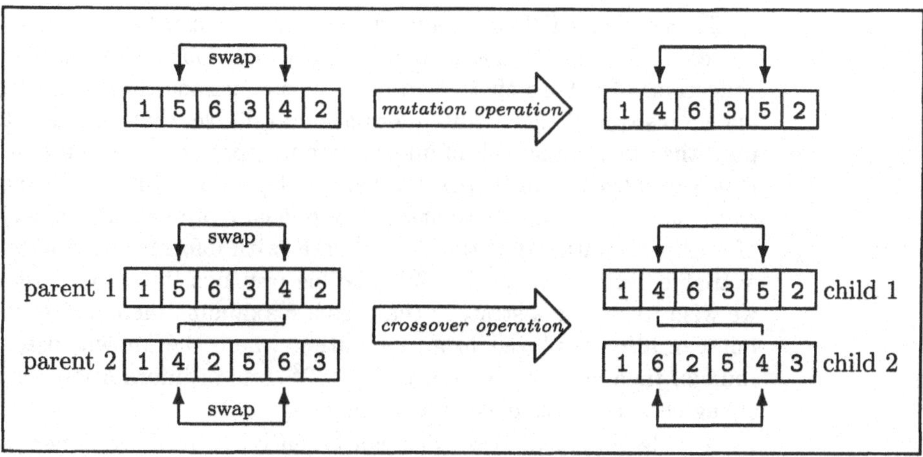

Figure 20.3 The crossover and mutation operations applied to candidate solutions of a combinatorial optimization problem

we find it in a second position. In a sense, the first parent asserts the hypothesis that "4" belongs in position 5 while the second parent asserts that "4" belongs in position 2. By swapping the characters in the second and fifth positions, we are combining the two parents in such a way that each offspring contains a piece of each parent: One offspring will be nearly identical to one parent, but it also shares at least one character with its other parent. One could easily extend this by applying multiple crossovers to a pair of parents at each generation, but care has to be taken that we don't destroy too much of what made the parents fit in the first place.

Using a population of ten strings, before the first generation my strings had an average fitness 23.1 and the best string had a score of 30. After twenty-three generations the GA found the same solution that the Hopfield neural network found. But after the twenty-sixth generation the GA found the optimal solution of 44, which required a single swapped pair from the neural network solution.

The Iterated Prisoner's Dilemma Our final example GA encoding is the iterated Prisoner's Dilemma (IPD), which we first studied in Chapter 17 (see pages 292 and 293 for introductions to the Prisoner's Dilemma and the iterated Prisoner's Dilemma). Toward the end of Chapter 17 we saw how different IPD strategies performed in different environments. The spatial and ecological IPD simulations hinted at how strategies similar to "Tit-for-Tat" could be viable, robust, and resistant to invasions. We can now explore these issues from an evolutionary point of view to see how cooperation can be evolved.

To encode an IPD strategy into a form that can be manipulated by a GA, we represent the strategies as strings that resemble lookup tables. The tables will have collections of entries that correspond to the actions that are to be taken, given a known history. If there is no information available, that is, this is the first round of play, then we need one bit of information to represent what our first move should be. But if we have at our disposal a history of one previous round, then we can base a move on our previous move and our opponent's previous move, which yields a total of four possibilities. For the general case, with information from r previous rounds available, we have a total of 2^{2r} possible previous states to consider. Therefore, if we wish to encode a strategy that has a maximum "memory" of r previous rounds but can also be played in any situation where the known history is less than r rounds, then we need a total of $\sum_{i=0}^{r} 2^{2i}$ bits of information (or table entries, or string characters) to encode a strategy.

A wide variety of strategies can be encoded in this manner. With r set to 0, we can encode only very simple strategies, such as "Always Cooperate" or "Always Defect." But with r set to 1, strategies that consider a very limited history, such as "Tit-for-Tat" and "Pavlov," can be represented. With even larger r it is possible to use sophisticated strategies that do "clever" things, such as probe an opponent to check if it is easily suckered or not. In the experiments that follow, we will use an r equal to 1, which still permits some interesting strategies but has the main advantage that the strings are short and thus the strategies can be easily understood. Therefore, a legal string for the GA to work on will consist of five letters with each character equal to a C or a D. The five characters, in order, represent (1) the move to make in the first round, and the moves to make given that in the previous round; (2) both players cooperated; (3) we cooperated and our opponent defected; (4) we defected and our opponent cooperated; and (5) both players defected.

To evaluate the strategies in the GA population, we must have each strategy play many other strategies during each generation so that we have a fair estimate of how a given strategy competes over all. The fitness, then, for a single strategy is simply the average score that it achieved over each round of each IPD contest. For every other GA problem that we have studied, fitness was a static function with a meaning that was independent of what the population looked like. But in this GA simulation, the fitness of any individual is going to be a function of what the rest of the population looks like. Hence, this GA simulation is subject to a greater degree of feedback than the other simulations.

Using a population of 100 individuals; fifty bouts per individual per generation, with each bout consisting of twenty IPD rounds; and starting the GA with random strategies, the GA converged to a stable solution after sixty generations. The average and best scores are shown in Figure 20.4. Initially, for the first fifteen generations or so, the most successful strategies are "mean," in that they start off with a defection and continue to defect in most circumstances. The mean strategies prey on the sucker strategies, which unconditionally cooperate. But by the sixteenth

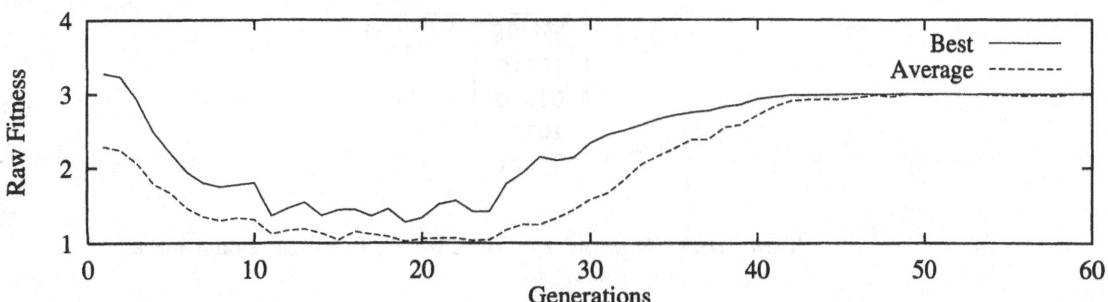

Figure 20.4 Average and best raw fitness scores for the IPD-playing GA

generation, the best strategy is encoded by the string "CCDCD" which is our old friend "Tit-for-Tat." At this point, the average fitness of the population is in a rather sickly state due to the rampant defections. But with no more suckers to prey on, the mean strategies are eventually overwhelmed by all of the Tit-for-Tat players. At the end, every member of the population uses "Tit-for-Tat."

Although the population reached a relatively stable strategy that was more or less resistant to invasions, with some modifications it would be possible for the GA population to never stop evolving, with each seemingly stable state exploitable by some other strategy. This is reminiscent of the Red Queen phenomenon, named after the Red Queen in Lewis Carroll's *Through the Looking-Glass*, who always moves but never passes anything because her environment is rushing along right beside her. With fitness being defined in terms of how an individual performs in the context of its environment, those that survive tend to change their environment, if only by being fit enough to reproduce. A changing environment implies a changing fitness function, which further means that what was once "fit" may no longer be. This last point is demonstrated by the fact that the IPD GA has a huge dip in the average fitness plot, which is a phenomenon not seen in the other GA simulations with static fitness functions. The situation gets much more complicated when competitive species and coevolution are factored in.

20.5 Schemata and Implicit Parallelism

All of the previous examples demonstrate the power of genetic algorithms, but there is another important attribute of GAs that warrants special attention. Genetic algorithms possess a property that Holland has referred to as *implicit parallelism*, which allows GAs to search for solutions more accurately than one would expect. The result is best explained by reexamining the fundamental problem that GAs are used to solve.

String	Fitness
10110	28
01010	70
10110	91
01001	62

Table 20.3 Four binary strings from a five-dimensional space

The goal in running a GA on any problem is to find the highest peak in the fitness function. For hard problems, which demand an encoding that uses very long strings (say, 100 characters or more), explicitly searching the entire space is impossible because the volume increases exponentially in the length of the strings. Yet we would still like to get an estimate of what the fitness function looks like with a subsample. By considering whole populations at once, a GA can exploit statistical properties of the strings with only a relatively small population size.

To explain the basic idea, consider a population of four binary strings, each of which has a length of five characters and a known fitness, as shown in Table 20.3.

By themselves, the strings tell us very little about what the whole fitness function looks like, but if we consider the similarities and differences among all of the strings, then much more information becomes available. To see why, we need to consider *schemata*, which are a type of template. A schema is a string that describes a whole class of strings. Schemata consist of the two binary symbols plus a wild card symbol denoted by "$\star$". The schema "$1\star\star\star\star$" represents all binary strings that start with a "1" and "$\star\star0\star\star$" represents all strings that have a "0" in the middle. In general, if a schema has x "$\star$" characters in it, then it represents exactly 2^x different strings.

If we knew the average fitness for a collection of strings represented by a single schema, then finding a peak of a fitness function becomes a little easier with the extra information. Looking back at Table 20.3, for n strings with length l ($n = 4$ and $l = 5$ in this case), there are between 2^l and $n2^l$ schemata. The exact number depends on the amount of variability in the population.

Since a GA allocates more reproductive trials to the fittest schemata, a fit schema will receive an exponentially increasing number of opportunities to reproduce. And since the each string belongs to 2^l different schemata, a GA can effectively process more schemata than there are strings in the population. Holland showed that, in general, the speedup due to implicit parallelism means that approximately n^3 schemata are processed in each generation with only n strings in the population. This means that performing n simultaneous searches is much more computationally efficient than performing n separate searches, which explains why evolutionary approaches are successful.

20.6 Other Evolutionary Inspirations

Besides genetic algorithms, there are a handful of other types of evolutionary-based problem-solving methods that either have been developed independently or can be thought of as offspring of the main approaches. What follows is a very brief summary of how these techniques relate to GAs and to each other.

Evolutionary Programming The idea behind an *evolutionary program* (EP) was introduced by Lawrence Fogel in 1960. EPs differ from GAs in three main ways. First, the representation of a solution in an EP follows directly from the problem and is not constrained to be in the form of a string of characters, as in a GA. Thus, to solve a multidimensional function approximation problem with an EP, we would encode a solution as a vector of floating-point numbers instead of as a binary string. The representation issues also relate to the second difference between GAs and EPs, which is that EPs do not attempt to closely model genetic operations. Consequently, the crossover operation is not used in an EP. Third, mutations take a different form in an EP. It is typical to use multivariate Gaussian perturbations instead of raw bit-flipping in an EP. Also, during the various stages of an EP, the rate of mutations is typically reduced as the optimal solution is approached. This means that exploration is at its highest at the initial stages—when it is most needed—and at its lowest toward the end, when one must be careful not to ruin a near optimal solution.

Evolutionary Strategies An *evolutionary strategy* (ES) is very similar to an EP, despite the fact that both techniques were developed completely independently of one another. The ES approach was first conceived in 1963 by Ingo Rechenberg and Hans-Paul Schwefel, whom were later joined by Peter Bienert. The ES and EP approaches differ slightly in the way selections are made and how mutations are performed. Also, a form of recombination is possible in an ES. Both ES and EP techniques are very similar in spirit to *simulated annealing*.

Genetic Programming More recently, John Koza pioneered the use of *genetic programs* (GP) as a technique for evolving whole programs to solve problems. GPs are similar to GAs—especially since they are a spin-off technique—but differ in that program fragments are used instead of strings. For example, the function $(a+b) \times c$ can be represented as a parse tree in which the leaves are the operands and the internal nodes are operators. With this representation, one can cross programs by swapping branches of the parse trees with other program branches. Since programs are manipulated under the GP approach, most practitioners use the Lisp programming language or a similar variant because it is easy to write Lisp programs that manipulate other Lisp programs. (See Section 3.3, page 30, for a brief introduction to Lisp.)

Classifier Systems Another type of adaptive system, conceived of by John Holland, is a *classifier system*, which is a sort of cross between a Post production system, a genetic algorithm, and a market economy. As such, classifier systems combine many methods of adaptation into a single form that possesses a type of learning and evolution. Because of the hybrid nature of classifier systems, we will devote all of the next chapter to them.

The techniques listed above are really just a small sample of the many biology-inspired problem-solving methods that are possible. In fact, the topics of evolutionary simulation and problem-solving are themselves subject to selective forces. We have some fundamental ideas developed in the GA and EP/ES paradigms that have been crossed, mutated, and otherwise borrowed from in order to create new and more powerful methods of problem-solving. Certainly, some of the current and future variations of evolutionary techniques will be selected against—which in the scientific community usually amounts to lost funding and/or lack of a publishing outlet—but future techniques will certainly combine some of the best features of each method in order to form new methods of artificial adaptation that surpass all of their predecessors.

20.7 Unifying Themes

Clearly, genetic algorithms and evolutionary simulations are powerful methods for demonstrating the adaptive power of evolution and natural selection. By simulating a few simple principles (crossover, mutation, reproduction, and selection), one can get a glimpse of how novel and creative innovations are made in nature. While this simulation approach to biology has yielded a tremendous number of insights into how nature works, the results have also been important to engineering and the applied mathematical sciences by inspiring non-biologists to rethink the way problems should be approached.

But, interestingly, every solved piece of the evolutionary puzzle seems to be replaced by two new puzzles, which is due, in part, to the complexity of the topic and the ubiquity of selective mechanisms. Some of the open topics lie at the heart of the philosophically "big questions" that we all ask. Why should evolution produce increasingly complex structures and organisms, with the human brain being the epitome? Stephen J. Gould has proposed that evolution tends to fill niches. With a world that consists entirely of some simple organism type, say bacteria, there are only so many innovations that can be made that improve fitness yet maintain the defining features of what it means to be a bacterium. But this kind of dances around the point, because it is misleading to imply that we are more fit than bacteria. The key idea here is that as the number of bacteria increases, it becomes easier to make a living as something that bacteria have not already mastered. Thus, the only action one could take to further this goal would be to become more complex. By extrapolating this line of reasoning, one can argue that all of the major innovations in nature are simply the consequences of species trying to find new room to grow, and the directions are limited to up and out.

Related to this issue is the question regarding the unit of selection. Richard Dawkins has persuasively argued that a surprisingly large number of biological phenomena can be accounted for as artifacts of the gene being the sole unit of selection. This argument is especially surprising, and yet is persuasive when applied to apparently altruistic animal behavior. If each of our genes is selfish in the sense that it exists solely for its own propagation, then how does one account for bees that sacrifice themselves for the benefit of the hive, birds that warn of predators, gazelles that do an eccentric dance to distract lions, and other such behaviors? If one does the math, it turns out that a gene actually improves its long-term survival rate if it encourages self-sacrifice for the benefit of other relatives that share the same gene.

While selfish genes are an elegant solution to a thorny issue, we also know that nature exploits the use of "chunks" by building up levels of complexity in hierarchies. For example, our cells are largely the result of a partnership of bacteria made a billion years ago; organelles that perform specific cell functions, such as metabolism and movement, are descendants of specialized bacteria that at one time existed independently of each other. In some cases organelles even possess their own DNA. Multicellular organisms such as humans, and super-organisms such as insect colonies, are further applications of nature's increasing complexity by using more complicated building blocks. In all three cases, there are vast quantities of shared genetic material with a limited distribution channel (nucleus, sperm or egg cells, and queen bee) that can be used to account for the overall cooperation of the system. Yet not all cooperative systems consist of entities that share DNA, which means that selfish genes cannot be the whole story when it comes to units of selection. One only needs to look at the delicate balance of resources found in ecosystems to see that species can be interconnected and selected for in highly complicated ways that cannot be explained by genes alone. On the far end of the selection spectrum is James Lovelock's Gaia hypothesis, which argues for a definition of life that includes Earth as a living organism. In many ways, this whole debate is a prime example of the reductionism versus holism conflict. But both extremes seem to be missing something.

Perhaps the most tantalizing feature of natural selection as an explanation of evolution is that it appears to have some explanatory power in non-biological systems as well. Richard Dawkins has coined the term *meme* to stand for a unit of cultural information. Dawkins explains:

> Examples of memes are tunes, ideas, catch-phrases, clothes fashions, ways of making pots or of building arches. Just as genes propagate themselves in the gene pool by leaping from body to body via sperms or

> eggs, so memes propagate themselves in the meme pool by leaping from brain to brain via a process which, in the broad sense, can be called imitation.

Reconsidering the equation **adaptation = variation + heredity + selection** as applied to non-biological things, it is easy to see how businesses, cultures, and ideas can vary and be selected for, but heredity in these cases takes on a whole new meaning. The so-called central dogma of biology posits that genetic information flows in one direction, that is, DNA codes RNA, and RNA codes protein, but protein does not code DNA. This idea is central to the current model of genetic heredity. An interesting historical footnote is that even though the science of genetics was unknown in Darwin's time, Jean Baptiste Lamarck (who coined the term "biology") proposed a method of heredity long before Darwin's work that is now known as *Lamarckism*. Lamarck had observed that organisms change in response to their environment, and proposed that organisms pass on these changes to their offspring. Thus, Lamarckism would suggest that a giraffe, by extending its neck to eat higher leaves, can endow its offspring with a longer neck solely through its efforts to stretch. We now know that Lamarckism is not directly applicable to biological heredity; nevertheless, Lamarck's ideas had considerable influence on Charles Darwin, who failed to come up with a more feasible method of heredity.

As ridiculous as Lamarckism may now sound for biological adaptation, it is a perfectly reasonable method of heredity for non-biological systems. This means that in some ways non-biological evolution can take shortcuts not available to biological systems because acquired improvements can be incorporated and passed along to offspring. This will be especially important in the next chapter when we combine ideas from evolution and cultural adaptation into a single adaptive mechanism.

20.8 Further Exploration

All of the programs highlighted in this chapter use essentially the same underlying GA engine. All of the command-line options are summarized in Table 20.4. The program code is very straightforward and can be used as a basis for your own GA programs. Modifying the GA code for another task will usually involve writing a mapping from the objects that you wish to optimize into a string, as well as writing a function that defines the fitness of one of your objects.

In addition to `gasurf`, which I used to maximize the surface, there is a program called `gabump` that is identical except that it attempts to find the maximum of a scalar function that consists of a single localized bump. You may want to play with this program in greater detail, since it is easier to understand how the GA search works in a single dimension. Both of these programs use the `-len` option to specify how many bits to use for each floating-point number. The `-power` option affects the

Option Name	Option Type	Option Meaning
Options Common to all GA programs		
-size	INTEGER	population size
-gens	INTEGER	number of generations
-seed	INTEGER	random seed
-crate	DOUBLE	crossover rate
-mrate	DOUBLE	mutation rate
Options Only for gastring		
-target	STRING	target string
Options Only for gabump and gasurf		
-len	INTEGER	DNA length
Options Only for gastring and gatask		
-pbase	DOUBLE	power base for fitness
Options Only for gaipd		
-bouts	INTEGER	bouts per generation
-rounds	INTEGER	rounds per bout
-hlen	INTEGER	history length
-noise	DOUBLE	chance of mistake in transaction
-CC	DOUBLE	reward payoff
-CD	DOUBLE	sucker's payoff
-DC	DOUBLE	temptation payoff
-DD	DOUBLE	punish payoff
-dump	SWITCH	print entire population at end?

Table 20.4 Command-line options for **gastring**, **gabump**, **gasurf**, **gatask**, and **gaipd**

scaling of the fitness functions for all of the programs except **gaipd**. As an exercise, you may wish to replace this with a linear scaling.

Finally, the **-noise** option for **gaipd** can be used to introduce errors into the IPD transactions. When there is noise in an IPD, strategies that retaliate harshly tend to suffer, so you can use this to encourage more forgiving strategies to evolve. I was able to evolve a more forgiving version of "Tit-for-Tat" that could correct itself if an error was made while playing another copy of itself. The **-hlen** option can be used to change the number of previous plays that are considered for each IPD strategy. Several researchers have performed similar simulations with variations on the memory length. Robert Axelrod and Stephanie Forrest found that a population of IPD players with a memory of three time steps was able to produce a strategy that attempted to bluff weak strategies but reverted to "Tit-for-Tat" when faced with a player that was not gullible.

20.9 Further Reading

Barlow, C. (1991). *From Gaia to selfish genes: Selected writings in the life sciences.* Cambridge, Mass.: MIT Press.

Bowler, P. J. (1996). *Charles Darwin: The Man and his influence.* Cambridge: Cambridge University Press.

Dawkins, R. (1976). *The selfish gene.* Oxford: Oxford University Press.

Dewdney, A. K. (1985). Computer Recreations: Exploring the field of genetic algorithms in a primordial computer sea full of flibs. *Sci. Am.*, 253(5): 21–32.

Goldberg, D. E. (1989). *Genetic algorithms in search, optimization, and machine learning.* Reading, Mass.: Addison-Wesley.

Holland, J. H. (1975). *Adaptation in natural and artificial systems.* Ann Arbor: University of Michigan Press.

Koza, J. R. (1992). *Genetic programming: On the programming of computers by natural selection.* Cambridge, Mass.: MIT Press.

Michalewicz, Z. (1996). *Genetic algorithms + data structures = evolution programs.* New York: Springer-Verlag.

Mitchell, M. (1996). *An introduction to genetic algorithms.* Cambridge, Mass.: MIT Press.

Ridley, M. (1995). *The red queen: Sex and the evolution of human nature.* New York: Macmillan.

Watson, J. D. (1991). *The double helix: A personal account of the discovery of the structure of DNA.* New York: New American Library.

Wesson, R. (1991). *Beyond natural selection.* Cambridge, Mass.: Bradford Books/MIT Press.

21 Classifier Systems

Mathematicians are inexorably drawn to nature, not just describing what is to be found there, but in creating echoes of natural laws.
— Roger Lewin

Plasticity is a double-edged sword: the more flexible an organism is the greater the variety of maladaptive, as well as adaptive, behaviors it can develop; the more teachable it is the more fully it can profit from the experiences of its ancestors and associates and the more it risks being exploited by its ancestors and associates.
— Donald Symons

Repetition is the only form of permanence that Nature can achieve.
— George Santayana

We ended the previous chapter with the idea that acquired traits and experience could aid systems in more rapidly adapting to an environment. In this chapter we will refocus on the themes of genetic algorithms in the context of direct environmental feedback and of simple reinforcement learning, so as to couple two types of adaptation into a form that more closely resembles the adaptation found in cultural, social, economic, and other competitive systems. The major focus of this chapter will be on *classifier systems*, yet another invention of John Holland, that combines all of these idea into an elegant framework for solving problems.

To explain the motivation behind classifier systems, we should first reexamine genetic algorithms in terms of how they interact with an environment. A GA produces several candidate solutions to a problem by making iterative improvements to existing solutions via the genetic operators. For most of the cases that we examined, a GA manipulated a string of characters that essentially encoded a location in a search space. The function optimization and string-matching problems are particularly clear examples of this. For the last example in Chapter 20, which entailed evolving strategies for the IPD, the strings represented lookup tables that specified moves to be made, given a particular history. Thus, we can think of the evolved strategies not just as being points in a search space but as being simple algorithms because they specify a mapping from environmental states (the previous IPD history) to actions (an appropriate move).

This observation gets at the heart of the issue regarding the limitations of GAs, their applicability to complex problems, and the motivation behind classifier systems. If an actual algorithm is needed, then a pure lookup table is a horribly poor way of encoding a program. Lookup tables, by definition, are programs that have no local memory and either must have an entry for every possible environmental state or must compress the state information in a manner that washes out much of the information. Neither alternative is attractive, especially because neither allows for the possibility of dealing with environmental states that cannot be anticipated. More sophisticated programs require memory and something akin to recursion or iteration. Classifier systems add both of these features to genetic algorithms.

Related to this issue is that adaptive systems must change at rates comparable with those of their environments. For example, every year all plants and animals experience the change of seasons and must compensate for the varying temperatures by scheduling their activities in conjunction with the weather. For organisms that have adapted to the change in weather in a predominantly evolutionary manner, short-term temperature fluctuations happen so fast relative to the machinery of evolution that there is little chance that they can successfully respond to the changes. Flowering plants, some of which have a relatively hardwired method for determining the time of year, can be fooled into releasing pollen too early by an unseasonably warm streak of winter weather. This is an example of a failure for evolution and lookup tables, since the instantaneous observable state of the environment (today's weather) is not always a good indication of the real state of the weather (midwinter). On the other hand, you and I and many other animals can base our decisions on the current state, remembered states, and remembered payoffs for previous behavior. Because of this, we can diverge from preprogrammed behavior and take actions that are more a function of our own experiences than of our ancestors' experiences. Similarly, classifier systems adapt on multiple time scales, which makes them responsive to both short-term and long-term events.

All of this is reminiscent of the "nature versus nurture" question, which is somewhat of a fallacy on its face because the question seems to imply that there is an either/or or yes/no answer to it. In reality, all sufficiently complex biological systems must adapt to the environment on several enormously different time scales. We have evolution, which adapts the species to long-term events; cultural adaptation, which preserves useful knowledge between the generations; and many different types of learning that adapt a single individual to very specific circumstances.

Great attention and respect are paid to the two extreme types of adaptation found in evolution and learning, but culture adaptation seems to get shortchanged in the comparison because, for whatever reason, it is easy for us to forget that twentieth-century humans have benefited from thousands of years of acquired knowledge. Yet, animals also possess a form of culture that goes beyond mere instinct. On one level, animal culture acts as a glue between instincts and learning. Birds may be born with the disposition and urge to sing, but the composition, imitation, and general acquisition of birdsongs are skills passed throughout an entire bird population. On rare occasions, animal innovations are witnessed by scientists just when they are discovered by other animals. One impressive instance of this was when some British tits found that they could peck their way through the metal tops of milk containers left on doorsteps. Other bird species were able to copy the act, and eventually the skill spread to continental Europe (Wesson, 1994).

In this chapter, we will see that classifier systems are basically general-purpose computing devices that are modified by both environmental feedback and an underlying genetic algorithm. In this way, classifier systems can be seen as a bridge between evolution and learning. Moreover, their behaviors, as well as their underlying mechanisms, resemble processes found in social, cultural, and economic systems, which is especially pleasing when one considers that these social phenomena span our own evolution and learning adaptive processes.

What follows is a brief introduction to some of the issues in control theory, which is followed by an overview of production, expert, and classifier systems. We will then consider Stewart Wilson's zeroth level classifier system, and finally play with two toy experiments that illustrate the ability of classifier systems to adapt.

21.1 Feedback and Control

For the purposes of this discussion, successful adaptation is best explained in terms familiar to engineers and control theorists. Figure 21.1 shows a simple diagram that defines the framework in which just about any adaptive system must work. The environment is represented by a single box that has a well-defined state that changes from one moment to the next. The current state of the environment is determined by both the previous state and the control signals by which an agent manipulates the environment. The agent is usually restricted in the amount of information it can observe at any time; hence, the visible features will usually correspond to a subset of the environment's state. Finally, how the agent behaves, that is, the actions that it performs when certain environmental features are observed, can adapt depending on the type of reinforcement received by the environment.

The difference between adaptive and nonadaptive systems, as well as the differences between the types of adaptation that can occur, are summed up by the single feedback arrow labeled "reinforcement" in Figure 21.1. In a strictly nonadaptive control system there is either no extra reinforcement information or the reinforcement is somehow trivially bundled into the observable state. A simple thermostat is a fair example of this because it can observe only the present temperature and

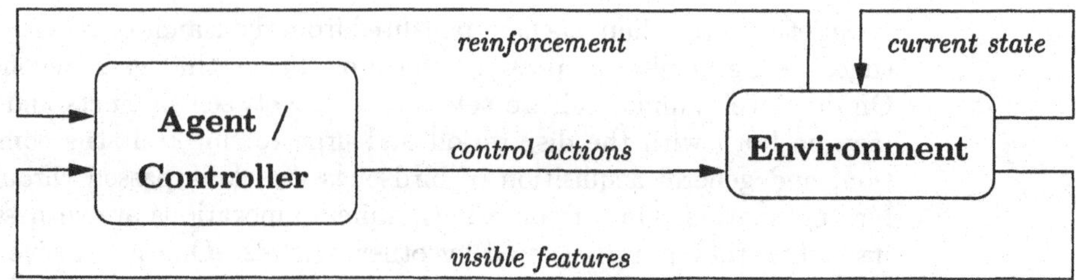

Figure 21.1 Adaptation through environmental reinforcement

can base its control actions solely on that information. In a truly adaptive system, actions that were unsuccessful in previous but similar states may be discarded in favor of actions that were more successful. In a sense, feedback allows for a complex adaptive system to reprogram itself.

Given the framework defined in Figure 21.1, there are many situations in which methods from linear control theory and traditional adaptive control theory can be successfully applied with little complication. These techniques, all of which owe something to Norbert Wiener and cybernetics, are well understood analytically and—when they work at all—work quite well. The caveat here is the same as in dynamical systems theory: Most things in nature are highly nonlinear and, as a result, control actions can have unpredictable results on an environment.

The general control problem—How does one find the optimal controller for a particular environment and objective function?—will never be completely solved because it is just too complicated as expressed. Things are further complicated when one factors in difficulties such as delayed rewards and punishments. In such a situation, a reward may be received only after a long sequence of actions has been taken. It is natural to associate the most recent action with the reward, but easy to lose sight of the fact that early actions may be just as crucial. Similarly, in other situations one may have to take a step backward, for instance, sacrifice a pawn in chess before a move forward (taking the queen) is possible. This means that any measure of success has to be flexible enough that long-term goals are not sacrificed in the interest of short-term goals. We will examine all of these problems in later, more detail.

21.2 Production, Expert, and Classifier Systems

Classifier systems, expert systems, and Post production systems all share a similar underlying structure. Because of this, we will briefly examine the latter two topics so as to better understand the first. All of these systems consist of simple rules of the form

if *condition* **then** *action*,

which has the same meaning as similar statements in most programming languages. If the *condition* portion of the statement is satisfied, then the *action* portion of the statement is executed. With many such rules, a single satisfied condition can trigger an action that causes other rules to be activated, forming a chain of execution that can carry out an arbitrary calculation. In fact, a Post production system is computationally equivalent to any other universal computing device.[1] This is an important distinction; since a classifier system is built with a Post production system beneath it, it is theoretically possible for a classifier system to represent any possible computation. If this were not the case, then classifier systems would be incapable, even in theory, of solving an infinite variety of problems.

An expert system is a special type of program that resembles a Post production system. Expert systems were prominently hailed as a major success of the symbolic artificial intelligence community in the 1980s, but the enthusiasm died down somewhat when the results did not keep pace with expectations. At this time, however, expert systems are slowly making a comeback due to new levels of sophistication in design and implementation, as well as rising CPU performance/price ratios. In any event, expert systems, and especially fuzzy expert systems, are a natural way of encoding expert knowledge into an automated form that nonexperts can use. An ideal home for expert systems is found in diagnostic applications. For example, doctors can consult a medical expert system by answering several questions concerning a patient with an undiagnosed condition. The questions could take the form of "Does the patient have a fever?" "What is the white blood cell count?" and so on. An expert system may even recommend specific tests to be performed. After being supplied with a sufficient amount of information, the expert system will follow the nested chain of expert rules to compute a probable diagnosis for a patient. In this way, the knowledge of one human expert can be put into a form that can be more easily distributed to the masses, so as to do the most good.

Perhaps the single most important reason why there are not as many expert systems in use today as there could be is that the task of embedding human expert knowledge into machine form is extremely difficult and time-consuming. If the human expert happens to diagnose problems through very logical and well-defined steps, then encoding this knowledge into a rule set may not be too trying. Unfortunately, this is rarely the case, since most humans aren't sure how they go about doing an intelligent task, which makes the "knowledge engineering" portion of building an expert system extremely difficult.

Classifier systems are not typically used on the same sorts of problems that expert systems are, though a handcrafted classifier system can always be built that emulates any expert system. Instead, classifier systems are most often applied to

[1]See Chapter 3, and in particular Section 3.2 on page 26, for other universal models of computations.

control-like problems, as defined in the previous section. Also, unlike Post production systems and expert systems, classifier systems are almost never "programmed" to solve a problem but are instead expected to discover working solutions on their own.

We will now examine classifier systems in more detail. There are several slight variations on the basic form of a classifier system, but I will use a stripped-down version that is true to Holland's original formulation of the idea. In general, a classifier system consists of a set of *classifiers* and a *message list*. The message list serves multiple functions. At each time step the message list will contain *messages* that describe the current observable state of the environment. The classifiers can post additional messages on the message list, making the list serve as a sort of temporary storage space. Also, specific messages may correspond to actions that an agent should perform.

A classifier system interacts with its environment through *detectors* and *effectors*. The detectors are like sensory organs in that they are responsible for posting the messages on the message list that correspond to the observable environment. The effectors can be thought of as hands and feet since they can be used to modify the environment. Stretching the analogy further, the message list is similar to short-term memory, while the classifiers themselves are akin to portions of an animal's nervous system. Figure 21.2 shows a basic schematic of a classifier system interacting with its environment.

As to the classifiers themselves, each consists of a triplet in the form

$$condition: message: strength.$$

The condition of the classifier is similar to the condition in the rules of a Post production system or expert system; however, classifier conditions are made up of the two binary digits and a special symbol, "#," which is a "don't care" symbol. A classifier's condition matches a message if, and only if, all of the symbols are an identical match with the corresponding characters in the message, or if the classifier has a "#" in an unmatched position. Thus, the "#" symbols are wild cards in that they match anything. With the "#" symbols, classifiers can match messages with varying amounts of specificity. On one extreme a classifier can be a perfect match for exactly one message. But with n "#" symbols, a classifier can potentially match 2^n different messages. With these details in place, we can now simulate a single cycle of how a classifier system interacts with its environment.

1. The detectors place messages on the message list that correspond to observable features in the environment.

2. A match set is formed from all classifiers whose conditions match any of the messages on the message list.

3. The classifiers bid against each other for the right to post their messages. The bids are always a function of the strength of the classifiers. Some classifier

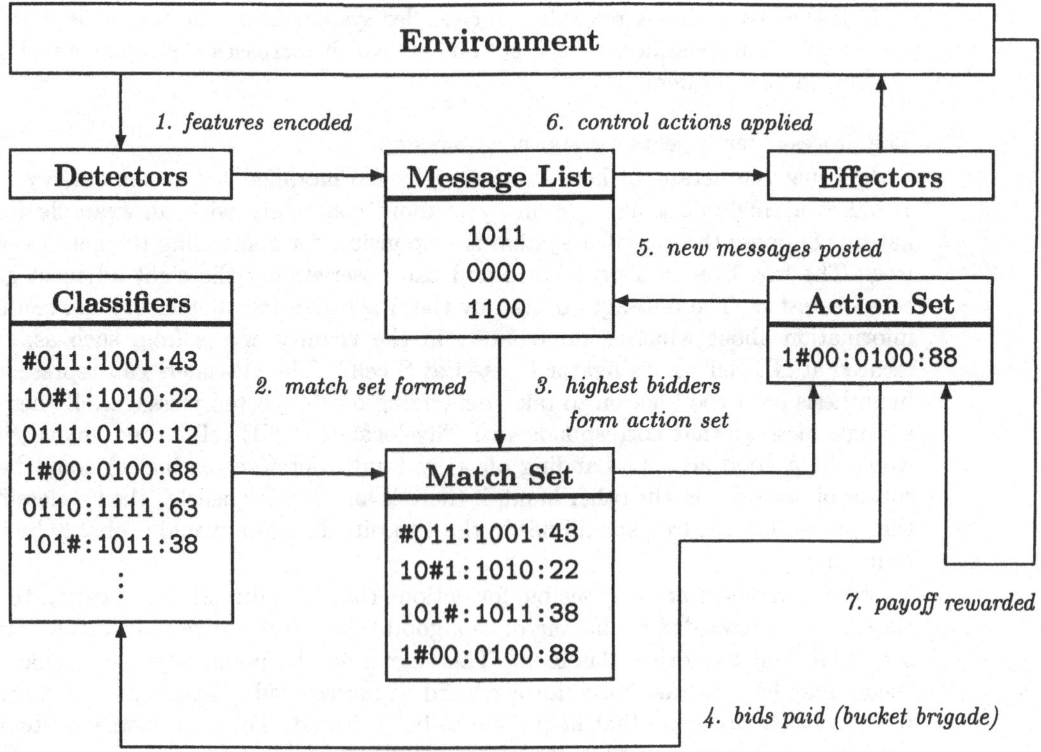

Figure 21.2 A classifier system interacting with its environment

systems incorporate the specificity of a condition into the bid, that is, the more specific a rule (the fewer the number of "#" characters), the greater the bid. An action set is formed from the highest bidders. There may be more than one winning classifier in the action set.

4. The classifiers in the action set pay a portion of their bids to the other classifiers (if any) that were responsible for posting the message that matched their condition. The paid classifiers have their strengths increased as a result.

5. The message list is erased and a new message list is formed from the message portions of all the classifiers in the action set.

6. If any of the new messages in the message list correspond to a real action, then the effectors process the action appropriately. (There may be need to resolve conflicting actions, e.g., "move left" versus "move right," etc.)

7. If the environment rewards the classifier system, then the reward is divided among the classifiers in the action set, which increases the strengths of the winning classifiers.

The process then repeats for another time step.

Ignoring the details of how the strengths are modified for a moment, we can visualize a single classifier system cycle more concretely with an example from nature. Suppose the classifier system is responsible for controlling the actions of a frog. The frog lives in a grid world and can observe only the eight adjacent grid cells nearest it. The messages posted by the frog's eyes (the detectors) can contain information about what is immediately in the vicinity of the frog, such as, "fly located at NE cell" or "alligator located at S cell." The classifiers can represent a hypothesis for a good action to take, depending on the posted messages. If there is a single message that corresponds with "fly located at NE cell," then "move NE" would be a good action. Landing on a fly (and, therefore, eating it) could be a source of reward. On the other hand, if there is an alligator nearby, then a classifier that posits that the frog should flee in the opposite direction would probably be the right choice.

When classifiers are responsible for actions that lead directly to rewards, those classifiers are rewarded for having done a good thing. But notice that in the fourth step, classifiers pay other classifiers. This allows for the possibility that a chain of events may have to take place for a reward to be received. Classifiers that do well will pay other classifiers that help them to be activated. Thus, a classifier system is a lot like an information economy where classifiers bid and make payouts to other classifiers, purchasing the right to be activated.

Holland has named the method by which classifiers pay other classifiers the "bucket brigade" algorithm, which gets its name from the fact that payments are passed down a line of classifiers, reinforcing all in the chain, in much the way an old-time fire brigade would pass buckets of water down a chain of people in order to get water to a fire. The bucket brigade algorithm works in much the same way, but passes information down a chain of classifiers instead.

We can see why these chains can be important by looking back to the frog example. Without chains, it would be possible to encode a simple but fairly successful classifier system that merely made decisions based on the most recent information from the detectors. Such a system would see an alligator, flee for one time step, and "forget" that there was an alligator in the direction it just came from. If a fly happened to come by at the wrong time and place, the frog would happily jump back toward danger just for a quick meal. Without memory, there is no other possible way for the frog to behave. But with a classifier system's message list, chains can actually represent the basis of a long-term memory.

We can see how this is possible by considering the frog in a dangerous situation again. Faced with the initial message "alligator located at S cell," a triggered

Immune Systems **Digression 21.1**

The main task of the immune system is to identify foreign material in an organism so that it can be removed. Antibodies assist by binding to foreign bodies that are then removed by macrophages. In order to accomplish all of this, human antibodies must be able to distinguish the approximately 10^5 types of proteins that may be found in a typical human body from the nearly infinite variety of foreign invaders. How all of this is done is mostly a mystery, but what is known about the immune system looks like a remarkable combination of evolution and learning.

Every antibody possesses a special region, known as the *paratope*, for identifying foreign molecules. If such a molecule has been identified, then the antibody can bind to it through a complementary site known as the *epitope*. As a long-term goal, immune systems must be able to bind to as large a number of foreign materials as possible. But on a short-term basis (say, during an infection), immune systems must produce vast quantities of a specific type of antibody. As to the first need, an unbelievably large number of the different antibody types can be made by combining a smaller number of building blocks coded in the DNA, but to meet specific needs, antibody production of a specific type is elevated by the very act of their binding to foreign materials, thus fulfilling both goals.

Doyne Farmer, Norman Packard, and Alan Perelson have made a compelling comparison between immune systems and classifier systems. New antibodies are produced by combining building blocks in a manner very similar to genetic crossing. It has also been shown that the mutation rate is elevated during this stage. Moreover, if one thinks of the paratope as a classifier's condition and the epitope as an action, then the concentration of the specific antibody types starts to resemble a classifier's strength. Through a novel mixture of adaptive processes, the immune system can guard against an amazing array of potential invaders.

classifier could post a message that amounted to "Danger at distance x, position y." This new message could then trigger two other classifiers, one that posts the message that triggers the effector to actually flee, and the other that posts a new message that amounts to "Danger at distance x', position y'," where x' and y' are estimates of the alligator's new location relative to the frog after the frog has moved. This last message will now be present on the next cycle of the classifier system, which means that the frog will "remember" that there was something dangerous recently encountered.

Up until this point we have ignored genetic algorithms, but it turns out that GAs play a very important role in the adaptation of a classifier system. When a classifier system starts interacting with its environment, it is typical for it to have randomly selected classifiers. Because of this, the initial behavior is likely to be close to random. Once the classifier system gets lucky and receives a reward, individual classifiers will be reinforced by having their strengths increased. After some time, it is likely that some classifiers will be strong while others will be relatively week. Moreover, we may find that there are not enough of the "right" classifiers to do the job. A GA can be used to weed out the weak classifiers and form new ones from the stronger classifiers. Because each classifier has a digital representation, it is a simple matter to use a GA to cross successful classifiers to form new and novel classifiers. Thus, GAs are responsible for removing bad classifiers and introducing new and potentially good classifiers, while the bucket brigade algorithm is responsible for doling out credit and strengthening those classifiers that help the whole system achieve a reward.

In this way, a classifier system can be thought of as a composition of partial hypotheses. Each classifier represents a single hypothesis that is applicable to a limited number of situations. No single classifier is in charge, yet the system as a whole can adapt and form an overall pattern of behavior that emerges from the competition and cooperation of the individual pieces.

21.3 The Zeroth Level Classifier System

In this section we will examine a simplification of Holland's classifier system proposed by Stewart Wilson. Wilson refers to this classifier system as a "Zeroth Level Classifier System" (ZCS) because it is in many ways the simplest type of classifier system that captures all of the essential pieces of Holland's ideas. Wilson performed many interesting experiments with classifier systems that gave him some insights into what are the most important features of a classifier system. ZCS is a particularly elegant design because it is easy to implement, and once it finds a solution, the solution can be easily understood.

All of the experiments in Section 21.4 will be performed on a ZCS; hence, we will examine the ZCS in enough detail to allow you to implement the system yourself. There are three major differences between a ZCS and a standard classifier system. First, a ZCS has no message list, which is to say that the message portion of all classifiers essentially corresponds to an action by the effector. Thus, for clarity, we will refer to this portion of the classifier as the action. This difference also means that there can be no long-term memory in a ZCS. We will look at a simple extension at the end of this section that incorporates memory into the scheme. Second, action strings do not have to have the same string length as the conditions. Conditions are matched to the state returned by the detectors; thus, conditions will have the same string length as the observed state (the input to the system) while actions will have a string length that corresponds to the number of actions the effector can perform. The final difference between the two schemes is that the ZCS uses what has been called an "implicit bucket brigade," which is a simplification of the original bucket brigade algorithm.

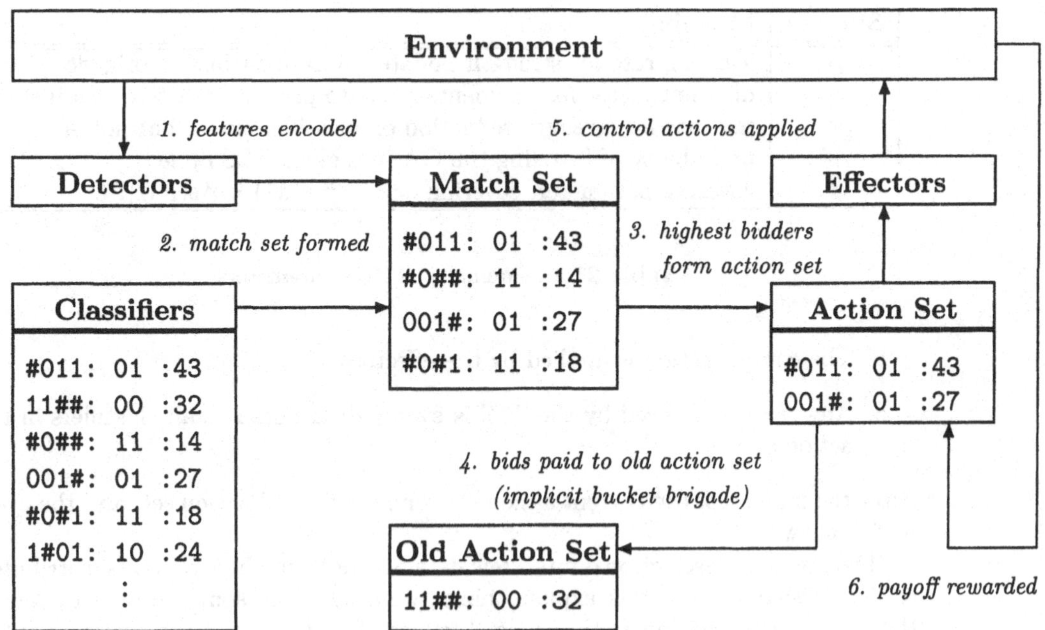

Figure 21.3 Wilson's zeroth level classifier system interacting with its environment (Wilson, 1994)

Figure 21.3 shows a ZCS system with its environment. A single cycle of a ZCS can be described as follows:

1. The features in the visible portion of the environment are encoded by the detectors. The result is a binary string (not shown in the figure, but equal to "0011") that is matched to the classifiers in the next step.

2. The match set is formed by comparing the condition of every classifier against the binary string returned by the detector. If no such classifier exists, then a special step (called "covering") is taken to add a new matching classifier to the ZCS.

3. Using a random roulette selection method on the strengths of all classifiers in the match set (identical to the roulette selection method described in Chapter 20), a single classifier is chosen. All classifiers in the match set that advocate the same action are then placed in the action set.

4. Every classifier in the action set pays a portion of its strength to every classifier in the previous action set (if it exists).

Symbol	Meaning
β	learning rate for strength updates in implicit bucket brigade
γ	discount factor for payments made to previously active classifiers
τ	tax rate for strength reduction on classifiers in M but not A
ρ	probability of invoking the GA in a given ZCS cycle
ϕ	covering parameter; covering occurs if $\mathrm{s}(M) < \phi\,\mathrm{s}(P)/\lvert P\rvert$.

Table 21.1 Summary of ZCS parameters

5. The control action is applied by the effectors.
6. Any reward received by the ZCS is evenly distributed to all classifiers in the action set.

After the final step, the current action set replaces the old action set, and the cycle begins anew.

The previous description omits a few details concerning how payoff is distributed to the classifiers. To further explain things, we need to use some symbols to denote the various sets and some other special values. Let P refer to the entire classifier population, M refer to the match set, A to the action set, and O to the old action set. Also, for any of the sets (A, for example), let the notation $\mathrm{s}(A)$ refer to the total strength of every classifier of the set and let $\lvert A\rvert$ refer to the number of classifiers in the set.

We can now more rigorously describe the credit assignment as follows. All of the system parameters are summarized Table 21.1. To start, a fraction, β, of the strength of each classifier in A is deducted from all members of A. This total amount, $\beta\,\mathrm{s}(A)$ is stored for a later step in a temporary holding place, which we will refer to as the "bucket" or b. Next, if the ZCS receives a reward of r after taking the action, then the strength of each member of A is increased by $\beta r/\lvert A\rvert$. Afterward, if O is not empty, then the strength of each member of O is increased by $\gamma b/\lvert O\rvert$, where b is the "bucket" used in the first step. Finally, all members of M that are not part of A have their strength reduced by τ, which can be thought of as a penalty or tax for having advocated a non-winning strategy.

The process of changing the strengths of the classifiers can be intuitively described by the following. Each classifier that contributes toward a specific action pays a portion of its strength to the classifiers that helped the ZCS get into the state that activated the action. That is why credit is passed from the current action set to the old action set. Next, each of the classifiers in the action set evenly shares in any reward received. Also note that at the next time step they will receive a share of the rewards at that time, but discounted by γ. Thus, classifiers pay those that help them and receive payment from those they help. The final step of the credit assignment, that is, the taxation step, makes the ZCS eventually more decisive. Wilson explains that the taxation reflects an explore/exploit tradeoff: A lower tax rate allows different actions to be tried while a higher tax rate encourages a specific action to be exploited.

The reinforcement algorithm can be combined with a GA as follows. Using a biased coin, the GA can be invoked at each cycle of the simulation with probability ρ. When the GA is invoked, exactly two parents are selected, via roulette selection on their strengths, that will have offspring that replace two other members of the population that are chosen by roulette selection on the inverse of their strengths. Thus, the strongest classifiers are most likely to reproduce and replace the weakest classifiers, but the whole process is stochastic, so anything can happen. This procedure is especially convenient because it keeps the population size constant and operates with a trivial amount of overhead at each cycle of the ZCS. As in the previous chapter, new offspring can be crossed and/or mutated. If they are crossed, then the average of the parents' strengths is used as the strength of the offspring.

In the second step of the performance cycle of the ZCS, it is possible for there to be no classifiers that match the current state returned by the detectors. When this happens, a special operation is invoked. The current state is used as a template to create a new classifier condition, "#" symbols are randomly sprinkled on the condition, the action of the new classifier is randomly set, and the strength of the classifier is set to the average strength of the population. The new classifier replaces an existing classifier that is chosen by roulette selection on the inverse of the strengths. Wilson refers to this as the "covering operation" and compares the process to rote memorization. Covering is also used if $\mathrm{s}(M)$ is less than some fraction of the population's average strength, which occurs when every member of the match set is relatively week.

21.4 Experiments with ZCS

We are now ready to put together everything from the last section to see how classifier systems can learn to solve problems. We will consider three problems in this section, all of which require us to simulate an artificial environment for the classifier system to interact with. The first two problems are test cases proposed by Wilson. The last problem is a standard test problem from the reinforcement learning community whose solution requires that the ZCS be augmented with a form of memory.

Woods1 Figure 21.4 shows an environment known as Woods1 that defines a rectangular grid world that a virtual creature (or "animat") is allowed to roam through. All of the actions of the creature are dictated by a ZCS. The ZCS can "see" only the eight cells that immediately surround it in its current location, and it is permitted to move only one step in one of the four compass directions at each time

```
.......................................................
.OOF..OOF..OOF..OOF..OOF..OOF..OOF..OOF..OOF..OOF..OOF.
.OOO..OOO..OOO..OOO..OOO..OOO..OOO..OOO..OOO..OOO..OOO.
.OOO..OOO..OOO..OOO..OOO..OOO..OOO..OOO..OOO..OOO..OOO.
.......................................................
.......................................................
.OOF..OOF..OOF..OOF..OOF..OOF..OOF..OOF..OOF..OOF..OOF.
.OOO..OOO..OOO..OOO*.OOO..OOO..OOO..OOO..OOO..OOO..OOO.
.OOO..OOO..OOO..OOO..OOO..OOO..OOO..OOO..OOO..OOO..OOO.
.......................................................
.......................................................
.OOF..OOF..OOF..OOF..OOF..OOF..OOF..OOF..OOF..OOF..OOF.
.OOO..OOO..OOO..OOO..OOO..OOO..OOO..OOO..OOO..OOO..OOO.
.OOO..OOO..OOO..OOO..OOO..OOO..OOO..OOO..OOO..OOO..OOO.
.......................................................
```

Figure 21.4 Environment of Wilson's Woods1: Shown are rocks ("O"), food ("F"), empty spaces ("."), and the ZCS's current position ("*")

step. The grid world wraps around so that as soon as the ZCS steps off one side, it is transported to the opposite edge; thus the grid world is infinite in size as far as the ZCS is concerned.

Grid cells in Woods1 either are empty ("."), contain food ("F"), or contain a rock ("O"). The ZCS can walk through empty space but cannot walk through rocks. If the ZCS lands on food, it receives a reward of 1000. The detector of the ZCS works by mapping the eight nearest cells into a binary string of sixteen characters. Food has a sensor code of "11," rocks are coded by "10" and a blank is represented by "00." The first two characters in the detector string correspond to the cell just north of the ZCS, and all other character pairs correspond to the remaining cells, working clockwise from the northern cell. Thus, for the displayed ZCS position in Figure 21.4, the detector would return the sixteen-bit string "0000000000101011."

Since the ZCS is rewarded only when it lands on a piece of food, its goal is to get food as quickly and as often as possible. The ZCS is trained by running several trial problems. A single problem consists of placing the ZCS at a random location in the grid world. The ZCS produces an action, and if it corresponds to moving to anything other than a rock, then the move is allowed. If the ZCS lands on food, then it receives its reward, the world is reinitialized to the initial configuration, and the ZCS is randomly relocated. In this way, the ZCS can experiment by trying many different actions under several different circumstances.

If the ZCS performed nothing more complicated than a random walk, then from a random starting position we could expect it to take approximately twenty-seven

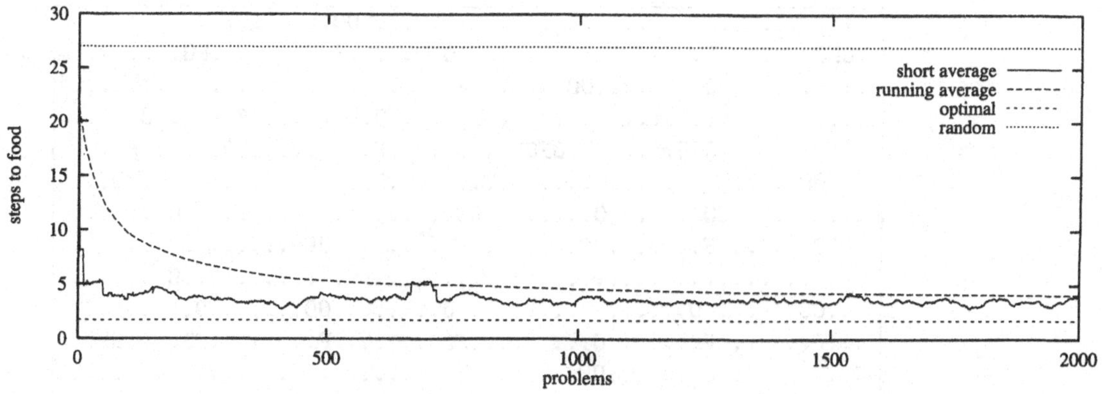

Figure 21.5 ZCS performance in Woods1: The "short average" plot is an average over the 50 most recent trials. The running average curve is over all past trials.

steps to find food. If the ZCS behaved perfectly and always proceeded by the shortest path to the nearest food, then it would require only about 1.7 steps on average. Using a population of 400 classifiers and parameter values described in Section 21.5, the ZCS starts off close to random and does very poorly, but after less than 100 trials it gets down to four steps. After several hundred more steps the performance is improved a bit more.

The overall performance for a single experiment is shown in Figure 21.5. As can be seen, the performance is far better than random, not quite as good as a perfect system but not so bad, considering that the solution was found automatically. Looking back to Figure 21.4, we can perform some hindsight analysis to see why the problem of traversing Woods1 is solvable. Woods1 has the property that no matter where one is located in it, it is always possible to tell where the nearest food is, based solely on the eight adjacent cells. This is due to two facts. First, Woods1 is perfectly periodic, so once you know what a small portion of the world looks like, you know the whole world. Second, regardless of where one stands in Woods1, there is always at least one observable feature that tells you exactly where you are standing relative to the rocks. This means that Woods1 is a relatively easy problem.

Woods7 Figure 21.6 shows Wilson's Woods7 environment, which is much more complicated than Woods1. From the map, it is pretty clear that it has neither of the two properties that made Woods1 an easy problem. Not only is it possible to get lost in Woods7, that is, there are many areas that look similar with limited perception, but the food and rocks are arranged in a nonuniform manner.

```
...........O.........................OO.........O.........
.OFO.......F........F.........O.......F.........FO........
...........O........OO.......F............................
............................O......O.........F......O.....
...F.......OFO........OFO..........F.........OO......F....
...OO..............................O..................O...
..........OO.......O........OO....................O.......
.OFO.......F.......OF........F.........OFO........F.......
..................................................O.......
...OO.......O.................O........OO.......O.........
...F.......F.......O.........FO........F........OF....OFO.
...........O.......OF.....................................
..O......................O............O......O.......O....
..F.......F...............F..........FO.......F......OF...
..O.......OO...............O...................O..........
.....................O.....................O..............
...F........OFO......F..........F.........F......OF.......
...OO................O..........OO.......O.......O........
```

Figure 21.6 Environment of Wilson's Woods7: Shown are rocks ("O"), food ("F"), and empty spaces (".")

The experimental results for a typical run using an identical setup for training a ZCS to traverse Woods7 as was used in Woods1 are shown in Figure 21.7. Once again, the ZCS does far better than random but not quite as well as the optimal solution. To be fair, the ZCS really doesn't stand a chance of coming close to the optimal solution because the ZCS has no memory and cannot, therefore, tell where it is located on the map. If you had memory, then after passing several distinctive features it would be possible to find your exact location; hence, the ZCS is really at a disadvantage.

In general, the ZCS will wander around in some general direction when it can see only blanks. When it comes directly adjacent to some food, it will eat it. But when the ZCS sees a rock, it will move around the rock, apparently looking for the expected morsel of food. Sometimes the ZCS gets confused and makes a bad turn, which accounts for some of its inefficiency. Nevertheless, it is impressive that the ZCS can learn the general pattern of the map that food always occurs near a rock.

The Cups Problem Our final experiment involves what is known as the "cups problem," which seems like a silly problem at first but turns out to be quite challenging (Whitehead & Lin, 1995). In the cups problem, a robot is placed on a linear

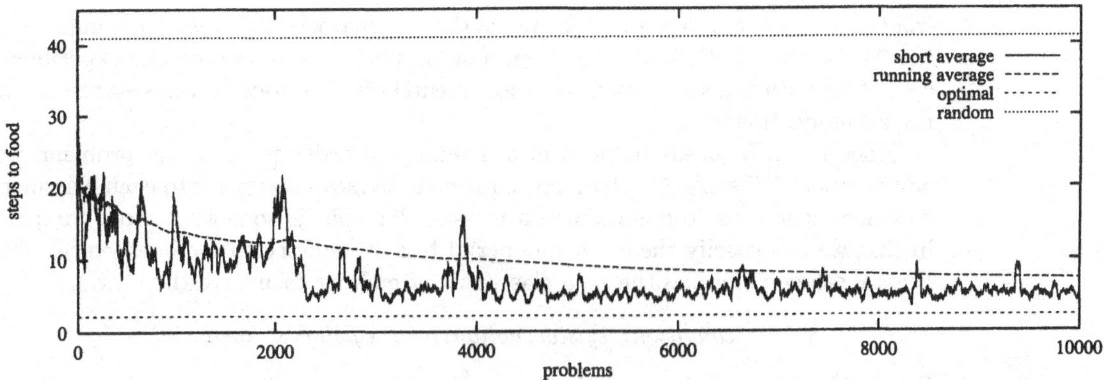

Figure 21.7 ZCS performance in Woods7: The "short average" plot is an average over the 50 most recent trials. The running average curve is over all past trials.

grid. The robot can do one of three things: It can move left, move right, or attempt to pick up a cup if it is standing above one. The sensory abilities of the robot are quite limited and are restricted to exactly four bits of information:

- Is there a cup to the immediate left of the robot?
- Is there a cup to the immediate right of the robot?
- Did the robot collide with a wall on the left?
- Did the robot collide with a wall on the right?

The robot cannot "see" walls. It knows that it is near one only if it runs into it. To make things worse, the robot cannot see what is directly beneath it, so to successfully pick up a cup, it must see it to one side, move on top of it, remember that it is on top of it, and pick it up.

The robot doesn't really know what any of these signals that it is receiving mean. It doesn't even know what the three possible control signals are. It just receives inputs and can send some output. The goal that the robot must achieve sounds amazingly simple: It must pick up two cups. But wait, it gets worse. The robot never receives any sort of feedback until it picks up the second cup. Thus, in order for the robot to know that it has done the right thing, it must go through an extremely complex and specific sequence of actions.

The exact configuration of the robot's world looks like

```
W..C*..CW
```

where the "W" characters stand for walls, the "C" characters represent the cups, and the "*" is the robot's initial location. For simplicity (and to keep the experiment consistent with the setup used by other researchers) the robot always starts out at the same location.

Since the ZCS needs some form of memory in order to solve the problem, we will augment Wilson's ZCS by incorporating a memory register into each classifier. This idea is similar to maintaining a message list, but is somewhat more compact in that we can specify the exact number of bits of memory to use in advance. The general scheme modifies the ZCS classifiers by making each have the form

condition: *register*: *action*: *new register*: *strength*.

What this means is that the classifier is considered a match only if the condition matches the environment description returned from the detector and the current register value matches *register*. If this classifier is acted upon, then *action* is performed by the effector, and the register is given the new value of *new register*. Thus, the classifiers can now be conditioned upon a certain memory being present and can also set the memory to a new value.

We could have made the problem easier for the ZCS by having the detector return twice as much information: one string for the current state and another string for the previous state. Encoding the information in this way is exactly the information that the ZCS needs to solve the problem (i.e., is it now on top of a cup?). But by being given only the current state and a single bit of memory, the ZCS must actually learn what feature is important to remember. Thus, *how* to remember is built into the system but *what* to remember is entirely up to the ZCS.

While it would be easier for the ZCS if we just gave it the information that it needs, it is educational to use the memory register instead. Why? For many problems, human designers simply do not know what information is required to solve a problem. By giving the ZCS the ability to form its own memories, we have removed one more design decision from the human. In a sense, we are forcing the ZCS to learn what to learn.

For this experiment I used 100 classifiers and a single bit for the register. As stated earlier, the problem requires four bits for the detector, and two bits for a control action ("10" means move left, "01" means move right, and "11" means pick up). Every experiment consisted of many trials, where a trial consists of starting the robot in the initial configuration and letting the whole thing run until both cups are picked up. In a typical experiment, the first 100 or so trials were extremely inefficient and often took hundreds of steps before the robot managed to pick up both cups simply by dumb luck. Afterward, the ZCS would eventually find a relatively efficient technique. Sometimes the ZCS could only learn how to pick up cups that were approached from the left side. Other times, the ZCS would only pick up the rightmost cup after running into the wall. Overall, the ZCS could usually be counted on to find a solution that took around ten steps or so.

Every now and then, the ZCS would manage to discover the optimal solution that takes exactly seven steps. This solution, as learned by the ZCS, can be implemented with four classifiers that roughly correspond to:

- If there is a cup to the left, then move to the left and turn the register on.
- If there is a cup to the right, then move to the right and turn the register on.
- If there is nothing to the left or right and the register is on, then pick up and turn the register off.
- If there is nothing to the left or right and the register is off, then move right.

Thus, the ZCS learned to associate the register with the fact that the robot was on top of a cup.

For all three example problems, the ZCS essentially had to learn a detailed path through a feature space. Somewhat counterintuitive is that each step in the path is learned in reverse order. When the ZCS just happens to find itself near a goal and when it just happens to make the right move to get to that goal, then that single classifier is reinforced. This has the effect of strengthening one classifier so that if the ZCS is in a similar situation, then it will be more likely to take the right path. But the bucket brigade algorithm (both implicit and explicit versions) will share strength with other classifiers that assist in getting the system back to the state that was near the goal. In this way, a classifier system learns how to make the very last step of a journey, followed by the next-to-last step, then the third-to-last step, and so on, ultimately learning as many partial solutions as possible in order to get to the final goal.

21.5 Further Exploration

Two programs were used for all experiments in this chapter. The first one is named simply `zcs`, and it can be used to train a classifier system to find food in an arbitrary environment. The second program, `zcscup` is a slight modification of the first program that I wrote especially for the cups problem. Both programs take identical options, as shown in Table 21.2.

The `-specs` option is used to specify a file that describes what the ZCS's world looks like. The specification files have a very simple text format that is obvious once you look at some of the examples. For the ZCS parameters described in Table 21.1, `-lrate` corresponds to β, `-drate` to γ, `-trate` to τ, `-grate` to ρ, and `-cover` to ϕ. All of the other options have the same meaning as they had in the GA examples from the previous chapter.

For all three experiments reported, the parameters used were the same as the default values for the programs. In fact, these values are identical to values reported

Option Name	Option Type	Option Meaning
`-specs`	STRING	file with world specs
`-steps`	INTEGER	number of simulated steps
`-seed`	INTEGER	random seed for initial state
`-size`	INTEGER	population size
`-sinit`	DOUBLE	initial classifier strength
`-lrate`	DOUBLE	BB learning rate
`-drate`	DOUBLE	BB discount rate
`-trate`	DOUBLE	tax rate for strength reduce
`-crate`	DOUBLE	GA crossover rate
`-mrate`	DOUBLE	GA mutation rate
`-grate`	DOUBLE	GA invocation rate
`-cover`	DOUBLE	covering factor
`-wild`	DOUBLE	probability of # in cover
`-avelen`	INTEGER	length of windowed average
`-inv`	SWITCH	invert colors?
`-xmag`	INTEGER	magnification factor for X Windows
`-term`	STRING	how to plot points

Table 21.2 Command-line options for `zcs` and `zcscup`

by Wilson. The only notable setting is that `zcscup` required a lower crossover rate (`-crate 0.1`) to solve the cups problem. This is most likely due to the "brittleness" of the problem, since crossing in this case will improve solutions only under extremely rare conditions.

21.6 Further Reading

Awad, E. M. (1996). *Building expert systems: Principles, procedures, and applications.* Minneapolis/St.Paul: West/Wadsworth.

Clark, W. R. (1995). *At war within: The double-edged sword of immunity.* New York: Oxford University Press.

Farmer, J. D., Packard, N. H., & Perelson, A. S. (1986). The immune system, adaptation & learning. *Physica D*, 22(1–3): 187–204.

Holland, J. H. (1976). Adaptation. In R. Rosen & F. M. Snell (Eds.), *Progress in theoretical biology IV* (pp. 263–293). New York: Academic Press.

Holland, J. H., Holyoak, K. J., Nisbett, R. E., & Thagard, P. R. (1989). *Induction: Processes of inference, learning and discovery.* Cambridge, Mass.: MIT Press.

Kaelbling, L. P. (Ed.). (1996). *Recent advances in reinforcement learning.* Boston: Kluwer Academic.

Lumsden, C. J. & Wilson, E. O. (1981). *Genes, mind, and culture: The coevolutionary process.* Cambridge: Harvard University Press.

Wesson, R. (1991). *Beyond natural selection.* Cambridge, Mass.: Bradford Books/MIT Press.

Whitehead, S. D. & Lin, L.-J. (1995). Reinforcement learning of a non-Markov decision process. *Art. Intell.*, 73(1–2): 271–306.

Wilson, S. W. (1994). ZCS: A zeroth level classifier system. *Evol. Comp.*, 2(1): 1–18.

22 Neural Networks and Learning

As a net is made up of a series of ties, so everything in this world is connected by a series of ties. If anyone thinks that the mesh of a net is an independent, isolated thing, he is mistaken. It is called a net because it is made up of a series of interconnected meshes, and each mesh has its place and responsibility in relation to other meshes.
— Buddha

If the brain were so simple we could understand it, we would be so simple we couldn't.
— Lyall Watson

I bet the human brain is a kludge.
— Marvin Minsky

A SHORT LIST of some mundane tasks that humans can effortlessly perform includes recognizing faces, understanding and speaking in a native language, walking upright while chewing gum, and manipulating objects with one or both hands. All of these tasks are easy to ignore, even when we do them simultaneously, most likely because we can do them without too much conscious thought involved. Despite this fact, "simple" tasks such as these represent some of the most challenging problems in computer science. Much has been spoken and written of how tasks that are "machine easy"—performing precise and complicated symbolic manipulation—are "human hard." The flip side to this is that many "human easy" tasks are "machine hard" since it is difficult to algorithmically describe such everyday skills.

Consider the hardware involved. Typical home computers can perform hundreds of millions of operations in a single second, while a single neuron can merely oscillate at a fraction of the same speed. Individual transistors that make up a CPU can propagate signals at speeds limited only by the speed of light and the physical distances between them, which is why silicon chips etched on smaller scales can be driven to higher clock speeds. On the other hand, neurons propagate electrical signals through a chemical medium that is sluggish in comparison. In fact, a single neuron can look clumsy compared with a pocket calculator.

How is it, then, that brains can easily do things that defy the abilities of the most sophisticated computers? The real power of the brain lies in massive parallelism. While a typical CPU has around 5 million transistors and a typical home computer around 100 million (10^8) transistors, the human brain has a staggering 10^{11} neurons, each of which may be connected to thousands of other neurons for a total of 10^{13} to 10^{14} synaptic connections. It is through this massive parallelism and connectivity that the human brain is able to perform such impressive feats of computation.

Using the brain as inspiration, researchers are now designing new types of computing devices that have many of the qualities contained in natural networks of neurons. Such devices, known as *artificial neural networks* or "neural nets," possess many simple processing units that are massively interconnected with each other. This departure from more traditional computer science methods has many potential benefits. First and foremost, neural nets are not programmed in the usual sense of the word but instead are trained with a *learning algorithm* that modifies neural connections based on the net's experience. Changing the way a neural net is wired changes the way it responds to inputs. Thus, the solutions to many different problems may differ only in the specifics of how a neural net is connected. By automating the whole process with a learning algorithm, researchers have been able to train neural nets to do tasks that have previously defied traditional approaches.

The second major benefit of using neural nets resides in massive parallelism. In a neural net, each neuron is conceptually identical. Each receives inputs and produces an output. The output response of a single artificial neuron is typically so simple that it can be computed with a hand-held calculator. If we think of each artificial neuron as a grossly simplified computer, it becomes possible to build hardware versions where all calculations are performed in parallel. This way, instead of simulating the same operation thousands of times in succession, each artificial neuron can perform its own calculation in parallel with all others in the network, thus reaping the same benefit that the brain does by doing many simple things at once.

In Chapter 18 we examined feedback neural networks whose weights were determined according to simple rules and left fixed. In this chapter, we will be considering *feedforward neural networks* having the property that no sequence of connections among neurons forms a loop, which means that no neuron can feed back directly or indirectly to itself. This architectural simplification makes it easier to design algorithms for automatically changing the weights. For example, in the case of Hebbian learning (see Section 18.2 on page 312), it was possible to set weights according to how the neurons were supposed to interact with each other. This chapter will highlight more general rules that extend the basic idea. The result is a technique for performing *supervised learning* that allows weights to be dynamically modified as new information is acquired by the neural network.

The history of neural networks is actually quite interesting, since the topic as a research area has had many high and low points. We will begin this chapter

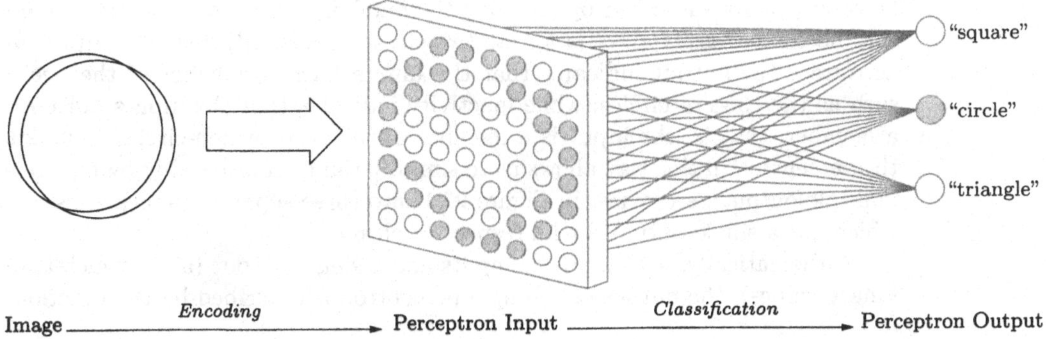

Figure 22.1 A stylized picture of a perceptron

with an introduction to the first feedforward neural network ever used, examine the problems that exposed its weaknesses, rediscover an extension that solved many of the earlier problems, consider some numerical examples, explore how neural networks can form internal representations of an input pattern, and finish off with some example applications.

22.1 Pattern Classification and the Perceptron

To summarize our exposure to the history of artificial neural networks so far, Chapter 18 introduced the McCulloch-Pitts neuron, originally proposed in the 1940s, and the Hopfield-Tank feedback neural network, an invention of the 1980s. Obviously there are some holes in this history. One of the greatest periods of activity in neural network research was in the 1960s. During this time, research was centered on Frank Rosenblatt's *perceptron*, a type of pattern classification device based on Rosenblatt's model of visual perception.

The basic idea behind the perceptron is illustrated in Figure 22.1, which shows that a perceptron can consist of multiple inputs and multiple outputs. Perceptrons are an example of feedforward networks because, unlike feedback networks, the activation of the network always propagates in one direction, starting from the inputs and ending at the outputs. The inputs are typically understood to represent visual information that is presented to an eyeball-like device, while the outputs represent the perception of the visual stimulus. For example, as seen in the figure, when the perceptron inputs are presented with a circular shape, the output with the label "circle" becomes activated, indicating the content of the input. This general type of problem goes by the name of *pattern classification* since the goal is to label or classify many different patterns into a smaller number of classes. The problem can be conceptually simplified by reducing the number of classes to two. A perceptron that needs to classify all objects into two classes needs only a single output. When activated, the output indicates that the inputs form a member of the one class, such as the class of circles, while inactivity indicates that the inputs did not form a member, that is, the input is a member of the class of non-circles. Thinking of the perceptron in this way allows us to simplify things considerably by breaking the multiple-output perceptron in Figure 22.1 into three separate perceptrons, each of which has a single output for its respective class.

Mathematically, with multiple inputs and a single output (all of which take 0/1 binary values), the output of a simple perceptron is described by the function

$$y = \Theta\left(\sum_{i=1}^{n} w_i x_i + b\right),$$

where x_i is a binary input, $\Theta(x)$ is the unit step function that is equal to 1 if $x > 0$ and 0 otherwise, w_i represents the synaptic strength of the connection from input i to the output, and b is a threshold or bias term.[1] For convenience, you can think of the w_i terms as being the lines in Figure 22.1 that connect the inputs to the outputs. The perceptron "fires" with a nonzero output whenever the weighted sum of the inputs multiplied by the weights is greater than the negation of the threshold.

"Neurons" in the perceptron consist of the outputs. We don't consider the inputs to be neurons because they simply pass information forward without processing it in any way. By way of comparison, the outputs form a weighted sum of the incoming signals and pass it through activation functions, thus performing a simple type of computation.

Clearly, a perceptron is a special type of function that maps binary inputs to a single binary output. To better understand how functions are represented by a perceptron, we will now consider some general features of binary functions and one simple example function in particular. If a perceptron has n inputs, then there are exactly 2^n different binary patterns that could be presented as input to the perceptron. For example, with two inputs there are four different input patterns: (0, 0), (0, 1), (1, 0), and (1, 1). With 2^n patterns, there are exactly 2^{2^n} functional mappings from the input pattern space to the space of binary numbers because each of the 2^n patterns can be labeled with either a 1 or a 0. With the two-input example, one such mapping could be the binary AND function, which is equal to 1 if and only if both inputs are 1.

Figure 22.2 shows three different ways of looking at a perceptron that represents the AND function. In Figure 22.2a we see weights and bias values that result in a perceptron behaving like an AND circuit, which you can check by verifying that $x_1 + x_2 - 1.5 > 0$ only when both binary inputs are 1. In Figure 22.2b, the gray

[1]The equation above is nearly identical to the McCulloch-Pitts neuron described in Figure 18.2 on page 310.

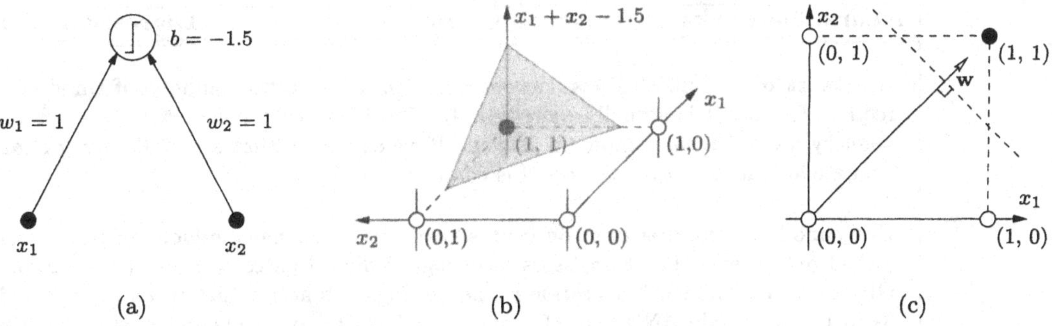

Figure 22.2 Three views of a perceptron solving the AND problem: (a) the perceptron with weights and bias shown; (b) the decision plane shown in three dimensions; (c) the decision line shown in two dimensions. Figure adapted from (Hertz et al., 1991)

region is a portion of the plane defined by $x_1 + x_2 - 1.5$, which we will refer to as the decision plane. Notice that the decision plane intersects the (x_1, x_2) plane, forming a diagonal line. The gray section of the decision plane corresponds to the region where $x_1 + x_2 - 1.5 > 0$ is true, while the region on the other side of the diagonal line (i.e., moving closer to (0, 0)) corresponds to where $x_1 + x_2 - 1.5 < 0$. Exactly on the diagonal line is where $x_1 + x_2 - 1.5 = 0$ is true, which is more clearly seen in Figure 22.2c. This diagonal line in two dimensions forms a linear decision boundary such that everything on one side belongs to one class and everything on the other side forms another class. Hence, having a perceptron compute the AND function is simply a matter of setting the weights such that a line separates (1,1) from the other three points. Implementing a perceptron that computes another function simply puts the decision boundary somewhere else.

In addition to the diagonal decision boundary, Figure 22.2c shows a vector labeled $\mathbf{w}$ that is formed by taking the two weights and the bias term to make a three-dimensional vector with components $[1,\ 1,\ -1.5]^T$. The decision boundary displayed in Figure 22.2c can be seen to be perpendicular to $\mathbf{w}$. Unfortunately, Figure 22.2c can show only two of the three dimensions, so the third component of $\mathbf{w}$ is essentially lost in the image. Nevertheless, it is often useful to visualize the decision boundary in this way.[2] In particular, when considering how small changes in the weight vector change the input-output response of a perceptron, it is crucial to think of all of the weight and bias terms of a perceptron as one composite object.

Now that we have seen how mappings can be represented by a perceptron, we can now look at the more interesting issue of how to automatically find a set of weights that implements a mapping of our choice. In the usual case, we may not

[2]Section 13.3, starting on page 207, gives a geometrical interpretation of the inner product, which may be helpful in visualizing the effect that weight vectors have on inputs.

Neural Networks as Universal Computers **Digression 22.1**

A network of McCulloch-Pitts neurons can form a universal computer if wired correctly. The proof is actually quite simple. We know that home PCs with infinite memory are universal computers as well. If we can show that a neural network can emulate a home PC, then the proof is complete.

Every modern computer is made from silicon chips that have millions of transistors etched onto them. The transistors form logical digital gates such as the AND and OR functions. The NOT operation is another logical function that turns 1s to 0s and 0s to 1s. With only AND and NOT gates, or just OR and NOT gates, it is possible to emulate any conceivable digital circuit. (Figure 22.6 on page 393 should give you a taste of how this can be done.) Therefore, if we can just show that a neural net can emulate AND and NOT or OR and NOT, then we know that a neural network is computationally universal.

We have already seen in this chapter how an AND circuit can be implemented as a perceptron. Emulating an OR circuit requires that a perceptron decision boundary separate (0, 0) from the other points. To compute a NOT gate, one only needs a weight of -1 and a threshold of $\frac{1}{2}$ in a simple perceptron. Therefore, a McCulloch-Pitts neural network or a multilayer perceptron with feedback connections could be wired up to emulate any conceivable digital circuit, including a home computer. This proves that neural networks are computationally universal, with the one caveat that total memory will be finite if we are limited to a finite number of neurons.

have a specific function like the AND function in mind, but will instead have a number of example inputs and target values that we want the perceptron to classify correctly. Our goal is to find some way of changing the behavior of a perceptron when it works incorrectly. In other words, we want it to learn based on feedback that a teacher would give it. In this setup, if you want a perceptron to recognize squares, then you would present the perceptron with labeled data that consist of images along with the correct class. The squares will be labeled as squares and circles, triangles, and other shapes as non-squares. With enough examples, in time the perceptron could learn to distinguish squares from non-squares on its own. And if things go truly well, your perceptron may even be able to generalize by correctly recognizing squares that it has never seen before.

The perceptron learning algorithm is more rigorously described by the following procedure, which is performed repeatedly until all patterns in a training set are correctly classified. The first step is to apply the input pattern to the perceptron. If the output of the perceptron is equal to the target value, t, then we move on to the next pattern. But if the perceptron's output differs from the target output, then we adjust the weights by

$$\begin{aligned} w_i^{\text{new}} &= w_i^{\text{old}} + \eta(t-y)x_i \text{ and} \\ b^{\text{new}} &= b^{\text{old}} + \eta(t-y), \end{aligned}$$

where η is a very small constant referred to as the *learning rate*.[3] The effect on the weights is relatively simple to understand. Assume for the moment that x_i is equal to 1 (if it is equal to 0, then the learning rule will not change the weight). The weight change is always proportional to $(t-y)$. If t is 1 and y is 0, then the weight is increased; otherwise the weight is reduced. In other words, if we want the output to be on when it is off, then making the weights more positive will help make that happen the next time around. But if the output is on when it is supposed to be off, pushing the weight in a more negative direction will reduce the perceptron's ability to fire.

As a disclaimer, the biological plausibility of the perceptron learning rule is somewhat debatable, since the idea of all biological neurons having target values is somewhat suspect. Nevertheless, the perceptron learning rule does resemble a form of behavioral adaptation, with the error term $(t-y)$ representing a form of negative feedback.

Another way of visualizing how the weights change over time is to think about how a perceptron can make mistakes. If the perceptron misclassifies a pattern, then it is natural to describe the error by $E = (t-y)^2$, which gets larger the more y differs from t. Ignoring for the moment the fact that both y and t are supposed to have binary values, the function $E = (t-y)^2$ is a quadratic function that defines a single valleylike surface in a multidimensional space. Since y is a function of the weights in the perceptron, we can look at how E changes when the weights are changed. Figure 22.3 shows the error surface with the optimal weight vector corresponding to the lowest point of the surface. The perceptron learning algorithm is a special case of a more general algorithm, known as *steepest descent*, that attempts to minimize error functions by always moving in a downhill direction. By thinking of the perceptron learning rule in this way, we can see how the weight changes correspond to taking a small step toward the bottom of the error valley. The step size is determined by η and the direction is determined by the negative feedback in $(t-y)$. Later on in this chapter, when we examine more complicated feedforward neural networks, you should keep this image in mind because it applies to the most complicated types of networks.

Rosenblatt and others showed that if a set of weights existed that solved a problem, then the perceptron learning algorithm would always find the correct weights in a finite number of steps. This positive result caused a sense of euphoria among neural researchers in the 1960s because it seemed to imply that perceptrons

[3]This learning rule actually was independently discovered many times and, as a result, it is known by several different names, such as the *delta rule*, the adaline rule, the Widrow-Hoff rule, and the LMS rule.

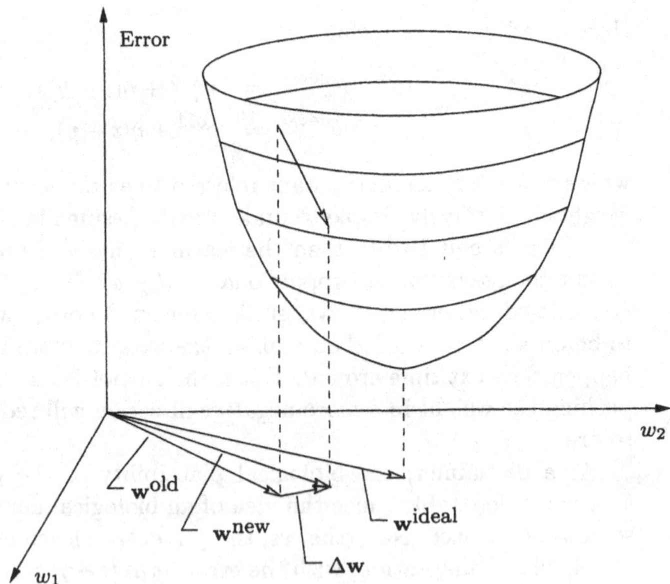

Figure 22.3 The delta rule as a steepest descent step in the error surface. Figure adapted from (Caudill & Butler, 1990).

could be used to magically solve all types of previously intractable problems. Think about it: Distinguishing circles from squares is one thing, but imagine that one could automatically distinguish dogs from cats, people you know from people you don't, or enemy aircraft from friendly aircraft. With this kind of discriminatory power all sorts of tasks that require human intervention could be automated. The problem with this conclusion is that success of the perceptron learning algorithm is conditioned on the existence of a solution in the first place. As it turns, out there are many extremely simple problems that can be proved to be beyond the powers of a perceptron.

22.2 Linear Inseparability

The most famous example of a simple problem that cannot be solved by a perceptron is the exclusive-or (XOR) problem. In the simplest version there are two binary inputs. The target output response is equal to 1 if and only if exactly one of the inputs is a 1. XOR is equivalent to the notion that the sum of the inputs is odd. A more general version of this problem is known as the n-bit parity problem, where the goal is to classify inputs according to whether they have an even or odd number of 1s; thus, the XOR problem is just a two-bit odd parity problem.

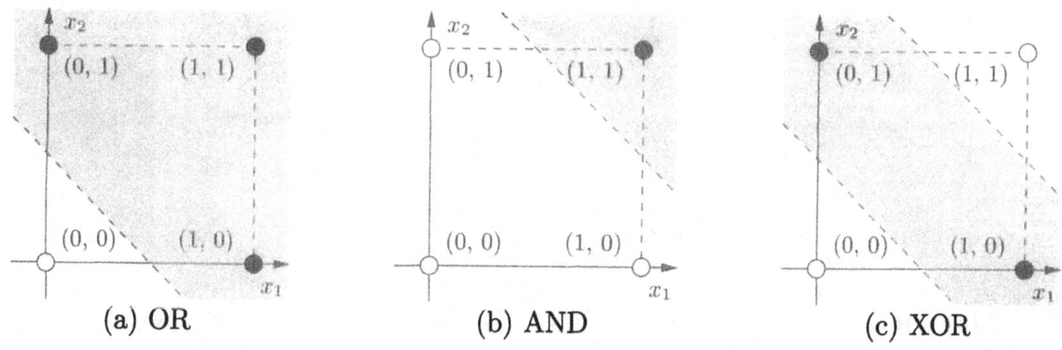

Figure 22.4 Three decision boundaries: Only the first two are linearly separable.

Figure 22.4 shows three different binary mappings and their associated decision boundaries. The first two problems, OR and AND, can be solved by a perceptron precisely because it is possible to draw a single line that divides the black points from the white points. For the XOR problem this is clearly not possible. OR and AND have the property that they are *linearly separable* while XOR is said to be *linearly inseparable*.

While Figure 22.4c shows that the patterns in the XOR problem cannot be correctly divided by a single line, thus making the point that perceptrons are ill-suited for some problems, it is still instructive to consider the more general n-bit parity problem to get an appreciation for some of the issues involved. The parity problem has the property that if you flip a single bit in an n-bit string, then the resulting string will always be in the opposite class from the first string. Why? Well, if the first string had an even number of 1s, then flipping a 0 to a 1 or a 1 to a 0 is going to change the number of 1s to an odd number. In other words, input patterns that are close to each other in a Euclidean sense are far away from each other in terms of their class. This means that in order to classify parity strings correctly, you can't just look at the inputs as individual bits; instead, you must look at the whole input string as one object in order to detect the higher-order patterns.

As mentioned earlier, the 1960s saw an almost reckless optimism in the faith that some practitioners had for perceptrons. Toward the end of the decade there was something of a backlash as many researchers began to voice skepticism. In 1969, Marvin Minsky and Seymour Papert published a book, entitled *Perceptrons*, that dealt the final blow to perceptrons as a research topic. In their book, they demonstrated that whole classes of problems were insolvable by any simple perceptron with any learning algorithm. Minsky and Papert also added some much-needed mathematical rigor to the area by giving detailed proofs for their claims. The effect

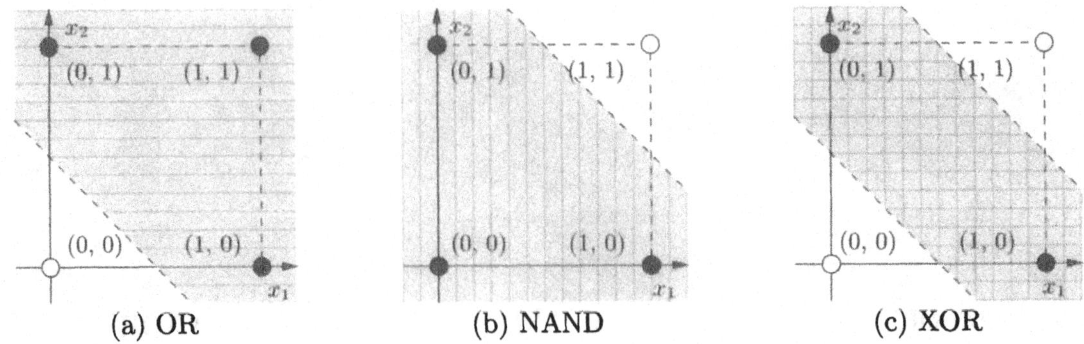

Figure 22.5 Forming XOR as a composition. The XOR set in (c) can be defined as the intersection of the sets in (a) and (b)

on the neural network community was nearly instantaneous. Research into neural networks would still continue, but it would take the area almost two decades to recoverer.

22.3 Multilayer Perceptrons

The fact that perceptrons cannot compute an XOR function clearly indicates that they have limited use in application areas; however, as a theoretical tool, perceptrons serve a useful role as the simplest example of what is now generally referred to as a feedforward neural network. We will see that the outright dismissal of neural networks in the late 1960s was in fact premature and a case of throwing out the baby with the bathwater. But first, let's look back to the XOR problem so that we can come up with a way to solve it with a more complicated type of perceptron.

Figure 22.5 shows another way of thinking about what it means for a point to be in the set for which XOR is true. If NAND is the set of all points that are not in AND, then XOR can be seen as the intersection between the sets defined by OR and NAND. This is an important clue to how a neural network should solve this problem. We know that a perceptron can compute the OR function, and NAND appears to be linearly separable as well. Hence, one perceptron could be wired to compute OR while another is used to compute NAND. If both of these perceptrons fire at the same time when given the same input, then we know that the input pattern belongs in the set defined by XOR.

Figure 22.6a shows a diagram for a digital circuit that computes XOR by first computing OR and NAND. In Figure 22.6b we see the same circuit, but this time it is realized as a *multilayer perceptron* (MLP) that computes intermediate values in order to compute the final value. Using multiple layers is the key to making

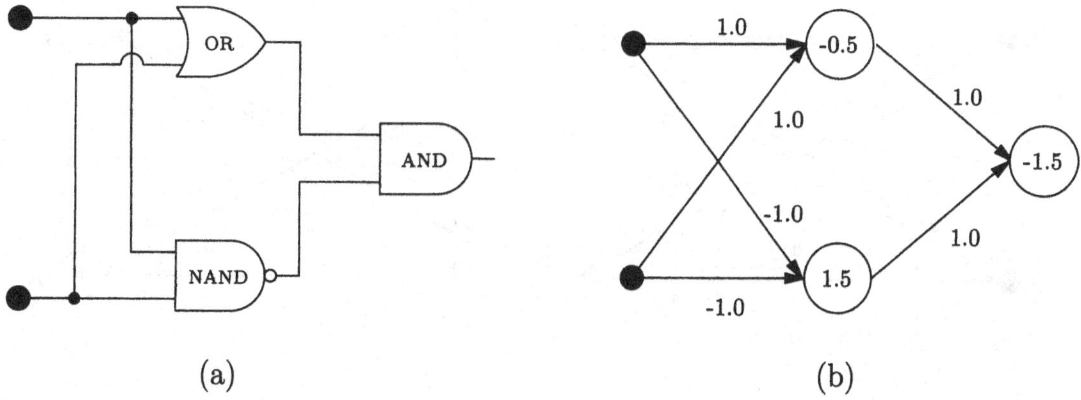

Figure 22.6 A two-layer perceptron solves XOR: (a) the solution as a digital circuit, and (b) weight and bias values for a perceptron that emulates the XOR circuit

perceptrons compute more powerful functions since multiple perceptrons can be composed through one another. Many researchers knew in the 1960s that this was the way to go in order to form more complicated neural nets. The problem was that no one knew how to train the things. Training the weights to an output neuron was never a problem, since the delta rule could always be used to compute appropriate weight changes. But how should one go about changing the weights that go into the "hidden neurons" in the middle of the network? The delta rule makes changes to the weights that are proportional to the difference between the target output value and the actual output value. We know what the actual output is for these hidden neurons, but we have no idea what the target values should be. In fact, it's not even clear what it means for hidden neurons to have target values.

22.4 Backpropagation

The solution to the problem of how to train hidden neurons had to be rediscovered several different times before the bulk of the research community took notice. The problem was solved somewhat independently by several individuals and groups: A. E. Bryson and Y.-C. Ho; Paul Werbos; D. B. Parker; and David Rumelhart, G. Hinton, and R. Williams. Rumelhart and his collaborators published a two-volume book that gained widespread attention and was largely responsible for ushering in a renaissance of research. The key to the solution is twofold: Replace the unit step function with a smooth sigmoidal function and generalize the delta rule so that error signals are passed backward through the hidden nodes. The resulting method for

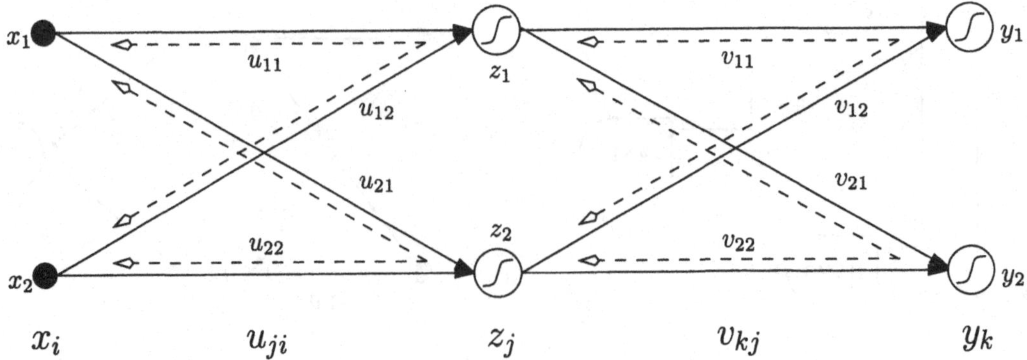

Figure 22.7 A labeled multilayer perceptron

computing weight changes is known as *backpropagation*[4] (or "backprop") because of the manner in which the error signals are passed backward through a network.

Before we look into the learning algorithm, we need to get some notational conventions out of the way. Figure 22.7 shows a multilayer perceptron with a single hidden layer. As before, the inputs into the system are denoted by the x_i terms and the outputs by the y_k terms, but this time there are hidden neurons whose outputs we will annotate with z_j terms. Each of these neurons computes a weighted sum and passes it through a sigmoidal activation function, $g(x)$.

To simplify the notation even further, we are going to ignore the threshold terms that were used earlier.[5] Since we have multiple layers of weights, it is notationally just easier to refer to them by two different base variables, u_{ji} and v_{kj}. But also note that there is no reason why you can't use a three- or thirty-layer perceptron as well. We are using the two-layer example (i.e., two layers of weights) of an MLP just because it is the simplest network with multiple layers. With these rules and caveats in place, the feedforward pass of a two-layer MLP is compactly described by

$$y_k = g\left(\sum_j v_{kj} z_j\right) = g\left(\sum_j v_{kj} g\left(\sum_i u_{ji} x_i\right)\right).$$

[4]Some practitioners of neural networks refer to the "backpropagation learning algorithm" or "backpropagation networks." Both terms are slightly incorrect since "backpropagation" really just refers to the method for computing the error gradient of a network. If you don't know what that last sentence means, don't worry about it. The point is that backpropagation is neither a type of network nor a learning algorithm, but a mathematical operation.

[5]We can do this without losing any mathematical details because the threshold term can be simulated by having an extra input that always has the value of 1. The weights coming from this auxiliary neuron play the same role that the threshold did in the earlier sections.

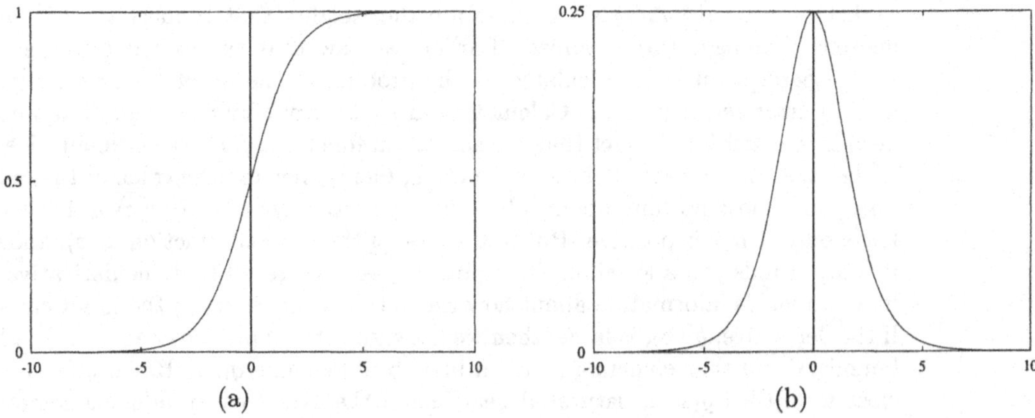

Figure 22.8 A sigmoidal activation function (a) and its derivative (b)

As for the activation function, $g(x)$, Figure 22.8a shows a plot of the sigmoid function that we first saw in Figure 18.5 (page 320). In this chapter we need to consider the mathematical properties of the sigmoid function in greater detail. In Figure 22.8b, the first derivative[6] of the sigmoid is shown. Notice that the tails of the derivative, where it goes to 0, correspond exactly to where the sigmoid saturates at either 0 or 1. Moreover, the highest point of the derivative is where the rate of change in the sigmoid is at its greatest. The sigmoid function is mathematically described by $g(x) = 1/(1 + \exp(-x))$. Computing the derivative of $g(x)$ turns out to be very easy because for this case it just happens to be equal to $g'(x) = g(x)(1 - g(x))$. Since this derivative is always computed with respect to a particular neuron, for example, an output neuron y_k or a hidden neuron z_j, it is more convenient to refer to it as $y'_k = y_k(1 - y_k)$ or $z'_j = z_j(1 - z_j)$, respectively.

We are now finally ready to see how backprop works. Our goal here is to fill in the blanks in the equations below:

$$\begin{aligned} u_{ji}^{\text{new}} &= u_{ji}^{\text{old}} + \eta \Delta u_{ji} \text{ and} \\ v_{kj}^{\text{new}} &= v_{kj}^{\text{old}} + \eta \Delta v_{kj}. \end{aligned}$$

That is, we need to come up with a way for specifying how to calculate weight changes so that learning can occur. The problem is: What should Δu_{ji} and Δv_{kj} be? The derivation of backprop can be a bit intimidating at first, but understanding it requires nothing more than knowledge of how summations and derivatives work. In the derivation that follows, I will primarily attempt to give an intuitive feel for how it works, and only then will we make things more mathematically rigorous.

[6]For an introduction to derivatives see Section 11.2 (page 165) or refer to a good calculus text.

Let's start with Δv_{kj} since these are the weights that connect to the output neurons that have target values. Earlier, we saw that the weight changes for a simple perceptron were calculated as the product of the input to the neuron, x_i, and an error term, $(t - y)$. Calculating Δv_{kj} is very similar except that we now need to account for the fact that the activation function, $g(x)$, is continuous instead of discrete. In the case of the step function, $\Theta(x)$, knowing the value of the output tells you almost nothing about what the input was, that is, if $\Theta(x)$ is 1, then we know only that x is positive. But in the case of the sigmoid function, $g(x)$, knowing its output tells you a lot about its input. To see why, recall that the derivative of a function yields information about how the output changes when the input changes. If the derivative, $g'(x)$, is large, then we know that the input was near the threshold boundary and that changing x just a little could change $g(x)$. But if $g'(x)$ is very close to 0, then $g(x)$ is saturated near one of the extremes—producing something close to 0 or 1.

In this light, the expression $g'(x)(t - y)$ contains many pieces of information. If it is close to 0, then we know that t is very close to y, $g'(x)$ is close to 0, or both of these conditions are true. In the first case, we don't want to change the way that the neuron fired because it gave the correct response. In the second case, the output may or may not be correct, but the weights are such that they would have to be changed a great deal in order to change the neuron's response; thus, perhaps it is better to leave them alone, since drastic changes could adversely affect other portions of the network. In the last case, with both terms close to 0, the neuron has fired correctly and is doing so unambiguously.

Now consider the opposite case, when $g'(x)(t-y)$ is far from 0. This tells us two important pieces of information. First, we know that the neuron fired incorrectly. The sign of $g'(x)(t-y)$ will tell us which way the neuron was wrong. (Did it output something close to 1 when it was supposed to yield a 0, or the other way around?) And with $g'(x)$ far from 0, we know that the neuron is firing near the middle of its activation area, that is, near $\frac{1}{2}$. This is very important. It means that changing the weights just a little bit can yield a dramatic improvement.

Putting all of this together, we can think of $g'(x)(t - y)$ as supplying us with the error correction information. As such, for an output neuron y_k, we will use the Greek letter delta with a subscript to represent the error correction information for output k, $\delta_{y_k} = y'_k(t_k - y_k)$, with the k subscript being used on all of the terms to indicate that we are talking about a specific output neuron with a specific target value. The weight change, Δv_{kj}, is now computed very similarly to the way the perceptron update rule worked. We set Δv_{kj} equal to $z_j\delta_{y_k}$, because z_j is the input connected to y_k via v_{kj}. Intuitively, this is very similar to the perceptron update rule, $x_i(t - y)$, but now all of the error correction information is in δ_{y_k} instead of just $(t - y)$.

We now turn our attention to the more difficult question of how to compute the updates for the hidden weights, Δu_{ji}. The short answer is that we will ultimately

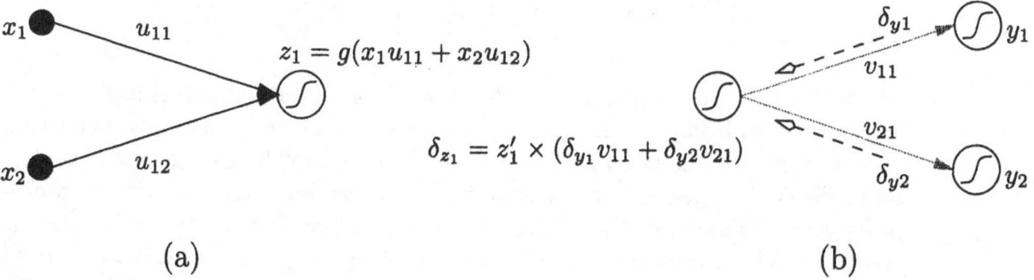

Figure 22.9 The MLP (a) feedforward pass compared with (b) the backpropagation pass

compute another delta term, δ_{z_j}, for the hidden neurons, which lets us set Δu_{ji} equal to $x_i\delta_{z_j}$, but this requires us to figure out what δ_{z_j} should be. Since each hidden neuron, z_j, sends its output to the y_k neurons via the v_{kj} weights, each hidden neuron can potentially contribute something to all of the y_k neurons. In other words, a hidden neuron's error correction term needs to be a function of the error correction terms that were calculated for the neurons that it connects to. The value of this term is equal to

$$\delta_{z_j} = z_j' \sum_k v_{kj}\delta_{y_k}.$$

Once again, the z_j' portion of the expression comes from the fact that we need to know how changing the net input into z_j changes its output. The summation takes all of the error correction terms from the output layer and sums them, weighted by the connection strengths.

Figure 22.9 shows both the forward and backward calculations for a single hidden neuron. We are already familiar with the forward pass in Figure 22.9a; however, the backward pass shown in Figure 22.9b illustrates how backprop is actually a reversed form of the forward pass. In the forward pass we are computing activation values, while in the backward pass we are computing correction terms. The forward pass goes left to right while the backward pass goes right to left. In each case, the value is calculated as part of a weighted sum of the terms that were computed in the earlier stage. The neat thing about backprop is that it is an efficient way to compute the error correction terms. It takes the same number of calculations as the forward pass, which is a surprising fact, considering that the values of the error correction terms are not as "obvious" to us as the activation values. Putting everything together, we now have

$$u_{ji}^{\text{new}} = u_{ji}^{\text{old}} + \eta x_i\delta_{z_j} \quad \text{and} \quad v_{kj}^{\text{new}} = v_{kj}^{\text{old}} + \eta z_j\delta_{y_k}, \text{ with}$$

$$\delta_{y_k} = y_k'(t_k - y_k) \quad \text{and} \quad \delta_{z_j} = z_j' \sum_k v_{kj} \delta_{y_k},$$

which completes the update rule. Because of the generic way in which the δ terms are computed, backpropagation is also referred to as the generalized delta rule.

The error surface of an MLP can look like a rugged landscape with many peaks and valleys. The peaks correspond to high error values where the MLP is producing incorrect outputs, while the valleys correspond to lower error rates and better output response. The backpropagation algorithm always adjusts the weights such that a very small step is taken in a downhill direction. Referring back to Figure 22.3 on page 390, given enough time and with a small enough step size, the weight updates suggested by backprop will always find a *local minimum* of the error surface that is a valleylike region having the property that any small adjustment of the weights can only hurt the MLP's performance. We know that a minimum will always be reached because each of the weight changes is always in the direction of the opposite of the error gradient. In other words, backprop is an efficient method for calculating how a change in each of the weights will change the error of its performance.

Unfortunately, the error surface of a complicated MLP trained to approximate a complicated function will almost always have many local minima that are suboptimal. Finding the *global minimum*, that is, the best minimum in the error surface, is the ultimate goal, but there is no guarantee that backprop will actually find it. In Section 22.9 we will discuss some of these issues in greater detail. None of this means that MLPs are poor at solving problems. In fact, as we will see in the next section, MLPs can solve some interesting problems. We simply need to recognize that there is no such thing as a free lunch. Perceptrons can be proved to converge to the best solution possible precisely because they are capable of forming only a very limited set of approximations. MLPs are much more powerful from a function approximation point of view and lack global convergence because each MLP can approximate many different types of functions.

22.5 Function Approximation

We are now ready to see how multilayer perceptrons can be trained to mimic other functions by looking at three simple problems. In the first example we will use an MLP with two hidden neurons to learn the XOR problem. In the second example we will train an MLP to emulate the logistic map, a chaotic system first discussed in Chapter 10. For the third example, we will build a model of the Hénon map, a more complicated chaotic system that was introduced in Chapter 11. Afterward, we will constructively see how it is possible for an MLP to approximate any function.

XOR For the XOR problem, we want the output of the MLP to correctly classify all possible input pairs. We start the MLP with random initial weights selected

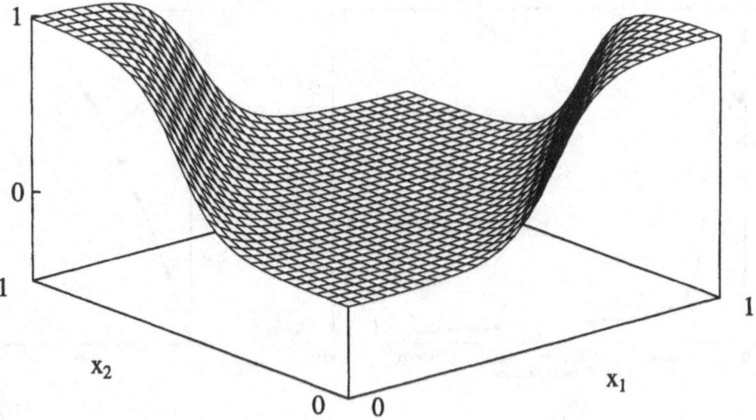

Figure 22.10 Output response surface of an MLP trained on the XOR data

from a -1 to 1 range. Random initialization is necessary because starting an MLP with all weights 0 can cause learning to proceed very slowly or not at all. Using backpropagation (plus some minor improvements discussed in Section 22.9), we train the network by randomly picking one of the four training patterns, adjusting the weights, then randomly picking another pattern, and so on, until the error drops to something close to 0. The total modeling error in this case is equal to the average of the partial errors produced for each pattern,

$$\text{Error} = \frac{1}{4}\sum_{p=1}^{4}(t^p - y^p),$$

where t^p represents the target value for pattern p and y^p is the MLP's output response when it is passed the inputs for pattern p.

After around 1000 or 2000 training iterations (which takes less than a second for my home PC to compute), the MLP has learned the correct mapping. Figure 22.10 shows the output response of the trained MLP. The x- and y-axes of the plot are labeled x_1 and x_2 for the two inputs, while the z-axis shows the MLP's output. As can be seen, the MLP has an output response that is elevated at the (0, 1) and (1, 0) corners but is depressed at the (0, 0) and (1, 1) corners. In between the four corners, the MLP interpolates things with a smooth, basinlike depression.

Logistic Map In the next example, the logistic map, we have a time series generated from the system while it is in the chaotic regime. We will train an MLP with one input and one output. The input to the MLP will be some point from the generated time series, labeled x_t, that has the target output of x_{t+1}. In other

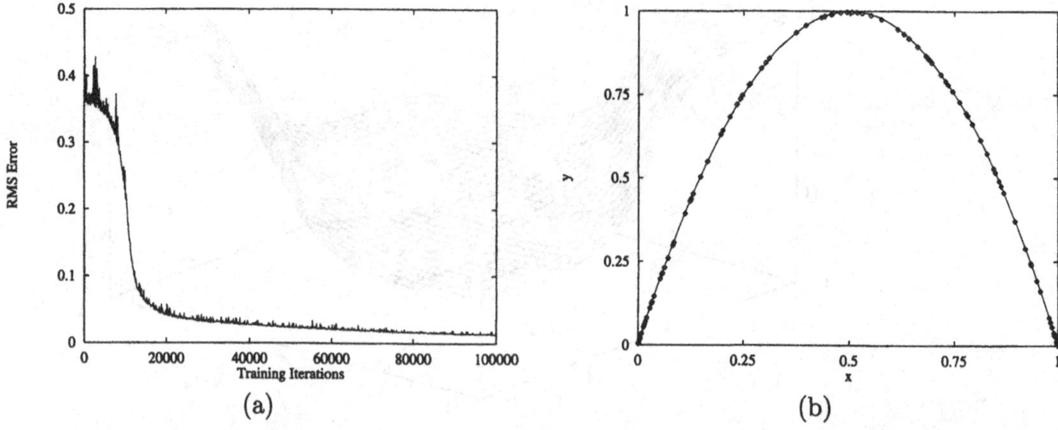

Figure 22.11 Training an MLP on chaos: (a) the training error as a function of the number of training iterations and (b) the target function (the logistic map) and the MLP's output response

words, given one point of the current portion of the chaotic series, we want the MLP to predict what the next point will be. Notice that our target values are no longer binary but may instead range anywhere from 0 to 1. Because of this, it is no longer appropriate to use a sigmoidal activation function on the output. Instead, we will simply use the identity function as a pseudo-activation function, that is, $g(x) = x$. This requires us to modify the backpropagation procedure slightly, by using $g'(x) = 1$ for the output neuron. The resulting values for the deltas are actually simpler than they were before, since δ_{y_k} is now equal to $(t_k - y_k)$. Other than this one change, everything stays the same.

Using two hidden neurons and 100 training patterns, Figure 22.11a shows the root mean squared error as related to the number of training iterations. It takes slightly more than 10,000 iterations to drop the error to an acceptable size, but I allowed the training to continue for a solid 1 million iterations just to illustrate the fact that learning slows down after a while.[7] The output response of the trained MLP is shown in Figure 22.11b. The solid line shows the actual target function, $x_{t+1} = 4x_t(1 - x_t)$, and the predicted points from the data set. As can be seen, the predictions are extremely accurate.

[7]This example also illustrates that MLPs may learn very slowly at times. In terms of rate of convergence, simple backprop is about the worst training procedure in existence. More sophisticated techniques like quasi-Newton's method or conjugate gradient offer learning speeds hundreds or even thousands of times faster. But these techniques are way beyond the scope of this book. Readers wishing to know more about advanced optimization routines should consult one of the neural network or numerical analysis texts in the bibliography.

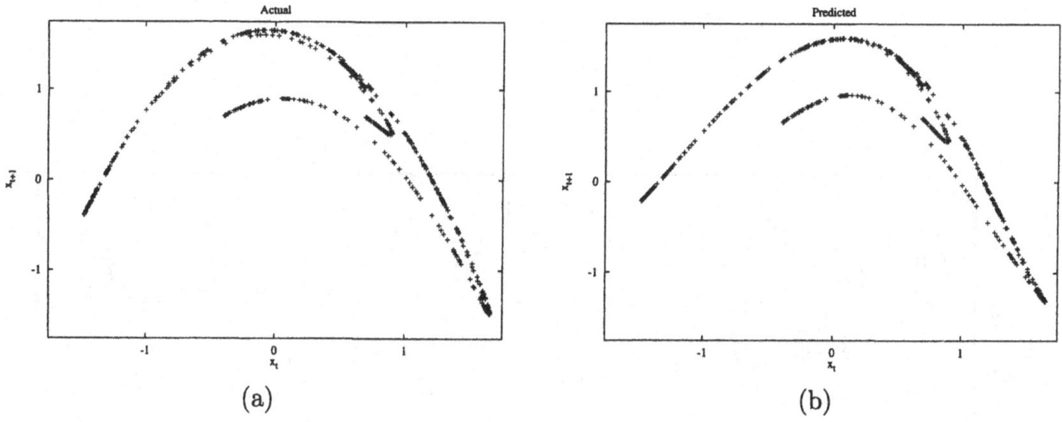

Figure 22.12 The reconstructed Hénon map: (a) the actual attractor plotted from the training points; (b) the attractor as approximated by an MLP

Hénon Map Our last example is a more complicated time series generated from the Hénon map. (See Section 11.1 on page 160 for an introduction to the Hénon map.) For this problem we must use two inputs that use two successive points from the time series, (x_t, x_{t+1}), while the target output is the next point, x_{t+2}. Since this time series is more complicated than any of the other examples, we will need more hidden neurons to increase the approximation power of the MLP. I used ten hidden neurons.

After 3000 training iterations the error drops considerably. The error could be reduced further with more training, but I would like this example to illustrate how an MLP could be slightly under-trained. Figure 22.12 shows the phase space of the actual Hénon map and the reconstructed attractor from the MLP. The approximation is very close, but some subtle differences are noticeable. The map in time series form is shown in Figure 22.13, which again reveals that the fit is very close but not perfect. Finally, Figure 22.14 shows the training error for the entire 3000 iterations.

All of these examples demonstrate that MLPs can learn mappings by just looking at training examples. What is not clear, however, is how the MLPs can form the correct output response. Multilayer perceptrons have a property known as *universal approximation*, which means that given any functional mapping, there exists an MLP that can approximate the mapping to an arbitrary accuracy. This does not necessarily mean that we can always find the weights to build that particular MLP; it just means that some values for the weights exist. MLPs with a single hidden layer of sigmoidal neurons are universal, but the proof of universality for this class

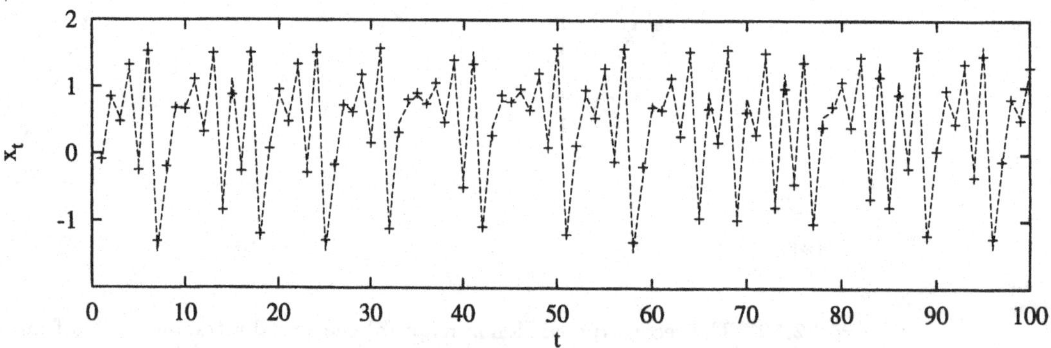

Figure 22.13 An actual and predicted portion of the Hénon map in time-series form: The lines are for the actual series and the points are the predicted values

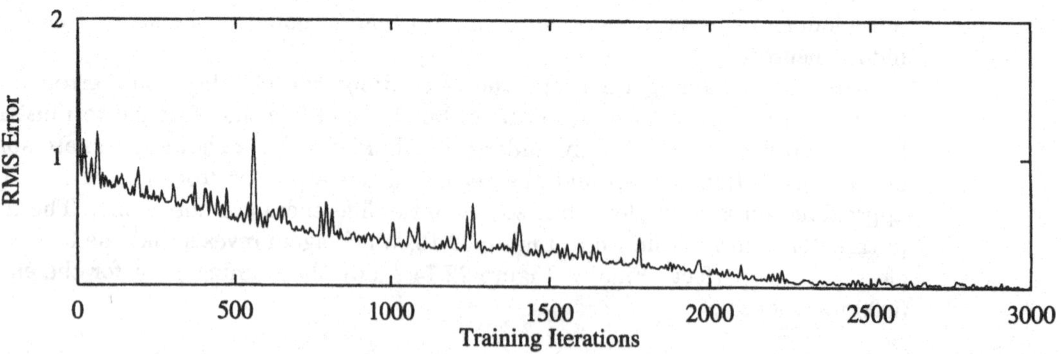

Figure 22.14 Training error for the Hénon map as a function of the number of training iterations

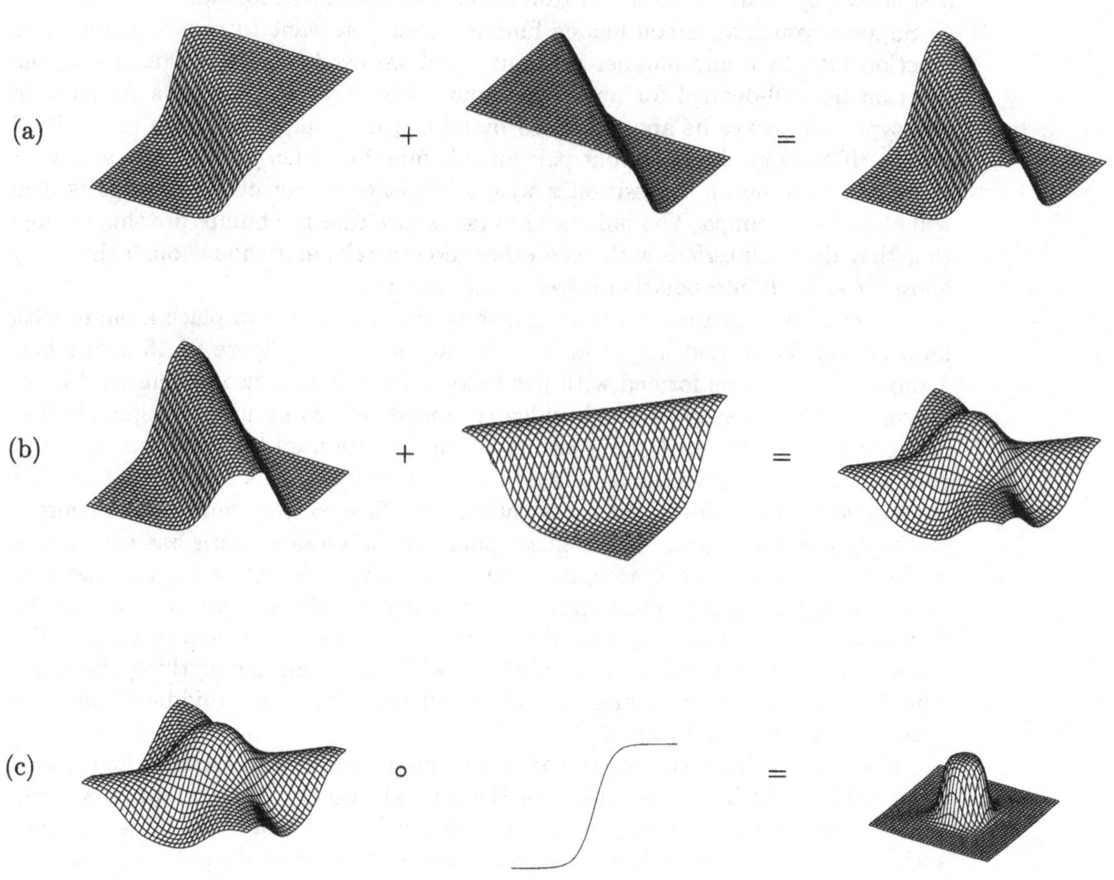

Figure 22.15 Forming bumps with 4 + 1 neurons: (a) two parallel but opposite sigmoids add up to form a single ridge; (b) two ridges form an elevated cross pattern with a peaked center; (c) the cross pattern is composed through a fifth sigmoid that filters out all but the peak, leaving a single local bump

of networks is not simple. With two hidden layers and a linear output, there is an elegant geometric proof for showing that MLPs are universal. The basic idea was first shown by Alan Lapedes and Rob Farber, and works as follows.

Suppose you have a continuous function that you want to approximate. The function may take any number of inputs. All we need is that the output of the function be well-defined for any legal input. The key idea is that a function of this type can always be approximated by adding up a large collection of localized bumps. If one legal input-output pair for this function is (x, y), then you will want to place a local bump at position x with a height of y. For other point pairs, you will place more bumps. You only need to make sure that the bumps are thin enough that they do not interfere with each other too severely, and wide enough that they allow for smooth interpolation between the bumps.

Universality is guaranteed if we can show that an MLP can place a bump with an arbitrary width and height at an arbitrary location. Figure 22.15 shows how a single bump can be formed with five hidden neurons in a two-dimensional input space. In the first stage, a single ridge is formed by adding up two sigmoids that are reflections of one another. Two more sigmoids are used to form a second ridge that is perpendicular to the first. Adding up the ridges yields a cross pattern that is elevated in the middle. The cross pattern was formed from four hidden neurons in the first hidden layer. The highest point in the cross pattern has a height of 4, the lowest points are near 0, and the ridges have a height of 2. The last step needed to form the bump is to pass the cross pattern through yet another hidden neuron in the second hidden layer of neurons. This final neuron acts as a filter. The weights coming into it squelch anything below 3.5, and amplify anything above 3.5. This has the affect of removing everything but the peak in the middle of the cross pattern, thus forming a bump.

By adjusting the weights, we can place this bump in any location and give it any height or width that we wish. For the general case of having n inputs, we need $2n + 1$ nodes to form a bump in an n-dimensional space. And by adding up many such bumps, it is possible to represent any conceivable input-output mapping with a multilayer perceptron.

22.6 Internal Representations

Since we have seen that MLPs can represent arbitrary functions, we will now consider a final example that shows how backpropagation can be used by an MLP to form an internal representation of a set of input patterns. This is a very subtle and important point, for if we are to expect a neural network to do something that seems intelligent, then it is necessary that a neural network can learn and exploit patterns within a set of data.

For example, suppose that we wish for a neural net to perform some task, be it function approximation, pattern classification, or some other generic type of prob-

Input Patterns							Target Patterns						
R	**S**	**S**	**S**	**S**	**F**	**F**	**R**	**S**	**S**	**S**	**S**	**F**	**F**
0	1	0	0	0	1	0	0	1	0	0	0	1	0
0	0	1	0	0	1	0	0	0	1	0	0	1	0
0	0	0	1	0	1	0	0	0	0	1	0	1	0
0	0	0	0	1	1	0	0	0	0	0	1	1	0
0	1	0	0	0	1	0	1	1	0	0	0	1	0
0	0	1	0	0	1	0	1	0	1	0	0	1	0
0	0	0	1	0	1	0	1	0	0	1	0	1	0
0	0	0	0	1	1	0	1	0	0	0	1	1	0
1	1	0	0	0	1	0	0	1	0	0	0	1	0
1	0	1	0	0	1	0	0	0	1	0	0	1	0
1	0	0	1	0	1	0	0	0	0	1	0	1	0
1	0	0	0	1	1	0	0	0	0	0	1	1	0
1	1	0	0	0	1	0	1	1	0	0	0	1	0
1	0	1	0	0	1	0	1	0	1	0	0	1	0
1	0	0	1	0	1	0	1	0	0	1	0	1	0
1	0	0	0	1	1	0	1	0	0	0	1	1	0
x_1	x_2	x_3	x_4	x_5	x_6	x_7	t_1	t_2	t_3	t_4	t_5	t_6	t_7

Table 22.1 Random, structured, and fixed data mixed into one data set: Columns labeled **R**, **S**, and **F** are effectively random, structured, and fixed, respectively

lem. Furthermore, let's also assume that the input data to the neural network contain things that are random, perfectly regular, and structured in some way. Our hope will be that the neural network will learn to ignore the randomness and regularity, but also discover the hidden order in the structured input data and be able to internally represent it in a more meaningful manner.

Put another way, the neural network and learning algorithm's task is a lot like what many people have to go through in order to pick a movie that they will like with high probability, based only on what a fixed set of movie reviewers say about the movie. Some reviewers seem to like everything ever put on film, so what they say about any movie is useless, in that it tells you nothing at all about whether or not you will like a movie. Other movie reviewers have such complex tastes that you may be hard pressed to ever guess what kind of movie they would like or dislike. However, if you find that your taste in science fiction films is similar to one particular critic's, or that your preferences for comedy films are exactly opposite to those of another critic, then these are both useful pieces of information for you to use when picking a movie.

To illustrate these issues further, Table 22.1 shows sixteen input and target patterns that we would like a neural network to reproduce (meaning that given

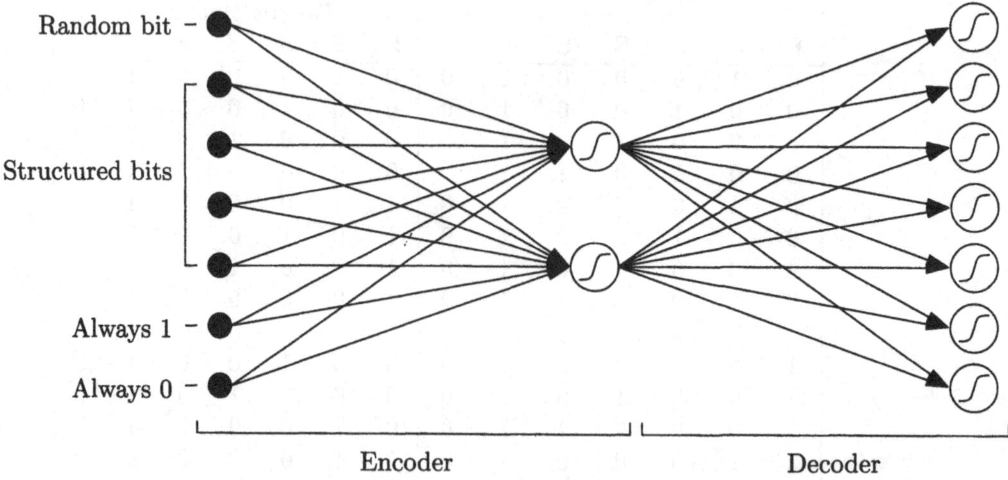

Figure 22.16 An encoder-decoder MLP that compresses a seven-bit input pattern into two bits, then decodes it with minimal information loss

an input vector from one row, we would like the neural network to reproduce the corresponding target vector from the same row). For the moment, we will ignore the neural network and just concentrate on the data in the table. The most obvious thing about the data is that inputs x_6 and x_7, along with targets t_6 and t_7, are perfectly regular in that they never change. This means not only that t_6 and t_7 are perfectly predictable, but also that x_6 and x_7 contain no information that would allow us to infer other things about other portions of the input or target vectors.

Note, however, that this is not the case for inputs x_2 through x_5 and targets t_2 through t_5. As with the fixed portions of the data set, the structured inputs are equal to their corresponding targets, but within the subset of these four inputs (or targets) there is a pattern, in that exactly one of the four inputs (or targets) is always on. Thus, if you know only which of the four inputs is on, you also know the value of the remaining three inputs as well as of the four targets.

Things are quite different for x_1 and t_1 which are labeled as "effectively random." For these two values there is no pattern to their values, since every combination of values is contained in the data set. For example, if you were to make any hypothesis concerning when or why x_1 or t_1 is 1 or 0 (as a function of the other inputs or targets), your hypothesis would have to be wrong, because whatever rule you try to construct could be disproved by a counter-example from another portion of the data set.

Putting this all together, we would like a neural network to discover the hidden order in the structured data but learn to ignore the fixed and random portions.

Moreover, our neural network will never "see" all of the data set at once, but only individual rows in isolation.

Figure 22.16 shows a special type of neural network that will be used for this problem. The network has seven inputs and targets that correspond to the dimensionalities of the data set. But also notice that there are only two hidden neurons. These two hidden neurons form an information bottleneck in that the network must learn to compress the information from the inputs into two values that can be decompressed by the right half of the network. The left portion of the network is an encoder because it encodes the seven inputs into two values, while the right half acts as a decoder that attempts to invert the encoding performed earlier.

While you and I have had the benefit of looking at the data set in its entirety beforehand, we also know that there is a structured pattern in four of the inputs and the targets. Since the neural network is randomly initialized, it has no preconceived notion about anything concerning the training data. It does not know what is regular, irregular, compressible, or incompressible. It has only one goal, and that is to reproduce the target values with the highest amount of accuracy. But to do this, it must learn to ignore the randomness and regularity because it is constrained to pass all of the information through only two hidden neurons. Thus, while we have explicitly constructed the network to minimize the redundancy of the input vectors, it must learn to do so almost as an implicit goal.

Training the network from Figure 22.16 on the data from Table 22.1 proceeds fairly rapidly for this problem. After only a few thousand training cycles it produces the output shown in Table 22.2 to within 10 percent. As can be seen, the structured and fixed target values are accurately reproduced while the random data are only statistically described by their mean. Things get interesting when we consider the hidden activation values that are produced for particular input values. What we find is that the network produces four distinct pairs of activation values that depend only on the structured data; thus, the network has learned to ignore both the fixed and the random data under all circumstances. The four distinct activation pairs for the hidden neurons represent the four types of input patterns for the structured data. The decoder portion of the network has learned to recover the structured data from the compressed versions in the hidden nodes, while the outputs corresponding to the fixed and random data are hardcoded in that they are produced independent of the hidden nodes. It is also interesting that the network settles on the mean of the data for both the random and the fixed data. For the fixed data this happens to be a perfect representation, but for the random data the mean is a slightly imperfect representation.

We should also note that the particular method of encoding and decoding the input vectors is somewhat arbitrary. For example, instead of the four activation pairs being (0, 1), (1, 0), (1, 1), and (0, 0), they could have just as easily been (1, 1), (0, 1), (0, 0), and (1, 0). The specifics of the encoding are not important. What is important is that the encoder and decoder agree on the representation.

Input Patterns							Hidden Units		Output Patterns						
R	**S**	**S**	**S**	**S**	**F**	**F**			**R**	**S**	**S**	**S**	**S**	**F**	**F**
0	1	0	0	0	1	0	0	1	0.5	1	0	0	0	1	0
0	0	1	0	0	1	0	1	0	0.5	0	1	0	0	1	0
0	0	0	1	0	1	0	1	1	0.5	0	0	1	0	1	0
0	0	0	0	1	1	0	0	0	0.5	0	0	0	1	1	0
0	1	0	0	0	1	0	0	1	0.5	1	0	0	0	1	0
0	0	1	0	0	1	0	1	0	0.5	0	1	0	0	1	0
0	0	0	1	0	1	0	1	1	0.5	0	0	1	0	1	0
0	0	0	0	1	1	0	0	0	0.5	0	0	0	1	1	0
1	1	0	0	0	1	0	0	1	0.5	1	0	0	0	1	0
1	0	1	0	0	1	0	1	0	0.5	0	1	0	0	1	0
1	0	0	1	0	1	0	1	1	0.5	0	0	1	0	1	0
1	0	0	0	1	1	0	0	0	0.5	0	0	0	1	1	0
1	1	0	0	0	1	0	0	1	0.5	1	0	0	0	1	0
1	0	1	0	0	1	0	1	0	0.5	0	1	0	0	1	0
1	0	0	1	0	1	0	1	1	0.5	0	0	1	0	1	0
1	0	0	0	1	1	0	0	0	0.5	0	0	0	1	1	0
x_1	x_2	x_3	x_4	x_5	x_6	x_7	z_1	z_2	t_1	t_2	t_3	t_4	t_5	t_6	t_7

Table 22.2 Results of training an encoder-decoder neural network: the network compresses the structured data, statistically describes the random data, and hard-codes the regular data. The shown values are only approximate

The key point to all of this is that the neural network learned to form an internal representation of the input patterns that ignored regularity and randomness, and compressed whatever could be compressed. It is never guaranteed that a neural network can do the same thing for any data set, but it is pleasing, nonetheless, that our network does the right thing for this example.

Forming internal representations is arguably one of the most important characteristics of any type of model. If we wish to train a neural network to perform pattern classification or to model a physical process, an internal representation for the data is useful in that it can often represent that which is truly important about the data. For the case of pattern classification, some patterns may be invisible to humans because they are visible only in some higher-dimensional space or they may exist only with respect to millions of individual data points. Having a model and a learning method that can automatically discover such hidden order is crucial to the goal of more compactly describing the phenomenon. Similarly, for the case of modeling a physical process, sometimes the most predictive part of state space does not reside in any individual input, but is instead some function of multiple inputs. Discovering the hidden function is, again, another facet of forming an internal representation.

22.7 Other Applications

The four example problems from the previous sections only scratch the surface of what it is possible to do with neural networks. Moreover, the multilayer perceptron is only one of many different types of neural networks in current use; it just happens to be the most popular type. In this section I will briefly list some applications in the hope of conveying the broad applicability of neural networks.

Pattern Recognition The general problem of pattern recognition can be applied to a nearly infinite number of problem areas. Some current applications include optical character recognition for human handwriting, facial recognition, sonar classification, credit card fraud detection, and electrocardiogram classification. In this application area the inputs to a neural network can consist of any digital form of information, such as an image, sound, spending record, or heartbeat.

Function Approximation Included here are all forms of time-series prediction, which include predicting the stock market and the weather. There are also many industrial processes that are not well understood analytically. Neural networks have been used to build data-based models that surpass in accuracy models built from physical first principles. Because a neural network has a well-defined structure, it is possible and often helpful to perform sensitivity analysis on a neural network trained to emulate a physical process. Doing so allows researchers to find out what measurements in a process have predictive power, which gives engineers greater insight into how a physical process works.

Signal Processing Many audio signals are continuously corrupted with noise. In a hearing aid, for example, background conversations, miscellaneous white noise, and spurious events like a loud bang can cause trouble for people who are wearing a device that amplifies these sounds as well as normal conversations. Neural networks are being used to selectively filter out different types of noise, thus enabling hearing aid users to perceive their environment more accurately. Similar applications can be found in cellular telephones and speaker phones.

Control Building models of processes can be difficult, but an even more challenging problem is controlling a process. Using techniques from reinforcement learning, neural networks have been trained to control many different systems. Current applications include neural networks that can drive a car down a highway, control chemical processes, or manipulate a robot arm. There are many different ways to build controllers with neural networks. One way is to model an ideal controller already in existence. The neural network controller essentially learns to duplicate the actions taken by another controller (say, a human). In other situations a technique known as model inversion can be used. Model-based control is a third technique that trains a controller to manipulate a second neural network that models some process. This last technique has been used to build controllers for processes that humans are incapable of controlling.

Compression and Correction Many data streams coming from sensors contain redundancy that can be exploited. In some cases it is possible to exploit this property by building an auto-associative neural network (similar to the encoder-decoder from the previous section) that merely produces an output vector that is equivalent to an input vector. The usefulness in this is that a hidden layer can be made to have fewer neurons than there are inputs or outputs. This means that the neural network must learn an efficient way to compress the data through the bottleneck of the hidden layer. In so doing, a neural network not only may compress the information into a more usable form, but also can correct for missing values in the input vector.

Soft Sensors From an engineering point of view, it is seldom possible to put as many sensors on a system as we would like. Consider detecting illegal emissions from an automobile engine. Installing complicated sensors on every car would contribute greatly to production costs. Researchers are working on building neural networks that can infer a difficult but needed measurement from readily available measurements. A neural network for this application would have things like engine temperature, gas consumption, and engine misfires as inputs and would output an approximation of the desired measurement, toxic emissions.

Anomaly Detection In this application area, a neural network is used to build a model of "typical" states of some system. Despite the fact that the network sees only the normal states, it is possible for a network to recognize anomalous conditions simply because they differ from the normal state. Automatically recognizing when anomalies occur can prevent component failures before they are too serious (say, in a helicopter), or even distinguish abnormal heartbeats from normal ones.

Because neural networks is such an active area of research, it is quite possible for this list to be out of date by the time this book is published. Nevertheless, as computing power increases and more data become available, it is likely that neural networks will be applied to hundreds of different applications.

22.8 Unifying Themes

Part of the opening discussion was unfair in its characterization of a single neuron. Much has been learned over the past thirty years about how neurons work, but there are still many puzzles to be solved. Sophisticated models of a single neuron that go way beyond the ideas in a perceptron neuron may contain hundreds of coupled nonlinear differential equations that can be only coarsely simulated in real time on a computer. While the research community is somewhat split as to how complete our understanding of a single neuron can ever be, the possibility remains that we may never have a perfect understanding of how a neuron works. But this does not stop us from using the things that we already know about how real neurons work. In fact, some have suggested that perfect knowledge of how biological neurons work is not strictly necessary for us to exploit them in simulations. This seems to be a reasonable hypothesis when we consider that computer scientists can safely ignore the quantum-level events that occur in real digital circuitry without losing any of the important details of how computation works in principle.

One of the more important parts of an artificial neuron is the nonlinear activation function. We were able to build more powerful neural networks by having intermediate hidden neurons produce values that were used by neurons further down the network. If a linear activation function were used, the resulting output of a multilayer perceptron would be yet another linear function of the inputs. In other words, an MLP with all linear activation functions can produce only the same class of functions that a single-layer linear perceptron can. This means that there would be no advantage in having multiple layers in a network. Thus, nonlinearity in a neuron is a a critical part of its power.

Also note that most researchers do not believe that the brain performs anything like backpropagation at the level of a neuron. A natural learning phenomenon that most closely resembles backprop is probably related to simple behavioral adaptation, which is a feedback process that adjusts behaviors to account for an environment.

We also know that human intelligence emerges from multiple levels of complexity. On the topmost level, intelligence may consist of many interacting yet partially modular components such as memory, feature recognition, and language processing, to name a few. On the lowest level lies the behavior of a single neuron. In between these two extremes lies the massive interconnectedness that glues the lower-level functions to higher-level functions. Intelligence may be an emergent phenomenon that can be best appreciated from a higher-level viewpoint, while neural interactions occupy the lower rung of the ladder. Because of this, researchers in learning must often attempt to straddle reductionist and holistic viewpoints simultaneously.

22.9 Further Exploration

A single program, `mlp`, was used for the four experiments in this chapter. The command-line options are summarized in Table 22.3. The program simulates an MLP with a single hidden layer of neurons. The number of neurons in the MLP is determined by the values used with the `-numin`, `-numhid`, and `-numout` options. The training data file is specified with the `-dfile` option. Data files should begin with a single number to indicate the number of training patterns, which is then followed by all of the patterns given as (input, target) vector pairs.

Option Name	Option Type	Option Meaning
`-dfile`	STRING	data file name
`-numin`	INTEGER	number of inputs
`-numhid`	INTEGER	number of hidden nodes
`-numout`	INTEGER	number of outputs
`-lrate`	DOUBLE	learning rate
`-mrate`	DOUBLE	momentum rate
`-winit`	DOUBLE	weight initialization factor
`-linout`	SWITCH	use linear outputs?
`-steps`	INTEGER	number of simulated steps
`-seed`	INTEGER	random seed for initial state
`-pdump`	SWITCH	dump patterns at end of run?
`-gdump`	SWITCH	dump `gnuplot` commands at end?
`-freq`	INTEGER	status printout frequency

Table 22.3 Command-line options for `mlp`

The `-winit` option specifies how big the initial weights will be. If w is the value passed to this option, then all weights will be randomly initialized in the $-w$ to w range with a uniform distribution. The `-seed` option is helpful if you wish to rerun an experiment with a different set of initial weights. If real-valued outputs are needed (as with the logistic map), the `-linout` switch should be set. The program trains the MLP for the number of iterations specified by `-steps`. With the `-freq` option, the printout frequency of the training can be controlled. Each of these printouts consists of the average error of the MLP computed over the entire training set.

With the `-pdump` option set, the program will print each input along with the MLP's output at the end of training. And with the `-gdump` option set, the program will create a file called `mlp.gnp` that contains specifications for the trained network represented as a `gnuplot` function. This is convenient if you want to plot the surface that represents the MLP's response to two inputs.

Finally, the learning rate or step size is controlled by the `-lrate` option. There is also an option called `-mrate` that controls a momentum factor that is used in the training. We did not talk about momentum prior to this section, but it is a simple modification to backprop that greatly increases performance. To explain how it works, for weight vector $\mathbf{w}$ with momentum rate μ, let the weight change determined by plain backprop be denoted by $\Delta\mathbf{w}^{\mathrm{bp}}$. The update rule used by backprop with momentum is

$$\begin{aligned}\Delta\mathbf{w}^{\mathrm{new}} &= \mu\Delta\mathbf{w}^{\mathrm{old}} + \eta\Delta\mathbf{w}^{\mathrm{bp}} \quad \text{and} \\ \mathbf{w}^{\mathrm{new}} &= \mathbf{w}^{\mathrm{old}} + \Delta\mathbf{w}^{\mathrm{new}},\end{aligned}$$

with μ taking a value between 0 and 1. This allows the program to retain a little bit of the previous step direction. If the MLP proceeds down an error surface like a ball rolling down a hill, momentum allows the ball to speed up over long downhill stretches as well as to jump over little potholes.

Those wishing to try their hand on more sophisticated neural architectures and learning algorithms should consult one of the texts listed in the next section or the bibliography.

22.10 Further Reading

Caudill, M. & Butler, C. (1990). *Naturally intelligent systems.* Cambridge, Mass.: MIT Press.

Haykin, S. (1994). *Neural networks: A comprehensive foundation.* New York: MacMillan.

Hertz, J., Krogh, A., & Palmer, R. G. (1991). *Introduction to the theory of neural computation.* Reading, Mass.: Addison-Wesley.

Minsky, M. & Papert, S. (1988). *Perceptrons* (expanded ed.). Cambridge, Mass.: MIT Press.

Nilsson, N. J. (1965). *Learning machines: Foundations of trainable pattern classifying systems.* New York: McGraw-Hill.

Press, W. H., Flannery, B. P., Teukolsky, S. A., & Vetterling, W. T. (1986). *Numerical recipes.* Cambridge: Cambridge University Press.

Rumelhart, D. E., Hinton, G. E., & Williams, R. J. (1986). *Parallel distributive processing.* Cambridge, Mass.: MIT Press.

23 Postscript: Adaptation

The sciences do not try to explain, they hardly even try to interpret, they mainly make models. By a model is meant a mathematical construct which, with the addition of certain verbal interpretations, describes observed phenomena. The justification of such a mathematical construct is solely and precisely that it is expected to work.
— John von Neumann

Breadth-first search is the bulldozer of science.
— Randy Goebel

The most extensive computation known has been conducted over the last billion years on a planet-wide scale: it is the evolution of life. The power of this computation is illustrated by the complexity and beauty of its crowning achievement, the human brain.
— David Rogers

IN THIS FINAL postscript we will dissect the general form of an adaptive system into three subsystems that are all deserving of study in their own right: an environment, a model of the environment, and a search procedure that attempts to adapt the model to the environment. We will see that all three components of an adaptive system are highly dependent on each other, in that each partially determines the other two. Our goal for this postscript is to see how this interdependence can be viewed from a computational viewpoint. As a consequence, all sophisticated adaptive procedures, including scientific methodology, are subject to the paradoxical attributes associated with self-reference and computability.

We will first compare and contrast learning, evolution, and cultural adaptation to examine the relationship between models and search methods, and also to see how all three processes are similar in their generality. We will then look at how an environment limits the types of feasible search procedures. This means that search methods can be adapted to tune models more effectively. This is followed by an examination of the relationship between models and environments that will highlight coadaptive processes that tune models and environments in a recursive manner. Putting all of these facts together, we will then consider how adaptation can be a "bootstrap" process by which adaptive systems spawn increasingly more sophisticated adaptive systems.

In the final section of this chapter, we will consider how the recursive framework of adaptive systems relates to Gödel's incompleteness and Chaitin's generalization of Turing's Halting Problem. In the end, we will find that these two computational results bring forth severe limitations on how well we can know and understand the universe.

23.1 Models and Search Methods

The term *model* can mean different things in different contexts, but for our purposes we will use a definition that is somewhat connected to the topics from this book part. With this in mind, we will use the term to mean a well-defined process that maps inputs to outputs but also happens to be parameterized in such a way that the model can be tuned by changing the parameters. The parameters may be discrete or continuous, but in either case they act as knobs that can be adjusted to change the input-output mapping that the model produces. As a simple example, we could model a periodic process by the equation

$$f(x; a, b, c) = a \sin(bx - c),$$

which has an output, a single input, x, and three parameters, a, b and c, that correspond to the amplitude, frequency, and phase of the sine wave, respectively. With this equation, we could adjust the three parameters to build a rough approximation of a frictionless pendulum, the average seasonal temperature, or the lunar cycle.

A *search procedure* is a method for choosing parameter values so that a model is made to closely approximate an environment. For the sine wave example, the model is so simple that for any environment, there is a best solution that can be found with a deterministic procedure. In this case, the simplicity of the model has simplified the search procedure for the parameters.

For most real-world systems that one could imagine modeling, a simple sine wave is completely inadequate as a representation of the environment. On the other hand, in principle classifier systems and neural networks can be used to model anything, because they are so general that virtually any process can be approximated with them.[1] But approximation power is somewhat of a curse as well. By using a more complicated model, we lose the bonus of having a search procedure that is guaranteed to work under all circumstances. Things are so bad that the general

[1]Including GAs in this statement is a little problematic, since GAs are really a type of search procedure, as we shall see shortly.

problem of optimizing a neural network or a classifier system is known to be NP-complete under many reasonable cases and intractable under some special cases.

This double-sided result is partially due to the modular nature of the models. Both classifier systems and neural networks derive their power from the fact that they are composed of many simple units that can be combined to form complex patterns. Doyne Farmer and others have made a more profound observation by noting that the similarities of these adaptive systems actually run quite deep. The following discussion is mostly inspired by Farmer's "Rosetta Stone" paper, which compares the aforementioned adaptive systems with immune and autocatalytic networks. Here, I will just give a summary of the comparison for neural networks and classifier systems, but afterward I will attempt to expand on the comparison to bridge the idea for evolution, culture, and learning.

Since the output of both a neural network and a classifier system is a composition of values computed at intermediate stages, both models need a form of working memory that allows these auxiliary values to be stored. For a neural network, this is simply a neuron that holds some value that is later passed to another neuron. The equivalent structure for a classifier system is a little more subtle because we haven't been in the habit of drawing classifier systems as networks. However, a message in a classifier system serves the same purposes despite the fact that it does not directly correspond to a tangible structure like a neuron. Messages are posted by classifiers on the message list, where they remain for a single time step. At the beginning of the next time step, the active messages trigger other classifiers; thus, the messages serve the role of holding an intermediate piece of information and triggering the production of other information.

Synapses in a neural network serve the role of transporting information from a source to a destination. They may also be associated with a strength. Classifiers serve a similar role since they are paired with a condition and a message, which act as a source and a destination, respectively. A synapse's strength is analogous to a classifier's strength; both strengths increase the probability that a message or signal will have a consequence when propagated further.

The net input of a neuron is computed as a weighted sum of other neuron activation values. In a classifier system, identical messages may be posted by more than one classifier. This is identical to having multiple neurons propagating signals to a single destination. Where a neural network uses a weighted sum to combine the signals, a classifier system will usually combine all of the identical messages into a single message that has an intensity proportional to the sum of the strengths of the original messages. Thus, both systems combine multiple signals into one in a weighted manner.

A neural network will additionally pass the net input of a neuron through a sigmoidal activation function, which has the effect of limiting the activation value to a well-defined range. Likewise, classifier systems do not propagate all messages on the message list at each iteration. Instead, only the strongest messages are able to trigger classifiers on the next time step. This selection method effectively treats a group of the strongest messages as active and thresholds all others to an inactive state. Hence, both systems pass information through thresholds that allow only a portion of the information to propagate.

One could continue this comparison to the point of showing that it is always possible to have these two model types mutually emulate one another in an efficient manner. However, the model types differ most in how they are tuned to their environment. For neural networks, a learning-like procedure is used to slightly change weights according to a error gradient measure, that is, if an error measure decreases in some direction of the weight space, then a small step is taken in that direction. Classifier systems use a related method for adjusting weights (the bucket brigade algorithm, or implicit bucket brigade) that assigns credit from one classifier to another in the form of payments. But also note that classifier systems additionally depend on a genetic algorithm to introduce new classifiers into the system. Thus, classifier systems are adapted with a learning-like procedure as well as an evolutionary-like procedure.

In the real world, cultural breakthroughs are made on time scales that are slow relative to learning but fast relative to evolution. In the simplest case, cultural adaptation is merely a process of imitation, as is the case with many animals. For humans, cultural adaptation has become far more significant because of the invention of language. For culture, language serves much the same role that far-reaching synapses do in a brain. Whenever an innovation can be passed only via imitation, propagation of the innovation can occur only at a very slow and localized rate. However, language, in particular writing, enables innovations to spread both far and wide. Whereas neurons serve the role of information holders in a neural network, humans act as the basic information repository in a cultural system. Under this view, synaptic strength starts to resemble the number and total influence of the holders of a particular idea. Individuals modify ideas with learning by incrementally improving on an idea that was acquired elsewhere. For example, Catholicism is an idea that has been around for quite a while. It is typically passed from parent to child, but on occasion it is transferred in a more evangelical manner. Influential members of the faith have incrementally modified the religion through their own efforts, as in the case of Thomas Aquinas, whose philosophical writings changed the way many Catholics interpreted the Bible. In other cases, the changes in Catholicism have resembled evolution more closely, as when the church accommodated new members by incorporating (memetic crossover?) pagan festivals as official holidays.

On a global scale, biological evolution starts to resemble culture and learning if we consider the species to be the basic type of information holder. Species are connected to each other through a web of interactions that may be competitive or cooperative. The population or total amount of genetic material resembles what we have been thinking of as the unit strength in the other models. Evolution performs a type of parameter search that stochastically samples nearby points in the genome. Genetic shifts that result in a more fit individual can move the entire species in a specific genetic direction. While this is not the same as a gradient-based search, stochastic sampling and gradient ascent are both examples of the hill-climbing search method.

All of this will be relevant in the next section, where we will see how search methods relate to environments and search spaces.

23.2 Search Methods and Environments

Since adaptive systems have parameters that can be modified, the space of all possible parameter settings defines a *search space*. For evolutionary systems, the search space consists of all conceivable DNA sequences, while for a neural network with n weights, the search space is equal to an n-dimensional hyperspace of weight settings. The purpose of adaptation is to move through the space from a region of poor fitness to one of good fitness. However, since fitness is a measure of how successfully a model is matched to its environment, the difficulty of the search problem is intimately tied to the environment. In this section, we will see that search methods may be adapted to an environment. In other words, we will see that phrases such as "learning to learn" or "evolving evolution" may refer to real processes.

To explain what is meant by a "search method," imagine that you have a very important meeting that is going to start promptly at midnight on the highest point of a mountain range. There is no way of getting to this point except to climb, and to make things worse, you do not have a map of the region nor do you have any idea where the peak is located. You have a flashlight to light your way, but there is a dense fog surrounding the mountain that permits you to see only about one foot in front of you. You have only three things working in your favor. First, this mountain range happens to be on a small planet with very low gravity, so you can make large leaps if you are certain that there is firm ground where you will land. Second, there are lots of little pebbles lying about, and being the current world champion in darts, you can throw the pebbles with perfect accuracy. Third, you have an altimeter and a compass to help you navigate.

You start at the base of the mountain. Since you can see only very small localized regions, your first move is to try to walk uphill. This works for a while, but eventually you reach a small peak. Your companions are not there, so you know that this is not the tallest peak. Scooping up a handful of pebbles, you methodically throw several pebbles in various directions, in an attempt to find a region that has a higher peak. At some point, one of your pebbles makes a sound that clearly indicates it has hit a peak that is higher than your current location. You then take

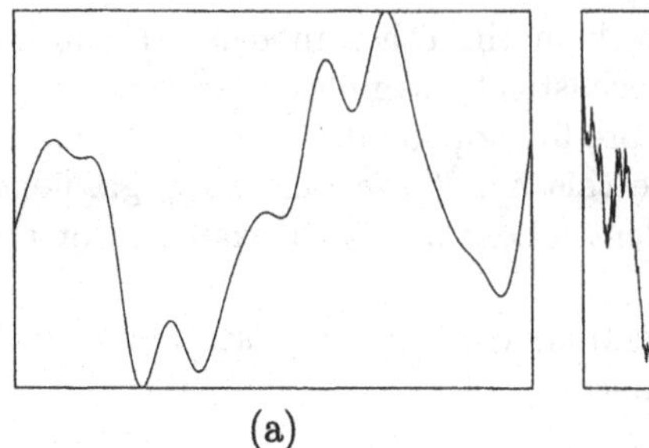
(a)

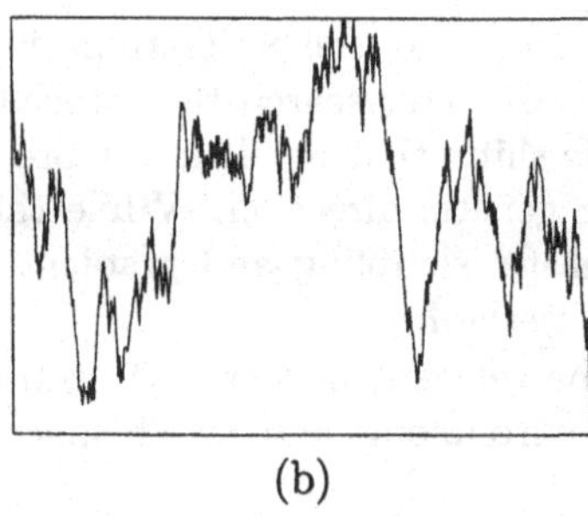
(b)

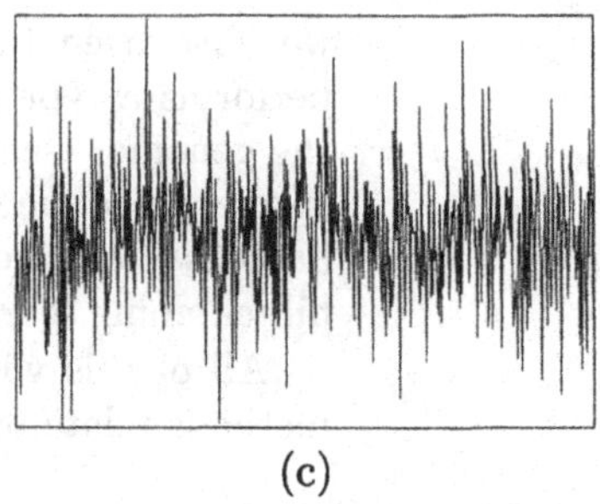
(c)

Figure 23.1 Three types of search spaces: (a) smooth, (b) neither smooth nor strictly random, and (c) random

advantage of the low gravity and leap to this new location. Once there, you start to climb in an uphill direction. This continues for some time, but you are running short of time. Fortunately, just before midnight, your friends hear your silly efforts, throw you a rope, and pull you up to your destination.

This little scenario illustrates how adaptation and search procedures must often proceed in a nearly blind manner, making tentative probes until progress is made. But there are other useful comparisons that can be made between search methods and this scenario. First, search methods can work in different ways. Sometimes a localized search makes sense. Other times, you are better off probing more distant areas with pebbles. Learning in artificial neural networks takes smooth steps, while genetic algorithms perform a very structured type of probing.

Figure 23.1 illustrates three types of search spaces. In Figure 23.1a we have a nice and smooth surface that lends itself to a learning-like procedure that makes small steps in an uphill direction. Some minor probing with the pebbles is necessary in order to find the largest peak, but one would expect to take more small steps than large probes for this search space. On the other hand, Figure 23.1c shows a surface that is completely random. Small and local steps are useless in a space such as this. The best search strategy for this surface is to randomly probe the entire region. Figure 23.1b shows a surface that is somewhat between the two extremes. While the surface has many irregular bumps, it contains a certain amount of continuity in that the height of a region is usually close to the height of nearby points. In a search environment such as this, you would need a mixture of local search steps and distant but structured probes to find the peak.

Knowing the type of search space that you may encounter is a huge advantage if you are limited to a fixed search method. But what should you do if the search space changes? There is much evidence that search methods in natural systems are adapted according to environments. As a first example, consider the different types of search probes that a fit population would make versus those of an unfit population. In biological systems "search probe" can be thought of as a mutation rate, with large and small mutations corresponding to large and small probes, respectively. Fit individuals have little to gain and much to lose from large mutations. Fit individuals are far better off taking small steps so as not to undo earlier progress. However, for an unfit population, small steps are usually useless. When your house is on fire, drinking some iced tea may make you momentarily feel better, but is clearly a case of the right idea applied in too small a proportion. Unfit individuals are better served by attempting large probes, for in times of trouble, big changes are needed. If the change makes things worse, well, things were bad already.

Biological systems have some sophisticated cellular machinery devoted to correcting replication errors in DNA. The level of sophistication varies between single-cell and multicellular animals as well as between the species, but it is present to some degree in all organisms. When bacteria are dangerously close to starving, the error correction machinery is inhibited to the degree that more drastic mutations are permitted. The advantages for bacteria in this case are significant: If a new mutation permits a bacterium to metabolize a new food source, then starvation can be avoided (Wills, 1989). Other examples of how evolution is evolved include the invention of sex in single-cell animals and sexual selection in the higher animals.

Human culture has experienced several major innovations that have altered the way in which information is passed through the generations. Many animals can communicate in ways such that information important to survival is passed from individual to individual. Birds declare territory and warn of predators with songs and chirps. Bees do a cute little jig that describes the location of a nectar cache. Otters teach their young how to smash open shells. But humans have taken communication to the unique extreme that our languages can express an infinite number of ideas. This innovation opened the door to a method of symbolically passing on information in a way that is distinct from imitation.

Another major milestone in human culture is the advancement of written language. The alphabet and the printing press have enabled us to make more or less permanent records of important knowledge. And of comparable importance was the invention of the scientific method. By defining a systematic way to ask and answer questions about nature, the scientific method has enabled humans to propel themselves to the point that human culture now far outweighs evolution in its affect on the world as a whole.

While evolution has produced increasingly complex animals, it has also adapted the process of adaptation. Hence, we have not only an advancement of physical structures but also an advancement of the functional structures of adaptation. Evolution produces simple adaptation, which allows for learning, which permits imitation, which spawns culture, which brings forth language, which gives birth to science, by which evolution is rediscovered.

23.3 Environments and Models

We have been speaking of models and environments as if they were two very distinct things that one could separate with a line. In reality, one creature's model is another creature's environment, which is to say that biological systems must adapt to other adapting biological systems. When multiple creatures simultaneously adapt to each other, the fitness of an organism becomes a function of how other organisms are behaving. The usual idea of evolution proceeding up a fitness landscape is no longer true in this case, for if a species stays still, that is, does not genetically change, and other species change, then the fitness landscape of the static species is altered despite its determination to stay still. This means that organisms often will have to continuously adapt just to stay at a comparable level of fitness. This is why Stuart Kauffman has often referred to fitness landscapes as being squishy: Taking a step deforms the terrain.

Coevolution encourages Red Queen scenarios that often result in biological arms races (as discussed in Chapter 20) that spawn adaptations that would never come about on their own. Danny Hillis and others have exploited coevolution as a means for improving the evolutionary optimization of genetic algorithms. But it is the mutual adaptation that changes both models and environments that is our main interest in this section.

Coadaptation relates to the search problem in a very unusual way. To see why, consider the No Free Lunch (NFL) theorem of David Wolpert and William Macready. Because there are so many different methods of performing search and optimization, one hot topic among researchers is the relative efficiency of the different methods. If one method could be clearly identified as being better than the others, then computer scientists could use the best method on any problem and no longer worry about finding a better technique. The NFL theorem states that over all possible search spaces, all methods perform equally well, including the simple technique of randomly guessing. Wolpert and Macready proved the NFL theorem by averaging a search score over every possible search space, which will contain well-behaved surfaces like Figure 23.1a as well as many random surfaces like Figure 23.1c.

At first glance the NFL theorem seems to be very disappointing in its implications. Under a strict interpretation it means that gradient-based learning and genetic algorithms are no better than a random guess. But Wolpert and Macready (as well as Stuart Kauffman) have pointed out that it may actually imply something far more interesting. Specifically, we know that evolutionary fitness landscapes are far from random. Kauffman has suggested that the NFL theorem actually highlights the importance of coadaptation. When an animal and its environment are mutually adapting to one another, the fitness landscapes (that is, the evolutionary search spaces) are molded to one another. Coadaptation squeezes the search spaces in such a way that they become highly nonrandom. One implication of this is that search methods may be optimally adapted for the space that they are used in. In other words, evolution may be evolved.

A similar property can be seen in learning systems as well. Training feedforward neural networks on a fixed set of input-output patterns is a relatively well-defined problem. Although finding the best weights for a feedforward network is known to be an NP-complete problem, there are many encouraging results that indicate that good solutions to challenging problems can be found. Parallel to the ideas in coevolution there are more complicated types of neural networks having recurrent connections that couple the network's output (or some internal states) to the network's input. Networks of this type are far more powerful than strictly feedforward nets (they are, in fact, capable of universal computation); however, the newly gained power comes at considerable expense. Specifically, finding the best set of weights for a recurrent network turns out to be an incomputable problem in the worst case, since the individual artificial neurons must adapt not only within the context of other neurons in the network but also in the context of the previous states of the neurons, making the whole problem hopelessly recursive. So, again, we find that once a system becomes self-referential, it must border a boundary between computability and incomputability. This means that no general technique can be used to solve the problem of training a recurrent neural network. Partial solutions must in some ways be adapted to the specifics of the problems. For systems of this type, "learning to learn" may be a more promising method.

23.4 Adaptation and Computation

In speaking of adaptation as a process of model-building, we have really been talking about ideas very central not just to computer science but to all of science.

In the end, scientific research is about building models. When we try to characterize a phenomenon by a set of equations or a program, it is a model that we are building. We interact with nature in many ways, but from a scientific perspective our interactions are characterized in two ways. First, we manipulate and observe nature so as to gather data. With this data we attempt to describe how nature works. For the second way, we use our descriptions of nature to make predictions of what nature will do at a later time. Our models are continuously adapted by new discoveries. And over time our models and our methods for adapting them become more sophisticated.

Curiously, the theory of computation has a lot to say about the limits of what we can do with science. As discussed in Chapters 9 and 14, Gregory Chaitin's extension of the Halting Problem proves that finding the smallest program (that is, a model) that explains a set of data (or observations) is in the general case undecidable. Considering that Occam's Razor is one of the foundations of the way we build our models, Chaitin's result implies that there may be phenomena that cannot be described more compactly than themselves.

From the opposite direction, Gödel's incompleteness and Turing's incomputability results (discussed in Chapters 4 and 3) tell us that even if we have a perfect model for some phenomenon, there are many interesting questions concerning the real phenomena that cannot be answered by looking at the model.

Is this a gloomy view of how far science can go toward describing the universe? I don't think so. To see why, read on.

23.5 Further Reading

Casti, J. L. (1989). *Alternate realities: Mathematical models of nature and man.* New York: John Wiley & Sons.

Farmer, J. D. (1990). Rosetta stone for connectionism. *Physica D*, 42(1–3): 153–187.

Hillis, W. D. (1992). Co-evolving parasites improve simulated evolution as an optimization procedure. In C. G. Langton, C. Taylor, J. D. Farmer, & S. Rasmussen (Eds.), *Artificial life II*, volume 10 of *Sante Fe Institute Studies in the Sciences of Complexity* (pp. 313–324). Redwood City, Calif.: Addison-Wesley.

Kauffman, S. (August 1991). Antichaos and adaptation. *Sci. Am.*, 265(2): 64–70.

Sarle, W. S. & Net Poohbahs (1994). Kangaroos and training neural networks. FAQ list available from `ftp://ftp.sas.com/pub/neural/kangaroos`.

Wills, C. (1989). *The wisdom of the genes.* New York: Basic Books.

Wolpert, D. H. & Macready, W. G. (1995). No free lunch theorems for search. Technical Report SFI-TR-95-02-010, The Santa Fe Institute, Santa Fe, N.M.

Epilogue

Recursion, which is the hallmark of computation, is an integral part of the structural and functional self-similarity of fractals and chaos. Parallel collections of simple things possess a similar form of recursion that comes about from local interactions. When interactions are permitted to change, systems can display collective behavior that is computationally profound.

The line between computability and incomputability defines a spectrum in which all natural phenomena exist. Things that reside at either of the two extremes are usually uninteresting because they are either too ordered or too disordered. Things in between the two operational extremes display a stunning variety of sophistication, complexity, and beauty that is directly related to the computable properties of these systems.

Because of the power of computation and the ubiquity of computational-like features in natural systems, a mixture of computability and incomputability forms an interface between the hierarchical partitions of natural systems. This, in turn, has deep implications for how closely humanity can understand nature.

24 Duality and Dichotomy

When two texts, or two assertions, perhaps two ideas, are in contradiction, be ready to reconcile them rather than cancel one by the other; regard them as two different facets, or two successive stages, of the same reality, a reality convincingly human just because it is complex.
— Marguerite Yourcenar

To see a World in a grain of Sand,
And a Heaven in a Wild Flower,
Hold Infinity in the palm of your hand,
And Eternity in an hour.
— William Blake

IN THE VARIOUS contexts of philosophy, religion, and science, humans have shown a fondness for classifying things in terms of absolutes, such as, black and white, good and evil, order and chaos, yin and yang, and so on. Absolutes are easy to comprehend and comfortable to our minds because they remove ambiguities and reinforce a sense of understanding. To be sure, there clearly exist domains in which binary rules not only work but also capture the essence of that which is being described. But for many things—and perhaps most things—reality blends the black-and-white absolutes into a beautiful melody of gray.

Just as life depends on an environment that allows water to exist in solid, liquid, and gaseous forms, so nature's most amazing and beautifully complex creations must exist at the juncture between computability and incomputability. On these two extremes scientific understanding is best pursued in the form of theory and experimentation, respectively. But at the interface between the two, both extreme approaches must give way to the grayness of reality.

In this final chapter, we will pull together all of the loose threads from the earlier chapters and attempt to reconcile conflicting themes into a single message. We will first consider issues of Chapter 1 and reexamine some of the commonalities that can be found in the diverse topics that have been covered in this book. Afterward, we

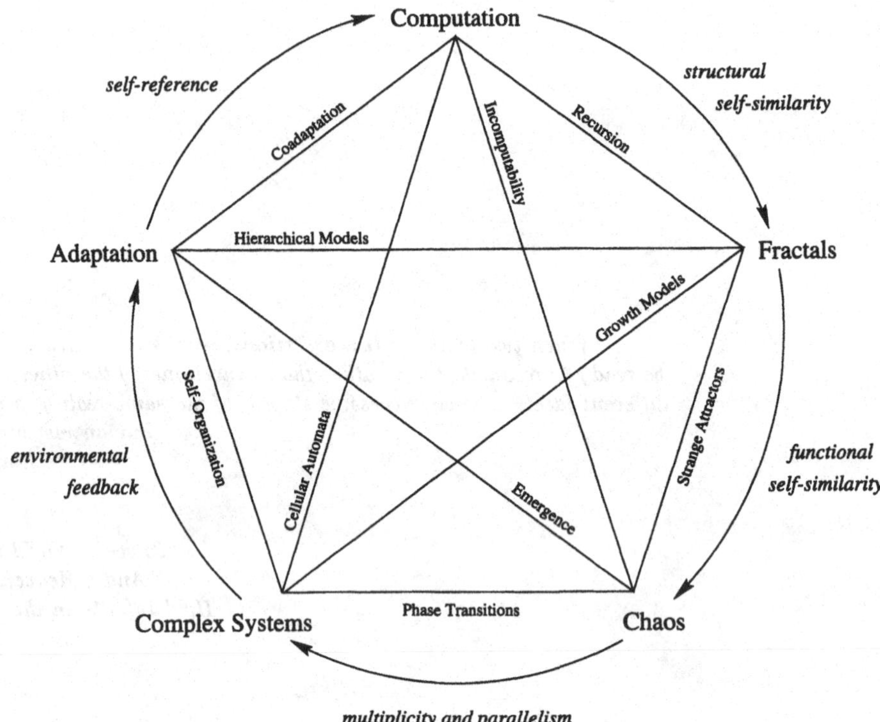

Figure 24.1 The relationships among computation, fractals, chaos, complex systems, and adaptation

will consider the boundary between computability and incomputability as it applies to the contents of this book and, in particular, the topics covered in the postscript chapters. We will then finish with a speculative discussion on how the grayness of this fundamental boundary is an integral part of the beauty of nature.

24.1 Web of Connections

Continuing with some of the themes first introduced in Chapter 1, the properties of recursion, parallelism, and adaptation play an interesting role as attributes of natural systems. For example, in order for the universe to move coherently from one state to the next, the universe must "remember" previous states, which means that recursion (and its close cousins, feedback and iteration) exists as a form of memory that binds locally occurring moments in time. Multiplicity and parallelism play a similar role that has to do with binding locally occurring points in space.

With this in mind, we can see how mixtures of recursion and multiplicity partially define and differentiate computation, fractals, chaos, complex systems, and adaptation. Figure 24.1, is a slightly revised version of Figure 1.1 that has a couple of extra labels to illustrate some of the relationships uncovered between the book parts. Starting from a computational framework, fractals are special "programs" that build self-similar structures. Chaotic systems are similar to fractals but also contain functional self-similarity that occurs at different scales. By adding multiplicity and parallelism to nonlinear systems, complex systems can be formed with only local interactions. And when complex systems are coupled to their environment with a feedback mechanism, systems can form implicit models of the environment, which is the basis of adaptation. Finally, when an adaptive system becomes so complex that it receives feedback from itself, a self-referential system is created that can potentially have all of the strengths and weaknesses of the computational basis that we started out with.

In this way, primitive computational systems can beget more sophisticated computational systems that build on previously built pieces. Looking at the organization of nature, we find that most interesting things are composed of smaller interesting things. This is evident when we consider that societies, economies, and ecosystems are made of animals, humans, and species, which are made of cells that consist of amazingly complicated organelles, which are themselves composed of an elaborate ensemble of autocatalytic chemical reactions. Each level is nearly a universe in itself, since all of them use and support types of structural and functional self-similarity, multiplicity and parallelism, recursion and feedback, and self-reference. Nature, then, appears to be a hierarchy of computational systems that are forever on the edge between computability and incomputability.

24.2 Interfaces to Hierarchies

We have seen in many examples that the novelty of a system is related to the indeterminacy of the computation that it performs. Static systems are boring because they settle down to steady-state behavior. Overactive systems lack the coherence to retain consistent patterns from one time step to the next. In between are systems that are forever changing but have a consistent underlying structure or function. Such nonequilibrium systems are analogous to a whirlpool of water; while the molecules of a whirlpool are forever moving and changing, the motion of the whirlpool contains a sufficient amount of constancy that it has functional persistence.

This behavior, which is best seen as being on the border between computability and incomputability, acts as an interface between the components of hierarchically organized structure. Tables 24.1 and 24.2 summarize some of the phenomena that can be characterized in this way. As can be seen in the table, this interface between computability and incomputability is relevant to mathematical, fractal, chaotic,

	Computable	**Partially Computable**	**Incomputable**
Sets	recursive	RE and CO-RE	not RE and not CO-RE
Numbers	rational	computable irrational	incomputable
Programs	trivially (never) halt	possibly halt	—
Proofs	true or false	profound statements	unprovable
NP-Complete Problems*	underconstrained	critically constrained	overconstrained
Deterministic Geometry	Euclidean	deterministic fractal	—
Stochastic Geometry	—	stochastic fractal	pure noise
AC	compressible	possibly incompressible	incompressible
Mandelbrot Set	white regions	border regions	black regions
Continuous Dynamics	fixed point or periodic	chaotic	high-dimensional chaos or stochastic
Discrete Dynamics	regular from over-sampling	complex at mid-sampling	irregular from under-sampling
Attractors	integral dimensions	strange	infinite dimensional
Mater*	solid	liquid	gas

Table 24.1 "Novelty" as a function of computability, part 1: Entries with a ⋆ are merely analogous. Not all entries listed as being "Partially Computable" are themselves technically incomputable, but instead represent a region between overly simple things and overly complex things.

complex, and adaptive systems. In each case, the most interesting types of behavior fall somewhere between what is computable and what is incomputable.

This raises an interesting point regarding the levels at which science tries to discover patterns in nature. The bottom-up reductionist approach is to describe the functions of the lowest-level structures and to infer the structure and function of higher-level things based on the known rules. This is a perfect approach when things are computable and can be described in a closed analytical form. In such simple systems, all higher-level behaviors can be predicted from a basic set of rules.

The top-down and somewhat holistic approach is to describe things from the opposite direction. Experiments are made and observations are noted. From this

	Computable	**Partially Computable**	**Incomputable**
Wolfram CA	class I or II	class IV	class III
Langton's λ	$\lambda < 1/3$	$\lambda \approx 1/2$	$\lambda > 2/3$
Agent Interactions	globally coordinated or always cooperative	locally coordinated or competitive and cooperative	uncoordinated or always competitive
NK Nets	$K = 1$	$K = 2$	$2 < K \leq N$
Sandpiles	flat and stable	critical	tall and unstable
Economics*	communism	free but regulated	unrestrained
Governments*	dictatorial	democracy	anarchy
Patterns	consistent	hidden order	inconsistent
Models	not self-referential	coadaptive or recurrent	hopelessly self-referential
Search Methods	local or greedy	hybrid	exhaustive
Search Spaces	smooth	complex structured	pathological

Table 24.2 "Novelty" as a function of computability, part 2: Entries with a ⋆ are merely analogous. Not all entries listed as being "Partially Computable" are themselves technically incomputable, but instead represent a region between overly simple things and overly complex things.

point, one is faced with the difficult task of deriving lower-level rules from upper-level behaviors. While both methods of investigation have a role in science (and in all scientific domains), the interface between levels of organization may be such that neither method is really up to the job. For novel phenomena, simulation becomes a crucial form of investigation.

24.3 Limitations on Knowledge

Figure 24.2 illustrates how science interacts with the universe. On the left side of the figure are natural processes that are recurrently coupled to themselves. On the right is human understanding that attempts to model the natural world. Experimentation consists of manipulating the environment and observing the changes that come about. Theorizing is the process of manipulating models to see if they make accurate predictions of future observations. Simulation resides between the two, and manipulates both models and environments.

As stated in the last postscript, Gödel's incompleteness result tells us that no theory or model can be used to make all of the predictions that we would like.

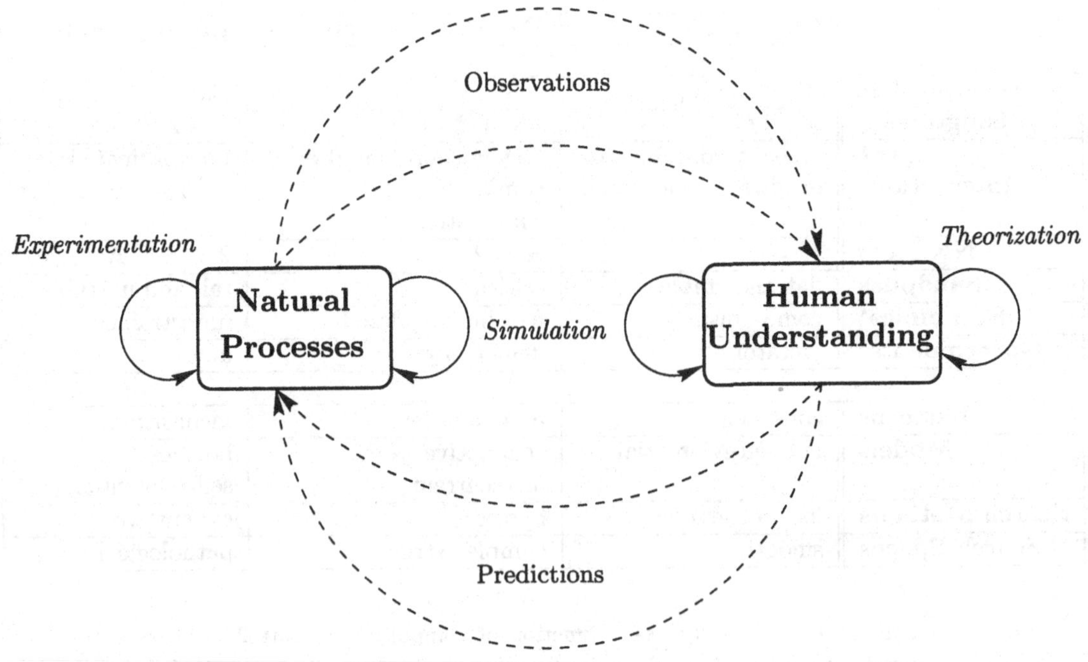

Figure 24.2 The universe of natural processes related to scientific understanding

Chaitin's extension of Turing's Halting Problem proves that there is no reliable way to build theories and models. Turing's incomputability shows us that simulations and natural processes may never halt, but also that we may never be able to prove this fact. Together, these three results rigorously prove that there are many things about nature that we will never be able to know with any amount of effort via experimentation, theorization, and simulation. This is truly wonderful.

Think back to Chapter 8, where we first constructed the Mandelbrot set. White pixels, that is, the background portions, correspond to points that we know must diverge under the Mandelbrot iterations, while black pixels correspond to points that we *suspect* will never diverge. While every white point corresponds to something that we are certain about, there are some black points (i.e., the main kidney-shaped section) that we can also color with certainty. On the border are black points that we merely suspect are colored correctly. It is impossible for us to determine the correct color of these points with perfect certainty. It is this region, between computability and incomputability, that contains all of the novelty and beauty of the M-set. If the rules for determining the colors of the M-set points lacked this pathological quality, the M-set would not be what it is. Instead, it would repeat itself, or worse yet, simply stop yielding any patterns. But as it is, the M-set contains an infinite amount of complexity and beauty that can never be exhausted.

We could make similar arguments about all of the other topics covered in the book. For example, these issues, as they pertain to mathematics and the theory of computation, mean that there is an infinite supply of programs and mathematical statements that will forever be just on the threshold of being understood. As soon as we understand them, there will remain a newly discovered and infinite collection of mysterious programs and mathematical statements. For the case of dynamical systems, while we may always make further progress in understanding particular systems, there will always be some processes that lie just beyond our abilities to predict. Similarly, for complex systems, parallel collections of simple nonlinear objects will always be able to produce behavior that is emergent and novel from the point of view that the collective behavior is far more interesting than the individual behaviors. And for adaptive systems, as long as perfect stability is never achieved, adaptation will build more complex models of environments, which further increases the complexity of the environments as well as the methods of adaptation.

Nature, being composed of all of these things, will always have novelty, richness, and beauty that can never be exhausted. As with the M-set, we can appreciate nature's beauty precisely because we can simulate it, but only to limited accuracy. If all natural phenomena were either perfectly describable or absolutely indescribable, not only would they be uninteresting, but life would be impossible.

Source Code Notes

The process of preparing programs for a digital computer is especially attractive, not only because it can be economically and scientifically rewarding, but also because it can be an aesthetic experience much like composing poetry or music.
— Donald E. Knuth

WHILE READING this book, you will have the opportunity to duplicate almost all of the figures and results by experimenting with the supplied programs. A link to an FTP site that contains the source code for the programs can be found at this book's homepage, located at:

```
http://mitpress.mit.edu/0262062003
```

The source code is written entirely in C and is known to work under Solaris, Linux, and Windows NT. This appendix gives a brief introduction on how to use the programs, tells where to find additional documentation, and gives a brief description of each program.

Input Interface In general, all programs have a command-line interface, meaning that all runtime parameters for the programs are specified on the same line in which the command name is typed. Command-line options will usually take a value that is either INTEGER, DOUBLE (a double precision floating-point number), or a STRING. An option that is a SWITCH takes no value since specifying the option on the command-line toggles an internal value in the program between "on" and "off." For example, the command:

```
prog -val 3.1415 -name "PI" -number 5 -flip
```

executes the program named `prog` and sets three value options (`-val`, `-name` and `-number`) to three values appropriate to their type and directly following the options on the command-line. The final option, named `-flip`, is a SWITCH and, therefore, takes no value.

`-term`	Driver	Notes
`vga`	Linux VGA	for Linux systems without X Windows
`x11`	X Windows	for most UNIX systems
`win`	Windows NT	may also work under Windows 95
`ps`	PostScript	best for line plots saved to a file
`pgm`	PGM	best for pixel plots saved to a file
`none`	—	inhibit all graphics
`raw`	—	outputs (x, y, color) triplets in ASCII

Table 25.1 Program terminal drivers

In no case does any program take interactive input. Some programs may need to operate on an entire set of input data (such as patterns to be remembered by a Hopfield network), in which case, the data is specified by a STRING option that denotes the input data filename.

Output Interface The output of a program is either plain text or graphical. If a program displays graphics (as most of them do), then you need to specify a value for the **`-term`** option that is appropriate for your computer system. This option tells the program which of the graphic terminal drivers to use. Table 25.1 contains a list of possible values to use with the **`-term`** option. Most programs that display graphics will have two more options named **`-width`** and **`-height`** that are used to specify the size of the graphics device. Additionally, the **`-inv`** SWITCH option will force reverse video, and **`-xmag`** can be used to increase the size of the X Windows display without increasing the resolution.

The PostScript and PGM graphic drivers do not actually display graphics but write the contents of the graphics in the specified file format. To save the output, the standard output of the program should be redirected to a file.

For programs that do not display graphics, some output may be sent to the standard output and standard error text streams. Periodic text output (such as the current error level of a neural network being trained) is usually sent to standard error and the final output of the program (such as the data points for a generated chaotic time series) is sent to standard output. Thus, by redirecting the standard output stream, the periodic output will still be displayed while the final output of the program can be stored in a file.

Documentation A minimal program description is given at the end of the chapters where the programs are mentioned. Detailed documentation is in the software distribution in the format of UNIX-style manual pages and HTML web documents. Moreover, programmers may wish to inspect the source code itself, since all of the documentation is automatically derived from the source code.

Program Descriptions The programs below are listed in the order in which they appear in the text.

`stutter` interprets simple lisp and only understands `car`, `cdr`, `cons`, `if`, `set`, `equal`, `quote`, and `lambda`, but is still Turing-complete. Uses stop-and-copy garbage collection and has an adjustable heap size. Examples that implement integer and floating-point arithmetic are provided. There is even an example `stutter` function to compute the square root of a floating-point argument with nothing but the primitives listed above.

`diffuse` Generates diffusion limited aggregate growth that looks like coral.

`lsys` Builds L-system fractals. Accepts multiple rules so that complicated fractals (such as a Penrose tiling) can be expressed. Great for generating plantlike fractals.

`mrcm` Uses the Multiple Reduction Copy Machine algorithm to generate affine fractals. Accepts an arbitrary number of transformations. Good for making snowflakes and mosaic patterns.

`ifs` Similar to `mrcm` but uses Iterated Functional Systems for finer granularity.

`mandel` Plots the famous Mandelbrot set. There are options for the displayed coordinates, zoom level, coloring schemes, etc.

`julia` Generates Julia sets, which are related to the Mandelbrot set. Has options similar to `mandel`.

`gen1d` Generates a time series from a one-dimensional map. Nothing fancy; it just shows how chaos can be seen in simple systems.

`bifur1d` Plots a bifurcation diagram for a one-dimensional map to illustrate how a change in a single parameter can move a system from fixed-point behavior, to periodic, and finally to chaos. Different regions can be zoomed in on.

`phase1d` Plots the phase space and trajectories of a one-dimensional map. Showing trajectories in the phase space more clearly illustrates why fixed-points and limit cycles occur. This can also be used to show the exponential divergence of nearby trajectories.

`henon` Plots the phase space of the Hénon map, a two-dimensional system with a fractal shape. Different regions can be zoomed in on.

henbif Plots a bifurcation diagram for the Hénon system. This is similar to `bifur1d` but shows that bifurcations apply to multidimensional systems as well.

henwarp Takes a square of a specified area and "warps" it a fixed number of times by the Hénon system. This illustrates the stretching and folding motion of chaotic systems as well as shows how points within an attractor's basin of attraction are eventually forced into a strange attractor.

lorenz Plots the phase space of the Lorenz system, a three-dimensional system described by differential equations with a fractal shape. Both plain phase-space plots and delayed state-space plots are possible.

rossler Similar to **lorenz**, but uses the Rossler system.

mg Plots a two-dimensional embedding of the phase space of the Mackey-Glass system, a delay-differential system, with arbitrary parameters.

gsw Simulates an individual-based three-species predator-prey ecosystem according to the specified parameters. The three species consist of plants, herbivores, and carnivores (grass, sheep, and wolves; hence the name, **gsw**). Updates are done synchronously, and each species has several parameters which can control their life cycles, from the ability to give birth, to the likelihood of starvation. Population statistics of the three species can be calculated over a subset of the entire grid.

predprey Plots the phase space of a three-species predator-prey system (described by differential equations) which may be fractal in shape. Both plain phase-space plots and delayed state-space plots are possible.

lotka Simulates the two-species Lotka-Volterra predator-prey system with a second-order Euler's method. This program serves as a simple introduction to differential equations.

hencon Controls the Hénon system with the OGY control law for arbitrary choices of the system parameters. The control law is analytically calculated based on the system parameters. The user can select times in which control is turned on and off so that time-to-control and transients can be observed. Gaussian noise can be injected into the system.

ca Simulates arbitrary one-dimensional cellular automata with an arbitrary choice of simulation parameters. Random rules can be generated and used with a desired lambda value.

life Simulates Conway's Game of Life with an arbitrary set of initial conditions. Input files need to be in the PBM file format.

`hp` Simulates and plots the time evolution of the hodgepodge machine according to specified parameters. With a proper choice of parameters, this system resembles the Belousov-Zhabotinsky reaction which forms self-perpetuating spirals in a lattice.

`termites` Simulates a population of termites which do a random walk while possibly carrying a wood chip. Under normal circumstances, the termites will self-organize and move the wood chips into piles without a global leader. The termites' behavior is dictated by the following set of rules: If a termite is not carrying anything and it bumps into a chip, then it picks it up, reverses direction, and continues with the random walk. If it is carrying a chip and bumps into another, it drops the chip, turns around, and starts walking again. Otherwise, it just does a random walk whether it is carrying a chip or not.

`vants` Simulates and plots a population of generalized virtual ants (vants). The behavior of the vants is determined by a bit string with length equal to the number of states that each cell in the vants' grid world can take. If a vant walks on a cell in state s, then the vant turns right if the s'th bit of the rule string is 1 and left if it is 0. As it leaves the cell the vant changes the state of the old cell to $(s+1)$ modulo the number of states.

`boids` Simulates a flock of boids according to rules that determine their individual behaviors as well as the "physics" of their universe. A boid greedily attempts to apply four rules with respect to its neighbors: It wants to fly in the same direction, be in the center of the local cluster of boids, avoid collisions with boids too close, and maintain a clear view ahead by skirting around others that block its view. Changing these rules can make the boids behave like birds, gnats, bees, fish, or magnetic particles.

`sipd` Simulates and plots the spatial iterated Prisoner's Dilemma over time according to the specified parameters. Each cell in a grid plays a specific strategy against its eight neighbors for several rounds. At the end of the last round, each cell copies the strategy of its most successful neighbor, which is then used for the next time step. Possible strategies include "Always-Cooperate," "Always-Defect", "Random," "Pavlov," and "Tit-for-Tat."

`eipd` Simulates the ecological iterated Prisoner's Dilemma over time according to the specified parameters. At every time step the population of each strategy is calculated as a function of the expected scores earned against all strategies weighted by the populations of the opponents. Possible strategies include "Always-Cooperate," "Always-Defect," "Random," "Pavlov," and "Tit-for-Tat."

`assoc` Attempts to reconstruct a corrupted image with a McCulloch-Pitts feedback neural network that acts as an associative memory. The weights of the network are determined via Hebb's rule after reading in multiple patterns. Weights can be pruned either by size, by locality, or randomly.

`hopfield` Solves a task assignment problem via a Hopfield neural network while plotting the activations of the neurons over time. The program uses the k-out-of-n rule for setting the external inputs and synapse strength of the neurons.

`gastring` Uses a genetic algorithm to breed strings that match a user-specified target string. This program illustrates how GAs can perform a type of stochastic search in a space of discrete objects. Reproduction of strings entails crossover and mutation with strings being selected based on fitness.

`gabump` Uses a genetic algorithm to find the maximum of a single-humped function that is centered at a user-specified location. This program serves as an example of how GAs can be used to optimize functions which take a floating-point argument.

`gasurf` Uses a genetic algorithm to find the maximum of a multi-humped function. This program serves as an example of how GAs can be used to optimize functions which take multiple floating-point arguments.

`gatask` Uses a genetic algorithm to solve a task assignment problem with user-specified costs. This program illustrates how GAs can perform combinatorial optimization. Reproduction of strings entails special crossover and mutation operations which preserve constraints on the form of feasible solutions.

`gaipd` Uses a genetic algorithm to evolve iterated Prisoner's Dilemma (IPD) strategies according to user-specified constraints. This program illustrates how GAs can demonstrate coevolution since IPD strategies can only be successful within the context of their likely opponents.

`zcs` Adapts a zeroth level classifier system (ZCS) with the implicit bucket brigade algorithm and a genetic algorithm so that the ZCS can traverse a two-dimensional terrain, avoid obstacles, and find food. At the beginning of each step the ZCS is placed at a random location of its world. It interacts with its environment until it finds food, which yields a reward. The simulation then restarts with the ZCS placed at a new random location. The progress of the ZCS is continuously plotted, while the statistics on the time to find food are calculated and displayed. At the end of the simulation the classifiers that make up the final ZCS are saved to a log file.

`zcscup` Trains a zeroth level classifier system (ZCS) to solve the cups problem with the implicit bucket brigade algorithm and a genetic algorithm. Solving this problem requires the ZCS to learn to remember important features from previous states, which makes this problem very challenging. The ZCS always starts in the same initial position. It interacts with its environment until it finds both cups, which (only at that point) yields a reward. The simulation then restarts with the ZCS placed at the original location. The progress of the ZCS is continuously plotted, while the statistics on the time to find both cups are calculated and displayed. At the end of the simulation the classifiers that make up the final ZCS are saved to a log file.

`mlp` Trains a multilayer perceptron with a single hidden layer of neurons on a set of data contained in a file using the backpropagation learning algorithm with momentum. Output units can be linear or sigmoidal, allowing you to model both discrete and continuous output target values.

Glossary

A

Activation The time-varying value that is the output of a NEURON.

Activation Function A FUNCTION that translates a NEURON'S NET INPUT to an ACTIVATION value.

Adaptive Subject to ADAPTATION; can change over time to improve fitness or accuracy.

Adaptation An internal change in a SYSTEM that mirrors an external event in the system's ENVIRONMENT.

Affine An equation that can be written in terms of MATRIX-VECTOR multiplication and vector addition.

Agent See AUTONOMOUS AGENT.

AI An abbreviation for ARTIFICIAL INTELLIGENCE.

Algorithm A detailed and unambiguous sequence of instructions that describes how a COMPUTATION is to proceed and can be implemented as a PROGRAM.

Algorithmic Complexity The size of the smallest PROGRAM that can produce a particular sequence of numbers. Regular patterns have low algorithmic complexity and RANDOM sequences have high algorithmic complexity.

Always Cooperate A PRISONER'S DILEMMA STRATEGY that cooperates with its opponent under all circumstances (the exact opposite of ALWAYS DEFECT).

Always Defect A PRISONER'S DILEMMA STRATEGY that never cooperates with its opponent under any circumstance (the exact opposite of ALWAYS COOPERATE).

Analog Having a CONTINUOUS value.

Analytical Can be symbolically represented in a closed form that does not require any of the complex aspects of a PROGRAM such as an ITERATIVE sum.

Analytical Solution An exact solution to a problem that can be calculated symbolically by manipulating equations (unlike a NUMERICAL SOLUTION).

Arms Race Two or more species experience ADAPTATION to one another in a COEVOLUTIONARY manner. This often seen in PREDATOR-PREY SYSTEMS.

Artificial Intelligence The science of making computers do interesting things that humans do effortlessly.

Artificial Life The study of life processes within the confines of a computer.

Associative Memory Memory that can be referenced by content, as opposed to location. HOPFIELD NETWORKS will act as associative memories when trained with the HEBBIAN LEARNING rule.

Asynchronous Describes events that occur independently of each other but on a similar time scale.

Attractor A characterization of the long-term behavior of a DISSIPATIVE DYNAMICAL SYSTEM. Over long periods of time, the STATE SPACE of some DYNAMICAL SYSTEMS will contract toward this region. Attractors may be FIXED POINTS, PERIODIC, QUASIPERIODIC, or CHAOTIC. They may also be STABLE or UNSTABLE.

Autonomous Agent An entity with limited perception of its ENVIRONMENT that can process information to calculate an action so as to be goal-seeking on a local scale. A BOID is an example of an autonomous agent.

Axiom A STATEMENT that is assumed to be true and can later be used along with THEOREMS to prove other theorems. Also, the starting configuration of an L-SYSTEM.

B

Backpropagation An ALGORITHM for efficiently calculating the error GRADIENT of a NEURAL NETWORK, which can then be used as the basis of LEARNING. Backpropagation is equivalent to the DELTA RULE for PERCEPTRONS, but can also calculate appropriate WEIGHT changes for the HIDDEN LAYER weights of a MULTILAYER PERCEPTRON by generalizing the notion of an error correction term. In the simplest case, backpropagation is a type of STEEPEST DESCENT in the SEARCH SPACE of the network weights, and it will usually CONVERGE to a LOCAL MINIMUM.

Basin of Attraction A region of STATE SPACE in which all included states of a DYNAMICAL SYSTEM ultimately lead into the ATTRACTOR.

Bias See THRESHOLD.

Bifurcation The splitting of a single mode of a SYSTEM'S behavior into two new modes. This usually occurs as a FUNCTION of a CONTINUOUSLY varying CONTROL parameter. A cascade of bifurcations will usually precede the onset of CHAOS.

Binary Written in a form that uses only 0s and 1s. A STRING of BITS.

Bit The smallest unit of information; the answer to a yes/no question; the outcome of a coin toss; a 0 or a 1.

Boid An AUTONOMOUS AGENT that behaves like a simplified bird but will display flocking patterns in the presence of other boids.

Boolean Taking only 0/1, true/false, yes/no values.

Bottom-Up A description that uses the lower-level details to explain higher-level patterns; related to REDUCTIONISM.

Brownian Motion A form of RANDOMNESS that is the result of cumulatively adding WHITE NOISE, to yield a RANDOM WALK pattern.

Bucket Brigade Algorithm A LEARNING ALGORITHM that is a method for adjusting the STRENGTHS of the CLASSIFIERS of a CLASSIFIER SYSTEM. "Winning" classifiers pay a portion of their earnings to other classifiers that assisted them in being activated, similar to an economic SYSTEM.

Byte Eight BITS. In programming, often used to store a single text character.

C

Cantor Set A simple FRACTAL SET composed of an UNCOUNTABLE INFINITY of dust-like points, but that also has 0 measure (meaning that the sum width of all points is 0). The Cantor set is constructed by removing the middle third of a unit line segment, and then RECURSIVELY removing the middle third of any remaining line segments, for an infinite number of steps.

Cellular Automaton (CA) A DISCRETE DYNAMICAL SYSTEM that is composed of an array of cells, each of which behaves like a FINITE-STATE AUTOMATON. All interactions are local, with the next state of a cell being a FUNCTION of the current state of itself and its neighbors. CONWAY'S GAME OF LIFE is a CA.

Chaos/Chaotic Irregular motion of a DYNAMICAL SYSTEM that is DETERMINISTIC, SENSITIVE to initial conditions, and impossible to predict in the long term with anything less than an infinite and perfect representation of ANALOG values.

Chomsky Hierarchy Four classes of languages (or computing machines) that have increasing complexity: regular (FINITE-STATE AUTOMATA), context-free (push-down automata), context-sensitive (linear bounded automata), and RECURSIVE (TURING MACHINES).

Classifier A rule that is part of a CLASSIFIER SYSTEM and has a condition that must be matched before its MESSAGE (or action) can be posted (or effected). The STRENGTH of a classifier determines the likelihood that it can outbid other classifiers if more than one condition is matched.

Classifier System An ADAPTIVE SYSTEM similar to a POST PRODUCTION SYSTEM that contains many "if ... then" rules called CLASSIFIERS. The state of the ENVIRONMENT is encoded as a MESSAGE by a DETECTOR and placed on the MESSAGE LIST from which the condition portion of the classifiers can be matched. "Winning" classifiers can then post their own messages to the message list, ultimately forming a type of COMPUTATION that may result in a message being translated into an action by an EFFECTOR. The STRENGTHS of the classifiers are modified by the BUCKET BRIGADE ALGORITHM, and new rules can be introduced via a GENETIC ALGORITHM.

Coevolution Two or more entities experience EVOLUTION in response to one another. Due to FEEDBACK mechanisms, this often results in a biological ARMS RACE.

Complement A SET composed of all elements that are not members of another set.

Combinatorial Optimization A class of problems in which the number of candidate solutions is combinatorial in size. Each possible solution has an associated cost. The goal is to find the solution with the lowest cost. Because of the vast numbers involved, explicit SEARCH an entire SEARCH SPACE is not always possible.

Complete Describes a FORMAL SYSTEM in which all STATEMENTS can be proved as being true or false. Most interesting formal systems are not complete, as proved in GÖDEL'S INCOMPLETENESS THEOREM.

Complex Number A number that has a REAL component and an IMAGINARY component and is characterized as a point on a plane (instead of the REAL NUMBER line).

Complex System A collection of many simple NONLINEAR units that operate in PARALLEL and interact locally with each other so as to produce EMERGENT behavior.

Complexity An ill-defined term that means many things to many people. Complex things are neither RANDOM nor regular, but hover somewhere in between. Intuitively, complexity is a measure of how interesting something is. Other types of complexity may be well defined; see the index for other references.

Compressible Having a description that is smaller than itself; not RANDOM; possessing regularity.

Computable Expressible as a yes/no question that can be answered in any case by a computer in finite time.

Computation The realization of a PROGRAM in a computer.

Connectivity The amount of interaction in a SYSTEM, the structure of the WEIGHTS in a NEURAL NETWORK, or the relative number of edges in a GRAPH.

Conservative System A DYNAMICAL SYSTEM that preserves the volume of its STATE SPACE under motion and, therefore, does not display the types of behavior found in DISSIPATIVE SYSTEMS.

Consistence In FORMAL SYSTEMS, having the property that all STATEMENTS are either true or false.

Continuous Taking a REAL value, i.e., not strictly DISCRETE. DYNAMICAL SYSTEMS may operate in continuous time or space.

Control Exerting actions to manipulate a SYSTEM or ENVIRONMENT in a goal-seeking manner.

Convergence For computers, halting with an answer; for DYNAMICAL SYSTEMS, falling into an ATTRACTOR; for SEARCHES (e.g., BACKPROPAGATION and GENETIC ALGORITHMS), finding a location that cannot be improved upon; for infinite summations, approaching a definite value.

Conway's Game of Life A CELLULAR AUTOMATON rule set that operates on a two-dimensional grid. Each cell changes its state according to the states of its eight nearest neighbors: dead cells come alive with exactly three live neighbors, and cells die if they have anything but two or three neighbors. The Game of Life can display complex patterns such as GLIDERS, FISH, and GLIDER GUNS, and is also capable of UNIVERSAL COMPUTATION.

Co-Recursively Enumerable (CO-RE) The COMPLEMENT of a SET that can be RECURSIVELY ENUMERATED.

Countable Infinity Having the same number of objects as the SET of NATURAL NUMBERS.

Crossover A genetic operator that splices information from two or more parents to form a composite offspring that has genetic material from all parents.

D

Darwinism The theory of EVOLUTION as proposed by Charles Darwin, which combined VARIATION of INHERITABLE traits with NATURAL SELECTION. After the discovery of the physical mechanism of genetics, this was further refined into NEO-DARWINISM.

Delta Rule The PERCEPTRON LEARNING rule that specifies that WEIGHT changes should be proportional to the product of a weight's input and the error (or delta) term for the perceptron.

Derivative An expression that characterizes how the output of a FUNCTION changes as the input is varied. Unlike INTEGRALS, derivatives can be calculated in an ANALYTICAL manner very easily.

Decision Problem A problem in which all questions take the form "Is something a member of a particular SET?" and all answers are either "yes" or "no."

Detector A sensor that translates the state of a CLASSIFIER'S ENVIRONMENT into a MESSAGE that is suitable for posting to the MESSAGE LIST of the CLASSIFIER SYSTEM.

Determinant A quantity of a MATRIX that characterizes the amount of expansion or contraction that the matrix inflicts on a VECTOR when that vector is multiplied by the matrix.

Deterministic Occurring in a non-RANDOM manner such that the next state of a SYSTEM depends only on prior states of the system or the ENVIRONMENT. Perfect knowledge of previous states implies perfect knowledge of the next state.

Diagonal Matrix A MATRIX that has 0 entries along all nondiagonal entries, i.e., only the main diagonal may have non-zero values.

Difference Equation An equation that describes how something changes in DISCRETE time steps. NUMERICAL SOLUTIONS to INTEGRALS are usually realized as difference equations.

Differential Equation A description of how something CONTINUOUSLY changes over time. Some differential equations can have an ANALYTICALLY SOLUTION such that all future states can be known without SIMULATION of the time evolution of the SYSTEM. However, most can have a NUMERICAL SOLUTION with only limited accuracy.

Differentiation The act of calculating a DERIVATIVE; the inverse operation of calculating an INTEGRAL.

Diffusion Limited Aggregation A type of STOCHASTIC FRACTAL formed by particles floating about in a RANDOM manner until they stick to something solid.

Discrete Taking only non-CONTINUOUS values, e.g., BOOLEAN or NATURAL NUMBERS.

Dissipative System A DYNAMICAL SYSTEM that contains internal friction that deforms the structure of its ATTRACTOR, thus making motion such as FIXED POINTS, LIMIT CYCLES, QUASIPERIODICITY, and CHAOS possible. Dissipative systems often have internal structure despite being far from EQUILIBRIUM, like a whirlpool that preserves its basic form despite being in the midst of constant change.

Diverge For ALGORITHMS or computers, to run forever and never halt; for ITERATIVE SYSTEMS (like the equations for the MANDELBROT SET), reaching a state such that all future states explode in size.

Dot Product The INNER PRODUCT of two VECTORS.

Dynamical System A SYSTEM that changes over time according to a set of fixed rules that determine how one state of the system moves to another state.

Dynamics/Dynamical Pertaining to the change in behavior of a SYSTEM over time.

E

Ecology The study of the relationships and interactions between organisms and ENVIRONMENTS.

Ecosystem A biological SYSTEM consisting of many organisms from different species.

Edge of Chaos The hypothesis that many natural SYSTEMS tend toward DYNAMICAL behavior that borders static patterns and the CHAOTIC regime.

Effector The part of a CLASSIFIER SYSTEM that can translate MESSAGES into actions that can manipulate a SYSTEM or an ENVIRONMENT.

Eigenvalue The change in length that occurs when the corresponding EIGENVECTOR is multiplied by its MATRIX.

Eigenvector A unit length VECTOR that retains its direction when multiplied to the MATRIX that it corresponds to. An $(n \times n)$ matrix can have as many as n unique eigenvectors, each of which will have its own EIGENVALUE.

Embedding A method of taking a SCALAR TIME SERIES and using delayed snapshots of the values at fixed time intervals in the past so that the DYNAMICS of the underlying SYSTEM can be observed as a FUNCTION of the previously observed states.

Emergent Refers to a property of a collection of simple subunits that comes about through the interactions of the subunits and is not a property of any single subunit. For example, the organization of an ant colony is said to "emerge" from the interactions of the lower-level behaviors of the ants, and not from any single ant.

Usually, the emergent behavior is unanticipated and cannot be directly deduced from the lower-level behaviors. COMPLEX SYSTEMS are usually emergent.

Entropy A measure of a SYSTEM'S degree of RANDOMNESS or disorder.

Environment If that which is under study is a SYSTEM, then the rest of the world is the environment.

Equilibrium A state of a SYSTEM that, if not subjected to PERTURBATION, will remain unchanged.

Ergodic The property of a DYNAMICAL SYSTEM such that all regions of a STATE SPACE are visited with similar frequency and that all regions will be revisited (within a small proximity) if given enough time.

Euclidean Pertaining to standard geometry, i.e., points, lines, planes, volumes, squares, cubes, triangles, etc.

Euler's Method The simplest method of obtaining a NUMERICAL SOLUTION of a DIFFERENTIAL EQUATION. There are many other numerical techniques that are more accurate; however, an ANALYTICAL SOLUTION (i.e., a closed form of an INTEGRAL) is always preferred but not always possible.

Evolution A process operating on populations that involves VARIATION among individuals, traits being INHERITABLE, and a level of FITNESS for individuals that is a FUNCTION of the possessed traits. Over relatively long periods of time, the distribution of inheritable traits will tend to reflect the fitness that the traits convey to the individual; thus, evolution acts as a filter that selects fitness-yielding traits over other traits.

Evolutionary Stable Strategy (ESS) In GAME THEORY and biology, a STRATEGY that, when possessed by an entire population, results in an EQUILIBRIUM such that MUTATION of the strategy can never result in an improvement for an individual. ALWAYS DEFECT is an ESS, while ALWAYS COOPERATE is not.

Excitatory Refers to a neural SYNAPSE or WEIGHT that is positive such that activity in the source NEURON encourages activity in the connected neuron; the opposite of INHIBITORY.

Experimentation One process by which scientists attempt to understand nature. A phenomenon is observed and/or manipulated so that changes in the phenomenon's state can be seen. The resulting data can be used to derive new MODELS of a process or to confirm an existing model. Experimentation is the complement of THEORIZATION. See also SIMULATION.

Expert System A special PROGRAM that resembles a collection of "if ... then" rules. The rules usually represent knowledge contained by a domain expert (such as a physician adept at diagnosis) and can be used to SIMULATE how a human expert would perform a task.

F

Feedback A loop in information flow or in cause and effect.

Feedback Neural Network A NEURAL NETWORK that has every NEURON potentially connected to every other neuron. The ACTIVATIONS of all neurons are updated in PARALLEL (SYNCHRONOUS or ASYNCHRONOUS order), unlike a FEEDFORWARD or RECURRENT NEURAL NETWORK.

Feedforward Neural Network A NEURAL NETWORK that is organized with separate layers of NEURONS. Connections in such a network are limited to one direction such that the ACTIVATIONS of the input neurons are updated first, followed by any HIDDEN LAYERS, and then finished with the outputs.

Feigenbaum Constant A constant number that characterizes when bump-like MAPS such as the LOGISTIC MAP will BIFURCATE.

Finite-State Automaton (FSA) The simplest computing device. Although it is not nearly powerful enough to perform UNIVERSAL COMPUTATION, it can recognize REGULAR EXPRESSIONS. FSAs are defined by a state transition table that specifies how the FSA moves from one state to another when presented with a particular input. FSAs can be drawn as GRAPHS.

Fish A simple object in CONWAY'S GAME OF LIFE that swims vertically or horizontally.

Fitness A measure of an object's ability to reproduce viable offspring.

Fitness Landscape A representation of how MUTATIONS can change the FITNESS of one or more organisms. If high fitness corresponds to high locations in the landscape, and if changes in genetic material are mapped to movements in the landscape, then EVOLUTION will tend to make populations move in an uphill direction on the fitness landscape.

Fixed Point A point in a DYNAMICAL SYSTEM'S STATE SPACE that maps back to itself, i.e., the system will stay at the fixed point if it does not undergo a PERTURBATION.

Formal System A mathematical formalism in which STATEMENTS can be constructed and manipulated with logical rules. Some formal systems are built around a few basic AXIOMS (such as EUCLIDEAN geometry) and can be expanded with THEOREMS that can be deduced through PROOFS.

Fractal An object with a FRACTAL DIMENSION. Fractals are SELF-SIMILAR and may be DETERMINISTIC or STOCHASTIC. See also CANTOR SET, DIFFUSION LIMITED AGGREGATION, IFS, JULIA SET, L-SYSTEMS, MRCM, MANDELBROT SET, and STRANGE ATTRACTOR.

Fractal Dimension An extension of the notion of dimension found in EUCLIDEAN geometry. Fractal dimensions can be non-integer, meaning that objects can be "more than a line but less than a plane" and so on. There is more than one way of computing a fractal dimension, one common type being the Hausdorff-Besicovich dimension. Roughly speaking, a fractal dimension can be calculated as the quotient of the logarithm of the object's size and the logarithm of the measuring scale, in the limit as the scale approaches 0. Under this definition, standard Euclidean objects retain their original dimension.

Function A mapping from one space to another. This is usually understood to be a relationship between numbers. Functions that are COMPUTABLE can be calculated by a UNIVERSAL COMPUTER.

Function Approximation The task of finding an instance from a class of FUNCTIONS that is minimally different from an unknown function. This is a common task for NEURAL NETWORKS.

G

Game Theory A mathematical formalism used to study human games, economics, military conflicts, and biology. The goal of game theory is to find the optimal STRATEGY for one player to use when his opponent also plays optimally. A strategy may incorporate RANDOMNESS, in which case it is referred to as a MIXED STRATEGY.

Gaussian Normally distributed (with a bell-shaped curve) and having a MEAN at the center of the curve with tail widths proportional to the STANDARD DEVIATION of the data about the mean.

Generalized Delta Rule Another name for BACKPROPAGATION.

Genetic Algorithm (GA) A method of SIMULATING the action of EVOLUTION within a computer. A population of fixed-length STRINGS is evolved with a GA by employing CROSSOVER and MUTATION operators along with a FITNESS FUNCTION that determines how likely individuals are to reproduce. GAs perform a type of SEARCH in a FITNESS LANDSCAPE.

Genetic Programming (GP) A method of applying simulated EVOLUTION on PROGRAMS or program fragments. Modified forms of MUTATION and CROSSOVER are used along with a FITNESS function.

Glider A simple object in CONWAY'S GAME OF LIFE that swims diagonally through the grid space.

Glider Gun An object in CONWAY'S GAME OF LIFE that builds and emits GLIDERS, which can then be collided in purposeful ways to construct more complicated objects.

Global Minimum (Maximum) In a SEARCH SPACE, the lowest (or highest) point of the surface, which usually represents the best possible solution in the space with respect to some problem.

Gödel Number A NATURAL NUMBER computed via a GÖDELIZATION procedure that uniquely corresponds to a STRING.

Gödelization A method for mapping arbitrary STRINGS to NATURAL NUMBERS such that the process is ONE-TO-ONE and INVERTIBLE. The process usually exploits the properties of PRIME NUMBERS. Since Gödelization can be defined as a COMPUTABLE FUNCTION, and since functions can be Gödelized, some functions (or PROGRAMS) can assert STATEMENTS about other functions or programs, or themselves.

Gödel's Incompleteness Theorem Any sufficiently interesting FORMAL SYSTEM can express true STATEMENTS for which there can be no PROOF in the original formal system.

Gödel's Statement Given the formal STATEMENT "There does not exist any PROOF for the statement with GÖDEL NUMBER x applied to x," which has it own Gödel number, g, Gödel's statement paraphrased is "There does not exist a proof of the statement with Gödel number g applied to itself." Gödel's statement is true, but cannot be proven true in the FORMAL SYSTEM in which it is constructed, which leads to GÖDEL'S INCOMPLETENESS THEOREM.

Gradient A VECTOR of partial DERIVATIVES of a FUNCTION that operates on vectors. Intuitively, the gradient represents the slope of a high-dimensional surface.

Graph A construct that consists of many nodes connected with edges. The edges usually represent a relationship between the objects represented by the nodes. For example, if the nodes are cities, then the edges may have numerical values that correspond to the distances between the cities. A graph can be equivalently represented as a MATRIX.

H

Halting Problem The problem of determining if a PROGRAM halts or doesn't halt on a particular input. This is an INCOMPUTABLE problem.

Halting Set The RECURSIVELY ENUMERABLE SET of GÖDEL NUMBERS that correspond to PROGRAMS that halt if given their own Gödel number as input.

Hebbian Learning A rule that specifies that the strength of a SYNAPSE between two NEURONS should be proportional to the product of the ACTIVATIONS of the two neurons.

Hénon Map A CHAOTIC SYSTEM (defined by the two equations $x_{t+1} = a - x_t^2 + by_t$ and $y_{t+1} = x_t$) that has a FRACTAL STRANGE ATTRACTOR and operates in DISCRETE time.

Hidden Layer In a FEEDFORWARD or RECURRENT NEURAL NETWORK, a layer of NEURONS that is neither the input layer nor the output layer but is physically between the two.

Hill-Climbing One of the simplest SEARCH methods that attempts to find a LOCAL MAXIMUM by moving in an uphill direction. It is related to STEEPEST ASCENT. Hill-climbing may use GRADIENT information, or RANDOM sampling of nearby points, in order to estimate the uphill direction.

Holism The idea that "the whole is greater than the sum of the parts." Holism is credible on the basis of EMERGENCE alone, since REDUCTIONISM and BOTTOM-UP descriptions of nature often fail to predict complex higher-level patterns. See also TOP-DOWN.

Hopfield Network A type of FEEDBACK NEURAL NETWORK that is often used as an ASSOCIATIVE MEMORY or as a solution to a COMBINATORIAL OPTIMIZATION problem.

I

IFS An iterated functional system; it constructs a FRACTAL by ITERATING a VECTOR quantity through an AFFINE equation that is RANDOMLY selected on each iteration.

Imaginary Number The square root of a negative number. The square root of -1 is often denoted as i for the purpose of writing out COMPLEX NUMBERS.

Implicit Parallelism The idea that GENETIC ALGORITHMS have an extra built-in form of PARALLELISM that is expressed when a GA SEARCHES through a SEARCH SPACE. Implicit parallelism depends on the similarities and differences between individuals in the population. The theory posits that GAs process more SCHEMATA than there are STRINGS in a population, thus getting something of a free lunch. See also NO FREE LUNCH.

Incomputable Something that cannot be characterized by a PROGRAM that always halts. SETS that are incomputable may be RECURSIVELY ENUMERABLE (like the HALTING SET), CO-RECURSIVELY ENUMERABLE (e.g., the halting set's COMPLEMENT), or NOT RECURSIVELY ENUMERABLE (which, if also not CO-RE, is a RANDOM set).

Incomputable Number A REAL NUMBER with an infinite decimal (or BINARY) expansion that cannot be enumerated by any UNIVERSAL COMPUTER.

Inheritable Refers to a trait that can be genetically passed from parent to offspring.

Inhibitory Refers to a neural SYNAPSE or WEIGHT that is negative such that activity in the source NEURON encourages inactivity in the connected neuron. The opposite of EXCITATORY.

Inner Product For two VECTORS of the same dimensionality, the sum of the pairwise products of the two vector components, $\sum_i x_i y_i$.

Integral The cumulative CONTINUOUS sum of a FUNCTION. The integral of a DIFFERENTIAL EQUATION represents the future state of a DYNAMICAL SYSTEM; however, most integrals do not have an ANALYTICAL SOLUTION, which means that they may only have NUMERICAL SOLUTIONS, an admittedly inexact process.

Integration The act of calculating an INTEGRAL, by either a NUMERICAL or an ANALYTICAL SOLUTION; the inverse operation of DIFFERENTIATION.

Invertible A FUNCTION is invertible (with a unique inverse) if the output uniquely determines the input (i.e., it is ONE-TO-ONE) and the set of legal outputs is equal to the set of legal inputs. The function x^2 is not strictly invertible, while x^3 has an inverse. For operations the definition is slightly looser. While INTEGRATION and DIFFERENTIATION are considered to be inverse operations, there are an infinite number of INTEGRALS that are valid results for integrating any function; thus, the process is not one-to-one.

Irrational Number A REAL NUMBER that cannot be represented as a fraction.

Iterated Prisoner's Dilemma The PRISONER'S DILEMMA game played in an ITERATIVE manner for a number of rounds that is unknown to both players.

Iterate/Iterative Doing something repeatedly. Doing something repeatedly. Doing something repeatedly. Doing something repeatedly. Doing something repeatedly.

J

Julia Set A SET of COMPLEX NUMBERS that do not DIVERGE if ITERATED an infinite number of times via a simple equation. The points form an extremely complex FRACTAL. There is an UNCOUNTABLE INFINITY of Julia sets, each of which corresponds to a particular complex number that appears as a constant in the iterative procedure. Julia sets are similar to CO-RECURSIVELY ENUMERABLE sets because only points that are not a members of the set can actually be identified as such. All of the Julia sets are related to the MANDELBROT SET.

K

Koch Curve A FRACTAL curve that looks like the edge of a snowflake. It has no DERIVATIVE at any point.

L

Lamarckism A method of heredity that does not apply to genetics but is applicable to social ADAPTATION. Lamarckism posits that acquired traits can be passed from parent to offspring.

Lambda Calculus A MODEL OF COMPUTATION that is capable of UNIVERSAL COMPUTATION. The LISP programming language was inspired by Lambda calculus.

Learning A process of ADAPTATION by which SYNAPSES, WEIGHTS of NEURAL NETWORK's, CLASSIFIER STRENGTHS, or some other set of adjustable parameters is automatically modified so that some objective is more readily achieved. The BACKPROPAGATION and BUCKET BRIGADE ALGORITHMS are two types of learning procedures.

LIFE See CONWAY'S GAME OF LIFE.

Limit Cycle A PERIODIC cycle in a DYNAMICAL SYSTEM such that previous states are returned to repeatedly.

Linear Having only a multiplicative factor. If $f(x)$ is a linear FUNCTION, then $f(a+b) = f(a) + f(b)$ and $cf(x) = f(cx)$ must both be true for all values of a, b, c, and x. Most things in nature are NONLINEAR.

Linearly (In)separable Two classes of points are linearly separable if a LINEAR FUNCTION exists such that one class of points resides on one side of the hyperplane (defined by the linear function), and all points in the other class are on the other side. The XOR mapping defines two SETS of points that are linearly inseparable.

Lisp A programming language designed to manipulate lists that was inspired by LAMBDA CALCULUS and was the inspiration for STUTTER.

Local Minimum (Maximum) The bottom of a valley or the top of a peak; a point in a SEARCH SPACE such that all nearby points are either higher (for a minimum) or lower (for a maximum). In a CONTINUOUS search space, local minima and maxima have a 0 GRADIENT VECTOR. Note that this particular valley (or peak) may not necessarily be the lowest (or highest) location in the space, which is referred to as the GLOBAL MINIMUM (MAXIMUM).

Logistic Map The simplest CHAOTIC SYSTEM that works in DISCRETE time and is defined by the MAP $x_t = 4rx_t(1-x_t)$. FEIGENBAUM'S CONSTANT was first identified for this map.

Lorenz System A system of three DIFFERENTIAL EQUATIONS that was the first concrete example of CHAOS and a STRANGE ATTRACTOR.

Lotka-Volterra System A two-species PREDATOR-PREY SYSTEM that in its simplest form can display only FIXED POINTS or LIMIT CYCLES. More complicated versions with three or more species can yield CHAOS.

L-System A method of constructing a FRACTAL that is also a MODEL for plant growth. L-systems use an AXIOM as a starting STRING and ITERATIVELY apply a set of PARALLEL string substitution rules to yield one long string that can be used as instructions for drawing the fractal. One method of interpreting the resulting string is as an instruction to a TURTLE GRAPHICS plotter. Many fractals, including the CANTOR SET, KOCH CURVE, and PEANO CURVE, can be expressed as an L-system.

M

Mackey-Glass System A delay DIFFERENTIAL EQUATION ($dx/dt = (ax(t-\tau))/(1 + x^{10}(t-\tau)) - bx(t)$) that can display a wide variety of behaviors via an adjustable delay term, τ. Even though this system generates a single SCALAR TIMES SERIES, it can be extremely CHAOTIC because its value at any time may depend on its entire previous history.

Mandelbrot Set An extremely complex FRACTAL that is related to JULIA SETS in the way that it is constructed and by the fact that it acts as a sort of index to the Julia sets. Like the Julia sets, the Mandelbrot set is calculated via an ITERATIVE procedure. Starting conditions that do not DIVERGE after an infinite number of iterations are considered to be inside the set. If, and only if, a COMPLEX NUMBER is in the Mandelbrot set, then the Julia set that uses that complex number as a constant will be connected; otherwise, the corresponding Julia set will be unconnected.

Map A FUNCTION that is usually understood to be ITERATED in DISCRETE time steps.

Matrix A rectangular two-dimensional array of numbers that can be thought of as a LINEAR operator on VECTORS. Matrix-vector multiplication can be used to describe geometric transformations such as scaling, rotation, reflection, and translation. They can also describe the AFFINE transformation used to construct IFS and MRCM FRACTALS.

Mean The arithmetical average of a collection of numbers; the center of a GAUSSIAN distribution.

Meme A unit of cultural information that represents a basic idea that can be transferred from one individual to another, and subjected to MUTATION, CROSSOVER, and ADAPTATION.

Message The basic unit of information in a CLASSIFIER SYSTEM that is stored in the MESSAGE LIST. A message may correspond to an external state of an ENVIRONMENT or an internal state of the classifier system.

Message List The portion of a CLASSIFIER SYSTEM that retains information in the form of MESSAGES.

Mixed Strategy In GAME THEORY, a STRATEGY that uses RANDOMNESS by employing different actions in identical circumstances with different PROBABILITIES.

Model In the sciences, a model is an estimate of how something works. A model will usually have inputs and outputs that correspond to its real-world counterpart. An ADAPTIVE SYSTEM also contains an implicit model of its ENVIRONMENT that allows it to change its behavior in anticipation of what will happen in the environment.

Model of Computation An idealized version of a computing device that usually has some simplifications such as infinite memory. A TURING MACHINE, the LAMBDA CALCULUS, and POST PRODUCTION SYSTEMS are all models of computation.

Monotonic The property of a FUNCTION that is always strictly increasing or strictly decreasing, but never both. The SIGMOIDAL ACTIVATION function of a MULTILAYER PERCEPTRON is monotonically increasing.

MRCM The Multiple Reduction Copy Machine ALGORITHM, which can be used to make AFFINE FRACTALS. MRCM fractals are related to IFS fractals in that they both use the same types of affine transformations. The MRCM algorithm performs several affine transformations of a seed image in PARALLEL to yield a secondary seed image. The output of the MRCM is RECURSIVELY passed back through to its input multiple times, to yield the fractal.

Multilayer Perceptron (MLP) A type of FEEDFORWARD NEURAL NETWORK that is an extension of the PERCEPTRON in that it has at least one HIDDEN LAYER of NEURONS. Layers are updated by starting at the inputs and ending with the outputs. Each neuron computes a weighted sum of the incoming signals, to yield a NET INPUT, and passes this value through its SIGMOIDAL ACTIVATION FUNCTION to yield the neuron's ACTIVATION value. Unlike the perceptron, an MLP can solve LINEARLY INSEPARABLE problems.

Mutation A RANDOM change in any portion of genetic material. For a GENETIC ALGORITHM, this means that a value in a BIT STRING is randomly set.

N

Nash Equilibrium In GAME THEORY, a pair of STRATEGIES for a game such that neither player can improve his outcome by changing his strategy. A Nash equilibrium sometimes takes the form of a SADDLE structure. Under some cases, when a strategy is at a Nash equilibrium with itself, the strategy resembles an EVOLUTIONARY STABLE STRATEGY.

Natural Number Any of the standard counting numbers; a positive integer.

Natural Selection The natural filtering process by which individuals with higher FITNESS are more likely to reproduce than individuals with lower fitness.

Neo-Darwinism A synthesis of DARWINISM with the mechanisms of genetics; the idea that ADAPTATION equals a combination of VARIATION, heredity, and selection. See also EVOLUTION, INHERITABLE, and NATURAL SELECTION.

Net Input The weighted sum of incoming signals into a NEURON plus a neuron's THRESHOLD value.

Neural Network (NN) A network of NEURONS that are connected through SYNAPSES or WEIGHTS. In this book, the term is used almost exclusively to denote an artificial neural network and not the real thing. Each neuron performs a simple calculation that is a FUNCTION of the ACTIVATIONS of the neurons that are connected to it. Through FEEDBACK mechanisms and/or the NONLINEAR output response of neurons, the network as a whole is capable of performing extremely complicated tasks, including UNIVERSAL COMPUTATION and UNIVERSAL APPROXIMATION. Three different classes of neural networks are FEEDFORWARD, FEEDBACK, and RECURRENT NEURAL NETWORKS, which differ in the degree and type of CONNECTIVITY that they possess.

Neuron A simple computational unit that performs a weighted sum on incoming signals, adds a THRESHOLD or bias term to this value to yield a NET INPUT, and maps this last value through an ACTIVATION FUNCTION to compute its own ACTIVATION. Some neurons, such as those found in FEEDBACK or HOPFIELD networks, will retain a portion of their previous activation.

Newton's Method An ITERATIVE method for finding 0 values of a FUNCTION.

Niche A way for an animal to make a living in an ECOSYSTEM.

No Free Lunch (NFL) A THEOREM that states that in the worst case, and averaged over an infinite number of SEARCH SPACES, all SEARCH METHODS perform equally well. More than being a condemnation of any search method, the NFL theorem actually hints that most naturally occurring search spaces are, in fact, not RANDOM.

Nonlinear A FUNCTION that is not LINEAR. Most things in nature are nonlinear. This means that in a very real way, the whole is at least different from the sum of the parts. See also HOLISM.

Not Recursively Enumerable (not-RE) An infinite SET that cannot be RECURSIVELY ENUMERATED. SETS of this type that are also not CO-RECURSIVELY ENUMERABLE are effectively RANDOM.

NP Nondeterministic polynomial time problems; a class of computational problems that may or may not be solvable in POLYNOMIAL time but are expressed in such a way that candidate solutions can be tested for correctness in polynomial time. See also TIME COMPLEXITY and NP-COMPLETE.

NP-Complete A problem type in which any instance of any other NP class problem can be translated to in POLYNOMIAL time. This means that if a fast ALGORITHM exists for an NP-complete problem, then any problem that is in NP can be solved with the same algorithm.

Numerical Solution A solution to a problem that is calculated through a SIMULATION. For example, solving the THREE BODY PROBLEM is not possible in the worst case; however, with the DIFFERENTIAL EQUATIONS that describe the motions of three bodies in space, one could simulate their movements by simulating each time step. Nevertheless, numerical solutions are usually error-prone due to SENSITIVITY and, therefore, can be used to estimate the future for only relatively short time spans, in the worst case.

O

Occam's Razor The principle that when faced with multiple but equivalent interpretations of some phenomenon, one should always choose the simplest explanation that correctly fits the data. Occam's Razor is useful for selecting competing MODELS for some phenomena.

One-to-One A FUNCTION or MAP that for every possible output has only one input that yields that particular output; if $f(a) = f(b)$, then $a = b$.

Optimization The process of finding parameters that minimizes or maximizes a FUNCTION.

Outer Product An operation on two VECTORS that yields a MATRIX. Given two vectors with the same dimensionality, the outer product is a square symmetric matrix that contains the product of all pairs of elements from the two vectors, i.e., $A_{ij} = x_i y_j$.

P

Parallel/Parallelism Many things happening at once.

Pattern Classification A task that NEURAL NETWORKS are often trained to do. Given some input pattern, the task is to make an accurate class assignment to the input. For example, classifying many images of letters to one of the twenty-six letters of the alphabet is a pattern classification task.

Payoff In GAME THEORY, the amount that a player wins, given the player's and his opponent's actions.

Peano Curve A FRACTAL SPACE-FILLING curve that can fill a plane even though it is a line of infinite length. Oddly enough, it has an integer FRACTAL DIMENSION of 2.

Perceptron The simplest type of FEEDFORWARD NEURAL NETWORK. It has only inputs and outputs, i.e., no HIDDEN LAYERS.

Periodic Refers to motion that goes through a finite number of regions, returns to a previous state, and repeats the same fixed pattern forever.

Perturbation A slight nudge.

Phase Space In this book, another name for STATE SPACE. In the scientific literature, "phase space" is used to denote the space of motion in a DYNAMICAL SYSTEM that moves in CONTINUOUS time, while STATE SPACE is often used for DISCRETE time SYSTEMS.

Phase Transition In physics, a change from one state of matter to another. In DYNAMICAL SYSTEMS theory, a change from one mode of behavior to another.

Planning In computer science, and particularly in ARTIFICIAL INTELLIGENCE, the task of determining a stepwise plan to accomplish a very specific task.

Polynomial A FUNCTION in which the output is the sum of terms that are the products of constant values and the input raised to some integer power. The polynomial of a polynomial is another polynomial. From a TIME COMPLEXITY point of view, polynomials are well-behaved.

Post Production System A MODEL OF COMPUTATION that resembles a collection of "if ... then" rules and is capable of UNIVERSAL COMPUTATION.

Predator-Prey System An ECOSYSTEM in which one portion of the population consumes another. With three or more species, simple predator-prey interactions can lead to CHAOS and biological ARMS RACES. See also LOTKA-VOLTERRA SYSTEM.

Prime Number A NATURAL NUMBER that can be evenly divided only by itself and 1.

Prisoner's Dilemma A non-ZERO-SUM GAME in which both players have incentive not to cooperate under any circumstances. Thus, the optimal GAME THEORY STRATEGY of ALWAYS DEFECT has the paradoxical property that both players would have a higher PAYOFF if they ignored the advice of game theory.

Probability The likelihood that a RANDOM event will occur.

Program An ALGORITHM that is written in a programming language for execution on a physical computer.

Proof A sequence of STATEMENTS in which each subsequent statement is derivable from one of the previous statements or from an AXIOM of a FORMAL SYSTEM. The final statement of a proof is usually the THEOREM that one has set out to prove.

Q

Quasiperiodic Refers to a form of motion that is regular but never exactly repeating. Quasiperiodic motion is always composed of multiple but simpler PERIODIC motions. In the general case, for motion that is the sum of simpler periodic motions, if there exists a length of time that evenly divides the frequencies of the underlying motions, then the composite motion will also be periodic; however, if no such length of time exists, then the motion will be quasiperiodic.

R

Random/Randomness Without cause; not COMPRESSIBLE; obeying the statistics of a fair coin toss.

Random Walk A walk in one or more dimensions that is dictated by the outcome of a coin toss. The direction of each step of the walk is specified by the coin toss. The resulting RANDOM motion is often referred to as BROWNIAN MOTION.

Rational Number A number that can be expressed as a fraction.

Real Number Any number that can be represented with a potentially infinite decimal expansion to the right of the decimal point. NATURAL, RATIONAL, IRRATIONAL, and INCOMPUTABLE numbers are all real numbers.

Recurrent Neural Network A network similar to a FEEDFORWARD NEURAL NETWORK except that there may be connections from an output or HIDDEN LAYER to the inputs. Recurrent neural networks are capable of UNIVERSAL COMPUTATION.

Recursive Strictly speaking, a SET or FUNCTION is recursive if it is COMPUTABLE; however, in the usual sense of the word, a function is said to be recursive if its definition make reference to itself. For example, factorial can be defined as $x! = x \times (x-1)!$ with the base case of 1! equal to 1. See also SELF-REFERENTIAL.

Recursively Enumerable (RE) A potentially infinite SET whose members can be enumerated by a UNIVERSAL COMPUTER; however, a universal computer may not be able to determine that something is not a member of a recursively enumerable set. The HALTING SET is recursively enumerable but not RECURSIVE.

Reductionism The idea that nature can be understood by dissection. In other words, knowing the lowest-level details of how things work (at, say, the level of subatomic physics) reveals how higher-level phenomena come about. This is a BOTTOM-UP way of looking at the universe, and is the exact opposite of HOLISM.

Regular Expression A definition for a class of STRINGS that can be recognized by a FINITE-STATE AUTOMATON. An example of a class of strings that is regular would be legal mathematical expressions using only "+" and digits. An example that is not regular is the same legal mathematical expressions as before, but with properly nested parentheses.

S

Saddle A type of surface that is neither a peak nor a valley but still has a 0 GRADIENT. Saddle points are situated such that moving in one direction takes one uphill, while moving in another direction would be downhill. Hence, saddles look like the things that cowboys ride on.

Scalar A single number, as opposed to a multidimensional VECTOR or MATRIX.

Schema/Schemata A similarity template used to analyze GENETIC ALGORITHMS. By using wild-card characters, a schema defines an entire class of STRINGS that may be found in a population.

Search/Search Method A method for finding a region of interest in a SEARCH SPACE. Usually, the interesting regions correspond to solutions to a specific problem. HILL-CLIMBING, STEEPEST DESCENT (ASCENT), SIMULATED ANNEALING, and GENETIC ALGORITHMS are all search methods.

Search Space A characterization of every possible solution to a problem instance. For a NEURAL NETWORK the search space is defined as all possible assignments to the network WEIGHTS; for a GENETIC ALGORITHM, it is every conceivable value assignment to the STRINGS in the population.

Selection See NATURAL SELECTION.

Self-Organization A spontaneously formed higher-level pattern of structure or FUNCTION that is EMERGENT through the interactions of lower-level objects.

Self-Organized Criticality (SOC) A mathematical theory that describes how SYSTEMS composed of many interacting parts can tune themselves toward DYNAMICAL behavior that is critical in the sense that it is neither STABLE nor UNSTABLE but at a region near a PHASE TRANSITION. SOC systems display events in a power-law distribution and are never quite at EQUILIBRIUM. See also EDGE OF CHAOS and SELF-ORGANIZATION.

Self-Referential Referring directly back to oneself through information flow, influence, or cause and effect. See SELF-REFERENTIAL.

Self-Similar An object that is structurally RECURSIVE in that a part will look like the whole. See also FRACTAL.

Sensitivity The tendency of a SYSTEM (sometimes CHAOTIC) to change dramatically with only small PERTURBATIONS.

Set A collection of things, usually numbers. Sets may be infinite in size.

Shadowing Lemma Implies that a numerical SIMULATION of CHAOS may "shadow" a real trajectory of a real CHAOTIC SYSTEM.

Sigmoidal An "S" shaped FUNCTION that is often used as an ACTIVATION FUNCTION in a NEURAL NETWORK.

Simulate/Simulation EXPERIMENTATION in the space of theories, or a combination of experimentation and THEORIZATION. Some numerical simulations are PROGRAMS that represent a MODEL for how nature works. Usually, the outcome of a simulation is as much a surprise as the outcome of a natural event, due to the richness and uncertainty of COMPUTATION.

Simulated Annealing A partially RANDOM method of SEARCH and OPTIMIZATION usually used for COMBINATORIAL OPTIMIZATION problems. The technique is modeled on how the molecular structure of metals is disordered at high temperatures but very ordered and crystalline at low temperatures. In simulated annealing, a problem instance is reformulated so that it loosely resembles disordered material. Gradually, the temperature is lowered such that the ordered states correspond to good solutions to a problem.

Space Complexity A FUNCTION that describes the amount of memory required for a PROGRAM to run on a computer to perform a particular task. The function is parameterized by the length of the program's input. See also TIME COMPLEXITY.

Space-Filling Refers to a curve that manages to twist and turn in such a way that it actually fills a space or volume. All space-filling curves are FRACTAL.

Special Function In LISP or STUTTER, a built-in FUNCTION that may or may not fully evaluate its arguments, such as the `if` primitive.

Stable Having a BASIN OF ATTRACTION that is non-zero in size; an ATTRACTOR that can withstand some form of PERTURBATION.

Standard Deviation A measure of the spread of a SET of data. For a GAUSSIAN distribution, the standard deviation hints at the width of the tails of the distribution FUNCTION.

Statement In a FORMAL SYSTEM, a STRING of characters that is formed according to well-defined rules such that it is legal for the language that is the formal system.

For example, in the formal system of arithmetic, the expression "$5+3\times(2-4)$" is a valid and well-formed statement, but "5+)3 × ×(2(−4)" is not.

State Space In this book, another name for the PHASE SPACE of a DYNAMICAL SYSTEM. Roughly speaking, if the DYNAMICS of a dynamical system can be described by n values, then the state space is the n-dimensional volume that the system moves through. SYSTEMS that are CONTINUOUS in time will form a smooth trajectory through this volume, while DISCRETE systems may jump to different locations on subsequent time steps. In either case, if a system ever returns to a previously visited location in the state space, then the system is in either a FIXED POINT or a LIMIT CYCLE. For CHAOTIC systems, or for PROGRAMS that never halt, the system will always be at a previously unvisited portion of the state space.

Steepest Descent (Ascent) A SEARCH METHOD that uses the GRADIENT information of a SEARCH SPACE and moves in the opposite direction from the gradient until no further downhill (or uphill) progress can be made. See also HILL-CLIMBING.

Stochastic Something that is RANDOM.

Strange Attractor An ATTRACTOR of a DYNAMICAL SYSTEM that is usually FRACTAL in dimension and is indicative of CHAOS.

Strategy In GAME THEORY, a policy for playing a game. A strategy is a complete recipe for how a player should act in a game under all circumstances. Some policies may employ RANDOMNESS, in which case they are referred to as MIXED STRATEGIES.

Strength For a CLASSIFIER SYSTEM, a CLASSIFIER'S relative ability to win a bidding match for the right to post its MESSAGE on the MESSAGE LIST.

String Any sequence of letters, numbers, digits, BITS, or symbols.

Stutter A silly programming language used in this book that is based on LISP and is capable of UNIVERSAL COMPUTATION.

Symmetric Matrix A MATRIX with the lower-left half equal to the mirror image of the upper-right half.

Synapse The junction between two NEURONS in which neural activity is propagated from one neuron to another. See also EXCITATORY, INHIBITORY, and WEIGHT.

Synchronous Acting in a lockstep fashion, with each event occurring in a precise order, or in such a way as to eliminate the notion of order entirely.

System Something that can be studied as a whole. Systems may consist of subsystems that are interesting in their own right. Or they may exist in an ENVIRONMENT that consists of other similar systems. Systems are generally understood to have an internal state, inputs from an environment, and methods for manipulating the environment or themselves. Since cause and effect can flow in both directions of a system and environment, interesting systems often posses FEEDBACK, which is SELF-REFERENTIAL in the strongest case.

T

Theorem A STATEMENT in a FORMAL SYSTEM that has PROOF.

Theorization A process by which scientists attempt to understand nature; it is the complement to EXPERIMENTATION. Theorization is the process of building mathematical MODELS for how things work. Scientists always desire theories that are simpler than the data they explain. See also OCCAM'S RAZOR and SIMULATION.

Three Body Problem The problem of determining the future positions and velocities of three gravitational bodies. The problem was proved unsolvable in the general case by Henri Poincaré, which forshadowed the importance of CHAOS. Although no ANALYTICAL SOLUTIONS are possible in the worst case, a NUMERICAL SOLUTION is sometimes sufficient for many tasks.

Threshold A quantity added to (or subtracted from) the weighted sum of inputs into a NEURON, which forms the neuron's NET INPUT. Intuitively, the net input (or bias) is proportional to the amount that the incoming neural ACTIVATIONS must exceed in order for a neuron to fire.

Time Complexity A FUNCTION that describes the amount of time required for a PROGRAM to run on a computer to perform a particular task. The function is parameterized by the length of the program's input. See also SPACE COMPLEXITY.

Time-Reversible A property of DYNAMICAL SYSTEMS that can be run unambiguously both forward and backward in time. The HÉNON MAP, LORENZ SYSTEM, and VANT CELLULAR AUTOMATA are all time-reversible, while the LOGISTIC MAP, the MACKEY-GLASS SYSTEM, and most other CELLULAR AUTOMATA are not. Time-reversible systems are described by FUNCTIONS that are INVERTIBLE.

Time Series A sequence of values generated from a DYNAMICAL SYSTEM over time. CHAOTIC SYSTEMS can be analyzed by examining the time series generated by a single portion of the SYSTEM. See also EMBEDDING.

Tit-for-Tat An effective STRATEGY for playing the ITERATED PRISONER'S DILEMMA. Tit-for-Tat starts by cooperating, and then does whatever its opponent did in the previous round of play.

Top-Down A method of examining things that first looks at higher-level phenomena and then tries to explain lower-level patterns in terms of the higher-level observations. This is the exact opposite of BOTTOM-UP. See also HOLISM and REDUCTIONISM.

Transpose An operation that flips a MATRIX about the main diagonal.

Turing Machine A MODEL OF COMPUTATION that uses an underlying FINITE-STATE AUTOMATON but also has an infinite tape to use as memory. Turing machines are capable of UNIVERSAL COMPUTATION.

Turtle Graphics A simple language for drawing graphics in which a "turtle" is used to make strokes on a plotting device. Typical commands include "move forward," "draw forward," and "turn left."

U

Uncountable Infinity An order of infinity that is larger than the number of NATURAL NUMBERS. The number of REAL NUMBERS is uncountably infinite.

Universal Approximation Having the ability to approximate any FUNCTION to an arbitrary degree of accuracy. NEURAL NETWORKS are universal approximators.

Universal Computation Capable of computing anything that can in principle be computed; being equivalent in computing power to a TURING MACHINE, the LAMBDA CALCULUS, or a POST PRODUCTION SYSTEM.

Universal Computer A computer that is capable of UNIVERSAL COMPUTATION, which means that given a description of any other computer or PROGRAM and some data, it can perfectly emulate this second computer or program. Strictly speaking, home PCs are not universal computers because they have only a finite amount of memory. However, in practice, this is usually ignored.

Unstable Having a BASIN OF ATTRACTION that is 0 in size; being such that the slightest PERTURBATION will forever change the state of a SYSTEM. A pencil balanced on its point is unstable.

V

Value Function A built-in FUNCTION in LISP or STUTTER that evaluates all of its arguments prior to being executed, e.g., `car`, `cdr`, and `cons`.

Vant A virtual ant; a type of CELLULAR AUTOMATON that vaguely emulates the activity of one or more ants.

Variation Genetic differences among individuals in a population.

Vector A one-dimensional array of numbers that can be used to represent a point in a multidimensional space.

W

Weight In a NEURAL NETWORK, the strength of a SYNAPSE (or connection) between two NEURONS. Weights may be positive (EXCITATORY) or negative (INHIBITORY). The THRESHOLDS of a neuron are also considered weights, since they undergo ADAPTATION by a LEARNING ALGORITHM.

White Noise Noise that uniformly distributed in the frequency domain; RANDOMNESS that is uniformly distributed; thus, a white noise process with a range of 0 to 1 would yield a random number in this range with PROBABILITY equal for all possible values. BROWN NOISE is a result of cumulatively adding white noise.

X

XOR The exclusive-or FUNCTION; given two BOOLEAN inputs, the output of XOR is 1 if and only if the two inputs are different; otherwise, the output is 0.

Z

Zero-Sum Game In GAME THEORY, a game in which a win for one player results in an equal but opposite loss for the other players.

Bibliography

Abelson, H., Sussman, G. J., & Sussman, J. (1996). *Structure and interpretation of computer programs.* Cambridge, Mass.: MIT Press.

Arbib, M. A. (1966). Self-reproducing automata—some implications for theoretical biology. In C. H. Waddington (Ed.), *Towards a theoretical biology*, volume 2 (pp. 204–226). Edinburgh: Edinburgh University Press.

Arneodo, A., Coullet, P., & Tresser, C. (1980). Occurrence of strange attractors in three-dimensional Volterra equations. *Phys. Lett. A*, 79A(4): 259–63.

Ashby, W. R. (1966). *An introduction to cybernetics.* New York: John Wiley & Sons.

Awad, E. M. (1996). *Building expert systems: Principles, procedures, and applications.* Minneapolis/St.Paul: West/Wadsworth.

Axelrod, R. (1984). *The evolution of cooperation.* New York: Basic Books.

Axelrod, R. & Hamilton, W. D. (1981). The evolution of cooperation. *Science*, 211(4489): 1390–1396.

Bai-Lin, H. (Ed.). (1984). *Chaos.* Singapore: World Scientific.

Bak, P. (1996). *How nature works: The science of self-organized criticality.* New York: Springer-Verlag.

Bak, P. & Chen, K. (January 1991). Self-organized criticality. *Sci. Am.*, 264(1).

Bak, P., Tang, C., & Wiesenfeld, K. (1988). Self-organized criticality. *Phys. Rev. A*, 38(1): 364–374.

Barlow, C. (1991). *From Gaia to selfish genes: Selected writings in the life sciences.* Cambridge, Mass.: MIT Press.

Barnsley, M. (1988). *Fractals everywhere.* New York: Academic Press.

Barnsley, M. (1989). Iterated function systems. In *Chaos and Fractals: The Mathematics Behind the Computer Graphics*, volume 39 of *Proc. Symposia Appl. Math.*, Providence, R.I. American Mathematical Society.

Beckmann, P. (1977). *A history of* π (Fourth ed.). Boulder, Colo.: Golem Press.

Benhabib, J. (Ed.). (1992). *Cycles and chaos in economic equilibrium.* Princeton: Princeton University Press.

Bennett, C. H., Gács, P., Li, M., Vitanyi, P. M. B., & Zurek, W. H. (1993). Thermodynamics of computation and information distance. In *Proceedings of the twenty-fifth annual ACM symposium on theory of computing*, (pp. 21–30)., San Diego. ACM Press.

Bennett, C. H. & Landauer, R. (July 1985). Fundamental physical limits of computation. *Sci. Am.*, 253(1): 48–56.

Berlekamp, E., Conway, J. H., & Guy, R. (1982). *Winning ways for your mathematical plays.* London: Academic Press.

Blum, L., Cucker, F., Shub, M., & Smale, S. (1995). Complexity and real computation: A manifesto. Technical Report TR-95-042, International Computer Science Institute, Berkeley, Calif.

Blum, L., Shub, M., & Smale, S. (1988). On a theory of computation over the real numbers; NP completeness, recursive functions and universal machines (extended abstract). In *29th annual symposium on foundations of computer science*, (pp. 387–397)., White Plains, N.Y. IEEE.

Bowler, P. J. (1996). *Charles Darwin: The Man and his influence.* Cambridge: Cambridge University Press.

Boyd, R. & Richerson, P. J. (1985). *Culture and the evolutionary process.* Chicago: University of Chicago Press.

Breder, C. M. (1951). Studies in the structure of the fish school. *Bull. Am. Mus. Nat. Hist.*, 98(3): 7ff.

Bremmerman, H. J. (1962). Optimization through evolution and recombination. In M. C. Yovits, G. T. Jacobi, & G. D. Goldstein (Eds.), *Self-organizing systems* (pp. 93ff). Washington, D.C.: Spartan Books.

Bryson, A. E. & Ho, Y. C. (1969). *Applied optimal control.* New York: Blaisdell.

Burks, A. W. (1961). Notes on John von Neumann's cellular self-reproducing automaton. Technical Report 108, Department of Computer Science, University of Illinois, Urbana.

Burks, A. W. (1974). Cellular automata and natural systems. In Keidel, W. D., Händler, W., & Spreng, M. (Eds.), *Cybernetics and bionics*, (pp. 190–204)., Munich. R. Oldenbourg.

Cairns-Smith, A. G. (1966). The origin of life and the nature of the primitive gene. *J. Theor. Biol.*, 10(1): 53–88.

Cairns-Smith, A. G. (1985). *Seven clues to the origin of life.* Cambridge: Cambridge University Press.

Capra, F. (1996). *The web of life: A new scientific understanding of living systems.* New York: Doubleday.

Casti, J. L. (1989). *Alternate realities: Mathematical models of nature and man.* New York: John Wiley & Sons.

Casti, J. L. (1994). *Complexification: Explaining a paradoxical world through the science of surprise.* New York: HarperCollins.

Caudill, M. & Butler, C. (1990). *Naturally intelligent systems.* Cambridge, Mass.: MIT Press.

Chaitin, G. J. (1966). On the length of programs for computing finite binary sequences. *J. ACM*, 13(4): 547–569.

Chaitin, G. J. (1969). On the simplicity and speed of programs for computing infinite sets of natural numbers. *J. ACM*, 16(3): 407–422.

Chaitin, G. J. (January 1970). To a mathematical definition of "life". *ACM SIGACT News*, 4: 12–18.

Chaitin, G. J. (1975). A theory of program size formally identical to information theory. *J. ACM*, 22(3): 329–340.

Chaitin, G. J. (1997). *The limits of mathematics: A course on information theory & limits of formal reasoning.* Singapore: Springer-Verlag.

Charles-Edwards, D. A. (1986). *Modelling plant growth and development.* New York: Academic Press.

Cheeseman, P., Kanefsky, B., & Taylor, W. M. (1991). Where the really hard problems are. In Mylopoulos, J. & Reiter, R. (Eds.), *Proceedings IJCAI-91*, (pp. 331–336)., Sydney.

Chomsky, N. (1956). Three models for the description of language. *IRE Trans. Info. Theory*, 1: 113–124.

Chomsky, N. (1959). On certain formal properties of grammars. *Info. and Control*, 2(2): 137–167.

Chomsky, N. & Miller, G. A. (1958). Finite state languages. *Info. and Control*, 1(2): 91–112.

Church, A. (1936). A note on the Entscheidungsproblem. *J. Symbol. Logic*, 1: 40–41 and 101–102.

Church, A. (1951). *The Calculi of Lambda-Conversion*, volume 6 of *Annals of Mathematical Studies.* Princeton: Princeton University Press.

Clark, W. R. (1995). *At war within: The double-edged sword of immunity.* New York: Oxford University Press.

Conrad, M. & Pattee, H. H. (1970). Evolution experiments with an artificial ecosystem. *J. Theor. Biol.*, 28(3): 393–409.

Cook, S. A. (1971). The complexity of theorem-proving procedures. In *Conference record of third annual ACM symposium on theory of Computing*, (pp. 151–158)., Shaker Heights, Oh. ACM.

Cowan, G., Pines, D., & Meltzer, D. (Eds.). (1994). *Complexity: Metaphors, models, and reality*, volume XIX of *Santa Fe Institute Studies in the Sciences of Complexity.* Reading, Mass.: Addison-Wesley.

Crutchfield, J. P. (1994). The calculi of emergence: Computation, dynamics and induction. *Physica D*, 75(1–3): 11–54.

Crutchfield, J. P. & Young, K. (1989a). Computation at the onset of chaos. In W. Zurek (Ed.), *Complexity, entropy and the physics of information.* Reading, Mass.: Addison-Wesley.

Crutchfield, J. P. & Young, K. (1989b). Inferring statistical complexity. *Phys. Rev. Lett.*, 63(2): 105–108.

Darwin, C. (1859). *On the origin of species.* London: John Murray.

DasGupta, B., Siegelmann, H., & Sontag, E. (1994). On the intractability of loading neural networks. In V. Roychowdhury, K.-Y. Siu, & A. Orlitsky (Eds.), *Theoretical advances in neural computation and learning.* Boston: Kluwer.

Dauben, J. W. (1990). *Georg Cantor: His mathematics and philosophy of the infinite.* Princeton: Princeton University Press.

Davis, M. (Ed.). (1965). *The undecidable.* New York: Raven Press.

Dawkins, R. (1976). *The selfish gene.* Oxford: Oxford University Press.

Dawkins, R. (1983). *The extended phenotype: The gene as a unit of selection.* Oxford: Oxford University Press.

Dawkins, R. (1986). *The blind watchmaker.* New York: W. W. Norton.

Dennett, D. C. (1978). *Brainstorms: Philosophical essays on mind and psychology.* Cambridge, Mass.: Bradford Books/MIT Press.

Derrida, B. & Pomeau, Y. (1986). Random networks of automata: A simple annealed approximation. *Europhys. Lett.*, 1(2): 45–49.

Descartes, R. (1987). *Méditations on first philosophy.* Cambridge: Cambridge University Press.

Dewdney, A. K. (1984). Computer Recreations: Sharks and fish wage an ecological war on the toroidal planet wa-tor. *Sci. Am.*, 251(6): 14–22.

Dewdney, A. K. (1985). Computer Recreations: Exploring the field of genetic algorithms in a primordial computer sea full of flibs. *Sci. Am.*, 253(5): 21–32.

Dewdney, A. K. (August 1988). The hodgepodge machine makes waves. *Sci. Am.*, 225(8): 104–107.

Dewdney, A. K. (1989). *The Turing omnibus: 61 excursions in computer science.* Rockville, Md.: Computer Science Press.

Dewdney, A. K. (1993). *200 percent of nothing: An eye-opening tour through the twists and turns of math abuse and innumeracy.* New York: John Wiley & Sons.

Doyle, J. C., Francis, B. A., & Tannenbaum, A. R. (1992). *Feedback control theory.* New York: MacMillan.

Edelman, G. M. (1987). *Neural darwinism: The theory of neuronal group selection.* New York: Basic Books.

Eigen, M. & Winkler, R. (1982). *The laws of the game: How the principles of nature govern chance.* New York: Harper Colophon.

Esbensen, B. J. & Davie, H. K. (1996). *Echoes for the Eye: Poems to celebrate patterns in nature.* New York: HarperCollins.

Faltings, G. (1995). The proof of Fermat's Last Theorem by R. Taylor and A. Wiles. *Notices Amer. Math. Soc.*, 42(7): 743–746.

Farmer, D. & Kauffman, S. (1988). Biological modelling: What's evolving in artificial life. *Nature*, 331(6155): 390–391.

Farmer, D., Toffoli, T., & Wolfram, S. (Eds.). (1983). *Cellular Automata: Proceedings of an Interdisciplinary Workshop*, Amsterdam. North-Holland.

Farmer, J. D. (1990). Rosetta stone for connectionism. *Physica D*, 42(1–3): 153–187.

Farmer, J. D., Lapedes, A., Packard, N. H., & Wendroff, B. (1986). *Evolution, games and learning.* Amsterdam: North-Holland.

Farmer, J. D., Ott, E., & Yorke, J. A. (1983). The dimension of chaotic attractors. *Physica D*, 7(1–3): 153–180.

Farmer, J. D., Packard, N. H., & Perelson, A. S. (1986). The immune system, adaptation & learning. *Physica D*, 22(1–3): 187–204.

Feigenbaum, M. J. (1978). Quantitative universality for a class of nonlinear transformations. *J. Stat. Phys.*, 19(1): 25–52.

Feigenbaum, M. J. (1979). The universal metric properties of nonlinear transformations. *J. Stat. Phys.*, 21(6): 669–706.

Field, R. J. & Noyes, R. M. (1974). Oscillations in chemical systems. V. Quantitative explanation of band migration in the Belousov-Zhabotinskii reaction. *J. Am. Chem. Soc.*, 96(7): 2001–2006.

Fogel, L. J., Owens, A. J., & Walsh, M. J. (1966). *Artificial Intelligence through Simulated Evolution.* New York: Wiley.

Forrest, S. & Mayer-Kress, G. (1991). Using genetic algorithms in nonlinear dynamical systems and international security models. In L. Davis (Ed.), *The genetic algorithms handbook* (pp. 166–185). New York: Van Nostrand Reinhold.

Fowler, D. R., Meinhardt, H., & Prusinkiewicz, P. (1992). Modeling seashells. *Comp. Graphics*, 26(2): 379–387.

Fredkin, E. & Toffoli, T. (1982). Conservative logic. *Int. J. Theor. Phys.*, 21(3–4): 219–253.

Gale, D. & Propp, J. (1994). Further ant-ics. *Math. Intell.*, 16(1): 37–42.

Gardner, M. (1961). *More mathematical puzzles and diversions.* New York: Penguin.

Gardner, M. (October 1970). Mathematical Games: The fantastic combinations of John Conway's new solitaire game 'Life'. *Sci. Am.*, 223(4): 120–123.

Gardner, M. (1971). Mathematical Games: On cellular automata, self-reproduction, the Garden of Eden and the game of "Life". *Sci. Am.*, 224(2): 112–117.

Gardner, M. (April 1978). Mathematical Games: White and brown music, fractal curves and 1/f fluctuations. *Sci. Am.*, 238: 16–32.

Gardner, M. (1983). *Wheels, life, and other mathematical amusements.* New York: W. H. Freeman.

Garey, M. R. & Johnson, D. S. (1979). *Computers and intractability: A guide to the theory of NP-completeness.* New York: W. H. Freeman.

Garfinkel, A., Spano, M. L., & Ditto, W. L. (1992). Controlling cardiac chaos. *Science*, 257(5074): 1230.

Gell-Mann, M. (1995). *The quark and the jaguar: Adventures in the simple and the complex.* New York: W. H. Freeman.

Gerhardt, M., Schuster, H., & Tyson, J. J. (1991). A cellular automaton model of excitable media IV. Untwisted scroll rings. *Physica D*, 50(2): 189–206.

Gleick, J. (1987). *Chaos.* New York: Viking.

Gödel, K. (1931). Über formal unentscheidbare Sätze der Principia mathematica und verwandter Systeme I. *Monats. für Math. und Phys.*, 38: 173–198.

Gödel, K. (1932). Ein spezialfall des entscheidungsproblem der theoretischen logik. *Ergebn. math. Kolloq.*, 2: 27–28.

Gödel, K. (1965). On intuitionistic arithmetic and number theory. In M. Davis (Ed.), *The undecidable* (pp. 75–81). New York: Raven Press.

Gödel, K. (1986). On completeness and consistency. In S. Feferman, J. W. Dawson, Jr., S. C. Kleene, G. H. Moore, R. M. Solovay, & J. Van Heijenoort (Eds.), *Kurt Gödel: Collected works*, volume 1 (pp. 235–237). Oxford: Oxford University Press.

Goldberg, D. E. (1989). *Genetic algorithms in search, optimization, and machine learning.* Reading, Mass.: Addison-Wesley.

Goldstine, H. H. (1993). *The computer from Pascal to von Neumann.* Princeton: Princeton University Press.

Gonick, L. & Smith, W. (1993). *The cartoon guide to statistics.* New York: HarperCollins.

Grebogi, C., Ott, E., & Yorke, J. A. (1987). Chaos, strange attractors, and fractal basin boundaries in nonlinear dynamics. *Science*, 238(4827): 632–638.

Hall, N. (Ed.). (1991). *Exploring chaos: A guide to the new science of disorder.* New York: W. W. Norton & Co.

Hamilton, W. (1964). The genetical evolution of social behavior. *J. Theor. Biol.*, 7: 1–31.

Haykin, S. (1994). *Neural networks: A comprehensive foundation.* New York: MacMillan.

Hebb, D. O. (1949). *The organization of behavior.* New York: Wiley & Sons.

Hènon, M. (1976). A two-dimensional mapping with a strange attractor. *Comm. Math. Phys.*, 50(1): 69–77.

Hertz, J., Krogh, A., & Palmer, R. G. (1991). *Introduction to the theory of neural computation.* Reading, Mass.: Addison-Wesley.

Hillis, W. D. (1992). Co-evolving parasites improve simulated evolution as an optimization procedure. In C. G. Langton, C. Taylor, J. D. Farmer, & S. Rasmussen (Eds.), *Artificial life II*, volume 10 of *Sante Fe Institute Studies in the Sciences of Complexity* (pp. 313–324). Redwood City, Calif.: Addison-Wesley.

Hirst, B. & Mandelbrot, B. (1995). *Fractal landscapes from the real world.* New York: Distributed Art Publishers.

Hodges, A. (1983). *Alan Turing: The enigma.* New York: Simon and Schuster.

Hofstadter, D. R. (1979). *Gödel, Escher, Bach: An eternal golden braid.* New York: Basic Books.

Hofstadter, D. R. (1985). *Metamagical themas: Questing for the essence of mind and pattern.* New York: Basic Books.

Hogeweg, P. (1988). Cellular automata as a paradigm for ecological modelling. *App. Math. & Comp.*, 27(1).

Hogg, T., Huberman, B. A., & McGlade, J. M. (1989). The stability of ecosystems. *Proc. Royal Soc. of London*, B237(1286): 43–51.

Hogg, T., Huberman, B. A., & Williams, C. P. (1996). Phase transitions and the search problem. *Art. Intell.*, 81(1–2): 1–15.

Holland, J. H. (1962). Outline for a logical theory of adaptive systems. *J. ACM*, 9: 297–314.

Holland, J. H. (1967). Nonlinear environments permitting efficient adaptation. In J. T. Tou (Ed.), *Computer and information sciences II.* New York: Academic Press.

Holland, J. H. (1975). *Adaptation in natural and artificial systems.* Ann Arbor: University of Michigan Press.

Holland, J. H. (1976). Adaptation. In R. Rosen & F. M. Snell (Eds.), *Progress in theoretical biology IV* (pp. 263–293). New York: Academic Press.

Holland, J. H., Holyoak, K. J., Nisbett, R. E., & Thagard, P. R. (1989). *Induction: Processes of inference, learning and discovery.* Cambridge, Mass.: MIT Press.

Holldobler, B. & Wilson, E. O. (1990). *The ants.* Cambridge, Mass.: Belknap Press of Harvard University Press.

Hopcroft, J. E. & Ullman, J. D. (1979). *Introduction to automata theory, languages, and computation.* Reading, Mass.: Addison-Wesley.

Hopfield, J. J. (1982). Neural networks and physical systems with emergent collective computational abilities. *Proc. Nat. Acad. Sci.*, 79(8): 2554–2558.

Hopfield, J. J. & Tank, D. W. (August 1986). Computing with neural networks: A model. *Science*, 233(4764): 625–633.

Hornik, K., Stinchcombe, M., & White, H. (1989). Multilayer feedforward networks are universal approximators. *Neural Networks*, 2(5): 359–366.

Isenberg, C. (1978). *The science of soap films and soap bubbles.* Avon, U.K.: Tiero.

Judd, J. S. (1990). *Neural network design and the complexity of learning.* Cambridge, Mass.: MIT Press.

Kaelbling, L. P. (Ed.). (1996). *Recent advances in reinforcement learning.* Boston: Kluwer Academic.

Kauffman, S. (August 1991). Antichaos and adaptation. *Sci. Am.*, 265(2): 64–70.

Kauffman, S. (1995). *At home in the universe: The search for laws of self-organization and complexity.* Oxford: Oxford University Press.

Kauffman, S. A. (1969). Metabolic stability and epigenesis in randomly constructed genetic nets. *J. Theor. Biol.*, 22(3): 437–467.

Kauffman, S. A. (1984). Emergent properties in random complex automata. *Physica D*, 10(1–2): 145–56.

Kauffman, S. A. (1986). Autocatalytic sets of proteins. *J. Theor. Biol.*, 119(1): 1–24.

Kauffman, S. A. (1993). *Origins of order: Self-organization and selection in evolution.* Oxford: Oxford University Press.

Kauffman, S. A. & Smith, R. G. (1986). Adaptive automata based on Darwinian selection. *Physica D*, 22(1–3): 68–82.

Kirchgraber, U. & Stoffer, D. (1990). Chaotic behaviour in simple dynamical systems. *SIAM Review*, 32(3): 424–452.

Kohonen, T. (1977). *Associative memory.* Berlin: Springer-Verlag.

Koiran, P., Cosnard, M., & Garzon, M. (1994). Computability with low-dimensional dynamical systems. *Theoret. Comp. Sci.*, 132(1): 113–128.

Kolmogorov, A. N. (1965). Three approaches to the quantitative definition of information. *Prob. Info. Trans.*, 1(1): 1–7.

Kolmogorov, A. N. (1968). Some theorems on algorithmic entropy and the algorithmic quantity of information. *UMN: Uspekhi Matematicheskikh Nauk*, 23.

Koza, J. R. (1992). *Genetic programming: On the programming of computers by natural selection.* Cambridge, Mass.: MIT Press.

Kuang, Y. (1993). *Delay differential equations with applications in population dynamics.* New York: Academic Press.

Langton, C. (1984). Self-reproduction in cellular automata. *Physica D*, 10(1–2): 135–144.

Langton, C. (1986). Studying artificial life with cellular automata. *Physica D*, 22(1–3): 120–149.

Langton, C. G. (Ed.). (1989). *Artificial Life*, volume 6 of *Santa Fe Institute studies in the sciences of complexity*, Reading, Mass. Addison-Wesley.

Langton, C. G., Taylor, C., Farmer, J. D., & Rasmussen, S. (Eds.). (1992). *Artificial Life II*, volume 10 of *Santa Fe Institute studies in the sciences of complexity*, Reading, Mass. Addison-Wesley.

Lapedes, A. & Farber, R. (1987). Nonlinear signal processing using neural networks: Prediction and system modelling. Technical Report LA-UR-87-2662, Los Alamos National Laboratory, Los Alamos, N.M.

Lapedes, A. & Farber, R. (1988). How neural nets work. In D. Z. Anderson (Ed.), *Neural information processing sytems* (pp. 442–456). New York: American Institute of Physics.

Levy, S. (1992). *Artificial life: A report from the frontier where computers meet biology.* New York: Vintage Books.

Li, T. Y. & Yorke, J. A. (1975). Period three implies chaos. *Am. Math. Monthly*, 82(10): 985–992.

Li, W., Packard, N., & Langton, C. G. (1990). Transition phenomena in CA rule space. *Physica D*, 45(1–3): 77–94.

Lin, L.-J. & Mitchell, T. M. (1992). Memory approaches to reinforcement learning in non-Markovian domains. Technical Report CMU//CS-92-138, Carnegie Mellon University, School of Computer Science, Pittsburgh, Pa.

Lindenmayer, A. (1968). Mathematical models for cellular interactions in development, I & II. *J. Theor. Biol.*, 18: 280–315.

Lindenmayer, A. & Rozenberg, G. (1972). Developmental systems and languages. In *Conference record, fourth annual ACM symposium on theory of computing*, (pp. 214–221)., Denver, Colorado.

Lorenz, E. N. (1963). Deterministic nonperiodic flow. *J. Atmos. Sci.*, 20: 130–141.

Lotka, A. (1910). Zur theorie der periodischen reaktionen. *Z. phys. Chemie*, 72: 508.

Lovelock, J. E. (1983). Daisy World: A cybernetic proof of the Gaia hypothesis. *CoEvol. Quart.*, 38(summer): 66–72.

Lumsden, C. J. & Wilson, E. O. (1981). *Genes, mind, and culture: The coevolutionary process.* Cambridge: Harvard University Press.

Mackey, M. C. & Glass, L. (1977). Oscillation and chaos in physiological control systems. *Science*, 2(4300): 287–289.

MacRae, N. (1992). *John von Neumann: The scientific genius who pioneered the modern computer, game theory, nuclear deterrence, and much more.* New York: Pantheon Books.

Mandelbrot, B. (1978). *Fractals: Form, chance, and dimension.* New York: W. H. Freeman.

Mandelbrot, B. (1983). *The fractal geometry of nature.* New York: W. H. Freeman.

March, R. H. (1995). *Physics for poets.* New York: McGraw-Hill.

Margolus, N. (1984). Physics-like models of computation. *Physica D*, 10(1–2): 81–95.

Margulis, L. (1981). *Symbiosis in cell evolution.* San Francisco: W. H. Freeman.

May, R. M. (1972). Limit cycles in predator-prey communities. *Science*, 177: 900–902.

May, R. M. (1974). Biological populations with nonoverlapping generations: Stable points, stable cycles, and chaos. *Science*, 186(4164): 645–647.

May, R. M. (1976). Simple mathematical models with very complicated dynamics. *Nature*, 261(5560): 459–467.

Mayer-Kress, G. (1992). Nonlinear dynamics and chaos in arms race models. In L. Lam & V. Naroditsky (Eds.), *Modeling complex phenomena* (pp. 153–183). Berlin: Springer.

Maynard Smith, J. (1975). *The theory of evolution* (third ed.). New York: Penguin.

Maynard Smith, J. (1982). *Evolution and the theory of games.* Cambridge: Cambridge University Press.

Maynard Smith, J. (1986). *The problems of biology.* Oxford: Oxford University Press.

McCarthy, J. (1960). LISP 1 programmer's manual. Technical report, Computation Center and Research Laboratory of Electronics, MIT, Cambridge, Mass.

McCulloch, W. S. & Pitts, W. (1943). A logical calculus of the idea immanent in nervous activity. *Bull. Math. Biophys.*, 5: 115–133.

Meinhardt, H. (1995). *The algorithmic beauty of sea shells.* New York: Springer.

Michalewicz, Z. (1996). *Genetic algorithms + data structures = evolution programs.* New York: Springer-Verlag.

Minsky, M. (1972). *Computation: Finite and infinite machines.* London: Prentice-Hall.

Minsky, M. (1979). The society theory of thinking. In P. H. Winston & R. H. Brown (Eds.), *Artificial intelligence: An MIT persective* (pp. 423–450). Cambridge, Mass.: MIT Press.

Minsky, M. (1987). *The society of mind.* London: Heinemann.

Minsky, M. & Papert, S. (1988). *Perceptrons* (expanded ed.). Cambridge, Mass.: MIT Press.

Mitchell, M. (1996). *An introduction to genetic algorithms.* Cambridge, Mass.: MIT Press.

Moore, C. (1990). Unpredictability and undecidability in dynamical systems. *Phys. Rev. Lett.*, 64(20): 2354–2357.

Moore, C. (1991a). Generalized one-sided shifts and maps of the interval. *Nonlinearity*, 4(3): 727–745.

Moore, C. (1991b). Generalized shifts: Unpredictability and undecidability in dynamical systems. *Nonlinearity*, 4(2): 199–230.

Moore, C. (1996). Recursion theory on the reals and continuous-time computation. *Theor. Comp. Sci.*, 162(1): 23–44.

Nicolis, G. & Prigogine, I. (1977). *Self-organization in nonequilibrium systems.* New York: John Wiley & Sons.

Nijhout, H. F. (November 1981). The color patterns of butterflies and moths. *Sci. Am.*, 245(5).

Nilsson, N. J. (1965). *Learning machines: Foundations of trainable pattern classifying systems.* New York: McGraw-Hill.

Nowak, M. & Sigmund, K. (1993). A strategy of win-stay, lose-shift that outperforms Tit-for-Tat in the Prisoner's Dilemma game. *Nature*, 364(6432): 56–58.

Nowak, M. A. & May, R. M. (1992). Evolutionary games and spatial chaos. *Nature*, 359(6398): 826–829.

Nowak, M. A., May, R. M., & Sigmund, K. (June 1995). The arithmetics of mutual help. *Sci. Am.*, 272(6): 76–81.

Omohundro, S. (1984). Modelling cellular automata with partial differential equations. *Physica D*, 10D(1–2): 128–134.

Ore, O. (1988). *Number theory and its history.* New York: Dover.

O'Rourke, J. (1994). *Computational geometry in C.* Cambridge: Cambridge University Press.

Ott, E., Grebogi, C., & Yorke, J. A. (1990a). Controlling chaos. *Phys. Rev. Lett.*, 64(11): 1196–1199.

Ott, E., Grebogi, C., & Yorke, J. A. (1990b). Controlling chaotic dynamical systems. In D. K. Campbell (Ed.), *Chaos—Soviet-American perspectives on nonlinear science* (pp. 153–172). New York: AIP.

Ott, E., Sauer, T., & Yorke, J. A. (1994). *Coping with chaos.* New York: Wiley.

Papert, S. (1980). *Mindstorms: Children, computers, and powerful ideas.* New York: Basic Books.

Peitgen, H.-O., Jürgens, H., & Saupe, D. (1992). *Chaos and fractals.* New York: Springer-Verlag.

Penrose, R. (1989). *The emperor's new mind.* Oxford: Oxford University Press.

Pickover, C. A. (1991). *Computers, pattern, chaos and beauty: Graphics from an unseen world.* New York: St. Martin's Press.

Poincaré, H. (1890). Sur les équations de la dynamique et le problème de trois corps. *Acta Math.*, 13: 1–270.

Póincare, H. (1952). *Science and hypothesis.* New York: Dover.

Poundstone, W. (1985). *The recursive universe.* New York: William Morrow.

Poundstone, W. (1992). *Prisoner's Dilemma.* New York: Doubleday.

Press, W. H., Flannery, B. P., Teukolsky, S. A., & Vetterling, W. T. (1986). *Numerical recipes.* Cambridge: Cambridge University Press.

Prusinkiewicz, P., Lindenmayer, A., Hanan, J. S., et al. (1990). *The algorithmic beauty of plants.* New York: Springer-Verlag.

Rand, D. A. (1994). Measuring and characterizing spatial patterns, dynamics and chaos in spatially extended dynamical systems and cologies. *Philos. Trans. Roy. Soc. A*, 348(1688): 497–514.

Rand, D. A. & Wilson, H. (1995). Using spatio-temporal chaos and intermediate-scale determinism to quantify spatially-extended ecosystems. *Proc. R. Soc. Lond. B*, 259(1355): 111–117.

Rapoport, A. & Chammah, A. M. (1965). *Prisoner's Dilemma.* Ann Arbor: University of Michigan Press.

Rechenberg, I. (1973). *Evolution strategy: Optimization of technical systems by means of biological evolution.* Stuttgart: Fromman-Holzboog.

Resnick, M. (1988). LEGO, logo, and life. In C. Langton (Ed.), *Artificial life* (pp. 397–406). Reading, Mass.: Addison-Wesley.

Resnick, M. (1994). *Turtles, termites, and traffic jams: Explorations in massively parallel microworlds.* Cambridge, Mass.: Bradford Books/MIT Press.

Reynolds, C. W. (1987). Flocks, herds, and schools: A distributed behavioral model. *Comp. Graph.*, 21(4): 25–34.

Ribenboim, P. (1991). *The little book of big primes.* New York: Springer-Verlag.

Richardson, L. F. (1961). The problem of contiguity: An appendix of statistics of deadly quarrels. *General Systems Yearbook*, 6: 139–187.

Ridley, M. (1995). *The red queen: Sex and the evolution of human nature.* New York: Macmillan.

Rosenblatt, F. (1962). *Principles of neurodynamics: Perceptrons and the theory of brain mechanisms.* Washington, D.C.: Spartan Books.

Rucker, R. (1995). *Infinity and the mind: The science and philosophy of the infinite.* Princeton: Princeton University Press.

Ruelle, D. (1980). Strange attractors. *Math. Intell.*, 2(3): 126–137.

Ruelle, D. (1993). *Chance and chaos.* Princeton: Princeton University Press.

Ruelle, D. & Takens, F. (1971). On the nature of turbulence. *Comm. Math. Phys.*, 20(3): 167–192.

Rumelhart, D. E., Hinton, G. E., & Williams, R. J. (1986). *Parallel distributive processing.* Cambridge, Mass.: MIT Press.

Sarle, W. S. & Net Poohbahs (1994). Kangaroos and training neural networks. FAQ list available from `ftp://ftp.sas.com/pub/neural/kangaroos`.

Schrödinger, E. (1944). *What is life?* Cambridge: Cambridge University Press.

Schroeder, M. (1991). *Fractals, chaos, power laws.* New York: W. H. Freeman.

Schwefel, H.-P. (1977). *Numerische optimierung von computer-modellen mittels der evolutionsstrategie.* Basel: Birkhäuser.

Shaw, E. (1962). The schooling of fishes. *Sci. Am.*, 206: 128–138.

Shinbrot, T., Ditto, W., Grebogi, C., Ott, E., Spano, M., & Yorke, J. A. (1992). Using the sensitive dependence of chaos (the "butterfly effect") to direct trajectories in an experimental chaotic system. *Phys. Rev. Lett.*, 68(19): 2863–2866.

Siegelmann, H. T. & Sontag, E. D. (1991). Turing computability with neural networks. *Appl. Math. Let.*, 4(6): 77–80.

Solomonoff, R. J. (1964a). A formal theory of inductive inference: Part I. *Info. and Control*, 7(1): 1–22.

Solomonoff, R. J. (1964b). A formal theory of inductive inference: Part II. *Information and Control*, 7(1): 224–254.

Stanley, H. E. & Ostrowsky, N. (Eds.). (1985). *On growth and form: Fractal and non fractal patterns in physics.* Kluwer Academic.

Sterman, J. D. (1984). Instructions for running the beer distribution game. Technical Report D-3679, System Dynamics Group, MIT, Cambridge, Mass.

Sterman, J. D. (1988). Modeling managerial behavior: Misperceptions of feedback in a dynamic decision making experiemnt. *Management Sci.*, 35(3): 321–339.

Stewart, I. (1990). *Does God play dice?: The mathematics of chaos.* Oxford: Blackwell.

Stewart, I. (July 1994). Mathematical Recreations: The ultimate anty-particles. *Sci. Am.*, 271(1): 104–107.

Stewart, I. (1995). *Nature's numbers: The unreal reality of mathematical imagination.* New York: Basic Books.

Stewart, I. (1996). *From here to infinity.* Oxford: Oxford University Press.

Stinson, D. R. (1995). *Cryptography: Theory and practice.* Boca Raton: CRC Press.

Strang, G. (1980). *Linear algebra and its applications.* San Diego: Harcourt Brace Jovanovich.

Strogatz, S. (1994). *Nonlinear dynamics and chaos.* New York: Addison Wesley.

Tagliarini, G. A. & Page, E. W. (1987). Solving constraint satisfaction problems with neural networks. In *Proceedings of the first international conference on neural networks,* San Diego.

Takens, F. (1980). Detecting strange attractors in turbulence. In D. A. Rand & L. S. Young (Eds.), *Dynamical systems and turbulence* (pp. 366–381). New York: Spinger-Verlag.

Tank, D. W. & Hopfield, J. J. (December 1987). Collective computation in neuronlike circuits. *Sci. Am.*, 257(6): 104–114.

Toffoli, T. (1977). Computation and construction universality of reversible cellular automata. *J. Comp. Sys. Sci.*, 15(2): 213–231.

Toffoli, T. (1984). Cellular automata as an alternative to (rather than an approximation of) differential equations in modeling physics. *Physica D*, 10(1–2): 117–127.

Toffoli, T. & Margolus, N. (1987). *Cellular automata machines.* London: MIT Press.

Tomita, K. & Tsuda, I. (1979). Chaos in Belousov-Zhabotinskii reaction in a flow system. *Phys. Lett. A*, 71(5–6): 489.

Tu, P. N. V. (1992). *Dynamical systems: An introduction with applications in economics and biology.* Berlin: Springer-Verlag.

Turing, A. M. (1936). On computable numbers, with an application to the Entscheidungsproblem. *Proc. London Math. Soc.*, 2(42): 230–265.

Turing, A. M. (1950). Can a machine think? *Mind*, 59(236): 433–460.

Turing, A. M. (1952). The chemical basis of morphogenesis. *Phil. Trans. Roy. Soc. London*, B(237): 37–72.

Turing, A. M. (1963). Computing machinery and intelligence. In E. A. Feigenbaum (Ed.), *Computers and Thought.* New York: McGraw-Hill.

Ulam, S. M. (1962). On some mathematical problems connected with patterns of growth of figures. *Proc. Symposia Appl. Math.*, 14: 215–224.

Ulam, S. M. & von Neumann, J. (1947). On combinations of stochastic and deterministic processes. *Bull. Am. Math. Soc.*, 53: 1120.

Vanecek, A. & Celikovsky, S. (1996). *Control systems: From linear analysis to synthesis of chaos.* New York: Prentice-Hall.

von Neumann, J. (1958). *The computer and the brain.* New Haven: Yale University Press.

von Neumann, J. (1966). *Theory of self-reproducing automata.* Urbana: University of Illinois Press.

von Neumann, J. & Morgenstern, O. (1944). *Theory of games and economic behavior.* Princeton: Princeton University Press.

Waldrop, M. M. (1992). *Complexity: The emerging science at the edge of order and chaos.* New York: Simon & Schuster.

Wang, H. (1987). *Reflections on Kurt Gödel.* Cambridge, Mass.: MIT Press.

Wassermann, G. D. (1997). *From Occam's Razor to the roots of consciousness: 20 essays on philosophy, philosophy of science and philosophy of mind.* Avebury.

Watson, J. D. (1991). *The double helix: A personal account of the discovery of the structure of DNA.* New York: New American Library.

Weinberg, R. (1970). Computer simulation of a primitive, evolving eco-system. Technical Report 03296-6-T, University of Michigan, Ann Arbor.

Werbos, P. (1974). *Beyond Regression: New Tools for Prediction and Analysis in the Behavioral Sciences.* PhD thesis, Harvard University, Cambridge, Mass.

Wesson, R. (1991). *Beyond natural selection.* Cambridge, Mass.: Bradford Books/MIT Press.

Whitehead, A. N. & Russell, B. (1910). *Principia mathematica.* Cambridge: Cambridge University Press.

Whitehead, S. D. & Lin, L.-J. (1995). Reinforcement learning of a non-Markov decision process. *Art. Intell.*, 73(1–2): 271–306.

Wickler, W. (1968). *Mimicry in plants and animals.* New York: World University Library.

Wiener, N. (1948). *Cybernetics, or control and communication in the animal and the machine.* New York: John Wiley.

Wills, C. (1989). *The wisdom of the genes.* New York: Basic Books.

Wilson, E. O. (1971). *The insect societies.* Cambridge, Mass.: Belknap Press of Harvard University Press.

Wilson, E. O. (1975). *Sociobiology: The new synthesis.* Cambridge, Mass.: Belknap Press of Harvard University Press.

Wilson, S. W. (1994). ZCS: A zeroth level classifier system. *Evol. Comp.*, 2(1): 1–18.

Wolfram, S. (1983). Statistical mechanics of cellular automata. *Rev. Mod. Phys.*, 55(3): 601–644.

Wolfram, S. (1984a). Cellular automata as models of complexity. *Nature*, 311(4): 419–424.

Wolfram, S. (1984b). Computation theory of cellular automata. *Comm. Math. Phys.*, 96(1): 15–57.

Wolfram, S. (1984c). Universality and complexity in cellular automata. *Physica D*, 10(1–2): 1–35.

Wolfram, S. (Ed.). (1986). *Theory and applications of cellular automata.* Singapore: World Scientific.

Wolfram, S. (1994). *Cellular automata and complexity.* Reading, Mass.: Addison-Wesley.

Wolpert, D. H. & Macready, W. G. (1995). No free lunch theorems for search. Technical Report SFI-TR-95-02-010, The Santa Fe Institute, Santa Fe, N.M.

Index

A

*Numbers in bold refer to glossary entries.

B

T

U

Production Notes

It would have been impossible to write this book without the vast collection of excellent software used by the author. In fact, this book was produced entirely with free software. Production and software development took place over three-plus years on a number of Intel-based personal computers running Linus Torvalds's Linux operating system, which had the X window system providing all GUI services. The bulk of the user-level commands under Linux were written as part of the GNU project. All editing was done with Richard Stallman's **emacs** editor. All programs were written with Stallman's gcc compiler. Additionally, Larry Wall's **perl** scripting language was extensively used for automating boring tasks.

Line drawings were made with **xfig**, all edited bit-mapped images were drawn with either xpaint or the **gimp** editor, and all plots were produced with **gnuplot**. A few figures derived from royalty-free clip art collections or royalty-free data sources. The book was typeset with LaTeX using BibTeX to produce the bibliography and **makeindex** for the index.

The author gratefully thanks and acknowledges the community of hackers who have made such excellent software available for free; without it producing this book would have been impossible.